W9-BCL-318

HANDBOOK

of CLINICAL

HEALTH

PSYCHOLOGY

Volume 1.
Medical Disorders and Behavioral Applications

HANDBOOK
of CLINICAL
HEALTH
PSYCHOLOGY

Volume 1.
Medical Disorders and Behavioral Applications

Editor-in-Chief
Thomas J. Boll

Volume Editors
Suzanne Bennett Johnson,
Nathan W. Perry, Jr., and Ronald H. Rozensky

AMERICAN PSYCHOLOGICAL ASSOCIATION

WASHINGTON, DC

Published by
American Psychological Association
750 First Street, NE
Washington, DC 20002
www.apa.org

To order
APA Order Department
P.O. Box 92984
Washington, DC 20090-2984

Tel: (800) 374-2721; Direct: (202) 336-5510
Fax: (202) 336-5502; TDD/TTY: (202) 336-6123
Online: www.apa.org/books/
Email: order@apa.org

In the U.K., Europe, Africa, and the Middle East, copies may be ordered from
American Psychological Association
3 Henrietta Street
Covent Garden, London
WC2E 8LU England

Typeset in Goudy by EPS Group Inc., Easton, MD

Printer: Sheridan Books, Ann Arbor, MI
Cover Designer: NiDesign, Baltimore, MD
Technical/Production Editor: Kristen R. Sullivan

The opinions and statements published are the responsibility of the authors, and such opinions and statements do not necessarily represent the policies of the American Psychological Association.

Library of Congress Cataloging-in-Publication Data
Handbook of clinical health psychology / edited by Suzanne Bennett Johnson, Nathan Perry, and Ronald H. Rozensky.—1st ed.
    p. cm.
  Includes bibliographical references and index.
  Contents: v. 1. Medical disorders and behavioral applications—
  ISBN 1-55798-909-5 (alk. paper)
  1. Clinical health psychology—Handbooks, manuals, etc.   2. Health behavior—Handbooks, manuals, etc.   I. Johnson, Suzanne Bennett.   II. Perry, Nathan W. III. Rozensky, Ronald H.

  R726.7 .H354 2002
  616.89—dc21

2002018260

British Library Cataloguing-in-Publication Data
A CIP record is available from the British Library.

Printed in the United States of America
First Edition

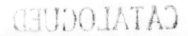

This book is dedicated to

Our patients, whose resilience in the face of pain and suffering is a tribute to the power of the human spirit;

Our students, whose intellectual curiosity and human compassion assures the future of health psychology as a science and a profession; and

Our families, whose love and support have made our successes a celebration and our failures bearable.

CONTENTS

CONTRIBUTORS

Deborah N. Ader, PhD, National Institute of Arthritis and Musculoskeletal and Skin Diseases, National Institutes of Health, Bethesda, Maryland

Elizabeth Balbin, BS, Department of Psychology, University of Miami, Coral Gables, Florida

Andrew Baum, PhD, Department of Behavioral Medicine and Oncology, University of Pittsburgh Cancer Institute

Cynthia D. Belar, PhD, Executive Director, Education Directorate, American Psychological Association, Washington, DC

Bruce G. Bender, PhD, Department of Behavioral Pediatrics, National Jewish Medical and Research Center, Denver, Colorado

Joshua I. Breier, PhD, Department of Neurosurgery and The Vivian L. Smith Center for Neurological Research, University of Texas–Houston, Health Science Center

Ronald T. Brown, PhD, ABPP, Departments of Pediatrics and Health Professions, Medical University of South Carolina, Charleston

Lisa M. Buckloh, PhD, Division of Psychology and Psychiatry, Nemours Children's Clinic, Jacksonville, Florida

Josee Casati, MEd, Research Associate, Women's Mental Health and Addiction Research Section, Centre for Addiction and Mental Health, Toronto, Ontario, Canada

Thomas L. Creer, PhD, Department of Psychology, Ohio University, Athens

Alan M. Delamater, PhD, ABPP, Department of Pediatrics, University of Miami School of Medicine, Miami, Florida

David DiLillo, PhD, Department of Psychology, University of Nebraska–Lincoln

Fonda Davis Eyler, PhD, Department of Pediatrics, College of Medicine, Division of Neonatology, University of Florida, Gainesville

Janet E. Farmer, Department of Health Psychology, University of Missouri–Columbia School of Medicine

Jack M. Fletcher, PhD, Department of Pediatrics and The Center for Academic and Reading Skills, University of Texas–Houston, Health Science Center

Catherine L. Grus, PhD, Department of Pediatrics, University of Miami School of Medicine, Miami, Florida

Brent N. Henderson, PhD, Department of Behavioral Medicine and Oncology, University of Pittsburgh Cancer Institute

Bruce A. Huyser, PhD, Behavioral Medicine Program, Albuquerque VA Medical Center, New Mexico

Gail Ironson, MD, PhD, Department of Psychology, University of Miami, Coral Gables, Florida

David S. Krantz, PhD, Department of Medical and Clinical Psychology, Uniformed Services University of the Health Sciences, Bethesda, Maryland

Deborah O. Lucas, MPH, Managed Care Division, Glaxo, Smith, Kline, Research Triangle Park, North Carolina

Michelle Y. Martin, PhD, Division of Preventive Medicine, Department of Medicine, University of Alabama at Birmingham

Raymond K. Mulhern, PhD, Division of Behavioral Medicine, St. Jude Children's Research Hospital and Department of Pediatrics, University of Tennessee College of Medicine, Memphis

Jerry C. Parker, PhD, Harry S. Truman Memorial Veterans' Hospital, Department of Physical Medicine and Rehabilitation, University of Missouri–Columbia School of Medicine

Lizette Peterson, PhD, Department of Psychological Sciences, University of Missouri–Columbia

Neil Schneiderman, PhD, Department of Psychology and Behavioral Medicine Research Center, University of Miami, Coral Gables, Florida, and Miami, Florida

Sonia Suchday, PhD, Ferkauf Graduate School of Psychology, Yeshiva University, Bronx, New York

Susan Simonian, PhD, Department of Psychology, College of Charleston, South Carolina

Robert J. Thompson, Jr., PhD, Department of Psychology: Social and Health Sciences, Duke University Medical Center, Durham, North Carolina

Brenda B. Toner, PhD, Head, Women's Mental Health and Addiction Research Section, CAMH Head, Women's Mental Health Program, Professor, Department of Psychiatry, University of Toronto, Ontario, Canada

Steven M. Tovian, PhD, ABPP, Department of Psychiatry and Behavioral Sciences, Evanston Northwestern Healthcare, Northwestern University Medical School, Evanston, Illinois

Dana L. Tucker, MS, Department of Medical and Clinical Psychology, Uniformed Services University of the Health Sciences, Bethesda, Maryland

Katherine J. Van Loon, BS, Department of Psychology: Social and Health Sciences, Duke University Medical Center, Durham, North Carolina

Mark A. Williams, PhD, Section of Neuropsychology, Department of Surgery, University of Alabama at Birmingham

Tim Wysocki, PhD, Division of Psychology and Psychiatry, Nemours Children's Clinic, Jacksonville, Florida

INTRODUCTION TO THE SERIES

THOMAS J. BOLL

The history of psychology in medicine predates the formal development of psychology. For the many millennia in which medicine has made a contribution to humankind, most of its contribution was in fact psychological. Until sometime in the middle part of the 20th century, medicine had very little of either science or technology to offer. For example, no general anesthetic existed until the end of the 19th century, and no antibiotics were available until the 20th century. Most of the miracles of surgical intervention and restoration occurred sometime after that. Prior to this time, common sense, diet, rest, and bedside manner were the doctor's stock-in-trade.

With the advent of "miracle medicine," a great deal has been gained and much has been lost. What has been gained is obvious. Medicine has allowed us to "fix" many disorders and conditions and make many once-fatal illnesses curable. It has also, however, placed the emphasis on the role of the physician as the sole person responsible for healing. This thinking, in turn, has to a considerable extent removed not only the patient's role but also the role of the interaction between doctor and patient. In many instances, patients are essentially passive recipients of pharmacological, surgical, and other biomechanical interventions. It was not until the end of the 20th and the beginning of the 21st centuries that what is now amusingly referred to as "alternative medicine" was rediscovered. Western allopathic procedures have become the mainstream, and all of the procedures that were for millennia the entire armamentarium of medicine are now only "alternative." Many of these procedures have roots in specific cultures and have continuously been in practice, whereas others are being re-recognized.

A positive effect of the biomedical revolution has been the prolonged life of many people with chronic illnesses. It is now common for individuals with diabetes, hypertension, hyperlipidemia, cerebral disorders, and coronary artery diseases to live not only long but also active and productive lives. At the same time, many early killers and limiters of life such as smallpox, whooping cough, and polio have been eliminated or largely controlled. However, this resulting longevity has led to the presence of increasing numbers of individuals with other illnesses of previously relatively small import (e.g., arthritis, dementing disorders), which has focused attention on the need for care of chronic illness and the elderly population.

Chronic care is an overbroad term that involves a return to nonbiomechanical interventions for individuals who simply cannot be "fixed." These individuals must, through their own participation as well as through the cooperation and active participation of significant others and a broad range of individuals in the "health care system," work to ameliorate symptoms, minimize dysfunction, increase capacity, and enhance quality in their lives. Much of this change was predicted by Nicholas Cummings and others in their seminal work at the Kaiser Foundation in the 1960s. Unfortunately, this knowledge is only recently gaining general acceptance with the health care community and general public. The remarkable work of Dean Ornish with end-stage cardiovascular disease demonstrates that behavioral interventions for "real" medical conditions work because they are "real" interventions. Time in the hospital, time for recovery after surgery, and amount of medication required for seizure management and pain management can all be reduced with behavioral and biobehavioral techniques. This reality seems, all too slowly, to be seeping into the awareness of physicians, the general patient population, and—even more slowly—third-party payers.

The purpose of the books in this series is to detail the contributions to scientific knowledge and effective evaluation and intervention of health psychology. Subsequent titles will be *Disorders of Behavior and Health* and *Models and Perspectives in Health Care Psychology*. The books covered by the *Handbook of Clinical Health Psychology* discuss the diagnoses contained in the *International Classification of Diseases, Ninth Revision* (World Health Organization, 1996) and the contributions of psychological and behavioral evaluation and intervention to each of these areas of medical disorder and dysfunction. Each major system of the body and the disorders attendant thereto are considered, as are lifestyle factors that affect health, in which health psychology has played a role in development and implementation of affective methods for health promotion as well as for primary, secondary, and tertiary illness prevention. These books also discuss a wide variety of specific disorders and crosscutting medical conditions (e.g., sleep problems, obesity) and delineate techniques, results, and interventions that have been found to be effective and continue to be developed. Finally, the theoretical underpinnings for each of these scientific advances and clinical applications are discussed.

All of this information makes these handbooks the first comprehensive effort to characterize the field of health psychology. The three volumes seek to describe the scientific basis of the endeavor; to delineate the specific techniques, technologies, and procedures for evaluation and intervention in the field; and to demonstrate the applications of health psychology to the full range of diagnostic entities recognized in medicine today.

REFERENCES

Cummings, N. A., & Follette, W. T. (1968). Psychiatric services and medical utilization in a prepaid health plan setting: Part II. *Medical Care, 6,* 31–41.

Follette, W. T., & Cummings, N. A. (1962). Psychiatry and medical utilization. An unpublished pilot project.

Follette, W. T., & Cummings, N. A. (1967). Psychiatric services and medical utilization in a prepaid health plan setting. *Medical Care, 5,* 25–35.

Ornish, D., Brown, S. E., Scherwitz, L. W., Billings, J. H., Armstrong, W. T., Ports, T. A., et al. (1990). Can lifestyle changes reverse coronary heart disease? *Lancet, 336,* 129–133.

World Health Organization. (1996). *International classification of diseases, ninth revision, clinical modification* (ICD–9–CM). Geneva: Author.

HANDBOOK
of CLINICAL
HEALTH
PSYCHOLOGY

Volume 1.
Medical Disorders and Behavioral Applications

INTRODUCTION TO VOLUME 1: MEDICAL DISORDERS AND BEHAVIORAL APPLICATIONS

SUZANNE BENNETT JOHNSON, NATHAN W. PERRY, JR.,
AND RONALD H. ROZENSKY

Volume 1 of this three-volume series focuses on health psychology's contributions to the management of specific diseases and disorders. For this reason, this volume is organized around the *International Classification of Diseases, Ninth Revision (ICD–9;* Hart, Schmidt, & Aaron, 1998). This is the coding system currently recognized by the U.S. Department of Health and Human Services and is commonly used worldwide.

The *ICD–9* organizes diseases and disorders into 17 categories or groupings: Infectious and Parasitic Diseases (codes 100–139); Neoplasms (codes 140–239); Endocrine, Nutritional and Metabolic Diseases, and Immunity Disorders (codes 240–279); Diseases of the Blood and Blood-Forming Organs (codes 280–289); Mental Disorders (codes 290–319); Diseases of the Nervous System and Sense Organs (codes 320–389); Diseases of the Circulatory System (codes 390–459); Diseases of the Respiratory System (codes 460–519); Diseases of the Digestive System (codes 520–579); Diseases of the Genitourinary System (codes 580–629); Complications of Pregnancy, Childbirth, and the Puerperium (codes 630–677); Diseases of the Skin and Subcutaneous Tissue (codes 680–709); Diseases of the Musculoskeletal System and Connective Tissue (codes 710–739); Congenital Anomalies (codes 740–759); Certain Conditions Originating in the Perinatal Period (codes 760–779); Symptoms, Signs and Ill-defined Conditions (codes 780–799); and Injury and Poisoning (codes 800–999). The chapters of this volume represent each of these groupings.

This organizational approach has both advantages and disadvantages. The ICD–9 is widely accepted in the United States and internationally. However, each category represents a large number of disorders that often include both pediatric and adult conditions; space limitations preclude a thorough discussion of behavioral applications relevant to each disorder within a category. Consequently, authors were asked to briefly describe the diseases and disorders that fell within their particular ICD–9 category, provide some epidemiological data relevant to these diseases and disorders, and describe health psychology's contributions to one or more of these conditions. Finally, authors were asked to highlight areas of opportunity: conditions that may have been largely ignored by health psychologists or areas that show particular promise. Authors often had expertise in one particular disease within a category; they were asked to broaden their approach to consider the category as a whole. If health psychology's primary contributions had been made in one or two particular diseases or disorders, this could be duly noted. However, authors were asked to comment on areas in which health psychology had made little impact, noting opportunities for new research and applications.

The ICD–9 system suffers from the mind–body dualism so common in Western medicine's approach to disease and its management. Musculoskeletal, respiratory, cardiovascular, skin, gastrointestinal, genitourinary, endocrine, or sense organ disorders that are "psychogenic" in etiology are to be classified under Mental Disorders (codes 306.0–306.7). In contrast, if an "organic" etiology is suspected, each disorder is classified under its respective grouping (e.g., Diseases of the Musculoskeletal System and Connective Tissue, Diseases of the Respiratory System). Headaches, for example, can be classified as a Mental Disorder (e.g., tension headaches, code 307.81), a Disorder of the Nervous System (e.g., migraine, code 346.0), or a Symptom Involving the Head (e.g., headache, code 784.0). We recognize that the ICD–9's reliance on a classification system that separates disorders by their "psychogenic" versus "organic" status is inimical to the biopsychosocial model that underlies health psychology as a science and as a profession. Health psychologists who conduct research and treat patients in medical settings face this issue every day. Until the larger health care system adopts the biopsychosocial model, we will continue to struggle with how best to present health psychology's role and contributions within the larger health care arena.

REFERENCE

Hart, A., Schmidt, K., & Aaron, W. (Eds.). (1998). *St Anthony's ICD–9 CM code book*. Reston, VA: St. Anthony Publishing.

1

HEALTH PSYCHOLOGY AND INFECTIOUS DISEASES

GAIL IRONSON, ELIZABETH BALBIN, AND NEIL SCHNEIDERMAN

Early investigations of the role of psychological factors and stress in human diseases focused primarily on coronary heart disease and cancer. However, more recently, the emerging field of psychoneuroimmunology has provided a framework for studying the role of psychological factors and stress in infectious disease (Cohen & Williamson, 1991). In addition, behavioral variables have assumed a critical role in the prevention of infectious diseases, especially sexually transmitted diseases. Prevention is especially important for diseases such as acquired immune deficiency syndrome (AIDS), which has no vaccine and no cure. This chapter presents an overview of health psychology and infectious diseases. The chapter focuses on six key questions: (1) Can stress increase susceptibility to disease? (2) Does stress affect the effectiveness of vaccines? (3) Can stress, distress, and coping alter the course of infectious disease progression? (4) Can stress influence reactivation of latent virus and thereby promote disease development? (5) Can stress management affect infectious disease progression? (6) Can health psychologists help prevent and treat infectious diseases (i.e., by helping patients change sexual behavior, adhere to medical regimens, and prevent transmission of tropical diseases)?

Worldwide, infectious diseases are an important cause of morbidity and mortality. According to the World Health Organization (WHO), six illnesses are the main killers (WHO, 1999). The top infectious diseases and number of deaths worldwide were as follows: respiratory diseases, including pneumonia and the flu (3.5 million); AIDS (2.3 million); diarrhea (2.2 million); tuberculosis (1.5 million); malaria (1.1 million); and measles (0.9 million). Malaria, tuberculosis, and AIDS combined have killed 150 million people since 1945—six times the number of soldiers and civilians killed in wars during the same period.

In the United States, the 10 nationally reportable infectious diseases with the most reported cases were chlamydia (520,164), gonorrhea (323,307), AIDS (58,492), salmonellosis (41,901), hepatitis A (30,021), shigellosis (23,217), tuberculosis (19,851), lyme disease (12,801), hepatitis B (10,416), and primary and secondary syphilis (8,540) (National Center for Health Statistics, 1999). Numbers of first-time consults with a physician were also high for other sexually transmitted diseases such as genital herpes (176,000), genital warts (145,000), and pelvic inflammatory disease (PID) (261,000). The actual number of people with these illnesses is estimated to be much higher than the reported cases. For example, the Centers for Disease Control and Prevention (CDC) estimates that in the United States, 3 to 5 million people have chlamydia, and an estimated 650,000 to 900,000 are infected with the human immunodeficiency virus (HIV) (Black, 1999).

STRESS AND SUSCEPTIBILITY TO DISEASE

When exposed to an infectious disease, only a proportion of people develop clinical symptoms of illness. Numerous studies have investigated whether stress can increase susceptibility to infectious disease. Illustrative examples are provided from three groups of infectious illnesses: upper respiratory infections, mononucleosis (Epstein-Barr virus [EBV]), and bacterial infections.

Upper Respiratory Infections

A series of naturalistic studies have examined the relationship between stress and the occurrence of subsequent upper respiratory infections (URIs). In one of the earliest studies, Meyer and Haggerty (1962) found that both disruptive daily events and chronic family stress were prospectively related to greater occurrence of URIs. In another prospective study (Graham, Douglas, & Ryan, 1986), 94 families indicated their levels of life stress and were monitored for 6 months, during which time they kept a diary of respiratory symptoms. The most highly stressed families experienced the most illness episodes as verified by nose and throat cultures. In addition, Stone, Porter, and Neale (1993) found that daily events and mood predicted the onset of respiratory illness episodes.

Another study measured stressful life events and family relationships in 58 families (246 individuals) before the start of flu season and found that stressed families ("rigid and chaotic") were more likely to get the flu than nonstressed ("balanced") families (Clover, Abell, Becker, & Crawford, 1989), although illness was not related to individual stressful life events. In another prospective study of flu susceptibility, Cluff, Canter, and Imboden (1966) measured 480 employees at a military research installation on hypochondriasis, morale loss, and ego strength with the Minnesota Multi-Phasic Inventory (MMPI) 6 months before an epidemic of Asian flu. Although they found a relationship between psychological vulnerability and illness reports, they found no relationship with actual infection rates (which were verified through antibody increases or viral isolation).

The issue of whether individual differences in physiological stress sensitivity could increase vulnerability to infection was addressed in two prospective studies of respiratory illness in children (Boyce et al., 1995). In one study, the physiological reactivity to stress of 137 children between the ages of 3 and 5 was measured by increases in heart rate and mean arterial pressure during developmentally challenging tasks. Environmental stress was measured in a childcare setting. Respiratory illnesses were measured for 6 months by a nurse.

Another study measured the physiological reactivity to stress of 99 5-year-olds through changes in immune parameters during the normative stressor of starting school. Environmental stress was measured by parent reports of family stressors. Respiratory illness incidence was measured by parent-completed reports done every 2 weeks for 12 weeks. Although environmental stress alone was not related to respiratory illnesses, the incidence of illness *was* related to an interaction: those children with high stress levels and physiological reactivity were more likely to develop respiratory illnesses.

One problem with the mentioned studies is that they do not control for exposure. For example, stressed people may seek more outside social contact and thus be exposed to more viruses. A few studies have intentionally exposed volunteers to specific viruses and then monitored the volunteers to determine who develops symptoms. In the most carefully conducted of these studies, 394 volunteers were exposed to one of five rhinoviruses and then quarantined to control for exposure to other viruses (Cohen, Tyrrell, & Smith, 1991). Those with the most stressful life events and highest levels of perceived stress and negative affect had a greater probability of developing cold symptoms. In a subsequent study of 276 volunteers inoculated with cold viruses and monitored for onset of colds, the presence of chronic, stressful life events (i.e., events lasting 1 month or longer, especially chronic underemployment or unemployment and enduring interpersonal difficulties) was associated with a significantly higher disease rate, although acute stressful events (i.e., events lasting less than 1 month) were not (Cohen et al., 1998). Two other viral challenge studies found that introverts had a greater probability of developing infections when exposed to rhinoviruses (Broadbent, Broadbent, Phillpotts, & Wallace, 1984; Totman, Kiff, Reed, & Craig, 1980).

Primary Infection With Epstein-Barr Virus: Mononucleosis

Most studies of stress and herpes viruses examine reactivation of the latent virus rather than first infection. However, one study (Kasl, Evans, & Niederman, 1979) examined primary infection with EBV, the causative agent for mononucleosis. A class of 1,400 West Point cadets was monitored prospectively for 4 years for the development of new infection (seroconversion as identified by the appearance of antibodies to EBV in previously uninfected cadets) and mononucleosis. Cadets with the combination of high motivation and poor academic performance were more likely to seroconvert and among those seroconverting were more likely to develop mononucleosis. They were also more likely to spend more time in the hospital if they had mononucleosis.

Bacterial Infections

Frequency of stressful life events has been related retrospectively to tuberculosis (Hawkins, Davies, & Holmes, 1957; Rahe, Meyer, Smith, Kjaer, & Holmes, 1964) and trenchmouth (Cohen-Cole et al., 1981). Prospectively, Canter (1972) conducted a bacterial challenge study in which 37 healthy volunteers were exposed to typhoidal-type tularemia, a plague-like disease characterized by inflammation of lymph nodes, headaches, chills, fevers, and vomiting. Psychologically vulnerable subjects were more likely to have severe illness (defined by number of hours with fever higher than 100 degrees and high self-reported symptom scores). Psychological vulnerability was defined by scoring above the median on three out of four psychological MMPI distress scales (hypochondriasis, morale, loss, and ego strength) and the Cornell Medical Index (CMI). Interestingly, 34 of the 37 subjects reported significant declines in positive mood and increases in negative mood at least 6 hours before the fever.

STRESS AND VACCINES

One method of preventing infectious illness is by immunization. Immunizations are particularly useful for viral illnesses because once a person gets the illness, antibiotics are not effective. Several studies have examined the effect of stress on the appearance of appropriate protective levels of antibodies after a vaccine is given. Evidence of a stress effect is presented for three infectious illness vaccines: flu, hepatitis B, and tetanus.

An influenza vaccine was given to a group with high stress (32 caregivers of Alzheimer's disease patients) and matched control subjects (Glaser, Kiecolt-Glaser, Malarkey, & Sheridan, 1998). A poorer antibody response to the vaccine and poorer virus-specific T-cell response following vaccination was found in the Alzheimer caregiver group compared with the control subjects as measured by fourfold increases in antibody titers to the vaccine and lower levels of virus-induced interleukin-2 (IL-2) levels in vitro.

The vaccine to hepatitis B is typically given in three doses. A study of the natural history of vaccination response showed that after the first dose, only 29% developed antibody levels to hepatitis B surface antigen at the level required for protection (>10 mlU/ml), whereas 94% developed this level after the third dose (Aspinall, Hauman, Bos, & Zulch, 1991). In a study of the effect of stress on vaccine administration, 48 medical students were given the three hepatitis B vaccine shots to coincide with the third day of exams. After the first injection, 12 of 48 medical students seroconverted; those with lower stress and lower anxiety were more likely to seroconvert. At the end of the third examination, students who reported lower stress and anxiety and higher social support had a higher antibody response to the vaccine and a more vigorous T-cell response to hepatitis B antigens (Glaser et al., 1992). In another study involving the hepatitis vaccine, Petrie, Booth, Pennebaker, Davison, and Thomas (1995) found that participants assigned to an emotional disclosure (of trauma) group had higher antibody titers to hepatitis B after the second and third injections compared with those assigned to a nondisclosure group. Another team (Jabaaij et al., 1996) showed that the negative influence of psychological stress on antibody formation after vaccination with recombinant deoxyribonucleic acid (rDNA) hepatitis B may develop only with a low dose of vaccine. When the higher dose was used, the subjects with more daily problems and neurotic symptoms had no difference in antibody titers than those with low stress levels.

In a study using an animal model, rhesus monkey levels of tetanus-specific antibodies were followed after prophylactic immunization with tetanus toxoid (Laudenslager, Rasmussen, Berman, Suomi, & Berger, 1993). Infant monkeys who were the most distressed (as shown by high levels of distress vocalizations) when under stress (when their mother resumed mating) several months before immunization had lower antibody titers to tetanus immunization when measured 2 weeks after immunization at approximately 1 year of age.

The results of the previous studies lend support to the notion that stress can play a role in the effectiveness of vaccines for flu, hepatitis, and tetanus. Practically speaking, this may suggest that it may be wise to check antibody levels to make sure people who are under a lot of stress at the time of vaccination are in the protective range.

DISEASE PROGRESSION: STRESS, DISTRESS, AND COPING

In this section, HIV is used as an example to illustrate that psychosocial variables may affect the course of disease.

Although biological factors such as HIV strain, genetic characteristics of the host, coinfection with sexually transmitted diseases, and medications are of key importance in disease progression of HIV, wide individual variability still remains. Psychosocial factors such as life stressors, depression, social support, and coping have been explored as possible predictors of disease progression that may account for some of this individual variability (for a review, see Balbin, Ironson, Solomon, Williams, & Schneiderman, 1999). Discovering which psychosocial factors may be related to slower disease progression may suggest targets for secondary prevention efforts and offer information for patients and health care providers.

Life Stressors

The clearest evidence for severe life stressors being related to faster disease progression of HIV has come from two studies done by the same group (Evans et al., 1997; Leserman et al., 1999). In the first study, Evans et al. monitored 93 initially asymptomatic gay men who were HIV positive every 6 months. They found higher life stress was associated with a fourfold increase in the odds of HIV progression in those monitored for at least 2 years. In their more recent report (Leserman et al., 1999), more cumulative life stress, more cumulative depression, and less cumulative social support were associated with faster disease progression to AIDS in 82 gay men who were HIV positive and monitored for up to 5.5 years. In contrast, Kessler, Foster, Joseph, Ostrow, and Chmiel (1991) failed to find a relationship between 24 stressor events and either the development of symptoms or CD4 declines. Similarly, Rabkin et al. (1991) failed to find a relationship between stress and CD4 changes during a 6-month period but did find a suggestive relationship between depression and symptom development. Interestingly, a life stressor may have more negative impact when it is combined with another factor. An example of this was found by Kemeny et al. (1994) and Reed, Kemeny, Taylor, and Visscher (1999) who noticed that bereavement was related to future CD4 declines and subsequent disease progression only when accompanied by negative expectancies.

Loss and Social Support

Loss of a loved one is one of the most stressful life events. In those with HIV infection, it has been related to the development of symptoms (Coates, Stall, Ekstrand, & Solomon, 1989), increases in serum neopterin (a marker of disease progression), with subsequent decreases in CD4 declines (Kemeny & Dean, 1995) and lower natural killer cell cytotoxicity (NKCC) and proliferative response to phytohemagglutinin (PHA) (Goodkin et al., 1996).

Although social support has had a positive effect on health in association with numerous diseases, the picture is more mixed for HIV, and some evidence suggests that the protective effects may be important only for sicker individuals. For example, Patterson et al. (1996) found large social network sizes were only associated with longevity for people with AIDS symptoms but not for others. Similarly, less social support was related to subsequent symptom development only in people with HIV infection who had lower CD4 numbers (Solano et al., 1993). Although more social support was related to slower subsequent drops in CD4 in a cohort of those with hemophilia (Theorell et al., 1995), opposite results were found by Miller, Kemeny, Taylor, Cole, and Visscher (1997); loneliness was related to slower CD4 declines and not associated with AIDS symptoms or death. Interestingly, the effects of less social support may be magnified when people have other life stressors and depression, as was noted previously in the Leserman et al. (1999) study. Finally, one study investigated social support in a primate model of AIDS (simian immune deficiency virus infection). Capitano and Lerche (1998) found that monkeys separated or relocated in the 90 days before SIV inoculation and the 30 days after inoculation had decreased survival rates.

Depression and Distress

Three major longitudinal studies have shown a clear relationship among psychosocial factors (e.g., depression, coping), disease progression, and HIV mortality (Ickovics et al., 2001; Leserman et al., 2000; Mayne et al., 1996). All three studies looked at multiple time points up to at least 7 years. Ickovics et al. (2001) observed 765 HIV infected women and found that those with chronic depression had twice the risk of death than those with limited or no depressive symptoms. Chronic depression was also significantly related to CD4 decline, controlling for clinical, substance use, treatment, and sociodemographic characteristics. Previously, Mayne et al. (1996) followed 402 homosexual or bisexual HIV infected men and also found a clear relationship between depression and mortality. Leserman et al. (2000) followed 82 HIV infected gay men and found that depression, stressful life events, denial coping, low social support, and elevated cortisol were all related to faster progression to AIDS. Similarly, Patterson et al. (1996) found that depression was related to shorter longevity. Kemeny et al. (1990) found that sustained depression (over a two-year period) was related to faster CD4 declines over 5 years when compared with non-chronically depressed people. Emotional distress also predicted disease progression in another cohort over 12 months (Vedhara et al., 1997). In a very short term study, however, Rabkin et al. (1991) found no relationship over a 6-month period between depression, distress, and stress on the one hand and CD4 or CD8 changes on the other, but they did find a suggestive relationship between depression and physical symptoms. In conclusion, there is convincing evidence relating depression to HIV disease progression when psychosocial variables are periodically monitored over several years.

Coping

Three studies have shown that active coping had a positive effect on health in those with HIV infection, and two studies have shown that denial predicted disease progression. Active confrontational coping predicted slower clinical progression in a group of gay men with HIV infection who were monitored for 1 year (Mulder et al., 1995). In another cohort of people with HIV infection and hemophilia, "active optimistic coping behavior" was related to lower mortality in 1 to 7 years (Blomkvist et al., 1994). Active problem-related coping (e.g., positive reappraisal, seeking social support) was related in those with HIV infection to a lesser chance of developing AIDS (Vassend, Eskild, & Halvorsen, 1997). Conversely, Solano et al. (1993) found that denial and repression were related to the development of AIDS symptoms at 6- and 12-month follow-ups, and Ironson et al. (1994) found that reacting to the news of being HIV seropositive with denial and behavioral disengagement was associated with the development of symptoms or death at a 2-year follow-up.

Cognitive Mind-Set

Fatalism and negative expectancies have been predictors of decreased survival time (Reed, Kemeny, Taylor, Wang, & Visscher, 1994) and progression to AIDS symptoms among initially asymptomatic gay men with HIV infection (Reed et al., 1999). Negative attributions (attributing negative events to self) significantly predicted CD4 decline during an 18-month period (Segerstrom, Taylor, Kemeny, Reed, & Visscher, 1996). Conversely, a sense of optimism, including anticipating future activities, was related to subsequent lower mortality (Blomkvist et al., 1994). In addition, finding meaning in response to an HIV-related stressor has been related to slower CD4 declines and lower mortality during 2- to 3-year periods (Bower, Kemeny, Taylor, & Fahey, 1998).

Other Variables

Another psychosocial variable that has been studied is disclosure (Cole, Kemeny, & Taylor, 1997; Cole, Kemeny, Taylor, & Visscher, 1996). Studies of long-term survivors of AIDS show that they have higher emotional expression (O'Cleirigh et al., 1999), higher life involvement (Balbin et al., 1998), lower depression and perceived stress (Balbin, Ironson, Solomon, Williams, et al., 1999), higher optimism, better coping, more religious coping (Ironson, Solomon, et al., 1995, 1998), and various other characteristics (Solomon, Temoshok, O'Leary, & Zich, 1987).

Summary

Evidence exists that some psychosocial variables predict progression (e.g., depression, life stressors, coping, cognitive mind-set), but it is more mixed for others (e.g., social support). More research is necessary monitoring large cohorts over long periods. Some suggestions from the literature include investigating combinations of variables such as life stressors, poor coping, and low social support. In addition, it would be useful to investigate mediators of improved health outcomes such as improved medication adherence, conscientiousness, or decreased levels of stress hormones. The stress–immune connection is also an important mediator and is reviewed in several sources in general (Herbert & Cohen, 1993; Rabin, 1999) and HIV in particular (Balbin et al., 1999).

STRESS AND REACTIVATION OF A LATENT VIRUS

Certain viruses such as herpes viruses remain latent in the host after initial exposure and infection. This section addresses the issue of whether stress is associated with the reactivation of latent viruses such as herpes viruses (herpes simplex virus [HSV] type 1 [HSV-1] and type 2 [HSV-2], EBV, cytomegalovirus [CMV], and varicella zoster virus [VZV]).

Numerous studies have investigated reactivation of latent viruses by measuring increases in antibody titers to the virus because reactivation of virus is necessary for disease recurrence. Glaser and colleagues (Glaser, Kiecolt-Glaser, Speicher, & Holliday, 1985; Glaser et al., 1987) found increases in antibody titers to HSV-1, EBV, and CMV in medical students during examination periods. In addition, lonely students were more likely to have higher titers to EBV. Other stressed groups have been found to have higher titers of antibodies to latent viruses when compared with normal control groups. Caregivers of patients with Alzheimer's disease were found to have higher antibody titers to EBV (Kiecolt-Glaser, Glaser, et al., 1987) and HSV-1 (Glaser & Kiecolt-Glaser, 1997). Older caregivers had higher titers to CMV (Pariante et al., 1997). Women recently separated from significant others were found to have elevated antibody titers to EBV (Kiecolt-Glaser, Fisher, et al., 1987). Divorced or recently separated men had elevated titers to both EBV and HSV-1 (Kiecolt-Glaser et al., 1988). In a study monitoring people prospectively for 6 months, it was found that stress-producing events during the previous week at work were associated with subsequent increases in antibody titers to CMV (Toro & Ossa, 1996). Finally, elevated titers to HSV-1 were found among residents living near the Three Mile Island nuclear plant (McKinnon, Weisse, Reynolds, Bowles, & Baum, 1989). In an interesting animal model, disruption of the social hierarchy within colonies of mice caused reactivation of HSV-1 in more than 40% of animals infected with the latent virus (Padgett et al., 1998).

Several studies have examined actual clinical diseases caused by reactivation of latent viruses (rather than just antibody titers). The most extensive studies have been done on HSV-1, the causative agent for oral herpes, and HSV-2, the causative agent for genital herpes. A few studies have been done on other viruses including VZV, the causative agent for shingles, and CMV.

Herpes Simplex Virus

Herpes Simplex Virus Type 1: Cold Sores

Retrospective and prospective studies of stress-related recurrence of cold sores are mixed. Two retrospective studies support a stress-recurrence association, and one reported no association. Depression and nervous troubles were related to self-reported recurrence in 1,133 medical and nursing students (Ship, Morris, Durocher, & Burket, 1960). In another study (Schmidt, Zyzanski, Ellner, Kumar, & Arnot, 1985), in the week before the appearance of a recurrence in 18 individuals, subjects were more likely to report increased numbers of daily hassles and stressful life events and higher state anxiety compared with the week before a dormant stage of infection. In contrast, in a study of 343 students and 242 hospital patients (Ship, Brightman, & Laster, 1967), no relationship was found between distress and verified ulcers.

Two prospective studies support a stress–illness relationship, and two were more negative. In a prospective study of HSV-1 and HSV-2 reactivation (Dalkvist, Wahlin, Bartsch, & Forsbeck, 1995), colds were the strongest predictor of recurrence of cold sores, and any possible effect of mood was overshadowed by the effect of colds. A study of 38 women monitored for a year during nursing school found those reporting chronically unhappy moods had more verified episodes of oral herpes (Katcher, Brightman, Luborsky, & Ship, 1973). However, an attempt to replicate these results in a sample of 43 student nurses monitored for 3 weeks failed

(Luborsky, Mintz, Brightman, & Katcher, 1976). Finally, a study monitoring 149 student nurses during 3 years found those reporting unpleasant moods at the beginning of the study had more recurrences (Friedman, Katcher, & Brightman, 1977).

Herpes Simplex Virus Type 2: Genital Herpes

Three retrospective studies and three prospective studies support an association between stress and the occurrence of genital herpes. One prospective study reported no association.

In a retrospective study, stressful life events were associated with the number of recurrences in the previous year in a sample of 59 volunteers with self-reported culture-positive genital herpes (VanderPlate, Aral, & Magder, 1988). This relationship held only for those infected less than 4 years previously. In another retrospective study, 39 patients with recurrent genital herpes were monitored for 6 months (Kemeny, Cohen, Zegans, & Conant, 1989). Depressive symptoms on the Profile of Mood States (POMS) scale were related to herpes recurrence but only for those without multiple recurrent infections. Neither stress (a linear combination of the five stressor and distress scales), hostility, nor anger were related to recurrence. A third retrospective study (Manne & Sandler, 1984) found an association between more symptoms of genital herpes and negative thoughts about herpes, higher depression (Beck Depression Inventory; BDI) scores, and more wishful thinking as a coping strategy. Another study reporting on cross-sectional data from 116 patients with a known history of genital herpes found that recurrences were more related to neuroticism on the Eysenck Personality Questionnaire rather than actual levels of stress (Cassidy, Meadows, Catal'an, & Barton, 1997).

One prospective study found that genital herpes infections could be predicted by "reduced and decreasing" emotional health beginning about 10 days before clinical symptoms appeared (Dalkvist et al., 1995). This relationship was stronger for women than men. Men noted they slept poorly 3 to 8 days before recurrence. Another prospective study (Goldmeier & Johnson, 1982) monitored 58 patients after first (verified) diagnosis of genital herpes for the next 28 weeks. Although recurrence was predicted by higher psychological distress at the onset of the study, 13 of the 29 patients without recurrences dropped out of the study. Therefore, it is possible that if more distressed people without recurrences dropped out of the study, the results could partly be a result of differential dropouts in the two groups. A third study monitored 16 patients with genital herpes before they began psychological therapy, 1 week after therapy, and 12 weeks after therapy. Anxiety (but not dysphoria) was higher during the 4 days before a recurrence than the 4 days after healing (McLarnon & Kaloupek, 1988). Finally, 64 participants with culture-verified genital herpes were followed prospectively for 1 to 3 months with daily questionnaires measuring stress (Rand, Hoon, Massey, & Johnson, 1990). Stress reported during the 6 days before a recurrence was no greater than on days not temporally related to recurrence.

Varicella Zoster Virus (VZV)

In a case control study in persons with VZV to determine whether stressful life events or major changes in spousal relationships were risk factors for an outbreak of herpes zoster, 101 people with zoster were compared with 101 matched (for age, sex, and race) control cases without zoster (Schmader, Studenski, MacMillan, Grufferman, & Cohen, 1990). The mean number of total life events 6 months (but not 2, 3, or 12 months) before was significantly higher in the zoster group (2.64 versus 1.82); case subjects also perceived more negative life events in the 2, 3, and 6 months before a zoster outbreak. In another study by the same group, a population-based prospective cohort study of more than 10,000 people older than age 65 found 167 new incident cases of herpes zoster (Schmader, George, Burchett, Hamilton, & Pieper, 1998). Negative life events increased the risk of zoster, but the result was borderline for statistical significance (relative risk = 1.38; p = .078). Social support was not related. Thus, limited support exists for a stress–zoster association.

In a study of stress, CMV antibody titers, and clinical disease, 11 healthy individuals who were CMV seropositive were monitored for 6 months for stress and CMV DNA in leukocytes (by polymerase chain reaction), urine and throat washings, and oral herpes lesions. An association was found among stress at work, CMV DNA, and oral herpes lesions (Toro & Ossa, 1996).

STRESS MANAGEMENT AND DISEASE PROGRESSION

Because psychological factors are related to disease progression in those with HIV/AIDS, one might reason that stress management and reduction of distress might slow disease progression. This section deals with the effects of stress management on immune markers and symptoms of one infectious disease, HIV/AIDS. The effects of stress management interventions on behavior change (including changes in sexual behavior and adherence) are covered in the next section.

Our group has been investigating the effects of a group-based, 10-week stress management intervention for gay men and more recently for minority women (Schneiderman, 1999). Goals of stress management include reduction of distress, stress, and disease severity and improvements in ability to relax, cope, and increase one's social support. Behavior changes including increasing adherence to complex medical regimens and practicing safer sex are also goals. Our first intervention was implemented for gay men first learning they were infected with HIV. We then extended the intervention to asymptomatic people who were HIV positive and later to those who were symptomatic. More recently, the protocol was extended to include minority women.

Our early work with a group cognitive behavior stress management (CBSM) intervention for gay men showed a buffering of the psychological and immunological sequelae of HIV serostatus notification (Antoni et al., 1991). The CBSM intervention was also associated with improved control of latent herpes viruses EBV and human herpes virus–type 6 (HHV-6) (Esterling et al., 1992). This is particularly important because the reactivation of herpes viruses in the presence of HIV can result in severe morbidity and mortality (Rinaldo, 1990). Treatment adherence (e.g., attending sessions, practicing relaxation) during the intervention was also associated significantly with health benefits, including decreases in the development of symptoms and death at a 2-year follow-up. Our recent work with symptomatic gay men has demonstrated the CBSM intervention to be of significant benefit in reducing depressed affect, anxiety, and distress (Lutgendorf et al., 1997); increasing cognitive coping strategies and social support (Lutgendorf et al., 1998); and improving surveillance of HSV-2 (Lutgendorf et al., 1997). With some modifications the CBSM intervention for African American women showed a buffering of CD4 decline and depressed affect in the intervention versus the control group (West-Edwards, Pereira, Greenwood, Antoni, & Schneiderman, 1997).

Although several other groups have found beneficial psychological and immune effects from stress management for those with HIV (for a review, see Ironson, Antoni, & Lutgendorf, 1995), one group has found beneficial effects on two markers of disease progression—CD4 and viral load. More specifically, Goodkin and colleagues (1998) found that a bereavement support group for gay men who had experienced a recent loss was associated with beneficial effects on CD4 counts and health care visits. Furthermore, the bereavement therapy group had a significant drop in viral load (Goodkin et al., 2001). Thus, stress management does have a role in reducing distress and may affect disease progression. As noted in the next section, group interventions can also help change behavior.

HEALTH PSYCHOLOGY: PREVENTION AND TREATMENT OF DISEASE

Various beliefs and behaviors are related to the prevention and spread of infectious diseases. Behaviors such as practicing safer sex, not sharing needles, selecting an AIDS-knowledgeable physician, and adhering to medical regimens are of key importance in the prevention of the spread of HIV. Thus, the first example of the way health psychologists can play an important role in the prevention and spread of infectious disease focuses on changing sexual behavior. This is of obvious relevance not only to HIV and AIDS but also to the spread of all sexually transmitted diseases. The second example focuses on adherence to medical regimens. In the infectious disease realm, this is important not only for the treatment of AIDS but also for the treatment of many infectious diseases. The final example of a relationship between psychosocial and sociocultural factors and infectious disease focuses on prevention of the transmission of tropical diseases. The broader view includes not only individual factors but also household, community, and broader societal conditions.

Changing Sexual Behavior

HIV causes AIDS and is transmitted by sexual contact or exposure to infected blood. Thus, HIV is spread primarily through sexual contact and the sharing of needles among drug users. HIV currently has no cure, and once infected with the virus it is expected that AIDS will eventually develop. HIV also has no vaccine, so it is of paramount importance to prevent the initial infection. Many factors are related to the risk of becoming infected with HIV, most of which are modifiable and many of which are behavioral. Increasing safe sex practices, decreasing drug and alcohol use, and enhancing knowledge, risk perception, self-efficacy, and support should all decrease the risk of infection (Coates, Stall, Catania, & Kegeles, 1988). Health psychology has played an important part in addressing the issue of behavior change. Thus, for example, in a study using individual counseling, fewer sexually transmitted diseases were observed in those who received counseling compared to those who received only didactic messages (Kamb, Fishbein, Douglas, Rhodes, & Rogers, 1998).

Media campaigns typically include information about HIV and AIDS, how the disease is spread, and how to reduce risk. This is especially useful because many people have numerous misconceptions about how one gets the disease and how to prevent infection. For example, a study of 1,326 students from 10 high schools in San Francisco (DiClemente, Zorn, & Temoshok, 1987) showed 26% were not sure whether the use of condoms would lower the risk of contracting HIV. However, although education about HIV and safe sex behavior has been shown to increase knowledge, it is a necessary but insufficient approach for behavior change (Leventhal & Cleary, 1980). Pairing education with provision of skills for behavior change is important. Prevention not only of the transmission of HIV but also of sexually transmitted diseases has focused on getting people to use condoms. Condoms have been shown to reduce the transmission of HIV (Conant, Hardy, Sernatinger, Spicer, & Levy, 1986). However, the use of condoms is often resisted by sexual partners. Thus, part of prevention efforts, including what psychologists do as part of a CBSM intervention, involves teaching people how to deal with resistance from their partner to using condoms. This may include determining the reasons for the partner's resistance, teaching negotiation through role plays, and assertiveness training. Programs pairing education about HIV with training on how to modify behavior have been successful in changing sexual behavior (Coates, 1990; Kelly & Murphy, 1992).

Other interventions focusing on increasing knowledge about HIV risk reduction and adopting less risky behaviors have reduced population rates of risky behavior in gay men (Kelly et al., 1997). A study of women at risk also showed initial reductions in risky behavior at a 3-month follow-up (Carey, Kalichman, Forsyth, & Wright, 1997). However another intervention that attempted to change behavior in men at risk failed to show maintenance of changes (Kalichman, Kelly, Hunter, Murphy, & Tyler, 1993).

Increasing a person's perception that they may be at risk is also an important prerequisite to behavior change. Goldman and Harlow (1993) and Kline and Strickler (1993) found that increasing people's perception of their risk while also changing their beliefs about being able to control their exposure to HIV has been a useful approach. Thus, motivation to change and developing the skills to insist on safer sex or avoid compromising situations is important (Fisher & Fisher, 1992; O'Keefe, Nesselhof-Kenall, & Baum, 1990).

Determining which groups to target (i.e., high-risk groups) has also been a part of prevention efforts. These groups include gay men in general, younger gay men who may consider HIV to be "an older gay man's disease," adolescent populations whose sexuality is emerging, and populations vulnerable because of poverty, such as certain ethnic minority groups, those who use intravenous drugs and share needles, and prostitutes. Identifying groups at high risk allows prevention efforts to be tailored to address their fears and resistance to change. It also can improve the motivation to change—for example, by increasing perception of risk and including opinion leaders in community efforts to change behavior.

Adherence to Medical Regimens

With the advent of combination therapies that include newer reverse transcriptase inhibitors and HIV-specific protease inhibitors (PI), or *highly active antiretroviral therapy* (HAART), significant improvements have been made in delaying the onset of AIDS and mortality (Sendi, Bucher, Craig, Pfluger, & Battegay, 1999). In fact, about 80% to 90% of individuals who adhere to a PI-containing regimen have undetectable plasma HIV viral loads in 6 to 12 months (Chaisson, 1998). Although these drugs are very successful, when even a few doses of the complex regimens are missed, resistant strains may develop (Van Hove, Shapiro, Winters, Merigan, & Blaschke, 1996). Adherence to medications also reduces viral load, and because viral load at the time of exposure is related to HIV transmission, proper adherence to medication can reduce transmission. However, failure to adhere to the strict medication regimens coupled with poor health behaviors such as unsafe sex can spell disaster and may cause the development and spread of resistant HIV strains. In work conducted at the University of Miami, Malow et al. (1998) found 48% adherence to combination medication therapy for HIV as measured by monthly refills for all medications in a sample of primarily African American men who lived in the inner city and abused drugs. An intervention consisting of an individual counseling session with a doctoral-level pharmacist increased refill rates to 75%. In addition, rates of going to scheduled clinic visits increased from 66% to 76%. Finally, 50% of the patients had viral load reductions of .5 logs or greater.

Our SMART intervention studies are currently examining whether teaching adaptive coping skills coupled with a counseling session by a pharmacist and decreases in distress that typically result from this treatment result in improved medication adherence.

For a long while, efforts have been made to predict and improve compliance and adherence to medical regimens, particularly for hypertension and diabetes. Much can be learned from this research, and it provides a potentially rich source for designing interventions to increase adherence to infectious disease treatments. Studies of treatment of a wide variety of illnesses indicate that between 40% and 70% of patients comply with their doctor's advice (Becker, 1991; Taylor, 1990; Taylor, Kemeny, Aspinwall, & Reed, 1992).

Factors related to compliance and adherence include (a) aspects of the medication regimen, particularly complexity, side effects, and cost; (b) social support from family and friends (Doherty, Schrott, Metcalf, & Iasiello-Vailas, 1983); (c) educational level and income (Strain, 1978); (d) physician's level of job satisfaction, the number of patients seen per week, and physician's tendency to answer questions (DiMatteo et al., 1993); (e) patient satisfaction with the health care provider (Francis, Korsch, & Morris, 1969; DiMatteo, Hays, & Prince, 1986; Morris & Schulz, 1993); (f) understanding of the medical regimen being prescribed; and (g) stress, which may interfere with adherence by increasing memory problems, decreasing satisfaction, or making it harder to adjust to treatment requirements (Brickman, Yount, Blaney, Rothberg, & De-Nour, 1996).

Several models have been proposed for predicting adherence, one of which is the health belief model (Becker, 1991; Rosenstock, 1974). It is proposed that three sets of factors need to be taken into consideration when predicting people's behavior. The first is the patient's readiness to act, which is determined by the patient's perception of the illness severity and the patient's perception of susceptibility to the illness. The second set of factors takes into account the costs and benefits of adherence and includes such considerations as side effects, perceived benefits, disruptiveness, and unpleasantness. A third factor in the model suggests the importance of a "cue to action" to motivate the patient for treatment. The development of mild symptoms of HIV or external stimuli such as health campaigns may be motivators.

A second model posits the construction of naive health theories by patients (Leventhal, Nerenz, & Leventhal, 1982). This model suggests that behavior is determined by the naive theory that a patient constructs around the disease. For example, if people who are hypertensive believe a headache is a sign of high blood pressure, they may only take their blood pressure medication when they have a headache and notice that it is high. However, research shows that having a headache does not reliably predict high blood pressure (Baumann & Leventhal, 1985). People with infectious diseases may have the naive theory that once their symptoms are gone, they no longer have to take their antibiotic for the prescribed length of time. This practice can be especially dangerous for a person with an infectious disease such as tuberculosis because the medication must be taken for an extended period.

Various attempts have been made to improve patients' adherence to medical regimens with varying success (Glasgow, 1995; Lemanek, 1995). Educational interventions in which health care providers offer information to patients about their treatment have met with some success (Dunbar-Jacob, 1993), although this approach is not sufficient. Tailoring regimens to fit into a person's lifestyle has had some positive results (Haynes, Taylor, & Sackett, 1979; Schneider & Cable, 1978), as has requiring patients to make verbal and written commitments to follow regimens (Putnam, 1994). Coaching health care professionals to become better communicators, more informative, and more warm and sensitive has also been tried (DiMatteo, 1994). Other behaviors targeted for improving the provider–patient relationship include focusing attention on patients' worries and concerns, providing clear information, and becoming more friendly and having a caring attitude (Korsch, Freeman, & Negrete, 1971). Many patients do not understand information given to them about taking prescribed medication (Ley, Bradshaw, Kincey, & Atherton, 1976). Improving communication between health providers and patients from the patient perspective has also been attempted. Specifically, getting patients to ask more questions gives them more information and increases satisfaction with the health care system, which can improve adherence (Roter, 1984). Supervision, or external monitoring, whereby patients regularly report to someone their adherence has proved useful—increasing adherence in some cases up to 60%—but it is expensive (Taylor, Sackett, & Haynes, 1978). Self-monitoring or keeping records can be useful but only in conjunction with external monitoring

(Haynes, 1976). Finally, encouraging family and social support through home visits or assigning family members a role in implementing health care can be helpful (Dickenson et al., 1981). Social support has also been positively associated with adherence to self-examinations for breast and testicular cancer (Finney, Hook, Friman, & Rapoff, 1993). Thus, various approaches to increasing adherence have been tried and somewhat successful.

Prevention of Tropical Disease Transmission

The transmission of infectious diseases worldwide involves a broad range of the factors influencing disease transmission and control. The transmission of tropical diseases is used to illustrate this multifactorial approach. Factors to be considered include not only those relevant to individuals, but also those relevant to household, community, and broader societal conditions (Rosenfield, 1990):

- In some areas, knowledge is blatantly lacking. For example, only 9.2% of those in rural Malaysia know of the relationship between mosquitoes and filariasis. One explanation for the disease, elephantiasis, is that it is caused by anger of the elephant goddess (Mohd, 1983).
- Although individual behavior is influenced by knowledge of disease, economic necessities may take precedence. In the Amazon region of Brazil, settlers know the risk of contracting malaria (an average of two cases per person per year) but continue to work clearing the jungle (Sawyer, 1986).
- Community hygiene is essential in preventing the spread of many tropical diseases such as guinea worm and schistosomiasis because the water can become contaminated with the parasite and become a source of infection.
- Control of mosquito-borne diseases such as malaria and filariasis must rely on community efforts (rather than individual efforts) by the elimination of breeding places and the maintenance of protected water supplies.
- Population participation in increasing availability of medications such as chloroquine may succeed if appropriate incentives and training are put into place (Kaseje, Sempebwe, & Spencer, 1987), but they may also fail. In Tanzania, local distributors were unavailable when mothers showed up for their drugs (MacCormack & Lwihula, 1983).
- Any community disease control program must be implemented in an acceptable manner or people will not use the services. For example, the attitude of the people doing spraying to control malaria is critical in determining whether spraying is accepted by individual households.

- Analyses of the underlying social and economic context are essential. Many of the tropical diseases of concern are closely linked to poverty, so very little can be done by an individual.
- It is critical to consider the structure of the society in which an intervention (such as vaccination against malaria) is to be implemented. The structure includes cultural, social, economic, and institutional factors (Bonair, Rosenfield, & Tengvald, 1989).

CONCLUSION

The beginning of this chapter posed the following six questions: (1) Can stress increase susceptibility to disease? (2) Does stress influence the effectiveness of vaccines? (3) Can stress, distress, and coping alter the course of infectious disease progression? (4) Can stress affect reactivation of latent viruses and thereby cause disease? (5) Can stress management affect infectious disease progression? (6) Can health psychologists help in the prevention and treatment of infectious disease? The answer to each of these questions seems to be a qualified *yes*. Thus, for most of the issues, both retrospective and prospective studies report positive findings, but negative ones exist as well. Given differences among studies in experimental design, measurement strategies, subject selection, and host vulnerabilities, it is not surprising that disparities exist.

Consider the putative relationship between stress and disease progression in those with HIV infection or AIDS. Whereas several studies have reported significant relationships between life stress, denial responses to stressors, depressed affect, or lack of social support and disease progression on the other, this has not inevitably been the case. First, life stressors have been measured in many ways and differ not only in psychological dimensions but also in intensity, cumulative duration, and quality. Second, the psychometric properties of the instruments have varied. Third, some studies have assessed individual differences in transactional variables such as coping strategies, whereas others have focused on mood or personality factors. Fourth, some studies have examined more than one biological dependent measure (e.g., CD4, viral load, symptoms, functional immune measures), whereas others have examined a single immune measure such as a CD4 count at two arbitrarily selected time points. Fifth, depression, or depressed affect, has been used as a measure of stress but has been measured in many ways and assessed at various stages of the disease process. Sixth, social isolation has also been considered to be related to stress and has been measured in numerous ways.

The measurement of stress responses and the assessment of psychosocial variables such as hostility, depression, anxiety, and social isolation fall within the purview of health psychology. To the extent that psychometric instruments are carefully chosen and reasonably applied, psychologists will have a better understanding of relationships among stressors, psychological predispositions, and such variables as disease susceptibility and progression.

A major contribution of psychology as a science has been the information it has provided concerning individual differences. The study of individual differences is important in the study of infectious diseases because it has long been known that not everyone exposed to an infectious disease becomes infected or develops symptoms. Even tuberculosis transmission depends on the existence of a vulnerable host. The ability of the tubercle bacillus to infect the host depends on multiple variables including host nutrition, actions of leukocytes, and responses of body tissues to counteract the bacillus at the site of potential infection.

The data that have been reviewed indicate that psychosocial factors such as stressful life events, perceived stress, and negative affect can play a role in determining host vulnerability with regard to the development of cold symptoms (Cohen et al., 1991). Conversely, the role of environmental stressors in promoting respiratory illness in children seems to be related to individual physiological sensitivities of the children to acute stressors (Boyce et al., 1995). Thus, the development and progression of infectious diseases depends on the presence of an infectious agent, environmental factors, and host vulnerability. Environmental factors and host vulnerability may involve psychosocial variables.

A particular strength of psychology as a discipline has been its use of theory in the development of study protocols. As previously mentioned, one of the first models developed to explain health behavior was the *health belief model* (Rosenstock, 1974). The model was originally developed to explain the adoption or nonadoption of preventive health behaviors such as checkups and immunizations but was later applied to various health-related behaviors. The model has generally been successful when used to predict the types of behavior for which it was originally intended (e.g., checkups, immunizations) but has been less successful in predicting more complex behaviors such as smoking initiation by adolescents (Flay, 1985).

To the extent that stress may affect health behaviors and disease processes, cognitive–behavioral therapy (CBT) has provided a theoretical model for teaching individuals to reduce their stress, evaluate their appraisals of potentially stressful situations more accurately, improve coping skills, and modify endocrine and immune responses (Antoni & Schneiderman, 1998). When used in a group format and combined with health education, CBT as part of a program of cognitive–behavioral self-management may be useful in facilitating social integration and reducing infectious disease transmission (Schneiderman, 1999).

Another influential model in health psychology has been the *transtheoretical model* of Prochaska and DiClemente (1984). The basic tenets of the model are that (a) different intervention approaches are needed for people at different stages of behavior change, and (b) different processes of change may occur at each stage. Thus, precontemplators need to receive information concerning the disadvantage of maintaining current risky behaviors and the advantages of changing behavior. On reaching a contemplation stage, people need to become motivated to make specific plans to change their behavior and set goals. Helpful interventions at this stage include those that increase self-efficacy, skills, and social support. Subsequently, at later stages, people need motivation and reinforcement to change and maintain behavior and deal with possible relapses.

At the precontemplation stage the emphasis is on providing credible information to large numbers of people. This is often best done at the community level. At subsequent stages in which skills learning, improved self-efficacy, and group process are important, interpersonal psychosocial interventions and community level efforts tend to reinforce one another.

Although the lay public often considers the control of infectious disease primarily in terms of the discovery of new medications, the control of infectious disease also depends on environmental factors, including psychosocial variables. In a provocative analysis, McKinlay and McKinlay (1997) observed that the precipitous decline in infectious disease rates in the United States preceded the development of immunizations and antibiotics by several decades. Based on the published work of McKeown (1976) and others, McKinlay and McKinlay attributed the decline in infectious disease rates to improved nutrition and decreased exposure to infection through improved hygiene. McKinlay and McKinlay concluded that only about 3.5% of the total decline in mortality since 1900 could be attributed to biological interventions.

Today, similar issues exist with regards to HIV and AIDS. No cure exists, so the best efforts focus on prevention. In this respect, psychosocial theories and interventions can be helpful because harm reduction (e.g., use of safer sex procedures, avoiding contaminated needles) depends on accurate information, skills, and the appropriate use of motivation and reinforcement. In terms of the management of people living with HIV and AIDS, medications can lower viral loads to undetectable levels. However, what are now needed are appropriate adherence programs that can help patients manage the complexities and difficulties of taking multiple pills each day, many of which have unpleasant side effects. Based on the available information, it is our belief that health psychologists can play an important role in the prevention and treatment of infectious diseases.

REFERENCES

Antoni, M. H., Baggett, L., Ironson, G., LaPerriere, A., August, S., Klimas, N., et al. (1991). Cognitive-behavioral stress management intervention buffers distress responses and immunologic changes following notification of HIV-1 seropositivity. *Journal of Consulting and Clinical Psychology, 59*, 906–915.

Antoni, M. H., & Schneiderman, M. (1998). HIV and AIDS. In A. Bellack & M. Herson (Eds.), *Comprehensive clinical psychology* (pp. 238–275). New York: Elsevier Science.

Aspinall, S., Hauman, C. H., Bos, P., & Zulch, R. N. (1991). Varying antibody response in dental health care workers vaccinated with recombinant hepatitis B vaccine. *Journal of the Dental Association of South Africa, 46*, 321–324.

Balbin, E., Ironson, G., O'Cleirigh, C., Pavone, J., Stivers, M., Ohata, J., et al. (1998). *Life involvement is associated with long term survival of patients with AIDS.* Poster presented at the annual meeting of the Society of Behavioral Medicine, New Orleans, LA.

Balbin, E., Ironson, G., & Solomon, G. (1999). Psychoneuroimmunology of HIV/AIDS. In M. Harbuz (Ed.), *Stress and immunity: The neuroendocrine link.* East Sussex, England: Balliere.

Balbin, E., Ironson, G., Solomon, G., Williams, R., & Schneiderman, N. (1999). Low perceived stress and depression as protective factors in asymptomatic HIV+ people with CD4 counts under 50. *Neuroimmunomodulation, 6*, 204.

Baumann, L. J., & Leventhal, H. (1985). I can tell when my blood pressure is up: Can't I? *Health Psychology, 4*, 203–218.

Becker, M. H. (1991). In hot pursuit of health promotion: Some admonitions. In S. M. Weiss, J. E. Fielding, & A. Baum (Eds.), *Perspectives in behavioral medicine: Health at work.* Hillsdale, NJ: Erlbaum.

Black, J. G. (1999). *Microbiology: Principles and explorations* (4th ed.). Upper Saddle, NJ: Prentice-Hall.

Blomkvist, V., Theorell, T., Jonsson, H., Schulman, S., Berntorp, E., & Stiegendal, L. (1994). Psychosocial self-prognosis in relation to mortality and morbidity in hemophiliacs with HIV infection. *Psychotherapy Psychosomatic, 62*, 185–192.

Bonair, A., Rosenfield, P., & Tengvald, K. (1989). Medical technologies in developing countries: Issues of technology development, transfer, diffusion and use. *Social Science and Medicine, 28*, 769–781.

Bower, J. E., Kemeny, M. E., Taylor, S. E., & Fahey, J. L. (1998). Cognitive processing, discovery of meaning, CD4 decline, and AIDS-related mortality among bereaved HIV-seropositive men. *Journal of Consulting and Clinical Psychology, 66*, 979–986.

Boyce, W. T., Chesney, M., Alkon, A., Tschann, J. M., Adams, S., Chesterman, B., et al. (1995). Psychobiologist's reactivity to stress and childhood respiratory illnesses. *Psychosomatic Medicine, 57*, 411–422.

Brickman, A. L., Yount, S. E., Blaney, N. T., Rothberg, S. T., & De-Nour, A. K.

(1996). Personality traits and long-term health status. The influence of neuroticism and conscientiousness on renal deterioration in type-I diabetes. *Psychosomatics, 37,* 459–468.

Broadbent, D. E., Broadbent, M. H. P., Phillpotts, R. J., & Wallace, J. (1984). Some further studies on the prediction of experimental colds in volunteers by psychological factors. *Journal of Psychosomatic Research, 28,* 511–523.

Canter, A. (1972). Changes in mood during incubation of acute febrile disease and the effects of pre-exposure psychological status. *Psychosomatic Medicine, 34,* 424–430.

Capitano, J. P., & Lerche, N. W. (1998). Social separation, housing relocation, and survival in simian AIDS: A retrospective analysis. *Psychosomatic Medicine, 60,* 235–244.

Carey, M. P., Kalichman, S., Forsyth, A., & Wright, E. (1997). Enhancing motivation to reduce the risk of HIV infection for economically disadvantaged urban women. *Journal of Consulting and Clinical Psychology, 65,* 531–541.

Cassidy, L., Meadows, J., Catal'an, J., & Barton, S. (1997). Are reported stress and coping style associated with frequent recurrence of genital herpes? *Genitourinary Medicine, 73,* 263–266.

Chaisson, R. E. (1998). The changing natural history of HIV/AIDS in the "HAART" era: Clinical implications. *Medscape HIV/AIDS, 4,* 7–12.

Clover, R. D., Abell, T., Becker, L. A., & Crawford, S. (1989). Family functioning and stress as predictors of influenza B infection. *Journal of Family Practice, 28,* 535–539.

Cluff, L. E., Canter, A., & Imboden, J. B. (1966). Asian influenza: Infectious disease and psychological factors. *Archives of Internal Medicine, 117,* 159–163.

Coates, T. J. (1990). Strategies for modifying sexual behavior for primary and secondary prevention of HIV disease. *Journal of Consulting and Clinical Psychology, 58,* 57–69.

Coates, T. J., Stall, R. D., Catania, J. A., & Kegeles, S. (1988). Behavioral factors in HIV infection. *AIDS, 2*(Suppl. 1), 239–246.

Coates, T. J., Stall, R., Ekstrand, M., & Solomon, G. (1989). *Psychological predictors as cofactors for disease progression in men infected with HIV: The San Francisco men's health study.* Paper presented at the V International AIDS Conference, Montreal, Canada.

Cohen, S., Frank, E., Doyle, W. J., Skoner, D. P., Rabin, B. S., & Gwaltney, J. M., Jr. (1998). Types of stressors that increase susceptibility to the common cold in healthy adults. *Health Psychology, 17,* 214–223.

Cohen, S., Tyrrell, D. A. J., & Smith, A. P. (1991). Psychological stress and susceptibility to the common cold. *New England Journal of Medicine, 325,* 606–612.

Cohen, S., & Williamson, G. M. (1991). Stress and infectious disease in humans. *Psychological Bulletin, 109,* 5–24.

Cohen-Cole, S., Cogen, R., Stevens, A., Kirk, K., Gaitan, E., Hain, J., et al.

(1981). Psychosocial, endocrine, and immune factors in acute necrotizing ulcerative gingivitis ("trenchmouth"). *Psychosomatic Medicine, 43*, 91.

Cole, S. W., Kemeny, M. E., & Taylor, S. E. (1997). Social identity and physical health: Accelerated HIV progression in rejection-sensitive gay men. *Journal of Personality and Social Psychology, 72*, 320–335.

Cole, S. W., Kemeny, M. E., Taylor, S. E., & Visscher, B. R. (1996). Elevated physical health risk among gay men who conceal their homosexual identity. *Health Psychology, 15*, 243–251.

Conant, M., Hardy, D., Sernatinger, J., Spicer, D., & Levy, J. A. (1986). Condoms prevent transmission of AIDS-associated retrovirus [Letter]. *Journal of the American Medical Association, 255*, 1706.

Dalkvist, J., Wahlin, T.-B. R., Bartsch, E., & Forsbeck, M. (1995). Herpes simplex and mood: A prospective study. *Psychosomatic Medicine, 57*, 127–137.

Dickinson, J. C., Warshaw, G. A., Gehlbach, S. H., et al. (1981). Improving hypertension control: Impact of computer feedback and physical education. *Medical Care, 19*, 843–854.

DiClemente, R. J., Zorn, R. J., & Temoshok, L. (1987). Acquired immune deficiency syndrome (AIDS) [Special issue]. The association of gender, ethnicity, and length of residence in the Bay area to adolescents' knowledge and attitudes about acquired immune deficiency syndrome. *Journal of Applied Social Psychology, 17*, 216–230.

DiMatteo, M. R. (1994). Communicating with patients about their medications [Special issue]. Enhancing medication adherence through communication and informed collaborative choice. *Health Communication, 6*, 253–265.

DiMatteo, M. R., Hays, R. D., & Prince, L. M. (1986). Relationship of physicians' nonverbal communication skill to patient satisfaction, appointment noncompliance, and physician workload. *Health Psychology, 5*, 581–594.

DiMatteo, M. R., Sherbourne, C. D., Hays, R. D., Ordway, L., Kravitz, R. L., McGlynn, E. A., et al. (1993). Physicians' characteristics influence patients' adherence to medical treatment: Results from the Medical Outcomes Study. *Health Psychology, 12*, 93–102.

Doherty, W. J., Schrott, H. G., Metcalf, L., & Iasiello-Vailas, L. (1983). Effect of spouse support and health beliefs on medication adherence. *Journal of Family Practice, 17*, 837–841.

Dunbar-Jacob, J. (1993). Contributions to the patient adherence: Is it time to share the blame? *Health Psychology, 12*, 91–92.

Esterling, B., Antoni, M., Schneiderman, N., LaPerriere, A., Ironson, G., Klimas, N., et al. (1992). Psychosocial modulation of antibody to Epstein-Barr viral capsid antigen and human herpes virus—Type 6 in HIV-1 infected and at-risk gay men. *Psychosomatic Medicine, 54*, 354–371.

Evans, D. L., Leserman, J., Perkins, D. O., Stern, R. A., Murphy, C., Zheng, B., et al. (1997). Severe life stress as a predictor of early disease progression in HIV infection. *American Journal of Psychiatry, 154*, 630–634.

Finney, J. W., Hook, R. J., Friman, P. C., & Rapoff, M. A. (1993). The overestimation of adherence to pediatric medical regimens. *Children's Health Care, 22, 297–304.*

Fisher, J. D., & Fisher, W. A. (1992). Changing AIDS-risk behavior. *Psychological Bulletin, 111, 455–474.*

Flay, B. R. (1985). Psychosocial approaches to smoking prevention: A review of findings. *Health Psychology, 4, 449–488.*

Francis, V., Korsch, B. M., & Morris, M. J. (1969). Gaps in doctor-patient communication. *New England Journal of Medicine, 280, 535–540.*

Friedman, E., Katcher, A. H., & Brightman, V. J. (1977). Incidence of recurrent herpes labialis and upper respiratory infection: A prospective study of the influence of biologic, social and psychologic predictors. *Oral Surgery, Oral Medicine and Oral Pathology, 43, 873–878.*

Glaser, R., & Kiecolt-Glaser, J. (1997). Chronic stress modulates the virus-specific immune response to latent herpes simplex virus type 1. *Annals of Behavioral Medicine, 19, 78–82.*

Glaser, R., Kiecolt-Glaser, J. K., Bonneau, R. H., Malarkey, W., Kennedy, S., & Hughs, J. (1992). Stress-induced modulation of the immune response to recombinant hepatitis B vaccine. *Psychosomatic Medicine, 54, 22–29.*

Glaser, R., Kiecolt-Glaser, J. K., Malarkey, W. B., & Sheridan, J. F. (1998). The influence of psychological stress on the immune response to vaccines. *Annals of the New York Academy of Science, 840, 649–655.*

Glaser, R., Kiecolt-Glaser, J. K., Speicher, C. E., & Holliday, J. E. (1985). Stress, loneliness, and changes in herpes virus latency. *Journal of Behavioral Medicine, 8, 249–260.*

Glaser, R., Rice, J., Sheridan, J., Fertel, R., Stout, J., Speicher, C. E., et al. (1987). Stress-related immune suppression: Health implications. *Brain, Behavior, and Immunity, 1, 7–20.*

Glasgow, R. E. (1995). Behavioral research on diabetes at the Oregon Research Institute. *Annals of Behavioral Medicine, 17, 32–40.*

Goldman, J., & Harlow, L. (1993). Self-perception variables that mediate AIDS-preventive behavior in college students. *Health Psychology, 12, 489–498.*

Goldmeier, D., & Johnson, A. (1982). Does psychiatric illness affect the recurrence rate of genital herpes? *British Journal of Venereal Disease, 54, 40–43.*

Goodkin, K., Baldewicz, T. T., Asthana, D., Khamis, I., Blaney, N. T., Kumar, M., et al. (2001). A bereavement support group intervention affects plasma burden of human immunodeficiency virus type 1. *Journal of Human Virology, 4, 44–54.*

Goodkin, K., Feaster, D. J., Asthana, D., Blaney, N. T., Kumar, M., Baldewicz, T., et al. (1998). A bereavement support group intervention is longitudinally associated with salutary effects on the CD4 cell count and number of physician visits. *Clinical and Diagnostic Laboratory Immunology, 5, 383–391.*

Goodkin, K., Feaster, D. J., Tuttle, R., Blaney, N. T., Kumar, M., Baum, M. K., et al. (1996). Bereavement is associated with time-dependent decrements in cellular immune function in asymptomatic human immunodeficiency virus type

1-seropositive homosexual men. *Clinical and Diagnostic Laboratory Immunology, 3*, 109–118.

Graham, N. M., Douglas, R. M., & Ryan, P. (1986). Stress and acute respiratory infection. *American Journal of Epidemiology, 124*, 389–401.

Hawkins, N. G., Davies, R., & Holmes, T. H. (1957). Evidence of psychosocial factors in the development of pulmonary tuberculosis. *American Review of Tuberculosis and Pulmonary Diseases, 75*, 768–780.

Haynes, R. B. (1976). A critical review of the "determinants" of patient compliance with therapeutic regimens. In D. L. Sackett & R. B. Haynes (Eds.), *Compliance with therapeutic regimens*. Baltimore: Johns Hopkins University Press.

Haynes, R. B., Taylor, D. W., & Sackett, D. L. (1979). *Compliance in health care*. Baltimore: Johns Hopkins University Press.

Herbert, T. B., & Cohen, S. (1993). Stress and immunity in humans: A meta-analytic review. *Psychosomatic Medicine, 55*, 364–379.

Ickovics, J. R., Hamburger, M. E., Valhov, D., Schoenbaum, E. E., Schuman, P., Boland, R. J., et al. (2001). Mortality, CD4 cell count decline, and depressive symptoms among HIV-seropositive women. *Journal of the American Medical Association, 285*, 1466–1474.

Ironson, G., Antoni, M., & Lutgendorf, S. (1995). Can psychological interventions affect immunity and survival? Present findings and suggested targets with a focus on cancer and human immunodeficiency virus. *Mind/Body Medicine, 1, 2*.

Ironson, G., Friedman, A., Klimas, N., Antoni, M., Fletcher, M. A., LaPerriere, A., et al. (1994). Distress, denial, and low adherence to behavioral interventions predict faster disease progression in gay men infected with human immunodeficiency virus. *International Journal of Behavioral Medicine, 1*, 90–105.

Ironson, G., Solomon, G., Balbin, E., O'Cleirigh, C., Stivers, M., Pavone, J., et al. (1998, March). *Characteristics of long term survivors of AIDS*. Paper presented at the annual meeting of the American Psychosomatic Society, Clearwater, FL.

Ironson, G., Solomon, G., Cruess, D., Barroso, J., & Stivers, M. (1995). Psychosocial factors related to long-term survival with HIV/AIDS. *Clinical Psychology and Psychotherapy, 2*, 249–266.

Jabaaij, L., van Hattum, J., Vingerhoets, J. J., Oostveen, F. G., Duivenvoorden, H. J., & Ballieux, R. E. (1996). Modulation of immune response to rDNA hepatitis B vaccination by psychological stress. *Journal of Psychosomatic Research, 41*, 129–137.

Kalichman, S. C., Kelly, J. A., Hunter, T. L., Murphy, D. A., & Tyler, R. (1993). Culturally tailored HIV-AIDS risk-reduction messages targeted to African American urban women: Impact on risk sensitization and risk reduction. *Journal of Consulting and Clinical Psychology, 61*, 291–295.

Kamb, M. L., Fishbein, M., Douglas, J. M., Rhodes, F., & Rogers, J. (1998). Efficacy of risk reduction counseling to prevent human immunodeficiency virus and sexually transmitted diseases: A randomized controlled trial. *Journal of the American Medical Association, 200,* 1161–1167.

Kaseje, D., Sempebwe, E., & Spencer, H. (1987). Community leadership and participation in the Saradidi, Kenya, Rural Health Development Programme. *Annals of Tropical Medicine and Parasitology* (Suppl. 81), 46–55.

Kasl, S. V., Evans, A. S., & Niederman, J. G. (1979). Psychosocial risk factors in the development of infectious mononucleosis. *Psychosomatic Medicine, 41,* 445–466.

Katcher, A. H., Brightman, V. J., Luborsky, L., & Ship, I. (1973). Prediction of the incidence of recurrent herpes labialis and systemic illness from psychological measures. *Journal of Dental Research, 52,* 49–58.

Kelly, J. A., & Murphy, D. A. (1992). Psychological interventions with AIDS and HIV: Prevention and treatment [Review]. *Journal of Consulting and Clinical Psychology, 60,* 576–585.

Kelly, J. A., Murphy, D. A., Sikkema, K. J., McAuliffe, T. L., Roffman, R. A., Solomon, L. J., et al. (1997). Randomized, controlled, community-level HIV-prevention intervention for sexual-risk behavior among homosexual men in U.S. cities. *Lancet, 350,* 1500–1505.

Kemeny, M. E., Cohen, F., Zegans, L. S., & Conant, M. A. (1989). Psychological and immunological predictors of genital herpes recurrence. *Psychosomatic Medicine, 51,* 195–208.

Kemeny, M. E., Duran, R., Taylor, S., Weiner, H., Visscher, B., & Fahey, J. (1990). *Chronic depression predicts CD4 decline over a five year period in HIV seropositive men.* Paper presented at the Sixth International Conference on AIDS, San Francisco, CA.

Kemeny, M. E., & Dean, L. (1995). Effects of AIDS-related bereavement on HIV progression among New York City gay men. *AIDS Education Prevention, 7*(Suppl.), 36–47.

Kemeny, M. E., Weiner, H., Taylor, S. E., Schneider, S., Visscher, B., & Fahey, J. L. (1994). Repeated bereavement, depressed mood, and immune parameters in HIV seropositive and seronegative gay men. *Health Psychology, 13,* 14–24.

Kessler, R. C., Foster, C., Joseph, J., Ostrow, J., & Chmiel, J. (1991). Stressful life events and symptom onset in HIV infection. *American Journal of Psychiatry, 148,* 733–738.

Kiecolt-Glaser, J. K., Fisher, L. D., Ogrocki, P., Stout, J. C., Speicher, C. E., & Glaser, R. (1987). Marital quality, marital disruption, and immune function. *Psychosomatic Medicine, 49,* 13–34.

Kiecolt-Glaser, J. K., Glaser, R., Shuttleworth, E. C., Kyer, C. S., Ogrocki, P., & Speicher, C. E. (1987). Chronic stress and immunity in family caregivers of Alzheimer's disease victims. *Psychosomatic Medicine, 49,* 523–535.

Kiecolt-Glaser, J. K., Kennedy, S., Malkoff, S., Fischer, L., Speicher, C. E., & Glaser, R. (1988). Marital discord and immunity in males. *Psychosomatic Medicine, 50,* 213–229.

Kline, A., & Strickler, J. (1993). Perceptions of risk for AIDS among women in drug treatment. *Health Psychology, 12,* 313–323.

Korsch, B. M., Freeman, B., & Negrete, V. F. (1971). Practical implications of doctor-patient interactions. Analysis for pediatric practice. *American Journal of Diseases of Children, 121,* 110–114.

Korsch, B. M., & Negrete, V. F. (1972). Doctor-patient communication. *Scientific American, 227,* 66–74.

Laudenslager, M. L., Rasmussen, K. L. R., Berman, C. M., Suomi, S. J., & Berger, C. B. (1993). Specific antibody levels in free-ranging rhesus monkeys: Relationships to plasma hormones, cardiac parameters, and early behavior. *Developmental Psychobiology, 26,* 407–420.

Lemanek, K. L. (1995). Commentary: Childhood asthma. Pediatric chronic disease [Special issue]. *Journal of Pediatric Psychology, 20,* 423–427.

Leserman, J., Jackson, E. D., Petitto, J. M., Golden, R. N., Silva, S. G., Perkins, D. O., et al. (1999). Progression to AIDS: The effects of stress, depressive symptoms, and social support. *Psychosomatic Medicine, 61,* 397–406.

Leserman, J., Petitto, J. M., Golden, R. N., Gaynes, B. N., Gu, H., Perkins, D. O., et al. (2000). Impact of stressful life events, depression, social support, coping, and cortisol on progression to AIDS. *American Journal of Psychiatry, 157,* 1221–1228.

Leventhal, H., & Cleary, P. D. (1980). The smoking problem: A review of the research and theory in behavioral risk modification. *Psychological Bulletin, 88,* 370–405.

Leventhal, H., Nerenz, D., & Leventhal, E. (1982). Feeling of threat and private views of illness: Factors in dehumanization in the medical care system. In A. Baum & J. E. Singer (Eds.), *Advances in environmental psychology* (Vol. 4). Hillsdale, NJ: Erlbaum.

Ley, P., Bradshaw, P. W., Kincey, J., & Atherton, S. T. (1976). Increasing patients' satisfaction with communication. *British Journal of Social and Clinical Psychology, 15,* 403–413.

Luborsky, L., Mintz, J., Brightman, V. J., & Katcher, A. H. (1976). Herpes simplex virus and moods: A longitudinal study. *Journal of Psychosomatic Research, 20,* 543–548.

Lutgendorf, S., Antoni, M., Ironson, G., Klimas, N., Kumar, N., Starr, K., et al. (1997). Cognitive behavioral stress management decreases dysphoric mood and herpes simplex virus Type-2 antibody titers in symptomatic HIV-seropositive gay men. *Journal of Consulting and Clinical Psychology, 65,* 31–43.

Lutgendorf, S. K., Antoni, M. H., Ironson, G., Starr, K., Costello, N., Zuckerman, M., et al. (1998). Changes in cognitive coping skills and social support during cognitive behavioral stress management intervention and distress outcomes in symptomatic human immunodeficiency virus (HIV)-seropositive gay men. *Psychosomatic Medicine, 60,* 204–214.

MacCormack, C. P., & Lwihula, G. (1983). Failure to participate in a malaria chemosuppression programme: North Mara, Tanzania. *Journal of Tropical Medicine and Hygiene, 86,* 99–107.

Malow, R., McPherson, S., Klimas, N., Antoni, M., Schneiderman, N., Penedo, F., et al. (1998). Adherence to complex combination antiretroviral therapies by HIV-positive drug abusers. *Psychiatric Services, 49,* 1021–1024.

Manne, S., & Sandler, I. (1984). Coping and adjustment to genital herpes. *Journal of Behavioral Medicine, 7,* 391–410.

Mayne, T. J., Vittinghoff, E., Chesney, M. A., Barrett, D. C., & Coates, T. J. (1996). Depressive affect and survival among gay and bisexual men infected with HIV. *Archives of Internal Medicine, 156,* 2233–2238.

McKeown, T. (1976). *The role of medicine: Dream, mirage or nemesis.* London: Nuffield Provincial Hospitals Trust.

McKinlay, J., & McKinlay, S. (1997). The questionable contribution of medical measures to the decline of mortality in the United States in the twentieth century. *Milbank Memorial Fund Quarterly, 55,* 405–428.

McKinnon, W., Weisse, C. S., Reynolds, C. P., Bowles, C. A., & Baum, A. (1989). Chronic stress, leukocyte subpopulations, and humoral response to latent viruses. *Health Psychology, 8,* 389–402.

McLarnon, L. D., & Kaloupek, D. G. (1988). Psychological investigation of genital herpes recurrence: Prospective assessment and cognitive-behavioral intervention for a chronic physical disorder. *Health Psychology, 7,* 231–249.

Meyer, R. J., & Haggerty, R. J. (1962). Streptococcal infections in families: Factors altering individual susceptibility. *Pediatrics, 29,* 539–549.

Miller, G. E., Kemeny, M. E., Taylor, S. E., Cole, S. W., & Visscher, B. R. (1997). Social relationships and immune processes in HIV seropositive gay and bisexual men. *Annals of Behavioral Medicine, 19,* 139–151.

Mohd, R. H. (1983). *Cultural factors in the epidemiology of filariasis due to* Brugia malayi *in an endemic community.* Final Report Project 810065, available from UNDP/World Bank/WHO Special Programme for Research and Training in Tropical Diseases, Geneva, pp. 137–149.

Morris, L. S., & Schulz, R. M. (1993). Medication compliance: The patient's perspective. *Clinical Therapeutics, 15,* 593–606.

Mulder, C. L., Antoni, M. H., Dulvenvoorden, H. J., Kauffmann, R. H., & Goodkin, K. (1995). Active confrontational coping predicts decreased clinical progression over a one-year period in HIV-infected homosexual men. *Journal of Psychosomatic Research, 39,* 957–965.

National Center for Health Statistics. (1999, August). *Monitoring the nation's health.* U.S. Department of Health and Human Services. Hyattsville, MD: CDC and National Center for Health Statistics.

O'Cleirigh, C. M., Ironson, G. H., Balbin, E. G., Ohata, J., Schneiderman, N., Fletcher, M. A., et al. (1999, April). *Emotional expression is associated with long-term survival of patients with AIDS.* Poster presented at the annual meeting of the Society of Behavioral Medicine, San Diego, CA.

O'Keefe, M. K., Nesselhof-Kenall, S., & Baum, A. (1990). Behavior and the prevention of AIDS: Bases of research and intervention. *Personality and Social Psychology Bulletin, 16,* 166–180.

Padgett, D. A., Sheridan, J. F., Dorne, J., Bernston, G. G., Candelora, J., & Glaser, R. (1998). Social stress and the reactivation of latent herpes simplex virus type 1. *Proceedings of the National Academy of Science, 95,* 7231–7235.

Pariante, C. M., Carpiniello, B., Orr'u, M. G., Sitzia, R., Piras, A., Farci, A. M., et al. (1997). Chronic caregiving stress alters peripheral blood immune-parameters: The role of age and severity of stress. *Psychotherapy and Psychosomatic, 66,* 199–207.

Patterson, T. L., Shaw, W. S., Semple, S. J., Cherner, M., McCutchan, J. A., Atkinson, J. H., et al. (1996). Relationship of psychosocial factors to HIV disease progression. *Annals of Behavioral Medicine, 18,* 30–39.

Petrie, K. J., Booth, R. J., Pennebaker, J. W., Davison, K. P., & Thomas, M. G. (1995). Disclosure of trauma and immune response to a hepatitis B vaccination program. *Journal of Consulting and Clinical Psychology, 63,* 787–792.

Prochaska, J. O., & DiClemente, C. C. (1984). *The transtheoretical approach: Crossing traditional boundaries of therapy.* Homewood, IL: Dow Jones Irwin.

Putnam, D. E. (1994). Enhancing commitment improves adherence to a medical regimen. *Journal of Consulting and Clinical Psychology, 62,* 191–194.

Rabin, B. S. (1999). *Stress immune function and health: The connection.* Pittsburgh, PA: Wiley-Liss.

Rabkin, J. G., Williams, J. B. W., Remien, R. H., Goetz, R., Kertzner, R., & Gorman, J. M. (1991). Depression, distress, lymphocyte subsets, and human immunodeficiency virus symptoms on two occasions in HIV-positive homosexual men. *Archives of General Psychiatry, 48,* 111–119.

Rahe, R. J., Meyer, M., Smith, M., Kjaer, G., & Holmes, T. H. (1964). Social stress and illness onset. *Journal of Psychosomatic Research, 8,* 35–44.

Rand, K., Hoon, E., Massey, J., & Johnson, J. (1990). Daily stress and recurrence of genital herpes simplex. *Archives of Internal Medicine, 150,* 1889–1993.

Reed, G. M., Kemeny, M. E., Taylor, S. E., & Visscher, B. R. (1999). Negative HIV-specific expectancies and AIDS-related bereavement as predictors of symptom onset in asymptomatic HIV-positive gay men. *Health Psychology, 18,* 354–363.

Reed, G. M., Kemeny, M. E., Taylor, S. E., Wang, H. J., & Visscher, B. R. (1994). Realistic acceptance as a predictor of decreased survival time in gay men with AIDS. *Health Psychology, 13,* 299–307.

Rinaldo, C. R. (1990). Immune suppression by herpes viruses. *Annual Review of Medicine, 41,* 331–338.

Rosenfield, P. L. (1990). Social determinants of tropical disease. In K. S. Warren & A. A. Mahmoud (Eds.), *Tropical and geographical medicine* (2nd ed.). New York: McGraw-Hill.

Rosenstock, I. M. (1974). The health belief model and preventive health behavior. *Health Education Monographs, 2,* 354–386.

Roter, D. L. (1984). Patient question asking in physician-patient interaction. *Health Psychology, 3*, 395–409.

Sawyer, D. R. (1986). Malaria on the Amazon frontier: Economic and social aspects of transmission and control. *Southeast Asian Journal of Tropical Medical Public Health, 17*, 342–345.

Schmader, K., George, L. K., Burchett, B. M., Hamilton, J. D., & Pieper, C. F. (1998). Race and stress in the incidence of herpes zoster in older adults. *Journal of the American Geriatric Society, 46*, 973–977.

Schmader, K., Studenski, S., MacMillan, J., Grufferman, S., & Cohen, H. J. (1990). Are stressful life events risk factors for herpes zoster? *Journal of the American Geriatric Society, 38*, 1188–1194.

Schmidt, D. D., Zyzanski, S., Ellner, J., Kumar, M. L., & Arnot, J. (1985). Stress as a precipitating factor in subjects with recurrent herpes labialis. *Journal of Family Practice, 20*, 359–366.

Schneider, P., & Cable, G. (1978). Compliance clinic: An opportunity for an expanded role for pharmacists. *American Journal of Hospital Pharmacy, 35*, 288–295.

Schneiderman, N. (1999). Behavioral medicine and the management of HIV/AIDS. *International Journal of Behavioral Medicine, 6*, 3–12.

Segerstrom, S. C., Taylor, S. E., Kemeny, M. E., Reed, G. M., & Visscher, B. R. (1996). Casual attributions predict rate of immune decline in HIV-seropositive gay men. *Health Psychology, 15*, 485–493.

Sendi, P. P., Bucher, H. C., Craig, B. A., Pfluger, D., & Battegay, M. (1999). Estimating AIDS-free survival in a severely immunosuppressed asymptomatic HIV-infected population in the era of antiretroviral triple combination therapy. *Journal of Acquired Immune Deficiency Syndromes and Human Retrovirology, 20*, 376–381.

Ship, I. I., Brightman, V. J., & Laster, L. L. (1967). The patient with herpes labialis: A study of two population samples. *Journal of the American Dental Association, 75*, 645–654.

Ship, I. I., Morris, A. L., Durocher, R. T., & Burket, L. W. (1960). Recurrent aphthous ulcerations and recurrent herpes labialis in a professional school student population. I. Experience. *Oral Surgery, 13*, 1191–1202.

Solano, L., Costa, M., Salvati, S., Coda, R., Aiuti, F., Mezzaroma, I., et al. (1993). Psychosocial factors and clinical evolution in HIV-1 infection: A longitudinal study. *Journal of Psychosomatic Research, 37*, 39–51.

Solomon, G., Temoshok, L., O'Leary, A., & Zich, J. (1987). An intensive psychoimmunologic study of long-surviving persons with AIDS. Pilot work, background studies, hypotheses, and methods. *Annals of the New York Academy of Sciences, 496*, 647–655.

Stone, A. A., Porter, L. S., & Neale, J. M. (1993). Daily events and mood prior to the onset of respiratory illness episodes: A non-replication of the 3–5 day "desirability dip." *British Journal of Medical Psychology, 66*, 383–393.

Strain, J. J. (1978). Noncompliance: Its origins, manifestations, and management. *The Pharos of Alpha Omega Alpha, 41*, 27–32.

Taylor, D. W., Sackett, D. L., & Haynes, R. B. (1978). Compliance with antihypertensive drug therapy. *Annals of the New York Academy of Science*, 390–403.

Taylor, S. E. (1990). Health psychology: The science and the field. *American Psychologist, 45*, 40–50.

Taylor, S. E., Kemeny, M. E., Aspinwall, L. G., & Reed, G. M. (1992). Optimism, coping, psychological distress, and high-risk sexual behavior among men at risk for acquired immunodeficiency syndrome (AIDS). *Journal of Personality and Social Psychology, 63*, 460–473.

Theorell, T., Blomkvist, V., Jonsson, H., Schulman, S., Berntorp, E., & Stigendal, L. (1995). Social support and the development of immune function in human immunodeficiency virus infection. *Psychosomatic Medicine, 57*, 32–36.

Toro, A. I., & Ossa, J. (1996). PCR activity of CMV in healthy CMV-seropositive individuals: Does latency need redefinition? *Research in Virology, 147*, 233–238.

Totman, R., Kiff, J., Reed, S. E., & Craig, J. W. (1980). Predicting experimental colds in volunteers from different measures of recent life stress. *Journal of Psychosomatic Research, 24*, 155–163.

Van Hove, G. F., Shapiro, J. M., Winters, M. A., Merigan, T. C., & Blaschke, T. F. (1996). Patient compliance and drug failure in protease inhibitor monotherapy. *Journal of the American Medical Association, 256*, 1955–1956.

VanderPlate, C., Aral, S. O., & Magder, L. (1988). The relationship among genital herpes simplex virus, stress, and social support. *Health Psychology, 7*, 159–168.

Vassend, O., Eskild, A., & Halvorsen, R. (1997). Negative affectivity, coping, immune status, and disease progression in HIV infected individuals. *Psychology and Health, 12*, 375–388.

Vedhara, K., Nott, K., Bradbeer, C., Davidson, E., Ong, E. L. C., Snow, M. H., et al. (1997). Greater emotional distress is associated with accelerated CD4$^+$ cell decline in HIV infection. *Journal of Psychosomatic Research, 42*, 379–390.

West-Edwards, C., Pereira, D., Greenwood, D., Antoni, M., & Schneiderman, N. (1997, August). *Stress management and relaxation training for HIV+ African-American women: Preliminary findings*. Paper presented at the annual meeting of the American Psychological Association, Chicago.

World Health Organization. (1999). *The World Health Report 1999: Making a difference*. Retrieved June 22, 1999, from www.who.int.

2

NEOPLASMS

BRENT N. HENDERSON AND ANDREW BAUM

Neoplasms comprise more than 100 types of cancer, each characterized by conditions in which somatic mutations accumulate and loosen restraints on cell proliferation. As a result, normal cells are altered and begin to grow uncontrollably, disrupting local tissue and often spreading to distant organ sites (Hanahan & Weinberg, 2000). These cancers contribute substantially to morbidity and mortality worldwide. In the United States, where cancer is the second leading cause of death (exceeded only by cardiovascular disease), there are more than a million new cancer diagnoses and over half a million cancer deaths each year (American Institute for Cancer Research, 1997). One in two American men will develop some form of cancer, the most common of which are prostate, lung, and colorectal. One in three American women will develop cancer, with breast, colorectal, and lung being the most common. Prognosis varies according to cancer type and severity. For men and women in the United States, lung cancer is the most common source of cancer mortality (American Cancer Society, 1994).

The overall burden of cancer increased dramatically during the 20th century, becoming more prominent as chronic diseases replaced infectious diseases as primary causes of death and disability in industrialized countries. Many factors were responsible for the increasing toll exacted by cancer.

With many traditional causes of premature mortality controlled, people lived longer and more people survived into adulthood. Cancer risk is strongly associated with age, and the aging population has contributed to growing cancer rates. Behavioral problems that are associated with cancer including obesity, sedentary lifestyles, tobacco use, and stress have increased or become more prominent. As the role of behavioral or psychosocial factors in cancer etiology became clearer, research on these issues has also increased. Growing effectiveness of early detection and cancer treatments has begun extending the survival of patients with cancer, making psychological adjustment and quality-of-life concerns more salient. In the past two decades, research into psychosocial and behavioral aspects of cancer has been sufficiently vigorous and productive to spawn a subspecialty of oncology, now known variously as *psychosocial oncology, biobehavioral oncology,* or *psycho-oncology.* This research has contributed to the understanding of the emotional, psychological, and social impact of cancer on patients and their families and has explored possible psychosocial and behavioral contributions to cancer risk and course.

This chapter summarizes this growing body of research, addressing the role of psychosocial or behavioral characteristics in the development of cancer or cancer course and survival. Evidence that psychosocial variables affect progression and recurrence of cancer has been more consistent than evidence about psychosocial influences on the slow development of cancer, but their impact may be greater than it seems. Furthermore, the effects of psychosocial interventions on disease outcomes are considered. The contribution of health psychology to understanding the psychosocial burden of cancer and how to best alleviate it is also discussed.

PSYCHOSOCIAL AND BEHAVIORAL FACTORS IN CANCER ETIOLOGY AND PREVENTION

Attempts to demonstrate relationships between psychosocial or behavioral factors and cancer incidence have been hampered by methodological difficulties common for research in this area. One such problem arises from variation in type or severity of cancer. As noted, cancer comprises more than 100 diseases, and tumors show considerable heterogeneity even within the subtypes. Because the predictability of disease course is associated with cancer type and severity, this heterogeneity adds variability to studies that do not control for it; adding such controls is expensive and often not feasible. For cancers that exhibit little deviation in patterns of disease progression, biological factors are thought to be sufficiently dominant to render psychosocial influences on disease course more or less negligible. Greater variability in prognosis may reflect psychosocial influences that affect vulnerability and resiliency, resulting in interactions among biological and psychosocial factors. Nevertheless, the role of psychosocial factors in cancer morbidity or mortality varies according to cancer site, type, and severity and according to personal risk factors such as age and family history, making it difficult or impossible to generalize about psychosocial contributions to the general set of diseases known as *cancer*.

Another important disease-related problem that makes research in this area difficult is the "silence" of the disease as it develops over a long time. Cancer involves many mutations and slow growth of neoplastic tissue. Consequently, it may be present for several years before it can be detected. Scientists are unable to pinpoint when a patient's neoplastic development began, when it reached critical stages of development, or even whether it is in its early stages. This problem adds further imprecision to reported temporal associations between disease onset and psychosocial events or states. Other methodological limitations have included failure to appropriately control for potential confounding variables such as smoking or diet, lack of or inappropriate use of control groups, lack of standardization of psychosocial measures, difficulties measuring possible interactions among the various psychosocial variables that are commonly measured, and difficulties assessing or controlling for interactions between psychosocial variables and biomedical risk factors. Such limitations have contributed to the lack of consistency in findings regarding the nature, strength, and significance of possible associations between psychosocial factors and cancer risk and outcomes.

The search to identify psychosocial variables that are associated with the risk of developing cancer has focused mainly on patients with breast cancer. One reason for this disproportionate emphasis is that breast cancer is a relatively common type of cancer that tends to exhibit a relatively large variance in course. Another reason is that breast cancer is known to be influenced by hormonal factors, which suggests a plausible pathway through which emotions could influence disease-relevant biological characteristics. Funding and sociopolitical issues have also increased the prominence of breast cancer as a psychosocial research target. As a consequence, our knowledge of psychosocial contributions to cancer onset is largely knowledge about how these variables affect the development of breast cancer. Personality, coping, social support, stress, and adjustment are among the most frequently studied influences on cancer development.

Personality

Anecdotal reports and some early evidence have suggested a possible relationship between personality styles and incidence of cancer. In a series of studies in England (e.g., Morris, Greer, Pettingale, & Watson, 1981), researchers found an association between diagnosis of breast cancer and a reported tendency to suppress or inhibit expression of anger and other emotions. These and other preliminary findings led to the conceptualization of a "cancer-prone," or "Type C," personality, described as cooperative, appeasing, unassertive, compliant, and unexpressive of anger and other negative emotions (e.g., Temoshok, 1987). In a meta-analysis, McKenna, Zevon, Corn, and Rounds (1999) concluded that individuals with a conflict-avoidant personality style were at significantly increased risk for breast cancer, although the small effect size warranted cautious interpretation of this finding. However, a lack of well-designed prospective studies that support a relationship between personality and cancer risk, combined with the presence of contradictory and negative findings (e.g., Persky, Kempthorne-Rawson, & Shekelle, 1987) and the small effect size in the meta-analysis, make it difficult to conclude that personality plays a significant role in the development of cancer.

Social Support

Although a great deal of interest has surrounded social factors related to cancer, unique methodological barriers have limited this effort. Social support is a multidimensional concept, and the way it has historically been operationalized and measured varies substantially (O'Reilly, 1988). This inconsistency has made it more difficult to draw conclusions about what specific aspects of the social environment may have health benefits. One important distinction is between structural and functional aspects of social support (Helgeson, Cohen, & Fritz, 1998). Structural components can include the size of a person's support network, the extent of a person's social integration, and marital status. Functional components refer to perceived availability of support or receipt of support, which is often further broken into emotional, informational, and instrumental forms. In addition to the conceptual value in making such distinctions, differences in type and source of support are relevant because different types of social support may be beneficial for different individuals or in different situations (Smith, Fernegel, Holcroft, Gerald, & Marien, 1994). These forms of social support may also convey variable benefits for different health outcomes (Ren, Skinner, Lee, & Kazis, 1999).

Despite the pervasive influence and general health benefits of social support (e.g., House, Landis, & Umberson, 1988), evidence has not supported a strong protective effect of social support on cancer development (Fox, 1998). Prospective studies (e.g., Reynolds & Kaplan, 1990; Vogt, Mullooly, Ernst, Pope, & Hollis, 1992) have not found consistent evidence of relationships between various social support dimensions and cancer incidence, although some suggestive relationships have been reported. For example, Reynolds and Kaplan (1990) studied more than 6,000 people for 17 years and found no association between social support and cancer incidence among men. However, isolation among women was associated with greater cancer incidence. Similarly, medical students in a cohort monitored for 24 years after graduation who developed cancer reported less closeness to parents at the start of the study (Thomas, Duszynski, & Schaffer, 1979). However, in general the data reflecting social support contributions to cancer onset are neither strong nor conclusive.

Stress

The relationship between stressful life events and the development of cancer is another area that has received considerable research attention but for which results have been equivocal. For example, Geyer (1993) interviewed 92 women with a suspicious breast lump and found that those who were later diagnosed with cancer were significantly more likely to have experienced severe stressors than were women with benign disease. However, other studies have failed to confirm this relationship, including one that used a national record-keeping database to compare more than 1,500 women with breast cancer to women of the same age without cancer (Ewertz, 1986). Loss of one's spouse by death or divorce in the 15-year period before diagnosis was not associated with increased breast cancer risk. Some studies that have reported significant associations between stressful events and cancer diagnoses used inappropriately brief reporting periods such as 5 years, which fails to capture the context for stress effects because this process may require considerably more time to unfold. In their meta-analysis, McKenna et al. (1999) concluded that a small but significant relationship exists between stressful life events and breast cancer risk, noting that well-designed prospective studies are needed to clarify this possible relationship. Identification and testing of possible pathways are also needed.

Depression

Studies of adjustment or mental health effects on cancer development have largely focused on depression, although some attention has been paid to schizophrenia and comorbid disorders. Meta-analytical reviews of this literature have found that depression is a marginally significant or an insignificant risk factor for cancer (McGee, Williams, & Elwood, 1994; McKenna et al., 1999). However, two prospective cohort studies provided stronger support for this relationship. In a study involving approximately 5,000 people, depression that lasted for at least 6 years was a significant independent risk factor for the development of cancer among those older than age 71 (Penninx et al., 1998). Similarly, in a cohort of approximately 3,000 women and men, those who experienced major depression had a significantly increased risk of developing breast and prostate cancer during the next 13 years (Gallo, Armenian, Ford, & Eaton, 2000).

As discussed, a meta-analysis suggested that a modest relationship may exist between the development of breast cancer and denial or repressive coping, separation or loss experiences, and stressful life events (McKenna et al., 1999). However, the relatively small effect sizes suggested that these psychosocial factors at best play a secondary role to biological factors in the development of breast cancer. Alternatively, it may not be possible to detect the relationships that could demonstrate links between psychosocial variables and cancer development. Until biomarkers of early disease are identified or other intermediate, nondisease variables can be measured, definitive answers to questions like this one may not be readily addressed. Further research is needed to clarify whether psychosocial factors such as personality, coping, depressed mood, stress, or social support have an impact on the development of breast cancer or other types of cancer.

Tobacco Use

Research has identified several behavioral factors that play a clearer role in increasing cancer risk. Tobacco use is the single largest cause of preventable premature death and illness in industrialized nations. In the United States, approximately 450,000 people die each year from tobacco-related diseases (McGinnis & Foege, 1999). Behavioral medicine and health psychology research have helped in the understanding of some of the psychological, behavioral, social, and biological factors that contribute to the initiation, maintenance, and relapse of cigarette-smoking behavior (e.g., Ockene et al., 2000). Modeling, social reinforcement, perceived cigarette availability, cost, and mental health all contribute to the initiation of smoking behavior, whereas maintenance of the behavior is largely a result of the addictive properties of nicotine (Gamberino & Gold, 1999) and biobehavioral factors related to continued use. Biological processes alone cannot explain the difficulties and failure rates of smoking cessation programs. Hiatt and Rimer (1999), adapting a more general biobehavioral model of health outcomes developed by Anderson (1998), proposed a biobehavioral framework for understanding the interaction of psychosocial and behavioral factors with genetic vulnerabilities to cause tobacco use, nicotine addiction, and cancer.

Diet and Other Behavior-Related Factors

Certain diets also increase the risk of some cancers (e.g., Willett, 1996). Epidemiological evidence has shown that diets low in fruits and vegetables are associated with greater risk for several types of cancers (Potter & Steinmetz, 1996). Laboratory research has investigated mechanisms that might mediate this relationship, suggesting that constituents of fruits and vegetables, including vitamins, fiber, and phytochemicals, may inhibit cancer initiation, promotion, progression, or all of these (Kelloff et al.,

1996). At the same time, constituents of meat or meat products, including animal fat, seem to contribute to certain cancers (Guthrie & Carroll, 1999). When a greater quantity of plant-based food is consumed, less meat is often consumed, changing dietary balance. Many people do not eat sufficient quantities of food derived from plants to establish optimally protective levels of key nutrients and may have an increased cancer risk as a result (American Institute for Cancer Research, 1997).

Dietary behaviors may also contribute to cancer risk by contributing to excess caloric intake relative to expenditure. Although more research is needed to clarify the relationship between obesity and cancer risk, obesity may promote breast cancer because of the effects of adipose tissue on epithelial cell growth (Guthrie & Carroll, 1999) or on the production of estrogen among postmenopausal women (Mezzetti et al., 1998). Obesity has also been associated with an increased risk of colon, endometrial, and gall bladder cancer (Ford, 1999; Pi-Sunyer, 1998). In addition, exercise may have independent protective effects associated with certain cancers (Longnecker, Gerhardsson le Verdier, Frumkin, & Carpenter, 1995; Thune, Brenn, Lund, & Gaard, 1997).

Sun exposure is another behavior-related factor that is known to increase cancer risk (Baum & Cohen, 1998). Basal-cell and squamous-cell skin cancers are associated with cumulative sun exposure, whereas melanomas are more strongly associated with infrequent, periodic sunburns. The effects of sun exposure depend on skin type and use of sunscreen, but the majority of skin cancers could be prevented by regular sunscreen use or other types of sun exposure management.

Together, these and other health-related behaviors may interact to significantly influence cancer risk. Stress may play an important role in many of these behaviors. Stress can alter cognitive functioning, mood, problem-solving ability, social relationships, task performance, attention, and quality of life, all of which can potentially influence health-related decisions or behaviors (Baum & Posluszny, 1999). The role of other psychosocial factors in contributing to cancer-related behaviors has also been studied. Psychosocial and sociodemographic characteristics are associated with significant variance in dietary behavior (De Castro, 1996; Messer, 1984), substance use (Ockene et al., 2000), exercise (Dishman, 1990; Owen & Vita, 1997), and immune processes (Cohen & Herbert, 1996) in ways that may be relevant for cancer risk. Consequently, psychosocial factors comprise the basis of prominent models of health behaviors (e.g., Conner & Norman, 1996).

The field of behavior genetics provides another important level of analysis in understanding behavioral contributions to cancer risk. For example, individual genetic differences seem to contribute to variance in diet and activity patterns (Faith, Johnson, & Allison, 1997; Reed, Bachmanov, Bauchamp, Tordoff, & Price, 1997), resting energy expenditure (Goran,

1997), and substance use (Heath & Madden, 1995) in ways that might influence cancer risk. Moreover, evolutionary theory may provide insight into the ultimate causes of genetically based biobehavioral disease vulnerabilities. Biobehavioral contributions to disease may reflect costs or by-products of adaptive systems, consequences of contact with an evolutionarily novel environment, or both (Henderson, Forlenza, & Baum, 2002).

Prevention

Although not a strong link, evidence has suggested that psychosocial variables contribute to cancer risk, and behaviors such as tobacco use and diet clearly affect this risk. One of the reasons this is so important is that unlike some risk factors, most psychosocial or behavioral contributors are modifiable and can be altered so that their contribution to overall cancer risk is reduced. Not surprisingly, many current cancer prevention strategies are based on epidemiological and surveillance research that point to particular behavioral contributions to cancer risk (Hiatt & Rimer, 1999). Considerable effort has been directed toward the reduction of morbidity (and mortality) through reducing or preventing such behaviors. Primary prevention efforts aim to reduce cancer morbidity by reducing exposure to carcinogenic foods, tobacco, and sun exposure. By removing these sources of disease risk, a person can reduce the likelihood that cancer will develop.

However, these changes are not easily achieved. Many of the behaviors that contribute to cancer risk are pleasurable or highly reinforcing. Because their contribution to cancer is slow and gradual, it may be difficult for people to give up these behaviors. Significant behavior changes are difficult to sustain, particularly when target behaviors are rewarding. Consistent with this idea, research has indicated that eliciting and maintaining health-promoting behavioral changes in diet is very challenging (Barnard, Akhtar, & Nicholson, 1995), although various nutrition education and behavioral counseling strategies have shown some promise (for a review, see Kumanyika et al., 2000). Reductions in sun exposure have also been difficult to achieve or document (Baum & Cohen, 1998). Likewise, efforts to curtail or prevent tobacco use (e.g., Ockene et al., 2000) and maintain long-term weight reductions (Jeffrey et al., 2000) have been met with mostly limited success. Public recognition that smoking is a behavioral risk factor for cancer in conjunction with public health and legislative efforts to curtail use has been associated with a significant decrease in smoking prevalence in the United States—from 45% in 1964 to less than 25% in 1995 (Centers for Disease Control and Prevention, 1997). However, obesity increased during this same period (Flegal, Carroll, Kuczmarski, & Johnson, 1998). Reductions in smoking have undoubtedly contributed to reductions in smoking-related cancer mortality, but more research is needed to develop individual, population, and macrolevel strategies to further reduce tobacco use (Orleans, 2000). Similarly, topics such as weight management, diet, and exercise should also be national research priorities.

PSYCHOSOCIAL AND BEHAVIORAL FACTORS IN CANCER PROGRESSION AND INTERVENTION

In contrast to the equivocal nature of data relating psychosocial variables to the initial development of cancer, much better evidence exists for psychosocial influences on cancer course. The same categories of variables have been studied in cancer progression investigations as are considered in studies of cancer etiology. The data may offer clearer evidence of psychosocial modulation of disease for several reasons. To some extent, the distinction between cancer onset and progression is arbitrary because it is not conceptually clear where initiation of cancer ends and promotion or progression of the disease begins. Traditionally, studies of cancer incidence have ended at the diagnosis and cover a large, diffuse, and hard-to-measure period of time preceding the identification of the disease. Studies of cancer course or progression have considered a more carefully documented period of time and have involved participants who can provide prospective data. It is possible that the clearer evidence of psychosocial influence on disease after diagnosis reflects the methodological advantages of studying this phase of the disease rather than more substantive differences.

Personality

Evidence has suggested that some personality or coping styles contribute to cancer progression or mortality. Greer, Morris, and Pettingale (1979) assessed psychological responses to breast cancer 3 months following initial surgical treatment for their breast cancer. Patients whose psychological responses were characterized by denial had a decreased recurrence-free disease survival rate 5 years later. In a prospective study among patients with breast cancer, Jensen (1987) found an association between a repressive personality style and metastases and death from breast cancer. In a prospective study involving patients with metastatic breast cancer, Derogatis, Abeloff, and Melisaratos (1979) found that patients who reported or communicated fewer negative feelings had a relatively shorter survival time. Other prospective studies examining related concepts such as avoidance (Epping-Jordan, Compas, & Howell, 1994) or reserved personalities (Stavraky, Donner, Kincade, & Stewart, 1988) provided further support for the notion that an avoidant, repressive, or unexpressive personality, coping style, or both is associated with poor disease course.

Social Support

Social support has been associated with longer survival or decreased disease recurrence in several studies of cancer. Maunsell, Brisson, and Deschenes (1995) found that the number of confidants with whom patients had discussed personal problems in the three months following the initial treatment was positively associated with survival among patients with metastatic breast cancer. In a large prospective cohort study, Reynolds and Kaplan (1990) found that women with the fewest social connections were at highest risk for cancer-related mortality. In a prospective study involving patients younger than age 55 with breast cancer, Waxler-Morrison, Hislop, Mears, and Kan (1991) found that more contact and support from friends and a higher number of supportive persons were significantly and positively associated with survival. Similarly, a higher degree of perceived emotional support from close relationships was associated with increased survival for patients with early-stage breast cancer (Ell, Nishomoto, Mediansky, Mantell, & Hamovitch, 1992). These and other studies form the basis of a growing literature and comprehensive reviews that conclude that degree of social support, quality of social support, or both affects cancer survival (Fox, 1998; Spiegel, Sephton, Terr, & Stites, 1998).

Not all studies, however, have found significant relationships between social support and cancer progression (e.g., Barraclough et al., 1992). The relationships that do exist likely vary according to disease type or severity. For example, Cassileth, Lusk, Strouse, et al. (1985) did not find relationships between various indexes of social support and survival among patients with Stage II breast cancer; intervention studies have found different effects of social support on various stages of disease as well (e.g., Helgeson, Cohen, Schulz, & Yasko, 1999). Although substantial evidence has suggested that social support is positively related to better cancer outcomes, further research is needed to confirm and clarify this relationship.

Stress

Stressful life events and perceived stress have also been associated with cancer progression (Funch & Marshall, 1983; Ramirez et al., 1989). For example, Ramirez and colleagues compared patients who had a breast cancer recurrence with patients who remained in remission. After matching the patients for prognostic pathological variables, the recurrence group was significantly more likely than the remission group to have experienced severe stressors such as a divorce or family member's death since initial treatment. However, other studies have not reported a significant relationship between stress and cancer progression (e.g., Barraclough et al., 1992). It may be that the influence of personality, coping styles, social support, or other potential stress-buffering factors (e.g., Smith et al., 1994) are more relevant than the actual stressful life events. Prospective studies of cancer-related stress and its interaction with other stressors are needed to isolate stress effects on disease course and to evaluate potential pathways by which these effects are conveyed. Evidence from psychosocial interventions that include stress management has also supported this relationship and the need for more research.

Depression

The majority of studies that have examined the role of distress or depression in cancer progression have not found significant associations (Wulsin, Valiant, & Wells, 1999). Methodological difficulties in these studies often include distinguishing between preexisting depression and depression that occurs either in response to the disease or as a side effect of cancer treatment. Nevertheless, better quality of life has predicted increased survival among patients with metastatic melanoma (Butow, Coates, & Dunn, 1999), suggesting that overall adjustment may contribute to survival.

Interventions and Early Detection

The notion that psychosocial factors may have the capacity to influence cancer course has led to the development and implementation of psychotherapeutic interventions aimed at increasing survival, adjustment, and quality of life by altering the psychological, emotional, and social milieu of patients with cancer. Interest in the possibility of extending cancer survival by group psychosocial intervention was heightened by a controversial study by Spiegel, Bloom, Kraemer, and Gottheil (1989) in which patients with metastatic breast cancer who received weekly group therapy for 1 year survived nearly twice as long as routine-care controls (36.6 months vs. 18.9 months). Fawzy and colleagues (1993) provided empirical support for this possibility as well, finding that a more time-limited structured psychosocial intervention was associated with longer survival among patients with malignant melanoma. Other studies suggested that these interventions increase aspects of immune system activity, quality of life, psychological adjustment, and overall well-being (Baum & Andersen, 2001). Whether they cost-effectively extend survival or delay relapse, these interventions clearly improve adjustment and quality of life and therefore contribute to enhanced well-being.

Intervention studies represent the most compelling evidence that psychosocial factors influence the course of cancer. However, in the absence of extensive and systematic replication of these findings, definitive conclusions about the value of psychosocial interventions and their capacity to extend survival cannot be yet drawn. Moreover, numerous studies have found no effect of psychosocial interventions on survival or disease course (e.g., Gellert, Maxwell, & Siegel, 1993; Goodwin et al., 2001; Ilnyckyj, Farber, Cheang, & Weinerman, 1994). Whether psychosocial interventions can reliably extend survival among patients with cancer currently remains open. Future research must consider that psychosocial effects will likely vary according to disease variables such as cancer type and severity and treatment variables such as modality and duration.

Early detection is clearly associated with better disease outcomes. Early detection increases the likelihood that treatment will begin in earlier stages, which increases the likelihood of successful treatment. Health psychologists have attempted to understand and harness factors that contribute to early detection behaviors, including adherence to surveillance regimens, and thus are joining other behavioral scientists who have studied this key public health variable for years.

The Health Belief Model (Janz & Becker, 1984; Rosenstock, 1974) has guided much of the research concerning possible psychosocial contributions to cancer screening practices. This model proposed that the combination of perceived disease susceptibility, perceived disease severity, perceived barriers to screening, perceived benefits to screening, and environmental signals to participate predict screening behavior. This model has been supported in numerous studies. Increased knowledge about the severity of cancer and the benefits of screening practices has been associated with better screening practices for various cancer types, including breast, prostate, colorectal, and cervical cancers (for a review, see DiPlacido, Zauber, & Redd, 1998). Perceived barriers to screening have also been reported and can be economic, logistic, or psychological (e.g., Rimer, Trock, Engstrom, Lerman, & King, 1991). A particular feature of cancer, namely its often asymptomatic nature, also seems to contribute to lack of optimal use of screening practices (e.g., Hart, Wicks, & Mayberry, 1995). Research involving high-risk populations, including women with a family history of breast cancer, has suggested that increased worry or anxiety associated with overestimated risk may be another barrier to screening behavior (Lerman, Kash, & Stefanek, 1994). Low socioeconomic status, advanced age, and poor linkages with the health care system have also been associated with infrequent secondary prevention practices (Rimer, 1992).

Other theoretical models for predicting and improving cancer screening practices have also been developed (for a review, see Curry & Emmons, 1994). Early detection of breast cancer can be achieved by increasing the use of mammography, clinical breast examinations, and self-examinations. Similar screening procedures are useful in detecting early stages of other cancers, and as biomarkers of early disease are developed, this effort may continue to increase. Since the advent of genetic screening techniques, researchers have begun to explore psychosocial effects or predictors of genetic testing practices (e.g., Baum, Friedman, & Zakowski, 1997). However, optimal use of these early detection tools requires that people use them, adhere to screening regimens, and respond appropriately to cancer risk evaluations; to a large extent this involves more effective behavior management.

Tertiary prevention includes reducing the delay between the recognition of disease symptoms and the initiation of medical help. This interval is relevant because the longer its duration, the more advanced the disease is likely to be before treatment is begun and the lower the chance is that treatment will be effective. Andersen and Cacioppo (1995) developed a model of patient delay that includes five stages: appraising symptoms, inferring illness, deciding to seek medical attention, scheduling an appointment, and treatment delay intervals. Each stage is believed to be governed by unique appraisal and decisional processes. Delay surrounding symptom interpretation accounts for most of the overall delay in beginning treatment. The complex, sometimes unpredictable dynamic symptom profile of many cancers, combined with their relatively low rate of occurrence (in comparison to other diseases), is believed to account for much of the delay in disease appraisal.

PATHWAYS LINKING PSYCHOSOCIAL AND BEHAVIORAL VARIABLES TO DISEASE

Until this point in the chapter, the discussion has focused on relating psychosocial and behavioral factors to cancer morbidity and mortality. Although these relationships are not firmly established, research has nevertheless explored possible underlying mechanisms. At least three general pathways through which psychosocial or behavioral factors may influence the development or progression of cancer have been identified: (a) direct effects of psychological processes on bodily systems, such as the nervous system, endocrine system, or immune system; (b) health-enhancing or health-impairing behaviors, such as diet, exercise, or smoking; and (c) responses to perceived or actual illness, such as screening behaviors or adherence with treatment recommendations. The latter two of these pathways are ultimately behavioral and were described in the previous section. The first of these pathways is considerably more complex, involving interactions among domains that have often been assumed to be separate. Study of the effects of psychosocial variables on physiological and biological processes comprises much of the basic research in biobehavioral oncology and warrants further discussion.

Neuroimmune and Neuroendocrine Pathways

Research has demonstrated that immune system activity can be influenced by various psychosocial and behavioral processes. Alterations in immune function have been associated with poor social support, loneliness, negative mood, disruption of marital relationships, bereavement, and various other types of stress (for a review, see Cohen & Herbert, 1996). Human and animal studies have demonstrated that the endocrine and central nervous systems (CNS) contain pathways through which psychosocial factors can affect immunity (Ader, Felten, & Cohen, 1991). The CNS has direct connections with the immune system through sympathetic innervation of various immune system components, including lymph nodes, the thymus, the spleen, and bone marrow (Maier, Watkins, & Fleshner, 1994). Neuroendocrine pathways may influence immunity through two primary systems: the sympathetic–adrenal–medullary (SAM) system and the hypothalamic–pituitary–adrenal–cortical (HPAC) system. Catecholamines released during SAM activity can influence immune activity, as can glucocorticoids involved in HPAC activity.

The ability of psychosocial factors to influence immune function by way of nervous and endocrine system alterations is fairly well established. On the other hand, the relevance of these immune changes for cancer onset or progression is not clear, particularly with respect to nonviral cancers (Brittenden, Heys, Ross, & Eremin, 1996). Although the clinical implications of stress-related immune changes have not been established, some stress-related immune changes have theoretical relevance for cancer incidence or progression (Andersen, Kiecolt-Glaser, & Glaser, 1994; Spiegel et al., 1998). Much research in this area has focused on alterations in natural killer cells, which may in some cases play an immunosurveillance role with respect to cancer (Whiteside & Herberman, 1995). In vitro, natural killer cells have been shown to lyse allogenic tumor cells without prior sensitization (Brittenden et al., 1996). It has been widely suggested that this might represent a mechanism by which psychosocial factors affect the development of new tumors or the growth of previously dormant or subclinical metastases (e.g., Spiegel et al., 1998). Stress has been associated with compromised natural killer activity (Herbert & Cohen, 1993), whereas social support has been linked to favorable natural killer activity (e.g., Levy et al., 1990). Changes in natural killer activity or other aspects of immune function thus represent one plausible biobehavioral pathway through which psychosocial factors may influence the development or progression of cancer.

Despite enthusiasm for the importance of immunosurveillance in control of cancer development or progression, some lines of evidence have called into question the relevance of this pathway (e.g., Somers & Guillou, 1994). Currently, the significance of immune surveillance seems most plausible with respect to the control of metastases or growth of nonsolid tumors (e.g., Garssen & Goodkin, 1999; Whiteside & Herberman, 1995). In any case, researchers are increasingly considering biological mechanisms that might mediate existing psychosocial effects on cancer (e.g., Forlenza & Baum, 2000).

DNA Damage and Repair

The impact of stress on deoxyribonucleic acid (DNA) damage and repair has been suggested as another biobehavioral pathway through which psychosocial factors might influence the development or progression of cancer (Pettingale, 1985). When DNA within human cells is damaged through either normal metabolic processes or exogenous factors, autonomous DNA repair mechanisms normally correct these abnormalities, curtailing the process of carcinogenesis by preventing the development of mutations. Research has suggested that stress may impair the body's ability to carry out these restorative functions (Kiecolt-Glaser et al., 1985). Alternatively, stress has also been associated with increased repair activity, implying that stress perhaps increases DNA damage, thus activating greater repair activity (Forlenza & Baum, 2000). Researchers are currently exploring whether these mechanisms influence cancer incidence or progression.

ADJUSTMENT TO CANCER

The experience of being diagnosed and treated for cancer is considered a major stressor, with potentially deleterious effects on psychological, emotional, family, social, and occupational aspects of patients' lives (e.g., Baum & Posluszny, 2001). A substantial body of research has documented the quality and severity of adjustment problems that often accompany a cancer diagnosis.

Impact of a Life Threat

Psychological responses of patients with cancer tend to resemble those of patients diagnosed with other life-threatening diseases (Casileth, Lusk, Miller, Brown, & Cross, 1985; Garofalo, 2000). The immediate psychological effects of a cancer diagnosis often include disbelief, shock, and emotional trauma (Weisman & Worden, 1976). Patients may report depression, hopelessness, anxiety, fear, anger, and rumination after receiving a cancer diagnosis (Meyerowitz, 1980). Rates of depression or depressed mood after receiving a cancer diagnosis have been estimated to range from approximately 15% to 25% (e.g., Massie & Holland, 1990). It is not clear how much of this distress represents long-term psychopathology and how much is more transient and characteristic of adjustment disorders. Consistent with this idea, a meta-analysis of 58 studies found no significant differences in major psychiatric morbidity between patients with cancer and the general population and concluded that patients with cancer more frequently exhibit subclinical depressive syndromes consistent with a diagnosis of adjustment disorder (Van't Spijker, Trijsburg, & Duivenvoorden, 1997).

Qualitative reviews have also concluded that many patients with cancer experience significant mood difficulties related to their disease, notably feelings of depression (e.g., McDaniel, Musselman, & Nemeroff, 1998). Some research has suggested that such disease-related mood difficulties are associated with intrusive thoughts related to illness and death, contributing to poor coping and negative expectations (Brewin, Watson, McCarthy, Hyman, & Dayson, 1998). However, with notable exceptions (e.g., Thompson & Shear, 1998), the distress reported by patients newly diagnosed with cancer generally seems manageable and declines over the course of their treatment and recovery, although broader psychosocial effects can linger for many years (e.g., Gotay & Muraoka, 1998).

Impact of Patient and Medical Factors

Various patient-related and medical factors seem to contribute to the severity of the emotional and psychological effects of cancer. Personal factors play a role. The type and degree of disruption in life-cycle tasks caused by cancer (e.g., marital, occupational, sexual, childbearing) varies according to the age and gender of the patient when the diagnosis occurs, which in turn affects the type and degree of threat or interruption to social and family-related tasks. For example, for women with breast cancer, threats to femininity, self-esteem, and sexuality may occur regardless of age but may be especially salient for younger women for whom attractiveness and reproductive potential may be of greater immediate psychological importance (Rowland & Massie, 1998). Premorbid psychological or psychiatric functioning, including a history of mental illness and an ability to cope with stress, are also important factors. Significant stressors such as cancer can trigger a psychiatric relapse in patients with a history of mood or adjustment disorders (Ganz, 1990). In addition, patients with other previous or concurrent stressors tend to have higher levels of distress (Maunsell, Brisson, & Deschenes, 1992). With respect to coping styles, some research has indicated that patients who use active, problem-solving coping strategies adjust better to cancer (e.g., Taylor et al., 1985), whereas those patients who use avoidant coping strategies fare more poorly (e.g., Bloom, 1982). Finally, the influence of social comparison (Gibbons, 1999) may be an important personal determinant of adjustment among patients with cancer. Van der Zee, Oldersma, Buunk, & Bos (1998) have shown that the emotional experience of some patients with cancer can be altered by how they compare themselves to their peers.

Medical and disease-related factors also contribute to the degree of distress experienced by patients, primarily because they affect the extent to which the diagnosis is perceived as life threatening, the type and extent of treatment that will follow, and the degree of physical disruption or impairment that will result from the disease and treatment (Holland, 1998). Cancer site, severity of disease, extent of spread, prognosis, and treatment options all affect the emotional and psychological impact of cancer. For example, patients who have had mastectomies reported greater distress related to body image and sexuality than patients receiving breast-conserving treatments such as lumpectomies (Margolis, Goodman, & Rubin, 1990). Cancers with a relatively good prognosis, including breast and gynecological cancers, have been associated with less psychological distress than have cancers with poorer prognoses or more severe treatments such as lung cancer or head and neck cancer (e.g., Sneed, Edlund, & Dias, 1992). Degree and quality of social support are also important factors. Patients with cancer who perceive that they have adequate support consistently show better adjustment than those who do not (e.g., Andersen, 1994; Funch & Mettlin, 1982). Medical staff members can also be an important source of support and a primary source for opportunities for discussing cancer-related issues (Henderson, Davison, Pennebaker, Gatchel, & Baum, in press).

Interventions

In light of evidence showing that psychosocial variables affect psychological and emotional adjustment to cancer, numerous interventions have been designed to promote better outcomes (Andersen, 1992). Many treatment approaches have been used, although controlled studies have typically relied on either cognitive–behavioral approaches or supportive–expressive group therapy. The first of these interventions is typically brief and includes relaxation training, stress management skills training, and problem-solving training. Supportive–expressive group formats are designed to promote the development of supportive relationships among group members, encourage expression of patients' feelings or anxieties that are related to their disease (including issues related to death and loss), and attempt to build meaning in the face of the disease. A meta-analysis of psychosocial interventions with adult patients with cancer, which included these approaches as well as basic informational and educational interventions and less standard techniques, indicated that psychosocial interventions are associated with small but significant positive effects on emotional adjustment, functional adjustment, and treatment- and disease-related symptoms (Meyer & Mark, 1995). Outcomes did not differ by treatment modality, although the authors acknowledged that their analysis was limited in its ability to detect such differences.

Research has also examined the connections between psychological and physiological variables in patients with cancer who are experiencing treatment-related pain, nausea, and sexual and neuropsychological impairments (for a review, see Redd et al., 1991). Psychological interventions have been developed with the aim of providing relief from such problems. A review of this literature indicates that some of these strategies, including progressive muscle relaxation and guided imagery, have been associated with significant reductions in the physical and psychological side effects of chemotherapy (Chambless & Hollon, 1998). Strategies aimed at reducing procedure-related pain among children and adolescents with cancer, particularly those with leukemia or lymphoma who are undergoing bone marrow aspirations and lumbar puncture procedures, have also been shown to be effective (for a review, see Powers, 1999). Cognitive–behavioral techniques, including relaxation, distraction, imagery, modeling, reinforcement and incentive, behavioral rehearsal, and other coping strategies result in consistent reductions in pain and distress in these populations.

Finally, research has also contributed to the development of better tools to measure and understand symptoms and side effects of disease and treatment-related outcomes including pain, fatigue, nausea, cognitive impairments, and mood disturbances.

CONCLUSION

The data described in the chapter suggest that psychological variables are important in several aspects of cancer research and cancer care. Despite severe methodological problems that greatly impair researchers' ability to identify significant relationships among variables such as stress and cancer outcome, some evidence has suggested that these variables affect the likelihood that people will develop cancer, the speed at which cancer progresses, the efficacy of various medical cancer treatments and prevention regimens, and the length of time people with cancer survive. Clear evidence has suggested that cancer has a substantial effect on mental health and psychological adjustment and that this psychological impact can affect a range of disease-related outcomes. Plausible behavioral and biobehavioral pathways linking these predictors and outcomes have been proposed and are under investigation, as are eclectic psychotherapeutic interventions and programs to prevent cancer and cancer-related distress. These developments offer considerable promise for the next decade as the mysteries of these feared and costly diseases are unraveled.

One important area for future investigation is identification of factors that contribute to individual differences in psychosocial adjustment to cancer. As Denollet (1999) noted, possibilities include differences in disease-related intrusive thoughts and related psychiatric syndromes (Andrykowski, Cordova, Studts, & Miller, 1998), development of depression (Van't Spijker et al., 1997), and the use of social comparison information (Van der Zee et al., 1998). Understanding these factors will help researchers identify and promote adjustment among patients at risk for psychological morbidity.

Another important and understudied area is that of ethnicity and the relationships among population subgroups, genetic predispositions, socio-economic status, and other factors affecting disease risk, prognosis, and well-being. The National Cancer Institute's Surveillance, Epidemiology, and End Results Program data have indicated that cancer incidence and outcomes vary according to ethnicity across cancer sites (Miller et al., 1996). Among various ethnic groups in the United States, African Americans have the highest incidence of cancer, which is primarily composed of high rates of lung and prostate cancer among African American men. Other groups, including Latinos, Asians, Native Americans, and Hawaiians, have varying risks for some cancers. Ethnicity is also associated with cancer survival (for a review, see Meyerowitz, Richardson, Hudson, & Leedham, 1998). African Americans tend to have poorer treatment outcomes, whereas Japanese Americans with cancer survive longer than most other ethnic groups with cancer.

On the basis of their empirical review, Meyerowitz and colleagues (1998) suggested a framework linking ethnicity to cancer outcomes. The authors proposed that the impact of ethnicity on cancer survival is likely partly a result of socioeconomic status, knowledge and attitudes, and treatment access and adherence. The role of ethnicity in psychosocial adjustment to cancer has not been well studied. Meyerowitz and colleagues (1998) offered recommendations to further explore this and other understudied areas involving ethnicity and cancer.

Clearly, developing better knowledge about pathways by which behavioral and psychosocial factors may affect the onset or progression of cancer is important. In addition, researchers need to understand the mechanisms mediating psychological and physical effects of psychosocial interventions and in particular to examine mechanisms other than neuroimmune effects that may mediate the influence of psychosocial factors on cancer progression. Management of symptoms, enhancing adjustment, otherwise improving the tolerability of cancer treatments, improving early detection efforts, and establishing strong prevention programs are issues that warrant immediate national attention.

Finally, as Hiatt and Rimer (1999) have emphasized, future efforts to reduce the cancer burden will profit from a synthesis of knowledge from basic research, intervention research, and epidemiological and surveillance research, translating into application and program delivery. Among other benefits, this should facilitate better and more cost-effective prevention and treatment strategies and should bring about the lasting behavioral changes necessary to reduce cancer morbidity and mortality.

REFERENCES

Ader, R., Felten, D., & Cohen, N. (1991). *Psychoneuroimmunology* (2nd ed.). New York: Academic Press.

American Cancer Society. (1994). *Cancer facts and figures—1994.* New York: Author.

American Institute for Cancer Research. (1997). *Food, nutrition, and the prevention of cancer: A global perspective.* Washington, DC: Author.

Andersen, B. L. (1992). Psychological interventions for cancer patients to enhance the quality of life. *Journal of Consulting and Clinical Psychology, 60,* 552–568.

Andersen, B. L. (1994). Surviving cancer. *Cancer, 74,* 1484–1495.

Andersen, B. L., & Cacioppo, J. T. (1995). Delay in seeking a cancer diagnosis: Delay stages and psychophysiological comparison processes. *British Journal of Social Psychology, 34,* 33–52.

Andersen, B. L., Kiecolt-Glaser, J., & Glaser, R. (1994). A biobehavioral model of cancer stress and disease course. *American Psychologist, 49,* 389–404.

Anderson, N. B. (1998). Levels of analysis in health science: A framework for integrating sociobehavioral and biomedical research. *Annals of the New York Academy of Sciences, 840,* 563–576.

Andrykowski, M. A., Cordova, M. J., Studts, J. L., & Miller, T. W. (1998). Post-traumatic stress disorder after treatment for breast cancer: Prevalence of diagnosis and use of the PTSD checklist–Civilian Version (PCL–C) as a screening instrument. *Journal of Consulting and Clinical Psychology, 66,* 586–590.

Barnard, N., Akhtar, A., & Nicholson, A. (1995). Factors that facilitate compliance to a low fat intake. *Archives of Family Medicine, 4,* 153–158.

Barraclough, J., Pinder, P., Cruddas, M., Osmond, C., Taylor, I., & Perry, M. (1992). Life events and breast cancer prognosis. *British Medical Journal, 304,* 1078–1081.

Baum, A., & Andersen, B. L. (Eds.). (2001). *Psychosocial interventions for cancer.* Washington, DC: American Psychological Association.

Baum, A., & Cohen, L. (1998). Successful behavioral interventions to prevent cancer: The example of skin cancer. *Annual Review of Public Health, 19,* 319–333.

Baum, A., Friedman, A. L., & Zakowski, S. G. (1997). Stress and genetic testing for disease risk. *Health Psychology, 16,* 8–19.

Baum, A., & Posluszny, D. (1999). Mapping biobehavioral contributions to health and illness. *Annual Review of Psychology, 50,* 137–163.

Baum, A., & Posluszny, D. M. (2001). Traumatic stress as a target for intervention with cancer patients. In A. Baum & B. L. Andersen (Eds.), *Psychosocial interventions for cancer* (pp. 143–174). Washington, DC: American Psychological Association.

Bloom, J. R. (1982). Social support, accommodation to stress, and adjustment to breast cancer. *Social Science and Medicine, 16,* 1329–1338.

Brewin, C. R., Watson, M., McCarthy, S., Hyman, P., & Dayson, D. (1998). Intrusive memories and depression in cancer patients. *Behavioral Research and Therapy, 36,* 1131–1142.

Brittenden, J., Heys, S. D., Ross, J., & Eremin, O. (1996). Natural killer cells and cancer. *Cancer, 77,* 1226–1243.

Butow, P. N., Coates, A. S., & Dunn, S. M. (1999). Psychosocial predictors of survival in metastatic melanoma. *Journal of Clinical Oncology, 17,* 2256–2263.

Cassileth, B. R., Lusk, E. J., Miller, D. S., Brown, L., & Cross, P. A. (1985). A psychological analysis of cancer patients and their next-of-kin. *Cancer, 55,* 72–76.

Cassileth, B. R., Lusk, E. J., Strouse, T. B., Miller, D. S., Brown, L. L., & Miller, C. (1985). Psychosocial correlates of survival in advanced malignant disease. *New England Journal of Medicine, 312,* 1551–1555.

Centers for Disease Control and Prevention. (1997). Cigarette smoking among adults—United States, 1995. *Morbidity and Mortality Weekly Report, 46,* 1217–1220.

Chambless, D. L., & Hollon, S. D. (1998). Defining empirically supported therapies. *Journal of Consulting and Clinical Psychology, 66,* 7–18.

Cohen, S., & Herbert, T. (1996). Health psychology: Psychological factors and physical disease from the perspective of human psychoneuroimmunology. *Annual Review of Psychology, 47,* 113–142.

Conner, M., & Norman, P. (Eds.) (1996). *Predicting health behaviour: Research and practice with social cognition models.* Buckingham, England: Open University Press.

Curry, S. J., & Emmons, K. M. (1994). Theoretical models for predicting and improving compliance with breast cancer screening. *Annals of Behavioral Medicine, 16,* 302–316.

De Castro, J. (1996). How can eating behavior be regulated in the complex environments of free-living humans? *Neuroscience and Biobehavioral Reviews, 20,* 119–131.

Denollet, J. (1999). Personality and cancer. *Current Opinions in Psychiatry, 12,* 743–748.

Derogatis, L. R., Abeloff, M. D., & Melisaratos, N. (1979). Psychological coping mechanisms and survival time in metastatic breast cancer. *Journal of the American Medical Association, 242,* 1504–1508.

DiPlacido, J., Zauber, A., & Redd, W. H. (1998). Psychosocial issues in cancer screening. In J. Holland (Ed.), *Psycho-oncology* (pp. 161–172). New York: Oxford University Press.

Dishman, R. (1990). Determinants of participation in physical activity. In C. Bouchard, R. J. Shepard, T. Stephens, J. R. Sutton, B. D. McPherson, et al. (Eds.), *Exercise, fitness, and health* (pp. 75–101). Champaign, IL: Human Kinetics Books.

Ell, K., Nishomoto, R., Mediansky, L., Mantell, J., & Hamovitch, M. (1992). Social relations, social support, and survival among patients with cancer. *Journal of Psychosomatic Research, 36*, 531–541.

Epping-Jordan, J. E., Compas, B. E., & Howell, D. C. (1994). Predictors of cancer progression in young adult men and women: Avoidance, intrusive thoughts, and psychological symptoms. *Health Psychology, 13*, 539–547.

Ewertz, M. (1986). Bereavement and breast cancer. *British Journal of Cancer, 53*, 701–703.

Faith, M. S., Johnson, S. L., & Allison, D. B. (1997). Putting the behavior into the behavior genetics of obesity. *Behavior Genetics, 27*, 423–439.

Fawzy, F., Fawzy, N. W., Hyun, C. S., Elashoff, R., Guthrie, D., Fahey, J. L., et al. (1993). Malignant melanoma. Effects of an early structured psychiatric intervention, coping, and affective state on recurrence and survival 6 years later. *Archives of General Psychiatry, 50*, 681–689.

Flegal, M. D., Carroll, R. J., Kuczmarski, R. J., & Johnson, C. L. (1998). Overweight and obesity in the United States: Prevalence and trends, 1960–1994. *International Journal of Obesity-Related Metabolic Disorders, 22*, 39–47.

Ford, E. (1999). Body mass index and colon cancer in a national sample of adult U.S. men and women. *American Journal of Epidemiology, 150*, 390–398.

Forlenza, M. J., & Baum, A. (2000). Psychosocial influences on cancer progression: Alternative cellular and molecular mechanisms. *Current Opinion in Psychiatry, 13*, 639–645.

Fox, B. (1998). Psychosocial factors in cancer incidence and progression. In J. C. Holland (Ed.), *Psycho-oncology* (pp. 110–124). New York: Oxford University Press.

Funch, D. P., & Marshall, J. (1983). The role of stress, social support and age in survival from breast cancer. *Journal of Psychosomatic Research, 27*, 77–83.

Funch, D. P., & Mettlin, C. (1982). The role of support in relation to recovery from breast surgery. *Social Science and Medicine, 16*, 91–98.

Gallo, J. J., Armenian, H. K., Ford, D. E., & Eaton, W. W. (2000). Major depression and cancer: The 13-year follow-up of the Baltimore Epidemiologic Catchment Area sample (United States). *Cancer Causes and Control, 11*, 751–758.

Gamberino, W., & Gold, M. (1999). Neurobiology of tobacco smoking and other addictive disorders. *Psychiatric Clinics of North America, 22*, 301–312.

Ganz, P. A. (1990). Current issues in cancer rehabilitation. *Cancer, 65*, 742–751.

Garofalo, J. P. (2000). Psychological adjustment in medical populations. *Current Opinions in Psychiatry, 13*, 647–653.

Garssen, B., & Goodkin, K. (1999). On the role of immunological factors as mediators between psychosocial factors and cancer progression. *Psychiatry Research, 85,* 51–61.

Gellert, G. A., Maxwell, R. M., & Siegel, B. S. (1993). Survival of breast cancer patients receiving adjunctive psychosocial support therapy: A 10-year follow-up study. *Journal of Clinical Oncology, 11,* 66–69.

Geyer, S. (1993). Life events, chronic difficulties and vulnerability factors preceding breast cancer. *Social Science and Medicine, 37,* 1545–1555.

Gibbons, F. X. (1999). Social comparison as a mediator of response shift. *Social Science and Medicine, 48,* 1517–1530.

Goodwin, P. J., Leszcz, M., Ennis, M., Koopmans, J., Vincent, L., Guther, H., et al. (2001). The effect of group psychosocial support on survival in metastatic breast cancer. *New England Journal of Medicine, 345,* 1719–1726.

Goran, M. (1997). Genetic influences on human energy expenditure and substrate utilization. *Behavior Genetics, 27,* 389–399.

Gotay, C. C., & Muraoka, M. Y. (1998). Quality of life in long-term survivors of adult-onset cancers. *Journal of the National Cancer Institute, 90,* 656–667.

Greer, S., Morris, T., & Pettingale, K. W. (1979). Psychological response to breast cancer. Effect on outcome. *Lancet, ii,* 785–787.

Guthrie, N., & Carroll, K. (1999). Specific versus non-specific effects of dietary fat on carcinogenesis. *Progress in Lipid Research, 38,* 261–271.

Hanahan, D., & Weinberg, R. (2000). The hallmarks of cancer. *Cell, 100,* 57–70.

Hart, A. R., Wicks, A. C. B., & Mayberry, J. F. (1995). Colorectal cancer screening in asymptomatic populations. *Gut, 36,* 590–598.

Heath, A., & Madden, P. (1995). Genetic influences on smoking behavior. In J. R. Turner, L. R. Cardon, & J. K. Hewitt (Eds.), *Behavior genetic approaches in behavioral medicine* (pp. 45–66). New York: Plenum Press.

Helgeson, V. S., Cohen, S., & Fritz, H. (1998). Social ties and cancer. In J. C. Holland (Ed.), *Psycho-oncology* (pp. 99–109). New York: Oxford University Press.

Helgeson, V., Cohen, S., Schulz, R., & Yasko, J. (1999). Education and peer discussion group interventions and adjustment to breast cancer. *Archives of General Psychiatry, 56,* 340–347.

Henderson, B. N., Davison, K. P., Pennebaker, J. W., Gatchel, R. J., & Baum, A. (in press). Disease disclosure patterns among breast cancer patients. *Psychology and Health.*

Henderson, B. N., Forlenza, M., & Baum, A. (2002). *An evolutionary framework for biobehavioral contributions to health and disease.* Unpublished manuscript.

Herbert, T. B., & Cohen, S. (1993). Stress and immunity in humans: A meta-analytic review. *Psychosomatic Medicine, 55,* 364–379.

Hiatt, R. A., & Rimer, B. K. (1999). A new strategy for cancer control research. *Cancer Epidemiology, Biomarkers and Prevention, 8,* 957–964.

Holland, J. (1998). Societal views of cancer and the emergence of psycho-oncology. In J. C. Holland (Ed.), *Psycho-oncology* (pp. 3–15). New York: Oxford University Press.

House, J. S., Landis, K. R., & Umberson, D. (1988). Social relationships and health. *Science, 241,* 540–545.

Ilnyckyj, A., Farber, J., Cheang, M. C., & Weinerman, B. H. (1994). A randomized controlled trial of psychotherapeutic intervention in cancer patients. *Annals of the Royal College of Physicians and Surgeons of Canada, 27,* 93–96.

Janz, N. K., & Becker, M. H. (1984). The health belief model: A decade later. *Health Education Quarterly, 11,* 1–47.

Jeffrey, R. W., Drewnowski, A., Epstein, L. H., Stunkard, A. J., Wilson, G. T., Wing, R. R., et al. (2000). Long-term maintenance of weight loss: Current status. *Health Psychology, 19,* 5–16.

Jensen, M. (1987). Psychobiological factors predicting the course of breast cancer. *Journal of Personality, 55,* 317–342.

Kelloff, G., Boone, C., Steele, V., Crowell, J., Lubet, R., Greenwald, P., et al. (1996). In B. W. Stewart, D. McGregor, & P. Kleihues (Eds.), *Principles of chemoprevention* (pp. 203–219). Lyon, France: International Agency for Research on Cancer.

Kiecolt-Glaser, J. K., Stephens, R. E., Lipetz, P. D., Speicher, C. E., & Glaser, R. (1985). Distress and DNA repair in human lymphocytes. *Journal of Behavioral Medicine, 8,* 311–320.

Kumanyika, S. K., Van Horn, L., Bowen, D., Perri, M. G., Rolls, B. J., Czajkowski, S. M., et al. (2000). Maintenance of dietary behavior change. *Health Psychology, 19,* 42–56.

Lerman, C., Kash, K., & Stefanek, M. (1994). Younger women at increased risk for breast cancer: Perceived risk, psychological well-being, and surveillance behavior. *Monographs of the National Cancer Institute, 16,* 171–176.

Levy, S. M., Herberman, R. B., Whiteside, T., Sanzo, K., Lee, J., & Kirkwood, J. (1990). Perceived social support and tumor estrogen/progesterone receptor status as predictors of natural killer cell activity in breast cancer patients. *Psychosomatic Medicine, 52,* 73–85.

Longnecker, M., Gerhardsson le Verdier, M., Frumkin, H., & Carpenter, C. (1995). A case-control study of physical activity in relation to risk of cancer of the right colon and rectum in men. *International Journal of Epidemiology, 24,* 42–50.

Maier, S. F., Watkins, L. R., & Fleshner, M. (1994). Psychoneuroimmunology: The interface between behavior, brain, and immunity. *American Psychologist, 49,* 1004–1017.

Margolis, G., Goodman, R., & Rubin, A. (1990). Psychological effects of breast-conserving cancer treatment and mastectomy. *Psychosomatics, 31,* 33–39.

Massie, M. J., & Holland, J. C. (1990). Depression and the cancer patient. *Journal of Clinical Psychiatry, 51,* 12–19.

Maunsell, E., Brisson, J., & Deschenes, L. (1992). Psychological distress after initial treatment of breast cancer. *Cancer, 70,* 120–125.

Maunsell, E., Brisson, J., & Deschenes, L. (1995). Social support and survival among women with breast cancer. *Cancer, 76,* 631–637.

McDaniel, J. S., Musselman, D. L., & Nemeroff, C. B. (1998). Cancer and depression: Theory and treatment. *Psychiatry Annuals, 27,* 360–364.

McGee, R., Williams, S., & Elwood, M. (1994). Depression and the development of cancer: A meta-analysis. *Social Science and Medicine, 38,* 187–192.

McGinnis, J., & Foege, W. (1999). Mortality and morbidity attributable to use of addictive substances in the United States. *Proceedings of the Association of American Physicians, 111,* 109–118.

McKenna, M. C., Zevon, M. A., Corn, B., & Rounds, J. (1999). Psychosocial factors and the development of breast cancer: A meta-analysis. *Health Psychology, 18,* 520–531.

Messer, E. (1984). Anthropological perspectives on diet. *Annual Review of Anthropology, 13,* 205–249.

Meyer, T. J., & Mark, M. M. (1995). Effects of psychosocial interventions with adult cancer patients: A meta-analysis of randomized experiments. *Health Psychology, 14,* 101–108.

Meyerowitz, B. E. (1980). Psychosocial correlates of breast cancer and its treatment. *Psychological Bulletin, 87,* 108–114.

Meyerowitz, B. E., Richardson, J., Hudson, S., & Leedham, B. (1998). Ethnicity and cancer outcomes: Behavioral and psychosocial considerations. *Psychological Bulletin, 123,* 47–70.

Mezzetti, M., La Vecchia, C., Decarli, A., Boyle, P., Talamini, R., & Franceschi, S. (1998). Population attributable risk for breast cancer: Diet, nutrition, and physical exercise. *Journal of the National Cancer Institute, 90,* 389–394.

Miller, B. A., Kolonel, L. N., Bernstein, L., Young, J. L., Swanson, G. M., West, D., et al. (Eds.). (1996). *Racial/ethnic patterns of cancer in the United States, 1988–1992* (National Institutes of Health Publication No. 96-4104). Bethesda, MD: U.S. Department of Health and Human Services & National Institutes of Health.

Morris, T., Greer, S., Pettingale, K. W., & Watson, M. (1981). Patterns of expression of anger and their psychological correlates in women with breast cancer. *Journal of Psychosomatic Research, 25,* 111–117.

Ockene, J., Emmons, K., Mermelstein, R., Perkins, K., Bonollo, D., Voorhees, C., et al. (2000). Relapse and maintenance issues for smoking cessation. *Health Psychology, 19,* 17–31.

O'Reilly, P. (1988). Methodological issues in social support and social network research. *Social Science and Medicine, 26,* 863–873.

Orleans, C. T. (2000). Promoting the maintenance of health behavior change: Recommendations for the next generation of research and practice. *Health Psychology, 19,* 76–83.

Owen, N., & Vita, P. (1997). Physical activity and health. In A. Baum et al. (Eds.), *Cambridge handbook of psychology, health and medicine* (pp. 154–157). Cambridge, England: Cambridge University Press.

Penninx, B. W., Guralnik, J. M., Pahor, M., Ferrucci, L., Cerhan, J. R., Wallace, R. B., et al. (1998). Chronically depressed mood and cancer risk in older persons. *Journal of the National Cancer Institute, 90,* 1888–1893.

Persky, V. W., Kempthorne-Rawson, J., & Shekelle, R. B. (1987). Personality and risk of cancer: 20-year follow-up of the Western Electric Study. *Psychosomatic Medicine, 49,* 435–449.

Pettingale, K. W. (1985). Towards a psychobiological model of cancer: Biological considerations. *Social Science and Medicine, 20,* 779–787.

Pi-Sunyer, F. X. (1998). NHLBI Obesity Education Initiative Expert Panel on the Identification, Evaluation, and Treatment of Overweight and Obesity in Adults—The evidence report. *Obesity Research, 6*(Suppl. 2), 51–209.

Potter, J. D., & Steinmetz, K. (1996). Vegetables, fruit and phytoestrogens as preventive agents. In B. W. Stewart, D. McGregor, & P. Kleihues (Eds.), *Principles of chemoprevention* (pp. 61–90). Lyon, France: International Agency for Research on Cancer.

Powers, S. W. (1999). Empirically supported treatments in pediatric psychology: Procedure-related pain. *Journal of Pediatric Psychology, 24,* 131–145.

Ramirez, A. J., Craig, T. K. J., Watson, J. P., Fentiman, I. S., North, W. R. S., & Rubens, R. D. (1989). Stress and relapse of breast cancer. *British Medical Journal, 298,* 291–293.

Redd, W. H., Silberfarb, P. M., Andersen, B. L., Andrykowski, M. A., Bovbjerg, D. H., Burish, T. G., et al. (1991). Physiologic and psychobehavioral research in oncology. *Cancer, 67*(3, Suppl.), 813–822.

Reed, D. R., Bachmanov, A. A., Bauchamp, G. K., Tordoff, M. G., & Price, R. A. (1997). Heritable variation in food preferences and their contribution to obesity. *Behavior Genetics, 27,* 373–387.

Ren, X. S., Skinner, K., Lee, A., & Kazis, L. (1999). Social support, social selection, and self-assessed health status: Results from the veterans health study in the United States. *Social Science and Medicine, 48,* 1721–1734.

Reynolds, P., & Kaplan, G. A. (1990). Social connections and risk for cancer: Prospective evidence from the Alameda County Study. *Behavioral Medicine, 16,* 101–110.

Rimer, B. K. (1992). Understanding the acceptance of mammography by women. *Annals of Behavioral Medicine, 14,* 197–203.

Rimer, B. K., Trock, B., Engstrom, P. F., Lerman, C., & King, E. (1991). Why do some women get regular mammograms? *American Journal of Preventive Medicine, 7,* 69–74.

Rosenstock. I. M. (1974). The health belief model: Origins and correlates. *Health Education Monograph, 2,* 336–353.

Rowland, J. H., & Massie, M. J. (1998). Breast cancer. In J. Holland (Ed.), *Psychooncology* (pp. 380–401). New York: Oxford University Press.

Smith, C. E., Fernegel, K., Holcroft, C., Gerald, K., & Marien, L. (1994). Meta-analysis of the associations between social support and health outcomes. *Annals of Behavioral Medicine, 16,* 352–362.

Sneed, N. V., Edlund, B., & Dias, J. K. (1992). Adjustment of gynecological and breast cancer patients to the cancer diagnosis: Comparisons with males and females having other cancer sites. *Health Care for Women International, 13,* 11–22.

Somers, S., & Guillou, P. J. (1994). Tumor cell strategies for escaping immune control: Implications for psychoimmunology. In C. E. Lewis, C. O'Sullivan, & J. Barraclough (Eds.), *The psychoimmunology of cancer: Mind and body in the fight for survival* (pp. 385–416). Oxford, England: Oxford Medical.

Spiegel, D., Bloom, J. R., Kraemer, H. C., & Gottheil, E. (1989). Effect of psychosocial treatment on survival of patients with metastatic breast cancer. *Lancet, 2,* 888–891.

Spiegel, D., Sephton, S. E., Terr, A. I., & Stites, D. P. (1998). Effects of psychosocial treatment in prolonging survival may be mediated by neuroimmune pathways. *Annals of New York Academy of Sciences, 840,* 674–683.

Stavraky, K. M., Donner, A. P., Kincade, J. E., & Stewart, M. A. (1988). The effect of psychosocial factors on lung cancer mortality at one year. *Journal of Clinical Epidemiology, 41,* 75–82.

Taylor, S. E., Lichtman, R. R., Wood, J. V., Bluming, A. Z., Dosik, G. M., & Leibowitz, R. L. (1985). Illness-related and treatment-related factors in psychological adjustment to breast cancer. *Cancer, 55,* 2506–2513.

Temoshok, L. (1987). Personality, coping style, emotion, and cancer: Towards an integrative model. *Cancer Surveys, 6,* 545–567.

Thomas, C. B., Duszynski, K. R., & Schaffer, J. W. (1979). Family attitudes reported in youth as potential predictors of cancer. *Psychosomatic Medicine, 41,* 287–302.

Thompson, D. S., & Shear, M. K. (1998). Psychiatric disorders and gynecological oncology: A review of the literature. *General Hospital Psychiatry, 20,* 241–247.

Thune, I., Brenn, T., Lund, E., & Gaard, M. (1997). Physical activity and the risk of breast cancer. *New England Journal of Medicine, 336,* 1269–1275.

Van der Zee, K., Oldersma, F., Buunk, B., & Bos, D. (1998). Social comparison preferences among cancer patients as related to neuroticism and social comparison orientation. *Journal of Personality and Social Psychology, 75,* 801–810.

Van't Spijker, A., Trijsburg, R. W., & Duivenvoorden, H. J. (1997). Psychological sequelae of cancer diagnosis: A meta-analytic review of 58 studies after 1980. *Psychosomatic Medicine, 59,* 280–293.

Vogt, T. M., Mullooly, J. P., Ernst, D., Pope, C. R., & Hollis, J. F. (1992). Social networks as predictors of ischemic heart disease, cancer, stroke and hypertension: Incidence, survival and mortality. *Journal of Clinical Epidemiology, 45,* 659–666.

Waxler-Morrison, N., Hislop, T. G., Mears, B., & Kan, L. (1991). Effects of social relationships on survival for women with breast cancer: A prospective study. *Social Science and Medicine, 33,* 177–183.

Weisman, A. D., & Worden, J. W. (1976). The existential plight in cancer: Significance of the first 100 days. *International Journal of Psychiatry in Medicine*, *7*, 1–15.

Whiteside, T. J., & Herberman, R. B. (1995). The role of natural killer cells in immune surveillance of cancer. *Current Opinions in Immunology, 7*, 704–710.

Willett, W. (1996). Can we prevent cancer by diet today? *Proceedings of the Annual Meeting of the American Association of Cancer Researchers, 37*, 644–645.

Wulsin, L. R., Valiant, G. E., & Wells, V. E. (1999). A systematic review of the mortality of depression. *Psychosomatic Medicine, 61*, 6–17.

3

ENDOCRINE, METABOLIC, NUTRITIONAL, AND IMMUNE DISORDERS

TIM WYSOCKI AND LISA M. BUCKLOH

This chapter surveys health psychology research on endocrine, metabolic, nutritional, and immune disorders that are represented by the ninth revision of the *International Classification of Diseases* (ICD–9; Medicode, 2001). Table 3.1 summarizes the many diagnostic entities that comprise this list. This chapter concentrates on four areas that have been studied heavily by health psychologists: (a) diabetes mellitus, (b) cystic fibrosis, (c) obesity, and (d) endocrine disorders. We focus on major findings that have achieved the status of consensus among experts, the clinical implications of the findings, and gaps in the research literature. Given the vast amount of literature on these topics, all relevant studies have not been discussed. Instead, the chapter includes a survey of the major research thrusts and their implications.[1]

---

[1]For prevalence rates and a more in-depth discussion of the other disorders covered by *ICD–9* codes 240 through 279.9, consult *Williams Textbook of Endocrinology* (Wilson, Foster, Kronenberg, & Larsen, 1998).

TABLE 3.1
Selected Diagnostic Categories in the *ICD–9* for Endocrine, Nutritional, Metabolic, and Immune Disorders

ICD–9 codes	Examples of diagnoses
240	Goiter
240.0	Simple goiter
241	Nontoxic nodular goiter
242	Thyrotoxicosis
243	Congenital hypothyroidism
244	Acquired hypothyroidism
245	Thyroiditis
246	Other disorders of thyroid
246.2	Cyst of thyroid
250	Diabetes mellitus
250.00	Diabetes mellitus Type 2 without complications
250.01	Diabetes mellitus Type 1 without complications
250.1	Diabetes with ketoacidosis
251	Other pancreatic disorders
252	Parathyroid disorder
252.0	Hyperparathyroidism
252.1	Hypoparathyroidism
253	Pituitary/hypothalamic disorders
253.2	Panhypopituitarism
253.3	Pituitary dwarfism—growth hormone deficiency
253.5	Diabetes insipidus
254	Diseases of thymus gland
254.0	Persistent hyperplasia of thymus
255	Adrenal gland disorders
255.0	Cushing's syndrome
255.2	Adrenogenital disorders—congenital adrenal hyperplasia
256	Ovarian dysfunction
257	Testicular dysfunction
258	Polyglandular dysfunction
258.0	Wermer's syndrome
259	Other endocrine disorders
259.0	Delay in sexual development
259.1	Sexual precocity
259.4	Psychosocial dwarfism
260	Kwashiorkor
261	Nutritional marasmus
263	Protein–calorie malnutrition
264	Vitamin A deficiency
265	Thiamine/niacin deficiency
266	B-complex deficiencies
267	Ascorbic acid deficiency
268	Vitamin D deficiency
268.0	Rickets, active
269	Other nutrition deficiency
269.0	Vitamin K deficiency
270	Disorders of amino acid transport and metabolism
270.0	Amino acid transport disorder
270.1	Phenylketonuria (PKU)
271	Disorders of carbohydrate transport and metabolism
271.0	Glycogenosis
271.1	Galactosemia

TABLE 3.1 *(Continued)*

ICD–9 codes	Examples of diagnoses
272	Disorders of lipid metabolism
272.0	Pure hypercholesterolemia
273	Disorders of plasma protein metabolism
273.0	Polyclonal hypergammaglobulinemia
274	Gout
275	Disorders of mineral metabolism
275.0	Disorders of iron metabolism
276	Disorders of fluid/electrolyte balance
276.0	Hyperosmolality
276.1	Hypo-osmolality
277.0	Cystic fibrosis
278	Obesity and other hyperalimentation
278.0	Obesity
279	Disorders involving immune mechanism
279.0	Deficiencies of humoral immunity
279.00	Hypogammaglobulinemia

DIABETES MELLITUS

Treatment of diabetes and its complications accounts for 12% to 14% of annual health care costs in the United States (National Diabetes Data Group, 1995). Type I diabetes mellitus results from autoimmune destruction of the pancreatic insulin-producing cells, resulting in insulin deficiency. Type 1 diabetes often has its onset in childhood and may be referred to as *juvenile-onset diabetes* or *insulin-dependent diabetes mellitus.* Prevalence is variable around the world but is estimated at 1 to 2 cases per 1,000 people in North America. Treatment consists of multiple daily insulin injections or use of an insulin pump, daily blood glucose testing, a constant carbohydrate diet, and exercise. Short-term complications of Type 1 diabetes are episodes of hypoglycemia that can require emergency care and diabetic ketoacidosis, which is the most common reason for hospitalization. Type 2 diabetes mellitus is the far more common form, with a prevalence of about 60 cases per 1,000. It often has its onset in adulthood and results from insulin resistance rather than insulin deficiency. It is estimated that about 5.4 million affected people in the United States are unaware that they have the disease. Treatment may consist of exercise and a special diet only, oral hypoglycemic drugs, or insulin injections. All forms of diabetes mellitus increase risks of damage to the heart, kidneys, nerves, eyes, and other organs.

The Diabetes Control and Complications Trial (Diabetes Control and Complications Trial [DCCT] Research Group, 1993) was a major National Institutes of Health (NIH) study designed to determine whether long-term maintenance of near-normal blood glucose decreased the onset and progression of diabetic complications. A sample of 1,441 patients with Type 1 diabetes were randomized to either intensive or conventional therapy and monitored for an average of 7 years. Intensive therapy was an effort to keep blood glucose near normal through more frequent insulin injections or use of an insulin pump; more frequent blood glucose monitoring; use of blood glucose data for insulin and diet adjustments; and access to a diabetes nurse, dietitian, and psychologist. Intensive therapy yielded significantly better diabetic control than did conventional therapy in each year of the study. Intensive therapy reduced the onset and progression of diabetic complications by 50% to 75%, even though few patients achieved consistent normoglycemia during the study. There was a linear relationship between average glycosylated hemoglobin (HbA_{1c}) and complication rates; any improvement in diabetic control reduced complications. Because the benefits of intensive therapy were achieved with extant medical tools, a key factor mediating its success was the capacity of patients, with the support of diabetes teams, to achieve and maintain long-term changes in self-care behaviors. The recent United Kingdom Prospective Diabetes Study (United Kingdom Prospective Diabetes Study [UKPDS] Group, 1998) results for Type 2 diabetes were similar to the DCCT findings for Type 1 diabetes. Thus, maintenance of tight glycemic control reduces the onset and slows the progression of long-term complications in both forms of diabetes.

Since the DCCT and UKPDS were carried out, diabetes management has evolved toward more intensive and aggressive treatment of patients of all ages. It is likely that patients will have a greater need for the skills of health psychologists in helping them to integrate this demanding regimen into their lives. Health psychologists should be familiar with the vast diabetes research literature and its implications, which are summarized in the following sections.

Knowledge, Skills, and Self-Efficacy

Patients with diabetes must learn about the disease and its treatment and master the necessary technical skills for self-management. Studies of diabetes knowledge have yielded the following primary conclusions:

- Diabetes knowledge and skills grow steadily during childhood and adolescence (e.g., Johnson et al., 1982; Wysocki et al., 1996b).
- Diabetes knowledge is necessary for adequate self-care, but it is not sufficient. Many studies have shown that diabetes knowledge is weakly related or unrelated to adherence and diabetic control (Clement, 1995; Johnson, 1995).
- Diabetes knowledge and skills tend to deteriorate over time unless periodic refresher training courses are offered (Delamater, Smith, Kurtz, & White, 1988; Johnson et al., 1982).

- A patient-centered model of diabetes education and care may be more acceptable than conventional education and have greater effects on patients' self-care behaviors (Anderson et al., 1995; Anderson, Funnell, & Arnold, 1996).

Health psychologists should appreciate not only that diabetes knowledge affects patients' psychological adjustment and disease management in multiple ways but also that it is but one of many psychological factors that merit consideration.

Treatment Adherence

The diabetes regimen may include daily insulin or an oral hypoglycemic agent, blood glucose testing, a constant carbohydrate diet, and regular exercise. Patients must also recognize and correct unwanted fluctuations in blood glucose levels by engaging in appropriate actions to either raise the level (e.g., by consuming carbohydrates) or lower the level (e.g., by taking more insulin, through exercise, by waiting to eat). Extensive research on adherence with this regimen has yielded the following broad conclusions:

- Adherence with the diabetes regimen is not related to a global or stable personality trait. Adherence with the various regimen components varies within and among patients, and a weak association often exists between measures of adherence with the various aspects of care (Glasgow, McCaul, & Schaefer, 1987; Johnson, Silverstein, Rosenbloom, Carter, & Cunningham, 1986).
- Perfect adherence with the regimen is uncommon; most patients have at least moderate difficulty integrating all of the treatment and monitoring demands into their daily lives (Anderson, 1996).
- Treatment adherence is difficult to maintain during adolescence (Johnson, 1995; Weissberg-Benchell et al., 1995), and this may be a common cause of preventable hospitalizations. Behavior therapy has been used successfully to treat this problem (e.g., Anderson, Wolf, Burkhart, Cornell, & Bacon, 1989; Delamater et al., 1990; Wysocki, Green, & Huxtable, 1989; Wysocki et al., 2000).
- Efforts to find a robust link between treatment adherence and diabetic control have often failed (Johnson, 1995). Although this seems counterintuitive, plausible explanations exist. Poor adherence to one treatment task can be offset by good adherence to another. Existing measures of adherence rely heavily on self-report, possibly resulting in inaccurate measure-

ment. If a patient's treatment regimen is not optimal, adherence to that regimen may not yield good glycemic control.

Inadequate treatment adherence is a common reason for referral of patients with diabetes to clinical health psychologists. However, improved treatment adherence does not guarantee improved diabetic control.

Self-Management and Problem Solving

The demands of diabetes pervade daily life, and patients often must respond to unwanted fluctuations in blood glucose levels. Numerous valuable findings have emerged from the study of these processes:

- Many patients with diabetes believe that they can estimate blood glucose levels accurately from subjective physical symptoms. Only a minority can do so reliably, yet many patients make treatment decisions that are based on these misconceptions. Cox et al. (e.g., 1985, 1995) have shown in an elegant series of studies that most patients can be trained to improve the accuracy of their blood glucose estimations.
- Severe hypoglycemia is predictable. Gonder-Frederick, Cox, Kovatchev, Schlundt, and Clarke (1997) have put forth a multivariate model of the behavioral and psychological processes that affect the risk of severe hypoglycemia.
- Many patients use their Self Monitoring of Blood Glucose (SMBG) data infrequently to guide treatment decisions (Delamater et al., 1989; Wysocki, Hough, Ward, Allen, & Murgai, 1992), yet insulin self-regulation predicts better diabetic control (Peyrot & Rubin, 1988), and training in the therapeutic use of SMBG data enhances diabetic control (Anderson et al., 1989; Delamater et al., 1990).

Using subjective physical symptoms rather than objective blood glucose tests to estimate blood glucose levels may lead to erroneous decisions. Improved adherence to blood glucose monitoring cannot improve diabetic control unless patients also learn to use effective diabetes problem-solving skills (Wing et al., 1985).

Stress

Patients who experience a great deal of stress or who cope ineffectively are at risk of poor diabetic control (Surwit, Schneider, & Feinglos, 1992). This may be a consequence of two different mechanisms:

- Stress may interfere with diabetes self-management by distracting the patient from careful monitoring and proactive self-care (Hanson & Pichert, 1986).
- Stress increases secretion of counter-regulatory hormones that block insulin action or transform stored glycogen into glucose for release into the bloodstream (Aiken, Wallander, Bell, & Cole, 1992; Chase & Jackson, 1981; Hanson, Henggeler, & Burghen, 1987).

The health psychologist must appreciate the influence of stress and coping on the patient's adjustment to diabetes. Evaluation of patients who have difficulty coping with diabetes should include assessment of the frequency and severity of recent stressful life events and minor daily stressors and the patients' ability to cope effectively with them. Various stress management interventions may be of help (Boardway, Delamater, Tomakowsky, & Gutai, 1993; Fowler, Budzynski, & Vandenbergh, 1978).

Social Context

Most events that affect diabetic control occur during patients' daily lives at home, work, and school. Not surprisingly, many studies have found that social variables can influence patients' psychological adjustment to diabetes, the effectiveness of diabetes self-care, and diabetic control (Anderson, 1996; Lorenz & Wysocki, 1991). The most robust findings related to the social context of diabetes are the following:

- The family environment is a potent determinant of adaptation to diabetes, particularly among adolescents (Anderson, 1996; Lorenz & Wysocki, 1991).
- Family interventions may promote adaptation to diabetes, but many more well-controlled intervention studies are needed (e.g., Satin, La Greca, Zigo, & Skyler, 1989; Wysocki et al., 2000).
- Other researchers have documented that effects of social support on diabetes management may be highly dependent on the context in which the support is offered (e.g., Fisher, LaGreca, Greco, Arfken, & Schneiderman, 1997; La Greca et al., 1995). Specific types of social support may be needed and therefore helpful under certain conditions but of little benefit otherwise.
- Training in diabetes-specific social skills and coping skills can yield benefits in terms of adherence and diabetic control (e.g., Gross, Heimann, Shapiro, & Schultz, 1983; Kaplan, Chadwick, & Schimmel, 1985).
- Evidence shows that excessive self-care autonomy may lead

to poor diabetes outcomes in youths (La Greca, Follansbee, & Skyler, 1990; Wysocki et al., 1996a).

The social context of diabetes carries the potential to enhance or impede adaptation to diabetes. Health psychologists should help patients to develop and rely on a supportive network of friends, relatives, and loved ones that balances self-care autonomy with helpful social support.

Concurrent Psychopathological Conditions

Diabetes has been associated with an increased incidence of certain psychiatric disorders. Patients who have diabetes and also a psychiatric disorder are at increased risk of poorer diabetes outcomes than are those without such disorders. Among the more robust findings in this area of research are the following:

- Diabetes increases the risks of depression and anxiety disorders. Kovacs, Goldston, Obrosky, and Bonar (1997) showed prospectively that 27% of youths had an episode of major depression during the 10 years after onset of diabetes, and 13% had anxiety disorders. Those with Type 2 diabetes also have an increased risk of depression (Lustman, Griffith, Gavard, & Clouse, 1992). Depression may impede treatment adherence, and its treatment may improve diabetic control (Lustman, Griffith, & Clouse, 1996).
- Anorexia nervosa and bulimia may be more common in young women with Type 1 diabetes than in the general population (Rodin & Daneman, 1992). Patients with eating disorders tend to have less diabetic control than those without eating disorders.
- Patients with diabetes may also experience subclinical depression and anxiety that warrant treatment. Polonsky et al. (1995) have validated the Problem Areas in Diabetes Scale, which can be used to evaluate diabetes-specific distress. Diabetes-specific quality of life measures have been validated for adults (DCCT Research Group, 1987) and for youths (Ingersoll & Marrero, 1991).

Health psychologists must be familiar with the types of psychopathology and coping problems that may affect patients with diabetes, sensitive to evidence that patients are exhibiting these symptoms, skilled in administration and interpretation of appropriate assessment tools, and capable of implementing interventions that have been empirically validated for these disorders.

Cognitive Sequelae

Substantial research shows that diabetes may have adverse cognitive effects on an acute and a chronic basis. Among the more robust findings in this area of research are the following:

- Children with early diabetes onset (about ages 5 to 7 years) are at risk for developing learning disabilities, although no consistent pattern of neuropsychological findings has emerged (Rovet & Fernandes, 1998; Ryan, 1997). Because diabetes duration, frequency of hypoglycemia, frequency of ketoacidosis, and chronicity of hyperglycemia are intercorrelated, it has been difficult to confirm that any of these etiological factors is causative.
- Even mild hypoglycemia leads to acute deterioration of mental acuity. Decreased cognitive function may be the first sign of hypoglycemia for some patients. Deterioration in cognitive function may persist for several days following severe hypoglycemia. However, Austin and Deary (1999) reported that they had no evidence showing that frequency of severe hypoglycemia was related to cognitive decline in DCCT patients.
- Older patients with Type 2 diabetes may experience accelerated cognitive declines. Diabetes may hasten aging; the types of cognitive impairments that have been identified tend to be typical of much older people (Perlmuter et al., 1984).

Many patients with diabetes merit evaluation of cognitive functioning. Patients who are at risk of diabetes-associated cognitive impairment (e.g., younger children, older adults) warrant efforts to minimize the frequency of hypoglycemia and of prolonged hyperglycemia. Health psychologists should consider cognitive impairment as a possible factor contributing to ineffective diabetes self-management.

CYSTIC FIBROSIS

Cystic fibrosis (CF) is the most common inherited lethal disease in White people, with an incidence of 1 in 2,000 to 2,500 live births in the United States (Stark, Jelalian, & Miller, 1995). The disease results from an inherited defect that causes the epithelia of the exocrine glands of the lungs, pancreas, and other organs to secrete viscous, sticky mucus. This mucus obstructs the function of affected organs, leading to irreversible damage. Chronic respiratory disease causes 90% to 95% of CF morbidity and mortality. Gene therapy holds promise for treatment of the central pathological factor of CF, but current therapy is essentially palliative. A typical regimen includes daily chest physiotherapy to clear mucus from the lungs, antibiotics to prevent respiratory infections, intake of pancreatic enzymes to improve digestion, and a high-fat diet that is 125% to 150% of usual daily caloric intake. Genetic screening can identify the 85% of CF carriers who have the most common genetic mutation, and prenatal diagnosis of CF is also possible. Although CF was previously uniformly fatal during adolescence, average life expectancy now exceeds 30 years.

Health psychology research on CF includes studies of the effects of CF on the adjustment of patients and their families, effects of CF on parenting, adaptation of families to the treatment burden, and adherence to the treatment regimen, especially with respect to caloric intake.

Effects on Patients' Psychological Adjustment

The stress associated with a lethal illness such as CF could manifest as psychopathological conditions (e.g., depression, anxiety disorders, eating disorders), so researchers have explored whether youths with CF are at increased risk of psychopathological conditions. The major conclusions of this research are as follows:

- Some studies report no more psychopathological symptoms among patients with CF than healthy control groups (e.g., Thompson, Hodges, & Hamlett, 1990), whereas others report that CF increases the risk of some forms of psychopathological symptoms (e.g., Simmons et al., 1987).
- Family function probably mediates the relationship between the psychological risks posed by CF and the development of childhood psychopathological conditions (e.g., Walker, Ortiz-Valdes, & Newbrough, 1989).
- Few studies have explored whether patients with CF and also psychological disorders are more likely to exhibit poor treatment adherence or poor health status. Studies that have focused on the interplay between disease management and childhood psychopathological conditions (e.g., Wilson, Fosson, Kanga, & D'Angelo, 1996) underscore the bidirectionality of these processes.

Most patients with CF are psychologically adjusted, but CF may increase the risk of certain forms of psychopathological conditions. Further, maladjusted patients may be more prone to poor disease outcomes. Health psychologists who work with patients with CF should be vigilant for anxiety, depression, and low self-esteem.

Relationship Between CF and Marital and Family Function

The fear of premature death of a child and the heavy CF treatment burden might adversely affect family function and the psychological status of family members. Research pertaining to these questions has yielded the following primary conclusions:

- Mothers bear the brunt of daily management of CF (Quittner, Opipari, Regoli, Jacobson, & Eigen, 1992). This may increase the risks of depression and marital dissatisfaction (Walker, Van Slyke, & Newbrough, 1992).
- Fathers are less distressed by CF than are mothers and are less prone to report adverse marital effects caused by CF (Quittner, DiGiralomo, Michel, & Eigen, 1992).
- No studies of the psychological status of healthy siblings of patients with CF have been published (Ievers & Drotar, 1996).
- Only a few studies have examined risk and resilience factors that influence family adaptation to CF (McCubbin et al., 1983; Mullins et al., 1991; Thompson, Gustafson, Hamlett, & Spock, 1992).
- Some studies suggest that better CF treatment adherence may increase the risk of maternal psychological distress (Eiser, Zoritch, Hiller, & Havermans, 1995; Geiss, Hobbs, Hammersley-Maercklein, Kramer, & Henley, 1992).

Just as CF may reveal psychopathological symptoms in a subset of patients, the psychological status of family members and family function may also be affected adversely. Health psychologists should assess families of patients with CF for marital and family dysfunction, especially for those who are adapting poorly to CF and its treatment.

Parents of Children With CF

Parents devote extra effort to the care of a child with CF. Because the child has a terminal illness, parents may distort their perspectives of their roles. Several studies have explored how CF affects parenting behavior:

- Studies on parenting of siblings of patients with CF have found no evidence of favoritism or permissiveness (Capelli, McGrath, MacDonald, Katsanis, & Lascelles, 1989; Goldberg, Washington, Morris, Fischer-Fay, & Simmons, 1990).
- One careful diary study showed that parents spend more time with patients with CF than their siblings, and CF families

spend less time in recreation compared with control families (Quittner & Opipari, 1994).

- Ecological assessments (e.g., telephone recall interviews, daily diaries) of family CF management offer promise of yielding information with direct clinical utility (Ievers & Drotar, 1996; Quittner et al., 1996).

Clinicians should recognize that some parents may treat a child with CF differently than they treat the child's siblings. Health psychologists should promote similar privileges and responsibilities for patients with CF and their healthy siblings.

Adherence With Treatment Regimen: Family Management of CF

The complex CF treatment regimen places significant demands on patients and families. Few patients show consistently perfect treatment adherence, and many endure chronic struggles with maintaining adequate adherence.

- Bartholomew, Sockrider, Seilheimer, Czyzewski, and Parcel (1993) validated 149 performance objectives for self-care for CF. These behaviors could serve as a standard for evaluating CF self-management behaviors.
- Other studies have explored psychological and social correlates of adherence to the CF regimen. Ricker, Delamater, and Hsu's (1998) telephone interview study indicated that higher self-esteem and younger age predict better adherence. Similarly, Gudas, Koocher, and Wypij (1991) reported that better adherence was associated with younger age, higher levels of optimism, and more knowledge of CF.

Consistent adherence to the CF treatment regimen is difficult to maintain. Families should be helped to recognize that perfect adherence may be laudable, but most patients struggle with doing all that is asked of them. Health psychologists should assist families with using behavioral contracts and behavior modification techniques to improve treatment adherence (Christophersen, 1994).

Promotion of Adequate Caloric Intake

Children with CF are expected to consume about 125% to 150% more calories daily than are their healthy peers. Research indicates that most patients with CF fail to achieve this goal, and health psychologists have much to offer in the assessment and treatment of inadequate caloric intake among these patients.

- Direct observation of mealtime interactions is an excellent method of identifying child and parent behaviors that contribute to poor eating and of evaluating interventions targeting these problems (e.g., Stark, Bowen, Tyc, Evans, & Pasero, 1990; Stark, Knapp, & Bowen, 1993; Stark, Powers, Jelalian, Rape, & Miller, 1994).
- One empirically validated treatment for poor eating habits of patients with CF is a behavioral approach consisting of instructions, feedback, modeling, and rehearsal of differential reinforcement of appropriate mealtime behavior. These studies report an average increase in caloric consumption of 1,000 kcal per day and clinically significant weight gain maintained for intervals as long as 2 years (Stark et al., 1990, 1993, 1994).

Direct observation of mealtime behavior is the most productive method of assessing the problem of inadequate caloric intake. Behavior modification has been soundly empirically validated as a treatment for poor eating habits of patients with CF.

OBESITY

Obesity is a disorder of energy balance that develops when energy intake exceeds energy expenditure (Epstein, 1993). Obesity is most commonly measured by using the body mass index (BMI; Jeffery et al., 2000), which is calculated by dividing weight in kilograms by height in meters squared. Almost 25% of children and adolescents in the United States are obese, an increase of more than 20% in the past decade (Troiano, Flegal, Kuczmarski, Campbell, & Johnson, 1995). In adults in the United States, the prevalence rates increased 33% in the 1980s (Williamson, 1995). More than one half of all U.S. citizens exceed the newest definition of obesity (BMI ≥ 25) (National Heart, Lung, and Blood Institute [NHLBI] Obesity Education Initiative Expert Panel, 1998).

Risk Factors

Obesity is a multifactorial trait that is influenced by social, behavioral, physiological, metabolic, cellular, and molecular variables (Bar-Or et al., 1998).

- The genetic contribution to obesity may be 25% to 40% of variance in body mass or body fat (Bouchard, 1994). Environmental factors that affect body fat may include energy intake, physical activity, smoking, and alcohol intake (Bar-Or et al., 1998).

- Risk for obesity is greater among older adults, women, and members of racial or ethnic minorities (Broussard et al., 1991; Sobel & Stunkard, 1989).
- About 40% of 7-year-olds and 70% of adolescents who are obese become obese adults (Mossberg, 1989; Stark, Atkins, Wolff, & Douglas, 1981). In addition, childhood obesity increases the risk for hypertension, hypercholesterolemia, hyperinsulinemia, decreased release of growth hormone, respiratory disorders, and orthopedic problems. Although being obese as a child increases the risk for obesity in adulthood, most adults who are obese were not obese as children. The relative risk for obesity increases with the age of the child, and the probability of growing out of obesity declines with age (Epstein, 1993).

Treatment of Childhood Obesity

Several excellent treatment outcome studies have shown both short-term and long-term effectiveness of treatment of children and adolescents who are obese. Successful programs have incorporated numerous basic treatment components:

- One basic component is to change the diet. The goal is to decrease caloric intake to promote weight loss while still providing enough calories to promote growth (Epstein, 1995). Epstein, Valoski, Wing, and McCurley (1994) taught children and their families to use the "traffic light" diet program. Foods are categorized as a *red* (stop), *yellow* (use caution), or *green* (go) light depending on their caloric content.
- Successful weight control programs also promote physical activity. Epstein and colleagues advocated a lifestyle activity approach rather than structured exercise, because the goal is to increase energy expenditure rather than promote fitness. They found that children who engage in lifestyle activities that are less sedentary lose more weight. Successfully decreasing the amount of time spent in sedentary activities such as watching television and playing video games improves weight loss more than structured attempts to increase physical activity (Epstein, 1995).
- Inclusion of the family in childhood obesity treatment is crucial. Epstein et al. (1994) found that family-based obesity treatment has produced long-term (10-year) changes in pre-

adolescents who are obese. A family-centered treatment approach encourages parents to reinforce and model good eating and exercise behavior and changes the child's environment to minimize cues for overeating and inactivity.

Treatment of Adult Obesity

Research has shown that short-term weight loss is clearly achievable for adults, but long-term weight loss has been more successful for children and adolescents. The natural history of weight loss resulting from behavioral programs is very consistent. Usually individuals lose weight rapidly for the first few months, with their maximum weight loss occurring at about 6 months. They then gradually gain weight until they stabilize at a weight somewhat below baseline levels (Jeffery et al., 2000).

- The rate of initial weight loss is an important determinant of the magnitude of long-term weight loss (Jeffery et al., 2000). Recently this area of research has emphasized finding ways to increase initial weight loss.
- Adult weight loss programs typically include diet and exercise, as do treatments for childhood obesity. Increasing the intensity of the program and using a very low-calorie diet (VLCD) can produce larger initial weight losses. However, little evidence shows that VLCDs enhance long-term maintenance of weight (Jeffery et al., 2000).
- The choice of one specific dietary prescription over another does not have much of an empirical basis. Dietary prescriptions that are based on fat intake versus total calorie intake have been equally effective for short-term and long-term weight loss. Adding a strong exercise component to behavioral treatment for obesity improves weight loss in the short-term and has potential for improving long-term weight maintenance (Pavlou, Krey, & Steffee, 1989; Sikand, Dondo, Foreyt, Jones, & Gotto, 1988).
- Longer treatment yields more weight loss (Perri, Nezu, Patti, & McCann, 1989). Some researchers have advocated a chronic disease treatment model of obesity rather than short-term treatment with minimal follow-up (Perri, Nezu, & Viegener, 1992). Perri (1998) reviewed seven studies that used extended contact schedules (at least biweekly) for between 20 and 52 weeks and found positive results.
- Enhancing motivation and teaching maintenance skills are other important components of successful weight loss programs (Jeffery et al., 2000).

- Small but significant short- and long-term benefits result from including spouses and friends in obesity treatment (Black, Gleser, & Kooyers, 1990).
- Medications have shown some promise in obesity treatment. The compound of fenfluramine and phentermine ("fen-phen") was removed from the market because a substantial minority of patients taking the drug developed valvular heart disease. However, other medications such as sibutramine (Meridia) and orlistat (Xenical) have been approved by the FDA. Sibutramine works by decreasing appetite via reuptake inhibition of serotonin, norepinephrine, and dopamine (*Physicians' Desk Reference [PDR]*, 2001). Orlistat works by inhibiting digestive enzymes, which reduces fat absorption by about 30% (*PDR*, 2001). Research with the hormone leptin, which is involved in the storage of fat, also may hold promise. Weight loss medications are most effective, however, when combined with behavioral programs (Jeffery et al., 2000).

Obesity is a complex trait influenced by social, behavioral, and physiological factors, and it has profound public health implications. The most successful treatment of obesity includes changing diet and exercise patterns. When treating children, family involvement is especially important. A chronic disease model of obesity should be considered because longer treatment is associated with better outcomes, and individuals tend to gain weight after treatment stops. Medications are a promising adjunctive treatment to behavioral programs.

ENDOCRINE DISORDERS

Any hormone can be produced in excess, produced insufficiently, or not produced at all. Many of these endocrine disorders have psychological effects, and health psychologists have done a substantial amount of research on these conditions. This section illustrates the breadth of this research by reviewing some key advances in the knowledge of the endocrine disorders that have been researched most heavily. Some of these disorders have a genetic etiology and are listed in other areas of the *ICD–9*, but all have significant endocrine involvement and are typically treated by endocrinologists.

Turner Syndrome

Turner syndrome (TS) is a genetic condition affecting females and is caused by the absence or abnormality of an X chromosome in at least some of the cells. The prevalence is about 1 in 2,500 to 5,000 female births (Hook & Warburton, 1983). Individuals with TS usually exhibit short stature and dysgenesis of the ovaries. Associated features may include a thick, short, webbed neck and many other medical problems (Sandberg & Barrick, 1995). Treatment of TS includes replacement of estrogen and growth hormone. In addition, individuals with TS have the following characteristics:

- Global intelligence of individuals with TS is typically in the average range (Rovet, 1990).
- Individuals with TS are at increased risk for impairments in visual–spatial processing (Rovet, 1990) and visual working memory (Buchanan, Pavlovic, & Rovet, 1998). They may also have deficits in executive function, memory, and attention and a higher incidence of hyperactivity and inattention (Rovet, 1993, 1994).
- Academic functioning, especially in mathematics, can be compromised as a consequence of cognitive weaknesses (Rovet, 1993).
- Individuals with TS have poorer relationships with peers than do peers with idiopathic short stature. They appear to have trouble accurately deciphering facial affect (McCauley, Kay, Ito, & Treder, 1987) and may appear socially immature.
- Individuals with TS are not at any greater risk for severe psychopathological symptoms than are others, but they are at risk for problems with psychosocial adaptation (Berch & McCauley, 1990; McCauley, 1990).

Patients with TS are at risk for cognitive and academic problems. They should be evaluated regularly to optimize school placement. They also are at risk for attention and social adjustment difficulties that may require intervention.

Klinefelter Syndrome

Klinefelter syndrome (KS) is a sex chromosomal variation that affects males. An extra X chromosome (chromosome 47, XXY) is present in 80% of the individuals, whereas the other 20% involve mosaic forms (e.g., chromosome 46, XY; chromosome 48, XXXY) and other chromosomal variations (Nielsen, 1991). KS occurs in about 1 in every 1,000 live male births, making it the most common chromosomal variation found in humans—and it is believed to be underdiagnosed.

Studies that are based on clinically referred samples may represent individuals with the most pronounced medical and psychological symptoms (Sandberg & Barrick, 1995). Individuals with KS display infertility; incomplete masculine body build; breast development (gynecomastia); and social, cognitive, and academic problems. They also may have small testes and penis sizes for their age, tall stature, disproportionately long legs (Ratcliffe, Butler, & Jones, 1990), and delays in puberty (Nielsen & Wohlert, 1990). Treatment of KS includes testosterone replacement therapy at approximately age 12. Individuals with prominent gynecomastia may undergo surgical correction. Additional important facts about KS include the following:

- Global intelligence of individuals with KS is normal and typically in the average range.
- Language disorders occur in about 50% of individuals with KS (Walzer, 1985) and include verbal distraction and deficits in articulation, comprehension, sequencing (Leonard, Landy, Ruddle, & Lubs, 1974), short-term memory, and reading skills (Bender, Puck, Salbenblatt, & Robinson, 1986).
- The most consistent finding in those with KS is poor school performance and lifelong language, reading, and spelling problems (e.g., Ratcliffe et al., 1990).
- Delays in gross and fine motor skills, coordination, speed, dexterity, and strength also have been noted (Mandoki & Sumner, 1991).
- Individuals with KS may exhibit increased anxiety, immaturity, passivity, withdrawal, poor peer relationships, academic underachievement, and low levels of activity (Robinson, Bender, & Linden, 1990; Sandberg & Barrick, 1995).

Boys with KS should be evaluated for possible language delays and receive appropriate academic remediation. They may need intervention for psychological problems, which may include social adjustment difficulties.

Congenital Hypothyroidism

Congenital hypothyroidism (CH) is a thyroid hormone deficiency that is present at birth. The thyroid secretes several hormones that regulate metabolism and growth. The effects of congenital hypothyroidism include stunted growth; if untreated, individuals can develop potentially severe mental retardation (Sandberg & Barrick, 1995).

CH occurs in 1 in 4,000 live births (Fisher, 1991). Since 1974, newborns have been screened for CH, enabling prompt hormone replacement therapy. Before then, early diagnosis was difficult because the symptoms of this condition (e.g., feeding problems, failure to thrive, constipation, hypotonia) take time to appear (Sandberg & Barrick, 1995). Some infants continue to be undertreated, resulting in cognitive deficits and lethargy (Fisher & Foley, 1989; New England Congenital Hypothyroidism Collaborative, 1990). Overtreatment of hypothyroidism can result in restlessness, distractibility, and anxiety (Wallace, MacCrimmon, & Goldberg, 1980). Additional key points about CH include the following:

- Major improvements in cognitive and academic development have occurred since 1974 (New England Congenital Hypothyroidism Collaborative, 1985).
- Findings regarding intellectual and academic functioning are mixed. Some studies have found global intelligence and academic achievement to be comparable to unaffected siblings or classmates (New England Congenital Hypothyroidism Collaborative, 1990). Other studies have revealed evidence of somewhat lower intellectual functioning in these children compared to control children (e.g., Rovet, Ehrlich, & Sorbara, 1992). The children most at risk for these complications are those with total absence of the thyroid gland (Fisher, 1991). Children without thyroid tissue resemble those with nonverbal learning disabilities with deficits in language acquisition, auditory perception, visual–spatial organization, and numerical abilities (Rovet et al., 1992).
- A large proportion of children (44% in one sample) with CH exhibit significant thyroid hormone deficiency as a result of inconsistent adherence with hormone replacement (New England Congenital Hypothyroidism Collaborative, 1994). Improvement in adherence has been associated with improvement in WISC–R Full Scale IQ (Wechsler, 1974).
- Some children with CH exhibit selective neurocognitive deficits, although little consensus exists about the type or extent of impairment. These deficits include speech and language delays (Rovet, Ehrlich, & Sorbara, 1987) and weaker perceptual–motor abilities (Rovet et al., 1987).

Adherence to hormone replacement is critical for individuals with CH but is problematic for many of them. Children without thyroid glands are at particular risk for cognitive deficits and should be targeted for early identification and intervention.

Congenital Adrenal Hyperplasia

Congenital adrenal hyperplasia (CAH) is an autosomal recessive disorder. The resulting deficiency in the adrenal 21-hydroxylase enzyme causes decreased glucocorticoid production (simple-virilizing CAH) or decreased mineralocorticoid production (salt-wasting CAH).

Females with CAH are exposed to an atypical amount of androgens during the prenatal and perinatal period. Individuals with CAH also are exposed to excessive adrenocorticotropic hormone (ACTH) and glucocorticoid precursors (e.g., progesterone), and those with salt-wasting CAH are exposed to excessive mineralocorticoid precursors (Nass & Baker, 1991a). The prevalence of CAH is 1 in 5,000 to 15,000 births (Miller & Levine, 1987). In addition, individuals with CAH have the following characteristics:

- Many studies show that patients with CAH have higher intelligence than control patients, but their intellectual abilities are similar to siblings and parents. It is unclear whether this effect is caused by genetic, hormonal, or socioeconomic factors (e.g., McGuire & Omenn, 1975).
- Patients with salt-wasting CAH may have lower IQ scores than those with the simple virilizing type (Nass & Baker, 1991a). Abnormal white matter typical in individuals with demyelination or gliosis after infarction has been found in patients with salt-wasting CAH (Haimes et al., 1989).
- Females with CAH may be at increased risk for learning disabilities because of prenatal androgen exposure (Nass & Baker, 1991b).
- Patients with simple virilizing CAH may be at greater risk for learning disabilities than those with salt-wasting CAH. Because of brain damage that can occur during a salt-wasting crisis, patients with salt-wasting CAH demonstrate generally decreased cognitive abilities rather than the specific learning disabilities that are caused by androgen effects in those with simple virilizing CAH (Nass & Baker, 1991a).

Clinicians should be aware that, although females with CAH have average to above-average intelligence, they may be at risk for learning disabilities. Their pattern of cognitive deficits may differ depending on their type of CAH.

Growth Hormone Deficiency

Growth hormone is produced by the anterior pituitary gland. Multiple congenital and acquired factors cause growth hormone deficiency (GHD). GHD can also be caused by environmental influences such as child abuse and neglect—the condition is known as psychosocial short stature (see below). The prevalence of GHD is about 1 in 3,500 to 5,000 births (Lindsay, Feldkamp, Harris, Robertson, & Rallison, 1994). Treatment includes daily injections of biosynthetic growth hormone for several years. Additional key points regarding GHD include the following:

- Overall, intelligence of those with GHD is in the average range.

- Some individuals with GHD may have specific cognitive deficits, including visual–motor (e.g., Siegel & Hopwood, 1986). Researchers have found some evidence of learning disabilities in this population (Stabler et al., 1994), but findings have been somewhat inconsistent, and sample sizes generally have been small.
- GHD may be a weaker predictor of adult educational attainment (i.e., last grade or degree completed) than academic achievement in the primary grades (e.g., Stabler, Siegel, & Clopper, 1991).
- Some studies have found children with GHD to be immature and have poor social problem-solving abilities (e.g., Siegel & Hopwood, 1986).

Although individuals with GHD are at risk for learning problems, the difficulties may not persist into adulthood. Those with GHD are at risk for social adjustment deficits such as social problem-solving difficulties that may require clinical intervention.

Psychosocial Short Stature

Psychosocial short stature (PSS) is characterized by growth retardation resulting from environmentally induced GHD. Reports of its prevalence vary widely. Children with PSS typically have abusive or neglectful caretakers (e.g., Blizzard & Bulatovic, 1992), and they commonly have marked developmental delays and behavioral disturbances.

Blizzard and Bulatovic (1992) identified two PSS types. Type I occurs in infants ages 2 years or younger. These infants usually show signs of nutritional deficiency, failure to thrive, and short stature. Parents of these children are often overwhelmed with responsibilities and lack effective coping skills but do not appear particularly rejecting. Infants with Type I PSS typically normalize in their growth once sufficient calories are provided. This type of PSS is thought to be quite common, although firm estimates of the incidence are not known (Blizzard & Bulatovic, 1992). Children with Type I PSS are treated by optimizing nutritional intake and teaching parents good coping and parenting skills.

Type II PSS usually occurs in children age 3 and older and includes a greater psychological component. These children are typically physically abused or neglected. The incidence of Type II PSS is unknown but is assumed to be underdiagnosed (Blizzard & Bulatovic, 1992). The endocrine, behavioral, and intellectual functioning of children with Type II PSS often normalizes when they are removed from their hostile environment and participate in other interventions. Treatment of these children includes improving their environment—which may mean removing them from the home—family therapy intervention, treatment of the parent's psychopathological symptoms, and treatment of the child's emotional and behavioral problems. Other characteristics of children with PSS include the following:

- Children with Type II PSS typically have a history of emotional disturbance and bizarre behaviors, with particularly abnormal eating and drinking behaviors.
- Children with PSS may exhibit a range of internalizing and externalizing behavior problems, including self-injury, disordered attachment, poor peer relationships, sleep problems, and insensitivity to pain (e.g., Blizzard & Bulatovic, 1992).
- Many children with PSS have developmental delays, which may include delayed language development, psychomotor retardation, and impaired cognitive functioning (i.e., IQs in the borderline to mentally retarded range; Annecillo, 1986).

Removal from or intensive amelioration of the home environment is warranted for children with PSS. In addition, the children may need psychological treatment for eating problems as well as other behavioral and emotional difficulties.

Intersexuality

Several rare endocrine disorders affect the developing reproductive organs, resulting in poorly developed or ambiguous genitalia. With disorders such as complete androgen insensitivity syndrome (CAIS), a genotypically male child is born with female external genitalia. These individuals are usually raised as female (Slijper, Drop, Molenaar, & de Muinck Keizer-Schrama, 1998).

However, in situations of hermaphroditism or pseudohermaphroditism with ambiguous genitalia, the issue of gender is complicated because there are no reliable criteria for sex assignment. Therefore, parents often must make this decision for their child. The child's genotype, penis length, and capacity to react to testosterone stimulation and to virilize in puberty, as well as the functionality of the male external genitalia in adulthood, are factors used to make the sex assignment decision (Slijper et al., 1998). Treatment for ambiguous genitalia usually involves surgical correction soon after the diagnosis is made. Vaginal plastic surgery and dilation usually are not performed until the individual is in the early teenage years (Slijper et al., 1998).

Individuals with intersexuality disorders are at increased risk for developing psychopathological symptoms. Although the majority of individuals with hermaphroditism are able to sustain their assigned gender, they are at risk for developing problems with gender identity, particularly if stigmatized (Money, Devore, & Norman, 1986; Money & Norman, 1987).

They also are at risk for developing depression and adjustment difficulties (Money & Norman, 1987; Slijpers et al., 1998).

Having a child with an intersex condition can be very confusing and stressful for families, especially as they consider the decision about the gender of their child with limited reliable criteria. It is important for health psychologists to be part of the treatment team for children with intersex conditions and their families to help them adjust to the condition during diagnosis and throughout childhood and adolescence. Given that these children may be at risk for gender identity problems and general psychopathological conditions, treatment should focus on early detection and prevention of psychological problems.

Precocious and Delayed Puberty

Precocious puberty is pubertal development before age 8 in girls and 9 in boys (Kaplan & Grumbach, 1990). Precocious puberty is associated with normal signs of puberty, including secondary sex characteristics, accelerated growth, and fertility. Many factors can cause precocious puberty, including central nervous system (CNS) abnormalities, adrenal gland dysfunction, lesions in the brain or endocrine glands, or a benign condition.

In girls, about 90% of cases are idiopathic. In contrast, about 80% of boys have a pathological cause (Lee, 1985). Precocious puberty is rare, occurring in approximately 1 in 20,000 children and about 8 times more frequently in girls than in boys (Mouridsen & Larsen, 1992). Precocious puberty usually is treated by medications that temporarily stop the influence of the pituitary gland on the gonads (Wheeler & Styne, 1991). The best results are achieved if treatment begins early to prevent premature growth, which can compromise adult height.

Puberty is considered delayed in girls without breast budding by age 13 and in boys lacking testicular enlargement by age 14 (Mansfield, 1999). Causes of delayed puberty include chronic illness, tumor, nutritional insufficiency, or endocrinopathy. Hormone replacement therapy is used in those with extremely delayed puberty (Mansfield, 1999). Other key points regarding delayed and precocious puberty include the following:

- Delayed and precocious puberty can affect social and emotional adjustment. The effects of early or late maturation differ by gender. In general, late-maturing boys and early maturing girls have the most difficulties (Gordon & Schroeder, 1995).
- Children with precocious puberty typically exhibit global intelligence in the average to above-average range (e.g., Rovet, 1983).

- Precocious puberty can affect adults' perceptions of these children, causing them to be perceived as slow learners or as socially immature (Sandberg & Barrick, 1995).
- Girls with precocious puberty have an incidence of psychopathological symptoms that is similar to the general population (e.g., Ehrhardt et al., 1984; Sonis et al., 1986). Children with precocious or delayed puberty are at risk for social adjustment problems.
- Parents and teachers are frequently concerned that children with precocious puberty will develop early sexual interests and behavior (Mazur & Clopper, 1991). However, the sexual behavior of children with precocious puberty does not differ from the normal sexual activity of age-matched peers (e.g., Money & Alexander, 1969; Money & Walker, 1971).

Children with precocious or delayed puberty, especially late-maturing boys and early maturing girls, are at risk for psychological adjustment difficulties. Those with precocious puberty do not generally show early sexual interest or behaviors, although this is a common parental fear.

CONCLUSION

Psychological variables play multiple roles in affecting the etiology, course, and outcome of endocrine, metabolic, and nutritional disorders, and health psychologists have made many significant contributions toward our understanding of these processes. This chapter has highlighted the most salient clinical implications of this research for psychologists who work with these patient populations in a clinical setting. Ideally, health psychologists should strive to maintain their familiarity with this ever-growing body of research literature. Although a great deal of research about the disorders covered in this chapter exists, many important questions remain to be investigated.

Examples of valuable future research topics include the following:

- Additional treatment outcomes studies that demonstrate that psychological interventions have both efficacy and cost benefits for patients with these medical conditions
- Further studies of interactions among psychiatric disorders and diseases of the endocrine, metabolic, nutritional, and immune systems
- Extension and replication of existing research to some of the more rare conditions in this spectrum—research that may require multicenter investigations
- Studies of psychological and behavioral factors that predict

benefits from newly emerging medical treatments for these disorders

- Research on the dissemination of interventions that have been empirically validated in patients who have these medical conditions.

REFERENCES

Aiken, J., Wallander, J., Bell, D., & Cole, J. (1992). Daily stress variability, learned resourcefulness, regimen adherence, and metabolic control in Type I diabetes mellitus: Evaluation of a path model. *Journal of Consulting and Clinical Psychology, 60*, 113–118.

Anderson, B. J. (1996). Involving family members in diabetes treatment. In B. J. Anderson & R. R. Rubin (Eds.), *Practical psychology for diabetes clinicians* (pp. 43–52). Alexandria, VA: American Diabetes Association.

Anderson, B. J., Wolf, F. M., Burkhart, M. T., Cornell, R. G., & Bacon, G. E. (1989). Effects of peer-group intervention on metabolic control of adolescents with IDDM: Randomized outpatient study. *Diabetes Care, 12*, 179–183.

Anderson, R. M., Funnell, M. M., & Arnold, M. S. (1996). Using the patient empowerment approach to help patients change behavior. In B. J. Anderson & R. R. Rubin (Eds.), *Practical psychology for diabetes clinicians* (pp. 163–172). Alexandria, VA: American Diabetes Association.

Anderson, R. M., Funnell, M. M., Butler, P., Arnold, M. S., Fitzgerald, J. T., & Feste, C. (1995). Patient empowerment: Results of a randomized, controlled trial. *Diabetes Care, 18*, 943–949.

Annecillo, C. (1986). Environment and intelligence: Reversible impairment of intellectual growth in the syndrome of abuse dwarfism. In B. Stabler & L. E. Underwood (Eds.), *Slow grows the child: Psychosocial aspects of growth delay* (pp. 168–177). Hillsdale, NJ: Erlbaum.

Austin, E. J., & Deary, I. J. (1999). Effects of repeated hypoglycemia on cognitive function: A psychometrically validated reanalysis of the Diabetes Control and Complications Trial data. *Diabetes Care, 22*, 1273–1277.

Bar-Or, O., Foreyt, J., Bouchard, C., Brownell, K. D., Dietz, W. H., Ravussin, E., Salbe, A. D., Schwenger, S., St. Jeor, S., & Torun, B. (1998). Physical activity, genetic, and nutritional considerations in childhood weight management. *Medicine and Science in Sports and Exercise, 30*, 2–10.

Bartholomew, L. K., Sockrider, M. M., Seilheimer, D. K., Czyzewski, D. I., & Parcel, G. S. (1993). Performance objectives for the self-management of cystic fibrosis. *Patient Education and Counseling, 22*, 15–25.

Bender, B. G., Puck, M. H., Salbenblatt, J. A., & Robinson, A. (1986). Dyslexia in 47, XXY boys identified at birth. *Behavior Genetics, 16*, 343–354.

Berch, D., & McCauley, E. (1990). Psychosocial functioning in individuals with sex chromosome abnormalities. In C. S. Holmes (Ed.), *Psychoneuroimmunology: Brain, behavior, and hormonal interactions* (pp. 164–183). New York: Springer-Verlag.

Black, D. R., Gleser, L. J., & Kooyers, K. J. (1990). A meta-analytic evaluation of couples weight-loss programs. *Health Psychology, 9,* 330–347.

Blizzard, R. M., & Bulatovic, A. (1992). Psychosocial short stature: A syndrome with many variables. *Balliere's Clinical Endocrinology and Metabolism, 6,* 687–712.

Boardway, R. H., Delamater, A. M., Tomakowsky, J., & Gutai, J. P. (1993). Stress management training for adolescents with diabetes. *Journal of Pediatric Psychology, 18,* 29–45.

Bouchard, C. (1994). Genetics of obesity: Overview and research directions. In C. Bouchard (Ed.), *The genetics of obesity* (pp. 223–233). Boca Raton, FL: CRC Press.

Broussard, B. A., Johnson, A., Himes, J. H., Story, M., Fichtner, R., Hauck, F., Bachman-Carter, K., Hayes, J., Frohlich, K., Gray, N., Valway, S., & Gohdes, D. (1991). Prevalence of obesity in American Indians and Alaska Natives. *American Journal of Clinical Nutrition, 53,* 15355–15425.

Buchanan, L., Pavlovic, J., & Rovet J. (1998). A reexamination of the visuospatial deficit in Turner syndrome: Contributions of working memory. *Developmental Neuropsychology, 14,* 341–367.

Capelli, M., McGrath, P. J., MacDonald, N. E., Katsanis, J., & Lascelles, M. (1989). Parental care and overprotection of children with cystic fibrosis. *British Journal of Medical Psychology, 62,* 281–289.

Chase, H. P., & Jackson, G. (1981). Stress and sugar control in children with insulin-dependent diabetes mellitus. *Journal of Pediatrics, 98,* 1011–1013.

Christophersen, E. R. (1994). *Pediatric compliance: A guide for the primary care physician.* New York: Plenum Press.

Clement, S. (1995). Diabetes self-management education. *Diabetes Care, 18,* 1204–1214.

Cox, D. J., Clarke, W. L., & Gonder-Frederick, L. A. (1985). Accuracy of perceiving blood glucose in IDDM. *Diabetes Care, 8,* 529–536.

Cox, D. J., Gonder-Frederick, L. A., Polonsky, W., Schlundt, D., Julian, D., & Clarke, W. L. (1995). A multicenter evaluation of blood glucose awareness training. *Diabetes Care, 18,* 523–528.

Delamater, A. M., Bubb, J., Davis, S. G., Smith, J. A., Schmidt, L., White, N. H., & Santiago, J. V. (1990). Randomized prospective study of self-management training with newly diagnosed diabetic children. *Diabetes Care, 13,* 492–498.

Delamater, A. M., Davis, S. G., Bubb, J., Smith, J. A., White, N. H., & Santiago, J. V. (1989). Self-monitoring of blood glucose by adolescents with diabetes: Technical skills and utilization of data. *The Diabetes Educator, 15,* 56–61.

Delamater, A. M., Smith, J. A., Kurtz, S. C., & White, N. H. (1988). Dietary skills and adherence in children with Type I diabetes mellitus. *The Diabetes Educator, 14,* 33–36.

Diabetes Control and Complications Trial Research Group. (1987). Reliability and validity of a quality of life measure for the Diabetes Control and Complications Trial. *Diabetes Care, 11*, 725–732.

Diabetes Control and Complications Trial Research Group. (1993). Diabetes Control and Complications Trial: The effect of intensive treatment of diabetes on the development and progression of long-term complications in insulin-dependent diabetes mellitus. *New England Journal of Medicine, 329*, 977–986.

Ehrhardt, A. A., Meyer-Bahlburg, H. F. L., Bell, J. J., Cohen, S. F., Healey, J. M., Stiel, R., et al. (1984). Idiopathic precocious puberty in girls: Psychiatric follow-up in adolescence. *Journal of the American Academy of Child Psychiatry, 23*, 23–33.

Eiser, C., Zoritch, B., Hiller, J., & Havermans, T. (1995). Routine stresses in caring for a child with cystic fibrosis. *Journal of Psychosomatic Research, 39*, 641–646.

Epstein, L. H. (1993). New developments in childhood obesity. In A. J. Stunkard & T. A. Wadden (Eds.), *Obesity: Theory and therapy* (3rd ed., pp. 301–312). New York: Raven Press.

Epstein, L. H. (1995). Management of obesity in children. In K. D. Brownell & C. G. Fairburn (Eds.), *Eating disorders and obesity: A comprehensive handbook* (pp. 516–519). New York: Guilford Press.

Epstein, L. H., Valoski, A., Wing, R. R., & McCurley, J. (1994). Ten-year outcomes of behavioral family-based treatment for childhood obesity. *Health Psychology, 13*, 373–383.

Fisher, D. A. (1991). Management of congenital hypothyroidism. *Journal of Clinical Endocrinology and Metabolism, 72*, 523–529.

Fisher, D. A., & Foley, B. L. (1989). Early treatment of congenital hypothyroidism. *Pediatrics, 83*, 785–789.

Fisher, E. B., La Greca, A. M., Greco, P., Arfken, C., & Schneiderman, N. (1997). Directive and nondirective social support in diabetes management. *International Journal of Behavioral Medicine, 4*, 131–144.

Fowler, J. E., Budzynski, T. H., & Vandenbergh, R. L. (1978). Effects of an EMG biofeedback relaxation program on the control of diabetes. *Biofeedback and Self-Regulation, 1*, 105–112.

Geiss, S. K., Hobbs, S. A., Hammersley-Maercklin, G., Kramer, J. C., & Henley, M. (1992). Psychosocial factors related to perceived noncompliance with cystic fibrosis treatment. *Journal of Clinical Psychology, 48*, 99–103.

Glasgow, R. E., McCaul, K. D., & Schaefer, L. C. (1987). Self-care behaviors and glycemic control in Type I diabetes. *Journal of Chronic Diseases, 40*, 399–412.

Goldberg, S., Washington, J., Morris, P., Fischer-Fay, A., & Simmons, R. J. (1990). Early diagnosed chronic illness and mother–child relationships in the first two years. *Canadian Journal of Psychiatry, 35*, 726–733.

Gonder-Frederick, L. A., Cox, D. J., Kovatchev, B., Schlundt, D., & Clarke, W. L. (1997). A biopsychobehavioral model of risk of severe hypoglycemia. *Diabetes Care, 20*, 661–669.

Gordon, B. N., & Schroeder, C. S. (1995). *Sexuality: A developmental approach to problems*. New York: Plenum Press.

Gross, A., Heimann, L., Shapiro, R., & Schultz, R. M. (1983). Children with diabetes: Social skills training and HbA$_{1c}$ levels. *Behavior Modification, 7,* 151–163.

Gudas, L. J., Koocher, G. P., & Wypij, D. (1991). Perceptions of medical compliance in children and adolescents with cystic fibrosis. *Journal of Developmental and Behavioral Pediatrics, 12,* 236–242.

Haimes, A., Heier, L., Speiser, P., Nass, R., New, M., & Deck, M. R. (1989). White matter abnormalities in congenital adrenal hyperplasia. *American Journal of Neuroradiology, 10,* 410.

Hanson, C. L., Henggeler, S. W., & Burghen, G. A. (1987). Social competence and parental support as mediators of the link between stress and metabolic control in adolescents with insulin-dependent diabetes mellitus. *Journal of Consulting and Clinical Psychology, 55,* 529–533.

Hanson, S., & Pichert, J. (1986). Perceived stress and diabetic control in adolescents. *Health Psychology, 5,* 439–452.

Hook, E. B., & Warburton, D. (1983). The distribution of chromosomal genotypes associated with Turner's syndrome: Live birth prevalence rates and evidence for diminished fetal mortality and severity in genotypes associated with structural X abnormalities or mosaicism. *Human Genetics, 64,* 24–27.

Ievers, C. E., & Drotar, D. (1996). Family and parental functioning in cystic fibrosis. *Journal of Developmental and Behavioral Pediatrics, 17,* 48–55.

Ingersoll, G., & Marrero, D. G. (1991). A modified quality of life measure for youths: Psychometric properties. *The Diabetes Educator, 17,* 114–118.

Jeffery, R. W., Epstein, L. H., Wilson, G. T., Drewnowski, A., Stunkard, A. J., Wing, R. R., et al. (2000). Long-term maintenance of weight loss: Current status. *Health Psychology, 19*(Suppl. 1), 5–16.

Johnson, S. B. (1995). Insulin-dependent diabetes mellitus in childhood. In M. C. Roberts (Ed.), *Handbook of pediatric psychology* (2nd ed., pp. 286–309). New York: Guilford Press.

Johnson, S. B., Pollak, J., Silverstein, J., Rosenbloom, A., Spillar, R., McCallum, M., & Harkavy, J. (1982). Cognitive and behavioral knowledge about insulin-dependent diabetes among children and parents. *Journal of Pediatrics, 69,* 708–713.

Johnson, S. B., Silverstein, J. H., Rosenbloom, A., Carter, R., & Cunningham, W. (1986). Assessing daily management of childhood diabetes. *Health Psychology, 5,* 545–564.

Kaplan, R. M., Chadwick, M. W., & Schimmel, L. E. (1985). Social learning intervention to improve metabolic control in Type I diabetes mellitus: Pilot experiment results. *Diabetes Care, 8,* 152–155.

Kaplan, S. L., & Grumbach, M. M. (1990). Pathophysiology and treatment of sexual precocity. *Journal of Clinical Endocrinology and Metabolism, 71,* 785–789.

Kovacs, M., Goldston, D., Obrosky, D. S., & Bonar, L. K. (1997). Psychiatric disorders in youths with IDDM: Rates and risk factors. *Diabetes Care, 20,* 36–44.

La Greca, A. M., Auslander, W. F., Greco, P., Spetter, D., Fisher, E. B., & Santiago, J. V. (1995). I get by with a little help from my friends: Adolescents' support for diabetes care. *Journal of Pediatric Psychology, 20,* 449–476.

La Greca, A. M., Follansbee, D. M., & Skyler, J. S. (1990). Developmental and behavioral aspects of diabetes management in youngsters. *Children's Health Care, 19,* 132–139.

Lee, P. (1985). Disorders of puberty. In F. Lifshitz (Ed.), *Pediatric endocrinology* (pp. 143–169). New York: Marcel Dekker.

Leonard, M. F., Landy, G., Ruddle, F. H., & Lubs, H. A. (1974). Early development of children with abnormalities of the sex chromosomes: A prospective study. *Pediatrics, 54,* 208–212.

Lindsay, R., Feldkamp, M., Harris, D., Robertson, J., & Rallison, M. (1994). Utah growth study: Growth standards and the prevalence of growth hormone deficiency. *Journal of Pediatrics, 125,* 29–35.

Lorenz, R. A., & Wysocki, T. (1991). From research to practice: The family and childhood diabetes. *Diabetes Spectrum, 4,* 260–292.

Lustman, P. J., Griffith, L. S., & Clouse, R. E. (1996). Recognizing and managing depression in patients with diabetes. In B. J. Anderson & R. R. Rubin (Eds.), *Practical psychology for diabetes clinicians* (pp. 143–152). Alexandria, VA: American Diabetes Association.

Lustman, P. J., Griffith, L. S., Gavard, J. A., & Clouse, R. E. (1992). Depression in adults with diabetes. *Diabetes Care, 15,* 1631–1639.

Mandoki, M. W., & Sumner, G. S. (1991). Klinefelter syndrome: The need for early identification and treatment. *Clinical Pediatrics, 3,* 161–164.

Mansfield, M. J. (1999). Delayed puberty. In R. A. Dershewitz (Ed.), *Ambulatory pediatric care* (3rd ed., pp. 521–525). Philadelphia: Lippincott-Raven.

Mazur, T., & Clopper, R. R. (1991). Pubertal disorders: Psychology and clinical management. *Endocrinology and Metabolism Clinics of North America, 20,* 211–230.

McCauley, E. (1990). Psychosocial and emotional aspects of Turner syndrome. In D. Berch & B. Bender (Eds.), *Sex chromosome abnormalities and human behavior: Psychological studies* (pp. 78–99). Boulder, CO: Western Press & American Association for the Advancement of Science.

McCauley, E., Kay, T., Ito, J., & Treder, R. (1987). The Turner syndrome: Cognitive discrimination and behavior problems. *Child Development, 58,* 464–473.

McCubbin, H. I., McCubbin, M. A., Patterson, J. M., Cauble, A. E., Wilson, L. R., & Warwick, W. (1983). CHIP: Coping Health Inventory for Parents: An assessment of parental coping patterns in the care of the chronically ill child. *Journal of Marriage and Family, 45,* 359–370.

McGuire, L., & Omenn, G. (1975). Congenital adrenal hyperplasia. I. Family studies and IQ. *Genetics, 5,* 165–173.

Medicode. (2001). *International classification of diseases, ninth revision, clinical modification, professional for physicians volumes 1 and 2* (6th ed.). West Valley City, Utah: Ingenix, Inc.

Miller, W. L., & Levine, L. S. (1987). Molecular and clinical advances in congenital adrenal hyperplasia. *Journal of Pediatrics, 111,* 1–17.

Money, J., & Alexander, D. (1969). Psychosexual development and absence of homosexuality in males with precocious puberty. Review of 18 cases. *Journal of Nervous and Mental Diseases, 148,* 111–123.

Money, J., Devore, H., & Norman, B. F. (1986). Gender identity and gender transposition: Longitudinal outcome study of 32 male hermaphrodites assigned as girls. *Journal of Sex and Marital Therapy, 12,* 165–181.

Money, J., & Norman, B. F. (1987). Gender identity and gender transposition: Longitudinal outcome study of 24 male hermaphrodites assigned as boys. *Journal of Sex and Marital Therapy, 13,* 75–92.

Money, J., & Walker, P. A. (1971). Psychosexual development, maternalism, non-promiscuity, and body image in 15 females with precocious puberty. *Archives of Sexual Behavior, 1,* 45–60.

Mossberg, H. O. (1989). 40-year follow-up of overweight children. *Lancet, 2,* 491–493.

Mouridsen, S. E., & Larsen, F. W. (1992). Psychological aspects of precocious puberty. *Acta Paedopsychiatrica, 55,* 45–49.

Mullins, L. L., Olson, R. A., Reyes, S., Bernary, N., Huszti, H. C., & Volk, R. J. (1991). Risk and resilience factors in the adaptation of mothers of children with cystic fibrosis. *Journal of Pediatric Psychology, 16,* 701–715.

Nass, R., & Baker, S. (1991a). Androgen effects on cognition: Congenital adrenal hyperplasia. *Psychoneuroendocrinology, 16,* 189–201.

Nass, R., & Baker, S. (1991b). Learning disabilities in children with congenital adrenal hyperplasia. *Journal of Child Neurology, 6,* 306–312.

National Diabetes Data Group. (1995). *Diabetes in America* (2nd ed., NIH Pub. No. 95-1468). Bethesda, MD: National Institutes of Health and National Institutes of Diabetes, Digestive, and Kidney Diseases.

National Heart, Lung, and Blood Institute Obesity Education Initiative Expert Panel. (1998). Clinical guidelines on the identification, evaluation, and treatment of overweight and obesity in adults—the evidence report. *Obesity Research, 6,* 51S–210S.

New England Congenital Hypothyroidism Collaborative. (1985). Neonatal hypothyroidism screening: Status of patients at 6 years of age. *Journal of Pediatrics, 107,* 915–919.

New England Congenital Hypothyroidism Collaborative. (1990). Elementary school performance of children with congenital hypothyroidism. *Journal of Pediatrics, 116,* 27–32.

New England Congenital Hypothyroidism Collaborative. (1994). Correlation of cognitive test scores and adequacy of treatment in adolescents with congenital hypothyroidism. *Journal of Pediatrics, 124,* 383–387.

Nielsen, J. (1991). *Klinefelter's syndrome: An orientation* (2nd ed.). Denmark: Novo Nordisk.

Nielsen, J., & Wohlert, M. (1990). Sex chromosome abnormalities found among 34,910 children: Results from a 13-year incidence study in Arhus, Denmark. In J. A. Evans, J. L. Hamerton, & A. Robinson (Eds.), *Children and young adults with sex chromosome aneuploidy* (Birth Defects: Original Article Series: Vol. 26, pp. 209–223). New York: Wiley-Liss.

Pavlou, K. N., Krey, S., & Steffee, W. P. (1989). Exercise as an adjunct to weight loss and maintenance in moderately obese subjects. *American Journal of Clinical Nutrition, 49,* 1115–1123.

Perlmuter, L. C., Hakami, M. K., Hodgson-Harrington, C., Gingsberg, J., Katz, J., Singer, D. E., et al. (1984). Decreased cognitive function in aging, non-insulin-dependent diabetic patients. *American Journal of Medicine, 77,* 1043–1048.

Perri, M. G. (1998). The maintenance of treatment effects in the long-term management of obesity. *Clinical Psychology: Science and Practice, 5,* 526–543.

Perri, M. G., Nezu, A. M., Patti, E. T., & McCann, K. L. (1989). Effect of length of treatment on weight loss. *Journal of Consulting and Clinical Psychology, 57,* 450–452.

Perri, M. G., Nezu, A. M., & Viegener, B. J. (1992). Improving the long-term maintenance of obesity: Theory, research, and clinical guidelines. In T. J. Boll (Series Ed.), *Wiley series on health psychology/behavioral medicine.* New York: Wiley.

Peyrot, M., & Rubin, R. R. (1988). Insulin self-regulation predicts better glycemic control [Abstract]. *Diabetes, 37*(Suppl. 1), 53.

Physicians' Desk Reference (55th ed.). (2001). Montvale, NJ: Medical Economics.

Polonsky, W. H., Anderson, B. J., Lohrer, P. A., Welch, G., Jacobson, A. M., & Schwartz, C. (1995). Assessment of diabetes-specific distress. *Diabetes Care, 18,* 754–760.

Quittner, A. L., DiGiralomo, A. M., Michel, M., & Eigen, H. (1992). Parental response to cystic fibrosis: A contextual analysis of the diagnosis phase. *Journal of Pediatric Psychology, 17,* 683–704.

Quittner, A. L., & Opipari, L. C. (1994). Differential treatment of siblings: Interview and diary analyses comparing two family contexts. *Child Development, 65,* 800–814.

Quittner, A. L., Opipari, L. C., Regoli, M. J., Jacobson, J., & Eigen, H. (1992). The impact of caregiving and role strain on family life. Comparisons between mothers of children with cystic fibrosis and matched controls. *Rehabilitation Psychology, 37,* 275–290.

Quittner, A. L., Tolbert, V. E., Regoli, M. J., Orenstein, D., Hollingsworth, J. L., & Eigen, H. (1996). Development of the Role Play Inventory for Situations and Coping Strategies (RISCS) for parents of children with cystic fibrosis. *Journal of Pediatric Psychology, 21,* 209–235.

Ratcliffe, S. G., Butler, G. E., & Jones, M. (1990). Edinburgh study of growth and development of children with sex chromosome abnormalities, IV. In J. A. Evans, J. L. Hamerton, & A. Robinson (Eds.), *Children and young adults with sex chromosome aneuploidy* (Birth Defects: Original Article Series: Vol. 26, pp. 1–44). New York: Wiley-Liss.

Ricker, J. H., Delamater, A. M., & Hsu, J. (1998). Correlates of regimen adherence in cystic fibrosis. *Journal of Clinical Psychology in Medical Settings, 5,* 159–172.

Robinson, A., Bender, B. G., & Linden, M. (1990). Summary of clinical findings in children and young adults with sex chromosome anomalies. In J. A. Evans, J. L. Hamerton, & A. Robinson (Eds.), *Children and young adults with sex chromosome aneuploidy* (Birth Defects: Original Article Series: Vol. 26, pp. 225–228). New York: Wiley-Liss.

Rodin, G. M., & Daneman, D. (1992). Eating disorders and IDDM: A problematic association. *Diabetes Care, 15,* 1402–1412.

Rovet, J. F. (1983). Cognitive and neuropsychological test performance of persons with abnormalities of adolescent development: A test of Waber's hypothesis. *Child Development, 54,* 941–950.

Rovet, J. F. (1990). The cognitive and neuropsychological characteristics of females with Turner syndrome. In D. B. Berch & B. G. Berger (Eds.), *Sex chromosome abnormalities and human behavior* (pp. 38–77). Boulder, CO: Westview.

Rovet, J. F. (1993). The psychoeducational characteristics of children with Turner syndrome. *Journal of Learning Disabilities, 26,* 333–341.

Rovet, J. F. (1994). School outcome in Turner syndrome. In B. Stabler & L. E. Underwood (Eds.), *Growth, stature, and adaptation: An international symposium on the behavioral, social, and cognitive aspects of growth delay* (pp. 165–180). Chapel Hill: University of North Carolina at Chapel Hill.

Rovet, J. F., Ehrlich, R. M., & Sorbara, D. L. (1987). Longitudinal perspective investigations of hypothyroid children detected by neonatal screening in Ontario. In B. L. Therell (Ed.), *Advances in neonatal screening* (pp. 99–103). Amsterdam: Elsevier.

Rovet, J. F., Ehrlich, R. M., & Sorbara, D. L. (1992). Neurodevelopment in infants and preschool children with congenital hypothyroidism: Etiological and treatment factors affecting outcome. *Journal of Pediatric Psychology, 17,* 187–213.

Rovet, J. F., & Fernandes, C. (1998). Insulin-dependent diabetes mellitus. In R.T. Brown (Ed.), *Cognitive aspects of chronic illness in children* (pp. 142–171). New York: Guilford Press.

Ryan, C. M. (1997). Effects of diabetes mellitus on neuropsychological function: A lifespan perspective. *Seminars in Clinical Neuropsychiatry, 2,* 4–14.

Sandberg, D. E., & Barrick, C. (1995). Endocrine disorders in childhood: A selective survey of intellectual and educational sequelae. *School Psychology Review, 24,* 146–170.

Satin, W., La Greca, A. M., Zigo, M., & Skyler, J. S. (1989). Diabetes in adolescence: Effects of multifamily support group intervention and parent simulation of diabetes. *Journal of Pediatric Psychology, 14,* 259–275.

Siegel, P. T., & Hopwood, N. J. (1986). The relationship of academic achievement and the intellectual functioning and affective conditions of hypopituitary children. In B. Stabler & L. E. Underwood (Eds.), *Slow grows the child: Psychosocial aspects of growth delay* (pp. 57–71). Hillsdale, NJ: Erlbaum.

Sikand, G., Dondo, A., Forcyt, J. P., Jones, P. H., & Gotto, A. M. (1988). Two-year follow-up of patients treated with a very-low-calorie diet and exercise training. *Journal of the American Dietetic Association, 88,* 487–488.

Simmons, R. J., Corey, M., Cowen, L., Keenan, N., Robertson, J., & Levison, H. (1987). Behavioral adjustment of latency-aged children with cystic fibrosis. *Psychosomatic Medicine, 49,* 291–301.

Slijper, F. M. E., Drop, S. L. S, Molenaar, J. C., & de Muinck Keizer-Schrama, S. M. P. F. (1998). Long-term psychological evaluation of intersex children. *Archives of Sexual Behavior, 27,* 125–144.

Sobel, J., & Stunkard, A. J. (1989). Socioeconomic status and obesity: A review of the literature. *Psychological Bulletin, 105,* 260–275.

Sonis, W. A., Comite, F., Pescovits, O. H., Hench, K., Rahn, W. C., Cutler, G. B., et al. (1986). Biobehavioral aspects of precocious puberty. *Journal of the American Academy of Child Psychiatry, 25,* 674–679.

Stabler, B., Clopper, R. R., Siegel., P. T., Stoppani, C., Compton, P. G., & Underwood, L. E. (1994). Academic achievement and psychological adjustment in short children. *Journal of Developmental and Behavioral Pediatrics, 15,* 1–6.

Stabler, B., Siegel, P. T., & Clopper, R. R. (1991). Growth hormone deficiency in children has psychological and educational co-morbidity. *Clinical Pediatrics, 30,* 156–160.

Stark, L. J., Bowen, A. M., Tyc, V. L., Evans, S., & Pasero, M. A. (1990). A behavioral approach to increasing calorie consumption in children with cystic fibrosis. *Journal of Pediatric Psychology, 15,* 309–326.

Stark, L. J., Jelalian, E., & Miller, D. L. (1995). Cystic fibrosis. In M. C. Roberts (Ed.), *Handbook of pediatric psychology* (2nd ed., pp. 241–263). New York: Guilford Press.

Stark, L. J., Knapp, L., & Bowen, A. M. (1993). Increasing calorie consumption in children with cystic fibrosis: Replication with two-year follow-up. *Journal of Applied Behavior Analysis, 26,* 435–450.

Stark, L. J., Powers, S. W., Jelalian, E., Rape, R. N., & Miller, D. L. (1994). Modifying problematic mealtime interactions of children with cystic fibrosis and their parents via behavioral parent training. *Journal of Pediatric Psychology, 19,* 751–768.

Stark, O., Atkins, E., Wolff, O. H., & Douglas, J. W. B. (1981). Longitudinal study of obesity in the National Survey of Health and Development. *British Medical Journal, 283,* 13–17.

Surwit, R., Schneider, M., & Feinglos, M. (1992). Stress and diabetes mellitus. *Diabetes Care, 15,* 1413–1422.

Thompson, R. J., Gustafson, K. E., Hamlett, K. W., & Spock, A. (1992). Stress, coping, and family functioning in the psychological adjustment of mothers of children with cystic fibrosis. *Journal of Pediatric Psychology, 17,* 573–585.

Thompson, R. J., Hodges, K., & Hamlett, K. W. (1990). A matched comparison of adjustment in children with cystic fibrosis in psychiatrically-referred and non-referred children. *Journal of Pediatric Psychology, 15,* 745–759.

Troiano, R. P., Flegal, K. M., Kuczmarski, R. J., Campbell, S. M., & Johnson, C. L. (1995). Overweight prevalence and tendencies for children and adolescents: The national health and nutrition examination surveys, 1963 to 1991. *Archives of Pediatric and Adolescent Medicine, 149,* 1085–1091.

United Kingdom Prospective Diabetes Study Group. (1998). Intensive blood glucose control with sulphonylureas or insulin compared with conventional treatment and risk of complications in patients with Type II diabetes (UKPDS 33). *Lancet, 352,* 837–853.

Walker, L. S., Ortiz-Valdes, J. A., & Newbrough, J. R. (1989). The role of maternal employment and depression in the psychological adjustment of chronically ill, mentally retarded, and well children. *Journal of Pediatric Psychology, 14,* 357–370.

Walker, L. S., Van Slyke, D. A., & Newbrough, J. R. (1992). Family resources and stress: A comparison of families of children with cystic fibrosis, diabetes, and mental retardation. *Journal of Pediatric Psychology, 17,* 327–343.

Wallace, J. E., MacCrimmon, D. J., & Goldberg, W. M. (1980). Acute hyperthyroidism: Cognitive and emotional correlates. *Journal of Abnormal Psychology, 80,* 519–527.

Walzer, S. (1985). X chromosome abnormalities and cognitive development: Implications for understanding normal human development. *Journal of Child Psychology and Psychiatry, 26,* 177–184.

Wechsler, D. (1974). *Manual for the Wechsler Intelligence Scale for Children—revised.* San Antonio, TX: The Psychological Corporation.

Weissberg-Benchell, J., Glasgow, A. M., Tynan, W. D., Wirtz, P., Turek, J., & Ward, J. (1995). Adolescent diabetes management and mismanagement. *Diabetes Care, 18,* 77–82.

Wheeler, M., & Styne, D. (1991). The treatment of precocious puberty. *Endocrinology and Metabolism Clinics of North America, 20,* 183–190.

Williamson, D. F. (1995). Prevalence and demographics of obesity. In K. D. Browned & C. G. Fairburn (Eds.), *Eating disorders and obesity* (pp. 391–395). New York: Guilford Press.

Wilson, J., Fosson, A., Kanga, J. F., & D'Angelo, S. L. (1996). Homeostatic interactions: A longitudinal study of biological, psychosocial, and family variables in children with cystic fibrosis. *Journal of Family Therapy, 18,* 123–139.

Wilson, J. D., Foster, D. W., Kronenberg, H. M., & Larsen, P. R. (Eds.). (1998). *Williams textbook of endocrinology* (9th ed.). Philadelphia: W. B. Saunders.

Wing, R. R., Lamparski, D., Zaslow, S., Betschart, J., Siminerio, L., & Becker, D.

(1985). Frequency and accuracy of self-monitoring of blood glucose in children: Relationship to glycemic control. *Diabetes Care, 8,* 214–218.

Wysocki, T., Green, L. B., & Huxtable, K. (1989). Blood glucose monitoring by diabetic adolescents: Compliance and metabolic control. *Health Psychology, 8,* 267–284.

Wysocki, T., Hough, B. S., Ward, K. M., Allen, A., & Murgai, N. (1992). Use of blood glucose data by families of children and adolescents with IDDM. *Diabetes Care, 15,* 1041–1044.

Wysocki, T., Miller, K. M., Harvey, L. M., Taylor, A., Elder-Danda, C., McDonell, K., et al. (2000). Behavior therapy for families of adolescents with diabetes: Effects on directly observed family interactions. *Behavior Therapy, 30,* 507–525.

Wysocki, T., Taylor, A., Hough, B., Linscheid, T. R., Yeates, K. O., & Naglieri, J. A. (1996a). Deviation from developmentally appropriate self-care autonomy: Association with diabetes outcomes. *Diabetes Care, 19,* 119–125.

Wysocki, T., Taylor, A., Meinhold, P. A., Barnard, M. U., Clarke, W. L., Bellando, B. J., et al. (1996b). Normative data for the Diabetes Independence Survey–Parent Version. *The Diabetes Educator, 22,* 587–591.

4

DISEASES OF THE BLOOD AND BLOOD-FORMING ORGANS

RONALD T. BROWN, RAYMOND K. MULHERN, AND SUSAN SIMONIAN

Diseases of the blood and blood-forming organs present challenges to health psychologists because of their wide array. The diseases include iron deficiency anemia, other deficiency anemias (e.g., pernicious anemia, anemia associated with nutritional deficiencies), hereditary hemolytic anemia (e.g., thalassemia, sickle cell anemia), acquired hemolytic anemia, aplastic anemia, coagulation defects (e.g., hemophilia, von Willebrand's disease), purpura and other hemorrhagic conditions (e.g., thrombocytopenia), diseases of the white blood cells (e.g., agranulocytosis, genetic anomalies of leukocytes, eosinophilia), other diseases of blood and blood-forming organs (e.g., high oxygen affinity, polycythemia, chronic lymphadenitis), and diseases of the spleen (Practice Management Information Corporation, 1999).

Health psychologist practitioners and researchers have focused efforts on hemophilia, sickle cell disease (SCD), and leukemia, so these three illnesses are discussed in this chapter. Although leukemia is technically a neoplasm, it involves blood-forming tissues and has been targeted by health psychologists and therefore is included in this chapter.

The chapter's focus is on the pathophysiological aspects of disease and the way neurocognitive and psychosocial functioning are affected. Also included is a review of medical management of the diseases and the way treatment is influenced. Findings are included about adjustment and quality of life of patients with the diseases and their families. When possible, a life-span perspective of the problems encountered in illness management is provided, drawing on literature from several developmental periods. However, most of the studies are from pediatric research because the significant gains made in improved prognosis and understanding of these diseases in children and adolescents have increased research in the area.

LEUKEMIA

Medical Aspects

Leukemia is a class of cancers characterized by the unrestricted proliferation of immature bone marrow cells. Leukemia tends to affect very young children and older adults. It is the most common form of cancer in children, with approximately 2,500 new cases each year in the United States (Weinstein & Tarbell, 1997). Acute lymphoblastic leukemia (ALL) is the most common leukemia subtype in children, with a peak incidence at age 4 years. ALL is more prevalent in males and is found more frequently in White individuals than in African American individuals. In adults the peak incidence of ALL and the more common acute myelogenous leukemia (AML) occurs after age 65.

The cause of most forms of childhood ALL is unknown, but some groups seem more susceptible. Children with Down syndrome are 10 to 20 times more likely to get leukemia than are normal children. Children with neurofibromatosis are also at greater risk for leukemia. No confirmed sources of prenatal or environmental risk have been established, but some children contract leukemia as a result of treatment of other cancers with particular types of chemotherapy (Weinstein & Tarbell, 1997). Environmental factors such as radiation exposure, smoking, and benzene exposure have been implicated in adult studies (Scheinberg, Maslak, & Weiss, 1997).

The most common presenting symptoms of ALL are fever or infection, malaise, leukemic blasts, bone pain, and bleeding that is found to result from bone marrow infiltration by malignant cells. From 5% to 10% of children also have central nervous system (CNS) involvement, which is indicated by blasts in their cerebrospinal fluid. In adults, gum involvement is more common.

ALL is fatal if untreated. Higher risk patients receive more aggressive and more toxic therapies. For adult and childhood leukemia, the treatment is usually divided into three phases. In remission induction, a 2-week multidrug chemotherapy is used to eradicate blasts from circulation. Continuation therapy must be implemented next to prevent relapse, and it may last 2 years or more. It involves intravenous and oral chemotherapy. If necessary, CNS prophylaxis, with intrathecal chemotherapy, cranial radiation therapy (CRT), or both, is administered last to rid the CNS of any occult leukemia, a serious source of relapses. This CNS treatment has been identified as a cause of learning difficulties, especially in young patients.

For children with ALL who relapse, as well as children with other forms of leukemia who relapse, bone marrow transplant is the treatment of choice (Weinstein & Tarbell, 1997). The bone marrow of the patient is ablated using extremely high-dose chemotherapy, with the rationale that the leukemic blasts are also killed. Preserved bone marrow from the patient (autologous transplant) or from a matched donor (allogenic transplant) is then intravenously reinfused into the patient.

Significant advances in the treatment of childhood leukemia have occurred over the past 25 years, resulting in an overall cure rate of 70% and an 80% cure rate for some types (Margolin & Poplack, 1997). These statistics are in sharp contrast to the cure rate of many adults, who initially respond to chemotherapy but then relapse and succumb to the disease.

Psychosocial Issues

Acute Procedural Pain and Distress

Patients with cancer frequently undergo invasive procedures such as venipunctures, bone marrow aspirations (BMAs), and lumbar punctures (LPs). BMAs and LPs are the most distressing and feared aspects of treatment (Jay, Ozolins, Elliott, & Caldwell, 1983), and many patients describe these procedures as worse than the disease itself (Hilgard & LeBaron, 1982). Hypnotic techniques have resulted in significant improvements in procedure-related distress in children as young as age 6 years (Hilgard & LeBaron, 1982; Zeltzer & LeBaron, 1986). Hypnotism generally involves intensively engaging the patient in a fantasy experience through suggestion, reframing, and altering the sensory experiences (Zeltzer & LeBaron, 1986).

Hypnotic interventions have been compared with cognitive strategies to determine the most effective method for reducing procedural distress. A comparison of hypnotic "imaginative involvement," behavioral distraction, and an attention–placebo–control condition for the reduction of pain and distress during BMAs showed that hypnotic procedures were effective but provided no substantial added benefit to cognitive strategies such as distraction and imagery (Kuttner, Bowman, & Teasdale, 1988). A series of studies on the efficacy of multicomponent, cognitive–behavioral treatment (CBT) programs for reducing procedural distress in children undergoing BMAs and LPs (Jay, Elliott, Katz, & Siegel, 1987; Jay, Elliott, Ozolins,

Olson, & Pruitt, 1985; Jay, Elliott, Woody, & Siegel, 1991). Such packaged interventions typically include modeling, relaxation training, breathing exercises, emotive imagery, behavioral rehearsal, and tangible reinforcers to increase motivation and compliance. CBT strategies are effective in reducing behavioral distress and self-reported pain (Broome, Lillis, McGahee, & Bates, 1992).

In a randomized crossover design, a CBT package, oral Valium, and an attention-control condition were compared for effectiveness (Jay et al., 1991). Patients receiving Valium showed reductions in anticipatory distress, but distress during procedures was not affected. The CBT group had significantly lower behavioral distress ratings, self-reported pain ratings, and pulse rates compared with the oral Valium and attention-control groups. The use of CBT plus oral Valium has also been compared with CBT alone. Both groups had reduced observed behavioral distress and self-reported pain scores after the intervention, but oral Valium was not as effective as CBT in alleviating distress during BMAs or LPs. Most recently, the efficacy of a CBT package was compared with general anesthesia (nitrous oxide and halothane) for alleviating distress of 18 patients with cancer undergoing BMAs (Jay, Elliott, Fitzgibbons, Woody, & Siegel, 1995). Results of the study were equivocal. No significant differences were found between the two groups in self-reported fear, pain, pulse, or anticipatory BMA anxiety. The most evolved intervention at this time is matching patients to the most individually appropriate intervention, which is based on predictive factors such as age, coping style, or preference (Zeltzer et al., 1990).

Chemotherapy-Induced Nausea and Vomiting

Nausea and vomiting are common aversive side effects for patients with cancer who are receiving chemotherapy. Although postchemotherapy side effects (postchemotherapy nausea and vomiting, or PNV) are more common, some patients develop anticipatory nausea and vomiting (ANV) before administration of chemotherapy agents. ANV aversions are hypothesized to be acquired through a classical conditioning process. Using this hypothesis, cues in the environment that are repeatedly paired with the infusion of emetogenic chemotherapy agents acquire the ability to elicit nausea and vomiting. Emetogenicity of the chemotherapy, severity of the postchemotherapy symptoms, and the number of treatment sessions can allow clinicians to predict ANV, supporting the conceptualization of ANV as a conditioned response (Blasco, 1994; Morrow & Dobkin, 1988). Patient variables such as high anxiety level, susceptibility to conditioned taste aversions, and increased autonomic reactivity have also been associated with ANV (Dolgin, Katz, McGinty, & Siegel, 1985; Dolgin & Katz, 1988; Dolgin, Katz, Zeltzer, & Landsverk, 1989).

Chemotherapy-induced nausea and vomiting have been greatly ameliorated with the introduction of serotonin (5-HT) antagonists (e.g., ondansetron), which offer antiemetic potency with fewer side effects. These new antiemetic agents are quite effective in preventing acute nausea and vomiting, but they are less effective in treating delayed nausea and vomiting (DeMulder et al., 1990). Patients whose symptoms remain refractory to antiemetics may benefit from psychological approaches.

Psychological interventions similar to those used for patients undergoing BMAs and LPs have been used to treat both PNV and ANV. In a study that included a no-treatment control group, 54 pediatric patients with cancer were randomly assigned to receive either hypnosis, nonhypnotic cognitive distraction, or an attention–placebo condition (Zeltzer, Dolgin, LeBaron, & LeBaron, 1991). The greatest reduction in observed and self-reported ANV, PNV, and distress occurred with hypnosis. The cognitive distraction intervention appeared to have a minimal effect, and the attention-placebo group participants progressively worsened.

Even though behavioral interventions such as progressive muscle relaxation training, systematic desensitization, biofeedback, and cognitive distraction have been effective in reducing chemotherapy distress in adults, the effect of these techniques with children has not been determined (Carey & Burish, 1988; Morrow & Dobkin, 1988). Dolgin and Katz (1988) reported that parenting practices may play a determining role in how pediatric patients cope with specific aversive medical events. The researchers found that children whose parents relied on threat of punishment were more likely to develop ANV, whereas children whose parents relied on modeling and reassurance were less likely to show these symptoms. Health psychologists can assist with parenting skills.

Patient and Family Adjustment

The psychosocial impact of leukemia affects the entire family. Early studies in this area focused only on the effect of cancer on family adjustment. Researchers now favor a systems perspective that recognizes reciprocal influences within the family, such as how the coping, adaptation, and illness-related behavior of one family member can affect those of other family members (Chesler & Barbarin, 1987; Horwitz & Kazak, 1990; Kazak, 1989).

Some of the first studies of family adaptation occurred at a time when childhood leukemia was almost invariably fatal, and the studies tended to report pathological responses by families (Bozeman, Orbach, & Sutherland, 1955; Friedman, Chodoff, Mason, & Hamburg, 1963; Karon & Vernick, 1968; Natterson & Knudson, 1960). As cure rates improved dramatically, researchers changed their focus to the healthy adaptation of families of children with leukemia (Kazak & Meadows, 1989; Sawyer, Crettenden, & Toogood, 1986). Varying levels of psychological distress clearly coexist with healthy reactions (Dolgin & Phipps, 1996).

The type of family environment may predict individual adjustment. Higher levels of family cohesion and support tend to be associated with lower levels of parental stress and improved marital functioning in parents of children with cancer (Noll, Gartstein, et al., 1995). The family environment can be a significant determinant of adjustment in the patient. Higher levels of family adaptability are related to the child's report of self-concept, particularly perceived social acceptance and scholastic competence (Kazak & Meadows, 1989). Family cohesion, expressiveness, and conflict are significant predictors of adjustment in children undergoing BMTs. Family cohesion and expressiveness were protective factors, promoting resilience to BMT-related stressors (Phipps & Mulhern, 1995). A similar relationship of adaptive family environment factors (e.g., cohesion, openness) and adjustment has been reported for siblings of pediatric patients with cancer (Dolgin & Phipps, 1996; Horwitz & Kazak, 1990).

One of the most consistent findings from the now classic family coping study of Kupst and colleagues (Kupst, 1993; Kupst et al., 1982; Kupst & Schulman, 1988) is the strength of the relationship between parental adjustment and the patient's adjustment to illness. This study led to the awareness that adequacy of coping is reciprocal, and the effectiveness of parents' and children's coping are directly related. Further evidence for this effect is that parental psychopathology and adjustment outcomes for children with leukemia and their siblings are strongly correlated (Blotcky, Raczynski, Gurwitch, & Smith, 1985; Brown, Kaslow, et al., 1993).

Adherence to Medical Treatment

Adherence to medically prescribed treatment, sometimes called *compliance*, is an important issue for patients with chronic illness conditions in general, but the consequences of decreased adherence to childhood cancer treatment may be more disastrous. However, inconsistent operational definitions of adherence and compliance in the literature have made measurement difficult. Differences in how adherence is measured (e.g., drug assay, behavioral observation, parent or patient report, physician ratings) also affect accuracy of estimates. Although global estimates of compliance have ranged as low as 50%, these estimates may not be accurate or have a significant impact on the success of cancer therapy. One frequently cited study (Tebbi et al., 1986) demonstrated that compliance with oral prednisone among newly diagnosed patients with ALL decreased from 80% to 60% within the first 20 weeks of treatment. Decreased compliance with oral prednisone is associated with a higher rate of relapse (Festa, Tamaroff, Chasalow, & Lanzkowsky, 1992).

Decreased adherence depends on numerous well-defined factors. Some evidence shows that the following factors increase noncompliance: drugs with adverse side effects, a long treatment duration, child or family psychological dysfunction before diagnosis (regardless of whether parents cope poorly with the diagnosis), poor socialization of the child, communication problems between the parents and the child's physician, and decreased family support for the patients during their therapy (Bearison, 1994). The effects of gender, ethnicity, and socioeconomic status have been equivocal or absent.

Noncompliance has been attributed in part to lack of knowledge on the part of the patient or caregivers and failure of health care professionals to communicate information about the disease and therapy in a way the patient and family can understand. However, noncompliance has rarely been solely attributed to knowledge deficits, and knowledge-based interventions have failed to show a consistent increase in adherence (Bearison, 1994). Other potential interventions include increased surveillance and monitoring of medication use. Behavioral interventions that encourage the patient to self-monitor and those that provide external incentives in the form of material rewards or privileges have also been proved effective (La-Greca, 1988).

Among the most problematic patients are preadolescents and adolescents who have not yet reached the legal age of consent but want to discontinue their treatment. Developmentally, most children between ages 11 and 14 years have the cognitive capacity to understand the objective risks and benefits of their therapy but do not have the cumulative life experiences that allow mature judgment. Normal adolescent rebellion and an increased need for autonomy may explain some of the underlying dynamics, and dysfunctional families may further intensify age-appropriate conflicts with authority figures about medications.

Neuropsychological Late Effects

Neuropsychological late effects, which are a subset of psychosocial late effects, are pathological changes in the CNS secondary to cancer or its treatment. The effects are manifested in stable changes in behavior. The most studied behavioral correlates are intellectual, cognitive, and academic performance in children. These issues are discussed in detail in several reviews (Armstrong & Mulhern, 1999).

Pathophysiology

Relevant sources of neuropathological features underlying neuropsychological deficits include chemotherapy and CRT for children with ALL. Although acute and subacute irradiation side effects such as anorexia, confusion, and somnolence are reversible within weeks of stopping treatment, late CNS effects may be irreversible even if not progressive. The severity of somnolence does not necessarily predict later neuropsychological decline

(Berg, Ch'ien, Lancaster, Williams, & Cummins, 1983). Radiation damage to normal CNS tissues may manifest as cortical atrophy, vascular damage (mineralizing microangiopathy), or white matter destruction (leukoencephalopathy; Price & Birdwell, 1978). Areas of involvement and severity are associated with the volume of brain irradiated, dose of irradiation per fraction, and total dose of irradiation received (Kun et al., 1984). Various forms of chemotherapy alone or in combination with CRT, administered intravenously or intrathecally, are used for CNS treatment of leukemia. Recently, efforts to eliminate the need for CRT have prompted the use of more intensive CNS chemotherapy, most often with methotrexate, in the hopes of avoiding the neurophysiological and neuropsychological adverse effects of irradiation. However, the potential neurotoxicity of methotrexate has been documented for at least the past 20 years (Meadows & Evans, 1976) and is especially problematic following CRT (Bleyer, 1990).

Global Neuropsychological Deficits

The most commonly used psychological index of neurotoxicity has been the IQ score or pattern of IQ subtest scores displayed by long-term patients. A meta-analysis of 30 studies published before 1988 concluded that children receiving CRT, children who are younger at the time of receiving CRT, and children who are farther from completion of their therapy with CRT show the greatest intellectual deficits, with an average of a 10-point decline in IQ (Cousens, Waters, Said, & Stevens, 1988).

Retrospective and longitudinal studies have demonstrated IQ declines over time and significantly lower IQs in irradiated compared with nonirradiated patients (Copeland et al., 1985; Mulhern et al., 1992; Ochs et al., 1991; Rubenstein, Varni, & Katz, 1990). It is generally accepted that the adverse effects of treatment on cognition are delayed 2 to 5 years (Mulhern et al., 1992; Rubenstein et al., 1990). Researchers indicate an inverse relationship between neuropsychological outcomes and the age of the patient at the time of CNS therapy (Jannoun & Chessells, 1987; Robison et al., 1984; Said, Waters, Cousens, & Stevens, 1989) with very poor outcomes in children less than 3 years old at the time of CRT (Sibler et al., 1992). Even among similarly irradiated children, differences in the amount and type of chemotherapy given may help to explain these discrepancies among studies (Mulhern, Fairclough, & Ochs, 1991). A younger age at treatment may place girls, but not boys, at greater risk (Brown et al., 1998; Waber et al., 1990). Although the mechanisms are not yet clear, at least some evidence suggests that girls are more likely to experience deleterious effects than boys (Mulhern et al., 1992; Robison et al., 1984; Waber et al., 1990).

Specific Neuropsychological Impairments

Investigators have begun to characterize deficits in terms of specific neuropsychological functions. The general consensus now emerging is that

IQ declines are secondary to one or more central processing deficits involving short-term memory, speed of processing, vasomotor coordination, or sequencing abilities (Cousens, Ungerer, Crawford, & Stevens, 1991). Verbal and nonverbal memory functions have been among the more frequently investigated deficits in this context (Brouwers & Poplack, 1990; Copeland et al., 1985). One study documented cognitive processing problems and learning disabilities in ALL survivors treated with chemotherapy alone (Brown et al., 1992).

Impact on Educational Attainment

Studies showing significant decreases in intellectual development as a result of treatment for ALL also show generally higher risk of school failure, special educational needs, and sometimes specific learning disabilities. A recent study of 593 former patients with ALL and 409 sibling controls showed former patients had more than a 3.5 times greater risk of learning disability placement in school (Haupt et al., 1994). The need for formal assessments of children at risk and for informing parents and teachers of potential signs and symptoms of these learning problems cannot be overemphasized (Armstrong & Horn, 1995). The standard of care for these children is a comprehensive psychoeducational evaluation and special measures of cognitive processing deficits commonly associated with cancer therapy. Evaluation results then guide the type and intensity of special educational interventions.

Summary

This section highlighted contemporary psychosocial issues in the acute and chronic care of patients with leukemia. Psychosocial research in oncology has promoted an understanding of the behavioral and social morbidities experienced by patients and their families. Regardless of the type of problem, significant variability is seen in the level of severity exhibited. This variability is explained by identifying medical and nonmedical risk factors associated with these morbidities, enabling particular patients or families to be targeted for interventions that prevent or minimize the impact of leukemia and its treatment. These descriptive and epidemiological studies have also been valuable in quantifying the psychosocial costs of cures, leading to increased efforts to maintain or improve leukemia cure rates while reducing the burden of acute and late toxicities (e.g., by reduction of BMAs and more selective use of CRT).

A smaller but equally important group of studies has attempted to translate descriptive findings into psychosocial interventions that may more directly affect problems encountered by patients and their families during the treatment experience and thereafter. These studies are labor intensive and have logistical problems when implemented in medical settings in which cancer treatment is the primary concern. Nevertheless, future psychosocial research will necessarily evolve in the direction of developing direct intervention strategies to improve the quality of life of patients and their families. In some selected areas, such as family coping and procedural distress, successful interventions are available that have defined contemporary standards of care. However, in other areas, such as health promotion and neuropsychological rehabilitation, the translation of descriptive data into studies that test the efficacy of psychosocial interventions is urgently needed. For more comprehensive discussion of these and other topics, refer to Holland (1998) for adult issues and Bearison and Mulhern (1994) for pediatric issues.

SCD

Medical Aspects

SCD is a group of genetic disorders characterized by the predominance of protein hemoglobin S (HbS) in red blood cells (Thompson & Gustafson, 1996). Hemoglobin transports oxygen and in healthy individuals consists of two alpha globulin chains and two beta globulin chains. In individuals with SCD, the beta globulin differs from normal globulin by the substitution of glutamic acid (Sickle Cell Disease Guideline Panel, 1993). This substitution produces a change in the shape of the red blood cell from a biconcave disc to a crescent, or sickle, shape. After repeated cycles of reoxygenation, the sickle cell becomes damaged and anemia results. All body tissues are then at significant risk for damage or ischemia because sickled red cells obstruct the flow of oxygenated blood cells.

Sickle cell disorders are classified according to genotype (Thompson & Gustafson, 1996). Hemoglobin type is determined by two beta globin genes that are located on chromosome 11 and four alpha globin genes that are located on chromosome 16. Individuals with sickle cell anemia (HbSS) are homozygous for the *SB* gene, which is the sickle beta globin gene. Patients with the heterozygous condition (HbSC) have two abnormal beta globin genes, *SB* and *SC*, that result in two abnormal hemoglobin genes, HbS and HbC. Individuals with sickle beta thalassemia have a *BS* gene and a gene that results in two types of beta thalassemia. When normal beta globin is produced by the thalassemia gene, the condition is called HbSB+ thalassemia; when no normal beta globin is produced, the condition is called HbSB0 thalassemia (Charache, Lubin, & Reid, 1989). HbS-beta thalassemia and HbSC disease are typically more benign than HbSS sickle cell anemia. SCD is different from sickle cell trait, in which individuals have both a normal beta globin gene (*BA*) and a sickle beta globin gene (BS). People with sickle cell trait do not have SCD, and they are rarely symptomatic. Sullivan (1993) estimated that more than 2 million African Americans have sickle cell trait, making the sickle cell gene widespread.

Two pathophysiological characteristics of SCD, anemia and vaso-occlusion, result from tissue injury as a result of ischemia and from obstruction in blood vessels from an accumulation of sickled red blood cells (Embury, Hebbel, Steinberg, & Mohandes, 1994; Thompson & Gustafson, 1996). Vaso-occlusion disrupts and impedes blood flow, which results in oxygen deprivation. Patients with SCDs often have damage to the bone marrow, heart, kidneys, spleen, and head of the femur because of tissue injury secondary to ischemia (Charache et al., 1989). Some symptoms are acute and short-lived, and others are chronic and lifelong. Vaso-occlusion also may cause increased sickling because cells tend to sickle when they are deoxygenated. Symptom display varies over time and may depend on such other factors as the presence of additional illnesses.

Hypoxia and ischemia result in pain episodes that frequently are precipitated by environmental factors such as dehydration, extreme cold, and high altitudes (for a review, see Brown, Doepke, & Kaslow, 1993). The most common pain crisis sites are musculoskeletal, abdominal, and lower back, with the symptoms typically lasting 4 to 6 days (Charache et al., 1989). Another common symptom of SCD is acute chest syndrome, with an etiology in the pulmonary vessels. It has symptoms similar to pneumonia, such as chest pain, fever, and prostration. Acute chest syndrome may be short term but if it is not properly managed, it can result in chronic lung disease. In some cases, it results in death.

Cerebral vascular accidents (CVAs), or strokes, also co-occur with SCD, particularly in individuals with HbSS disease. CVAs affect 6% to 12% of patients with SCD (Charache et al., 1989). Most CVAs occur in the first 2 decades of life but after this period, the prevalence gradually increases with age. Recent evidence indicates that "silent" CVAs, which are detectable on neuroimaging examinations but not on routine physical examinations, also frequently affect those with HbSS disease (Armstrong et al., 1996; Brown et al., 2000). CVAs may cause alterations in mental status and impairments in cognitive functioning and may require substantial rehabilitation therapy. CVAs and silent infarcts place children and adolescents at marked risk for academic difficulties and failure in school.

Other medical complications that frequently occur with SCD include progressive kidney disease that begins during the first decade of life and continues throughout life. Priapism, or persistent painful penile erection, may occur in adolescent and adult males. In addition, when anemia reduces oxygen, the heart must compensate with increased output. Thus, lifelong cardiac functioning is affected. Cardiac disease may occur in adults in the form of myocardial infarction, arrhythmias, and congestive heart failure, whereas cardiomegaly and cardiac murmurs are especially common in children with sickle cell anemia. Leg ulcers occur in approximately 10% to 20% of patients with SCD, occurring most frequently in males. Also common are bone lesions that are attributable to infarction. These bone lesions manifest themselves in hand–foot syndrome in young infants and children and in aseptic necrosis of the femoral head in adults.

Significant advances in the management of SCD in recent years have resulted in more favorable prognoses. More children survive the disease well into adulthood, and some patients survive into their fifth, sixth, and even seventh decades (Midence, Fuggle, & Davies, 1993). Platt and colleagues (1994) studied nearly 4,000 patients with SCD ranging from newborn to age 66 in the Cooperative Study of Sickle Cell Disease (CSSCD). The individuals studied were from 23 clinical centers across the United States. Findings from this longitudinal investigation were that 85% of individuals with sickle cell anemia (HbSS) and 95% of those with HbSC survived to age 20 (Leikin et al., 1989).

Platt and associates (1994) reported that the median ages of death for children and adults with SCD were 42 years for men and 48 years for women, which are 25 to 30 years less than average in the African American population. For individuals with HbSC disease, the median age of death was 60 years for men and 68 years for women. In 33% of deaths, an acute pain episode, stroke, or acute chest syndrome was the immediate precipitant. Renal failure was the most likely cause when death resulted from organ failure.

SCD affects 1 of 400 African Americans, and sickle cell anemia (HbSS) affects approximately 50,000 individuals in the United States. This high prevalence is due paradoxically to the protection the sickle cell trait historically offered against malaria (for review, see Lemanek, Buckloh, Woods, & Butler, 1995). After African Americans, SCD is most frequently diagnosed in Hispanics from the Caribbean, Central America, and parts of South America (Charache et al., 1989). These researchers also found SCD in Africans, Mediterraneans (including Greeks and Italians), Indians, and Middle Easterners. SCD affects approximately 1 of 10,000 individuals who are not African American (Davis, 1995).

Disease Management

Medical management of SCD is lifelong and varies depending on severity of the disease and age of the individual. Newborn screening helps reduce morbidity and mortality in young children because prophylactic therapies to prevent pneumococcal sepsis can be implemented (Lemanek et al., 1995). In addition, increased understanding of the natural history of SCD has helped enhance the prognosis of individuals with the disease. Systematic approaches that educate patients and families on strategies to prevent the onset of a vaso-occlusive crisis and warning signs of disease exacerbation have improved prognosis.

Bone marrow transplantation still remains the only demonstrated cure for SCD, but it carries risks that include an associated mortality of 10% (Kirkpatrick, Barrios, & Humbert, 1991). The procedure is costly and because suitable donors are not always available, bone marrow transplants are not an option for all individuals. More recently, hydroxyurea has shown some promise in decreasing painful episodes and increasing fetal hemoglobin in individuals affected with SCD. This approach also has risks, and it is not yet clear if its long-term efficacy outweighs its adverse effects. The use of fatty substances like fish oils and butyrate, a fatty substance naturally produced by the body, is also a treatment possibility, primarily because of the lesser side effects. Clearly, the most promising treatment for SCD is the genetic manipulation of the responsible genes (Ledley, 1992), and it is hoped that such gene therapy will be part of routine medical care in the next decade.

Pain and Associated Management

A hallmark of SCD is the recurrent vaso-occlusive episodes resulting from the abnormal shape of the cells (Charache et al., 1989). Because clinicians have no means of preventing or controlling these pain episodes, medical therapy has been primarily supportive and aimed at managing symptoms. Emphasis has included analgesia, adequate hydration from regular intake of fluids, and warmth. Analgesic agents that most commonly manage the pain crises associated with SCD include Demerol or morphine, although they are primarily used in an inpatient setting. More recently, the use of nonsteroidal anti-inflammatory agents has increased because they have fewer side effects (Tarnowski & Brown, 1995; Tarnowski, Brown, Dingle, & Dreelin, 1998).

The painful episodes may require repeated hospitalizations, missed days from work and school, and disruptions in family and personal activities (Bonner, Gustafson, Schumacher, & Thompson, 1999). Painful events are frequently accompanied by negative emotions, including anxiety, depressive symptoms, and hopelessness, and they sometimes result in negative behaviors. Health care providers are concerned about the possibility of adverse effects associated with narcotic analgesia, such as drug dependence, respiratory depression, urinary retention, and anticholinergic effects (e.g., dry mouth, constipation). These grave issues sometimes result in providers withholding analgesia, which the patients desperately want. The contingencies available to the patient and the degree to which the pain is able to be controlled are part of a complex situation for both the provider and the patient (Tarnowski & Brown, 1995; Tarnowski et al., 1998).

Psychological Aspects

Several investigations examining the psychological ramifications of SCD on the adjustment of individuals with this illness and their families have been conducted with children and adolescents. Findings ranged from poor adjustment to few difficulties with adjustment and adaptation. Illness severity (e.g., hemoglobinopathy, hemoglobin, number of disease-related complications, frequency of pain episodes) does not predict psychological adjustment in individuals with SCD.

Previous studies on psychosocial adjustment showed poor adjustment and adaptation, but more recent studies have suggested adequate adaptation. The more recent studies focused on variables that predict successful disease adaptation, including specific coping strategies for adjusting to the stressors associated with a chronic illness (Midence et al., 1993). Included in this research have been variables related to resiliency and vulnerability and how these factors predict psychological adjustment and overall disease adaptation.

Social, Emotional, and Behavioral Adaptation

In two studies examining social competence and peer relationships of preschool and school-age children (Lemanek et al., 1995) and adolescents (Noll, Ris, Davies, Bukowski, & Koontz, 1992) with SCD, teachers and parents rated ill children and adolescents the same as their healthy peers on dimensions of sociability, leadership, or aggression. Additional research is needed examining peer relationships of children with SCD. A range of both externalizing (disruptive behaviors) and internalizing (anxiety, depression) symptoms has been reported for children, adolescents, and adults with SCD (Brown, Kaslow, Doepke, et al., 1993). Findings from specific studies have revealed that children and adolescents exhibited more externalizing and internalizing problems at home, at school, and with peers relative to healthy controls (Brown, Doepke, & Kaslow, 1993; Lemanek et al., 1995; Thompson & Gustafson, 1996). Children with SCD have been at high risk for depression relative to other chronic illness groups (Bennett, 1994). Vichinsky, Johnson, and Lubin (1982) reported depression and anxiety as frequent symptoms in adults with SCD. Williams, Earles, and Pack (1983) observed that depression may be associated with the chronicity of SCD or the fatal nature of the disease. Thompson, Gil, Burbach, Keith, and Kinney (1993) found that nearly one half of their adult sample met diagnostic criteria for an internalizing psychiatric disorder (e.g., anxiety, obsessive–compulsive disorder), whereas some patients met criteria for an externalizing disorder (e.g., oppositional defiant disorder; Thompson, Gustafson, & Gil, 1995).

Adolescent boys display more overactive, immature, and somatic behaviors than their younger female counterparts (Hurtig & White, 1986). Thompson and associates (1995) suggested that some externalizing symptoms may increase with age, particularly disruptive behavior disorders. This increase is attributed to delayed physical growth, posited to affect male adolescents as a result of the social importance of physical strength. Consistent with these findings, Adedoyin (1992) surveyed adolescent boys and noted that a significant number of them worried about their inability to engage in athletic activities.

Leavell and Ford (1983) reported significant variation in the adjustment of adults with SCD, ranging from normal to severe psychopathological symptoms. Their scores on a measure of anxiety did not, however, differ from general medical patients. Barrett et al. (1988) found that adult patients with SCD reported fewer problems on a psychosocial screening instrument than did adult patients with other chronic illnesses. However, Damlouji, Kevess-Cohen, Charache, Georgopoulous, and Folstein (1982) reported higher rates of psychiatric disorders in patients with SCD than in patients with insulin-dependent diabetes mellitus. These findings underscore apparent age effects in externalizing behaviors in children and adolescents with SCD, with older youth having a higher frequency of behavioral problems. Anxiety, phobias, and depressive symptoms also have been reported, even when controlling for somatic symptoms. The findings are less clear for adults, although SCD is associated with some adjustment difficulties like depression and anxiety. Depression has been posited to be associated with the frequency and unpredictability of pain episodes.

Thompson, Gil, Abrams, and Phillips (1992) examined a transactional model of psychological adjustment to chronic illness in 109 adults with SCD. Good psychological adjustment was associated with lower levels of perceived daily stress and stress regarding SCD illness-related tasks. It was also associated with higher efficacy expectations, less use of palliative coping methods, and less use of negative thinking and passive adherence pain-coping strategies. Family functioning characterized by high levels of support and low levels of conflict and control was associated with good psychological adjustment. This model accounted for nearly 50% of the variance in psychological adjustment of adults with SCD. In contrast to the studies of children and adolescents that showed age-related adjustment difficulties, no differences were reported by Thompson's 1992 group as a function of age. In a follow-up investigation examining the role of child and maternal processes in the psychological adjustment of children with SCD, Thompson and colleagues (1993) found that maternal anxiety accounted for up to one third of the variance in mother-reported behavior problems in their children. These findings support a family systems approach to the management of adjustment difficulties for children with SCD.

Coping

As noted previously, coping strategies are important predictors of psychological adjustment in individuals with SCD, with an association between styles of coping and health-seeking behaviors. Children with SCD who scored higher on negative thinking and passive adherence were less active in school and in social situations and used more health care services (Gil, Williams, Thompson, & Kinney, 1991). In addition, they reported higher frequencies of psychological distress during painful episodes. The frequency of active coping attempts was associated with higher levels of school, household, and social activity during painful periods, and passive adherence and negative thinking were related to more frequent contacts with health care providers. Similarly, Thompson's 1993 group found that children's pain coping strategies characterized by negative thinking accounted for 20% of the variance in mothers' reports of children's externalizing behavior problems.

An association also has been found between parents' coping strategies and children's behavior (Gil, Williams, Thompson, & Kinney, 1991). Parents who scored high on passive adherence and negative thinking had children who were less active and had more internalizing and externalizing behavioral symptoms. In a 10-month follow-up of children's coping and management of pain, Thompson, Gil, Keith, et al. (1994) found that children's coping strategies for pain accounted for a significant amount of the variance in symptoms reported by the child and internalizing problems reported by mothers. These symptoms were more than the contribution of illness and demographic parameters. Palliative coping or passive types of coping strategies accounted for nearly one third of the variance in mothers' adjustment ratings of children with SCD. These findings were sustained at the 16-month follow-up assessment (Thompson, Gil, Gustafson, et al., 1994).

Family Factors

The significant role of the family system in mediating the adjustment of individuals with SCD is becoming clearer. Social support and the family's knowledge of SCD have been identified as contributors to positive family relationships. Social class, family structure, and illness severity did not predict parental adjustment (Hurtig, 1994). An association has been demonstrated between parents' knowledge about SCD, stability and availability of their social network, parental coping methods, and children's self-esteem (Tarnowski & Brown, 2000). Increased family cohesion and organization have been associated with resilience and coping competency, and high levels of family conflict and control have been associated with negative coping in adolescent females and poor coping in mothers (Thompson et al., 1993). In addition, stress related to daily problems and disease-related stressors have been associated with the adjustment of mothers. Families of girls with SCD have more positive family relationships, suggesting a possible gender influence on family functioning (Hurtig, 1994).

Neurocognitive and Academic Functioning

Findings related to neuropsychological functioning in children with SCD have been variable, which has been largely attributed to methodological limitations in some of the earlier studies (Bonner et al., 1999; Brown, Armstrong, & Eckman, 1993). The studies that are more recent and methodologically sound are reviewed here. The sequelae of CVAs for individuals with SCD are similar to those of individuals with traumatic brain injury (Cohen, Branch, McKie, & Adams, 1994; Hariman, Griffith, Hurtig, & Keehn, 1991). These studies mark the adverse neurocognitive sequelae for children and adolescents who have sustained a CVA. The specificity and degree of impairment differs depending on the location of the infarction, with those who sustain left hemisphere infarcts having more adverse sequelae including aphasia and constructional praxis (Cohen et al., 1994).

Children with SCD but without any overt signs or symptoms of a CVA may still be at significant risk for cognitive impairment. For example, Fowler and colleagues (1988) and Swift and associates (1989) reported that, relative to healthy and comparison sibling controls, children with SCD but without overt symptoms of a CVA still scored lower on tests of intellectual functioning and academic achievement. Wasserman, Wilimas, Fairclough, Mulhern, and Wang (1991) compared sibling controls to 43 children with SCD ages 8 to 16 years with no overt neurological dysfunction. The children with SCD still scored lower on measures of intelligence, although no differences were found in the area of academic achievement. In addition, children ages 12 years or younger showed language-based deficits. Brown, Buchanan, et al. (1993) used a battery of neurocognitive measures to compare children and adolescents with SCD but without CVAs or overt neurological dysfunction to healthy siblings. Children with SCD performed more poorly than siblings on measures of sustained attention, and hemoglobin levels contributed significantly to intelligence and achievement measures when controlling for age and social class. These findings are consistent with those of Rodgers, Clark, and Kessler (1984), who found evidence of altered metabolism in the frontal lobe area on positron emission tomography (PET) scans for adult patients with SCD. These studies indicate the likelihood of deficits in attention and executive functioning in patients with SCD, including those with overt CVAs (Brown et al., 2000; DeBaun et al., 1998; Rodgers et al., 1984; Schatz et al., 1999) and those with no documented evidence of infarcts (Brown, Buchanan, et al., 1993; Goonan, Goonan, Brown, Buchanan, & Eckman, 1994). As Bonner et al. (1999) pointed out, the studies offer evidence of the possible mechanisms (reduced oxygen delivery, CVAs) that underlie the cognitive deficits associated with SCD. That a significant percentage of children with SCD (11% to 20%) with no evidence of overt neurological disease on physical examination may have cerebral infarction detectable only by magnetic resonance imaging (MRI) also has been investigated (Armstrong et al., 1996; Brown et al., 2000; Pavlakis et al., 1988). The most current definitive investigation of silent cerebral infarction with neuropsychological data has been a subset of the CCSCD (Armstrong et al., 1996). Participants in this large, multisite, collaborative clinical research program included 194 children with SCD, 135 of whom had HbSS type. The incidence of CNS abnormalities identified on MRI was 17%, with more than 10% of the sample being categorized as having a silent infarct. Children with a clinical history of a CVA were compared on neurocognitive functioning to those with MRI evidence of a silent infarct or no MRI abnormality. Children with a clinical stroke as revealed on MRI showed the highest frequency of neurocognitive deficits, including impairments in intellectual functioning, language abilities, visual–motor and visual–spatial processing, academic achievement, and sequential memory. Children with silent infarcts did not show problems as severe or pervasive as those with overt CVAs. However, they did perform more poorly than those children with no MRI abnormality on visual–motor speed and coordination, and academic achievement. Brown et al. (2000), in a similar design, found that children with both silent and overt CVAs performed more poorly than children without infarcts on measures of attention and executive functioning.

Pain Management

Acute and chronic pain are symptoms that differentiate SCD from many other chronic illnesses (Tarnowski & Brown, 2000). Gil (1989) concluded that individuals vary in their capacity to cope with pain, and this coping capacity influences functional activity, psychological adjustment, and disease adaptation. Gil, Abrams, Phillips, and Keefe (1989) studied pain-coping strategies of 79 adults with SCD. Pain-coping strategies characterized by negative thinking and passive adherence (e.g., catastrophizing, fear self-statements, resting, taking fluids) were associated with more severe pain episodes, less activity during episodes of pain, more frequent contacts with medical personnel, and greater psychological distress.

To delineate more specifically the mechanism underlying negative thoughts and reports of pain, Gil and associates (1995) studied 58 adults with SCD who completed a finger pressure experimental pain induction task. Individuals who reported more negative thoughts had a greater tendency to report pain during noxious stimulation, even to stimuli of relatively low intensity. Negative thoughts were not associated with sensory discrimination. The researchers suggested that motivation and attitude factors rather than sensory factors are involved in adults' interpretations of pain. In a similar investigation with pediatric populations, Walco and Dampier (1990) examined pain perception in children. Children with SCD had lower pain thresholds for finger pressure than did their healthy peers. The researchers suggested that disease processes affect sensory systems and that psychological factors associated with a chronic illness influence reports of pain threshold levels. The studies by Gil and associates (1995) and Walco and Dampier (1990) suggested that pain is not merely a sensory experience and that psychological factors significantly contribute to interpretations of pain by adults and children with SCD.

In an investigation of strategies of coping with pain in children with SCD, Gil and colleagues (Gil et al., 1991) assessed parent- and child-reported psychological distress, parent-reported child activity during periods of pain episodes, and health care utilization. Consistent with the adult findings, children's pain-coping strategies characterized by passive adherence and negative thinking (e.g., catastrophizing, self-statements of fear and anger) were associated with psychological and functional impairment. Specifically, negative thinking was associated with fewer activities during painful episodes and higher levels of self-reported distress. In addition, and consistent with adult findings, use of passive coping strategies was associated with more frequent visits to the emergency room and fewer activities during periods of pain. Active coping strategies, including behavioral and cognitive coping strategies like diverting attention, calming self-statements, and reinterpreting pain sensations, were associated with fewer visits to the emergency room and a greater number of activities during painful episodes. Baseline pain-coping strategies also were found to be predictive of adjustment 9 months later.

These studies have implications for intervention programs. Specifically, the overall adjustment of adults and children with SCD may be enhanced by replacing pain-coping strategies characterized by negative thinking patterns with active coping strategies (Gil et al., 1991; Thompson et al., 1992; Thompson et al., 1993). We hope these and another intervention study (Gil, 1989) that taught active coping strategies and showed increased adult and child adjustment will experimentally validate investigations that have primarily been correlational.

Summary

SCD is a group of genetic disorders that primarily affect hemoglobin of the blood. The disease is prevalent primarily in African Americans and individuals of Mediterranean descent. The effect of SCD on the body is widespread and ranges from frequent pain episodes that are the result of vaso-occlusive episodes to extensive organ involvement that may eventually result in death. The prognosis of the disease has improved significantly as a result of newborn screening and the use of prophylactic penicillin for young children, but medical management continues to be lifelong and there are no cures for the disease. Social and emotional adaptation to the disease are variable and in part have been found to be associated with social class, chronological age, and styles of coping. Style of coping also is an important predictor in managing pain episodes. There are significant cognitive and academic difficulties associated with SCD, usually as a result of CVAs. Successful pain management is strongly associated with coping and psychological adjustment. Individuals who use more active strategies to cope with pain use fewer medical resources than individuals who have more passive maladaptive coping styles.

HEMOPHILIA

Medical Aspects

Hemophilia is the most common hereditary coagulation disorder, affecting approximately 20,000 males in the United States (Hoyer, 1994). Hemophilia transcends ethnic and geographic boundaries and has an overall incidence approaching 1 in 5,000 male births (Rosendaal, Smit, & Briet, 1991; World Health Organization, 1991). In about one third of newly diagnosed patients, there is no known family history of clotting disorder (Hoyer, 1994). Hemophilia A, "classic hemophilia," is a diminished blood-clotting ability caused by the absence, deficiency, or malfunctioning of plasma coagulation factor VIII. Factor VIII circulates in association with von Willebrand factor (vWF), which helps to stabilize Factor VIII (Weiss, Sussman, & Hoyer, 1977). Hemophilia B, "Christmas disease," is a deficiency of partial thromboplastin (factor IX) and also results in deficient blood-clotting ability (Bloom, 1987). The clinical features of hemophilia B are similar to those of hemophilia A, but the incidence of hemophilia B is only about one fourth that of hemophilia A.

Hemophilia A and B share the same genetic inheritance pattern (Bloom, 1987). Clotting factors VIII and IX are linked to the X chromosome. Men with hemophilia transmit the disorder to their daughters, who become carriers. In each pregnancy involving a female carrier, chances are 50% that a male child will inherit the disorder and 50% that a female child will be a carrier. The incidence of hemophilia in females is rare, but a carrier mother and a father with hemophilia can produce a daughter with the disorder.

Hemophilia is a clinically heterogeneous disorder, meaning that the sites and severity of bleeding are related to the variability of clotting factor present in the blood. The distinction of severe (<1% factor VIII/IX), moderate (1% to 5% factor VIII/IX), and mild (6% to 25% factor VIII/IX) dictates the clinical management of the disease (Lanzkowsky, 1995). Children with mild hemophilia may have no history of significant bleeding and may be identified only after they experience a significant trauma or surgery that reveals dysfunctional clotting (Hoyer, 1994). Individuals with severe hemophilia, on the other hand, are at significant risk for repetitive joint and tissue bleeding even with minimal or no obvious injury (spontaneous hemorrhage). Although abnormal hemorrhages may occur at any site in the body, the most common sites of bleeding are the knee, elbow, ankle, shoulder, and hip joints. Hemarthroses (bleeding in the joint) is associated with pain, swelling, and limitation of joint motion. Untreated hemarthroses may result in hemophilic arthropathy, narrowing of joint space, small bone cysts, and limited motion. Muscle hemorrhage is also common, and if not treated early, permanent muscle damage and paralysis can occur. Other potentially serious sites of bleeding associated with hemophilia are the CNS and the kidneys. Intracranial bleeding represents a significant mortality risk for individuals with hemophilia. The risk of CNS bleeding is highest for individuals with severe hemophilia and hemophilia B (Lanzkowsky, 1995).

Before the early 1960s, the treatment for bleeding episodes was the infusion of frozen plasma. With the discovery of more specific and effective factor replacement therapy, highly purified factor VIII concentrates have become the treatment of choice. Treatment with factor VIII concentrates has resulted in advances in the prevention or rapid reversal of bleeding episodes (Hoyer, 1994). In addition, hemophilia home care programs have allowed for home-based treatment with factor replacement therapy. Home-based care has been associated with decreased hospitalizations, with no difference in the rate of medical complications when compared to traditional hospital-based treatment (Strawczynaki, Stachewitsch, Morgen-Stern, & Shaw, 1973). These improvements in the medical management of hemophilia and the availability of home-based intervention have had a profound effect on both the life expectancy (Ikkala et al., 1982) and the quality of life (Kaufert, 1980) of patients with hemophilia.

Prior to 1985 there was no system of widespread donor screening or viral inactivation for blood products, and pooled coagulation-factor concentrates were a significant source of infection with the human immunodeficiency virus (HIV). An estimated 60% to 75% of patients with hemophilia who received blood products prior to 1985 were infected with HIV (Evatt, Gomperts, McDougal, & Ramsey, 1985). Jason, Stehr-Green, Holman, Evatt, and the Hemophilia–AIDS Collaborative Study Group (1988) reported in 1985 that 88% of pediatric and 94% of adult patients with hemophilia A were seropositive. The recognition of HIV infection in blood products also resulted in the identification of hepatitis B, non-A, and C in patients who had received transfusions. The treatment of blood products through heating or chemical treatment has resulted in what is believed to be an elimination of the transmission of HIV and hepatitis B and C. Recent focus has been on recombinant DNA technology, which virtually eliminates the potential for transmitting any virus present in human plasma (Hoyer, 1994).

In response to the increased focus on the medical, psychosocial, and behavioral issues germane to hemophilia, the U.S. Department of Health and Human Services, Division of Maternal and Child Health provided funding for the development of Regional Hemophilia Diagnostic and Treatment Centers (HTCs). This system of comprehensive care targeted medical care to address hematological issues and orthopedic sequelae, preventive counseling to address child and parent safety behaviors, and genetic counseling as three major areas of intervention. In a survey of psychosocial services for children with hemophilia and their families, data from providers at 53 HTCs showed that general information and support to parents and patients were the most frequently provided psychosocial services (Drotar, Agle, Eckl, & Thompson, 1997).

Complications from soft-tissue hemorrhages and hemarthroses remain a critical medical and behavioral issue even with treatment advances. Hemarthroses is especially problematic because it is associated with degenerative hemophilic arthropathy and chronic arthritic pain. Even the prompt treatment of hemarthroses may not prevent the development of painful joint changes (Guenther, Hilgartner, Miller, & Vienne, 1980; Helske, Ikkala, Myllyla, Nevallinna, & Rasi, 1982), and most children and adults with hemophilia experience chronic pain associated with degenerative hemophilic arthropathy (Dietrich, 1976). The management of pain in hemophilia, therefore, should focus not only on the acute pain associated with a discrete episode of bleeding but also on the chronic pain associated with joint degeneration. Spitzer (1993) asserted that pain allows children with hemophilia to monitor changes in their health (i.e., acute pain signals the presence of an intra-articular bleeding episode) and alert their caregivers to intervene quickly. However, the management of chronic pain in hemophilia is essential in that chronic pain is associated with analgesic dependence and impaired functioning in daily life activities (Varni & Gilbert, 1982). Varni and colleagues (Varni, 1981; Varni, Gilbert, & Dietrich, 1981; Varni, Katz, & Dash, 1982) conducted a series of investigations of cognitive–behavioral interventions for management of chronic arthritic pain in populations of adults and children with hemophilia. The self-regulation program involving a combination of progressive muscle relaxation, meditative breathing exercises, and guided imagery was found to be effective in modulating chronic arthritic pain and reducing the use of pharmacological interventions for pain. Most important, the overall reduction in pain perception did not affect the pain-based knowledge of the occurrence of an acute bleed.

The general management of hemophilia in pediatric populations involves avoidance of high-risk situations (i.e., any situation in which the child has a risk for physical injury) and prompt intravenous factor infusion to manage hemorrhage. A regimen of prevention and timely factor treatment can often control minor bleeding episodes and is thought to increase a sense of control of the disease (Warren & McMillan, 1986). Van Sciver, D'Angelo, Rappaport, and Woolf (1995) investigated treatment compliance, treatment attitude, and illness-related family stress in boys with hemophilia, sickle cell disease, or asthma. The researchers hypothesized that the high level of symptom control afforded by factor replacement therapy and the clear relationship between prompt intervention and favorable outcomes in hemophilia would result in compliance, positive attitudes toward treatment, and more moderate levels of illness-related family stress in boys with hemophilia as compared to the other pediatric groups. Measurement of health care provider ratings of compliance in the groups with hemophilia included indices of response to emergency situations, participation in maintenance behaviors related to home care, performance of preventive behaviors, and willingness to participate in medical tests critical to health status monitoring. Boys with hemophilia were rated by their health care professionals as "somewhat compliant" in the areas of emergency care, home care participation, and medical tests. However, they were rated as "resistant" to medical advice about prevention, which included the avoidance of contact sports and other physical restrictions to prevent injury. Boys with hemophilia had treatment attitudes that were significantly more positive than boys with either sickle cell disease or asthma. However, mothers of children in all three participant groups reported disease-related elevated levels of family and social stress.

Psychosocial Issues

Early investigations suggested that stress was a precipitating factor of bleeding in individuals with hemophilia (Garlinghouse & Sharp, 1968; Heisel, Ream, Raitz, Rappaport, & Coddington, 1973). More recently, Perrin, MacLean, Janco, and Gortmaker (1996) studied 97 children and adolescents with hemophilia for 6 months. The relationship between stress and incidence of bleeding with and without injury received focus, and elevated parent daily stress ratings during a 4-day period were associated with increased likelihood of their son's injury-related bleeding during the subsequent day. No significant relationship was found between boys' daily mood measures and subsequent increases in bleeding. Perrin and colleagues reasoned that stress may indirectly promote bleeding by increasing the likelihood of an injury. However, variations in clotting factor levels were much stronger predictors of bleeding episodes than any of the stress-related variables.

The presence of a chronic medical condition in children is associated with increased risk for psychological adjustment problems (Wallander, Varni, Babani, Banis, & Wilcox, 1988). Wallander et al. assessed the presence of internalizing and externalizing child behavior problems in hemophilia, juvenile diabetes, chronic obesity, juvenile rheumatoid arthritis, spina bifida, and cerebral palsy. Few significant disease-specific differences were found, and no differences were found in relation to hemophilia. Behavior patterns and social adjustment of children with chronic illnesses were more positive than in children referred to mental health clinics, but children with chronic illnesses showed more externalizing and internalizing behavior problems and less social competency than the normative sample. No specific pattern of maladjustment was evident other than elevated frequency of somatic concerns.

Although Wallander et al. (1988) found no disease-specific patterns of maladjustment associated with hemophilia versus other chronic pediatric conditions, the medical, social, educational, and lifestyle repercussions of hemophilia may be related to the long-term psychological functioning of those with hemophilia and their families. A significant stressor for adults and children with hemophilia is HIV infection. Many investigations before 1985 found elevated rates of psychosocial stress in children with hemophilia and their parents (Agle, Gluck, & Pierce, 1987; Mattsson, 1984), but HIV status was not used as a variable in these adjustment studies. In addition, many of the earlier studies were hampered by the lack of objective and comprehensive measurement of psychosocial functioning (Drotar et al., 1997).

Later studies began to incorporate HIV status. Bussing and Burket (1992) investigated the prevalence of anxiety disorders and intrafamilial stress in children with hemophilia, children with asthma, and healthy children. Boys with hemophilia who tested positive for HIV had significantly more total anxiety diagnoses than healthy children. Boys with hemophilia who tested negative for HIV had fewer anxiety disorders than children with asthma but significantly more total diagnoses than the healthy control group. However, children with hemophilia and their parents reported low levels of subjective stress irrespective of HIV status. Bussing and Burket questioned whether the low subjective stress ratings were related to a pattern of denial developed to assist patients in coping with the pain associated with the hemophilia.

To address this issue, Drotar, Agle, Eckl, and Thompson (1995) investigated the relationship between a repressive personality style and psychological distress in children and adolescents with hemophilia who tested positive or negative for HIV. Highly defensive children and adolescents with hemophilia, regardless of HIV status, reported lower levels of depression than nondefensive children and adolescents with hemophilia. Both groups self-reported similar levels of anxiety. However, mothers of children and adolescents with a repressive personality style reported that their children were more anxious and depressed than did mothers of nondefensive children. Using the risk and resistance framework proposed by Wallander et al. (1989), Drotar and colleagues (1997) examined psychological distress in mothers of children and adolescents who tested positive or negative for HIV. Data indicated that stressful life events were associated with increased levels of maternal distress, whereas family support was associated with lower levels of distress. Contrary to the risk and resistance model, the severity of hemophilia was not related to maternal distress. The nature of the relationship between these risk and resistance factors and maternal distress was comparable for mothers of children who tested positive or negative for HIV. However, stressful life events were more strongly related to distress in mothers of children and adolescents who tested positive for HIV than of those who did not. The researchers suggested that the accumulation of multiple stressors adversely affected maternal vulnerability to stress. Additional studies that identify the protective and risk factors present in specific aspects of family relationships, social support, life events, and disease-related factors are warranted. The relationship between parental psychological adjustment and child psychological variables in families of children with hemophilia is only somewhat documented. Handford, Mayes, Bagnato, and Bixler (1986) found that children with hemophilia who had accepting mothers scored more positively on seven of eight personality traits, including intelligence, enthusiasm, and security. Mayes, Handford, Kowalski, and Schaefer (1988) investigated personality variables in 22 boys with hemophilia and the child-rearing attitudes and parenting behaviors of their parents over 6 years. Personality variables changed in a positive direction, with the boys becoming more enthusiastic and self-reliant over time. No negative personality pattern changes were found, and all other personality variables remained within the normal range with the exception of a positive increase in the intelligence trait shown during the duration of the investigation. Overall interaction patterns indicated that positive child personality changes were associated with positive parental attitudes.

HIV in individuals with hemophilia makes adjustment to potentially stressful medical and behavioral management regimens more difficult. Another concern is the neurodevelopmental effects of HIV in children and adolescents with hemophilia. Loveland et al. (1994) conducted a longitudinal investigation of children and adolescents involved in the Hemophilia Growth and Development Study (HGDS), a multicenter study of children and adolescents with hemophilia and HIV infection. At baseline, no differences were found in neuropsychological performance with regard to HIV status. Children with and without HIV infection performed in the average range across multiple neuropsychological, academic, and behavioral indexes, consistent with data from Whitt et al. (1993), but the combined sample showed a pattern of lesser adaptive skills and academic achievement relative to intelligence. These data, similar to the baseline data, suggest that the pattern of academic and adaptive performance deficits is not specific to HIV-related brain disease but to hemophilia. In addition, data indicate that the HIV disease development process in children with hemophilia who were infected postnatally resembles the lengthy disease course in adults instead of the more rapid development in children with congenitally transmitted HIV infections (Tovo et al., 1992).

Sirois et al. (1998) measured HGDS participant performance on numerous neuropsychological measures; MRI and electroencephalogram (EEG) data were collected. Children and adolescents were categorized into three groups according to HIV status: HIV negative, HIV positive with CD4 count ≥200, and HIV positive with CD4 count <200. Abnormal or equivocal MRI findings and diffuse atrophy were found more frequently in children and adolescents with CD4 counts of less than 200. Performance on measures of coordination and gait was lower for children with abnormalities on the neuropsychological examination, regardless of HIV status. Abnormal MRI and neurological findings were not associated with decrements in neuropsychological performance unless they were considered in an interaction with coordination or gait abnormalities, a history of head trauma, and parental education. These findings may indicate that cognitive performance in children with hemophilia is adversely affected by a combination of neuropsychological and environmental variables. These data and previous investigations (Loveland et al., 1994; Whitt et al., 1993) indicate that hemophilia itself, regardless of HIV status, may adversely affect cognitive performance, coordination, and gait.

In general, investigations of academic, behavioral, and social functioning of individuals with hemophilia and HIV and those who only have hemophilia suggest that many of the difficulties are related to hemophilia. However, most studies focused on children and adolescents whose HIV had not progressed to acquired immunodeficiency syndrome (AIDS). AIDS is associated with deleterious effects on the CNS, so it is likely that a pattern of neuropsychological sequelae will emerge in these children and adolescents as their disease progresses.

Olch (1971) and Markova and McDonald (1980) pointed out discrepancies between academic achievement and intellectual abilities linked to a pattern of school absences in boys with hemophilia. Woolf et al. (1989) showed poor academic achievement relative to intelligence, as well as significant absenteeism, but did not support a strong correlation between number of absences and achievement test scores. Colegrove and Huntzinger (1994) found a 15% absenteeism rate in their sample of 37 school-age boys with hemophilia, approximately one half of whom were infected with HIV. Teacher ratings in all areas of academic and social competence were inversely related to absenteeism, but teacher ratings, parent ratings, and self-ratings of behavioral and social competence were all within the normal range. The overall sample showed a pattern of low academic achievement compared to intellectual potential. In general, no differences in intellectual and academic performance were found based on HIV status. Similarly, Mayes et al. (1996) found that despite higher than normal mean IQ, boys with hemophilia had disproportionately high rates of learning disabilities (LDs), graphomotor weakness, and attention deficit hyperactivity disorder (ADHD). School absenteeism was high but not significantly related to grade point average, achievement test scores, IQ/achievement discrepancy score, or clinical diagnosis of ADHD or LD. Boys with hemophilia who were also infected with HIV were absent more frequently than boys with hemophilia who were not infected, but academic achievement scores and grades were not significantly different between the two groups.

Summary

Hemophilia treatment has advanced remarkably in the past 2 decades. Factor replacement therapy has allowed for more effective and time-efficient treatment of acute bleeding, and home care programs have changed the long-term management of orthopedic sequelae. In addition, the risk of viral transmission has been minimized through the systematic application of screening and treatment of blood products. Still, the treatment and management of hemophilia remains complex, involving multiple medical and behavioral issues. Adjustment to the demands of a chronic illness, familial stress associated with demands imposed by frequent medical treatments, and preventive behaviors are critical features for individuals with hemophilia and their families.

CONCLUSION AND DIRECTIONS FOR FUTURE RESEARCH

Health psychologists have contributed to research and clinical efforts on psychological factors associated with diseases of the blood and blood-forming tissues. Leukemia, SCD, and hemophilia have received the most focus in this disease category. The problems associated with these illnesses are lifelong and, without strong medical and psychological intervention, can result in diminished quality of life. Most research studies related to these diseases have been with pediatric populations, but as life expectancies for some of the diseases increase, additional empirical efforts with adult populations will be a focus.

The contributions of health psychologists to treatment of these diseases mirror contributions of health psychologists to other physical disorders reviewed in this volume. In general, they pertain to measurement of adjustment and most efficacious intervention for several disease-related concerns. These include the understanding of adherence to treatment and how adherence may best be assessed and enhanced, family systems issues, and the influence of disease on family functioning and adaptation to disease. This chapter also included reviews of the effects of the various blood disorders on the CNS, as well as associated treatment toxicities on CNS functioning. Health psychologists have contributed through neuropsychological assessments of these CNS effects, studies of the psychological as well as the sensory components of pain and how these components interact, and the study of psychotherapies and pharmacotherapies used to manage acute and chronic pain. Psychological adaptation to and coping with the disease process and how these factors affect overall psychological adjustment and quality of life for individuals and their families are issues that have been studied.

These advances are important to the field of health psychology and also represent significant contributions to the field of hematology. For example, cognitive toxicities are associated with chemotherapy and radiation for children receiving prophylactic treatment for leukemia. As a result of health psychology research, it is now standard care to obtain baseline and ongoing neurocognitive assessments. These tests assess current and late cognitive effects that might be associated with either prophylactic chemotherapy or radiation (for a review, see Armstrong & Mulhern, 1999). The selection of a cancer treatment protocol involves evaluating any significant differences among various chemotherapy regimens. The National Cancer Institute (Armstrong & Mulhern, 1999) maintains that the overall quality of life for the patient is the deciding variable in choosing the best medical therapy. For example, in the area of SCD, assessment of cognitive, academic, developmental, and psychosocial functioning has been recommended by the American Academy of Pediatrics (1996) as part of the practice parameter and standard of care. These are the tasks that have been well researched and profitably implemented by health psychologists.

Health care providers routinely turn to the psychological literature for assessment of adherence and interventions that increase adherence. Some research has resulted in significant changes in prescribing practices and in some cases even the pharmaceutical industry. For example, researchers have shown that carefully educating patients about compliance issues and minimizing the number of pharmacotherapies prescribed improve adherence, as does minimizing the number of doses that are self-administered by the patient without supervision. Now these interventions are standard care. New health-related journals report psychological research that recognizes the influence of chronic or life-threatening illnesses on family functioning, as well as the role of the family in providing social support that enhances psychological adaptation.

Health psychologists have contributed to more appropriate and humane management of pain (for a review, see Walco, Sterling, Conte, &

Engle, 1999). The major organizations setting practice standards on assessment and management of pain and appropriate analgesia have now developed important practice parameters and standards of care for both procedurally related and chronic pain. As recently as 25 years ago, medical personnel erroneously believed that children did not experience pain because of their immature CNS. Today, as a result of medical and psychological research, most clinics provide sedation, analgesia, or a combination for children and adolescents who undergo painful procedures (e.g., lumbar punctures, spinal taps) or who must endure pain associated with a chronic disease due to the diminished concern regarding addiction and adverse effects of pain analgesia for chronic illness.

The well-researched significant variability in individual response to the stressors of a lifelong or life-threatening disease has afforded the development and testing of psychological models to understand issues associated with psychological adjustment and adaptation. Regression equations and the more recent structural equation modeling allow identification of factors that are apt to place individuals at risk for poor adjustment. More important, researchers have learned much from patients who have adapted successfully to stressful life events. These data are used to develop intervention programs for individuals who have less optimal outcomes. It is hoped that research will verify experimentally what has been learned from studies that have been primarily correlational in nature.

Behavioral and biological sciences are coordinating in the laboratory and in clinical medicine to make important contributions to the well-being of individuals who must endure the chronic and sometimes life-threatening disorders of the blood and blood-forming organs. Identification of genes that may underlie some blood disorders and novel medical treatments such as bone marrow transplantation and hydroxyurea are examples of biological and medical contributions. Such medical treatments may provide patients greater hope in a more favorable prognosis and perhaps even a cure for their disease. With such developments come associated psychological maladjustments and other psychological issues that are concomitant with increased life expectancy, which is similar to the current view of HIV as a chronic illness rather than a harbinger of rapid death. Health psychologists must continue efforts in both the research and clinical arena. It is their responsibility to provide training to the next generation of health psychologists so that they may be equipped to negotiate some of the complex issues in health care. Despite the financial complexities in the delivery of health care, the performance of health psychologists over the past 2 decades indicates that important clinical research contributions will be made. These efforts should continue into the next century and enhance the quality of life for individuals with chronic and life-threatening diseases and their families.

REFERENCES

Adedoyin, M. A. (1992). Psychosocial effects of sickle cell disease among adolescents. *East African Medical Journal, 69,* 370–372.

Agle, D., Gluck, H., & Pierce, G. F. (1987). The risk of AIDS: Psychologic impact on the hemophilic population. *General Hospital Psychiatry, 9,* 11–17.

American Academy of Pediatrics Committee on Genetics. (1996). Health supervision for children with sickle cell disease and their families. *Pediatrics, 98,* 467–473.

Armstrong, F. D., & Horn, M. (1995). Educational issues in childhood cancer. *School Psychology Quarterly, 10,* 292–304.

Armstrong, F. D., & Mulhern, R. K. (1999). Acute lymphoblastic leukemia and brain tumors. In R. T. Brown (Ed.), *Cognitive aspects of chronic illness in children* (pp. 47–77). New York: Guilford Press.

Armstrong, F. D., Thompson, R. J., Wang, W., Zimmerman, R., Pegelow, C. H., Miller, S., et al. (1996). Cognitive functioning and brain magnetic resonance imaging in children with sickle cell disease. *Pediatrics, 97,* 864–870.

Barrett, D., Wisotzek, I., Abel, G., Rouleau, J., Platt, A., Pollard, W., et al. (1988). Assessment of psychosocial functioning of patients with sickle cell disease. *Southern Medical Journal, 81,* 745–750.

Bearison, D. J. (1994). Medication compliance in pediatric oncology. In D. J. Bearison & R. K. Mulhern (Eds.), *Pediatric psychooncology* (pp. 84–98). New York: Oxford University Press.

Bearison, D. J., & Mulhern, R. K. (1994). *Pediatric psychooncology.* New York: Oxford University Press.

Bennett, D. S. (1994). Depression among children with chronic medical problems: A meta-analysis. *Journal of Pediatric Psychology, 19,* 149–170.

Berg, R., Ch'ien, L. T., Lancaster, W., Williams, S., & Cummins, J. (1983). Neuropsychological sequelae of postradiation somnolence syndrome. *Developmental and Behavioral Pediatrics, 4,* 103–107.

Blasco, T. (1994). Anticipatory nausea and vomiting: Are psychological factors adequately investigated? *British Journal of Clinical Psychology, 33,* 85–100.

Bleyer, W. A. (1990). Acute lymphoblastic leukemia in children: Advances and prospectus. *Cancer, 65,* 689–695.

Bloom, A. L. (1987). Inherited disorders of blood coagulation. In A. Bloom & D. Thomas (Eds.), *Haemostasis and thrombosis* (2nd ed., pp. 393–436). Edinburgh, Scotland: Churchill Livingstone.

Blotcky, A. D., Raczynski, J. M., Gurwitch, R., & Smith, K. (1985). Family influences on hopelessness among children early in the cancer experience. *Journal of Pediatric Psychology, 10,* 479–493.

Bonner, M., Gustafson, K., Schumacher, E., & Thompson, R. J., Jr. (1999). The impact of sickle cell disease on cognitive functioning and learning. *School Psychology Review, 28,* 182–193.

Bozeman, M. F., Orbach, C., & Sutherland, M. (1955). Psychological impact of cancer and its treatment: The adaptation of mothers to the threatened loss of their children through leukemia: Part I. *Cancer, 8,* 1–19.

Broome, M. E., Lillis, P. P., McGahee, T. W., & Bates, T. (1992). The use of distraction and imagery with children during painful procedures. *Oncology Nursing Forum, 19,* 499–502.

Brouwers, P., & Poplack, D. (1990). Memory and learning sequelae in long-term survivors of acute lymphoblastic leukemia: Association with attention deficits. *American Journal of Pediatric Hematology/Oncology, 12,* 174–181.

Brown, R. T., Armstrong, F. D., & Eckman, J. R. (1993). Neurocognitive aspects of pediatric sickle cell disease. *Journal of Learning Disabilities, 26,* 33–45.

Brown, R. T., Buchanan, I., Doepke, K., Eckman, J. R., Baldwin, K., Goonan, B., et al. (1993). Cognitive and academic functioning in children with sickle cell disease. *Journal of Clinical Child Psychology, 22,* 207–218.

Brown, R. T., Davis, P. C., Lambert, R., Hsu, L., Hopkins, K., & Eckman, J. (2000). Neurocognitive functioning and magnetic resonance imaging in children with sickle cell disease. *Journal of Pediatric Psychology, 25,* 503–513.

Brown, R. T., Doepke, K. J., & Kaslow, N. J. (1993). Risk–resistance–adaptation model for pediatric chronic illness: Sickle cell syndrome as an example. *Clinical Psychology Review, 13,* 119–132.

Brown, R. T., Kaslow, N. J., Doepke, K., Buchanan, I., Eckman, J., Baldwin, K., et al. (1993). Psychosocial and family functioning in children with sickle cell syndrome and their mothers. *Journal of the American Academy of Child and Adolescent Psychiatry, 32,* 545–553.

Brown, R. T., Kaslow, N. J., Madan-Swain, A., Doepke, K., Sexson, S. B., & Hill, L. (1993). Parental psychopathology and children's adjustment to leukemia. *Journal of American Academy of Child and Adolescent Psychiatry, 32,* 554–561.

Brown, R. T., Madan-Swain, A., Pais, R., Lambert, R. G., Sexson, S. B., & Ragab, A. (1992). Chemotherapy for acute lymphocytic leukemia: Cognitive and academic sequelae. *Journal of Pediatrics, 121,* 885–889.

Brown, R. T., Madan-Swain, A., Walco, G., Cherick, I., Ievers, C. E., Conte, P. M. et al. (1998). Cognitive academic late effects among children previously treated for acute lymphocytic leukemia receiving chemotherapy as CNS prophylaxis. *Journal of Pediatric Psychology, 23,* 219–228.

Bussing, R., & Burket, R. C. (1992). Anxiety and intrafamilial stress in children with hemophilia after the HIV crisis. *Journal of the American Academy of Child and Adolescent Psychiatry, 32,* 562–567.

Carey, M. P., & Burish, T. G. (1988). Etiology and treatment of the psychological side effects associated with cancer chemotherapy: A critical review and discussion. *Psychological Bulletin, 104,* 307–325.

Charache, S., Lubin, B., & Reid, C. D. (1989). *Management and therapy of sickle cell disease* (NIH Pub. No. 89-2117). Washington, DC: National Institutes of Health.

Chesler, M. A., & Barbarin, O. A. (1987). *Childhood cancer and the family*. New York: Brunner/Mazel.

Cohen, M. J., Branch, W. B., McKie, V. C., & Adams, R. J. (1994). Neuropsychological impairment in children with sickle cell anemia and cerebrovascular accidents. *Clinical Pediatrics, 33*, 517–524.

Colegrove, R. W., Jr., & Huntzinger, R. M. (1994). Academic, behavioral, and social adaptation of boys with hemophilia/HIV disease. *Journal of Pediatric Psychology, 19*, 457–473.

Copeland, D. R., Fletcher, J. M., Pfefferbaum-Levine, B., Jaffe, N., Reid, H., & Maor, M. (1985). Neuropsychological sequelae of childhood cancer in long-term survivors. *Pediatrics, 75*, 745–753.

Cousens, P., Ungerer, J. A., Crawford, J. A., & Stevens, M. M. (1991). Cognitive effects of childhood leukemia therapy: A case for four specific deficits. *Journal of Pediatric Psychology, 16*, 475–488.

Cousens, P., Waters, B., Said, J., & Stevens, M. (1988). Cognitive effects of cranial irradiation in leukemia: A survey and meta-analysis. *Journal of Child Psychology and Psychiatry, 29*, 839–852.

Damlouji, N. F., Kevess-Cohen, R., Charache, S., Georgopoulos, A., & Folstein, M. F. (1982). Social disability and psychiatric morbidity in sickle cell anemia and diabetes patients. *Psychosomatics, 23*, 925–931.

Davis, C. (1995). Sickle cell anemia: An overview posing an employment quandary. *Vocational Evaluation and Work Adjustment Bulletin, 28*, 20–23.

DeBaun, M. R., Schatz, J., Siegel, M. J., Koby, M., Craft, S., Resar, L., et al. (1998). Cognitive screening examinations for silent cerebral infarcts in sickle cell disease. *Neurology, 50*, 1678–1682.

DeMulder, P. H. M., Seynaeve, C., Vermorken, J. B., van Liessum, P. A., Mols-Jevdevic, S., Allman, E. L., et al. (1990). Ondansetron compared with high-dose metroclopramide in prophylaxis as acute and delayed cisplatin-induced nausea and vomiting. *Annals of Internal Medicine, 113*, 834–840.

Dietrich, S. L. (1976). Musculoskeletal problems. In M. W. Higartner (Ed.), *Hemophilia in children*. Littleton, MA: Publishing Sciences Group.

Dolgin, M. J., & Katz, E. R. (1988). Conditioned aversions in pediatric cancer patients receiving chemotherapy. *Developmental and Behavioral Pediatrics, 9*, 82–85.

Dolgin, M. J., Katz, E. R., McGinty, K., & Siegel, S. E. (1985). Anticipatory nausea and vomiting in pediatric cancer patients. *Pediatrics, 75*, 547–552.

Dolgin, M. J., Katz, E. R., Zeltzer, L. K., & Landsverk, J. (1989). Behavioral distress in pediatric patients with cancer receiving chemotherapy. *Pediatrics, 84*, 103–110.

Dolgin, M. J., & Phipps, S. (1996). Reciprocal influences in family adjustment to childhood cancer. In L. Baider, C. L. Cooper, & A. K. DeNour (Eds.), *Cancer and the family* (pp. 73–92). West Sussex, England: Wiley.

Drotar, D. D., Agle, D. P., Eckl, C. L., & Thompson, P. (1995). Psychological response to HIV-positivity in hemophilia. *Pediatrics, 96*, 1062–1069.

Drotar, D. D., Agle, D. P., Eckl, C. L., & Thompson, P. A. (1997). Impact of the repressive personality style on the measurement of psychological distress in children and adolescents with chronic illness: An example from hemophilia. *Journal of Pediatric Psychology, 21,* 282–293.

Embury, S. H., Hebbel, R. P., Steinberg, M. H., & Mohandes, N. (1994). Pathogenesis of vasoocclusion. In S. H. Embury, R. P. Hebbel, N. Mohandes, & M. H. Steinberg (Eds.), *Sickle cell disease: Basic principles and clinical practice* (pp. 311–326). New York: Raven Press.

Evatt, B. L., Gomperts, E. D., McDougal, S. S., & Ramsey, R. B. (1985). Coincidental appearance of LAV/HTLV-III antibodies in hemophiliacs and the onset of the AIDS epidemic. *New England Journal of Medicine, 312,* 483–490.

Festa, R., Tamaroff, M. H., Chasalow, F., & Lanzkowsky, P. (1992). Therapeutic adherence to oral medication regimens by adolescents with cancer: I. Laboratory assessment. *Journal of Pediatrics, 120,* 807–811.

Fowler, M. G., Whitt, J. K., Nash, K. B., Atkinson, S., Wells, R. J., & McMillan, C. (1988). Neuropsychological and academic functioning of children with sickle cell anemia. *Developmental and Behavioral Pediatrics, 9,* 213–230.

Friedman, S. B., Chodoff, P., Mason, J. W., & Hamburg, D. A. (1963). Behavioral observations on parents anticipating the death of a child. *Pediatrics, 32,* 610–625.

Garlinghouse, J., & Sharp, L. J. (1968). The hemophilic child's self-concept and family stress in relation to bleeding episodes. *Nursing Research, 17,* 32–37.

Gil, K. M. (1989). Coping with sickle cell disease pain. *Annals of Behavioral Medicine, 11,* 49–57.

Gil, K. M., Abrams, M. R., Phillips, G., & Keefe, F. J. (1989). Sickle cell disease pain: Relation of coping strategies to adjustment. *Journal of Consulting and Clinical Psychology, 57,* 725–731.

Gil, K. M., Phillips, G., Webster, D. A., Martin, N. J., Abrams, M., Grant, M., et al. (1995). Experimental pain sensitivity and reports of negative thoughts in adults with sickle cell disease. *Behavior Therapy, 26,* 273–293.

Gil, K. M., Williams, D. A., Thompson, R. J., Jr., & Kinney, T. R. (1991). Sickle cell disease in children and adolescents: The relation of child and parent pain coping strategies to adjustment. *Journal of Pediatric Psychology, 16,* 643–663.

Goonan, B. T., Goonan, L. J., Brown, R. T., Buchanan, I., & Eckman, J. R. (1994). Sustained attention and inhibitory control in children with sickle cell syndrome. *Archives of Clinical Neuropsychology, 9,* 89–104.

Guenther, E. E., Hilgartner, M. W., Miller, C. H., & Vienne, G. (1980). Hemophilic arthropathy: Effect of home care on treatment patterns and joint disease. *Journal of Pediatrics, 97,* 378–382.

Handford, H. A., Mayes, S. D., Bagnato, S. J., & Bixler, E. O. (1986). Relationships between variations in parents' attitudes and personality traits of hemophilic boys. *American Journal of Orthopsychiatry, 56,* 424–434.

Hariman, L. M. F., Griffith, E. R., Hurtig, A. L., & Keehn, M. T. (1991). Functional outcomes of children with sickle cell disease affected by stroke. *Archives of Physical Medicine and Rehabilitation, 72*, 498–502.

Haupt, R., Fears, T. R., Robison, L. L., Mills, J. L., Nicholson, H. S., Zeltzer, L. K., et al. (1994). Educational attainment in long-term survivors of childhood acute lymphoblastic leukemia. *Journal of the American Medical Association, 272*, 1427–1432.

Heisel, J. S., Ream, S., Raitz, R., Rappaport, M., & Coddington, R. D. (1973). The significance of life events as contributing factors in the diseases of children. *Journal of Pediatrics, 83*, 119–123.

Helske, T., Ikkala, E., Myllyla, G., Nevallinna, H. R., & Rasi, V. (1982). Joint involvement in patients with severe hemophilia A in 1957–59 and 1978–79. *British Journal of Haematology, 51*, 643–647.

Hilgard, J. R., & LeBaron, S. (1982). Relief of anxiety and pain in children and adolescents with cancer: Quantitative measures and clinical observations. *International Journal of Clinical and Experimental Hypnosis, 30*, 417–442.

Holland, J. C. (1998). *Psycho-oncology*. New York: Oxford University Press.

Horwitz, W. A., & Kazak, A. E. (1990). Family adaptation to childhood cancer: Sibling and family system variables. *Journal of Clinical Child Psychology, 19*, 221–228.

Hoyer, L. (1994). Medical review: Hemophilia A. *New England Journal of Medicine, 330*, 38–47.

Hurtig, A. L. (1994). Relationships in families of children and adolescents with sickle cell disease. Psychosocial aspects of sickle cell disease: Past, present, and future directions of research [Special issue]. *Journal of Health and Social Policy, 5*, 161–183.

Hurtig, A. L., & White, L. S. (1986). Psychosocial adjustment in children and adolescents with sickle cell disease. *Journal of Pediatric Psychology, 11*, 411–427.

Ikkala, E., Helske, T., Myllyla, G., Nevanlinna, H. R., Pitkanen, P., & Rasi, V. (1982). Changes in the life expectancies of patients with severe hemophilia A in Finland in 1930–79. *British Journal of Haematology, 52*, 7–12.

Jannoun, L., & Chessells, J. M. (1987). Long-term psychological effects of childhood leukemia and its treatment. *Pediatric Hematology/Oncology, 4*, 293–308.

Jason, J. M., Stehr-Green, J., Holman, R. C., Evatt, B. L., & Hemophilia–AIDS Collaborative Study Group. (1988). Human immunodeficiency virus infection in hemophilic children. *Pediatrics, 82*, 565–570.

Jay, S., Elliott, C. H., Fitzgibbons, I., Woody, P., & Siegel, S. (1995). A comparative study of cognitive behavior therapy versus general anesthesia for painful medical procedures in children. *Pain, 62*, 3–9.

Jay, S. M., Elliott, C. H., Katz, E., & Siegel, S. (1987). Cognitive–behavioral and pharmacologic interventions for children's distress during painful medical procedures. *Journal of Consulting and Clinical Psychology, 55*, 860–865.

Jay, S. M., Elliott, C. H., Ozolins, M., Olson, R., & Pruitt, S. (1985). Behavioral management of children's distress during painful medical procedures. *Behavior Research and Therapy, 23,* 513–552.

Jay, S. M., Elliott, C. H., Woody, P. D., & Siegel, S. (1991). An investigation of cognitive–behavior therapy combined with oral Valium for children undergoing painful medical procedures. *Health Psychology, 10,* 317–322.

Jay, S. M., Ozolins, M., Elliott, C., & Caldwell, S. (1983). Assessment of children's distress during painful medical procedures. *Health and Psychology, 2,* 133–147.

Karon, M., & Vernick, J. (1968). Approaches to emotional support of fatally ill children. *Clinical Pediatrics, 7,* 274–280.

Kaufert, J. M. (1980). Social and psychological responses to home treatment of hemophilia. *Journal of Epidemiology and Community Health, 34,* 194–200.

Kazak, A. E. (1989). Families of chronically ill children: A systems and social–ecological model of adaptation and challenge. *Journal of Consulting and Clinical Psychology, 57,* 25–30.

Kazak, A. E., & Meadows, A. T. (1989). Families of young adolescents who have survived cancer: Social–emotional adjustment, adaptability, and social support. *Journal of Pediatric Psychology, 14,* 175–191.

Kirkpatrick, D. V., Barrios, N. J., & Humbert, J. H. (1991). Bone marrow transplantation for sickle cell anemia. *Seminars in Hematology, 28,* 240–243.

Kun, L. E., Camitta, B. M., Mulhern, R., Lauer, S., Kline, R., Caspter, J., et al. (1984). Treatment of meningeal relapse in childhood acute lymphoblastic leukemia. I. Results of craniospinal irradiation. *Journal of Clinical Oncology, 2,* 359–364.

Kupst, M. J. (1993). Family coping: Supportive and obstructive factors. *Cancer, 71,* 3337–3341.

Kupst, M. J., & Schulman, J. L. (1988). Long-term coping with pediatric leukemia. *Journal of Pediatric Psychology, 13,* 7–22.

Kupst, M. J., Schulman, J. L., Honig, G., Maurer, H., Morgan, E., & Fochtman, D. (1982). Family coping with childhood leukemia. *Journal of Pediatric Psychology, 7,* 157–174.

Kuttner, L., Bowman, M., & Teasdale, M. (1988). Psychological treatment of distress, pain, and anxiety for young children with cancer. *Developmental and Behavioral Pediatrics, 9,* 374–381.

LaGreca, A. (1988). Adherence to prescribed medical regimens. In D. K. Routh (Ed.), *Handbook of pediatric psychology* (pp. 299–320). New York: Guilford Press.

Lanzkowsky, P. (Ed.). (1995). *Manual of pediatric hematology oncology.* New York: Churchill Livingstone.

Leavell, S. R., & Ford, C. V. (1983). Psychopathology in patients with sickle cell disease. *Psychosomatics, 24,* 23–25, 28–29, 32.

Ledley, F. D. (1992). The application of gene therapy to pediatric practice. *International Pediatrics, 7,* 7–15.

Leikin, S. L., Gallagher, D., Kinney, T. R., Sloane, D., Klug, P., & Rida, W. (1989).

Mortality in children and adolescents with sickle cell disease. *Pediatrics, 84*, 500–508.

Lemanek, K. L., Buckloh, L., Woods, G., & Butler, R. (1995). Diseases of the circulatory system: Sickle cell disease and hemophilia. In M. Roberts (Ed.), *Handbook of pediatric psychology* (pp. 286–309). New York: Guilford Press.

Loveland, K. A., Stehbens, J., Contant, C., Bordeaux, J. D., Sirois, P., Bell, T. S., et al. (1994). Hemophilia growth and development study: Baseline neuro-developmental findings. *Journal of Pediatric Psychology, 19*, 223–239.

Margolin, J. F., & Poplack, D. G. (1997). Acute lymphoblastic leukemia. In P. A. Pizzo & D. G. Poplack (Eds.), *Principles and practice of pediatric oncology* (3rd ed., pp. 409–462). Philadelphia: Lippincott–Raven.

Markova, I., & McDonald, K. (1980). Integration of hemophilic boys into normal schools. *Child: Care, Health and Development, 6*, 101–109.

Mattsson, A. (1984). Hemophilia and the family: Life-long challenges and adaptation. *Scandinavian Journal of Haematology, 33*, 65–74.

Mayes, S. D., Handford, H. A., Kowalski, C., & Schaefer, J. H. (1988). Parent attitudes and child personality traits in hemophilia: A six year longitudinal study. *International Journal of Psychiatry in Medicine, 18*, 339–355.

Mayes, S. D., Handford, H. A., Schaefer, J. H., Scogno, C. A., Neagley, S. R., Michael-Good, L., et al. (1996). The relationship of HIV status, type of coagulation disorder, and school absenteeism to cognition, educational performance, mood, and behavior of boys with hemophilia. *Journal of Genetic Psychology, 157*, 137–151.

Meadows, A. T., & Evans, A. E. (1976). Effects of chemotherapy on the central nervous system: A study of parenteral methotrexate in long-term survivors of childhood acute lymphoblastic leukemia. *Cancer, 37*, 1079–1985.

Midence, K., Fuggle, P., & Davies, S. (1993). Psychosocial aspects of sickle cell disease in childhood and adolescence: A review. *British Journal of Clinical Psychology, 32*, 271–280.

Morrow, G. R., & Dobkin, P. L. (1988). Anticipatory nausea and vomiting in cancer patients undergoing chemotherapy treatment: Prevalence, etiology, and behavioral interventions. *Clinical Psychology Review, 8*, 517–556.

Mulhern, R. K., Fairclough, D., & Ochs, J. (1991). A prospective comparison of neuropsychologic performance of children surviving leukemia who received 18-Gy, 24-Gy or no cranial irradiation. *Journal of Clinical Oncology, 9*, 1348–1356.

Mulhern, R. K., Kovnar, E. H., Langston, J., Carter, M., Fairclough, D., Leigh, L., et al. (1992). Long-term survivors of leukemia treated in infancy: Factors associated with neuropsychological status. *Journal of Clinical Oncology, 10*, 1095–1102.

Natterson, J. M., & Knudson, A. G., Jr. (1960). Observations concerning fear of death in fatally ill children and their mothers. *Psychosomatic Medicine, 22*, 456–465.

Noll, R. B., Gartstein, M. A., Hawkins, A., Vannatta, K., Davies, W. H., & Bukowski, W. M. (1995). Comparing parental distress for families with children who have cancer and matched comparison families without children with cancer. *Family Systems Medicine, 13,* 11–28.

Noll, R. B., Ris, M. D., Davies, W. H., Bukowski, W. M., & Koontz, K. (1992). Social interactions between children with cancer or sickle cell disease and their peers: Teacher ratings. *Developmental and Behavioral Pediatrics, 13,* 187–193.

Ochs, J., Mulhern, R., Fairclough, D., Mauer, A., Simone, J., Parvey, L., et al. (1991). Comparison of neuropsychologic functioning and clinical indicators of neurotoxicity in long-term survivors of childhood leukemia given cranial radiation or parenteral methotrexate: A prospective study. *Journal of Clinical Oncology, 9,* 145–151.

Olch, D. (1971). Effects of hemophilia upon intellectual growth and academic achievement. *Journal of Genetic Psychology, 119,* 63–74.

Pavlakis, S. G., Bello, J., Prohovnik, I., Sutton, M., Ince, C., Mohr, J. P., et al. (1988). Brain infarction in sickle cell anemia: Magnetic resonance imaging correlates. *Annals of Neurology, 23,* 125–130.

Perrin, J. M., MacLean, W. E., Jr., Janco, R. L., & Gortmaker, S. L. (1996). Stress and incidence of bleeding in children and adolescents with hemophilia. *Journal of Pediatrics, 128,* 82–88.

Phipps, S., & Mulhern, R. K. (1995). Family cohesion and expressiveness promote resilience to the stress of pediatric bone marrow transplant: A preliminary report. *Journal of Developmental and Behavioral Pediatrics, 16,* 257–263.

Platt, O. S., Brambilla, D. J., Rosse, W. F., Milner, P. F., Castro, O., Steinberg, M. H., et al. (1994). Mortality in sickle cell disease: Life expectancy and risk factors for early death. *New England Journal of Medicine, 330,* 1639–1644.

Practice Management Information Corporation. (1999). *International classification of diseases.* Los Angeles: Author.

Price, R. A., & Birdwell, D. A. (1978). The central nervous system in childhood leukemia. III. Mineralizing microangiopathy and dystrophic calcification. *Cancer, 35,* 717–728.

Robison, L. L., Nesbit, M. E., Sather, H. N., Meadows, A. T., Ortega, J. A., & Hammond, G. D. (1984). Factors associated with IQ scores in long-term survivors of childhood acute lymphoblastic leukemia. *American Journal of Pediatric Hematology/Oncology, 6,* 115–121.

Rodgers, G. P., Clark, C. M., & Kessler, R. M. (1984). Regional alterations in brain metabolism in neurologically normal sickle cell patients. *Journal of the American Medical Association, 256,* 1692–1700.

Rosendaal, F. R., Smit, C., & Briet, E. (1991). Hemophilia treatment in historical perspective: A review of medical and social developments. *Annals of Hematology, 62,* 5–15.

Rubenstein, C. L., Varni, J. W., & Katz, E. R. (1990). Cognitive functioning in long-term survivors of childhood leukemia: A prospective analysis. *Developmental and Behavioral Pediatrics, 11,* 301–305.

Said, J. A., Waters, B. G. H., Cousens, P., & Stevens, M. M. (1989). Neuropsychological sequelae of central nervous system prophylaxis in survivors of childhood acute lymphoblastic leukemia. *Journal of Consulting and Clinical Psychology, 57,* 251–256.

Sawyer, M., Crettenden, A., & Toogood, I. (1986). Psychological adjustment of families and adolescents treated for leukemia. *American Journal of Pediatric Hematology/Oncology, 8,* 200–207.

Schatz, J., Craft, S., Koby, M., Siegel, M. J., Resar, L., Lee, R., et al. (1999, June). Neuropsychological deficits in children with sickle cell disease and cerebral infarction: Role of lesion site and volume. *Child Neuropsychology, 5*(2), 92–103.

Scheinberg, D. A., Maslak, P., & Weiss, M. (1997). Acute leukemias. In V. T. DeVita, S. Hellman, & S. A. Rosenberg (Eds.), *Cancer: Principles and practice of oncology* (pp. 2293–2343). New York: Lippincott–Raven.

Sibler, J. H., Radcliff, J., Peckham, V., Perilongo, G., Kishmani, P., Friedman, M., et al. (1992). Whole-brain irradiation and decline in intelligence: The influence of dose and age on IQ score. *Journal of Clinical Oncology, 10,* 1390–1396.

Sickle Cell Disease Guideline Panel. (1993). Sickle cell disease: Screening, diagnosis, management, and counseling in newborns and infants. *Clinical practice guideline* (No. 6, AHCPR Pub. No. 93-0562). Rockville, MD: Agency for Health Care Policy and Research Public Health Service, U.S. Department of Health and Human Services.

Sirois, P. A., Usner, D. W., Hill, S. D., Mitchell, W. G., Bale, J. F., Loveland, K. A., et al. (1998). Hemophilia growth and development study: Relationships between neuropsychological, neurological, and MRI findings at baseline. *Journal of Pediatric Psychology, 23,* 45–56.

Spitzer, A. (1993). The significance of pain in children's experiences of hemophilia. *Clinical Nursing Research, 2,* 5–18.

Strawczynaki, H., Stachewitsch, A., Morgen-Stern, G., & Shaw, E. (1973). Delivery of care to hemophilia children: Home care versus hospitalization. *Pediatrics, 51,* 986–991.

Sullivan, L. W. (1993). The risks of sickle cell trait: Caution and common sense. *New England Journal of Medicine, 317,* 830–831.

Swift, A. V., Cohen, M. J., Hynd, G. W., Wisenbaker, J. M., McKie, K. M., Makari, G., et al. (1989). Neuropsychological impairment in children with sickle cell anemia. *Pediatrics, 84,* 1077–1085.

Tarnowski, K. J., & Brown, R. T. (1995). Pediatric pain. In R. T. Ammerman & M. Hersen (Eds.), *Handbook of child behavior therapy in the psychiatric setting* (pp. 453–476). New York: Wiley.

Tarnowski, K. J., & Brown, R. T. (2000). Psychological aspects of pediatric disorders. In M. Hersen & R. T. Ammerman (Eds.), *Advanced abnormal child psychology* (2nd ed., pp. 131–150). Mahwah, NJ: Erlbaum.

Tarnowski, K. J., Brown, R. T., Dingle, A. D., & Dreelin, E. (1998). Pediatric pain. In R. T. Ammerman & J. V. Campo (Eds.), *Handbook of pediatric psychology and psychiatry* (Vol. 2, pp. 453–476). Mahwah, NJ: Erlbaum.

Tebbi, C. K., Cummings, K. M., Zevon, M. A., Smith, L., Richards, M., & Mallon, J. (1986). Compliance of pediatric and adolescent cancer patients. *Cancer, 58,* 1179–1184.

Thompson, R. J., Jr., Gil, K. M., Abrams, M. R., & Phillips, G. (1992). Stress, coping, and psychological adjustment of adults with sickle cell disease. *Journal of Consulting and Clinical Psychology, 60,* 433–440.

Thompson, R. J., Jr., Gil, K. M., Burbach, D. J., Keith, B. R., & Kinney, T. R. (1993). Psychological adjustment of mothers of children and adolescents with sickle cell disease: The role of stress, coping methods, and family functioning. *Journal of Pediatric Psychology, 18,* 549–559.

Thompson, R. J., Jr., Gil, K. M., Gustafson, K. E., George, L. K., Keith, B. R., Spock, A., et al. (1994). Stability and change in the psychological adjustment of mothers of children and adolescents with cystic fibrosis and sickle cell disease. *Journal of Pediatric Psychology, 19,* 171–188.

Thompson, R. J., Jr., Gil, K. M., Keith, B. R., Gustafson, K. E., George, L. K., & Kinney, T. R. (1994). Psychological adjustment of children with sickle cell disease: Stability and change over a 10-month period. *Journal of Consulting and Clinical Psychology, 62,* 856–860.

Thompson, R. J., Jr., & Gustafson, K. E. (1996). *Adaptation to chronic childhood illness.* Washington, DC: American Psychological Association.

Thompson, R. J., Jr., Gustafson, K. E., & Gil, K. M. (1995). Psychological adjustment of adolescents with cystic fibrosis or sickle cell disease and their mothers. In J. Wallander & L. Siegel (Eds.), *Advances in pediatric psychology: II. Behavioral perspectives on adolescent health* (pp. 232–247). New York: Guilford Press.

Tovo, P. A., DeMartino, M., Gabiano, C., Cappello, N., D'Elia, R., Loy, A., et al. (1992). Prognostic factors and survival of children with perinatal HIV-1 infection. *Lancet, 339,* 1249–1253.

Van Sciver, M. M., D'Angelo, E. J., Rappaport, L., & Woolf, A. D. (1995). Pediatric compliance and the roles of distinct treatment characteristics, treatment attitudes, and family stress: A preliminary report. *Journal of Developmental and Behavioral Pediatrics, 16,* 350–358.

Varni, J. W. (1981). Self-regulation techniques in the management of chronic arthritic pain in hemophilia. *Behavior Therapy, 12,* 185–194.

Varni, J. W., & Gilbert, A. (1982). Self-regulation of chronic arthritic pain and long-term analgesic dependence in a hemophiliac. *Rheumatology and Rehabilitation, 21,* 171–174.

Varni, J. W., Gilbert, A., & Dietrich, S. L. (1981). Behavioral medicine in pain and analgesia management for the hemophilic child with Factor VIII inhibitor. *Pain, 11,* 121–126.

Varni, J. W., Katz, E. R., & Dash, J. (1982). Behavioral and neurochemical aspects of pediatric pain. In D. C. Russo & J. W. Varni (Eds.), *Behavioral pediatrics: Research and practice* (pp. 177–223). New York: Plenum.

Vichinsky, E. P., Johnson, R., & Lubin, B. H. (1982). Multidisciplinary approach to pain management in sickle cell disease. *American Journal of Pediatric Hematology/Oncology, 4,* 328–333.

Waber, D. P., Urion, D. K., Tarbell, N. J., Niemeyer, C., Gelber, R., & Sallan, S. E. (1990). Late effects of central nervous system treatment of acute lymphoblastic leukemia in childhood are sex dependent. *Developmental Medical Child Neurology, 32,* 238–248.

Walco, G. A., & Dampier, C. D. (1990). Pain in children and adolescents with sickle cell disease: A descriptive study. *Journal of Pediatric Psychology, 15,* 643–658.

Walco, G. A., Sterling, C. M., Conte, P. M., & Engle, R. G. (1999). Empirically supported treatment in pediatric psychology: Disease-related pain. *Journal of Pediatric Psychology, 24,* 155–167.

Wallander, J. L., Varni, J. W., Babani, L., Banis, N. T., DeHaan, C. B., & Wilcox, K. T. (1989). Disability parameters, chronic strains, and adaptation of physically handicapped children and their mothers. *Journal of Pediatric Psychology, 14,* 33–42.

Wallander, J. L., Varni, J. W., Babani, L., Banis, N. T., & Wilcox, K. T. (1988). Children with chronic physical disorders: Maternal reports of their psychological adjustment. *Journal of Pediatric Psychology, 13,* 197–212.

Warren, M. S., & McMillan, C. W. (1986). Hemophilia. In M. J. Hochenberry & D. K. Coody (Eds.), *Pediatric oncology and hematology: Perspectives on care* (pp. 252–272). St. Louis, MO: Mosby.

Wasserman, A. L., Wilimas, J. A., Fairclough, D. L., Mulhern, R. K., & Wang, W. (1991). Subtle neuropsychological deficits in children with sickle cell disease. *American Journal of Pediatric Hematology/Oncology, 13,* 14–20.

Weinstein, H. J., & Tarbell, N. J. (1997). Leukemias and lymphomas of childhood. In V. T. Devita, S. Hellman, & S. A. Rosenberg (Eds.), *Cancer: Principles and practice of oncology* (pp. 2145–2165). New York: Lippincott–Raven.

Weiss, H. J., Sussman, I. I., & Hoyer, L. W. (1977). Stabilization of factor VIII in plasma by the von Willebrand factor: Studies on post-transfusion and dissociated factor VIII and in patients with von Willebrand's disease. *Journal of Clinical Investigation, 60,* 390–404.

Whitt, J. K., Hooper, S., Tennison, M., Robertson, W., Gold, S., Burchinal, M., et al. (1993). Neuropsychologic functioning of human immunodeficiency virus-infected children with hemophilia. *Journal of Pediatrics, 122,* 52–59.

Williams, I., Earles, A. N., & Pack, B. (1983). Psychological considerations in sickle cell disease. *Nursing Clinics of North America, 18,* 215–229.

Woolf, R. W., Rappaport, L., Reardon, P., Cibrorowski, J., D'Angelo, E., & Besette, J. (1989). School functioning and disease severity in boys with hemophilia. *Journal of Developmental and Behavioral Pediatrics, 10,* 81–85.

World Health Organization. (1991). *Prevention and control of hemophilia: Memorandum from a joint WHO/WFH meeting*. Geneva, Switzerland: Author.

Zeltzer, L., Altman, A., Cohen, D., LeBaron, S., Munuksela, E. L., & Schecter, N. L. (1990). Report of the subcommittee on the management of pain associated with procedures in children with cancer. *Pediatrics, 86*, 826–831.

Zeltzer, L. K., Dolgin, M. J., LeBaron, S., & LeBaron, C. (1991). A randomized controlled study of behavioral intervention for chemotherapy distress in children with cancer. *Pediatrics, 88*, 34–42.

Zeltzer, L., & LeBaron, S. (1986). Hypnosis and nonhypnotic techniques for reduction of pain and anxiety during painful procedures in children and adolescents with cancer. *Journal of Pediatrics, 101*, 1032–1035.

5

MENTAL DISORDERS

ROBERT J. THOMPSON, JR., AND KATHERINE J. VAN LOON

This chapter addresses the contribution of health psychology to the understanding and treatment of mental disorders—a task that is not only daunting but also paradoxical. The primary focus of health psychology has not been on disorders classified as "mental disorders," rather it has been on psychological and behavioral factors as they relate to physical health and illness. Accomplishing the task and resolving the paradox requires delineation about what is essential and distinctive about health psychology.

For some time, the distinction between mental and physical disorders has been recognized as an unwarranted consequence of the division of labor spawned by Cartesian dualism. This is acknowledged even in the fourth edition of the *Diagnostic and Statistical Manual of Mental Disorders (DSM–IV)*:

> The term *mental disorder* unfortunately implies a distinction between "mental" disorders and "physical" disorders that is a reductionistic anarchism of mind/body dualism. A compelling literature documents that there is much "physical" in "mental" disorders and much "mental" in "physical" disorders. (American Psychiatric Association, 1994, p. xxi)

Changes in conceptual models within psychology and medicine have facilitated a more holistic view of human functioning. It is of particular interest to trace these developments from 1950 when Dennis published *Current Trends in the Relation of Psychology to Medicine*. In addition to recognizing the contributions that psychology had made to health care, Dennis made two observations that have turned out to be prescient: "The application of learning principles to the prevention and cure of disease remains primarily for the future" (p. 6), and "It may be that our most basic contribution will not be a specific discovery, but rather the promulgation of an objective approach to human behavior" (p. 7). Two decades later, Schofield (1969) developed the view of psychology as a life science and envisioned psychology expanding out of the confines of mental health to the broader purview of health. Schofield argued that the unique contributions of psychologists were those "evolving from our expertise in the study of complex behaviors and from our fundamental commitment to critical evaluation" (p. 578).

Concurrently within the medical field, there was growing recognition of the limits of the biomedical model that incorporates assumptions of mind–body dualism and attempts to explain illness in terms of single-factor biological malfunction with little attention to behavioral and psychosocial processes. Engel (1977) advocated a biopsychosocial model as a way to "broaden the approach to disease to include the psychosocial without sacrificing the enormous advantages of the biomedical approach" (p. 131). The biopsychosocial model maintains that health and illness are caused by multiple factors, and the operation of biological, psychological, and social processes must be considered simultaneously in terms of etiology and treatment.

Thus, by the end of the 20th century, the emergence of the biopsychosocial model and multifactorial approaches to the pathogenesis of disease enabled the linkage between the behavioral and the biomedical sciences. "The concern now is to determine how biological and psychosocial processes act together in health and illness across the life span" (Thompson, 1991, p. 14). The distinctiveness of the contribution of health psychology continues to be its behavioral science approach and the application of learning principles to health and illness.

This chapter is organized into six sections. The first section addresses issues regarding the nature, types, and classification of mental disorders, and various systems of estimating prevalence are identified. The second section addresses several specific mental disorders that are common across the spectrum of primary care, secondary or specialty clinics, and tertiary health care settings. The third section addresses cognitive–mediational and biological theories of stress as a specific mechanism of effect for the major mental disorders. In turn, cognition and physiology and the relationship between them serve as salient treatment targets. The fourth section considers psychological treatments for mental disorders for which there is empirical support of efficacy. The fifth section addresses the manifestations, cognitive and biological etiological models, and empirically supported treatments for four disorders: depression in adults, generalized anxiety disorder (GAD) in adults, depression in adolescents, and obsessive–compulsive disorder (OCD) in children. The sixth section concludes the chapter with a consideration of research and clinical challenges and opportunities.

CLASSIFICATION OF MENTAL DISORDERS

Advances in medical science and health care are facilitated by the ability to describe and group patients according to homogenous categories. Uniformity of definition and systems of classification are essential. The World Health Organization (WHO) formulates and revises approximately every 10 years a uniform nomenclature known as the *International Classification of Diseases (ICD)*. WHO members are required to use the *ICD* classification system for reporting morbidity and mortality statistics (Kramer, 1994). The *ICD* has been adapted as a nomenclature for various medical specialties; it also has been modified to accommodate the diagnostic concepts and classification systems used in other countries. Specific efforts have been made to ensure compatibility of the *ICD* with the *Diagnostic and Statistical Manual of Mental Disorders* (DSM; American Psychiatric Association, 1994), which is the most frequently used classification system in the United States.

The *ICD* is organized into 17 major sections of disorders according to eclectic axes of classification, including topographical and etiological. The fifth section, mental disorders, is subdivided into four major categories: organic psychoses conditions; other psychoses; neurotic disorders, personality disorders, and other nonpsychotic mental disorders; and mental retardation.

Cooper (1994) has shown that the major psychiatric classification systems have a common structure; 16 major groups of mental disorders can be derived from the 30 three-digit categories of the *ICD–9*, and the same 16 can be derived from the *DSM* system. Furthermore, these 16 groups can be condensed into three major categories. This three-category structure of mental disorders and the relevant subcategories for this chapter are presented in Exhibit 5.1.

Although they have a common structure and efforts have been made to maintain compatibility, national systems such as the *DSM* more rapidly incorporate new developments than international systems such as the *ICD*. For example, unlike the *ICD–9*, the recent editions of the *DSM* incorporate a multiaxial system of classification that addresses not only the disorder but also other attributes of people and their interactions with the social environment; the *DSM* also includes research diagnostic criteria that

EXHIBIT 5.1
ICD–9 Classification of Mental Disorders

Severe (psychotic) mental disorders
Dementias (290)
Disorders due to alcohol (291) and drugs (292)
Transient and symptomatic organic disorders (293–294)
Schizophrenic disorders (295)
Affective disorders (296)
   Manic disorder (296.0–296.1)
   Major depressive disorder (296.2–296.3)
   Bipolar affective disorder (296.4–296.7)
Paranoid, acute, and other disorders (297)

Neurotic, stress, and personality disorders
Neurotic (anxiety) disorders (300.00)
   Panic disorder (300.01)
   Generalized anxiety disorder (300.02)
   Hysteria (300.1)
   Phobic disorders (300.2)
   Obsessive–compulsive disorders (300.3)
   Neurotic depression (300.4)
   Neurasthenia (300.5)
   Hypochondrias (300.7)
   Somatization disorder (300.81)
Personality disorders (301)
Physiological malfunction arising from mental factors (306)
Stress reactions and adjustment disorders (307.00)
   Anorexia nervosa (307.1)
   Specific disorders of sleep of nonorganic origin (307.4)
   Other disorders of eating (307.5)
     Bulimia (307.51)
   Enuresis (307.6)
   Encopresis (307.7)
   Psychalgia (307.8)
     Tension headache (307.81)
   Acute reaction to stress (308)
   Adjustment reaction (309)

Disorders of childhood, adolescence, and development
Overanxious disorder (313.0)
Hyperkinetic syndrome of childhood (314.0)
Specific delays in development (315.0)
Mental retardation (317–319)

are not included in *ICD–9* (Cooper, 1994). The *DSM–IV* (American Psychiatric Association, 1994) also attempts to reflect the mutual influence of mental and physical disorders through the use of the following specific categories.

- The category *mental disorders due to a general medical condition* refers to mental symptoms with an etiology that is related to a general medical condition by a known physiological mechanism.

- The category *psychological factors affecting medical condition* refers to mental disorders, personality disorders, and behavioral factors that have a clinically significant effect on the course or outcome of a general medical condition or significantly increase the risk for an adverse outcome.
- The category *somatoform disorders* refers to physical symptoms that cannot be explained by a known medical condition, but the symptoms are not under voluntary control. The various subcategories are distinguished by the number and type of a person's physical symptoms. For example, a person with *somatization disorder* refers to multiple chronic somatic complaints, whereas a person with conversion disorder refers to motor or sensory symptoms or deficits. Stress is assumed to play a central role in somatoform disorders.
- The category *factitious disorders* refers to physical or psychological symptoms that are intentionally produced. Factitious disorders differ from acts of *malingering* in which symptoms are motivated by external incentives such as avoiding work or securing compensation. Patients with factitious disorders are motivated to assume the sick role allows patients to get the attention, support, and care of others. Although rare, a particular subtype of factitious disorder called *Munchausen's syndrome by proxy* has received considerable attention. People with this disorder cause illness, injure, or produce physical symptoms in another person. They indirectly satisfy their own needs by assuming the sick role through another person.

From a behavioral science perspective the *DSM* system has several limitations (Follette & Houts, 1996). First, the *DSM* acknowledges that the classification of mental disorders lacks a consistent operational definition with regard to which phenomena are "mental" and what constitutes the boundaries between normalcy and pathological behavior. Second, the *DSM* is primarily a topographic, or structural, description of behavior in which clusters of covarying symptoms or behaviors are organized into syndromes.

> The *DSM* makes no provision for understanding behavior in a context. Rather, behaviors are just to be counted for the purpose of making a diagnosis. The diagnosis, in most cases, tells one little about etiology, course, or response to treatment. (Follette, 1996, p. 1118)

It has been cogently argued that the structural approach of the *DSM* has to be supplemented with a functional analysis that delineates the controlling and contextual variables and the antecedent and consequent events that elicit and sustain specific target behaviors (Scotti, Morris, McNeil, & Hawkins, 1996). Third, there is "no agreed upon way to determine how categories are to be evaluated" (Follette & Houts, 1996, p. 1126). Decisions about the inclusion or exclusion of categories are not made on the basis of supporting or refuting evidence but apparently with regard to appeasing interest groups (Follette & Houts, 1996).

These concerns about the *DSM* classification system have led to a call for more explicit competition among approaches to classification (Follette, 1996). From a behavioral science perspective, the development of taxonomies that are based on different theoretical formulations is needed. However, until a more scientifically sound system is developed, the *DSM* is the system that will be used by clinicians and researchers. The challenge is to use the system with a critical understanding of its limitations. In this regard, the dualistic thinking about etiology and the basis for diagnostic categories are most problematic.

Mental and Physical: Mutual Influence

The confluence of psychological and physical functioning is readily apparent across the settings in which health care is provided—from the general medical or primary care office to specialty clinics to tertiary care hospitals. It is estimated that the incidence of psychiatric disorders is approximately 15% in outpatient medical populations; approximately 60% of psychiatric disorders are treated by primary care health providers, whereas only 20% to 25% are treated by mental health professionals; psychological distress is a factor in up to 40% of patients' decisions to make an appointment with a physician; 30% of all primary care visits involve counseling for psychosocial stress; and primary care physicians spend 23% of their time with mental health problems (Cavanaugh & Zalski, 1998). The most prevalent mental disorders and symptoms in outpatient medical populations include major depressive disorders (4%) and minor depressive disorders (10%); anxiety disorders (4% to 8%); anxiety symptoms, depressive symptoms, or both (20%); somatoform disorders (4%); and drug and alcohol dependence (7% to 12%) or abuse (10%; Cavanaugh & Zalski, 1998).

Compared with people who do not have psychological distress, people with psychological distress experience more physical symptoms, have more functional disabilities, appraise their global health status less favorably, may have a higher prevalence of chronic disease, and use health care services at a higher rate (Von Korff, Katon, & Lin, 1990). It is estimated that "these 'distressed high-utilizers' use two to three times the average outpatient services" and 10 times the specialty and inpatient services (Cavanaugh & Zalski, 1998, p. 20). In addition, the introduction of mental health services into medical services can decrease inappropriate health care utilization by 30% to 70% (Cavanaugh & Zalski, 1998).

Diabetes is an example of a physical disorder that affects and is affected by psychological functioning. The prevalence of concurrent depression in adults with diabetes was found to range from 8.5% to 27.3% (mean = 14%) in controlled studies and 11% to 19.9% (mean = 15.4%) in uncontrolled studies, which is at least three times the 3% to 4% prevalence of major depression found in the general population (Lustman & Gavard, 1995). However, no consistent relationship has been found between depression and diabetes severity (Lustman & Gavard, 1995). Similarly, anxiety disorders were also found to be common in patients with diabetes, and one study reported a prevalence of GAD in adults with insulin-dependent and non−insulin-dependent diabetes that was approximately six times greater than the estimated base rate of 5% in the general population (Lustman, 1988). In addition, GAD was associated with poor glucose control and the reporting of hypoglycemic and hyperglycemic symptoms (Lustman, 1988).

The influence of psychological processes on physical functioning is reflected in the application of psychological interventions to prepare patients for surgical procedures. The finding of a meta-analysis (Johnston & Vogele, 1993) of properly controlled studies indicates that eight major areas benefit significantly: negative affect, pain, pain medication, length of stay, behavioral recovery, clinical recovery, physiological indices, and satisfaction. The specific interventions used include sensory information, procedural information, behavior instruction, cognitive intervention, relation, hypnosis, and emotion-focused intervention. In terms of differential effectiveness, procedural information and behavioral instruction produced benefits in each of the eight areas. Cognitive interventions seem to have a specific effect on negative affect, pain, pain medication, and clinical recovery. Little support was found for the effectiveness of sensory information, hypnosis, or emotion-focused approaches.

Health psychologists typically become involved in the care of patients when physical symptoms cannot be explained entirely on the basis of a diagnosable medical condition. The assumption is that if a medical explanation cannot be confirmed, the problem must be psychological. This "either−or" thinking is problematic in both conceptualization and practice: The absence of an organic explanation does not indicate the presence of a psychological explanation. Stress and learning paradigms postulate the interaction of psychological and physiological processes in the development and maintenance of physical symptoms. This interaction suggests a need for combined approaches in the management of physical conditions in which psychological and behavioral factors are deemed to play a significant role. Diathesis−stress models have been formulated as a way to transcend dualistic thinking and reflect the way physiological, genetic, environmental, and psychosocial processes continuously interact to influence functioning.

Prevalence of Mental Disorders

Estimating the prevalence of mental disorders is a difficult task given the described conceptual and definitional problems. Furthermore, differences in rates occur as a function of sample composition and assessment methods used. O'Leary and Norcross (1998) bring together three sources of lifetime prevalence rates of mental disorders in the general population: The National Comorbidity Study (NCS; Kessler et al., 1994); the National Institute of Mental Health (NIMH) Epidemiological Catchment Area (ECA) Study (Robbins & Reiger, 1991); and the *DSM–IV* (American Psychiatric Association, 1994). The NCS prevalence rates are based on a national probability sample of noninstitutionalized individuals across the 48 continental states. The ECA prevalence data are based on structured interviews of more than 20,000 adults in five cities across the United States. The *DSM–IV* prevalence rates are based on epidemiological and clinical studies reported in the literature. Throughout this chapter, prevalence estimates are based on these sources.

SELECTED MENTAL DISORDERS

Although the distinction between mental disorders and physical disorders and the classifications of mental disorders are problematic, it is generally accepted that mental disorders involve dysfunctions in cognition or thought process, affect, the interactions between process and affect, or all of these. *Psychoses* are major impairments in thought processes, whereas mood disorders are dysfunctions of affect and are primarily classified as depression. *Neurotic* and *stress disorders* involve anxiety-based dysfunction.

It is beyond the scope of this chapter to discuss all mental disorders. Instead, the focus is on the two disorders—depression and anxiety—that are most commonly the symptoms of a primary mental disorder, a consequence of a physical disorder, or a contributor to a physical disorder. In addition, three other specific mental disorders are discussed that have major contributions from health psychology research: sleep disorders, eating disorders, and pain.

Depressive Disorders

Depression typically involves a constellation of symptoms including a sad or irritable mood; loss of interest or pleasure; cognitions involving hopelessness, worthlessness, and interpretive distortions; and somatic symptoms involving sleep, appetite, and psychomotor functioning. Diagnostic distinctions are sometimes made on the basis of severity and duration. For example, the *DSM–IV* has separate diagnostic criteria for *major depressive episode* and *dysthymic disorder*.

In terms of prevalence for major depressive disorder, NCS reported 17.1% overall—12.7% of men and 21.3% of women; *DSM–IV* reported 5% to 12% of men and 10% to 25% of women; and ECA reported 6.4% overall, 3.6% of men, and 8.7% of women. In terms of dysthymic disorder, NCS reported 6.4% overall, 4.8% of men, and 8% of women; *DSM–IV* reported 6.0% overall; and ECA reported 3.3% overall, 2.2% of men, and 4.1% of women.

Anxiety Disorders

Excessive anxiety and worry that an individual finds difficult to control is the central feature of an array of disorders such as GAD and OCD. Panic attacks can occur in people with these disorders. The attacks include a combination of somatic and cognitive symptoms such as palpitations, accelerated heart rate, sweating, sensations of shortness of breath, feelings of depersonalization, and a fear of "going crazy."

In terms of prevalence for GAD, NCS reported 5.1% overall, 3.6% of men, and 6.6% of women; *DSM–IV* reported 5.0% overall; and ECA reported 5.8% overall, 4.5% of men, and 6.8% of women. In terms of prevalence for OCD, *DSM–IV* reported 2.5% overall, and ECA reported 2.6% overall, 2% of men, and 3% of women.

Sleep Disorders

Sleep disturbances are reported by 35% of adults and are generally grouped into three categories: (a) disorders of initiating and maintaining sleep (insomnia), (b) disorders of excessive daytime sleepiness (hypersomnias), (c) and abnormal sleep behaviors (parasomnias; Singer & Sack, 1997). Of the three, insomnia is most prevalent, occurring in 36% of adults. It increases with age and is more common in women and those with chronic illnesses (Jain, 1998). Sleep problems can have multiple etiologies including psychological disorders, alcohol and drug use, neurodegenerative diseases, and other medical disorders (Singer & Sack, 1997).

Sleep disorders and psychological disorders are associated. Problems with sleep have been reported in 90% of patients with affective disorders (Jain, 1998). Major depression has been reported in 14% of patients with insomnia and in 10% of patients with hypersomnia, and anxiety disorders have been reported in 25% of patients with insomnia and hypersomnia (Jain, 1998). Treatment of sleep disorders typically involves addressing the underlying causes. Cognitive–behavioral treatment approaches use stress management techniques to reduce anxiety, stimulus control techniques to eliminate conditioned associations and arousals that interfere with sleep, and behavior change techniques to develop good sleep habits, such as avoiding caffeine and alcohol (Jain, 1998).

Eating Disorders

Eating disorders constitute a spectrum of clinical syndromes that result not from a single cause but from the interplay of psychological, biological, and sociocultural factors (Romano & Halmi, 1997). Specific disorders include anorexia nervosa, bulimia nervosa, and binge eating. Obesity is also included among the eating disorders but is not considered a mental disorder (Erickson, Yager, & Seeger, 1998).The severity of obesity is defined in terms of body weight percentage higher than that recommended for a person's age and height: mild is 20% to 40% higher, moderate is 40% to 100% higher, and morbid is more than 100% higher (Erickson et al., 1998).

Anorexia nervosa has a prevalence of less than 1% and predominately affects girls and women (Romano & Halmi, 1997). The diagnostic criteria is a body weight that is 15% less than expected for age and height brought about through the reduction of caloric intake, an irrational fear of becoming fat, and a distorted body image (Erickson et al., 1998). General weight loss can be associated with numerous medical and psychiatric disorders, but this type of weight loss is not characterized by the morbid fear of becoming fat and the pursuit of thinness that is specific to anorexia nervosa (Romano & Halmi, 1997). Psychiatric comorbidity is high, with major depression occurring in about half the patients and a 25% lifetime prevalence of OCD (Erickson et al., 1998).

Bulimia nervosa has a prevalence of 2% to 3% in women and 0.2% in men (Romano & Halmi, 1997) and is characterized by binge eating, or the consumption of large quantities of food in a short period, followed by compensatory behavior such as purging through self-induced vomiting, use of laxatives, fasting, or excessive exercise. It is estimated that "as many as 75% of those with bulimia suffer from a concurrent major depression or anxiety disorder" (Erickson et al., 1998, p. 222).

Treatments for eating disorders typically involve a combination of medical and psychological interventions. Medical treatment focuses on the associated and at times life-threatening medical complications. Psychological treatments use cognitive and behavioral therapies that focus on the distortions in thoughts and feelings that are associated with maladaptive eating behaviors. Cognitive behavior therapy (CBT) is considered a well-established treatment for bulimia (Chambless et al., 1998).

Pain

Pain is a normal experience in everyday life but can be a symptom of an underlying injury or illness. Pain has two components: nociception —the sensory component—and the response to the nociception, which is influenced by a complex interaction of physical, psychological, and social factors. Three types of pain have been identified. *Acute pain* has adaptive value, serving as a warning signal that directs attention or action and is rarely psychogenic. *Chronic pain* does not have adaptive value and is associated with a constellation of reactive behaviors such as compensatory posturing or restrictions of daily activities and can be associated with secondary gains by eliciting nurturance and attention or avoidance of responsibilities (Thompson & Gustafson, 1996). Examples of chronic pain include migraine headaches and low back pain. *Recurrent pain* is repetitive episodes of pain that alternate with pain-free periods and is associated with chronic illnesses in terms of recurrent medical procedures and disease processes, such as arthritis or sickle cell disease.

Approaches to pain management include analgesics, behavioral intervention, or a combination of these. Health psychologists have focused attention on the role of cognitive and affective interpersonal factors and sociocultural factors in the perception, interpretation, and behavioral responses to pain. Efforts to enhance coping with pain, whether acute pain associated with invasive medical procedures or chronic pain, use cognitive–behavioral approaches to regulate pain perception and modify social and environmental processes that affect the behavioral expression of and response to pain. Coping strategies characterized by passive adherence and catastrophic thinking and thoughts of fear and anger are associated with functional impairment. Coping strategies characterized by multiple cognitive and behavior techniques including diverting attention, calming thoughts, reinterpreting pain sensations, and various relaxation methods such as progressive muscle relaxation, breathing methods, and visual imagery are associated with less functional impairment (Thompson & Gustafson, 1996). In particular, biofeedback has been used to teach patients to alter their physiological responses (e.g., alter blood flow or muscle contractions to reduce pain associated with vascular or muscle-contraction headaches). In terms of pain behaviors, the role of caregivers in providing discriminative cues and selective reinforcement and modeling has been recognized and incorporated into efforts to foster active coping strategies, maintain activity levels, and engage tasks and relationships. Considerable empirical support has been provided for the effectiveness of CBT for the treatment of chronic pain conditions such as back pain and persistent disease-related pain conditions such as arthritis; CBT is considered a well-established treatment for headaches and chronic pain (Chambless et al., 1998).

BIOPSYCHOSOCIAL MODEL AND MECHANISMS OF STRESS

The mutual influences of psychosocial processes and biological processes can be appreciated by considering *stress*. The delineation of possible mechanisms of effect for the postulated mutual influences provides the basis for combined psychological and pharmacological treatment approaches. This discussion requires a brief overview of the interaction of the nervous system and endocrine system in situations that are perceived to be threatening.

The nervous and endocrine systems have mutual influences. One structural connection is through the pituitary gland, which is the part of the brain that serves as an endocrine gland. The pituitary gland produces adrenocorticotropic hormone (ACTH), which in turn stimulates the adrenal glands to release into the bloodstream three types of hormones, corticosteroids, catecholamines, and endorphins. These hormones play a role in response to stress.

Biological Model

Stress activates two neuroendocrine systems. One system has become known as the hypothalamic–pituitary–adrenal cortex axis (HPA). The paraventricular nucleus in the hypothalamus releases corticotropin-releasing hormone (CRH). Various neuronal and hormonal agents can stimulate the release of corticotropin, including serotonin, epinephrine, norepinephrine, emotions, pain, and changes in blood pressure (Felker & Hubbard, 1990). In turn, CRH stimulates the anterior pituitary gland to release ACTH, which then stimulates the adrenal cortex to release corticosteroids into the bloodstream. The glucocorticoids elevate blood sugar, cortisol conserves stores of carbohydrates and reduces inflammation, and endorphin decreases pain and suppresses the immune system.

Stress also activates the sympathoadrenal (SA) system. Sympathetic centers are located in the hypothalamus and the brainstem, particularly the locus coeruleus. Norepinephrine is the neurotransmitter for the locus coeruleus projections throughout the brain. Sympathetic fibers directly innervate the adrenal medulla, which produces the catecholamines norepinephrine and epinephrine. These hormones serve to increase or decrease heart rate, blood pressure, breathing rate, and digestion. The direct sympathetic innervation affects primarily norepinephrine. Epinephrine production is stimulated by an enzyme in the blood flow from the adrenal cortex, which is released under the influence of ACTH produced in the pituitary gland. Researchers are trying to determine whether specific and different neuroendocrine patterns are elevated by different emotions—for example, whether increased norepinephrine, noradrenaline, and plasma testosterone are associated with anger; whether increased epinephrine and adrenaline are associated with anxiety; and whether increased cortisol and decreased testosterone are associated with depression (Henry, 1990).

The SA and HPA innervate one another, so activation of one system automatically leads to activation of the other (Felker & Hubbard, 1990). CRH stimulates the locus coeruleus, which produces norepinephrine, promoting the release of CRH (Felker & Hubbard, 1990). The knowledge about these interrelated systems has led to neurotransmitter and neuroendocrine hypotheses about the etiology of mental disorders, thus influencing treatment. This chapter includes a discussion of the application of these hypotheses to adult depression.

Cognitive–Mediation Model

The theory of cognitive mediation became dominant in the field of psychology in the 1970s (Lazarus, 1999). Thoughts are considered to be occurring between an event or stimulus and the behavioral response. Thus thoughts, reflecting beliefs about the self and the world, and motivations are viewed as having a causal influence on responses. The application of cognitive mediation to stress enables the consideration of a basic mechanism of effect for dysfunctional behavior and for the mutual influence of biological and psychosocial processes.

The cognitive process of appraisal is a core concept in Lazarus's (1999) cognitive–mediational theory of stress. Differences in responses to similar situations over time within and among individuals demonstrate that stress is not inherent in a situation or event. Lazarus's theory focuses on the role of the mind in evaluating and making judgments about the significance of what is happening (primary appraisal) and of coping options (secondary appraisal). "It is the meaning constructed by a person about what is happening that is crucial to the arousal of stress reactions" (Lazarus, 1999, p. 55). The personal meaning that is constructed through the appraisal process is the proximal cause of a stress reaction. The appraisal process can be deliberative and conscious or intuitive, unconscious, and automatic and relatively instantaneous. The appraisal process can be influenced by environmental variables such as social demands or pressures to behave in prescribed ways, and personal variables such as motivation, values, beliefs, and resources, including social skills, support of family and friends, physical attractiveness, and intelligence.

The process of *coping* involves the cognitive and behavioral efforts to manage stress. Two broad types of coping have been identified that are based on two different but interrelated functions. *Problem-focused coping* refers to actions directed at the self or the environment that change the person–environment relationship. *Emotion-focused coping* refers to reappraisal of the meaning of the emotion reaction, which Lazarus (1999) also referred to as *cognitive coping*. Thus, the initial appraisal of the event and the reappraisal of the event as a coping method are cognitive mediators of stress.

A substantial body of research has yielded numerous robust findings about the cognitive–mediational theory of stress and coping (Lazarus, 1999, pp. 119–122). First, in any single stressful encounter, people use a variety of coping strategies. Second, the consistency in use of a specific coping strategy varies by situation and strategy. Third, coping is a process, which means that stressful events are not unitary, and coping strategies change as the encounter unfolds. Fourth, the type of coping strategy used relates to the appraisal of whether the conditions of stress are changeable —that is, controllable. Situations appraised to be controllable are associated with use of problem-focused coping strategies, whereas those appraised to be uncontrollable are associated with use of emotion-focused strategies. Fifth, "no universally effective or ineffective coping strategies exist" (Lazarus, 1999, p. 111). The two types of coping strategies are not discrete action types but two functions that are essential parts of the coping process. "It is the fit between thinking and action—that is, the balance between them and the environmental realities—which makes coping efficacious or not" (p. 124).

EMPIRICALLY SUPPORTED TREATMENTS

One manifestation of the distinctive behavioral science approach of psychology is the effort through the Division of Clinical Psychology of the American Psychological Association to delineate empirically supported psychological treatments for the major mental disorders affecting adults and children. The Task Force on Promotion and Dissemination of Psychological Procedures (1995) established separate criteria for two categories of empirically validated treatments: (a) well-established treatments and (b) probably efficacious treatments. To be classified as *well-established*, at least two group design studies with random assignment to groups conducted by different investigatory teams were required. Furthermore, the treatment had to be shown to be superior to an alternative treatment or placebo or equivalent to an already established treatment. As an alternative, a large series of single-case design studies ($n > 9$) could provide the necessary evidence. A further requirement was that treatment manuals be used for the intervention. *Probably efficacious* interventions were demonstrated to be superior to no treatment, or a smaller series ($n > 3$) of single-case design experiments could be used as evidence. The Task Force on Effective Psychosocial Interventions: A Life Span Perspective expanded the criteria to children, adolescents, and older adults (Lonigan, Elbert, & Johnson, 1998).

The efforts to establish empirically supported treatments were facilitated by the advent of treatment manuals that provided the main principles and precise definition of treatment techniques, methods, and procedures for a specific patient problem. Treatment manuals enabled sufficient standardization of treatment, which was necessary for replication. A compendium of current psychotherapy treatment manuals by type of disorder has been compiled (Lambert, Chiles, Kesler, & Vermeersch, 1998).

Two points of clarification are important. First, the task forces focused on studies of efficacy rather than effectiveness or clinical utility. Efficacy studies attempt to establish whether an intervention reduces symptoms in a well-controlled, experimental study usually with nonreferred participants without comorbid disorders. Effectiveness studies attempt to determine how well an intervention works under conditions in which treatment typically occurs in the community (Lonigan et al., 1998). Second, efficacy of interventions was not determined in general but rather in relation to specific problems or disorders. The prevailing premise was that "no treatment will work for all problems, and it is essential to verify which treatments work for which type of disorders" (Task Force on Promotion and Dissemination of Psychological Procedures, 1995, p. 4).

REPRESENTATIVE DISORDERS: MANIFESTATIONS, ETIOLOGIES, AND TREATMENTS

The references cited in the previous paragraphs provide evidence for the effectiveness of numerous psychological interventions, primarily cognitive–behavioral interventions, for the major mental disorders. The underlying rationale, in terms of theories of etiology, and specific treatment methods are considered in more detail for cognitive–behavior therapy (CBT) for four disorders that are representative of depression and anxiety disorders in adults and children.

Depression in Adults

Depression as a clinical syndrome includes a heterogeneous group of symptoms. The diagnosis of depression can be challenging for the clinician given its highly variable symptoms. The diagnosis of depression in patients with a primary medical illness can be additionally challenging because many of its common symptoms (e.g., weight loss, apathy, insomnia) may be symptoms of a medical condition or complications of a medical treatment.

According to the DSM–IV, severe depression is designated as a major depressive disorder to emphasize the psychological and somatic symptoms that are associated with the syndrome. DSM–IV criteria require that five out of nine specified symptoms must be present for a period of at least 2 weeks for a diagnosis of depression to be made. In addition, those five

symptoms must include either depressed mood or loss of interest or pleasure.

Etiology

The cognitive model identifies the presence of early maladaptive
schemas as an important predisposing factor for many patients with depression (Young, 1990). Early maladaptive schemas refer "to extremely stable and enduring themes that develop during childhood and are elaborated
upon throughout the individual's lifetime" (p. 9). The schemas are experienced as (a) a priori truths about oneself or the environment, (b) self-
perpetuating and resistant to change, (c) dysfunctional, (d) often triggered
by a change in the environment, (e) associated with high levels of affect
when activated, and (f) the result of an ongoing conflict between the
child's innate temperament and dysfunctional developmental experiences
(Young, 1990).

The cognitive model also identifies the interpretations or meaning a
person ascribes to events as another predisposing factor. In addition to the
role of appraisal of stressfulness and perceptions of control, explanations
regarding the cause of stressful events have been related to psychological
distress. Three dimensions of causal attributions have been identified. The
cause may be internal or external to the person, stable or transient over
time, and either limited to the specific event or global—that is, cause a
variety of events (Peterson & Seligman, 1984). The specific explanatory
style of habitually attributing positive events to causes that are external,
unstable, and specific and attributing negative events to causes that are
internal, stable, and global has been associated with cognitive, motivational, and emotional deficits termed *learned helplessness* (Peterson &
Seligman, 1984). The cognitive deficits are reflected in an inability to
perceive or recognize opportunities to control outcomes. Motivational deficits are reflected in passivity—that is, lowered response initiation and
persistence. Emotional deficits are reflected in lowered self-esteem and sadness. The diathesis–stress model postulates that individuals who exhibit
this explanatory style are predisposed to helplessness in the face of negative
events. A substantial body of research with adults and children supports
the role of causal attributions as a risk factor for distress, particularly depression, in the face of stressful events (Peterson & Seligman, 1984).

Biologically based models of depression begin with recognition of evidence for heritability of affective disorders. Various hypotheses have been
proposed regarding more proximal "causes" for the development of the
clinical syndrome. Among these, the catecholamine and neuroendocrine
hypotheses have garnered empirical support, although no single hypothesis
accounts for the onset, cause, and moderating or exacerbating processes.
In terms of neurotransmitters, depression has been associated with de-

creased levels of norepinephrine and serotonin. The neuroendocrine hypothesis is based on the role that the hypothalamus plays in regulating eating, pleasure, and sexual desires, which are also functions that are disrupted in persons with depression. In particular, the HPA is the system that moderates stress by promoting attention and arousal and inhibiting of functions such as eating. The neurotransmitters also mediate endocrine functions (Shuchter, Downs, & Zisook, 1996).

Treatment

The cognitive model of depression assumes that cognition, behavior, and biochemistry are all substantial components of major depressive disorders. These three factors are not viewed as competing theories of depression but rather as three mutually independent levels of analysis, each of which has its own "focus of convenience" (Young, Beck, & Weinberger, 1993). The pharmacotherapist intervenes at the biochemical level, and the cognitive–behavior therapist likewise intervenes at the cognitive, affective, and behavioral levels. Cognitive therapy and imipramine pharmacotherapy were found to be comparably effective in the treatment of depressed outpatients, regardless of initial severity, and combined treatment was not superior to either single modality alone (Hollon et al., 1992).

CBT, found to be a well-established treatment for depression (Chambless et al., 1998), specifically addresses the negatively biased information processing that is reflected in the *cognitive triad of depression*: Patients with depression typically have a negative perception of the self, the environment, and the future (Beck, Freeman, & Associates, 1979). To accommodate their negative views, patients with depression often have distorted perceptions of events in their lives. Cognitive theory suggests that CBT works by helping patients to learn to systematically test their beliefs and alter maladaptive processing techniques (Beck et al., 1979). The focus of CBT is on changing automatic and maladaptive ways of thinking and behaving (Beck et al., 1979). Treatment is designed to assist patients with learning to think more adaptively and thus to experience improvements in affect, motivation, and behavior.

The general approach is to guide patients through several structured learning experiences (Butler & Beck, 1995). Patients are first taught to identify maladaptive patterns. They are then taught to monitor and record their negative thoughts and mental images and learn to recognize the associations among thoughts, emotions, physiology, and behavior. Thus, patients learn to assess the validity and utility of these cognitions, to evaluate their cognitions empirically, and to change the dysfunctional cognitions to reflect a more adaptive perspective. In later stages of therapy, patients learn to identify, evaluate, and alter underlying assumptions and dysfunctional beliefs that may predispose them to depressive reactions. Patients are taught coping skills and are assisted in overcoming inertia and encouraged to expose themselves to potentially rewarding experiences (Butler & Beck, 1995).

Treatment typically consists of 14 to 16 sessions, although severe cases of major depressive disorder may require additional sessions. Patients typically require a minimum of eight sessions to master the cognitive model and the involved skills and to exhibit a significant reduction in symptoms. Remaining sessions are used to assess and modify dysfunctional beliefs that impair functioning, learn skills to prevent future depressive episodes, build relapse prevention skills, and discuss termination issues. Maintenance of therapeutic advances is enhanced by periodic booster sessions during the first year subsequent to termination (Butler & Beck, 1995).

Pharmacotherapy studies have provided substantial support for the efficacy of antidepressants, including monoamine oxidase inhibitors (MAOIs), tricyclic antidepressants (TCAs), and selective serotonin reuptake inhibitors (SSRIs), in the treatment of depression (Shuchter et al., 1996). In accordance with the catecholamine hypothesis, MAOIs and TCAs increase the functional effects of norepinephrine and serotonin, and SSRIs (e.g., fluoxetine) increase levels of serotonin in the brain (Shuchter et al., 1996). Administration of psychostimulants (e.g., methylphenidate, dextroamphetamine) enhances dopamine transmission and was found to be particularly efficacious in the treatment of secondary depression in patients with acute medical or surgical conditions (Masand, Pickett, & Murray, 1991).

Early antidepressant medications such as MAOIs and TCAs have a broad spectrum of action—that is, they affect both the norepinephrine and serotonin systems—and result in undesirable side effects (Shuchter et al., 1996). Newer drugs, such as the SSRIs have "increased specificity of many of their actions and, as corollary, the relative absence of anticholinergic, antihistaminergic, and anti-alpha-adrenergic side effects" (Shuchter et al., 1996, p. 21).

Depression in Adolescents

The *DSM–IV* does not incorporate a developmental perspective into its criteria for depressive disorder in adolescents; thus, the criteria for a major depressive disorder in adolescents are almost identical to those for adults. In light of this failure to account for children's cognitive, affective, and social competencies and biological maturation, many clinicians advocate a developmental psychopathological perspective for the diagnosis of mood disorders in youth (Cicchetti & Schneider-Rosen, 1986). Epidemiological studies indicate that the point and lifetime prevalence rates of adolescent depression are comparable to adult levels, ranging from 2.9% to 8.3% (Robbins & Reiger, 1991). Characteristics of the depressed mid-adolescent to older adolescent tend to include (a) a history of psychopathological symptoms, (b) elevated levels of problematic behaviors as well as physical symptoms and illnesses, (c) a depressotypic cognitive style, (d) a negative body image and poor self-esteem, and (e) excessive emotional dependence (Lewinsohn, Clarke, Rohde, Hops, & Seeley, 1996). There is no evidence of sex differences in prepubescent youth; however, by age 15, girls are twice as likely as boys to receive a depressive diagnosis (Nolen-Hoeksema & Girgus, 1994). The duration of major depressive disorder episodes in adolescents varies widely and is, in general, shorter than these episodes in adults (Lewinsohn, Rohde, & Seeley, 1994). Conversely, the comorbidity of depression with other psychiatric disorders (both lifetime and concurrent) has been reported to be higher in adolescents than in adults (Rohde, Lewinsohn, & Seeley, 1991).

Etiology

Significant evidence for a family history of depression, associated with onset in offspring, implicates the biological causes for the disorder. The cognitive–behavioral perspective is based on research indicating that the cognitive patterns of depressed children are similar to their adult counterparts (Kaslow, Deering, & Racusin, 1994). According to this perspective, youths who are depressed, compared with their counterparts who are not depressed, have the following characteristics: impaired information processing; cognitive distortions; a negative view of themselves, the world, and the future; a perception of themselves as unable to control the events in their lives; a depressogenic attribution style (the tendency to attribute negative events to more internal, stable, and global causes and attribute positive events to more external, unstable, and specific causes); and deficits in self-appreciation and self-evaluation (Kaslow et al., 1994).

Treatment

From a cognitive–behavioral perspective, multicomponent treatments consisting of fewer than 20 sessions and administered in a group format in a school setting have received the most consistent empirical support. The treatment formulated by Lewinsohn et al. (1996) has been classified as *probably efficacious* according to criteria for empirically supported treatments for youths who are depressed (Kaslow & Thompson, 1998).

Lewinsohn's approach is CBT that is based on premises of the Coping with Depression (CWD) course for adults. The therapy is modified to address the issues and adaptations of adolescents. The CWD for adolescents is a 14-session, multiple-component intervention and focuses on experiential learning and skills training, paying particular attention to increasing pleasant activities, training in relaxation, controlling depressive thoughts, improving social interactions, and developing conflict resolution skills. Parents cooperatively participate in a seven-session intervention program designed to enhance their ability to reinforce the adolescent's adaptive changes, thereby increasing the maintenance of treatment effects.

TCAs and SSRIs are the most frequently prescribed antidepressants for major depressive disorder in adolescents (Kronenberger & Meyer, 1996). However, the efficacy of TCAs and SSRIs remains questionable. Although open trial studies of TCAs and SSRIs indicate that both are independently effective in decreasing depressive symptoms among prepubescent youth (Harrington, 1993), double-blind studies do not support these findings because neither type of antidepressant yields results that are significantly different from those of placebo treatments (Apter et al., 1994).

GAD in Adults

GAD is referred to as the *basic* anxiety disorder because the core process of *anxious apprehension* is a fundamental component of all anxiety disorders (Barlow, 1988). Anxious apprehension is defined as a mood state in which one focuses primarily on the future and becomes ready to attempt to cope with upcoming negative events. Anxious apprehension is associated with a state of high negative affect and chronic overarousal, a sense of uncontrollability, and an attentional focus on threat-related stimuli.

In defining GAD, the *DSM–IV* emphasizes the process of apprehensive expectation (i.e., worry). To designate worry as *excessive*, the *DSM–IV* specifies that the intensity, duration, and frequency of the worry is out of proportion to the likelihood or impact of the feared event, and the individual perceives the worry as difficult to control. Diagnostic criteria require manifestations of at least three of the following six symptoms: (a) restlessness, or feeling "keyed up" or "on edge," (b) being easily fatigued, (c) difficulty concentrating, (d) irritability, (e) muscle tension, and (f) sleep disturbance. Symptoms must be present consistently on most days for at least 6 consecutive months and must significantly interfere with the person's social, occupational, or other areas of normal functioning.

Patients with GAD tend to respond to psychological stress with autonomic inflexibility; thus, they exhibit diminished variability in autonomic responses compared with their nonanxious counterparts (Hoehn-Saric & McLeod, 1988). Symptoms of motor or psychic tension also serve as important discriminating features of GAD. Tension is viewed as a state of motor readiness to respond to threat.

Etiology

From a cognitive–behavioral perspective, the symptoms of GAD (e.g., tension, vigilance, a sense of uncontrollability) could emerge from early life experiences and thereby enhance one's vulnerability to the later development of a variety of other emotional disorders. Consistent with this finding, patients with GAD often have a long history of generalized anxiety, and many are unable to report a specific time of onset (Barlow, Blanchard, Vermilyea, Vermilyea, & DiNardo, 1986).

Biological models, which are based on neuroanatomical, neurotransmitter, and neuroendocine studies, identify possible brain mechanisms for anxiety. The septohippocampal region of the limbic system is activated during anxiety states and in turn affects the cortex, hypothalamus, thalamus, and anterior pituitary, which are hypothesized to produce the symptomatic manifestations (Klerman et al., 1993). The noradrenergic theory postulates that anxiety is related to increased activity or reactivity of the neurotransmitter system. More specifically, anxiety is associated with increased levels of norepinephrine, which can be produced through activation of the locus ceruleus, the primary source of noradrenergic (i.e. norepinephrine-releasing) neurons (Klerman et al., 1993). The serotonergic theory postulates that anxiety is related to increased activity of serotonergic neurons from the midbrain (Klerman et al., 1993). Medications used in the treatment of anxiety, such as tricyclic antidepressants and MAOIs, inhibit activation of the locus ceruleus by corticotropin-releasing factor. The benzodiazepines and tricyclic antidepressants decrease serotonin levels (Klerman et al., 1993).

Treatment

The cognitive and somatic symptoms of GAD reviewed in the previous paragraphs are most frequently treated with CBT—a *well-established* treatment—and some form of relaxation treatment—a *probably efficacious* treatment (Chambless et al., 1998). Specifically, the two principal components that are the targets of a treatment intervention for GAD are excessive, uncontrollable worry and its associated persistent overarousal, which results in tension-related, central nervous system symptoms.

An example of CBT applied to the treatment of GAD is the Mastery of Your Anxiety and Worry (MAW) program (Zinbarg, Craske, & Barlow, 1993). The first module of MAW is designed to restructure faulty misconceptions of the nature, processes, and consequences of anxiety and worry. Cognitive restructuring is used to foster the awareness and replacement of negative and anxious thought processes. The second module involves somatic control exercises and focuses on progressive muscle relaxation training. Relaxation therapy directly targets the physiological arousal and tension that are a core component of GAD. The third module uses controlled and methodical exposure to worry to evoke those worries most concerning to the patient. Repeated exposures to the primary worries provide increased control over the worry process. Confrontation and challenges are used to help the patient focus on replacing cognitive avoidance techniques with cognitive modification techniques.

Because the process of worrying suppresses the generation of imagery, particularly those aspects of imagery that generate efferent commands to the autonomic system, it is important to include somatic response elements as part of worry exposure (Borkovec, Shadick, & Hopkins, 1991). Worry exposure initially involves simulation activities and later progresses to everyday, routine activities. The fourth module involves in vivo exposure to those situations that are being avoided. Response prevention of excessive cautiousness and "safety" or "checking" behaviors is included in this module. Cognitive restructuring and relaxation are introduced and implemented before conducting in vivo exposure exercises and response prevention.

Many patients experiencing worry and tension who are referred to mental health professionals are already taking psychotropic medication, most often prescribed by primary care physicians. More than 50% of these prescriptions are low doses of benzodiazepines or other minor tranquilizers. Another subset of prescriptions is for tricyclic antidepressants or SSRIs (Zinbarg et al., 1993).

A review of studies indicated that CBT was more effective than waiting-list or pill placebo control conditions and nondirective therapy (Chambless & Gillis, 1993). In addition, CBT and other therapies including pharmacotherapy lead to changes in cognition that are related to reduction of anxious symptoms and to the persistence of treatment gains at follow-up (Chambless & Gillis, 1993). CBT is generally well received by patients with GAD, as reflected in an estimated premature termination rate of 14% (Chambless & Gillis, 1993).

OCD in Children

The symptoms of OCD in children are similar to those in adults because both groups have obsessions, compulsions, or both. *Obsessions* are persistent thoughts, ideas, images, or impulses that are inappropriate and intrusive and create marked distress or anxiety. *Compulsions* are repetitive behaviors or mental acts that are performed because they reduce or prevent distress or anxiety, not because they are inherently pleasurable (Kronenberger & Meyer, 1996). The most frequent obsessions observed in children and adolescents with OCD involve concerns about contamination, fears that harm may come to them or others, and excessive scrutiny of their thoughts or actions (March, Leonard, & Swedo, 1995). The most frequent compulsions are washing, repeating, checking, touching, counting, arranging, and hoarding (March et al., 1995). Children are often able to suppress the obsessive thoughts or compulsive behaviors when away from the home, only to regress back into these thoughts and behaviors on their return to the home. To warrant a diagnosis of OCD, the symptoms must significantly interfere with normal functioning because of the high level of distress experienced or the time that is allocated to committing compulsive acts (American Psychiatric Association, 1994).

One third to one half of adults with OCD report that the onset occurred by age 15 (Rapoport, 1988). Evidence shows a gender difference in age of onset. The typical age of male onset is between ages 6 and 15, and the typical age of female onset is between ages 20 and 29 (American Psychiatric Association, 1994). The onset age of childhood OCD follows the same pattern, with younger onset for boys than for girls, and OCD is more common in boys than in girls, with the youngest age of onset being predominantly male (Swedo, Rapoport, Leonard, Lenane, & Cheslow, 1989). Onset is sometimes acute, so children can occasionally recall when they initially began to experience OCD symptoms (Rapoport, 1988). One epidemiological study indicated approximately 0.3% of the general child and adolescent population has OCD (Rapoport, 1988).

The course of OCD is not consistent. Some children reported that obsessions and compulsions subside for certain periods, whereas others reported the symptoms to be continuous (Kronenberger & Meyer, 1996). In general, symptoms usually change over time, beginning with a single obsession or compulsion that persists for a certain period, with a gradual shift to a new symptom (Swedo et al., 1989). Keeping busy is temporarily helpful in suppressing symptoms, and stress aggravates symptoms (Swedo et al., 1989).

Etiology

According to biological theory, genetics and neurotransmitter and neuroendocrine abnormalities have a role in the etiology of OCD. Support for the role of genetics comes from the relationship between OCD and Tourette's syndrome, as well as from reports of OCD in first-degree relatives —such as the 25% reported by Swedo and colleagues (1989). Treatment and challenge studies provide support for the role of serotonergic dysregulation in OCD. In addition, the association of OCD with Tourette's syndrome and the exacerbation of OCD symptoms with psychostimulants support the role of dopaminergic dysregulation in some patients (March et al., 1995). Hypotheses of serotonin involvement are grounded in clinical responses to serotonin reuptake inhibitors (Kronenberger & Meyer, 1996). Abnormalities in the basal ganglia are implicated by the association of OCD and Sydenham's chorea, the presence of obsessive–compulsive symptoms in Tourette's syndrome, and OCD's association with postencephalitic Parkinson's disease (Leonard et al., 1991).

According to behavioral theories, anxiety relief is the motivating factor for obsessions and compulsions. Whereas resisting an obsession increases a child's anxiety and stress levels, giving in to the obsession is reinforced by the relief of anxiety (Kronenberger & Meyer, 1996). Behavioral theories explain the maintenance but not the emergence of OCD.

Treatment

"Cognitive–behavioral therapy is routinely described as the psychotherapeutic treatment of choice for children and adolescents with OCD" (March et al., 1995, p. 261). The core elements of the treatment include exposure-based treatment with response prevention, which have been found to be well-established treatments (Chambless et al., 1998), and anxiety management training (March et al., 1995). Anxiety management training involves a variety of techniques including relaxation training, breathing control training, and cognitive restructuring and can facilitate the management of the exposure process (March et al., 1995). *Exposure procedures* gradually or suddenly expose a child to obsessions or compulsions or situations associated with the obsessions or compulsions. Presumably, techniques such as desensitization, flooding, and satiation reduce the anxiety associated with a symptom or situation by coupling relaxation (or a lack of negative feedback) with the symptom or situation. Exposure must be used until habituation has occurred and OCD symptoms are reduced (Kronenberger & Meyer, 1996).

Response prevention therapy integrates blocking approaches to reduce the frequency of obsessive thoughts or compulsive behaviors. Techniques include thought stopping, covert sensitization, and aversion therapy. Response prevention therapy typically begins with restricting a child to a single compulsive act or obsessive thought and then eventually phasing it out. Restriction can be achieved through the patient's self-control, altering the environment, or both (Kronenberger & Meyer, 1996).

Pharmacotherapy for adults and children with OCD relies on SSRIs. Clomipramine is the most thoroughly studied SSRI in the pediatric populations (March et al., 1995). Findings from the National Institute of Mental Health multicenter collaborative study showed that clomipramine produces a 30% reduction in OCD symptoms, but on average it is not a panacea, as indicated by participants remaining in the mildly to moderately ill range at the completion of the trial (DeVeaugh-Geiss et al., 1992). Several other SSRIs, including fluoxetine (Prozac), sertraline (Zoloft), and paroxetine (Paxil) "have been approved by the Food and Drug Administration (FDA) for the treatment of depression in adults," and fluvoxamine (Luvox) "is considered a likely candidate for treatment of OCD in youth" (March et al., 1995, p. 264).

The most efficacious treatment for OCD may be a combination of exposure and response prevention therapy with clomipramine (Abel, 1993), because each of these three treatments affects a different aspect of OCD symptoms. Exposure with response prevention exhibits the highest long-term efficacy (Marks & O'Sullivan, 1988) and demonstrates the most profound effect on alleviating compulsive rituals. Clomipramine, on the other hand, has significant short-term effects (Marks & O'Sullivan, 1988) and has a greater overall effect among individuals who experience obsessions only (Kronenberger & Meyer, 1996). Because of evidence on side effects and relapses during drug cessation, medication is not recommended as the primary line of treatment for OCD (Marks & O'Sullivan, 1988); however, the incorporation of pharmacotherapy will likely make therapy more efficient by providing quicker symptom relief and therefore increasing patient compliance.

CONCLUSION

This chapter has addressed the major contributions of health psychology to the understanding and treatment of mental disorders. What is clear is that the combination of biopsychosocial model, life span perspective, and behavioral science approaches that characterize health psychology has resulted in substantive gains in knowledge and clinical practice. Thus, this essential triad of characteristics should be maintained when confronting future challenges and opportunities.

One fundamental challenge is facing the increasing recognition of the relative absence of main effects and the myriad interactions of biological, psychological, and social process that constitute risk and resilience factors for psychological and physical functioning. In clinical practice and the research on which practice is founded, clinicians must persist in carrying out the fundamental work of delineating the process that mediates and moderates the etiology and treatment of disorders. Thus, the challenge that Paul (1967) framed for psychology more than 30 years ago remains salient for both the researcher and the clinician: to determine "*what* treatment, by *whom*, is most effective for *this* individual with that *specific* problem, under which *set* of circumstances" (p. 111).

Another challenge is to continue the process of moving beyond the convenience of dualism. As behavioral scientists, psychologists have an approach and a body of knowledge that allows them to contribute to collaborative efforts with their biomedical colleagues. The focus needs to be maintained on the interface of mind and brain, mental and physical, and not on the general superiority of the cognitive or biological models. Thus, more controlled, longitudinal, outcome studies of combinations of cognitive and biologically based treatment approaches are needed.

On the other hand, another major challenge and opportunity is to engage in the explicit competition among approaches to classification advocated by Follette (1996). The limitation of the *DSM* system, with its nontheoretical, nonempirical, appeasement approach, is increasingly clear. Psychologists need to seriously engage in the competition of ideas, which is fundamental to advancement of knowledge.

Finally, a major challenge for psychology is to maintain its commitment to a behavioral science approach, even though it may be threatening to the economic interests of practitioners in this era of managed care. The efforts to delineate empirically supported treatments are illustrative of the tensions, vulnerabilities, and countervailing forces that must be traversed. In this regard, the limitations of the classification system associated with the appeasement approach of the American Psychiatric Association should be instructional for psychology's efforts to develop effective treatments. Competition of approaches, not appeasement, is the basis for developing effective interventions.

REFERENCES

Abel, J. L. (1993). Exposure with response prevention and serotonergic antide-pressants in the treatment of obsessive–compulsive disorder: A review and implications for interdisciplinary treatment. *Behavior Research and Therapy, 31*, 463–478.

American Psychiatric Association. (1994). *Diagnostic and statistical manual of mental disorders* (4th ed.). Washington, DC: Author.

Apter, A., Ratzoni, G., King, R., Weizman, A., Iancu, I., Binder, M., et al. (1994). Fluovoxamine open-label treatment of adolescent inpatients with obsessive–compulsive disorder or depression. *Journal of the American Academy of Child and Adolescent Psychiatry, 33*, 342–348.

Barlow, D. H. (1988). *Anxiety and its disorders: The nature and treatment of anxiety and panic.* New York: Guilford Press.

Barlow, D. H., Blanchard, E. B., Vermilyea, J. A., Vermilyea, B. B., & DiNardo, P. A. (1986). Generalized anxiety and generalized anxiety disorder: Description and reconceptualization. *American Journal of Psychiatry, 143*, 40–44.

Beck, A. T., Freeman, A., & Associates. (1979). *Cognitive therapy of personality disorders.* New York: Guilford Press.

Borkovec, T. D., Shadick, R. N., & Hopkins, M. (1991). The nature of normal and pathological worry. In R. M. Rapee & D. H. Barlow (Eds.), *Chronic anxiety and mixed anxiety–depression* (pp. 29–51). New York: Guilford Press.

Butler, A. C., & Beck, A. T. (1995). Cognitive therapy for depression. *The Clinical Psychologist, 48*, 3–5.

Cavanaugh, S., & Zalski, A. (1998). Psychiatric diagnosis. In L. S. Goldman, T. N. Wise, & D. S. Brody (Eds.), *Psychiatry for primary care physicians* (pp. 19–40). Chicago: American Medical Association.

Chambless, D. L., Baker, M. J., Baucom, D. H., Beutler, L. E., Calhoun, K. S., Crits-Christoph, P., et al. (1998). Update on empirically validated therapies, II. *The Clinical Psychologist, 51*, 3–16.

Chambless, D. L., & Gillis, M. M. (1993). Cognitive therapy of anxiety disorders. *Journal of Consulting and Clinical Psychology, 61*(2), 248–260.

Cicchetti, D., & Schneider-Rosen, K. (1986). An organization approach to childhood depression. In M. Rutter, C. E. Izard, & P. B. Read (Eds.), *Depression in young people: Developmental and clinical perspectives* (pp. 71–134). New York: Guilford Press.

Cooper, J. E. (1994). The structure and presentation of contemporary psychiatric classifications, with special reference to *ICD–9* and *ICD–10*. In J. E. Mezzich, M. R. Jorge, & I. M. Salloum (Eds.), *Psychiatric epidemiology: Assessment concepts and methods* (pp. 103–115). Baltimore: Johns Hopkins University Press.

Dennis, W. (1950). Interrelations of psychology and medicine. In W. Dennis (Ed.), *Current trends in the relation of psychology to medicine* (pp. 1–10). Pittsburgh, PA: University of Pittsburgh Press.

DeVeaugh-Geiss, J., Moroz, G., Biederman, J., Cantwell, D., Fontaine, R., Greist, J. H., et al. (1992). Clomipramine hydrochloride in childhood and adolescent obsessive compulsive disorder multicenter trial. *Journal of the American Academy of Child and Adolescent Psychiatry, 31,* 45–49.

Engel, G. L. (1977). The need for a new medical model: A challenge for biomedicine. *Science, 196,* 129–136.

Erickson, B., Yager, J., & Seeger, K. (1998). Eating disorders. In L. S. Goldman, T. N. Wise, & D. S. Brody (Eds.), *Psychiatry for primary care physicians* (pp. 217–230). Chicago: American Medical Association.

Felker, B., & Hubbard, J. R. (1990). Influence of mental stress on the endocrine system. In J. Hubbard & E. Workman (Eds.), *Handbook of stress medicine: An organ system approach* (pp. 69–85). New York: CRC Press.

Follette, W. C. (1996). Introduction to the special section on the development of theoretically coherent alternatives to the *DSM* system. *Journal of Consulting and Chemical Psychology, 64,* 1117–1119.

Follette, W. C., & Houts, A. C. (1996). Models of scientific progress and the role of theory in taxonomy development: A case study of the *DSM*. *Journal of Consulting and Clinical Psychology, 64,* 1120–1132.

Harrington, R. (1993). *Repressive disorder in childhood and adolescence.* West Sussex, England: Wiley & Sons.

Henry, J. P. (1990). Stress, neuroendocrine patterns, and emotional response. In J. D. Noshpita & R. D. Coddington (Eds.), *Stressors and the adjustment disorders* (pp. 477–496). New York: Wiley & Sons.

Hoehn-Saric, R., & McLeod, D. R. (1988). The peripheral sympathetic nervous system: Its role in normal and pathological anxiety. *Psychiatric Clinics of North America, 11,* 375–386.

Hollon, S. D., DeRubeis, R. J., Evans, M. D., Wiemer, M. J., Garvey, M. J, Grove, W. M., et al. (1992). Cognitive therapy and pharmacotherapy for depression: Singly and in combination. *Archives of General Psychiatry, 49,* 774–781.

Jain, B. (1998). Sleep disorders. In L. S. Goldman, T. N. Wise, & D. S. Brody (Eds.), *Psychiatry for primary care physicians* (pp. 181–195). Chicago: American Medical Association.

Johnston, M., & Vogele, C. (1993). Benefits of psychological preparation for surgery: A meta-analysis. *Annuals of Behavioral Medicine, 15,* 245–256.

Kaslow, N. J., Deering, C. G., & Racusin, G. R. (1994). Depressed children and their families. *Clinical Psychology Review, 14*, 39–59.

Kaslow, N. J., & Thompson, M. P. (1998). Applying the criteria for empirically supported treatments to studies of psychosocial interventions for child and adolescent depression. *Journal of Clinical Child Psychology, 27*, 146–155.

Kessler, R. C., McGonagle, K. A., Zhao, S., Nelson, C. B., Hughes, M., Eshleman, S., et al. (1994). Lifetime and 12-month prevalence of *DSM–III–R* psychiatric disorders in the United States: Results from the National Comorbidity Study. *Archives of General Psychiatry, 51*, 8–19.

Klerman, G. L., Hirschfeld, R. M. A., Weissman, M. M., Pelicier, Y., Ballenger, J. C., Costa e Silva, J. A., et al. (Eds.). (1993). *Panic anxiety and its treatments*. Washington, DC: American Psychiatric Press.

Kramer, M. E. (1994). The history of the international classification of diseases. In J. E. Mezzich, M. R. Jorge, & I. M. Salloum (Eds.), *Psychiatric epidemiology: Assessment concepts and methods* (pp. 91–97). Baltimore: Johns Hopkins University Press.

Kronenberger, W. G., & Meyer, R. G. (1996). Anxiety disorders. In *The child clinician's handbook*. Boston: Allyn and Bacon.

Lambert, M. J., Chiles, J. A., Kesler, S. R., & Vermeersch, D. A. (1998). Compendium of current psychotherapy treatment manuals. In G. P. Koocher, J. C. Norcross, & S. S. Hill III (Eds.), *Psychologists' desk reference* (pp. 202–209). New York: Oxford University Press.

Lazarus, R. S. (1999). *Stress and emotion: A new synthesis*. New York: Springer.

Leonard, H. L., Swedo, S. E., Rapoport, J. L., Koby, E. V., Lenane, M. C., Cheslow, D. L., et al. (1991). Treatment of obsessive–compulsive disorder with clomipramine and desipramine in children and adolescents: A double-blind crossover comparison. In S. Chess & M. E. Hertzing (Eds.), *Annual progress in child psychiatry and child development, 1990* (pp. 467–480). New York: Brunner/Mazel.

Lewinsohn, P. M., Clarke, G. N., Rohde, P., Hops, H., & Seeley, J. R. (1996). A course in coping: A cognitive–behavioral approach to the treatment of adolescent depression. In E. Hibbs & P. S. Jensen (Eds.), *Psychosocial treatments for child and adolescent disorders* (pp. 109–135). Washington DC: American Psychological Association.

Lewinsohn, P. M., Rohde, P., & Seeley, J. R. (1994). Psychosocial risk factors for future adolescent suicide attempts. *Journal of Consulting and Clinical Psychology, 62*, 297–305.

Lonigan, C. J., Elbert, J. C., & Johnson, S. B. (1998). Empirically supported psychosocial interventions for children: An overview. *Journal of Clinical Child Psychology, 27*, 138–145.

Lustman, P. J. (1988). Anxiety disorders in adults with diabetes mellitus. *Psychiatric Clinics of North America, 11*, 419–431.

Lustman, P. J., & Gavard, J. (1995). Psychosocial aspects of diabetes in adult populations. In M. Harris (Ed.), *Diabetes in America* (2nd ed.; pp. 507–517). NIH Publication No. 95.

March, J. S., Leonard, H. L., & Swedo, S. E. (1995). Obsessive–compulsive disorder. In J. March (Ed.), *Anxiety disorders in children and adolescents* (pp. 251–275). New York: Guilford Press.

Marks, I., & O'Sullivan, G. (1988). Drugs and psychological treatments for agoraphobia/panic and obsessive–compulsive disorders: A review. *The British Journal of Psychiatry, 153,* 650–658.

Masand, P., Pickett, P., & Murray, G. B. (1991). Psychostimulants for secondary depression in medical illness. *Psychosomatics, 32,* 203–208.

Nolen-Hoeksema, S., & Girgus, J. S. (1994). The emergence of gender differences in depression during adolescence. *Psychological Bulletin, 115,* 424–443.

O'Leary, B. J., & Norcross, J. C. (1998). Lifetime prevalence of mental disorders in the general population. In G. P. Koocher, J. C. Norcross, & S. S. Hill III (Eds.), *Psychologists' desk reference* (pp. 3–6). New York: Oxford University Press.

Paul, G. L. (1967). Strategy of outcome research in psychotherapy. *Journal of Consulting and Clinical Psychology, 31,* 109–118.

Peterson, C., & Seligman, M. E. P. (1984). Causal explanations as a risk factor for depression: Theory and evidence. *Psychological Review, 91,* 347–374.

Rapoport, J. L. (1988). Childhood obsessive–compulsive disorder. In S. Chess, A. Thomas, & M. E. Hertzing (Eds.), *Annual progress in child psychiatry and child development, 1987* (pp. 437–445). New York: Brunner/Mazel.

Robbins, L. N., & Reiger, D. A. (Eds.). (1991). *Psychiatric disorders in America: The Epidemiological Catchment Area study.* New York: Free Press.

Rohde, P., Lewinsohn, P. M., & Seeley, J. R. (1991). Comorbidity with unipolar depression II: Comorbidity with other mental disorders in adolescents and adults. *Journal of Abnormal Psychology, 99,* 264–271.

Romano, S. J., & Halmi, K. A. (1997). Eating disorders. In M. D. Feldman & J. F. Christensen (Eds.), *Behavioral medicine in primary care: A practical guide* (pp. 157–162). Stamford, CT: Appleton & Lange.

Schofield, W. (1969). The role of psychology in the delivery of health services. *American Psychologist, 24,* 564–584.

Scotti, J. R., Morris, T. L., McNeil, C. B., & Hawkins, R. P. (1996). DSM–IV and disorders of childhood and adolescence: Can structural criteria be functional? *Journal of Consulting and Clinical Psychology, 64,* 1177–1191.

Shuchter, S. R., Downs, N., & Zisook, S. (1996). *Biologically informed psychotherapy for depression.* New York: Guilford Press.

Singer, C., & Sack, R. L. (1997). Sleep disorders. In M. D. Feldman & J. F. Christensen (Eds.), *Behavioral medicine in primary care: A practical guide* (pp. 157–162). Stamford, CT: Appleton & Lange.

Swedo, S. E., Rapoport, J. L., Leonard, H., Lenane, M., & Cheslow, D. (1989). Obsessive–compulsive disorder in children and adolescents: Clinical phenomenology of 70 consecutive cases. *Archives of General Psychiatry, 46,* 335–341.

Task Force on Promotion and Dissemination of Psychological Procedures. (1995). Training in and dissemination of empirically validated psychological treatments. *Clinical Psychologist, 48,* 3–23.

Thompson, R. J., Jr. (1991). Psychology and the health care system. In J. Sweet, R. H. Rozensky, & S. M. Tovian (Eds.), *Handbook of clinical psychology in medical settings* (pp. 11–25). New York: Plenum Press.

Thompson, R. J., Jr., & Gustafson, K. E. (1996). *Adaptation to chronic childhood illness.* Washington, DC: American Psychological Association.

Von Korff, M., Katon, W., & Lin, E. (1990). Psychological distress, physical symptoms, utilization and the cost-offset effect. In N. Sartorius, D. Goldberg, G. de Girolamo, J. Costa e Silva, Y. Lecrubier, & V. Wittchen (Eds.), *Psychological disorders in general medical settings* (pp. 159–169). Toronto: Hogrefe & Huber Publishers.

Young, J. E. (1990). *Cognitive therapy for personality disorders: A schema-focused approach.* Sarasota, FL: Professional Resource Exchange.

Young, J. E., Beck, A. T., & Weinberger, A. W. (1993). Depression. In D. H. Barlow (Ed.), *Clinical handbook of psychological disorders* (pp. 240–277). New York: Guilford Press.

Zinbarg, R. E., Craske, M. G., & Barlow, D. H. (1993). *Therapist's guide for the Mastery of Your Anxiety and Worry Program.* San Antonio: Psychological Corporation.

6

DISEASES OF THE NERVOUS SYSTEM AND SENSE ORGANS

JOSHUA I. BREIER AND JACK M. FLETCHER

This chapter addresses diseases of the nervous system (brain, spinal cord, peripheral nerves) and sensory organs (eyes and ears). The organization of this chapter involves several decisions about coverage relative to the ninth edition of the *International Classification of Diseases* (ICD–9; World Health Organization, 1991). The *ICD–9* classification of nervous system and sensory organ diseases has six major subclassifications. Three involve the central nervous system (CNS): (a) *inflammatory diseases*, (b) *hereditary and degenerative diseases*, and (c) *other disorders*. One involves disorders of the peripheral nervous system (PNS), and two involve disorders of the eye or ear. However, disorders in all six subclassifications are linked with and may involve the CNS. For example, the eyes and ears are sensory organs that require the CNS to operate. The peripheral nerves are connected to the CNS. The distinction that is made within this section of *ICD–9* is the primary locus of the disorder: in the brain or spinal cord (CNS, autonomic nervous system [ANS]), nerves in other parts of the body that carry out CNS directives (PNS), and primary sensory organs involved in vision and hearing. Other disorders involving touch, smell, and proprioception are addressed in the other four subclassifications of this section of *ICD–9*.

DISORDERS OF THE CNS

Psychologists who work in the health care system could potentially be involved with patients from any of the six subclassifications. However, most of the work occurs with patients who experience CNS disorders. Some psychologists work with people who have severe vision and hearing problems, but these psychologists are highly specialized professionals whose primary focus is typically not health psychology. Many of the sensory disorders involve impairment or disease of the eye or ear that would typically require treatment by a specialized medical practitioner (e.g., an ophthalmologist). Eye disorders include full or partial blindness, retinitis, and various forms of inflammation. Ear disorders range from full or partial deafness to mastoiditis, otitis media, and various infections. If the eye or ear disorders had consequences involving mental status, family adjustment, pain, language development, or behavioral issues, a health psychologist might become involved—but not specifically because the disorder involved a sensory organ. Thus, this chapter does not review these sensory organ disorders.

Disorders of the PNS involve problems such as peripheral neuropathy, cranial nerve disorders such as Bell's palsy that are often painful, and neuromuscular disorders such as myasthenia gravis and the muscular dystrophies. Psychologists in the health care system do not often work with patients with PNS disorders unless the disorders have other behavioral and health consequences. For example, the pain experienced by a patient with trigeminal nerve disease, Bell's palsy, or even carpal tunnel syndrome might result in interactions with a health psychologist. The identification and treatment of pain is addressed in Volume 2 of this series (see Raczynski, Bradley, & Leviton, in press). Similarly, identification and treatment of the effects of these disorders on emotional and family adjustment would be generic and not specific to these disorders, although patients would receive information about the disease. Psychologists in the health care system rarely work with children who have muscular dystrophy or adults with myasthenia gravis unless issues involving intellectual level, learning skills, or psychosocial adjustment are involved. Thus, these disorders are briefly reviewed.

In contrast, psychologists in the health care system, especially clinical neuropsychologists, are commonly involved with patients who experience CNS disorders. Except for the inflammatory diseases category, which largely involves different types of bacterial and viral forms of meningitis and encephalitis, the groupings within these three subclassifications are quite diverse. In the other two subclassifications, a wide variety of CNS disorders is covered, and no simple classification relevant to health care psychology is possible. The disorders range from childhood degenerative disorders such as leukodystrophy to specific dementias, Parkinson's disease, various ataxias, multiple sclerosis (MS), epilepsy, migraines, and many other disorders.

Other CNS disorders that commonly involve psychologists in the health care system, such as stroke, traumatic brain injury, and tumors, are classified in other parts of the *ICD–9* and therefore covered elsewhere in the book. Thus, the classification of a disorder of the CNS into this part of the *ICD–9* has little relationship to disorders that would involve a psychologist, much less a relationship with behavioral factors or cognitive outcomes. In some disorders, such as dementia, involvement of a psychologist is essential for diagnosis. In disorders such as epilepsy, psychologists are less involved in diagnosis but play key roles in treatment planning, including neurosurgical interventions, and habilitation of the patient. In others, such as MS, the role of the psychologist is largely consultative; questions may arise concerning the effects of the disease on daily functioning, psychosocial factors, and the need for generic psychological interventions with the patient or family.

In the remainder of this chapter, disorders in the four subclassifications of diseases of the nervous system involving the CNS and PNS are reviewed. Not all disorders are covered, but representative examples are used. Disorders such as epilepsy and dementia, which commonly involve psychologists, are given more coverage.

INFLAMMATORY DISEASES

Diseases that are subclassifications of inflammatory disorders largely involve different brain infections caused by bacterial, viral, parasitic, and toxic factors. Determining the cause of the infection is critical for treatment. However, the classification and symptomatology depend on the site of the infection. If the infection involves the brain meninges (membranes that surround the brain), it is classified as meningitis. If the infection involves the brain, it is encephalitis if the brain infection is diffuse (i.e., is not specific to any localized, or focal, area of the brain). If the infection is localized, it is an abscess, which is the third type of disorder in this subclassification (Pryse-Phillips & Murray, 1986).

The neurobehavioral sequelae of brain infections are varied and depend on the severity of the infection, the development of secondary consequences (e.g., diffuse or localized swelling of the brain, seizures), and the efficacy of treatment. The diagnosis of brain infections involves neuroimaging to establish the site of infection and analysis of cerebrospinal fluid, blood, or both to establish that the disorder is an infection and to identify treatable causes for bacterial disorders. The next section includes discussions on meningitis and encephalitis. (Abscesses are simply localized infections that are classified according to the site of infection—brain or spine.)

Meningitis

Meningitis is usually either viral or bacterial. Viral meningitis is more prevalent than bacterial meningitis and typically has a sudden (acute) onset. It can be related to various viral diseases, including herpes simplex, mumps, and human immunodeficiency virus (HIV). The type of virus is usually apparent after a review of the patient's history and an analysis of cerebrospinal fluid (Pryse-Phillips & Murray, 1986). The prognosis is generally good (except for patients infected with HIV), and neurobehavioral sequelae are not significant when secondary symptoms are controlled.

In contrast, bacterial forms of meningitis often have a slower onset and can be fatal if not detected early in the disease process. This form of meningitis affects mostly young children and older adults. The most well-known type of meningitis is caused by the bacteria *Haemophilus influenzae* and is relatively common in infants and preschoolers (Menkes, 1995). Before the advent of antibiotics, it was usually fatal; if the child survived, significant neurobehavioral deficits were common. With antibiotics, the disease is less frequently fatal, and neurobehavioral sequelae are less disabling. Mortality rates now vary widely depending on the organism that causes the infection and the timing of treatment (Anderson & Taylor, 2000). Taylor et al. (1990; Anderson & Taylor, 2000) conducted a series of longitudinal follow-up studies of infants and preschoolers who had survived *H. influenzae* meningitis. They found that significant neurobehavioral sequelae were infrequent and occurred largely in children who had focal neurological deficits (e.g., hemiplegia). On average, the children performed more poorly on measures of fine motor skills and had lower than expected IQ scores and academic performance relative to control siblings. These outcomes are consistent with a diffuse CNS disorder, with little specificity of sequelae for individual children.

Encephalitis

Viruses cause more than 90% of all forms of encephalitis. The infection is usually characterized by a sudden onset of symptoms, particularly a severe headache. Viruses are often carried by insects (mosquitoes) and parasites (ticks), so this type of encephalitis is common in the summer and early fall (Davis, 1994). There are no antiviral treatments for these causes of encephalitis, so the primary treatment is for the inflammation and swelling of the brain that results from the diffuse infection, as well as for seizures and other complications. Blood tests are essential for diagnosis (Pryse-Phillips & Murray, 1986).

In contrast, encephalitis caused by the herpes simplex virus is a latent infection that can be treated with antiviral agents. A brain biopsy is the only conclusive diagnostic test. This form of encephalitis is often fatal (i.e., in 20% of those infected) and is significantly handicapping, with more than half of the patients having focal neurological deficits (Davis, 1994). In some cases, the limbic system and hippocampus are severely damaged, leaving the patient completely amnestic and sometimes with severe behavioral disorders.

In contrast, the prognosis for other forms of encephalitis varies with the source of the infection (e.g., type of mosquito), and sequelae depend on the management of the symptoms associated with brain swelling, increased intracranial pressure, and seizures (Davis, 1994). Neurobehavioral sequelae vary, reflecting the diffuse nature of the infectious process. Finally, when encephalitis occurs with another disease (e.g., mumps, syphilis), it is classified with the primary disease. Nonetheless, a diffuse infection of the brain is involved, which is why it is classified as encephalitis.

HEREDITARY AND DEGENERATIVE DISEASES

Disorders in this section include various diseases that often have a genetic basis and are progressive, degenerating disorders. In many instances, the degenerative nature of the disease involves dementia, which is the point of contact with a psychologist in the health care system. The disorders include (a) various childhood disorders, (b) cortical degenerative disorders, (c) Parkinson's disease (which is discussed in the context of subcortical dementia), (d) other extrapyramidal disorders, (e) degenerative disorders involving the spine and cerebellum, (f) disorders involving components of the motor neural system, and (g) disorders involving the ANS.

The various childhood disorders, such as leukodystrophy and the cerebral lipidoses, are progressive, associated with severe degeneration of motor functions, and eventually fatal. Psychologists in the health care system are not routinely involved with these patients, so these disorders are not further discussed.

The cortical degenerative disorders include dementia caused by Alzheimer's disease, and dementia is discussed in detail. For the sake of coherence, the forms of dementia not classified in this section of the ICD–9 are often mentioned.

The other extrapyramidal disorders include an assortment of problems involving the motor system that lead to tics, choreoathetoid movements, and symptoms associated with degeneration of the extrapyramidal motor system. Huntington's chorea is discussed in the context of dementia as an example of this disorder.

The degenerative disorders involving the spine and cerebellum include Friedrich's ataxia and cerebellar ataxia. These disorders have in common the involvement of the cerebellum, which is often manifested in an ataxic (wide-based, shuffling) gait. Other signs of cerebellar dysfunction are often apparent, such as difficulties with precise fine motor movements. These disorders are not further discussed.

Disorders involving components of the motor neural system include motor neuron diseases such as amyotrophic lateral sclerosis (ALS) and pseudobulbar palsy. ALS is discussed as an example.

Disorders involving the ANS include hereditary peripheral neuropathy. The symptoms include loss of sensation (e.g., touch) and parethesias (e.g., tingling sensations) caused by a disorder of the ANS. These disorders are not discussed in this chapter, but other disorders with similar symptoms are discussed in the section on PNS disorders.

In the remainder of this section, disorders in this subclassification commonly involving health psychologists are reviewed largely from the viewpoint of dementia, which is associated with virtually all of these disorders. The classification does not correspond exactly to the ICD–9, but its use is necessary for a full understanding of these disorders.

Dementia

Dementia is an acquired, persistent impairment of cognitive abilities severe enough to interfere with daily functioning and quality of life. Diagnosis requires the presence of a memory deficit in addition to a deficit in one or more cognitive functions: aphasia (language disturbance), apraxia (impaired ability to carry out learned motor sequences in the presence of intact motor functioning), agnosia (failure to recognize objects despite intact sensory function), or disturbance in executive function (reduction in the ability to plan, organize, make abstractions, or all). The requirement that deficits be acquired distinguishes dementia from mental deficiency, and it is important to establish that *deficits* represent a significant change from a prior level of functioning. The requirement of *persistence* distinguishes dementia from acute states of confusions, lasting hours to days, secondary to traumatic brain injury, and metabolic or toxic disorders. The requirement of *multiple deficits* rules out patients with isolated focal cortical deficit.

Cummings and Benson (1992) stated that deficits in three areas of function must be present for a diagnosis of dementia; however, they did not state that a memory deficit must be present for diagnosis. They added visuo–spatial difficulties and problems with emotional or personality function to the list of possible deficits. Elimination of the memory deficit requirement and adding the possibility of a personality change forms a classification that is consistent with other dementia conditions, such as Pick's disease or frontotemporal dementia, in which deterioration in social–emotional function may be prominent and memory may be relatively preserved until later stages of the disorder. Similarly, in those with vascular dementia, the memory disorder varies and may or may not be prominent.

Dementia occurs primarily in later life, with an incidence of approximately 1% at age 60, which doubles every 5 years to 30% to 50% at age 85 (Evans, Funkenstein, & Albert, 1989; White, Cartwright, Cornoni-Huntley, & Brock, 1986). Approximately 6% of individuals older than age 65 exhibit severe dementia—12% including mild cases (Jorm, Korten, & Henderson, 1987). As the proportion of adults older than 65 continues to increase substantially, it is expected that the absolute numbers of individuals affected with dementia will rise significantly.

Numerous pathological processes can result in dementia, many of which are addressed in this section of the *ICD–9*. Although many of these processes are degenerative and irreversible, some are reversible and others are becoming increasingly treatable, making accurate diagnosis imperative. Although brain imaging and laboratory tests are of great importance in this diagnosis, characterization of cognitive deficits using neuropsychological testing is a very important element in the diagnostic process. The cognitive deficit pattern provides salient information regarding underlying structural or functional abnormalities caused by a specific process (Absher & Cummings, 1994). In addition, changes in memory and rate of information processing are part of the normal aging process. However, the nature of the cognitive and neurobiological alterations associated with age-related change is quite different from that in a dementing illness, and neuropsychological testing is often essential for distinguishing between the effects of dementia and normal aging.

Several factors affect the expression of any dementing disorder, including genetic predisposition, education, gender, age-related changes, and medical and psychiatric comorbidity. However, despite this variance in expression, syndromes of dementia fall into two general categories with distinguishable patterns of cognitive dysfunction: (a) cortical and (b) frontal/subcortical. Cortical syndromes involve impairment in one or more of the modular cortical systems that subserve language, memory, visuo–spatial, and executive function. Subcortical disorders affect the frontal/subcortical circuits that modulate cortical activity; in addition to prominent motor abnormalities, they may be accompanied by cognitive deficit or dementia (Absher & Cummings, 1994). Psychiatric dysfunction can occur in the context of either. Table 6.1 summarizes the profile of cognitive deficits associated with the most common cortical, subcortical, and "other" (mixed) dementias, as well as dementia resulting from depression for comparison purposes.

TABLE 6.1
Dementia Syndromes and Effects on Functioning

Function	Alzheimer's disease	Diffuse Lewy body disease	Frontotemporal dementia	Parkinson's disease	Dementia secondary to depression	Vascular dementia
Language functions	Initial naming and word-finding difficulty progressing to fluent, transcortical sensory aphasia (intact repetition, poor comprehension, and paraphasic production) and eventually to minimal and rote repetition of phrases (echolalia, pallilalia) or parts of words (logoclonia)	Initial naming and word-finding difficulty	Initial economical or sparse speech or possibly pressured speech, progressing to stereotyped, echolalic or perseverative speech and ultimately mutism	Generally intact	Generally intact, although speech may be slowed and sparse in content	Dysarthria more likely than aphasia, although residual aphasia can result from left hemispheric cortical infarction
Memory functions	Impaired learning and recall of new material early, progressing to an amnestic disorder in the middle and latter stages	Early memory impairment that is variable; memory deficits usually emerging over time	Relatively spared initially	Characterized by mild to moderate "forgetfulness" and poor retrieval processes. Recognition memory often intact.	Memory dysfunction related to reduced encoding and poor effortful retrieval. Recognition memory intact.	Memory deficits usually present, although often not as severe or prominent as in AD.
Visuo–spatial functions	Impaired early; may cause person to become lost following unfamiliar routes or disoriented in familiar surroundings and may create difficulties dressing (dressing apraxia)	Impaired early; may cause person to become lost following unfamiliar routes or disoriented in familiar surroundings	Relatively spared initially	Impaired	Intact	Frequently impaired

Executive functions	Focused attention, tively spared, however, may involve early impairment of divided attention, working memory, and mental flexibility, although not as severe as in Diffuse Lewy Body Disease or Frontal Lobe Dementia	May affect attention, working memory, and mental flexibility early; causes executive deficits, including decreased verbal fluency, which are more severe at an earlier stage than in AD	Early impairment of working memory and ability to establish, shift, and maintain	Possible impairment of attention, working memory, and mental flexibility; may have significant executive deficits, including decreased verbal fluency	Possible impairment of attention, working memory, and mental flexibility; may have significant executive deficits, including decreased verbal fluency	—
Psychomotor speed	Initially relatively spared	Slowed	Slowed	Slowed	Often very slowed	Slowed, particularly in subcortical vascular diseases
Personality changes	Poor personal hygiene, reduced initiation, lack of insight into deficits (anosognosia), and psychosis in up to 50% of patients, including delusions and hallucinations (Absher & Cummings, 1994); may cause sadness or demoralization, but major depressive episodes are rare; may cause euphoria, but mania is rare (Wragg & Jeste, 1989)	Possible visual hallucinations	Early deterioration in social judgment; early appearance of inappropriate and disordered social behavior; early emotional blunting and loss of insight; possible early preoccupation with somatic symptoms; eventual stereotyped behavior and inertia	Apathy and depression	—	—
Other	Anosognosia, apraxia, acalculia (may appear early)	—	—	Micrographia; motor perseveration	Negative response bias	In multi-infarct dementia, any number of residua of stroke syndromes depending on location

Cortical Dementia

Alzheimer's disease. Alzheimer's disease, which is included in the cortical dementia section of the *ICD–9*, is by far the most common of the degenerative dementias that primarily affect cortical functions. It is the single most common dementing illness, accounting for approximately 70% of dementias in most industrialized nations (American Psychiatric Association, 1994). The prevalence rate is less than 1% for those younger than age 65, but it reaches nearly 3% by age 79 and more than 10% for those older than age 80 (Adams, Victor, & Ropper, 1997). It is estimated that the disease currently affects approximately 4 million people in the United States, a number that is expected to rise dramatically over the next 50 years (Geldmacher & Whitehouse, 1997). The only definite risk factors for Alzheimer's disease are age and familial aggregation. The latter accounts for less than 1% of all cases.

The etiology of Alzheimer's disease is unknown and there are no pathognomic laboratory findings (Cummings & Benson, 1992). The diagnosis is made on the basis of clinical features and is by postmortem examination, which reveals numerous consistent neuropathological features. Brains are generally grossly atrophic, with atrophy most evident in temporoparietal, anterior frontal, and medial temporal regions (Harasty, Halliday, Kril, & Code, 1999; Jack et al., 1999). Histological examination reveals several neuronal abnormalities, including the presence of neurofibrillar tangles (abnormal proteinaceous inclusions within the cell), neuritic plaques (amorphous material composed of a core of amyloid protein surrounded by residua of degenerated neuronal terminals), and granulovacuolar degeneration of neurons (Price et al., 1998).

The predilection of the pathological processes in Alzheimer's disease for certain brain areas and the temporal order of degeneration account for the nature and timing of the deficits that emerge. Medial temporal areas, including the hippocampi, are affected early in the progression of the disease directly and by interference with cholinergic neurons in the septal nuclei (Frisoni et al., 1999). The resulting deficits in learning and consolidation of new material early in the illness progress to an amnestic state in the middle and latter stages.

As the disease progresses from medial temporal to association areas in lateral temporal cortex, linguistic deficits develop. Initially, naming and word-finding difficulties become evident, resulting in circumlocutory speech, or "beating around the bush." This progresses to a transcortical sensory aphasia that is characterized by empty content; semantic paraphasia; and use of one-word, nonspecific circumlocutions (e.g., "thing") with relatively intact repetition. Finally, production is limited to repetition of phrases (echolalia, pallilalia) or word parts (logoclonia). Early visuo–spatial dysfunction may be related to involvement of parietal areas. As difficulties with spatial orientation become more prominent, patients get lost even in familiar surroundings and have difficulty dressing (dressing apraxia). As parietal areas become progressively more involved, difficulty with calculations (acalculia) and learned motor routines (apraxia) arise. With increasing involvement of frontal lobe areas, initiation is affected and patients may become unmotivated or disinterested. Hygiene deteriorates and patients may need to be fed. The course of the illness varies; however, although evidence shows that mild cognitive deficit may be present for numerous years before they become severe enough to lead to diagnosis (Linn et al., 1995), the duration between presentation and death is approximately 10 years (Jost & Grossberg, 1995).

Creutzfeldt–Jakob disease. Creutzfeldt–Jakob disease, or subacute spongiform encephalopathy, is a rapidly progressive degenerative disease affecting primarily the cortex and cerebellum. The incidence is 1 to 2 cases per million. It is a transmissible disease and invariably fatal. Its effects on brain tissue are characterized by widespread neuronal loss and the striking spongy state of affected tissue. Psychiatric symptoms are prominent and develop early, with confusion, hallucinations, and agitation occurring early in many instances (Adams et al., 1997). Creutzfeldt–Jakob disease is a form of cortical dementia but is covered in the part of the *ICD–9* addressing infectious diseases, not in any subclassification in this part of the *ICD–9*.

Frontal/Subcortical Dementia

Many disorders that affect the extrapyramidal motor systems may result in dementia and movement disorders. Parkinson's disease and Huntington's chorea are two examples, both involving the basal ganglia and its connections. They are included in the frontal/subcortical dementia subclassification of the *ICD–9* and are discussed in the context of dementia because it involves health psychologists. Although these disorders affect somewhat different subcortical systems, the behavioral deficits that result are quite similar and are summarized in Table 6.1.

Parkinson's disease. Parkinson's disease affects about 1% of individuals older than age 65. The disease is a degenerative disorder of unknown etiology affecting the pigmented brain stem nuclei (substantia nigra, locus ceruleus) that modulate movement through the activity of specific neurotransmitters (dopamine, norepinephrine) in projections to the basal ganglia. Resultant motor abnormalities include a masklike facial expression, a stooped posture, resting tremors, and gait abnormalities. Bradykinesia (slowness in initiation and production of movement), micrographia, and hypophonic speech are common as the disorder progresses. Idiopathic and postencephalitic forms of the illness can occur. The incidence of Alzheimer's disease increases in those people with Parkinson's disease.

Huntington's chorea. Huntington's chorea is an inherited, autosomal dominant degenerative disorder affecting subcortical structures including the caudate nucleus and putamen. Overall frequency is 4 to 5 per million but increases to 30 to 70 per million among White people of northern European ancestry (Adams et al., 1997). Motor abnormalities involve excessive choreathetoid movements, or jerking movements of the face, tongue, limbs, and trunk (Pryse-Phillips & Murray, 1986). Psychiatric dysfunction, which may develop before motor symptoms, can include major depressive disorder; psychotic disorders with paranoia, delusions, and hallucinosis; anxiety symptoms; sleep disorders; sexuality disorders; and behavioral symptoms including apathy, irritability, and aggression (Leroy & Michalon, 1998). Progressive mental deterioration and dementia accompany the loss of motor control.

Other Dementia Syndromes

Psychiatric dysfunction can be accompanied by changes in mental status, which is an essential component of the evaluation of possible dementia. Although the term *pseudodementia* has been used to describe these changes, Cummings and Benson (1992) pointed out that the cognitive deficits experienced by these patients are in no way "pseudo-", so the term *pseudodementia* is inappropriate. Caine (1981) suggested that the following four criteria be used during the assessment of dementia resulting from a psychiatric disorder: (a) patients with a primary psychiatric disorder should also have an intellectual impairment, (b) the profile of deficits should resemble those present in patients with a degenerative neurological disorder, (c) the impairment should be reversible, and (d) no identifiable CNS dysfunction should better account for the cognitive deficits.

Although numerous psychiatric disorders are accompanied by cognitive dysfunction, including Ganser syndrome, depression, schizophrenia, conversion disorder, and anxiety, the most common etiology is depression (Cummings & Benson, 1992). The onset of mental slowness, poor memory secondary to reduced attention and effort in processing, loss of hygiene, lability, difficulty sleeping, intermittent disorientation, and weight loss in older adults can be mistaken for the effects of a degenerative neurological disorder. Further complicating the picture are the prevalence of depressive symptomatology associated with numerous neurological disorders and the presence of age-related changes on neuroimages. Vulnerability to depression in older adults may be affected by age-related structural and biochemical changes, effects of bereavement and other psychological losses, and increased incidence of somatic disease (Palsson & Skoog, 1997; Salloway et al., 1996; Snowden, 1997).

Dementia resulting from depression. In contrast to those with progressive dementia, individuals with dementia resulting from depression often overestimate their cognitive dysfunction. Individuals with Alzheimer's disease often are unaware of deficits (anosognosia). They may tend to take a negative response bias rather than the positive or confabulatory bias sometimes shown by those with Alzheimer's disease. Although free recall may worsen, recognition is often intact in those with dementia caused by depression, whereas it is not in those with Alzheimer's disease. In addition, cortical signs such as agnosia, apraxia, and significant anomia are generally not present. Individuals with dementia due to depression may have symptoms similar to those with subcortical dementias, and subcortical dysfunction may indeed be involved, at least in a subgroup of individuals (Hickie, Scott, Wilhelm, & Brodaty, 1997; Salloway et al., 1996).

Frontotemporal degeneration. The term *frontotemporal degeneration* (FTD) is used to describe the anatomical focus of any primary degenerative process that affects primarily frontal and anterior temporal regions (Neary, 1997). FTD is the third most common cause of cortical dementia after Alzheimer's disease and diffuse Lewy body disease (Neary et al., 1998). Onset is generally before age 65, is rarely after age 70, and may account for up to 10% of dementia cases in some series of cases (Brun & Gustafson, 1998). Pick's disease is a pathophysiologically distinct process that may represent up to 20% to 25% of frontotemporal degenerative disorders (Mendez, Selwood, Mastri, & Frey, 1993). However, other processes can affect the same areas, resulting in clinical symptoms that are similar to Pick's disease, including dementia with a characteristic pattern of deficits (see Table 6.1).

The pathophysiology of FTD is not well known. The disease is characterized by progressive atrophy of frontal and often anterior temporal areas (Brun & Gustafson, 1998). Hypometabolism is often evident in metabolic studies of these areas. In individuals with Pick's disease, prominent lobar atrophy of gray and white matter and argentophilic intranuclear inclusions called *Pick bodies* are both prominent in frontotemporal areas. "Ballooning" of frontal neurons with gliotic changes and spongiosis are common in these areas as well.

FTD and Pick's disease are distinguished from Alzheimer's disease by the initial relative sparing of memory function, the early appearance of florid behavioral difficulties, and the nature and progression of the language disturbance (see Table 6.1). Changes in personality including disinhibition, loss of social awareness, hyperorality (overeating and inappropriate eating), executive dysfunction including perseverative and stereotyped behavior, and mental inflexibility are early behavioral disturbances. Depression, anxiety, and delusions are common, as are hypochondriasis and bizarre somatic preoccupation. If speech areas of the dominant hemisphere, including the frontal and temporoparietal areas, are predominantly involved, semantic aphasia may occur separately from the behavioral symptoms (semantic dementia). In this case, speech becomes progressively empty although fluent, with loss of word meaning. If homologous areas of the nondominant hemisphere are involved, speech difficulties may be accompanied by or supplanted by an inability to recognize familiar faces (prosopagnosia) or impaired visual recognition of objects despite intact visuo–spatial abilities (agnosia).

Dementia associated with Lewy bodies. Dementia associated with Lewy bodies is characterized by abnormalities associated with Alzheimer's disease and Parkinson's disease. It is a primary progressive dementia accounting for up to 25% of dementing illnesses (Salmon et al., 1996). The brain exhibits cerebral atrophy with a frontal or frontotemporal predominance. Parietal areas are also involved. The core feature is the presence of cortical and subcortical eosinophilic interneuronal inclusion bodies, or Lewy bodies. Cell loss in the substantia nigra and locus ceruleus with Lewy bodies in the remaining neurons is common. The latter changes are quite similar to those observed in individuals with Parkinson's disease and likely account for the parkinsonian aspects of the disease. The typical Alzheimer's disease distribution of senile plaques and neurofibrillar tangles is present as well (Salmon et al., 1996). Generally a combination of subcortical and cortical deficits occurs, often with less severe initial memory difficulty and more severe executive dysfunction (see Table 6.1).

Vascular dementia. *Vascular dementia* is associated with cerebrovascular disease and is the second most common cause of dementia after vascular dementia (Tatemichi, 1995). It is discussed in this section because it is a form of dementia that must be differentiated from Alzheimer's disease. Approximately 25% of stroke victims may exhibit vascular dementia; vascular dementia and Alzheimer's disease may be comorbid in up to 18% of patients (Markesbery, 1998). Estimates regarding prevalence vary widely depending on the population studied (Kase, 1991). In some countries, such as Japan, China, and Russia, vascular dementia may be the leading cause of dementia (Markesbery, 1998). An overall mean of 17% of all dementia cases is reported in one review of the literature (Markesbery, 1998) but may be more on the order of 10% (Kase, 1991). Other studies reported overall prevalence rates on the order of 2% to 5% (Markesbery, 1998).

Vascular dementia can be a difficult entity to diagnose. Behavioral changes may be similar to those seen in Alzheimer's disease and other dementias, and white matter changes identified by magnetic resonance imaging (MRI) and computed tomography (CT) may be present in those with Alzheimer's disease, those with vascular dementia, and healthy older adults. For this reason, numerous attempts have been made to establish clinical diagnostic criteria for those with vascular dementia. The Hachinski Ischemic Scale (Hachinski et al., 1975) used abrupt onset, stepwise deterioration, fluctuating course, nocturnal confusion, hypertension, and a history of neurological symptoms as distinguishing features. The NINDS–AIREN group (Roman et al., 1993) has published clinical criteria that emphasize (a) the heterogeneity of vascular dementia syndromes and their symptoms, (b) specific clinical findings early in the course (e.g., gait disorder, incontinence, mood and personality changes) that show evidence of a vascular rather than a degenerative cause, (c) the need to establish a temporal relationship between stroke and dementia onset for a secure diagnosis, (d) the importance of brain imaging to support clinical findings, (e) the value of neuropsychological testing to document impairments in multiple cognitive domains, and (f) a protocol for neuropathological evaluations and correlative studies of clinical, radiological, and neuropsychological features.

Separately or together, multiple cortical or subcortical infarcts can result in vascular dementia. The nature of the deficits in vascular dementia depend on location and degree of infarction and are summarized in Table 6.1. When primarily cortical areas are involved, the clinical symptoms are more like those for cortical dementia. When subcortical areas are primarily involved (multiple lacunar strokes or Binswanger's disease), the symptoms are more like subcortical dementia, with executive dysfunction and memory deficits that are based on reduced retrieval ability.

ALS

The discussion of dementia addressed the most important diseases in the *ICD–9* subclassification. ALS, or Lou Gehrig disease, is one example of a progressive neuromuscular disorder not commonly addressed by psychologists except during generic interventions involving the patient and family.

ALS is a progressive degenerative disorder of motor neurons in the spinal cord, brainstem, and motor cortex. Muscle weakness and atrophy are prominent. Incidence rate is 0.4 to 1.76 per 100,000 population. Men are affected somewhat more frequently than women. The age at onset is generally older than 50, and incidence increases with age. In a small percentage of cases, the disease is familial. An increased frequency of ALS has been found in Japan and Guam, and dementia and parkinsonism may occur in conjunction with the illness. Decreases in fine motor dexterity, stiffness of the hands or fingers, and muscle wasting are common early signs. The disease is progressive, with 90% of patients dying within 6 years (Adams et al., 1997). In the Guam variant of ALS, when dementia is present, it is generally in association with parkinsonism. In these individuals, dementia is usually an early sign; severe; and characterized by memory decline, difficulty with abstraction and calculation, poor reasoning, and disorientation and personality changes, including apathy, depression, and aggression (Lishman, 1998). Psychologists are often called on to help the patient and family adjust to the fact that the disease is progressive and fatal, that the patient will lose mentation and motor function, and to address severe behavior changes that may occur.

Other Disorders of the CNS

As the title *other disorders of the CNS* implies, this section of the *ICD–9* is a miscellaneous collection of disorders. No unifying characteristics were used to group these disorders together other than the fact that they do not fit well elsewhere. The primary disorders that involve psychologists in the health care system are (a) multiple sclerosis and other progressive neuromuscular disorders, (b) epilepsy, (c) cerebral palsy, and (d) migraines and related forms of headaches. Other disorders in this subclassification are an odd assortment of problems that are classified elsewhere when the cause is known; for example, hemiplegia, which is usually caused by cerebrovascular disease; cysts, but not neoplasms; and cerebral edema, or brain swelling, which is usually caused by another disorder such as a brain infection or trauma. The next sections focus on the first four disorders because they are the primary diseases that involve psychologists.

Multiple Sclerosis

MS is an inflammatory disorder that primarily affects the neuronal sheath. About 300,000 people have MS in North America. Almost 70% of patients manifest symptoms between ages 21 and 40, and women are affected more often than men (Lishman, 1998). Incidence varies with latitude and is 2 to 6 times more common in northern than southern states in the United States. Studies indicate a rate of 30 to 60 per 100,000 in northern latitudes, and 5 to 15 per 100,000 in southern latitudes (Adams et al., 1997). The incidence of MS in first-degree relatives is 20 times higher than in the general population. Therefore, both genetic and environmental factors seem to be important in disease expression (Adams et al., 1997; Hogancamp, Rodriguez, & Weinshenker, 1997).

MS involves the demyelination of the neuronal sheaths in white matter of the cerebral hemispheres, brainstem, optic nerves, cerebellum, and spinal cord. The cause is unknown. Demyelination results in characteristic multiple lesions, or plaques, consisting of demyelinated neurons within the white matter. MRI indicates sclerotic plaques, often most evident in the periventricular border, cerebral and cerebellar white matter, and brainstem (Stewart, Houser, Baker, O'Brien, & Rodriguez, 1987).

Demyelination impedes nerve conduction. Therefore, sensorimotor disturbances are prominent early in the disease progression. Visual disturbance may be an early symptom in a substantial portion of patients (Adams et al., 1997). Approximately 40% to 65% of patients with MS experience some form of significant cognitive dysfunction (Rao, 1995) and because MS generally affects white matter, the pattern of cognitive dysfunction that emerges is subcortical in nature. Deficits in short-term memory, sustained attention, verbal fluency, conceptual reasoning, and visuo–spatial perception (Rao, 1995; Rao, Leo, Bernardin, & Unverzagt, 1991) are common. Depression is a not infrequent concomitant of MS (Rodgers & Bland, 1996), and bipolar disorder occurs more in those with MS than in the general population (Mahler, 1992).

Epilepsy

Epilepsy is a condition characterized by recurrent paroxysmal events, or seizures, which are associated with stereotypical changes of behavior, movement, or sensation. Numerous pathological processes, including trauma, infection, stroke, metabolic disorders, and neoplasms, may cause disordered brain function and give rise to epilepsy. A wide variety of clinical phenomena are also considered to be seizures, including generalized tonic–clonic seizures, partial or complex partial seizures, absence seizures, myoclonic seizures, and atonic seizures. Specific epileptic syndromes have been identified by their characteristic seizure type and associated clinical features, such as electroencephalographic findings, age at onset, pattern of occurrence, concomitant neurological and other signs, and familial occurrence (Engel & Pedley, 1997).

The overall prevalence of epilepsy is estimated at 4 to 10 people in 1,000 (International League Against Epilepsy [ILAE] Commission Report, 1997). Incidence is high in the youngest age groups—particularly in the first few months of life—is lowest during the early and middle adult years and then rises sharply beginning at age 60 (Hauser, 1997). Incidence and prevalence is somewhat higher in males than females, even when risk factors such as head injury are controlled (Hauser, 1997).

The common features in the epilepsy syndromes are the development of neuronal hyperexcitability and hypersynchronous discharge in one or more regions of the CNS. This may be the result of a known lesion or other identifiable etiology, in which case seizures are termed *symptomatic* or presumed to be secondary to a currently unknown etiology, in which case seizures are *cryptogenic*. *Idiopathic* epilepsies are not associated with a brain lesion or other neurological abnormality and are presumed to be genetic in origin (Dreifuss, 1996). The pathophysiology of the different seizure types is a matter for intense research. Although much has been learned regarding basic cellular mechanisms in animal models and in vitro studies of human tissue, the mechanisms of seizures in humans have not been completely characterized. The *ICD–9* essentially classifies epilepsy into types that are based on seizure patterns.

Generalized convulsive seizures. Generalized convulsive seizures (sometimes called *grand mal seizures*) are one of the generalized seizure disorders in *ICD–9*. Generalized convulsive seizures represent approximately 23% of all seizure types in incidence studies (Hauser, 1997). The term *generalized* indicates that clinical changes (e.g., motor movements, as shown by electroencephalography [EEG]) provide no evidence for anatomical localization or focal onset (ILAE Commission Report, 1997), a characteristic that distinguishes generalized convulsive seizures from seizures that begin with focal onset and then secondarily generalize (i.e., partial seizures). That is, both hemispheres are initially involved. Generalized convulsive seizures typically begin with sudden loss of consciousness followed by tonic contraction of muscles. The patient may cry out briefly if respiratory muscles are involved. Clonic convulsive movements follow for a varied time. Cyanosis, salivation, tongue biting, and incontinence are common. The patient may gain consciousness slowly after the seizure or after a period of sleep during a variable postictal period (Rifkin & Dravet, 1997). Although generalized convulsive seizures can be a symptom of serious brain disease, they are generally associated with syndromes, and patients have a good prognosis for seizure control and normal development (Rifkin & Dravet, 1997).

Partial seizures. Partial seizures, with or without impairment of consciousness, by definition involve only one of the cerebral hemispheres, although they may become generalized tonic–clonic seizures. Partial seizures may be simple, which means the patient does not lose consciousness, or complex, which means the patient loses consciousness. Partial seizures represent approximately 50% of all seizure types in incidence studies (Hauser, 1997), with complex partial seizures representing 36% of all seizure types. Although complex partial seizures can originate elsewhere, temporal lobe seizures are the most common form of complex partial seizures and the most common form of epilepsy in adults (Williamson & Engel, 1997). Most temporal lobe seizures begin in the mesiotemporal areas. A typical mesiotemporal lobe seizure begins with an aura, which is sometimes a visceral sensation and represents a simple partial seizure. The seizures may occur in isolation, but they are more often followed by a variable reduction in awareness, a fixed stare, and oral–alimentary automatisms (e.g., lip smacking, chewing, swallowing). Patients may react to stimuli inappropriately or may not react at all. Head and eye deviations and tonic–dystonic posturing can occur and may provide information regarding the laterality and location of the focus, as do auras.

Absence seizures. Absence seizures (also called *petit mal seizures*) are generalized seizures that are characterized by sudden loss of awareness in association with a motionless stare and interruption of ongoing activity. Events are brief (2 to 10 seconds) with limited motor activity. Some patients may be motionless only for a short time; others may have brief clonic fine motor movement of the eyelid, facial, or other muscles. Absence seizures represent approximately 6% of all seizure types in incidence studies (Hauser, 1997). Absence seizures generally occur in children of school age, although they can occur in adults as well (Stefan & Snead, 1997).

Although a diagnosis of epilepsy is compatible with normal cognitive and psychosocial development, it does carry with it an increased risk for cognitive (Glosser, Cole, French, Saykin, & Sperling, 1997; Holmes, 1991) and psychological (Mendez, 1996) dysfunction. The nature and degree of cognitive dysfunction depends on a complex interaction of various factors, including seizure variables (etiology, epilepsy syndrome and seizure type, seizure frequency, age at onset, duration of seizure disorder, severity of EEG abnormality), laterality and location of seizure focus, effects of anticonvulsive medications, and numerous psychosocial variables (Giordani, 1996).

Some epilepsy syndromes, such as Lennox–Gastaux syndrome or infantile spasms, are often accompanied by mental retardation. Other syndromes, such as childhood absence seizures, are not usually associated with intellectual deficiency. Of the epilepsy syndromes, cognitive dysfunction has been most thoroughly studied in mesiotemporal sclerosis. As the mesiotemporal lobes are intimately involved in memory function and are the most common site of seizure onset, memory disability is common in this syndrome. Mesiotemporal sclerosis is usually accompanied by structural changes in the hippocampus in the affected hemisphere, termed *hippocampal sclerosis*, which consists of cell loss and atrophy. When the left hemisphere is involved, verbal memory is usually affected, whereas hippocampal sclerosis may affect nonverbal memory in the right hemisphere, although the latter finding is more variable. Left hemisphere seizure onset in mesiotemporal lobe sclerosis may be accompanied by language deficits including decreased naming, verbal fluency (Hermann, Seidenberg, & Davies, 1997), and comprehension (Hermann, Seidenberg, Haltiner, & Wyler, 1992). Executive dysfunction has also been noted in at least a subgroup of patients with mesiotemporal lobe sclerosis (Hermann, Wyler, & Richey, 1988), whereas attention difficulties are not generally salient (Hermann et al., 1997).

When considering psychiatric disorders in patients with epilepsy, it is important to distinguish among the *ictal* (during the seizure), *periictal* (just before [*preictal*] and after [*postictal*] the seizure), and *interictal* (in-between seizures) periods. An aura during the preictal period may also occur in the form of depression, irritability, anxiety, or insomnia. Ictal mood changes may occur in the form of auras (simple partial seizures) and include subjective feelings of anxiety or depression that patients will remember. These are usually but not always followed by a complex partial seizure. Ictal automatisms during complex partial seizures may include crying, laughing, or (rarely) aggressive behavior. The latter is more commonly associated with postictal psychosis (Kanemoto, Kawasaki, & Mori, 1999). Patients generally do not have memories of these events. Postictal psychosis, depression, or agitation also occur (Mendez, 1996). These disorders are circumscribed temporally and are tied to seizure activity.

Depression is the most common interictal psychiatric disorder in mixed epilepsy groups and may occur in up to 75% of patients (Mendez,

1996). This is generally a chronic, mild disorder, although patients with epilepsy have an increased risk of hospitalization for depression (Mendez, 1996). Evidence shows a relationship between the effects of seizures on brain function and depression (Altshuler, Devinsky, Post, & Theodore, 1990) as well as psychosocial variables (Hermann & Whitman, 1989). Patients with epilepsy, particularly those with mesiotemporal lobe sclerosis, may also be at increased risk for a chronic psychosis resembling schizophrenia (Tandon & DeQuardo, 1994). Risk factors include severe and intractable epilepsy, epilepsy of early onset, secondary generalization of seizures, certain anticonvulsant drugs, and temporal lobectomy (Sachdev, 1998).

Cerebral Palsy

The inclusion of cerebral palsy in this section *(hereditary and degenerative diseases)* of the *ICD–9* is puzzling because cerebral palsy is not a degenerative disease and commonly has a perinatal origin. Cerebral palsy refers to a consolidation of abnormalities of muscle tone and postural reflexes that begins early in development (Menkes, 1995) and reflects problems involving the nervous system around the time of birth. It often begins with lack of tone in the newborn, which progresses to various forms of spasticity and other motor anomalies later in life. The prevalence varies but ranges from 2 to 6 infants per 1,000 births (Menkes, 1995).

Classification of cerebral palsy in the *ICD–9* focuses on the nature of the spasticity, which may involve one arm (hemiplegia), two legs (diplegia), or both of the upper and lower limbs (quadraplegia). Some manifestations of cerebral palsy do not involve paralysis but actually involve uncontrollable exptrapyramidal (athetoid) movements or ataxia. Abnormal postures, weakness, and other symptoms may be apparent. Although cerebral palsy is typically classified in the *ICD–9* and elsewhere according to the involvement of the limb, it is a CNS disorder.

Cerebral palsy has other manifestations of CNS disorders. Neuroimaging through ultrasonography and MRI commonly show abnormalities such as periventricular leukomalacia, which is damage to the white matter of the brain around the ventricles. When unilateral hemiplegia is apparent, there may be some lateralization of the periventricular leukomalacia or a cyst. Determining whether cerebral palsy is associated with perinatal hypoxia is a controversial topic (Nelson & Ellenberg, 1986), but it is clear that cerebral palsy is more likely to occur in premature, low-birthweight infants. Maternal infection during gestation is increasingly being considered a prominent cause of cerebral palsy. Many children with cerebral palsy have learning deficiencies with no specificity relating to the disorder. Treatment of cerebral palsy involves a combination of occupational and physical therapy as well as interventions addressing the educational needs of the child.

Migraines

Headaches are chronic, potentially disabling, and affect most people. The headache component of the *ICD–9* involves *primary headaches*, which are migraine and cluster headaches. These types of headaches do not have any consistently identified neurological cause. Migraines are severe headaches that are usually characterized by whether they occur with an aura (Saper, 1994). An aura occurs in a phase before the onset of a headache and is usually characterized by physiological changes in visual, motor, or sensory experiences (e.g., a perception of a flashing light). When the aura recedes, a pulsating, usually unilateral pain begins that may last for hours to days. The pain is typically intense. Migraines are sometimes associated with acute onset of neurological deficits (e.g., hemiplegia). When a migraine occurs without an aura, the onset is not well defined, although the patient may experience discomfort a few hours before onset. The headache is typically either unilateral or bilateral, is severely painful, and most commonly affects the eyes and specific portions around the brain. Regardless of the form of migraine, symptoms vary and the patterns are rarely the same. A significant heritability component is involved in migraines, and migraines occur in childhood through adulthood. The cause is not clear. Vascular hypotheses have been prominent, but more recent studies have examined the relationship of different neurotransmitters as a cause of migraines. Available pharmacological treatments can be preventative but are typically symptomatic (e.g., the use of anticonvulsants). Nonpharmacological treatments of migraines include biofeedback and other related methods (see Raczynski, Bradley, & Leviton, in press).

Cluster headaches clearly have a vascular origin (Saper, 1994). They are called *cluster* headaches because they are a series of distinct, brief headaches that occur over a period of weeks to months and are typically followed by a period of remission. As with migraines, symptomatic and preventative pharmacological treatments are common. Cluster headaches often produce excruciating pain that is usually unilateral and occurs around the eyes.

DISORDERS OF THE PNS

The PNS includes the components of the nervous system that are not in the CNS (i.e., the brain and spinal chord). The PNS is connected to CNS structures and may be affected by the same types of disease processes that affect the CNS. However, some diseases primarily affect the PNS, including disorders of the cranial nerves, spinal nerves, peripheral nerves, and parts of the ANS outside the brain and spinal chord. All PNS disorders share in common a reduction or loss of sensorimotor functions.

This subclassification of the *ICD–9* involves (a) disorders of the 12 cranial nerves; (b) peripheral neuropathies involving the upper and lower limbs (e.g., carpal tunnel syndrome) or resulting from hereditary, inflammatory, toxic, or unknown causes; and (c) certain neuromuscular disorders, including myasthenia gravis and the muscular dystrophies. Following is a brief description of each of these large classes of disorders, reflecting the fact that specific involvement of psychologists in the health care system is not common.

Cranial Nerve Disorders

The 12 cranial nerves control various sensorimotor functions involving the head (Pryse-Phillips, & Murray, 1986). Table 6.2 lists the 12 cranial nerves and their primary functions. Trauma or infection can impair a cranial nerve, resulting in partial or full loss of the nerve's function. These types of problems are identified through a formal neurological examination. Bell's palsy, for example, refers to unilateral facial paralysis caused by impairment of cranial nerve VII, which is the facial nerve (see Table 6.2). The origin is not well understood but may be infectious. Bell's palsy is common (occurring in 20 people per 100,000 yearly), occurs acutely, and typically recovers spontaneously. The condition can be quite painful, which may result in referral to a health psychologist for nonpharmacological intervention. In contrast, trauma may damage cranial nerve I, leading to anosmia, or a reduction or loss of the sense of smell.

Peripheral Neuropathies

Except for the facial nerves, any damage to a nerve not in the CNS may lead to loss of motor or sensory function. The *peripheral neuropathies*

TABLE 6.2
Cranial Nerves and Their Functions

Cranial nerve	Name	Function
I	Olfactory	Smell
II	Optic	Central vision
III	Oculomotor	Ocular/pupillary motility
IV	Trochlear	Ocular/pupillary motility
V	Trigeminal	Facial sensation, corneal reflex
VI	Abducens	Ocular/pupillary motility
VII	Facial	Facial movements
VIII	Auditory/vestibular	Hearing, balance
IX	Glossopharyngeal	Swallowing
X	Vagus	Swallowing
XI	Spinal accessory	Head, shoulder movement
XII	Hypoglossal	Tongue control

section of the *ICD–9* does not involve all forms of peripheral neuropathy, but it does seem to include those that involve the nerve roots and plexus, movements of the upper and lower limbs, and neuropathological symptoms caused by hereditary, inflammatory, toxic, and unknown causes. The classification depends on the part of the body that is involved, reflecting involvement of the peripheral nerves in that area. In addition to loss of sensory or motor function, neuropathies may lead to parathesias, such as tingling sensations and pain. They are identified through neurological examination and electromyography (EMG), which measures conduction velocities in the nerves. Many neuropathies reflect an underlying progressive disease process (e.g., Guillain–Barré syndrome), so identifying the nature and cause of the neuropathy is essential (Pryse-Phillips & Murray, 1986).

Other Neuromuscular Disorders

Many neuromuscular disorders exist, some of which are covered in other parts of the overall classification of *other disorders of the CNS* (e.g., ALS, leukodystrophy). In the *other neuromuscular disorders* section, disorders of the neuromuscular junction (e.g., myasthenia gravis) and muscle (e.g., muscular dystrophy) are included.

Myasthenia Gravis

Myasthenia gravis is an autoimmune disorder (as is MS) associated with a defect in the neurotransmitter receptor for acetylcholine. It occurs most frequently in women in their 30s and men in their 50s. The disorder is characterized by weakness and fatigue in musculature across the body, with prominent ocular, facial, and truncal symptoms. Vision becomes blurred, speech is difficult, and postural control is gradually lost. As with MS, symptoms progress but fluctuate over time. Treatments, such as steroids, help slow the progression and severity of the disease.

Muscular Dystrophy

Muscular dystrophy is a class of disorders that affects children and adults. In children the two most common forms are Duchenne's and Becker's dystrophy. Both forms are associated with progressive loss of function that is apparent when a child begins to walk. These disorders are genetically determined, progressive, and by middle childhood result in an inability to walk. Mental deficiency is common. The weakness usually extends to basic respiratory functions, resulting in death in the late teens. Intervention is oriented toward enhancement of quality of life (Menkes, 1995).

In contrast, myotonic dystrophy affects adults. This involves disease of distal muscles, especially in the face. A patient usually maintains walking ability but finds speech and swallowing difficult. Myotonic dystrophy is a genetic disorder associated with problems in other organ systems, mental deficiency, and behavioral difficulties (Fisher, 1994).

CONCLUSION

The authors of this chapter are clinical neuropsychologists. As such, when asked to write a chapter on diseases of the nervous system, we accepted with eagerness but without much awareness of how brain-related disorders are classified in the *ICD–9*. We were dismayed to realize that disorders commonly under the purview of a clinical neuropsychologist, especially vascular disease (stroke) and traumatic brain injury, were not covered in this part of the *ICD–9*. This made our task rather difficult and led us into topics, such as peripheral neuropathies, that require a working knowledge for differentiated diagnosis, but in which our specific expertise is not often needed. It is essential to know about disorders involving, for example, the cranial nerves and peripheral nerves because of their impact on a diagnostic evaluation and the development of an intervention plan. Other disorders, such as dementia and epilepsy, require the clinical neuropsychologist in diagnostic evaluations and multiple components of intervention.

The key for a successful interface with the health care system is a thorough understanding of the CNS and its disorders. Such an understanding extends far beyond this section of the *ICD–9* and is vital for participation in the care and treatment of people with disorders of the nervous system. As such, clinical neuropsychologists require expertise that extends beyond the administration and interpretation of a neuropsychological test battery. Division 40 of the American Psychological Association (Clinical Neuropsychology) and other professional organizations (e.g., the National Academy of Neuropsychology, the International Society of Neuropsychology) have collaborated on the development of guidelines for training in clinical neuropsychology that include specific predoctoral and postdoctoral experiences (Hannay et al., 1998). The only defining credential for a clinical neuropsychologist, however, is board certification from the American Board of Clinical Neuropsychology, American Board of Professional Psychology.

Other health care professionals, such as those who provide nonpharmacological intervention for pain, interact with people who have nervous system disorders. However, generic forms of assessment and intervention are also essential. The identification of a nervous system disorder is potentially devastating. Many disorders, such as MS, are associated with a high rate of affective disorders; management problems may be associated with other disorders such as dementia. Psychologists in the health care system need to address these difficulties.

Finally, habilitation and quality of life are important issues. Psychologists must be prepared to work with other delivery systems designed to habilitate individuals with nervous system disorders. These systems include public schools—both regular and special education, rehabilitation centers, and specialized care facilities such as nursing homes. These examples make it clear that providing services to people with nervous system disorders extends far beyond traditional diagnostic evaluations associated with these types of disorders.

REFERENCES

Absher, J. R., & Cummings, J. L. (1994). Cognitive and noncognitive aspects of dementia syndromes: An overview. In A. Burns & R. Levy (Eds.), *Dementia* (pp. 59–76). London: Chapman & Hall.

Adams, R. D., Victor, M., & Ropper, A. H. (1997). Degenerative diseases of the nervous system. In R. D. Adams, M. Victor, & A. H. Ropper (Eds.), *Principles of neurology* (6th ed.). New York: McGraw-Hill.

Altshuler, L. L., Devinsky, O., Post, R. M., & Theodore, W. (1990). Depression, anxiety, and temporal lobe epilepsy. Laterality of focus and symptoms. *Archives of Neurology, 47,* 284–288.

American Psychiatric Association. (1994). *Diagnostic and statistical manual of mental disorders* (4th ed.). Washington, DC: Author.

Anderson, V. A., & Taylor, H. G. (2000). Meningitis. In K. O. Yeates, M. D. Ris, & H. G. Taylor (Eds.), *Pediatric neuropsychology: Research, theory, and practice* (pp. 117–148). New York: Guilford Press.

Brun, A., & Gustafson, L. (1998). Frontal lobe degeneration of the non-Alzheimer's type and dementia in motor neuron disease. In W. R. Markesbery (Ed.), *Neuropathology of dementing disorders* (pp. 158–169). New York: Arnold.

Caine, E. D. (1981). Pseudodementia. Current concepts and future directions. *Archives of General Psychiatry, 38,* 1359–1364.

Cummings, J. L., & Benson, D. F. (1992). *Dementia: A clinical approach.* Boston: Butterworth-Heinemann.

Davis, L. E. (1994). Central nervous system infection. In W. J. Weimer & C. G. Goetz (Eds.), *Neurology for the non-neurologist* (3rd ed., pp. 145–170). Philadelphia: Lippincott.

Dreifuss, F. E. (1996). Epileptic syndromes. In J. C. Sakellares & S. Berent (Eds.), *Psychological disturbances in epilepsy* (pp. 3–11). Boston: Butterworth-Heinemann.

Engel, J., Jr., & Pedley, T. A. (1997). Introduction: What is epilepsy? In J. Engel, Jr. & T. A. Pedley (Eds.), *Epilepsy: A comprehensive textbook* (pp. 1–7). Philadelphia: Lippincott–Raven.

Evans, D. A., Funkenstein, H. H., & Albert, M. S. (1989). Prevalance of Alzhei-mer's disease in a community population of older persons: Higher than pre-viously reported. *Journal of the American Medical Association, 262,* 2551–2556.

Fisher, M. (1994). Peripheral neuropathy. In W. J. Weimer & C. G. Goetz (Eds.), *Neurology for the non-neurologist* (3rd ed., pp. 154–170). Philadelphia: Lippin-cott.

Frisoni, G. B., Laakso, M. P., Beltramello, A., Geroldi, C., Bianchetti, A., Soini-nen, H., et al. (1999). Hippocampal and entorhinal cortex atrophy in fronto-temporal dementia and Alzheimer's disease. *Neurology, 52,* 91–100.

Geldmacher, D. S., & Whitehouse, P. J. (1997). Differential diagnosis of Alzhei-mer's disease. *Neurology, 48*(Suppl. 6), 2–9.

Giordani, B. J. (1996). Intellectual and cognitive disturbances in epileptic patients. In J. C. Sackellares & S. Berent (Eds.), *Psychological disturbances in epilepsy* (pp. 45–98). Boston: Butterworth-Heinemann.

Glosser, G., Cole, L. C., French, J. A., Saykin, A. J., & Sperling, M. R. (1997). Predictors of intellectual performance in adults with intractable temporal lobe epilepsy. *Journal of the International Neuropsychological Society, 3,* 252–259.

Hachinski, V. C., Cliff, L. D., Zilhka, E., Du Boulay, G. H., McAllister, V. L., Marshall, J., et al. (1975). Cerebral blood flow in dementia. *Archives of Neu-rology, 32,* 632–637.

Hannay, H. J., Bieliauskas, L. A., Crosson, B. Hammeke, Hamsher, K. deS., & Koffler, S. (1998). Proceedings of the Houston Conference on Specialty Ed-ucation and Training in Clinical Neuropsychology [Special Issue]. *Archives of Clinical Neuropsychology, 13,* 2.

Harasty, J. A., Halliday, G. M., Kril, J. J., & Code, C. (1999). Specific temporo-parietal gyral atrophy reflects the pattern of language dissolution in Alzhei-mer's disease. *Brain, 122*(Pt. 4), 675–686.

Hauser, W. A. (1997). Incidence and prevalence. In J. Engel, Jr., & T. A. Pedley (Eds.), *Epilepsy: A comprehensive textbook* (pp. 47–57). Philadelphia: Lippincott–Raven.

Hermann, B. P., Seidenberg, M., & Davies, K. (1997). Neuropsychological char-acteristics of the syndrome of mesial temporal lobe epilepsy. *Archives of Neu-rology, 54,* 369–376.

Hermann, B. P., Seidenberg, M., Haltiner, A., & Wyler, A. R. (1992). Adequacy of language and verbal memory performance in unilateral temporal lobe ep-ilepsy. *Cortex, 38,* 423–433.

Hermann, B. P., & Whitman, S. (1989). Psychosocial predictors of interictal de-pression. *Journal of Epilepsy, 2,* 231–237.

Hermann, B. P., Wyler, A. R., & Richey, E. T. (1988). Wisconsin Card Sorting Test performance in patients with complex partial seizures of temporal-lobe origin. *Journal of Clinical and Experimental Neuropsychology, 10,* 467–476.

Hickie, I., Scott, E., Wilhelm, K., & Brodaty, H. (1997). Subcortical hyperin-tensities on magnetic resonance imaging in patients with severe depression —A longitudinal evaluation. *Biological Psychiatry, 42,* 367–374.

Hogancamp, W. E., Rodriguez, M., & Weinshenker, B. G. (1997). The epidemiology of multiple sclerosis. *Mayo Clinic Proceedings, 72,* 871–878.

Holmes, G. L (1991). Do seizures cause brain damage? *Epilepsia,* (Suppl. 5), 14–28.

International League Against Epilepsy Commission Report. (1997). The epidemiology of the epilepsies: Future decisions. *Epilepsia, 38,* 614–618.

Jack, C. R., Petersen, R. C., Xu, Y. C., O'Brien, P. C., Smith, G. E., Ivnik, R. J., et al. (1999). Prediction of AD with MRI-based hippocampal volume in mild cognitive impairment. *Neurology, 52,* 1397–1403.

Jorm, A. F., Korten, A. E., & Henderson, A. S. (1987). The prevalence of dementia: A quantitative integration of the literature. *Acta Psychiatrica Scandinavica, 76,* 465–479.

Jost, B. C., & Grossberg, G. T. (1995). The natural history of Alzheimer's disease: A brain bank study. *Journal of the American Geriatrics Society, 43,* 1248–1255.

Kanemoto K., Kawasaki J., & Mori, E. (1999). Violence and epilepsy: A close relation between violence and postictal psychosis. *Epilepsia, 40,* 107–109.

Kase, C. S. (1991). Epidemiology of multi-infarct dementia. *Alzheimer's Disease and Associated Disorders, 5*(2), 71–76.

Leroy, I., & Michalon, M. (1998). Treatment of the psychiatric manifestations of Huntington's disease: A review of the literature. *Canadian Journal of Psychiatry, 43,* 933–940.

Linn, R. T., Wolf, P. A., Bachman, D. L., Knoefel, J. E., Cobb, J. L., Belanger, A. J., et al. (1995). The "preclinical phase" of probable Alzheimer's disease. A 13-year prospective study of the Framingham cohort. *Archives of Neurology, 52,* 485–490.

Lishman, W. A. (1998). *Organic psychiatry* (3rd ed.). Malden, MA: Blackwell Science.

Mahler, M. E. (1992). Behavioral manifestations associated with multiple sclerosis. *Psychiatric Clinics of North America, 15,* 427–438.

Markesbery, W. R. (1998). Vascular dementia. In W. R. Markesbery (Ed.), *Neuropathology of dementing disorders* (pp. 293–311). New York: Arnold.

Mendez, M. F. (1996). Disorders of mood and affect in epilepsy. In J. C. Sackellares & S. Berent (Eds.), *Psychological disturbances in epilepsy* (pp. 125–141). Boston: Butterworth-Heinemann.

Mendez, M. F., Selwood, A., Mastri, A. R., & Frey, W. H. 2d. (1993). Pick's disease versus Alzheimer's disease: A comparison of clinical characteristics. *Neurology, 43,* 289–292.

Menkes, J. H. (1995). *Textbook of child neurology* (5th ed.). Baltimore: Williams & Wilkins.

Neary, D. (1997). Frontotemporal degeneration, Pick disease, and corticobasal degeneration. One entity or 3? *Archives of Neurology, 54,* 1425–1427.

Neary, D., Snowden, J. S., Gustafson, L., Passant, U., Stuss, D., Black, S., et al.

(1998). Frontotemporal lobar degeneration: A consensus on clinical diagnostic criteria. *Neurology, 51,* 1546–1554.

Nelson, K. B., & Ellenberg, J. H. (1986). Antecedents of cerebral palsy: Multivariate analysis of risk. *New England Journal of Medicine, 315,* 81–86.

Palsson, S., & Skoog, I. (1997). The epidemiology of affective disorders in the elderly: A review. *International Clinical Psychopharmacology, 12*(Suppl. 7), 3–13.

Price, D. L., Thinakaran, G., Borchelt, D. R., Martin, L., Crain, B. J., Sisodia, S. S., et al. (1998). Neuropathology of Alzheimer's disease and animal models. In W. R. Markesbery (Ed.), *Neuropathology of dementing disorders* (pp. 121–141). New York: Arnold.

Pryse-Phillips, W., & Murray, T. J. (1986). *Essential neurology* (3rd ed.). New York: Elsevier.

Raczynski, J., Bradley, L., & Leviton, L. (Eds.). (in press). *Handbook of clinical health psychology: Volume 2. Disorders of behavior and health.* Washington, DC: American Psychological Association.

Rao, S. M. (1995). Neuropsychology of multiple sclerosis. *Current Opinion in Neurology, 8,* 216–220.

Rao, S. M., Leo, G. J., Bernardin, L., & Unverzagt, F. (1991). Cognitive dysfunction in multiple sclerosis. I. Frequency, patterns, and prediction. *Neurology, 41,* 685–691.

Rifkin, B., & Dravet, C. (1997). Generalized convulsive seizures. In J. Engel, Jr. & T. A. Pedley (Eds.), *Epilepsy: A comprehensive textbook* (pp. 567–576). Philadelphia: Lippincott–Raven.

Rodgers, J., & Bland, R. (1996). Psychiatric manifestations of multiple sclerosis: A review. *Canadian Journal of Psychiatry, 41,* 441–445.

Roman, G. C., Tatemichi, T. K., Erkinjuntti, T., Cummings, J. L., Masdeu, J. C., Garcia, J. H., et al. (1993). Vascular dementia: Diagnostic criteria for research studies. Report of the NINDS–AIREN International Workshop. *Neurology, 43,* 250–260.

Sachdev, P. (1998). Schizophrenia-like psychosis and epilepsy: The status of the association. *American Journal of Psychiatry, 155,* 325–336.

Salloway, S., Malloy, P., Kohn, R., Gillard, E., Duffy, J., Rogg, J., et al. (1996). MRI and neuropsychological differences in early- and late-life-onset geriatric depression. *Neurology, 46,* 1567–1574.

Salmon, D. P., Galasko, D., Hansen, L. A., Masliah, E., Butters, N., Thal, L. J., et al. (1996). Neuropsychological deficits associated with diffuse Lewy body disease. *Brain and Cognition, 31,* 148–165.

Saper, J. R. (1994). Chronic headache: Current concepts in diagnosis and treatment. In W. J. Weimer & C. G. Goetz (Eds.), *Neurology for the non-neurologist* (3rd ed., pp. 68–83). Philadelphia: Lippincott.

Snowden, J. (1997). Epidemiologic questions on mood disorders in old age. *Clinical Neurosciences, 4,* 3–7.

Stefan, H., & Snead, O. C. (1997). Absence seizures. In J. Engel, Jr. & T. A.

Pedley (Eds.), *Epilepsy: A comprehensive textbook* (pp. 579–588). Philadelphia: Lippincott–Raven.

Stewart, J. M., Houser, O. W., Baker, H. L., Jr., O'Brien, P. C., & Rodriguez, M. (1987). Magnetic resonance imaging and clinical relationships in multiple sclerosis. *Mayo Clinic Proceedings, 62,* 174–184.

Tandon, R., & DeQuardo, J. R. (1994). Psychoses and epilepsy. In J. C. Sackellares & S. Berent (Eds.), *Psychological disturbances in epilepsy* (pp. 171–190). Boston: Butterworth-Heinemann.

Tatemichi, T. K. (1995). Dementia. In J. Bogousslavsky & L. Caplan (Eds.), *Stroke syndromes* (pp. 169–181). Cambridge, England: Cambridge University Press.

Taylor, H. G., Mills, E. L., Ciampi, A., DuBerger, R., Watters, G. V., Gold, R., et al. (1990). The sequelae of *Haemophilus influenzae* meningitis in school-age children. *New England Journal of Medicine, 223,* 1657–1663.

White, L. R., Cartwright, W. S., Cornoni-Huntley, J., & Brock, D. B. (1986). Geriatric epidemiology. *Annual Review of Gerontology and Geriatrics, 6,* 215–311.

Williamson, P. D., & Engel, J., Jr. (1997). Complex partial seizures. In J. Engel, Jr. & T. A. Pedley (Eds.), *Epilepsy: A comprehensive textbook* (pp. 557–566). Philadelphia: Lippincott–Raven.

World Health Organization. (1991). *The international classification of diseases, ninth revision.* Salt Lake City, UT: Med-Index Publications.

Wragg, R. E., & Jeste, D. V. (1989). Overview of depression and psychosis in Alzheimer's disease. *American Journal of Psychiatry, 146,* 577–587.

7

DISEASES OF THE CIRCULATORY SYSTEM

SONIA SUCHDAY, DANA L. TUCKER, AND DAVID S. KRANTZ

Chronic circulatory diseases are a major public health problem and the leading cause of death in Western countries (Higgins & Luepker, 1988; National Heart, Lung, and Blood Institute [NHLBI], 1994). Diseases of the circulatory system include acute rheumatic fever; chronic rheumatic heart diseases; hypertension; ischemic heart disease; pulmonary heart disease; cerebrovascular disease; diseases of the arteries, arterioles, and capillaries; and diseases of the veins, lymphatic vessels, and lymph nodes. Circulatory disorders have received increased attention in the public health arena because of their far-reaching impact and also because the occurrence of these disorders is influenced by lifestyles and health habits. The limited success of some public health interventions to promote healthier lifestyles has led public health educators to turn to psychology for a better understanding of the principles of behavior change (Ewart, 1991). Despite the difficulties of implementing health behavior changes, lifestyle changes—when coupled with medical interventions—have led to a decline in circulatory disease-related mortality over the past 30 years (Higgins & Luepker, 1988; NHLBI, 1994). The circulatory diseases that have been most extensively studied by behavioral scientists—coronary heart disease (CHD) and essential hypertension (EH)—are discussed in detail in this chapter. Raynaud's disease, stroke, and rheumatic fever, which have been less subject to behavioral science research, are considered briefly.

CHD

Pathophysiology

Atherosclerosis, characterized by the accumulation of fatty substances in the arteries, develops unnoticed over many years (Krantz & Lundgren, 1998). Some of the end-stage consequences of clinically important atherosclerosis can be angina pectoris, myocardial ischemia, myocardial infarction, and sudden cardiac death. *Myocardial ischemia* is caused by insufficient coronary blood flow for the heart's metabolic demands. *Angina pectoris* refers to chest pain that sometimes accompanies myocardial ischemia. Frequent occurrences of myocardial ischemia may lead to disturbances of the cardiac rhythm, which in turn can result in sudden cardiac death. Prolonged or severe ischemia, a complete blockage in the coronary arteries surrounding the heart, or both, caused by rupture of unstable arterial plaque, results in myocardial infarction or a heart attack.

Standard Risk Factors

As noted previously, behavioral factors and lifestyle variables play an important role in predisposing individuals to developing heart disease. The risk of developing CHD increases synergistically with the presence of multiple risk factors (Higgins & Luepker, 1988), which may be classified as either modifiable or nonmodifiable. Risk factors that cannot be modified include chronological age and gender; risk of CHD increases with age, but at younger ages (especially before the age of female menopause) men are more susceptible to CHD than are women. A family history of CHD is another risk factor that cannot be modified (Glueck et al., 1975; Nicolosi & Schaefer, 1992).

Potentially modifiable risk factors include EH, cigarette smoking, high blood levels of low-density lipoprotein cholesterol and low levels of high-density lipoprotein, diabetes, obesity, a sedentary lifestyle, and psychosocial risk factors (Ockene & Ockene, 1992). Often patients have several of the aforementioned risk factors, which increases the risk of developing CHD.

Psychosocial Risk Factors

Assessment of risk involves not only an assessment of standard risk factors but also of a set of psychosocial risk factors that increase vulnerability to the development of CHD. Psychosocial factors include individual predispositions, such as responsivity to stress, and characteristics of the social and physical environment. Psychosocial factors that have been demonstrated to increase CHD risk include responses to chronic and acute stressors in the environment, individual responses to stressors, and psychological traits.

Chronic and Acute Stress

Evidence has suggested that chronic and acute stress play an important role in the development and prognosis of CHD. *Chronic stress* refers to "subacute stress" that may result from the presence of life stressors for months or years (Rozanski, Blumenthal, & Kaplan, 1999). Three aspects of chronic stress that may affect the development of CHD are work-related stress, stress from the home and family, and environmental stress caused by low socioeconomic status.

Acute stressors, in contrast to chronic stressors, describe provocations in the environment that require the individual to expend considerable effort to cope. Among susceptible individuals with preexisting atherosclerosis, acute physical and mental stress can trigger acute clinical cardiovascular events such as myocardial infarction and sudden cardiac death (Muller, Tofler, & Stone, 1989). In this regard, recent laboratory-based evidence has indicated that acute behavioral stress can trigger episodes of myocardial ischemia in daily life and in the laboratory (Deanfield et al., 1984; Gottdiener et al., 1994).

Acute Stress and Anger

Recent research evidence suggests that in addition to acute stress, intense negative emotions such as anger may trigger myocardial infarction and sudden death among individuals with preexisting disease (Muller, 1999; Willich, 1999). Using a retrospective interview format, it has been demonstrated that intense episodes of anger may trigger myocardial infarction among patients with an underlying pathological condition (Mittleman et al., 1995). In this study the "toxic" anger episodes occurred within 2 hours before the onset of the myocardial infarction. The frequency with which episodes of anger triggered myocardial infarction was substantially lower among regular users of aspirin (Mittleman et al., 1995). An explanation proposed by Mittleman and his colleagues is that myocardial infarction in response to anger is triggered by the disruption of atherosclerotic plaque by hemodynamic responses to anger provocation; aspirin may interfere with this plaque disruption.

Acute Stress and Sudden Cardiac Death

Acute stress may also serve as a trigger for sudden cardiac death. Early studies in this area focused on the occurrence of a catastrophic event (e.g., death of a spouse) during the 24 hours preceding the cardiac event (Cottington, Matthews, Talbott, & Kuller, 1980). However, these early observations were subject to the alternative explanation of biased recall of stressful events by friends and family. In addition to personal traumas, the occurrence of natural and human-made disasters is also associated with an increased rate of myocardial infarction and sudden cardiac death. For example, after the Iraqi missile strikes in Israel in 1991, the residents of Tel Aviv and the surrounding areas had an increased incidence of myocardial infarction and sudden cardiac death (Meisel et al., 1991). Natural disasters such as earthquakes are also associated with an increase in cardiac-related mortality. On the day of the Northridge, California, earthquake in 1994, there was a significant increase in sudden cardiac death compared with deaths during the preceding week (Leor, Poole, & Kloner, 1996).

Stress and Cardiac Ischemia

Even regular daily life stress—both physical and mental—may trigger transient episodes of myocardial ischemia among cardiac patients. The continuous monitoring of the electrocardiogram during daily life to detect the presence of ischemia has made it possible to assess the link among daily life stressors, emotions, and myocardial ischemia. Myocardial ischemia seems to occur most frequently during intense physical activities and stressful mental activities, including during intense episodes of anger (Gabbay et al., 1996; Gullette et al., 1997). Among mental stress tasks, provocation of anger is a particularly potent trigger of ischemia (Ironson et al., 1992).

Moreover, evidence also suggests that ischemia in the laboratory induced by physical and mental stress can predict future cardiac events among patients with CHD (Jain, Burg, Soufer, & Zaret, 1995; Jiang et al., 1996; Krantz, Kop, Santiago, & Gottdiener, 1996). Usually, these studies are conducted by monitoring ischemia in the laboratory while participants are engaged in acutely stressful tasks such as anger recall, giving a speech to people in the laboratory, and a math task involving serial 7 subtractions. Ischemia induced by mental stress is usually painless and occurs at lower heart rates than, but at similar blood pressure elevations as, exercise-induced ischemia.

Occupational Stress

Research on occupational stress has focused on the impact of various occupations on the development of CHD and on identifying specific job characteristics that have a toxic impact on cardiovascular health. Evidence has indicated that men and women may be differentially affected by occupational stress. Among men, low control and high job demands (Karasek & Theorell, 1990) predict cardiovascular disease and mortality. Among women, the impact of job characteristics vary depending on work and family demands. Women who have low-control jobs (e.g., clerical positions), unsupportive bosses, and high family demands (e.g., children) seem more likely to develop CHD (Haynes & Feinleib, 1980).

Scarcity of Resources

Lack of social and economic resources, insufficient social support, and social isolation can increase the risk of developing CHD (Shumaker & Cjakowski, 1994). *Social support* refers to aid received from social ties and other sources in the community and can refer to different dimensions of aid including instrumental, emotional, and informational (Cohen & Wills, 1985). Social support might affect the development of heart disease at two levels. First, it can serve as a moderator or buffer between stress and the development of disease (Krantz & Lundgren, 1998). Second, it may serve a more practical function such as providing access to available resources or increasing medical compliance (Krantz & Lundgren, 1998).

In developed countries, socioeconomic status is inversely correlated with risk of CHD morbidity, cardiovascular disease mortality, and all-cause mortality (Kaplan & Keil, 1993). This relationship is graded and applies to all levels of the gradient (Adler, Boyce, Chesney, & Cohen, 1994).

Social factors, including social support and socioeconomic status, seem to synergistically affect the development of CHD. In one study, participants with low economic resources (reflected in a low education level) and insufficient social resources (i.e., more social isolation) had a decreased chance of survival after the first myocardial infarction (Ruberman, Weinblatt, Goldberg, & Chaudhary, 1984). In other studies of patients who had cardiac disease, unmarried male and female patients without a close confidant had an increased risk of mortality over a 5-year period (Case, Moss, Case, McDermott, & Eberly, 1992; Williams et al., 1992).

The impact of low economic resources on the development of CHD is sometimes exacerbated by personality variables such as hostility. For example, it has been suggested that hostile individuals frequently corrode the social support in their environment (Smith, 1992). It remains unclear whether low social support gives rise to high hostility or vice versa. However, the presence of high hostility and low social resources are likely to contribute to a poor prognosis for CHD (Smith, 1992).

Insights From Animal Studies

Animal models have been used to assess the impact of chronic stress on the development of coronary atherosclerosis. Specifically, cynomolgus monkeys, whose disease pathology and social behavior are analogous to the disease pathology and social behavior of humans, have been studied (Manuck, Kaplan, & Matthews, 1986). A series of studies has shown that in dominant male monkeys, unstable social conditions induced by introducing new monkeys into already established hierarchies led to the development of extensive coronary atherosclerosis (Manuck et al., 1986). Among female monkeys, the opposite pattern was observed, and submissive females rather than dominant females developed atherosclerosis (Kaplan, Adams, Clarkson, & Koritnick, 1984). Hence, male and female monkeys have increased susceptibility to CHD after exposure to chronic environmental stress. However, the effects of social stress are affected by an animal's dominance or submissiveness, with different patterns evident in male and female animals.

In summary, evidence has suggested that environmental or social stress interacts with individual characteristics to affect the development of CHD.

Individual Characteristics and Personality Variables

Individual characteristics, such as personality variables or traits, can have an influence on health, perhaps by determining individuals' responses to provocations occurring during daily life. Personality may also affect health by influencing the health behavior choices that people make. For example, hostile individuals are more likely to engage in harmful health habits such as smoking and drinking alcohol (Smith, 1992). Although personality may develop from an interaction of genetic predispositions and the environment, over time personality variables may also determine the type of environments in which individuals choose to live and work.

Type A Behavior Pattern

The *Type A behavior pattern* is defined by a constellation of behaviors, including competitiveness, anger, hostility, impatience, and certain speech stylistics (emphatic and vigorous speech), that are assessed by a structured interview developed by Friedman and Rosenman (1974). Although initial evidence supported the validity of the Type A behavior pattern as a risk factor for CHD (Haynes, Feinleib, & Kannel, 1980; Jenkins, Rosenman, & Zyzanski, 1974), subsequent studies did not find evidence linking this pattern with CHD (Ragland & Brand, 1988; Shekelle, Hulley, & Neaton, 1985). These inconsistent findings led to a focus on assessing and identifying which, if any, of the Type A component characteristics are critical, or "toxic."

Anger and Cynical Hostility

A reanalysis by Matthews and colleagues (Matthews, Glass, Rosenman, & Bortner, 1977) of data from the Western Collaborative Group

Study (Rosenman et al., 1975), in which the Type A behavior pattern was positively correlated with the development of CHD, showed that potential for hostility, vigorous speech characteristics, and frequently reported anger and irritation were the most consistent predictors of the occurrence of new CHD incidence over an 8.5-year period. Subsequently, a self-report measure of hostility derived from the Minnesota Multiphasic Personality Inventory—the Cooke Medley Hostility Inventory (Cook & Medley, 1954) —was found to also be related to incidence of CHD as well as to all-cause mortality (Barefoot, Dahlstrom, & Williams, 1983).

Cynical hostility is operationally defined as an attitude of suspiciousness and cynicism, comprising a negative worldview that considers others' behaviors as frustrating and provocative (Smith, 1992). Hostile people also demonstrate a high degree of self-absorption because of their inability to trust other people (Williams, 1987). Although the preponderance of studies have implicated hostility in the development and exacerbation of CHD, findings from both prospective and cross-sectional studies have been mixed, with methodological problems noted in some studies (Rozanski et al., 1999; Smith, 1992). Evidence also has suggested that hostility might influence the development of CHD through its correlation with the tendency to adopt unhealthy lifestyles (i.e., the standard risk factors), as well as with enhanced autonomic responses to stress (Rozanski et al., 1999). In general, hostile individuals also tend to corrode the social support of friends and family because of their negative and suspicious behaviors (Smith, 1992).

Clinical Depression

Clinical depression is defined by symptoms of affective distress; decreased interest in life; changes in appetite and sleep patterns; difficulty concentrating; fatigue and exhaustion; dysphoria; and, in extreme cases, hopelessness, helplessness, and suicidal ideation. Evidence has suggested that depression may be experienced by one of five patients who have had a heart attack (Frasure-Smith, Lesperance, & Talajic, 1993). The presence of a major depressive episode in patients with CHD is associated with poor psychosocial rehabilitation and increased cardiac morbidity (Carney, Rich, & Jaffe, 1995). In addition to clinical depression, subclinical depression is itself equally common among these patients (Hance, Carney, Freedland, & Skala, 1996) and is also associated with increased risk for cardiac events (Anda et al., 1993). Hopelessness and fatigue have received particular attention as being particularly toxic manifestations of depression (Rozanski et al., 1999). Hopelessness has also been shown to independently predict the development of CHD (Everson et al., 1996).

Appels and colleagues (Kop, Appels, Mendes de Leon, de Swart, & Bar, 1994) have identified a syndrome of fatigue or exhaustion called *vital exhaustion,* which overlaps with some of the symptoms of depression. Vital exhaustion is a syndrome characterized by excessive tiredness and low energy, increased irritability, and a sense of demoralization (Appels, 1997). It has been suggested that hypoactivity of the hypothalamic–pituitary–adrenal axis associated with chronic stress and sleep disturbances may be responsible for some of these symptoms (Nicolson & van Diest, 2000). Research has indicated that vital exhaustion is also predictive of the development or worsening of cardiovascular disease. Furthermore, the predictive value of fatigue or exhaustion cannot be explained solely by the effects of illness on mood or energy levels (Kop et al., 1994).

The possible physiological and behavioral mechanisms responsible for the association among depression, fatigue, and CHD include more unhealthy lifestyles, hypercortisolemia, impaired platelet function, reduced heart rate variability, and impaired vagal tone in patients who are depressed (Rozanski et al., 1999). Studies are currently underway to assess whether risk of death and recurrence in patients who have had a heart attack can be decreased by treating symptoms of depression with either cognitive–behavioral or pharmacological means.

Responsiveness (Reactivity) to Acute Stress

It has been known for some time that individual physiological reactions to stress vary widely. More recent research has suggested that cardiovascular and endocrine responses to stress may be implicated as a risk factor or risk marker for the development of CHD, high blood pressure, or both (Krantz & Manuck, 1984; Rozanski et al., 1999). *Cardiovascular reactivity* refers to changes in heart rate, blood pressure, or other cardiovascular measures in response to stress, as opposed to the sole measurement of resting levels of cardiovascular function. Some individuals display large changes in cardiac measures in response to laboratory stressors or challenging tasks, whereas others show very little or no change at all.

Keys et al. (1971) monitored a group of initially healthy men for 23 years and found that the magnitude of their diastolic blood pressure reactions to a cold pressor test (immersing the hand in cold water) was a good predictor of subsequent cardiac events; in fact, it was a better predictor than many of the standard risk factors. However, a later attempt to replicate these findings was unsuccessful (Coresh, Klag, Mead, Liang, & Whelton, 1992). Other studies have shown that heightened reactivity to laboratory stressors is associated with presence of ischemia induced by mental stress and with ischemia during daily life (Blumenthal, Jiang, et al., 1995), with the occurrence of future cardiac events in patients with coronary disease (Krantz et al., 1996), or both.

Risk Factor Summary

In general, the risk factors for the development of CHD include individual characteristics such as race and sex, and personality characteristics such as hostility and acute and chronic stress. A combination of individual and environmental stress variables may exponentially increase the risk of developing CHD. For example, heart disease risk is greatest among African American men (race and sex variables) residing in high-stress, poor neighborhoods (environmental variables) (Polednak, 1998). Because multiple risk factors, ranging from multiple environmental stressors to individuals' responses to these stressors, are implicated in the development and exacerbation of CHD, multiple treatment options are also available that target various aspects of the illness. Treatments range from medical and surgical treatments targeting the pathophysiological mechanisms of the diseases to interventions aimed at changing lifestyles to decrease the impact of acute and chronic environmental stress.

Treatment

Treatment options for CHD include drug treatments and medical and surgical revascularization procedures (e.g., coronary angioplasty, coronary artery bypass graft [CABG]) that restore blood flow to cardiac tissue. Behavioral treatments (e.g., cognitive–behavior therapy, meditation techniques) have also been used as an adjunct to medical and surgical approaches.

A comprehensive cardiac rehabilitation program consists of multiple components aimed at reducing the standard risk factors and reducing psychological and physiological distress associated with having CHD, thereby preventing reoccurrence of disease and preventing death (Dafoe & Huston, 1997). In general, cardiac rehabilitation programs aim to optimize the patient's functioning in all areas of life. In recent years, rehabilitation programs have combined physical rehabilitation with psychoeducational components and have demonstrated success in ameliorating cardiac morbidity and mortality and in modifying proximal risk factors (e.g., blood pressure, cholesterol, body weight, smoking, amount of exercise, eating behaviors; Dusseldorp, van Elderen, Maes, Meulman, & Kraaij, 1999). The various components of cardiac rehabilitation programs are described in the following section, although cardiac rehabilitation programs may differ in their emphasis on the various components.

Medical and Surgical Treatment Options

Many medical and surgical options are available for treating patients with CHD, ranging from bypass surgery to pharmacological treatments with anti-ischemic drugs (e.g., beta blockers, calcium-channel blockers), nitrates, lipid-lowering drugs, and aspirin. Usually, pharmacological treatments improve cardiac function and blood flow and lower blood pressure. Other common interventions include CABG and percutaneous transluminal angiography (PTCA), the latter of which is a nonsurgical invasive procedure conducted by cardiologists. Both CABG and PTCA are revascularization procedures used to restore blood flow to areas in the heart that were previously deprived of blood. Research results have indicated that CABG improves functional status and ameliorates anginal pain among patients with CHD (Coronary Artery Surgery Study [CASS] Principal Investigators, 1984). Whereas both PTCA and CABG are effective revascularization procedures, CABG tended to provide a more favorable long-term health outcome (Hara et al., 1996), and patients who have had PTCA generally required repeat surgery and had a higher probability of cardiac events compared to patients who had CABG (Carrie et al., 1997).

Exercise and Behavioral Components of Cardiac Rehabilitation

Important components of an effective cardiac rehabilitation program include aerobic exercise training, smoking cessation, weight loss, and diet modification. Successful implementation of each of these components requires significant lifestyle changes and attention to behavioral issues such as promoting behavior change and treatment adherence and maintenance. Treatment approaches that incorporate social factors may be more successful in producing long-term lifestyle changes (Ewart, 1991). Each component of the rehabilitation process affects another, and they are synergistic in their impact on health. For example, regular aerobic exercise also leads to weight loss, lowering of blood pressure, and lower cholesterol. Moreover, individuals who are physically fit have lower hemodynamic and neuroendocrine responses to behavioral stress (Blumenthal & Wei, 1993).

A review of rehabilitation programs revealed that participation in programs that include an exercise component are associated with a decline in total mortality and cardiac-related mortality and a repeat infarction among patients with a history of myocardial infarction (O'Connor et al., 1989). However, the beneficial effects of standard cardiac rehabilitation programs on mortality are often relatively small and require very large samples to demonstrate.

Despite the multiple studies that have been conducted on the efficacy of cardiac rehabilitation programs in prolonging life and preventing recurrence of cardiac events, the impact of rehabilitation programs has been difficult to assess because rehabilitation programs are multimodal, making it difficult to determine specifically which components account for the programs' effects; in addition, large sample sizes are needed to reveal effects. Meta-analytical studies have amassed sufficient sample sizes to report reductions in mortality among patients assigned to rehabilitation programs in comparison with control groups (Fletcher, 1996).

Frequently, social relationships also play a significant role in determining which lifestyle changes the patient is able to make. Sometimes a spouse or partner in a healthy relationship may impede important lifestyle changes that the patient seeks to make because that lifestyle change interferes with important daily life interactions between the patient and the person (Ewart, 1991). Whereas improvements in participation of patients in exercise programs can be increased with increases in social support, maintenance of behavioral changes is difficult (Blumenthal & Emery, 1988). Maintenance of behavioral changes is aided by integration of lifestyle change into everyday functioning.

Psychosocial Treatment Approaches

A recent meta-analysis by Linden, Stossel, and Maurice (1996) observed that psychosocial approaches to treating CHD lead to an amelioration of psychological distress (mainly depression and anxiety) and physiological endpoints such as blood pressure, heart rate, and serum cholesterol levels. About half of the 23 studies used in this meta-analysis reported an increased rate of mortality and morbidity among patients with CHD not receiving psychosocial follow-up in the first 2 years after a coronary event. Interestingly, positive effects of psychosocial interventions were observed among interventions that differed on quantitative and qualitative dimensions (Linden et al., 1996), suggesting that any psychosocial intervention was better than no psychosocial intervention. Typical psychosocial interventions include interventions aimed at modifying specific psychosocial components such as the Type A behavior pattern, hostility, stress, social support, and lifestyles. Table 7.1 presents a more recent review of psychological intervention trials for CHD as reviewed by Rozanski et al. (1999).

Modifying hostility and Type A behavior. Cardiac rehabilitation programs aimed at modifying the Type A behavior pattern are based on the premise that Type A and hostility behaviors are significant risk factors for disease (Blumenthal & Emery, 1988). Evidence from an ambitious large-scale project—the Recurrent Coronary Prevention Project—has demonstrated that modification of hostility and Type A behavior pattern leads to a significantly lower rate of recurrence of myocardial infarction among patients who participated in the behavior modification group compared with patients receiving the usual cardiac care (Friedman et al., 1986). However, findings from other studies of the impact of Type A behavior modification on CHD recurrence are inconsistent (Allan & Scheidt, 1996). In light of the negative evidence regarding Type A behavior, it is possible that the positive findings obtained by Friedman et al. (1986) may reflect a generalized effect of psychosocial interventions in reducing distress and increas-

TABLE 7.1
Impact of Psychosocial Intervention Trials on Cardiac Events

Study	Type of patients	No. of patients Control group	No. of patients Intervention group	Follow-up (years)	Type of intervention	Reduction in psychosocial factors?	Cardiac end points	Reduction in events?
Rahe et al., 1979	s/p MI	22	39	3	Group education and support	Yes (for overwork, time urgency)	CD/MI	Yes ($p < .05$)
Stern et al., 1983	s/p MI	20	35	1	Group counseling	Yes (for depression)	ACM; MI	No
Friedman et al., 1984	s/p MI	270	592	4.5	TABP modification and group counseling	Yes (for TABP)	CD/MI	Yes ($p < .005$)
Horlick et al., 1984	s/p MI	33	83	0.5	Hospital-based education program (6 wk)	No (for anxiety, depression)	CD	No
Patel et al., 1985	≥2 RF	93	99	4	Breathing, muscle relaxation, meditation	Not assessed	Angina, MI-1, CD	Small sample
Maeland et al., 1987	s/p MI	1,115	137	3.3	Educational program	No (for anxiety, depression)	ACM	No*
Dixhoorn et al., 1987	s/p MI	46	42	2.5	Physiological relaxation (e.g., breathing, exercise)	Not assessed	CD, MI, UAP, CABG	Yes ($p = .05$)
Frasure-Smith et al., 1989	s/p MI	229	232	5	Home-based nursing intervention	Yes (for GHQ)	MI, CD	Yes ($p = .04$ for MI†)

Study	Population	Intervention n	Control n	Length of intervention (yr)	Intervention	Psychological benefit	Endpoints	Cardiac benefit
Thompson et al., 1990	60 s/p MI	30	30	0.5	Group counseling	Yes (for anxiety and depression)	ACM	Small sample
Neison et al., 1994	s/p MI	20	20	0.5	Physiological stress management (e.g., breathing)	Yes (for ability to handle "stress")	MI, ACM	Small sample
Burell et al., 1994	s/p MI	24	23	2	TABP modification	Yes (for TABP)	CD/MI	Small sample
Jones et al., 1996	s/p MI	1,155	1,159	1	Group sessions (7 wk) for stress management and counseling	No (for anxiety, depression)	ACM, CD	No
Blumenthal et al., 1997	CAD with EII	40	33	5	Structured group instruction with multiple stress reduction components	Yes (for GHQ scores and hostility)	CD, MI, PTCA, CABG	Yes RR = 0.26 (0.07–0.90)
Frasure-Smith et al., 1997	s/p MI	684	692	1	Home-based nursing intervention to decrease transient increase in distress	No (for anxiety, depression)	CD	No

Note. RF = risk factors; EII = exercise-induced ischemia; TABP = type A behavior pattern; MI-1 = undocumented myocardial infarction; UAP = unstable angina pectoris. From "Impact of Psychological Factors on the Pathogenesis of Cardiovascular Disease and Implications for Therapy," by A. Rozanski, J. A. Blumenthal, and J. R. Kaplan, 1999, *Circulation, 99*, p. 2209. Copyright 1999 by American Heart Association. Adapted with permission of the author and Lippincott, Williams, & Wilkins.
*At 6 months of follow-up, short-term lower anxiety and death rate (*p* < 0.05) in intervention group.
†At 1 year (length of intervention), *p* = 0.07 for CD reduction in intervention group.

ing social support among patients. In addition, interventions that modify Type A behavior may be successful at improving cardiac health because they are successful at specifically modifying the toxic component—hostility—of the Type A behavior pattern. A recent report of modification of the hostility and time urgency components of the Type A behavior pattern revealed a significant decline in ischemic episodes among patients with CHD (Friedman et al., 1996).

Other stress management and psychosocial interventions. In addition to interventions designed to decrease hostility and Type A behavior pattern, other types of stress management and social support interventions have also been proved successful in reducing CHD-related morbidity and mortality (Blumenthal et al., 1997). For example, a cost-effective alternative to modifying Type A behavior is monitoring and modifying life stress and symptoms of distress. This approach was used in the Ischemic Heart Disease Life Stress Monitoring Program (Frasure-Smith & Prince, 1987, 1989). Results indicated that male patients who participated in the program experienced fewer recurrences of myocardial infarction and had decreased mortality following their participation in the program. However, other evidence showed that monitoring and modifying psychological distress combined with supportive interventions actually had a negative impact on the prognosis for women and no impact on prognosis for men (Frasure-Smith et al., 1997). Another study by Jones and West (1996), which included a group stress management and counseling component, showed no decrease in CHD-related morbidity and mortality. Blumenthal et al. (1997) reported that participation in a group stress management program reduced the occurrence of myocardial ischemia, lowered serum cholesterol, reduced self-reported distress, and lowered the risk of subsequent cardiac events over a year.

One possible reason for the inconsistent findings could be that different interventions are focusing on modifying different aspects of stress and social support and are using different methods of stress management. Standardizing stress management interventions and identifying the key components of a successful intervention may help assess their effectiveness in reducing the risk of CHD. The NHLBI has sponsored an ongoing intervention trial, the Enhanced Recovery in Coronary Heart Disease trial, in which patients with clinical depression who are deemed to be socially isolated are assigned to either a stress reduction program or to a usual care group. This study is still in progress at the time of writing this chapter.

Effects of lifestyle changes on cardiac morbidity and mortality. The Lifestyle Heart Trial (Ornish et al., 1990) was an intensive program to modify risk factors in a small group of patients with CHD. Components of this trial included a low-fat vegetarian diet, stress management (using yoga) and group support, smoking cessation, and a program of moderate exercise training. Results demonstrated a regression (reduction) in the extent of stenosis or blockage in program participants compared to a usual care control group. Although this study is impressive in its effectiveness with behavioral interventions, it may be criticized because it is difficult to assess the value of each of the treatment components (such as diet vs. stress management). Furthermore, applicability of the sample to the general population is an issue. The participants were selected for their high levels of motivation and compliance, so it could be argued that most patients would lack the desire or will power to follow through on such an intensive and a demanding intervention. Nevertheless, this study demonstrates clinically important and significant improvements in CHD status as a result of intensive lifestyle modification.

A review of interventions to modify lifestyles (Rozanski et al., 1999) reported both negative and positive findings from studies in this area and concluded that efficacy of interventions designed to promote lifestyle changes may be enhanced by adding a component modifying the psychosocial aspects of patients' functioning. Additionally, interventions tailored to meet the needs of the individual patient and specific aspects of patient functioning are suggested to more likely be effective in promoting rehabilitation rather than interventions that are geared toward a group of patients and that intervene on multiple risk factors (Rozanski et al., 1999).

Treatment Summary

It is clear from the previous discussion that diverse treatment options, including medical, psychosocial, and behavioral approaches, can have a beneficial impact on the prevention and prognosis of CHD. Medical interventions include surgical options such as CABG and PTCA and pharmacological treatment with anti-ischemic drugs, nitrates, and lipid-lowering drugs. Promising psychosocial interventions include interventions focusing on exercise, lifestyle changes, modification of individual characteristics such as the Type A behavior pattern and hostility, depression, and social support. Further research is needed to identify the specific components of psychosocial treatment approaches that are most effective for patients with cardiac disease.

EH

EH, or *high blood pressure*, is a condition in which blood pressure remains chronically elevated in the absence of a clearly definable physiological etiology. The underlying physiological mechanisms for EH differ during the earlier and later stages and also with the severity of the disease. Individuals with borderline EH, early stages of EH, or both experience an increased output of blood from the heart but no evidence of increased resistance to blood flow in the body's vasculature. However, in older individuals with established EH, the opposite pattern is observed—the output from the heart is normal, but resistance to blood flow is elevated (Julius & Esler, 1975).

High blood pressure increases the risk for stroke, heart attack, and kidney and vascular diseases but, because the disorder is asymptomatic, EH can sometimes remain undiagnosed or untreated for long periods. Risk factors for development of hypertension include age, a family history of hypertension, borderline high blood pressure, excessive dietary intake of salt in susceptible individuals, and obesity. Thus, like CHD, EH is a multifaceted disorder with many psychosocial factors involved with genetic and biological factors in its etiology and progression.

Effects of the Environment

Race

The impact of the environment on the development of EH is shown by the high rate of EH among African Americans (Ng-Mak, 1999). As a group, African Americans in the United States have high rates of EH, and the rates of disease are higher among African Americans with a lower socioeconomic status than among those with a higher status (Harburg et al., 1973; Young, Waller, & Kahana, 1991). The specific roles of genes and the environment are controversial, and it is unclear whether the observed differences are a function of genes or a result of the different experiences of people belonging to each of the two cultures (Anderson & Armstead, 1995). One intriguing avenue of research evidence showed that darker skin color is positively correlated with higher blood pressure (Gleiberman, Harburg, Frone, Russell, & Cooper, 1995). This association could be a function of environmental discrimination caused by skin color or a marker of genetic origins that increase susceptibility to elevated blood pressure (Gleiberman et al., 1995). Further research needs to closely examine the specifics of the ethnic experience from the genetic influences on the development of disease by studying the details of disease development within each of the groups (African Americans, Latinos, Asian Americans, and White Americans) in addition to the experience of ethnicity in the culture (Anderson & Armstead, 1995).

Stress and Behavioral Factors

Environmental factors that affect the development of EH include neighborhoods where people live and places where people work (Cobb & Rose, 1973). A recent review of the environmental influences on health (e.g., Wandersman & Nation, 1998) defined multiple levels at which the environment influences health, including structural levels or neighborhood indexes such as poverty, neighborhood disorder or physical decay and social incivility (e.g., the number of abandoned buildings in the neighborhood), and environmental level or transient environmental stressors such as noise (Fleming, Baum, Davidson, Rectanus, & McArdle, 1987). Environmental influences on health at each of these levels are moderated by personal, social, and community resources (Wandersman & Nation, 1998).

Living in areas with *high residential stress*, which is defined by high residential mobility, a high crime rate, a high population density, a low socioeconomic status, and high marital break-up rates, is associated with higher blood pressure levels, especially among African Americans (Harburg et al., 1973). Social factors, which include experiences with social incivility such as racism, may contribute further to elevated blood pressure levels among African Americans (Krieger & Sidney, 1996). In addition to environments in which people live, work environments can also contribute to elevated blood pressure levels (Cobb & Rose, 1973). As noted previously in the section on CHD, characteristics that contribute to increased stress at work include high demands accompanied by low levels of autonomy (Karasek & Theorell, 1990). The impact of environmental factors can be further complicated by social interactions (Ewart, 1991). For example, health habits of spouses are usually similar, therefore it can be difficult for one spouse to make health-related habit changes without support from the other spouse.

The impact of environmental stress may also be exacerbated by behavioral factors and lifestyles such as exercise and diet. For example, high salt intake during periods of elevated stress can lead to blood pressure elevations (Haythornthwaite, Pratley, & Anderson, 1992). In addition, among people residing in high-stress inner-city areas, engaging in health practices such as walking in the neighborhood may not be an option.

Personality

A wide range of personality characteristics have been reported to be associated with EH, including suppressed hostility or anger (Dunbar, 1943; Harburg et al., 1973), neuroticism and anxiety (Markovitz, Matthews, Kannel, Cobb, & D'Agostino, 1993), and submissiveness (Esler et al., 1977). These traits may play a causal role in the development of EH (Jern, 1987), may reflect a tendency to seek medical care and therefore be diagnosed with EH (Irvine, Garner, Olmsted, & Logan, 1989), or may reflect an underlying physiological mechanism such as central and sympathetic nervous system arousal (Weder & Julius, 1987) that could itself predispose a person to develop hypertension. It is also possible that psychological traits such as hostility and suppressed anger influence the development of EH through indirect pathways such as the erosion of social support (Smith, 1992).

Salt Intake

Excessive salt intake may cause the kidneys to increase the volume of blood and result in a subsequent increase in blood pressure. Additionally, the impact of salt intake can be compounded by environmental factors. For example, salt intake is low among underdeveloped tribal societies, as is the prevalence of EH (Page, Danion, & Moellering, 1970). Acculturation to Western societies leads to an increase in salt intake and an increase in the prevalence of EH. Environmental factors also influence salt intake by changes in eating patterns during periods of high stress, which may lead to blood pressure elevations. Research has suggested that the combination of excessive salt intake and stress related to medical school examinations produce chronic blood pressure elevations (Haythornthwaite et al., 1992). Animal studies have corroborated these results by demonstrating that prolonged exposure to salt and stress can induce EH in previously normotensive animals, and the effects of salt intake and environmental stress are synergistic in elevating blood pressure (Anderson, 1984).

Obesity

Obesity is also a risk factor for EH, one that is independent of dietary variables such as sodium intake (Reisin et al., 1978). Obesity increases the risk of EH among men and women (Stamler, Stamler, Riedlinger, Algera, & Roberts, 1978). In addition to obesity, the pattern of fat distribution also increases the risk of hypertension. Specifically, the risk of developing EH is greater in people with abdominal obesity (Wiensier et al., 1985). Although the precise reasons or mechanisms by which obesity leads to an increased risk for EH remain unclear (Shapiro, 1983), controlling obesity is obviously an important behavioral management strategy in controlling high blood pressure.

Nonpharmacological Treatment

Because lifestyle variables seem to play an important role in the development and maintenance of high blood pressure, treatment of this disorder should include a combination of behavioral lifestyle changes and pharmacological approaches. Accordingly, a comprehensive set of lifestyle changes including weight loss, reduced salt intake, and exercise are initially recommended for patients with hypertension. Pharmacological interventions are sought if these approaches are not successful in normalizing blood pressure (Joint National Committee on Detection, Evaluation, and Treatment of High Blood Pressure [JNC], 1993). Typically, many of the drugs used to treat CHD are also used to treat high blood pressure; these include beta-blockers, calcium-channel blockers, and angiotensin converting enzyme inhibitors. Additionally, new classes and variations of drugs are continuously being developed to treat EH.

Weight Loss and Dietary Salt Restriction

Weight loss and decreased salt intake have a beneficial impact on blood pressure. Even a moderate weight loss can have a beneficial impact (Dubbert, 1995). In addition, decreasing dietary intake of salt can also lead to reductions in blood pressure, although the effects tend to be smaller than those gained from weight loss (Dubbert, 1995).

Exercise Training

Although meta-analyses have suggested that exercise lowers blood pressure (Kelley & McClellan, 1994), the impact of exercise on treating hypertension seems to be confounded by the benefits of weight loss. According to existing evidence, it is unclear whether blood pressure is lowered as a function of exercise or the accompanying weight loss. Randomized controlled trials are needed to assess whether exercise, weight loss, or exercise and weight loss combined is actually responsible for lowering blood pressure (Blumenthal, Thyrum, Gullette, Sherwood, & Waugh, 1995). The mechanism by which exercise and weight loss may affect blood pressure is also unclear and needs to be determined (Blumenthal, Thyrum, et al., 1995).

Reduced Alcohol Intake

Reduction of alcohol among those who drink heavily may play a beneficial role in treating hypertension (Dubbert, 1995). Generally, reducing alcoholic intake to no more than two drinks a day has become standard recommended practice in EH treatment (JNC, 1993).

Stress Management, Biofeedback, and Other Cognitive Interventions

Because stress seems to interact with biological variables in the development of EH, it makes intuitive sense that techniques to reduce the experience of stress would be effective in treating or preventing hypertension. Unfortunately, despite early reports to the contrary, use of stress management, other cognitive treatments, or a combination have not been proved effective in recent studies. Specifically, techniques such as biofeedback and relaxation training have been effective only in achieving small but statistically significant decreases in blood pressure (reviewed by Dubbert, 1995). Disappointingly, other meta-analytic reviews (Dubbert, 1995; Eisenberg et al., 1993) have reported that these modest gains are likely a function of nonspecific factors or result from repeated blood pressure measurements and may not necessarily be explained by the specific behavioral or stress management treatment being implemented.

Nevertheless, given that the small blood pressure reductions obtained as a result of cognitive treatments occur with minimal side effects, they may be still useful as adjuncts to drug treatments for EH rather than as alternates to drug treatments. Additionally, behavioral interventions may sometimes assist in enhancing adherence to medical regimens by helping patients cope with the side effects of pharmacological treatments. The possible secondary or adjunctive role of stress management interventions warrants further study.

Adherence to Antihypertensive Medication Regimens

The chronic, asymptomatic course of EH and the range of possible side effects associated with pharmacological treatment of EH (including impotence, depression, and fatigue) make adherence to treatment particularly problematic. Information about compliance is often hard to assess because it cannot be accurately measured. Typically used methods to measure compliance, including patient self-reports, physician reports, and pill count, are frequently inaccurate. Research has suggested that compliance differs based on treatment settings, with family practices reporting greater compliance than hospital clinics (Dunbar-Jacob, Wyer, & Dunning, 1991). Factors such as increasing provider and family support, simplifying the regimen, and behavioral self-management strategies may be effective in increasing compliance. Involvement of family members, especially significant others, may also help in obtaining accurate information about adherence to medical regimens.

Summary

Environmental and lifestyle variables, such as stress, diet, exercise, and obesity, seem to interact with genetic predispositions in the development of hypertension. Pharmacological treatment of EH, which is highly effective, is often complicated by side effects of the medications and consequent nonadherence to medical regimens. Behavioral treatments to reduce obesity, increase exercise, and reduce salt intake in conjunction with pharmacological treatments have been effective in reducing EH. However, results for various cognitive–behavioral stress management approaches have been less encouraging. Given the importance of treatment compliance in ensuring the effectiveness of drug and lifestyle treatments for high blood pressure, the development of improvements in the ability to enhance long-term adherence warrant considerable attention from behavioral scientists.

RAYNAUD'S DISEASE

Symptomatology

The primary manifestations of Raynaud's phenomenon and Raynaud's disease consist of vasospasms of the fingers or toes provoked by exposure to cold or emotional stress (Freedman & Ianni, 1983). These attacks generally last for several minutes and often involve three phases of color change in the affected extremities. The three phases that may occur in some vasospasm attacks include (a) whitening (blanching) of the affected areas, indicating powerful vasoconstriction; (b) blue coloration (cyanosis) of the affected areas, which is thought to be caused by pooling of blood in venules caused by the vasoconstriction; (c) and red coloration (hyperemia) of the affected areas, resulting from a rebound vasodilation. Although the most commonly affected areas are the fingers and toes, the vasospasm attacks may also affect the tips of the nose and ears (Marcus, Weiner, Suzuki, & Kwan, 1991).

Raynaud's symptomatology is usually separated into primary Raynaud's disease and secondary Raynaud's phenomenon. Secondary Raynaud's phenomenon usually has more severe symptoms and is caused by an underlying organic disease, with the patient often having an organic change in the arteries, arterioles, or surrounding connective tissue. Primary Raynaud's disease is a type of digital vasospasm that has no recognized underlying cause (Sedlacek & Taub, 1996).

Pathophysiology and Mechanisms

Raynaud (1888) hypothesized that overactivity of the sympathetic nervous system produces peripheral vasoconstriction. A theory presented by Lewis (1929) suggested that a "local fault" causes small peripheral blood vessels to be hypersensitive to local cooling. Freedman and colleagues (see Freedman, 1995, for a review) performed numerous studies and concluded that the pathophysiology of Raynaud's disease and the vasospastic attacks do not result from sympathetic nervous system hyperactivity. Along the lines of the Lewis theory, Freedman et al. stated that the peripheral vascular α_2-adrenergic receptors are likely to be hypersensitive to cooling. They further suggested that peripheral vascular adrenoreceptors are hypersensitive in the basal state. The consequence of these hypersensitivities is that normal catecholamine elevations produced by emotional stress or reflex cooling can trigger vasospasm attacks. Of note, these explanations of pathophysiology apply only to the study of Raynaud's disease and not necessarily to secondary Raynaud's phenomenon. The mechanisms for secondary Raynaud's phenomenon are less well understood, and behavioral and medical treatments for the phenomenon have met with less success (Belch et al., 1983; Freedman, Ianni, & Wenig, 1983).

Treatment Options

Numerous treatments for Raynaud's disease have been developed and implemented with varying amounts of success. Among the behavioral or psychological treatments, thermal biofeedback treatments have received the most support (Freedman, 1995; Sedlacek & Taub, 1996). Other non-behavioral or nonpsychological methods of treatments have included pharmacological management (reviewed by Coffman, 1991) and surgery (Marcus et al., 1991; Porter, Rivers, Anderson, & Baur, 1981).

Temperature Biofeedback

As noted previously, of the psychological and behavioral treatments for Raynaud's disease, temperature biofeedback treatment seems to be the most efficacious. The actual conducting of temperature biofeedback sessions generally follows these guidelines: Each participant receives 10 to 20 biweekly training sessions (Freedman, 1995; Sedlacek & Taub, 1996). Each session consists of 10 minutes of adaptation, a 16-minute resting baseline, and 16 minutes of feedback or instructions. Patients listen through headphones to a sinusoidal tone with a pitch that varies inversely with the temperature of the middle finger of their dominant hand. The volume of the tone gradually increases from zero at the beginning of each feedback period to avoid startling the patient. Patients are told to increase the temperature of their fingers as much as possible using the tone as a guide. They are also instructed to practice raising their digital skin temperature at home without any tapes or feedback instruments.

Patients given temperature biofeedback training in several group outcome studies achieved symptom frequency reductions ranging from 67% to 92% and reported that these reductions were maintained through 2- and 3-year follow-ups (for a review, see Freedman, 1995). Addition of other procedures such as progressive relaxation therapy or autogenic training (self-suggestion of warm imagery) provided no added benefits or produced less symptom frequency reduction. For comparison, pharmacological studies using nifedipine, a calcium-channel blocker, decreased frequency, duration, and intensity of vasospasm attacks in about two thirds of patients with primary and secondary Raynaud's (Coffman, 1991). Other reports have suggested less impressive numbers of 15% to 40% reductions of vasospasm attacks (Marcus et al., 1991; Rodehoffer, Rommer, Wigley, & Smith, 1983; Sarkozi, Bookman, & Mahon, 1986; Smith & McKendry, 1982); in addition, consideration should be given to side effects of medication such as lightheadedness, headache, edema, and constipation.

A different pharmacological treatment approach using ketanserin, a serotonergic S_2 antagonist, reduced vasospasm attack frequency 34%, compared with a placebo rate of 18% (Coffman et al., 1989). The patients had no changes in severity or duration of vasospasm attacks. Surgical sympathectomies have been used to abolish reflex sympathetic activity, but vascular tone generally recovers within a few weeks (Robertson & Smithwick, 1951). Furthermore, conducting a sympathectomy is a questionable approach given the findings that vasospasm attacks can occur in patients with primary and secondary Raynaud's despite a digital nerve blockade (Freedman, 1995).

Summary

A review of the research suggests that up to 80% to 90% of people with Raynaud's disease can obtain substantial relief through the use of 10 to 20 sessions of temperature biofeedback over 3 to 6 months, with minimal follow-up sessions in the following years. Sedlacek and Taub (1996) recommended the use of inexpensive home biofeedback equipment to aid in the training and monitoring of skin temperature self-regulation. Findings have suggested that without proper training and equipment, the therapeutic results of temperature biofeedback sessions are minimized. In these cases, results are similar to those from other forms of therapy, such as autogenic training, progressive muscle relaxation, verbal relaxation training, or pharmacotherapy, with 10% to 40% of patients showing a clinical improvement (i.e., at least a 50% reduction in vasospasm attacks). Temperature biofeedback seems to be a valuable treatment for Raynaud's disease in view of the cost, side effects, and limited success of other methods of treatment.

STROKE

Stroke is the third leading cause of death in the United States and the leading cause of disability among adults. About 550,000 people have strokes each year, and 150,000 of them die from the strokes within the year. There are currently about 3 million stroke survivors with varying degrees of neurological impairment. Brain infarctions account for about 75% of strokes, and intracerebral or subarachnoid hemorrhages account for about 15%. Stroke frequency increases with age, the incidence of stroke doubling every decade after age 55. Men experience more strokes than women, and African Americans experience strokes more frequently than White people. Mortality from stroke has declined in recent years because of a combination of better acute care (such as the wider use of thrombolytics), reduced stroke severity, and earlier and more accurate diagnosis.

Important modifiable risk factors include EH, cigarette smoking, atrial fibrillation, left ventricular hypertrophy, and transient ischemic attacks (Post-Stroke Rehabilitation Guideline Panel [PSRGP], 1995). Thus, the role of behavior modification for risk factors such as hypertension and smoking is important for stroke as well.

Impairments, Disabilities, and Rehabilitation

Hemiparesis, a muscular weakness or partial paralysis affecting one side of the body, is experienced by 75% of patients who have had strokes. Acute neurological impairments frequently resolve spontaneously, but in 25% to 50% of individuals who survived a stroke, persisting disabilities lead to partial or total dependence in activities of daily living (PSRGP, 1995). The World Health Organization (WHO) conceptualized the disablement associated with stroke in terms of impairment (organ dysfunction), disability (difficulty with tasks), and handicap (social disadvantage). The rehabilitation process is oriented as a restorative and learning process that hastens and maximizes recovery from stroke by treating the resulting impairments, disabilities, and handicaps (PSRGP, 1995). The overarching goal of the rehabilitation process is to help the patient regain freedom of movement and functional independence and to reintegrate as much as possible into community life.

Health Psychology and Stroke Prevention

Health psychologists may contribute to assessment, intervention, and consultation for stroke in numerous ways. Primary prevention and reducing the possible impact of risk factors is of key importance, with the risk factors of EH and smoking being ideal candidates for targeting by health psychologists. Behavioral treatments relevant to EH were addressed previously in the chapter. Current recommendations regarding smoking cessation programs typically involve both behavioral or counseling treatments combined with pharmacological approaches such as nicotine transdermal patches or other forms of nicotine replacement (Agency for Health Care Policy and Research, 1997).

Clinical Practice Guidelines

A role for health psychologists in stroke rehabilitation is suggested as part of an interdisciplinary team in recent clinical practice guidelines from the U.S. Department of Health and Human Services (PSRGP, 1995). Various assessment tools can be used by health psychologists at different stages in the rehabilitation process, from the beginning of screening for rehabilitation and choice of initial setting to the endpoint of transition to the community. Abilities to perform activities of daily living should be assessed. Some of the further important facets of continuing assessment throughout the rehabilitation include management of cognitive and perceptual deficits and diagnosis and treatment of depression.

The treatment of depression is also of major importance, not only for reduction of the patients' sadness and distress but also because depression is often accompanied by cognitive difficulties that cloud post-stroke assessments and can hinder patients' progress in the rehabilitation process. The U.S. Department of Health and Human Services clinical practice guidelines call for further research into (a) the development and validation of standardized tests for use in monitoring post-stroke rehabilitation, (b) research determining the characteristics of patients most likely to benefit from rehabilitation interventions, and (c) the most effective specific behavioral treatments or combinations of treatments to reduce impairments and improve function (PSRGP, 1995).

Studies have examined the post-stroke pharmacological treatment of depression (Andersen, 1997; Miyai & Reding, 1998; Palomaeki et al., 1999). In these studies, attention has been paid not only to the direct treatment of depression but also to the side effect profiles of the medication, particularly as they relate to the overall process of rehabilitation. In general, the studies found that among the classes of antidepressants, the newer selective serotonergic agents are as effective as other classes but are associated with better functional recovery and a more favorable side effect profile (Miyai & Reding, 1998). Among other types of treatment for depression, Lincoln and colleagues reported on a pilot study of cognitive–behavioral therapy for stroke patients with depression that resulted in decreased depression levels but noted no significant benefits in functional abilities (Lincoln, Flannaghan, Sutcliffe, & Rother, 1997).

Researchers have studied other treatment methods to deal with various aspects of post-stroke rehabilitation. Rimmer and Hedman (1998) presented a health promotion strategy for rehabilitation constructed with three major components of exercise, nutrition, and health behavior. Taub, Crago, and Uswatte (1998) developed a therapy that is based on neuroscience and behavioral psychology directed towards increasing use of an affected upper extremity via restriction of the contralateral arm and training the affected arm, which they called *constraint-induced movement therapy*. Another researcher, who has studied motor aspects of stroke rehabilitation, approached the process of rehabilitation from the standpoint of motor learning principles (Majsak, 1997). Techniques for dealing with memory impairments have included memory notebook training to lessen reliance on caregivers for day-to-day information (Squires, Hunkin, & Parkin, 1997). Occupational therapy was found to decrease the number of readmissions to hospital during the rehabilitation period following stroke (Corr & Bayer, 1996).

Summary

Treatment for stroke needs to address patients' needs at the level of regaining functional independence in daily living skills and reintegration into social and community networks, as well as making long-term lifestyle changes in diet, exercise, and smoking-related behaviors to prevent future strokes. Given the multidimensional services needed by those who have had strokes, a multidisciplinary team of rehabilitation specialists may be required, with behavioral medicine specialists playing a prominent role.

ACUTE RHEUMATIC FEVER

Symptomatology and Medical Guidelines

Acute rheumatic fever is an inflammatory sequela to streptococcal infection. Occurring most commonly among individuals ages 5 to 17 and equally across genders, the risk factors for this health problem include crowding, poor medical care, poor nutrition, and positive family history of the disease. Treatment for the disease includes initially eliminating the streptococcal infection by penicillin or an equally effective antibiotic and then treating with bed rest, salicylates, and adrenal corticosteroids. Recommendations for prophylaxis include penicillin injections, with a shift to oral penicillin once the patient reaches a sufficient maturity level (Reitman, 1998).

Health Psychology Contributions to Treatment and Prevention

Very little research has been done on the role of behavior in rheumatic fever. However, possible areas in which health psychology contributes to the understanding of the disease include identification and eradication of the modifiable risk factors (e.g., crowding, poor medical care, poor nutrition). From intervention and consultation points of view, assessing patients' understanding of the prophylaxis program and implementing behavioral programs to ensure compliance are ways in which health psychologists may contribute to understanding and treating the disease. This field does not currently have an extensive research literature.

CONCLUSION

Development of circulatory disorders may be considered a function of biological predispositions, environmental context, and individual characteristics. Whereas it is hard to modify biological predispositions, the environment and individual characteristics are more amenable to modification. An impressive body of research demonstrates that modifying psychosocial and individual characteristics may have a beneficial impact on the development and exacerbation of circulatory disorders, especially CHD and EH. A significant role for behavioral scientists has emerged in the treatment and prevention of CHD and hypertension, particularly with respect to the role of lifestyle modification (e.g., dietary changes, exercise, smoking cessation, weight management). In addition, psychosocial and stress management treatments have also been shown to be clinically important in the treatment of patients with CHD.

The evidence for the role of individual and psychosocial characteristics in the development of circulatory disorders other than CHD and EH (e.g., stroke) is more sparse; however, it is likely that leading a healthy lifestyle in relatively low-stress environments may have a beneficial impact on the prevention and exacerbation of circulatory disorders other than CHD and EH as well.

REFERENCES

Adler, N. E., Boyce, T., Chesney, M. A., & Cohen, S. (1994). Socioeconomic status and health: The challenge of the gradient. *American Psychologist, 49*, 15–24.

Agency for Health Care Policy and Research. (1997). *Clinical practice guidelines on smoking cessation, No. 18*. Rockville, MD: Agency for Health Care Policy and Research.

Allan, R., & Scheidt, S. (1996). Empirical basis for cardiac psychology. In R. Allan & S. Scheidt (Eds.), *Heart and mind: The practice of cardiac psychology* (pp. 63–124). Washington, DC: American Psychological Association.

Anda, R., Williamson, D., Jones, D., Macera, C. A., Eaker, E. D., Glasman, A., et al. (1993). Depressed affect, hopelessness, and the risk of ischemic heart disease in a cohort of U.S. adults. *Epidemiology, 4*, 285–294.

Andersen, G. (1997). Post-stroke depression and pathological crying: Clinical aspects and new pharmacological approaches. *Aphasiology, 11*, 651–664.

Anderson, D. E. (1984). Interactions of stress, salt, and blood pressure. *Annual Review of Physiology, 46*, 143–153.

Anderson, N. B., & Armstead, C. A. (1995). Toward understanding the association of socioeconomic status and health: New challenges for the biopsychosocial approach. *Psychosomatic Medicine, 57*, 213–225.

Appels, A. (1997). Why do imminent victims of a cardiac event feel so tired? *International Journal of Clinical Practice, 51*(7), 447–450.

Barefoot, J. C., Dahlstrom, W. G., & Williams, R. B. (1983). Hostility, CHD incidence and total mortality: A 25-year follow-up study of 255 physicians. *Psychosomatic Medicine, 45,* 59–63.

Belch, J. J., Newman, P., Drury, J. K., McKenzie, F., Capell, H., Leiberman, P., et al. (1983). Intermittent epoprostenol (prostacyclin) infusion in patients with Raynaud's syndrome. *Lancet, 1,* 313–315.

Blumenthal, J. A., & Emery, C. F. (1988). Rehabilitation of patients following myocardial infarction. *Journal of Consulting and Clinical Psychology, 56,* 374–381.

Blumenthal, J. A., Jiang, W., Reese, J., Frid, D. J., Waugh, R., Morris, J. J., et al. (1995). Mental stress-induced ischemia in the laboratory and ambulatory ischemia during daily life: Association and hemodynamic features. *Circulation, 92,* 2102–2108.

Blumenthal, J. A., Thyrum, E. T., Gullette, E. D., Sherwood, A., & Waugh, R. (1995). Do exercise and weight loss reduce blood pressure in patients with mild hypertension? *North Carolina Medical Journal, 56,* 92–95.

Blumenthal, J. A., & Wei, J. (1993). Psychobehavioral treatment in cardiac rehabilitation. *Cardiology Clinics, 11,* 323–331.

Blumenthal, J. A., Wei, J., Babyak, M., Krantz, D. S., Frid, D., Coleman, R. E., et al. (1997). Stress management and exercise training in cardiac patients with myocardial ischemia: Effects on prognosis and on markers of myocardial ischemia. *Archives of Internal Medicine, 157,* 2213–2223.

Carney, R. M., Rich, M. W., & Jaffe, A. S. (1995). Depression as a risk factor for cardiac events in established coronary heart disease: A review of possible mechanisms. *Annals of Behavioral Medicine, 17,* 142–149.

Carrie, D., Elbaz, M., Puel, J., Fourcade, J., Karouny, E., Fournial, G., et al. (1997). Five-year outcome after coronary angioplasty versus bypass surgery in multivessel coronary artery disease: Results from the French Monocentric Study. *Circulation, 96*(Suppl.), 11–16.

Case, R. B., Moss, A. J., Case, N., McDermott, M., & Eberly, S. (1992). Living alone after myocardial infarction. *Journal of the American Medical Association, 267,* 515–519.

Cobb, S., & Rose, R. M. (1973). Hypertension, peptic ulcer, and diabetes in air traffic controllers. *Journal of the American Medical Association, 224,* 489–492.

Coffman, J. D. (1991). Raynaud's phenomenon. An update. *Hypertension, 17,* 593–602.

Coffman, J. D., Clement, D. L., Creager, M. A., Dormandy, J. A., Janssens, M. M., McKendry, R. J., et al. (1989). International study of ketanserin in Raynaud's phenomenon. *American Journal of Medicine, 87,* 264–268.

Cohen, S., & Wills, T. A. (1985). Social support and the buffering hypothesis. *Psychological Bulletin, 98,* 310–357.

Cook, W. W., & Medley, D. M. (1954). Proposed hostility and pharisaic virtue scales for the MMPI. *Journal of Applied Psychology, 38,* 414–418.

Coresh, J., Klag, M. J., Mead, L. A., Liang, K. Y., & Whelton, P. K. (1992).

Vascular reactivity in young adults and cardiovascular disease. A prospective study. *Hypertension*, *19*, 414–418.

Corr, S., & Bayer, A. (1996). Occupational therapy for stroke patients after hospital discharge: A randomized controlled trial. *Clinical Rehabilitation*, *9*, 291–296.

Cottington, E. M., Matthews, K. A., Talbott, E., & Kuller, L. H. (1980). Environmental events preceding sudden death in women. *Psychosomatic Medicine*, *42*, 567–574.

Dafoe, W., & Huston, P. (1997). Current trends in cardiac rehabilitation. *Canadian Medical Association Journal*, *156*, 527–532.

Deanfield, J. E., Shea, M., Kensett, M., Horlock, P., Wilson, R. A., de Landsheere, C. M., et al. (1984). Silent myocardial ischemia due to mental stress. *Lancet*, *2*, 1001–1005.

Dubbert, P. M. (1995). Behavioral (life style) modification in the prevention and treatment of hypertension. *Clinical Psychology Review*, *15*, 187–216.

Dunbar, H. F. (1943). *Psychosomatic diagnosis*. New York: Harper & Brothers.

Dunbar-Jacob, J., Wyer, K., & Dunning, E. J. (1991). Compliance with antihypertensive regimen: A review of the research in the 1980s. *Annals of Behavioral Medicine*, *13*, 31–39.

Dusseldorp, E., van Elderen, T., Maes, S., Meulman, J., & Kraaij, V. (1999). A meta-analysis of psychoeducational programs for coronary heart disease patients. *Health Psychology*, *18*, 506–519.

Eisenberg, D. M., Delbanco, T. L., Berkey, C. S., Kaptchuk, T. J., Kupelnick, B., Kuhl, J., et al. (1993). Cognitive behavioral techniques for hypertension: Are they effective? *Annals of Internal Medicine*, *188*, 964–972.

Esler, M., Julius, S., Zweifler, A., Randall, O., Harburg, E., Gardiner, H., et al. (1977). Mild high renin essential hypertension. Neurogenic human hypertension? *New England Journal of Medicine*, *296*, 405–411.

Everson, S. A., Goldberg, D. E., Kaplan, G. A., Cohen, R. D., Pukkala, E., Tuomilehto, J., et al. (1996). Hopelessness and risk of mortality and incidence of myocardial infarction and cancer. *Psychosomatic Medicine*, *58*, 113–121.

Ewart, C. (1991). Social action theory for a public health psychology. *American Psychologist*, *46*, 931–946.

Fleming, I., Baum, A., Davidson, L. M., Rectanus, E., & McArdle, S. (1987). Chronic stress as a factor in physiologic reactivity to challenge. *Health Psychology*, *6*, 221–237.

Fletcher, G. F. (1996). The antiatherosclerotic effect of exercise and development of an exercise prescription. *Cardiology Clinics*, *14*, 85–96.

Frasure-Smith, N., Lesperance, F., Prince, R. H., Verrier, P., Garber, R. A., Juneau, M., et al. (1997). Randomised trial of home-based psychosocial nursing intervention for patients recovering from myocardial infarction. *Lancet*, *350*, 473–479.

Frasure-Smith, N., Lesperance, F., & Talajic, M. (1993). Depression following myocardial infarction: Impact on 6-month survival. *Journal of the American Medical Association, 270,* 1819–1825.

Frasure-Smith, N., & Prince, R. (1987). The Ischemic Heart Disease Life Stress Monitoring Program. *Psychosomatic Medicine, 5,* 485–513.

Frasure-Smith, N., & Prince, R. (1989). Long-term follow-up of the Ischemic Heart Disease Life Stress Monitoring Program: Possible therapeutic mechanisms. *Psychology and Health, 1,* 273–285.

Freedman, R. R. (1995). Raynaud's disease and phenomenon. In A. J. Goreczny (Ed.), *Handbook of health and rehabilitation psychology* (pp. 117–131). New York: Plenum Press.

Freedman, R. R., & Ianni, P. (1983). Role of cold and emotional stress in Raynaud's disease and scleroderma. *British Medical Journal, 287,* 1499–1502.

Freedman, R. R., Ianni, P., & Wenig, P. (1983). Behavioral treatment of Raynaud's disease. *Journal of Consulting and Clinical Psychology, 151,* 539–549.

Friedman, M., Breall, W. S., Goodwin, M. L., Sparagon, B. J., Ghandour, G., & Fleischmann, N. (1996). Effect of type A behavioral counseling on frequency of episodes of silent myocardial ischemia in coronary patients. *American Heart Journal, 132,* 933–937.

Friedman, M., & Rosenman, R. H. (1974). *Type A behavior and your heart.* New York: Knopf.

Friedman, M., Thorese, C., Gill, J., Ulmer, D., Powell, L., Price, V., et al. (1986). Alteration of type A behavior and its effects on cardiac recurrences in post myocardial infarction patients: Summary results of the recurrent coronary prevention project. *American Heart Journal, 112,* 653–665.

Gabbay, F. H., Krantz, D. S., Kop, W. J., Hedges, S. M., Klein, J., Gottdiener, J. S., & Rozanski, A. (1996). Triggers of myocardial ischemia during daily life in patients with coronary artery disease: Physical and mental activities, anger, and smoking. *Journal of the American College of Cardiology, 27,* 585–592.

Gleiberman, L., Harburg, E., Frone, M. R., Russell, M., & Cooper, M. L. (1995). Skin colour, measures of socioeconomic status, and blood pressure among blacks in Erie County, NY. *Annals of Human Biology, 22,* 69–73.

Glueck, C. J., Fallat, R. W., Millett, F., Gartside, P., Elston, R. C., & Go, R. C. (1975). Familial hyperalphalipoproteinemia: Studies in eighteen kindreds. *Metabolism, 24,* 1243–1265.

Gottdiener, J. S., Krantz, D. S., Howell, R. H., Hecht, G. M., Klein, J., Falconer, J. J., et al. (1994). Induction of silent myocardial ischemia with mental stress testing: Relationship to the triggers of ischemia during daily life activities and to ischemic functional severity. *Journal of the American College of Cardiology, 24,* 1645–1651.

Gullette, E. C., Blumenthal, J. A., Babyak, M., Jiang, W., Waugh, R. A., Frid, D. J., et al. (1997). Effects of mental stress on myocardial ischemia during daily life. *Journal of the American Medical Association, 277,* 1521–1526.

Hance, M., Carney, R. M., Freedland, K. E., & Skala, J. (1996). Depression in patients with coronary heart disease. A 12-month follow-up. *General Hospital Psychiatry, 18,* 61–65.

Hara, K., Suma, H., Kozuma, K., Horii, T., Wanibuchi, Y., Yamaguchi, T., et al. (1996). Long-term outcome of percutaneous transluminal coronary angioplasty and coronary bypass surgery for multivessel coronary artery disease. *Japanese Circulation Journal, 60,* 940–946.

Harburg, E., Erfurt, J. C., Hauenstein, L. S., Chape, C., Schull, W. J., & Schork, M. A. (1973). Socioecological stress, suppressed hostility, skin color, and Black–White male blood pressure: Detroit. *Psychosomatic Medicine, 35,* 276–296.

Haynes, S. B., & Feinleib, M. (1980). Women, work, and coronary disease: Prospective findings from the Framingham Heart Study. *American Journal of Public Health, 700,* 133–141.

Haynes, S. B., Feinleib, M., & Kannel, W. B. (1980). The relationship of psychosocial factors to coronary heart disease in the Framingham Study. III. Eight-year incidence of coronary heart disease. *American Journal of Epidemiology, 3,* 37–58.

Haythornthwaite, J. A., Pratley, R. E., & Anderson, D. E. (1992). Behavioral stress potentiates the blood pressure effects of a high sodium intake. *Psychosomatic Medicine, 54,* 231–239.

Higgins, M. W., & Luepker, R. V. (1988). *Trends in coronary heart disease mortality.* New York: Oxford University Press.

Ironson, G., Taylor, C. B., Boltwood, M., Bartzokis, T., Dennis, C., Chesney, M., et al. (1992). Effects of anger on left ventricular ejection fraction in coronary artery disease. *American Journal of Cardiology, 70,* 281–285.

Irvine, M. J., Garner, D. M., Olmsted, M. P., & Logan, A. G. (1989). Personality differences between hypertensive and normotensive individuals: Influence of knowledge of hypertension status. *Psychosomatic Medicine, 51,* 537–549.

Jain, D., Burg, M., Soufer, R., & Zaret, B. L. (1995). Prognostic implications of mental stress-induced silent left ventricular dysfunction in patients with stable angina pectoris. *American Journal of Cardiology, 76,* 31–35.

Jenkins, C. D., Rosenman, R. H., & Zyzanski, S. J. (1974). Prediction of clinical coronary heart disease by a test for the type A coronary prone behavior pattern. *New England Journal of Medicine, 290,* 1271–1275.

Jern, S. (1987). Specificity of personality factors found in hypertension. In S. Julius & D. R. Basset (Eds.), *Handbook of hypertension: Vol. 9. Behavioral factors in hypertension* (pp. 150–161). Amsterdam: Elsevier.

Jiang, W., Babyak, M., Krantz, D. S., Waugh, R. A., Caleman, R. E., Hanson, M. M., et al. (1996). Mental stress-induced myocardial ischemia and cardiac events. *Journal of the American Medical Association, 275,* 1651–1656.

Joint National Committee on Detection, Evaluation, and Treatment of High Blood Pressure. (1993). The fifth report of the Joint National Committee on Detection, Evaluation, and Treatment of High Blood Pressure (JNC–V). *Archives of Internal Medicine, 153,* 154–183.

Jones, D. A., & West, R. R. (1996). Psychological rehabilitation after myocardial infarction: Multicenter randomized control trial. *British Medical Journal, 313,* 1517–1521.

Julius, S., & Esler, M. (1975). Autonomic nervous cardiovascular regulation in borderline hypertension. *American Journal of Cardiology, 36,* 685–696.

Kaplan, G. A., & Keil, J. E. (1993). Socioeconomic factors and cardiovascular disease: A review of the literature. *Circulation, 88,* 1973–1998.

Kaplan, J. R., Adams, M. R., Clarkson, T. B., & Koritnick, D. R. (1984). Psychosocial influences on female "protection" among cynomolgus macaques. *Atherosclerosis, 53,* 283–295.

Karasek, R. A., & Theorell, T. G. (1990). *Health work, stress, productivity, and the reconstruction of working life.* New York: Basic Books.

Kelley, G., & McClellan, P. (1994). Antihypertensive effects of aerobic exercise. A brief meta-analytic review of randomized controlled trials. *American Journal of Hypertension, 7,* 115–119.

Keys, A., Taylor, H. L., Blackburn, H., Brozeck, J., Anderson, J., & Simonson, E. (1971). Mortality and coronary heart disease among men studied for 23 years. *Archives of Internal Medicine, 128,* 201–214.

Kop, W. J., Appels, A. P., Mendes de Leon, C. M., de Swart, H. B., & Bar, F. W. (1994). Vital exhaustion predicts new cardiac events after successful coronary angioplasty. *Psychosomatic Medicine, 56,* 281–287.

Krantz, D. S., Kop, W. J., Santiago, H. T., & Gottdiener, J. S. (1996). Mental stress as a trigger of myocardial ischemia and infarction. *Cardiology Clinics, 14,* 271–287.

Krantz, D. S., & Lundgren, N. R. (1998). Cardiovascular disorders. In A. S. Bellack & M. Hersen (Eds.), *Comprehensive clinical psychology* (pp. 189–216). New York: Pergamon Press.

Krantz, D. S., & Manuck, S. B. (1984). Acute psychophysiologic reactivity and risk of cardiovascular disease: A review and methodological critique. *Psychological Bulletin, 96,* 435–464.

Krieger, N., & Sidney, S. (1996). Racial discrimination and blood pressure: The CARDIA study of young Black and White adults. *American Journal of Public Health, 86,* 1370–1378.

Leor, J., Poole, W. K., & Kloner, R. A. (1996). Sudden cardiac death triggered by an earthquake. *New England Journal of Medicine, 334,* 413–419.

Lewis, T. (1929). Experiments relating to the peripheral mechanism involved in spasmodic arrest of the circulation in the fingers, a variety of Raynaud's disease. *Heart, 15,* 7–101.

Lincoln, N. B., Flannaghan, T., Sutcliffe, L., & Rother, L. (1997). Evaluation of cognitive behavioural treatment for depression after stroke: A pilot study. *Clinical Rehabilitation, 11,* 114–122.

Linden, W., Stossel, C., & Maurice, J. (1996). Psychosocial interventions for patients with coronary artery disease: A meta-analysis. *Archives of Internal Medicine, 156,* 745–752.

Majsak, M. J. (1997). Application of motor learning principles to the stroke population. *Topics in Stroke Rehabilitation, 3*, 27–59.

Manuck, S. B., Kaplan, J. R., & Matthews, K. A. (1986). Behavioral antecedents of coronary heart disease and atherosclerosis. *Atherosclerosis, 6*, 2–14.

Marcus, S., Weiner, S., Suzuki, S., & Kwan, L. (1991). Raynaud's syndrome. *Postgraduate Medicine, 89*, 171–187.

Markovitz, J. H., Matthews, K. A., Kannel, W. B., Cobb, J. L., & D'Agostino, R. B. (1993). Psychological predictors of hypertension in the Framingham Study: Is there tension in hypertension? *Journal of the American Medical Association, 270*, 2439–2443.

Matthews, K. A., Glass, D. C., Rosenman, R. H., & Bortner, R. W. (1977). Competitive drive pattern A and coronary heart disease: A further analysis of some data from the Western Collaborative Group Study. *Journal of Chronic Diseases, 30*, 489–498.

Meisel, S. R., Kutz, I., Dayan, K. I., Pauzner, H., Chetboun, I., Arbel, Y., et al. (1991). Effect of Iraqi missile war on incidence of acute myocardial infarction and sudden death in Israeli civilians. *Lancet, 338*, 660–661.

Mittleman, M. A., Maclure, M., Sherwood, J. B., Mulry, R. P., Tofler, G. H., Jacobs, S. C., et al. (1995). Triggering of acute myocardial infarction onset by episodes of anger. *Circulation, 92*, 1720–1725.

Miyai, I., & Reding, M. J. (1998). Effects of antidepressants on functional recovery following stroke: A double-blind study. *Journal of Neurologic Rehabilitation, 12*, 5–13.

Muller, J. E. (1999). Circadian variation and triggering of acute coronary events. *American Heart Journal, 137*, S1–S8.

Muller, J. E., Tofler, G. H., & Stone, P. H. (1989). Circadian variation and triggers of onset of acute cardiovascular disease. *Circulation, 79*, 733–743.

National Heart, Lung, and Blood Institute. (1994). *Report of the task force on research in epidemiology and prevention of cardiovascular diseases.* Bethesda, MD: Author.

Ng-Mak, D. S. (1999). A further analysis of race differences in the National Longitudinal Mortality Study. *American Journal of Public Health, 89*, 1748–1751.

Nicolosi, R. J., & Schaefer, E. J. (1992). Pathobiology of hypercholesterolemia and atherosclerosis: Genetic and environmental determinants of elevated lipoprotein levels. In I. S. Ockene & J. K. Ockene (Eds.), *Prevention of coronary heart disease* (pp. 69–102). Boston: Little, Brown.

Nicolson, N. A., & van Diest, R. (2000). Salivary cortisol patterns in vital exhaustion. *Journal of Psychosomatic Research, 49*(5), 335–342.

Ockene, I. S., & Ockene, J. K. (Eds.). (1992). *Prevention of coronary heart disease.* Boston: Little, Brown.

O'Connor, G. T., Buring, J. E., Yusuf, S., Goldhaber, S. Z., Olmstead, E. M., Paffebarger, R. S., et al. (1989). An overview of randomized trials of rehabilitation with exercise after myocardial infarction. *Circulation, 80*, 234–244.

Ornish, D., Brown, S. E., Scherwitz, L. W., Billings, J. H., Armstrong, W. T., Ports,

T. A., et al. (1990). Can lifestyle changes reverse coronary heart disease? *Lancet, 336,* 129–133.

Page, L., Danion, A., & Moellering, R. C. (1970). Antecedents of cardiovascular disease in six Solomon Island societies. *Circulation, 49,* 1132–1140.

Palomaeki, H., Kaste, M., Berg, A., Loenqvist, R, Loenqvist, J., Lehtihalmes, M., et al. (1999). Prevention of poststroke depression: 1-year randomised placebo controlled double blind trial of mianserin with 6 month follow up after therapy. *Journal of Neurology, Neurosurgery and Psychiatry, 66,* 490–494.

Polednak, A. P. (1998). Mortality among Blacks living in census tracts with public housing projects in Hartford, Connecticut. *Ethnicity and Disease, 8,* 36–42.

Porter, J. M., Rivers, S. P., Anderson, C. J., & Baur, G. M. (1981). Evaluation and management of patients with Raynaud's syndrome. *American Journal of Surgery, 142,* 183–189.

Post-Stroke Rehabilitation Guideline Panel. (1995). *Post-stroke rehabilitation.* Rockville, MD: U.S. Department of Health and Human Services.

Ragland, D. R., & Brand, R. J. (1988). Type A behavior and mortality from coronary heart disease. *New England Journal of Medicine, 318,* 65–69.

Raynaud, M. (1888). *New researches on the nature and treatment of local asphyxia of the extremities* (T. Barlox, Trans., Selected Monographs, Vol. 121). London: New Sydenham Society.

Reisin, E., Abel, R., Modan, M., Silverberg, D. S., Eliahou, H. E., & Modan, B. (1978). Effect of weight loss without salt restriction on the reduction of blood pressure in overweight hypertensive patients. *New England Journal of Medicine, 298,* 1–6.

Reitman, M. (1998). Cardiac infection and inflammation: Rheumatic fever, endocarditis, and myocarditis. In S. B. Friedman (Ed.), *Comprehensive adolescent health care* (2nd ed., pp. 288–291). St. Louis, MO: Mosby.

Rimmer, J. H., & Hedman, G. (1998). A health promotion program for stroke survivors. *Topics in Stroke Rehabilitation, 5,* 30–44.

Robertson, C., & Smithwick, R. (1951). The recurrence of vasoconstrictor activity after limb sympathectomy in Raynaud's disease and allied vasomotor states. *New England Journal of Medicine, 245,* 317–320.

Rodehoffer, R. J., Rommer, J. A., Wigley, R., & Smith, C. R. (1983). Controlled double blind trial of nifedipine in the treatment of Raynaud's phenomenon. *New England Journal of Medicine, 308,* 880–883.

Rosenman, R. H., Brand, R. J., Jenkins, D., Friedman, M., Straus, R., & Wurm, M. (1975). Coronary heart disease in Western Collaborative Group Study. Final follow-up experience of 8½ years. *Journal of the American Medical Association, 233,* 872–877.

Rozanski, A., Blumenthal, J. A., & Kaplan, J. R. (1999). Impact of psychological factors on the pathogenesis of cardiovascular disease and implications for therapy. *Circulation, 99,* 2192–2217.

Ruberman, W., Weinblatt, E., Goldberg, J. D., & Chaudhary, B. S. (1984). Psychosocial influences on mortality after myocardial infarction. *New England Journal of Medicine, 311,* 552–559.

Sarkozi, J., Bookman, A., & Mahon, W. (1986). Nifedipine in the treatment of idiopathic Raynaud's syndrome. *Journal of Rheumatology, 13,* 331–336.

Sedlacek, K., & Taub, E. (1996). Biofeedback treatment of Raynaud's disease. *Professional Psychology: Research and Practice, 27,* 548–553.

Shapiro, A. P. (1983). The non-pharmacologic treatment of hypertension. In D. S. Krantz, A Baum, & J. E. Singer (Eds.), *Handbook of psychology and health: Vol. 3. Cardiovascular disorders and behavior* (pp. 277–293). Hillsdale, NJ: Erlbaum.

Shekelle, R. B., Hulley, S. B., & Neaton, J. (1985). The MRFIT behavior pattern study. II. Type A behavior and incidence of coronary heart disease. *American Journal of Epidemiology, 122,* 559–570.

Shumaker, S. A., & Cjakowski, S. M. (Eds.). (1994). *Social support and cardiovascular disease* (Plenum Series in Behavioral Psychophysiology and Medicine). New York: Plenum Press.

Smith, C. D., & McKendry, R. J. (1982). Controlled trial of nifedipine in the treatment of Raynaud's phenomenon. *Lancet, 2,* 1299–1301.

Smith, T. M. (1992). Hostility and health: Current status of a psychosomatic hypothesis. *Health Psychology, 11,* 139–150.

Squires, E. J., Hunkin, N. M., & Parkin, A. J. (1997). Take note: Using errorless learning to promote memory notebook training. In A. J. Parkin (Ed.), *Case studies in the neuropsychology of memory.* Hove, England: Psychology Press/Erlbaum.

Stamler, R., Stamler, J., Riedlinger, W. F., Algera, G., Roberts, R. H. (1978). Weight and blood pressure. Findings in hypertension screening of one million Americans. *Journal of the American Medical Association, 240,* 1607–1610.

Taub, E., Crago, J. E., & Uswatte, G. (1998). Constraint-induced movement therapy: A new approach to treatment in physical rehabilitation. *Rehabilitation Psychology, 43,* 152–170.

Wandersman, A., & Nation, M. (1998). Urban neighborhoods and mental health: Psychological contributions to understanding toxicity, resilience, and interventions. *American Psychologist, 53,* 647–656.

Weder, A. B., & Julius, S. (1987). Behavior, blood pressure variability and hypertension: A research agenda. In S. Julius & D. R. Basset (Eds.), *Handbook of hypertension: Vol. 9. Behavioral factors in hypertension.* Amsterdam: Elsevier.

Wiensier, R. L., Norris, D. J., Birch, R., Bernstein, R. S., Wang, J., Yang, M. U., et al. (1985). The relative contribution of body fat and fat pattern to blood pressure level. *Hypertension, 7,* 578–585.

Williams, R. B. (1987). Psychological factors in coronary artery disease: Epidemiologic evidence. *Circulation, 76,* 117–123.

Williams, R. B., Barefoot, J. C., Califf, R. M., Haney, T. L., Saunders, W. B., Pryor, D. B., et al. (1992). Prognostic importance of social and economic resources among medically treated patients with angiographically documented coronary artery disease. *Journal of the American Medical Association, 267,* 559–560.

Willich, S. N. (1999). Circadian variation and triggering of cardiovascular events. *Vascular Medicine, 4,* 41–49.

Young, R. F., Waller, J. B., Jr., & Kahana, E. (1991). Racial and socioeconomic aspects of myocardial infarction recovery: Studying confounds. *American Journal of Preventive Medicine, 7,* 438–444.

8

DISEASES OF THE RESPIRATORY SYSTEM

THOMAS L. CREER, BRUCE G. BENDER, AND DEBORAH O. LUCAS

Globally, the number, variety, and prevalence of respiratory disorders and diseases pose a major health concern. Many of the causes of these disorders can be linked to two human-generated factors: air pollution and cigarette smoking. Air pollutants, for example, adversely affect the health of 4 to 5 billion people throughout the world. Polluted air is harmful to patients with respiratory disorders, particularly asthma, because it can trigger attacks or exacerbate them. The problem of air pollution will only continue to increase because of the expanding world population, the burning of fossil fuels, and the increased amount and array of industrial chemicals being released into the air (Pimental et al., 1998).

Cigarette smoking is discussed by Fisher (in press). However, the association between smoking and respiratory disorders merits a brief comment. Cigarette smoking is a significant risk factor for chronic obstructive pulmonary disease (COPD). For example, China has the largest number of tobacco-related deaths in the world. Liu et al. (1998) pointed out that 45% of the deaths in China are caused by respiratory illness, specifically COPD. If current smoking rates in China persist, Liu and his colleagues estimated that tobacco will kill about 100 million of the 0.3 billion male population now between ages 0 and 29 years, with half of the deaths occurring in middle age and half occurring in old age. Predictions are that by 2020, tobacco will result in 10 million deaths worldwide each year (Murray & Lopez, 1996).

Tuberculosis is caused by a potentially deadly bacteria. Tuberculosis was a leading cause of death in the United States until the 1940s, when the development of antibodies effectively controlled the disease. However, in recent years, tuberculosis has returned with a vengeance unmatched by any other recurring disease. Approximately 8 million people have tuberculosis in the world; an estimated 2 million people die from the disease each year (World Health Organization [WHO], 1999). One particular strain—multidrug-resistent tuberculosis (MDRTB)—has been rapidly proliferating on five continents. The four drugs used to treat MDRTB result in high cure rates in areas of low drug resistance; however, curing this strain is more difficult in areas that have high levels of drug resistance, such as in poorer regions of the world (Centers for Disease Control and Prevention [CDC], 1999). These areas, also burdened by HIV and AIDS, do not have the resources to also combat TB.

However, tuberculosis can no longer be considered a disease endemic to developing or Third World countries. With increased globalization (e.g., Kombe & Darrow, 2001), tuberculosis is fast becoming a concern for developed countries. For example, in Japan the number of new patients with tuberculosis increased in 1999 for the third straight year. The infection rate—38.1 per 100,000 people—was the highest among industrialized nations. The surge in tuberculosis in Japan was thought to result from its aging population, a weak economy that has aggravated the health problems of poor people, and the widespread ignorance about the long-forgotten disease. Furthermore, Abe, Hirano, Wada, and Aoyagi (2001) found that resistance of *Mycobacterium tuberculosis* (MTB) to first-line antituberculosis drugs was high, particularly in those patients requiring retreatment. The findings accentuate the point that controlling and eradicating tuberculosis throughout the world will require unparalleled cooperation and a concerted effort by medical and behavioral scientists.

BEHAVIORAL PSYCHOLOGY'S CONTRIBUTIONS TO RESPIRATORY HEALTH

In the past three decades, a shift in the approach taken to treat chronic physical conditions, including respiratory diseases and disorders, has occurred. The switch is actually a shift in treatment paradigms (e.g., Creer, 2000) and involves moving away from a multidisciplinary team approach toward an interdisciplinary team approach. *Multidisciplinary team* refers to the independent activities taken by professionals who represent a number of disciplines involved with a patient (Melvin, 1980; Varni, 1983). In a multidisciplinary team, health care professionals work in an uncoordinated fashion in that professionals only need to know and execute skills specific to their own discipline. For example, psychologists may have expertise in changing behavior but may lack the medical knowledge of the other team members such as physicians or nurses. Physicians and nurses may know how to medically treat a condition but may be unaware that behavioral scientists could help enhance patient adherence to a prescribed treatment regimen. The *interdisciplinary* model takes a different approach: It assumes that physicians, nurses, psychologists, physical therapists, social workers, and other health care professionals have a working knowledge of the skills and expertise of each member of the team. Thus, Varni (1983) concluded, "The approach is synergistic, integrating the knowledge and skills from the various disciplines into a coordinated plan for patient care" (p. 5). However, Creer, Holroyd, Glasgow, and Smith (in press) suggested that synergy arising from an interdisciplinary approach remains more of a goal than a consistent and measurable outcome.

Three major respiratory diseases or conditions are discussed in this chapter: tuberculosis, COPD, and asthma. The conditions can be differentiated not only physiologically from one another but also by the extent to which behavioral scientists have been involved in the treatment and research of the conditions. Although the presentation can be construed as an unbalanced discussion of the three disorders, it delineates the context within which psychologists have been able to apply their skills and expertise. Because psychologists have mainly been onlookers in the treatment of tuberculosis, this chapter includes a description of the disease and problems generated by its treatment.

The discussion reveals the potential for using behavioral skills to help abolish the disease and argues that behavioral expertise is integral to any success attained in curtailing, treating, and controlling tuberculosis. The role of behavioral scientists in treating COPD is better defined because psychologists are increasingly integrated into treatment and research teams for the disorder. The success of a collaborative approach by medical and behavioral scientists to COPD treatment and problems that require behavioral input are discussed. The bulk of the discussion focuses on asthma. The decision to highlight asthma was made not only because of the prevalence of the disease but because psychologists have long been included as members of treatment and research teams for the disorder. Therefore, a considerable amount of research data, particularly regarding childhood asthma, exists. Finally, the chapter includes a discussion of the levels of behavioral techniques, particularly self-management, that have been proved applicable to asthma. In doing so, the discussion highlights the potential use of these procedures for patients with COPD and patients with tuberculosis.

TUBERCULOSIS

A comprehensive survey of the global burden of tuberculosis was reported by Dye, Scheele, Dolin, Pathania, and Raviglione (1999), who presented data gathered in 1997 from 212 countries by the WHO Global Surveillance and Monitoring Project. The data indicated that the global prevalence of tuberculosis and MTB continues to escalate. The MTB infection was found in 32%, or 1.86 billion, people in the world. Although the infection remains dormant in most patients, approximately 10% of those infected will develop active tuberculosis (Broughton & Bass, 1999). Broughton and Bass pointed out that all cases of tuberculosis are acquired through person-to-person contact via droplet nuclei. Infection can be prevented by use of ultraviolet radiation in a patient's room or by patients covering their mouth and nose by wearing a mask or a handkerchief. A patient with tuberculosis may infect 10 to 15 other people, so anyone has the potential to become infected, including individuals in developed countries.

Once detected, tuberculosis can be controlled only through aggressive medical treatment. The predominant treatment strategy—direct observed therapy (DOT)—is practiced in more than 100 countries throughout the world; WHO (1999) has estimated that 1 million patients have been treated with DOT. DOT calls for patients with tuberculosis to report to a medical facility and receive treatment directly from health care personnel, an approach Garner (1998) referred to as "supervised swallowing." The approach does not involve asking patients with tuberculosis to accept the program, a factor that undermines patient compliance (Heyman, Sell, & Brewer, 1998), or even to accept any responsibility for self-care (Garner, 1998). The acceptance of DOT as a gold standard for the treatment of tuberculosis is senseless for the reasons in the following paragraphs, which include several enumerated by Creer et al. (in press).

Optimal treatment and control of tuberculosis is not occurring anywhere in the world (WHO, 1999). Progress has been much too slow—1 million patients have been treated, but almost half a billion could end up with tuberculosis. WHO credits this failure to a lack of political commitment in countries with a high rate of the disease. The global burden falls disproportionately on developing countries with limited financial resources (e.g., Asia and sub-Saharan Africa); however, more than a political commitment is required to control tuberculosis.

Studies on the cost effectiveness of DOT are suspect. Early results with DOT are mixed (e.g., Palmer, Miller, Halpern, & Geiger, 1998), particularly because they were not based on randomized clinical trials. Different approaches, including a decision analysis by Burman, Dalton, Cohn, Butler, and Reves (1997), have suggested that DOT is more effective than self-administered therapy (SAT). Other investigators (e.g., Gourevitch,

Alcabes, Wasserman, & Arno, 1998; Snyder et al., 1999) echo these findings. However, no data on SAT were gathered and analyzed in these studies. The truth, Garrett (1994) contended, is that no nation does a worse job than the United States in identifying tuberculosis cases, successfully treating these cases, and tracking the outcomes.

Noncompliance to DOT is common throughout the world; in only half of the cases do patients with tuberculosis complete treatment (Volmink & Garner, 2001). In the United States, nonadherence occurs particularly among alcoholics and the homeless population (Burman et al., 1997). Approaches taken to improve adherence range from sending the noncompliant person to jail (Gasner, Maw, Feldman, Fujiwara, & Frieden, 1999), where tuberculosis is spread to inmates and jail personnel or, as has been done in a few isolated cases, applying behavioral techniques to enhance compliance. In one of the few studies that used behavioral techniques, Tulsky and her colleagues (2000) found that a $5 biweekly cash incentive improved adherence to tuberculosis regimens. The application of behavioral technology is certainly a more palliative approach to promote adherence to tuberculosis regimens than sending noncompliant patients with tuberculosis to jail, where they infect others.

Two recent investigations compared DOT to SAT in randomized controlled trials. Zwarenstein, Schoeman, Vundule, Lombard, and Tatley (1998) found that treatment of tuberculosis was more successful among patients who performed SAT (60%) than among those treated with DOT (54%). Retreatment patients had significantly greater treatment success with SAT (74%) than with DOT (42%); the finding is of significance given the rate of noncompliance in patients with tuberculosis. Zwarenstein and his colleagues concluded that SAT achieved equivalent outcomes to clinic-based DOT at a lower cost. In a second study, Walley, Khan, Newell, and Khan (2001) randomly assigned 497 adults with tuberculosis to one of three groups: (a) 170 patients were assigned to DOT by health workers, (b) 165 patients were assigned to DOT by family workers, and (c) 162 patients were assigned SAT. Health-worker DOT, family-member DOT, and SAT had similar outcomes, with cure rates of 64%, 55%, and 62%, respectively; cure or treatment completion rates were 67%, 62%, and 65%, respectively. The findings led Walley and colleagues to declare that none of the three strategies was superior to the others and that DOT did not give any additional improvement in cure rates. An introduction to the *Lancet* article read, "Is DOT not so hot?"

The Cochrane Collaboration is composed of experts who regularly review the literature for specific diseases and disorders. In their most recent update of interventions for promoting adherence to tuberculosis management, Volmink and Garner (2001) analyzed 14 trials. They concluded that reminder cards sent to defaulters, a combination package of a monetary incentive and health education, and more supervision of clinic staff increased the number of people completing tuberculosis treatment. The rate of return to the clinic for reading of a tuberculin skin test was increased by monetary incentives, assistance by lay health workers, contracts, and telephone prompts.

No single strategy, specifically DOT, has been responsible for decreasing tuberculosis infection in various regions of the world. For example, Farmer, Becerra, and Kim (1999) reported that several interventions were used in New York City, "including more rapid diagnosis, active case finding in epicenters of transmission, more rapid detection and treatment of MDR–TB, and, for a minority of patients, directly observed therapy" (p. 176). The CDC (2001) was more forthright in suggesting that state and local tuberculosis control programs collaborate with public health and behavioral scientists to develop methods for tracing, testing, and treating contacts, particularly patients with tuberculosis. Studies could then tailor the strategy that would be most appropriate for individuals with tuberculosis.

Few people in the world are immune from the scourge of tuberculosis. The potential of the disease to spread rapidly and ubiquitously presents a major risk to the health and development of all nations (Kombe & Darrow, 2001). Tuberculosis affects both developing and developed nations, in part, because of increased globalization of the world. Rodriguez-Garcia (2001) reported that global travel has grown from 25 million people in 1950 to 500 million people in 1995. Estimations are that by 2010, 1 billion people will travel each year. The result, noted Rodriguez-Garcia, is increased vulnerability to the domino-type spread of old, new, and reemerging infectious diseases such as tuberculosis.

Finally, WHO can be faulted for advocating DOT as the gold standard of treatment without comparing DOT to SAT in randomized clinical trials. As we described, data gathered in two such trials indicate that SAT not only is equally effective but also is superior in some instances. The finding by Zwarenstein et al. (1998) that SAT is more effective for patients requiring retreatment is significant given the high rate of nonadherence among patients with tuberculosis (e.g., Volmink & Garner, 2001). A second proclivity of WHO is to insist that the tuberculosis and the human immunodeficiency virus (HIV) epidemics are "inextricably linked" (WHO, 2001, p. 2). Although this is indeed the case in developing areas of the world, particularly among inhabitants of Asia and sub-Saharan Africa, it is not the case among patients with tuberculosis in developed countries such as Japan. The insistence on linking tuberculosis with HIV does little but create a false sense of being immune to tuberculosis among people in developed countries when in reality they could be a cough away from the disease.

In summary, the discussion of tuberculosis suggests a leading role must be played by psychologists and other behavioral scientists in abolishing the infection. Although tuberculosis is a condition that can be controlled only with appropriate medical treatment, the need for behavioral input in primary prevention (e.g., helping to prevent tuberculosis by changing patient behaviors) and secondary prevention (e.g., helping design and implement self-management programs) is equally important.

COPD

COPD is "a disease state characterized by airflow limitation that is not fully reversible. The airflow limitation is usually both progressive and associated with an abnormal inflammatory response of the lungs to noxious particles or gases" (National Institutes of Health [NIH], 2001, p. 2). Approximately 80% to 90% of those at risk for COPD smoke cigarettes (American Thoracic Society, 1995). The risk of COPD, in turn, increases as a function of the number of cigarettes a person smokes daily. Smoking is associated with three types of disease conditions: emphysema, small airway inflammation and fibrosis, and mucus gland hyperphasia (Senior & Anthonisen, 1998). Although defined in behavioral parameters (i.e., the amount of coughing that occurs during a certain number of months each year), chronic bronchitis can also be produced by smoking. Chronic bronchitis, in addition to emphysema, is a major form of COPD.

Epidemiology

Epidemiological data on COPD are hard to collect because the disorder is usually not diagnosed until it is clinically apparent and moderately advanced. Nevertheless, the worldwide prevalence of COPD in 1990 was estimated to be 9.34 men per 1,000 and 7.33 women per 1,000 (NIH, 2001). In the United States, the Joint ACCP/AACVPR Evidence-Based Guidelines on Pulmonary Rehabilitation (1997) estimated that the overall prevalence of COPD in adult White populations in the United States is 4% to 6% men and 1% to 3% women; in people older than age 55, COPD is recognized in approximately 10% to 15% of individuals. Available data suggest that morbidity from COPD increases with age and is greater in men than in women. COPD is responsible for a significant number of physician visits, emergency room visits, and hospitalizations.

In 1990, COPD emerged as the fourth leading cause of death in the world; further increases in the prevalence and mortality of the disorder are predicted in the coming decades because of the prevalence of cigarette smoking. In the United States, COPD death rates are low among people younger than age 45, but the rates increase with age. COPD is the fourth or fifth leading cause of death among those older than age 45 (NIH, 2001).

Behavioral Treatment

In addition to medications, two behavioral approaches comprise the triumvirate of treatment for COPD: smoking cessation and rehabilitation of patients.

Smoking Cessation

"Smoking cessation is the single most effective—and cost-effective—intervention to reduce the risk of developing COPD and stop its progression" (NIH, 2001, p. 9). To achieve this goal, brief tobacco dependence treatment is recommended for every tobacco user. In addition, three types of counseling—practical counseling, social support as part of treatment, and social support outside of treatment—are recommended as approaches to take in curbing smoking. If these prove ineffective alone, the NIH has suggested that effective pharmacotherapies be combined with counseling if needed and in the absence of contraindications.

The suggestions offered by NIH on smoking cessation are too general to be of value to most behavioral scientists. They are akin to the advice, "Take two aspirin and call me in the morning," in the way they ignore the complexity involved in changing the behaviors needed to attain smoking cessation. As noted by Fisher (in press), smoking cessation is far easier said than done. For example, cigarette smoking in the United States is the single most preventable cause of disease and death. According to the U.S. Department of Health and Human Services (U.S. DHHS, 2000), smoking results in more deaths each year in the United States than the combined total from acquired immune deficiency syndrome (AIDS), alcohol, cocaine, heroin, homicide, suicide, motor vehicle crashes, and fires. On the positive side, Ockene et al. (2000) pointed out that 70% of smokers want to stop smoking. However, Ockene and colleagues also noted that 88% of smokers who stop smoking eventually relapse and resume smoking. Smokers with a long-standing smoking habit, such as patients with COPD, are likely to be among those patients who relapse. In the reports by the DHHS (2000) and by Ockene and colleagues (2000), it is obvious that changing behaviors required for smoking cessation and maintaining these changes remains a possible yet highly elusive outcome.

Rehabilitation

The report by the NIH (2001) emphasized the importance of rehabilitation in the treatment of patients with COPD. In the report, it is noted that "the principle goals of pulmonary rehabilitation are to reduce symptoms, improve quality of life, and increase physical and emotional participation in everyday activities" (p. 15). The report continued by suggesting that the achievement of these goals requires resolving a range of nonpulmonary problems, including exercise deconditioning, social isolation, altered mood states (e.g., depression), muscle wasting, and weight loss. At all stages of COPD, patients benefit from exercise training programs; they improve with respect to exercise tolerance, symptoms of dyspnea, and fatigue. Although authors of the report suggested that these benefits can be sustained even after a single pulmonary rehabilitation program conducted in inpatient, outpatient, and home settings, they are ambiguous in their descriptions of the way the goals are to be attained. Thus, although they noted that pulmonary rehabilitation should involve several types of health professionals, they do not mention that rehabilitation requires both behavioral skills and the establishment of behavioral goals (e.g., halting smoking, attaining increasingly higher levels of exercise).

Initial attempts to rehabilitate patients with COPD have centered around providing exercise training to improve physical function and quality of life. In part because of methodological weaknesses in these studies, the efficacy of exercise as an adjunctive treatment for COPD was initially regarded as controversial and inconclusive (Barry & Walschlager, 1998). However, a meta-analysis of pulmonary rehabilitation and COPD found positive benefits were attained in programs in which exercise was the main rehabilitative component (Lacasse et al., 1996). The development of a package of various components for the rehabilitation of patients with COPD has paralleled what has occurred with other chronic respiratory conditions, particularly asthma. Programs that offer various options that can be selected and tailored for individual patients have met with overall success (e.g., Bendstrup, Ingemann, Jensen, Holm, & Bengtsson, 1997; Cambach, Wagenaar, Koelman, van Keimpema, & Kemper, 1999; Scherer, Schmieder, & Shimmel, 1998; Young, Dewse, Fergusson, & Kolbe, 1999).

Numerous investigators have described the benefits of rehabilitation for patients with COPD, including improved exercise tolerance, the perception of dyspnea, and quality of life (e.g., Fogio et al., 1999; Goldstein, Gort, Stubbing, Avendano, & Guyatt, 1994; Young et al., 1999). Toshima, Kaplan, and Ries (1990) described improvements in self-efficacy that were correlated with improvements in exercise, and Janelli, Schrer, and Schmieder (1991) recommended that pulmonary rehabilitation programs teach appropriate coping strategies to patients with COPD.

Other investigators have been more multidisciplinary and oriented toward using behavioral skills and expertise in rehabilitation programs for COPD. Such programs of pulmonary rehabilitation blend medical and behavioral tools and skills to address the multiple needs of patients with COPD (Ries, Kaplan, Limberg, & Prewitt, 1995; Tiep, 1997). The approach expands treatment beyond traditional medical care by attempting to alter disabling features of chronic and progressive lung disease. The skills described by Tiep (1997) are familiar to behavioral scientists regardless of the chronic condition they treat. The skills include self-management, exercise promotion, functional training, building and enhancement of social skills, and techniques designed to optimize the medical management of COPD (e.g., medication adherence). Other components of successful rehabilitation programs for COPD include patient and family education (Ferguson, 1998), training in coping with the condition (Young et al., 1999), and development of self-efficacy in patients (Scherer et al., 1998). Kaptein (1997) suggested that all these techniques are beneficial in the rehabilitation of patients with COPD.

In summary, several challenges remain in the implementation of rehabilitation programs for patients with COPD (Creer et al., in press). First, smoking cessation must remain at the forefront of any rehabilitative effort (e.g., Celli, 1998). However, a brief review by Fisher (in press) accentuates the difficulties encountered in attaining this goal. Second, rehabilitation from COPD is often regarded as a one-time intervention instead of as an ongoing effort that takes place over time. As a result, Tiep (1997) complained, any benefits from many brief rehabilitation programs are likely to fade quickly. Participation of health care providers in an ongoing partnership with their patients is required to strengthen rehabilitation outcomes in patients with COPD. Such relationships would also increase the chance of maintenance and generalization of change, a point Mahler (1998) cited as important for future rehabilitation programs. Third, Mahler highlighted the need to establish levels of training intensity, particularly with respect to exercise, during formal training and in the later maintenance of behavioral skills. Considering the number of rehabilitation programs being developed and implemented for COPD, these levels may soon be established. Finally, rehabilitation is available to only a small percentage of patients with COPD. Tiep (1997) insisted that optimal disease management requires the redesigning of standard medical care for COPD to integrate components of rehabilitation into a system centered around patient self-management and regular exercise. As is mentioned in the discussion of asthma, it also requires a greater synthesis of patient and health care provider skills than has heretofore been present in the pulmonary rehabilitation of patients with COPD.

ASTHMA

Definition and Characteristics

Asthma has always been hard to define, although accurate descriptions of the disorder extend back to Hippocrates (Pearce, Beasley, Burgess, & Crane, 1998). The reason for confusion in defining asthma is that, as Busse and Reed (1988) explained, those working with asthma tend to define the disorder according to their specific needs. Clinicians working with asthma, for example, want a different definition than epidemiologists who study patient populations or immunologists who investigate the pathogenesis of the condition. Despite difficulties in defining asthma, numerous panels composed of asthma experts have issued guidelines for the treatment of the disorder.

A definition of asthma that has served to unify interdisciplinary health care teams was provided by the initial set of treatment guidelines disseminated for asthma in the United States: "Asthma is a lung disease with the following characteristics: (1) airway obstruction (or airway narrowing) that is reversible (but not completely so in some patients) either spontaneously or with treatment; (2) airway inflammation; and (3) airway hyperresponsiveness to a variety of stimuli" (NIH, 1991, p. 1). Elements of this definition highlight the characteristics of asthma. The importance of the characteristics to behavioral scientists is as follows.

Intermittency

The frequency of attacks varies from patient to patient and for each individual patient. Intermittency of attacks presents several problems to behavioral scientists (Creer & Bender, 1995). First, the unique pattern of each patient's asthma makes it difficult to make clinical decisions about the proper way to treat patients. Because physicians are uncertain about the outcomes of some decisions, potential outcomes of treatment options should be viewed in terms of probabilities. In other words, physicians take actions that are most likely to result in a given outcome. The same view must be practiced by patients, a common characteristic found in those labeled "gold standard patients" and "gold standard physicians" in making decisions for treating asthma (Creer, 1990). Second, the intermittency of asthma makes it difficult to recruit and to maintain patients in research. Patients can be enthusiastic volunteers during exacerbations of their asthma; however, when asymptomatic, they lose interest. Finally, the intermittency of attacks generates a wide range of expectancies in patients (Renne & Creer, 1985). For example, patients with persistent or perennial asthma know they are likely to experience asthma throughout the year, so they may be more adherent to a treatment regimen. Depending on the frequency of attacks, patients with intermittent asthma may go long periods without attacks. Consequently, they often forget how to treat an attack and are unprepared to manage one when it occurs (Creer, 1991).

Variability

Variability refers to severity of a patient's asthma and of discrete asthma attacks. Use of the term has not always been clear, so saying a person has *severe asthma* is not always clear. Does a patient's overall status vary, or does a given asthma attack vary? Fortunately, treatment guidelines contain a general classification for asthma severity and an outline for defining an attack as mild, moderate, or severe (NIH, 1991, 1997).

Reversibility

As noted in the definition, asthma is characterized by airway obstruction that remits either spontaneously or with treatment, but this definition has exceptions (Creer & Bender, 1995). First, as with emphysema, reversibility of airflow obstruction may be relative. Most patients achieve reversibility with proper treatment; however, other patients do not achieve complete reversibility even with intensive treatment. Why asthma is irreversible in some patients has recently been of interest to scientists who suggest that airway modeling may occur. The term describes the dynamic processes that may lead to structural changes in the airways of patients with severe asthma (e.g., Fish & Peters, 1999). The changes are thought to result in an irreversible component in the airway obstruction that occurs in asthma and perhaps in the development of airway hyperresponsiveness. Fish and Peters suggested that "the dynamic processes underlying these structural changes are viewed as injury repair processes driven by airway inflammation" (p. 509). However, Fish and Peters cautioned that it should be recognized that airway modeling remains just a concept. The problem of irreversibility can make it difficult to determine whether a patient has asthma or COPD. Indeed, many medical scientists insist that the conditions overlap (e.g., American Thoracic Society, 1995). Second, the fact that attacks remit spontaneously makes it impossible to prove a cause–effect relationship between changes in a patient's asthma and treatment for the condition. A chance always exists that spontaneous reversibility unrelated to a medical treatment accounted for any changes observed in a patient's asthma (Creer, 1982).

Airway Hyperresponsiveness

Airway hyperreactivity, or hyperresponsiveness, is ubiquitous in asthma. It is an exaggerated airway response called *bronchoconstriction* that occurs when the airways are exposed to numerous and various stimuli. Bronchoconstriction is the action that constitutes an asthma attack or persistent asthma. It consists of a reduction in the airway opening caused by small muscle spasms, mucosal swelling or edema, mucosal inflammation, increased mucus secretion, or a combination of these factors. Stimuli that produce bronchoconstriction include (a) viral respiratory infections; (b) allergens such as pollen, dust mites, mold, cat dander, and cockroach parts; (c) irritants such as tobacco smoke, air pollution, or strong odors; (d) drugs such as aspirin; (e) exercise; (f) weather changes; and (g) emotional reactions such as laughing or crying too hard. Behavioral scientists may be asked to teach patients to avoid exposing themselves to stimuli that produce bronchoconstriction (e.g., allergens) and thus prevent asthma attacks.

Airway Inflammation

Although airway inflammation has been recognized as a factor in asthma since the 1800s (Pearce et al., 1998), the mechanism by which inflammation occurs and the way it interacts with bronchial hyperresponsiveness are unknown. However, it is believed that inflammation is not caused by a single cell or single inflammatory mediator but results from complex interactions among inflammatory cells, mediators, and the cells and tissues present in the airways (NIH, 1991).

Epidemiology

Prevalence

During 1993 and 1994, an estimated 13.7 million people in the United States had asthma. From 1980 to 1994 the prevalence of self-reported asthma in the United States increased 75% (CDC, 1998b). Also in 1998 a state-specific estimate of asthma reported that the disorder affected an estimated 17.3 million people in the United States, which is 6.4% of the current population in the United States and an increase of 10.6 million since 1980 (CDC, 1998a).

The prevalence of asthma provides a baseline for those working with the disorder. Undoubtedly, such a baseline has an impact on the way data are analyzed and interpreted. For example, prevalence data have been used to support the contention that work-related asthma is underestimated (Jajosky et al., 1999). The conclusion warrants a more intensive approach being taken to identify those with work-related asthma. On the other hand, other data on the prevalence of asthma result in a different interpretation. Keeley and Silverman (1999) suggested that pediatric asthma may be overdiagnosed. They concluded that physicians should avoid the indiscriminate use of an asthma diagnosis and the consequences that often accompany such a diagnosis. For behavioral scientists, prevalence data must be carefully considered as they are a major ingredient in the decisions they make regarding treatment options (Garb, 1998) in patients with asthma.

Mortality

For the first half of the 20th century, deaths from asthma were rare. Instead of considering it a fatal disease, patients and health care providers believed the following oft-quoted statement by the eminent physician, Sir William Osler (1892): "The asthmatic patient pants into old age." The implication was that although people with asthma may have difficulty breathing throughout their lives, few will die from the condition. However, thoughts regarding asthma mortality changed in the 1960s with the significant increase in asthma deaths, particularly in New Zealand and Australia. Although the exact cause of the increase in asthma mortality was not found, several factors, including the introduction of some inhaled asthma drugs, changes in disease classification, improved accuracy of death certificates, and advances in diagnostic procedures for confirming asthma were correlated with the trend (e.g., Pearce et al., 1998).

The rate of death from asthma in the United States increased from 0.8 per 100,000 in the general population from 1977 to 1978 to 2 per 100,000 in 1989. The rate remained stable until the slight increase in deaths to 2.1 per 100,000 in 1994 (Sly & O'Donnell, 1997). However, these latter rates are still 50% higher than those of 1979. The exact number of deaths from asthma in the United States ranged from 1,674 in 1977 to 5,487 in 1994. Sly and O'Donnell pointed out that rates of death were much higher for African American than White people, and rates among White people increased more for women than men. Although low compared with other diseases or disorders such as heart conditions, cancer, and COPD, the increase in asthma mortality is inexcusable given the fact that the condition can generally be controlled.

Morbidity

The real impact of asthma is found in analyses of morbidity data. Pediatric asthma is the major cause of school absenteeism caused by chronic physical conditions and is the leading cause of hospitalizations of children. In 1990, children between ages 5 and 17 years missed more than 10 million days of school, had an estimated 160,000 hospitalizations, and made 860,000 emergency room visits because of asthma (Weiss, Gergen, & Hodgson, 1992). More recent data show that the rate of absenteeism among children with asthma has decreased, although respiratory conditions, particularly asthma, remain the most common cause of childhood disability (Newacheck & Halfon, 1998).

Fewer asthma morbidity data are available for adults. However, ample evidence has suggested the magnitude of occupational asthma is greatly underestimated (Blanc, Eisner, Israel, & Yelin, 1999; Jajosky et al., 1999), hospitalization for patients older than age 45 is more expensive (Stanford, McLaughlin, & Okamoto, 1999), and there is a lower probability that asthma can be reversed in older patients (Reed, 1999). More data on the impact of asthma in adults should be reported in the future, particularly given the increase in pollution and work-site triggers of the disorder (e.g., Pearce et al., 1998).

Finally, the cost of treating asthma continues to climb. Weiss and his colleagues (1992) reported that the economic costs of asthma in the United States were an estimated $6.2 billion in 1990. Other estimates (e.g., Smith et al., 1997; Stempel, Sturm, Hedblom, & Durcannin-Roberts, 1995) reinforced the data presented by Weiss and his colleagues. Asthma is an expensive disorder not only for patients and their families but also, as are all chronic health conditions, for society.

Psychological Factors in Patients With Asthma

Adults

In the past, asthma was often thought of as a pediatric disorder. For this reason, far less attention has been focused on the psychological and behavioral sequelae of adults with the disorder than on children with asthma. Nevertheless, Mathison (1998) succinctly summarized behavioral problems common in adults with the condition, including many issues common for children with asthma. The problems they noted were anxiety, including panic, depression, and marital or family discord. Like children, adults can trigger an asthma attack or exacerbate an ongoing attack through behavioral patterns, particularly hyperventilation and anger, or specific behaviors, such as laughing or crying too hard.

All of these problems are amenable to change through the application of behavioral intervention (Creer, 1979). Adults are often willing participants in behavioral interventions such as educational and self-management programs because many of them, particularly women, experience late-onset asthma. Once adults begin to have their normal activities curtailed by asthma, they often make every effort to regain the health and quality of life they experienced before they developed the condition. Their willingness to partner with their health care providers and accept greater responsibility for their condition makes them ideal participants for asthma self-management training (Kotses et al., 1995).

Although adults and children with asthma have some similar problems, the amount of research done with adults is simply not comparable to research done with children (e.g., Renne & Creer, 1985). The impact of watching a child with asthma struggle to breathe is likely a partial cause of the research disparity, particularly when the people watching are a child's parents. For this reason, many innovations for the treatment of asthma such as the development and implementation of self-management programs were well-established with children before they were introduced to adults (e.g., Kotses et al., 1995). Following is a thorough review of what researchers have learned during the past few decades of childhood asthma investigations. It is hoped that the discussion will stimulate research on adults with the disorder, patients who have not received the attention they deserve from behavioral scientists.

Children and Families

Although impressive, epidemiological data fail to convey the potential influence of asthma on psychological, social, and cognitive development of children. Conclusions about the psychological consequences of pediatric asthma are inconsistent and controversial; in many instances, these conclusions largely reflect variations in research methodologies. Because of the key role played by behavioral scientists in research on childhood asthma, this section reviews and critiques studies on the psychological consequences of asthma and explores important mediating variables regarding psychology and asthma.

Psychological development. As we noted previously, childhood asthma has often been associated with psychological disorders (Bussing, Halfon, Benjamin, & Wells, 1995; Graham, Rutter, Yule, & Pless, 1967; Hamlett, Pelligrini, & Katz, 1992; Kashani, Konig, Shepperd, Wilfley, & Morris, 1988; Lavigne & Faier-Routman, 1992; MacLean, Perrin, Gortmaker, & Pierre, 1992; McNicol, Williams, Allan, & McAndrew, 1973; Norrish, Tooley, & Godfrey, 1977; Padur et al., 1995; Perrin, MacLean, & Perrin, 1989; Steinhausen, Schindler, & Stephan, 1983). Anxiety and depressive affect in children with asthma and distress in their families have been the most frequently documented disorders (Austin, 1989; Bender, Ilke, DuHamel, & Tinkelman, 1998; Kashani et al., 1988). The research has implied that a large portion of children with asthma have been psychologically compromised by the illness and, therefore, are in need of mental health services (Bussing et al., 1995). However, inconsistencies in the findings obscure the conclusions that can be drawn from the studies. For example, although some experimenters reported a relationship between disease severity and psychological distress (Bussing et al., 1995; Graham et al., 1967; Klinnert, 1997; McNicol et al., 1973; Norrish et al., 1977; Perrin et al., 1989), others did not (Hamlett et al., 1992; Kashani et al., 1988; Lavigne and Faier-Routman, 1992; Padur et al., 1995).

Variations in the studies' sampling and methodology likely contributed to the inconsistencies and confusion about the relationship between asthma and psychological adaptation in children. Two methodological shortcomings are found in many of these studies (Annett & Bender, 1994; Bender & Klinnert, 1998). First, most investigators relied on parental reports of asthma diagnosis, severity, medication use, and symptom control but included no documentation of pulmonary test results, medical chart reviews, or physician verifications of findings. Second, many investigators recruited samples of convenience (Lavigne & Faier-Routman, 1992). In particular, the demographic and illness characteristics of certain single-site samples may not be representative of the larger population of children with asthma.

Some of the discrepancy in findings regarding the relationship between disease severity and psychological adaptation can be traced to differences in researchers' definitions of asthma severity. In a few instances the decision about whether to include a participant in a study was based only on a diagnosis of asthma reported by a parent; no severity-related assessment by health care providers was included (Lavigne & Faier-Routman, 1992; Padur et al., 1995). In other cases in which illness severity was assessed by pulmonary function measures, frequency of asthma attacks, or medication use, no direct relationship was found between illness and psychopathology (Kashani et al., 1988; MacLean et al., 1992; Steinhausen et al., 1983). However, measures of functional control, such as days of asthma-related school absence (Graham et al., 1967; Klinnert, 1997; Stein & Jessop, 1984) or activity restriction (Bussing et al., 1995), were frequently associated with children's psychological adaptation as measured by standardized parent report questionnaires. In all cases, this illness and adaptation relationship remained relatively weak, and all variables were less significant determinants of psychological adaptation than characteristics of the family, such as parental psychopathology (Steinhausen et al., 1983), exposure to stressful life events (MacLean et al., 1992), family conflict (Perrin et al., 1989), and maternal social support (Hamlett et al., 1992).

Evidence from the largest study conducted on pediatric asthma has indicated that mild or moderate asthma does not result in an increase in cognitive, emotional, or behavioral problems. One thousand children in eight cities in North America were monitored in the Childhood Asthma Management Program (CAMP, 1999). Baseline psychological testing found no score increases that were indicative of behavioral problems (according to the Child Behavior Checklist), depression (according to the Children's Depression Inventory), or anxiety (according to the Revised Children's Manifest Anxiety Scale; Bender, 1998). Furthermore, results from intelligence and school achievement tests revealed a distribution of scores that was no different from those of a normative, age-matched population of children (Annett, 1996).

Psychological distress. Pediatric asthma is distressing for children and their families. The data from CAMP (1999) have indicated that most children with asthma do not have psychological disorders; however, asthma can be difficult and stressful. Asthma interferes with normal physical and social activity (MacLean et al., 1992) because children with asthma are often restricted in their ability to play and participate in sports. Peer interactions can be impeded, and the natural evolution of childhood friendships interrupted. These experiences, in turn, can produce a sense of loss and of self-doubt.

Families and distress. As mentioned, children with asthma have activity limitations and may often be absent from school. In addition, chronic illness and the resulting need for medical care create financial burdens, force parents to miss work, and interfere with family vacations (Donnelly,

1994; Donnelly, Donnelly, & Thong, 1987). Marital conflict may increase, and siblings may receive less attention (Nocon & Booth, 1989–1990). Recommended environmental control measures include intense cleaning of the interior of home, replacement of carpeting, and restricted access to pets, which can be difficult and expensive for families.

The stress that asthma creates for patients and their families directly affects quality of life. Although difficult to measure, the concept of quality of life captures the notion that chronic illnesses can interfere with the satisfaction and enjoyment of daily life. Quality-of-life questionnaires may reflect a degree of the stress brought on by the illness but have little or no demonstrable capacity to assess significant psychological changes or disorders (Bender, 1996).

Without question, some children with asthma develop psychological disorders. Which circumstances determine whether a child with asthma is vulnerable to psychopathology? Disease severity, presence of other stressful life events, illness, school absenteeism, and medication side effects are all potential mediators of the relationship between asthma and psychological disorders. These factors are examined in the following sections.

Disease severity and other illnesses. Severe asthma increases distress, which adds significantly to the psychological burden of children and their families. The level of debilitation and activity restriction increases, financial burdens grow, and interruptions of family life dramatically increase. Discomfort, pain, suffering, and a gnawing anxiety about the possibility of death intrude on the entire family's sense of well-being. Most evidence has supported the conclusion that psychological disorders are more likely to occur in children with asthma only when their asthma is severe (Graham et al., 1967; McNichol et al., 1973), although some investigators have reported no severity-mediated relationships between the disorder and psychological adaptation (MacLean et al., 1992; Stein & Jessop, 1984; Steinhausen et al., 1983). Inaccuracies in the assessment of asthma severity may be found in such studies because they rely on parent report measures, include no objective disease measures, and fail to include those with severe asthma. The lack of an observed relationship between severity and psychopathology may reflect the absence of patients with severe asthma.

The psychological adaptation of children who have other illnesses in addition to asthma may be further compromised. Results from the 1988 U.S. National Health Interview Survey on Child Health found that the most common pediatric chronic illnesses were respiratory disorders, which included asthma and allergies (Newacheck & Stoddard, 1994). About 20% of the sampled children had one chronic condition. The 5% of children who had two or more chronic health conditions were three times more likely to develop learning difficulties and be absent from school. Children with more than one physical illness (Kopp & Krakow, 1983) or physical disability (Cadman, Boyle, Szatmari, & Offord, 1987) are more likely to develop psychopathology than children with only one such condition. In a study of 551 children with asthma, those with asthma and another chronic medical condition demonstrated more behavioral and psychological problems than children with asthma only (Bussing et al., 1995).

Poverty and urban minority groups. Sociological variables involving poverty and being a member of a minority group correlate with more severe asthma and more frequent attacks. Asthma mortality and hospitalization rates are greater among non-White patients (Sly, 1988) and patients with low incomes (Wissow, Gittelsohn, Sazklo, Starfield, & Mussman, 1988). These individuals may have less access to health care; may fail to use asthma medications appropriately, may not recognize illness severity; may poorly adhere to treatment regimens; and may be more exposed to respiratory infections and environmental conditions that tend to exacerbate asthma such as air pollution, dust mites, indoor molds, and cigarette smoke (Marder, Targonski, Orris, Persky, & Addington, 1992). Low socioeconomic status (SES) in children with asthma has been found to be associated with increased prevalence of psychological disorders (Steinhausen et al., 1983) and decreased academic performance (Gutstadt et al., 1989).

Stressful life events. Stressful life events such as frequent moves, parental job loss, or loss of a family member increase the psychological duress for a child with a chronic illness. In a study of behavior problems and social competence of 81 children with asthma ages 6 to 14, these negative life events predicted the increased behavioral problems reported on the "internalizing" score from the Child Behavior Checklist. Lower socioeconomic status and high illness severity were predictive of less optimal adjustment (MacLean et al., 1992). "Undesirable life events" also predicted psychopathology in a study of 36 children with asthma. The events played a greater role in predicting psychopathology than did other factors including illness severity (Steinhausen et al., 1983).

Garmezy (1985) identified a child's disposition, or temperament, as a primary predictor of risk. Children with difficult or irritable temperaments are more likely than other children to be the targets of parental hostility or criticism (Rutter, 1987). Children with asthma and an irritable temperament, a temperament that is frequently caused by the illness itself, may similarly distress their parents more than would healthy children. One group of investigators compared temperament profiles of children with asthma to children with other chronic illnesses and healthy children and found that the children with asthma had significantly lower rhythmicity, lower adaptability, lower reaction intensity, more negative mood, and lower persistence (Kim, Ferrara, & Chess, 1980). Parents of children with asthma have been found to be more critical of their children than parents of healthy children (Hermann, Florin, Dietrich, Rieger, & Hahlweg, 1989; Schobinger, Florin, Zimmer, Lindemann, & Winter, 1992). Illness improvements are often greater when children (Purcell et al., 1969) or adolescents with asthma (Wamboldt, Wamboldt, Gavin, Roesler, & Brugman, 1995) are not in the presence of critical or overprotective parents for treatment.

School absences. Many children with asthma have numerous school absences; children with asthma miss school more often than do children without a chronic illness. One study revealed that children with asthma in one school district were absent for 7% of school days, whereas the remaining children missed 2% of school days (Parcel, Gilman, Nader, & Bunce, 1979). Frequent school absenteeism interrupts the process of learning and interferes with children's social interactions and participation in extracurricular activities. However, increased school absenteeism is associated neither with decreased achievement nor increased asthma severity. A study of 99 children with moderately severe or severe asthma found no statistical correlation between academic performance and school absenteeism. It was further noted that the mean achievement of the group with asthma was average or above average despite the fact that the children were absent from school 20% of the days in the semester before testing (Gutstadt et al., 1989). A Connecticut-based study found that in one school district, the incidence of asthma or chronic bronchitis was 7.1% among kindergarten through 12th graders (Weitzman, Klerman, Lamb, Menary, & Alpert, 1982). In this asthma group, absenteeism was higher and significantly associated with lower grades but not decreased achievement scores. In noting that the grades of children with asthma remained above average, the investigators concluded that the children with asthma in that study required no special education intervention. These findings indicate that school absences may temporarily interrupt the acquisition of new skills and knowledge without permanently impeding academic progress.

It might be assumed that the frequency of school absenteeism correlates with the severity of asthma, but this does not seem to be the case. One large study of 773 children with asthma and 773 control children found that severity of asthma was not correlated with increased school absences. The investigators concluded that school absences cannot serve as a marker of morbidity in childhood asthma (McCowan, Bryce, Neville, Crombie, & Clark, 1996). Parents of children with asthma vary greatly in when they choose to keep their children home from school for asthma symptoms. Thus, frequency of school absence may be more of a reflection of parental protectiveness than asthma severity.

A survey of parents of children with asthma living in the inner city found that 40% of the children were having difficulty in their school progress because of frequent absenteeism (Freudenberg et al., 1980). The reported findings suggest that children with asthma who live in the inner city may have a greater problem with school absences than other children. However, a subsequent study reported that low SES did not predict absence frequency for children with chronic illnesses such as asthma (Fowler, Johnson, & Atkinson, 1985).

Allergy-mediated neuropsychological changes. Some investigators suggested the possibility that the presence of childhood asthma or allergies may result in or be associated with specific brain changes. If this were true, then academic difficulties would increase, and specific associated learning disabilities would be identified in children with asthma and allergies. Research examining these questions has been plagued by methodological problems that, at times, have led to erroneous conclusions. For instance, scientists in one study reported results of a parent questionnaire indicating that almost 40% of children with asthma had difficulty in school, particularly with reading (Freudenberg et al., 1980). However, surveys of select groups of parents did not provide objective information about the incidence of learning problems in children with asthma. Studies that used larger groups of children with asthma and standardized tests of educational achievement have not found that the children had lesser academic skills than children without asthma. In a school-based study of mild and moderately ill children with asthma, standardized achievement test scores from 255 children with asthma in Iowa were found to be no different from those of classmates without asthma (Lindgren et al., 1992). In the largest study of children with asthma that included 1,041 patients in eight cities, mean IQ, cognitive, and achievement test scores were normally distributed (Annett, 1996). Even among children with more severe asthma, no clear evidence exists for an increased risk for learning disability or lagging academic skills. In a study of 99 children who had been hospitalized with moderately severe or severe asthma, average scores on the Slosson Intelligence Test, Woodcock Reading Mastery Test, Woodcock-Johnson Psychoeducational Battery, and Key Math Diagnostic Arithmetic Test were well above the 50th percentile relative to age-based norms (Gutstadt et al., 1989).

The possibility of a learning disability mediated by immune and autoimmune diseases has been raised (DeFries, Olson, Pennington, & Smith, 1991; Geschwind & Galaburda, 1987; Hugdahl, Synnevag, & Satz, 1990). One widely disseminated hypothesis suggested that the prevalence of autoimmune and allergic disorders was higher among children with dyslexia (Pennington, Smith, Kimberling, Green, & Haith, 1987), thus supporting the contention that changes in the immune system may be associated with alterations in normal brain development that affect specific learning or behavioral problems (Geschwind & Galaburda, 1987). Other investigators suggested that children with allergies experience difficulties with auditory and visual perception (Havard, 1975) and an increased prevalence of hyperkinetic (Kaplan, McNichol, Conte, & Moghadam, 1987) or attention deficit disorders (Roth, Beyreiss, Schlenzka, & Beyer, 1991). Havard (1975) concluded that many children with hyperactivity, language disabilities, learning disabilities, minimal brain damage, or emotional disturbances may in fact have allergy problems that play a role in their disability.

Theories proposing a direct link among allergic disorders, brain function, and learning disabilities have not been validated in subsequent research. When samples of children with hyperactivity were evaluated, an increased incidence of allergic disorders was not found (McGee, Stanton, & Sears, 1993; Mitchell, Aman, Turbott, & Manku, 1987). Achievement levels among children with allergies were no lower than those of children without allergies (McLoughlin et al., 1983). The association among reading disabilities, immune disorders, and left-handedness proposed by Geschwind (Geschwind & Galaburda, 1987) was, for the most part, not supported by subsequent research (Biederman, Milberger, Faraone, Guite, & Warburton, 1994; Gilger, Pennington, Green, Smith, & Smith, 1992).

The hypothesis that attention deficit hyperactivity disorder (ADHD) is associated with asthma has been similarly disputed. In one study, the illness histories were compared of 140 children with ADHD ages 6 to 17 years and both their first-degree relatives and 120 unaffected control boys. Although ADHD and asthma rates were higher among relatives—likely reflecting a genetic component—the absence of evidence refuted the existence of a relationship between them (Biederman et al., 1994). McGee and colleagues similarly documented that they found no association among parent, teacher, or self-reported ADHD and history of allergic disorders in children (McGee et al., 1993).

Hypoxia-induced brain damage. On rare occasions, a child with severe asthma may experience a complete respiratory arrest. Such arrests typically follow a rapid increase in airway obstruction that requires emergency room assistance for resuscitation of the child, possibly by the insertion of a tube into the airway to reestablish breathing (i.e., intubation). These episodes are traumatic and life threatening. Because respiratory arrest prevents the brain from receiving vital oxygen, such events can be accompanied by seizures and neurological damage. Individual case reports have documented significant neuropsychological changes after asthma-induced respiratory arrest (Bierman, Pierson, Shapiro, & Simons, 1975; Nellhaus, Newman, Ellis, & Pirnat, 1975).

One group of investigators argued that as a consequence of oxygen deprivation, children with asthma demonstrated significant neuropsychological impairment (Dunleavy, 1981; Dunleavy & Baade, 1980). A neuropsychological test battery was administered to 20 children attending a summer asthma camp. These investigators argued that 7 (35%) of the children tested demonstrated evidence of neuropsychological impairments. The researchers concluded that hypoxia causes brain damage in a significant proportion of children with asthma. However, this study was criticized for lack of inappropriate control groups and misinterpretation of test results (Annett & Bender, 1994; Suess & Chai, 1981) and seems to have greatly exaggerated the incidence of hypoxia-induced brain damage in children with asthma.

A subsequent study involved the administration of a battery of cognitive and neuromotor tests to 67 children hospitalized with severe asthma (Bender, Belleau, Fukuhara, Mrazek, & Strunk, 1987). Thirteen of the children had histories of respiratory arrest accompanied by seizures, thus placing them at risk for hypoxia-induced brain damage. However, mean scores in this sample did not differ from others in the group who had not experienced seizures. The authors concluded that most children with asthma who have experienced a respiratory arrest do not have resulting cognitive impairments or learning problems. Rare instances of brain damage can result from respiratory arrests, but the majority of children with asthma do not have permanent changes related to hypoxia.

Medication side effects. Medication side effects may be yet another perturbation to the psychological adaptation of children with asthma. Because children with severe, poorly controlled asthma are likely to receive more medications at larger doses, risk factors increase to the greatest degree in this segment of the population with asthma. Although the psychological effects of theophylline are not as severe as once believed (Rachalefsky et al., 1986), the caffeine-like effects of theophylline have been documented and include a slight trend toward more anxiety and hand tremor in treated versus untreated children. These behaviors are accompanied by slightly increased attention, verbal memory, or both (Bender, Lerner, & Poland, 1991; Bender & Milgrom, 1992; Schlieper, Adcock, Beaudry, Feldman, & Leikin, 1991). Classic antihistamines, such as diphenhydramine, have been found to cause drowsiness in some children (Vuurman, Veggel, Uiterwijk, Leutner, & O'Hanlon, 1993), although a recent study found that classic, sedating antihistamines and nonsedating antihistamines had no differences in their effects on children's learning (Bender, Milgrom, & McCormick, 2001). Individual case studies have shown an association between sympathomimetics and various unusual behaviors in children, including aggressiveness and visual hallucinations (Bender & Milgrom, 1995).

Children with asthma stabilized with high doses of oral corticosteroids (40–80 mg per day) can experience significant depression, anxiety, and long-term memory impairment compared with children receiving low maintenance doses of corticosteroids (2–20 mg per day; Bender, Lerner, & Kollasch, 1988). However, the steroid-induced psychosis reported in adults has not been documented in children. Of particular interest is the finding that children with a preexisting history of emotional difficulties were more likely to become anxious and depressed while receiving high doses of prednisone than children without such histories (Bender et al., 1991). This finding further supports the conclusion that a combination of risk factors heightens the potential for maladaptation. Inhaled steroids have not been associated with cognitive or behavioral changes in children with asthma (Bender et al., 1998).

Summary

In summary, evidence has indicated that, although asthma is a stressful and disruptive chronic illness, the psychological development of most children with mild to moderate asthma is not significantly altered. The risk of developing a psychological disorder increases for children who have severe asthma or are exposed to heightened stress, live in poverty, or belong to a racial or ethnic minority group. Other factors hypothesized to alter the developmental course for children with asthma—school absences, hypoxia, allergy-mediated changes in brain functions, and medication side effects—have been found to have little impact.

Behavioral Approaches to Asthma Management

For most of the 20th century, patients with asthma were treated with traditional psychotherapy to resolve whatever psychological problems they were experiencing. However, the development of behavioral techniques in the 1960s and 1970s shifted the focus of intervention toward modifying asthma-related psychological and behavioral problems. Initial efforts were directed toward changing such problems as fear or panic generated by asthma, noncompliance to medication regimens, incorrect inhaler use, and inappropriate overuse of hospital facilities (Creer, 1979, 1982, 1991). Research was also directed toward increasing involvement of patients in their treatment through the use of negotiation and written contracts between health care providers and their patients (Creer, 1979). Many of these methods are still state-of-the-art techniques with respect to the management of asthma, particularly pediatric asthma (Creer & Levstek, 1998). Indeed, they are usually integrated into self-management programs designed to help manage the disorder.

Self-Management Programs

In the late 1970s, four factors came together to spur the development and testing of intervention programs for asthma, particularly pediatric asthma (Creer, 2000). First, it was widely recognized that control over asthma required an interdisciplinary approach that included patients' involvement in their health care. This was partly prompted by concerns regarding compliance to medication regimens and failure to establish environmental control over triggers of asthma.

Second, the techniques of self-management had already been developed and tested, many in the previous decade (Creer, 1979; Decker & Kaliner, 1988). Processes that seemed necessary for the self-management of asthma included (a) goal setting, a joint process of patients and their health care workers; (b) information collection, particularly information gathered through the use of peak flow meters, asthma diaries, and reports of attacks; (c) information processing and evaluation; (d) decision making; (e) action; and (f) self-reaction (Creer & Holroyd, 1997).

Third, the rising prevalence of the disorder and its consequences indicated that patients needed to become partners with health care providers in the management of their asthma. This need was prompted by the rising tide of the cost of asthma treatment and changes in asthma morbidity, including increased rates of hospital use, emergency room visits, and school absenteeism.

Finally, organizations involved with asthma (e.g., the American Lung Association) and the federal government prompted and provided financial support for behavioral and medical scientists to develop and test asthma self-management programs. As a consequence, a wide array of self-management programs was designed and implemented for asthma, particularly pediatric asthma. Despite some methodological flaws, typical of comprehensive first-generation intervention programs, results from these programs demonstrated that forming an active partnership with health care providers produced significant results. These results included reductions in frequency of attacks, decreases in hospital and emergency room visits for asthma, increased school and work attendance, improved medication use, and reduced asthma costs (Wigal, Creer, Kotses, & Lewis, 1990). Later application of these techniques to adults with asthma produced similar results, and most patients were continuing to practice the skills 5 years or longer after training (Caplin & Creer, 2001). An unexpected finding in the study by Caplin and Creer was that many patients who performed few self-management tasks reported that they no longer needed these skills because their asthma had gone into remission. The response result raises another issue—whether the patients who continued to perform self-management techniques also experienced periods of asthma remission or quiescence.

Asthma Guidelines

The initial set of guidelines for asthma management was issued in 1991 (NIH, 1991). The guidelines became invaluable to physicians and other health care personnel as a benchmark for comparing the treatment they were providing patients with asthma (Creer, Winder, & Tinkelman, 1999). Of equal significance, the guidelines served to stimulate consideration of the role patients should play in the treatment and control of their asthma. Thus, by the time a second set of guidelines was issued (NIH, 1997), the role of patients and health care providers in the treatment of asthma was clearly spelled out. Key points are summarized in Exhibit 8.1.

EXHIBIT 8.1
Key Points in Providing Educational and Other Services to Patients
With Asthma

- Patient education should begin at the time of diagnosis and be integrated into every step of clinical asthma care.
- It is essential that education be provided by all members of the health care team.
- Teach asthma self-management, tailoring the approach to the needs of each patient. Be sensitive to cultural beliefs and practices.
- Use every opportunity to teach and reinforce the following:
  (a) Basic facts about asthma
  (b) Roles of asthma medications, including the difference between controller and reliever drugs
  (c) Patient skills such as self-monitoring and using the inhaler, spacer and holding chamber
- Jointly develop treatment goals.
- Encourage an active partnership with patients. Provide all patients with a written daily self-management plan and an action plan for asthma attacks or exacerbations. Provide patients with a daily asthma diary.
- Encourage adherence by promoting open communication; individualizing, reviewing, and adjusting plans as needed; emphasizing goals and outcomes; and encouraging family involvement.

Note. From *Highlights of the Expert Panel Report 2: Guidelines for the Diagnosis and Management of Asthma,* National Institutes of Health, 1997, Bethesda, Maryland. Copyright 1997 by National Institutes of Health, National Heart, Lung, and Blood Institute.

As noted, the points are aimed at making certain everyone, including patients, become cooperating members of an interdisciplinary treatment team. Although the guidelines were developed specifically for asthma, they could serve as a starting point for the development and introduction of intervention programs for all respiratory disorders, particularly COPD and tuberculosis. The guidelines are useful because behavioral scientists are asked to apply their skills within the structure and confines of managed care. As integration increases, it is imperative to have knowledge of the various strategies that can be taken.

The following section provides a brief overview and discussion of several levels of intervention that can be taken when applying educational and behavioral change procedures to asthma. The levels may be followed in sequence and tailored to fit the needs of particular patients (according to resources of each given situation).

Managed Care and Disease Management

Although managed care has a long history (Knight, 1998), it only became a major player in health care in the past two decades. Basically, managed care is a spectrum of health delivery systems that tries to control the cost of, the quality of, and access to health care. Conditions that are expensive, chronic, complex, and likely to have large variations in practice patterns are often targeted for intensive management; these conditions include asthma. The way asthma has often been treated is through *disease management*, a "systematic, population-based approach to identifying persons at risk, intervening with specific programs of care, and measuring clinical and other outcomes" (Epstein & Sherwood, 1996, p. 838). Despite the wide acceptance of applying "best practices" to asthma treatment, many patients with asthma fail to receive optimal treatment. In addition, patients also may not take medications correctly or flounder at monitoring their asthma, which may cause exacerbations of the condition.

Most organizations related to health care and groups with a vested interest in health promotion provide information to patients with asthma designed to help them understand asthma, form a partnership with their health care provider, and take appropriate self-initiated actions to manage their condition. In addition, many of these organizations offer educational services to health care providers to improve the treatment of asthma. The organizations include managed care and disease management organizations, health care providers, employers, employer coalitions, pharmaceutical companies, government agencies, volunteer health organizations, schools, clinics, and hospitals. Educational services provided for patients with asthma range from increasing patients' awareness of asthma to providing on-call assistance in disease management programs. Educational services and change programs developed for providers range from education about treatment guidelines to improving communication and from preceptorships to office-based processes for implementation of best practices. The goals and expected outcomes from each type of services differ. For purposes of this discussion, the services are divided into three levels of intensity: low, moderate, and high. The advantages and disadvantages of each approach are listed in Exhibit 8.2. Issues to consider when deciding which type of educational or intervention services to develop and implement for people with asthma are described in the following sections.

Low-intensity educational approaches. Educational elements are developed to increase awareness and knowledge of different respiratory disorders. It is also anticipated that education will motivate the people with the disorders and health care providers to consider how to change behavior for better asthma control. Elements can be developed for various types of media, including print, audiotape, videotape, Web site, radio, and television. Provider pieces for asthma typically integrate parts of the Expert Panel Report 2 (NIH, 1997), described in Exhibit 8.1 in full or a condensed form. In many cases, the information includes tools such as asthma action plans, reference cards on the diagnosis and severity classification of asthma, trigger checklists, and types of medications. Educational pieces for patients with asthma often include a readiness-to-change survey and materials on the nature of asthma, how to identify triggers, how to manage asthma, and the purpose of an asthma action plan. Low-intensity educational ap-

EXHIBIT 8.2
Advantages and Disadvantages: Three Approaches of Patient Services Developed for Health Care Providers

Low-intensity educational approaches
Advantages
- Low cost
- Possible wide distribution

Disadvantages
- Promotes little if any behavioral change
- Promotes little if any change in treatment of asthma by patient or provider

Moderate-intensity educational approaches
Advantages
- Allows for two-way interactions between patients and health care providers
- May produce changes consistent with better treatment and management of asthma

Disadvantages
- Moderate cost
- Requires more resources to implement program
- Less participation

High-intensity educational approaches
Advantages
- Sustained behavior change
- Produces positive outcomes related to improvement in asthma care
- Produces positive return on investment

Disadvantages
- Limited participation by those targeted for program
- High initial cost to develop, implement, and evaluate program
- Human resource intensive

proaches rarely produce sustained behavior change; however, they are a relatively inexpensive way to provide information on chronic conditions to a broad audience. They also provide an excellent starting point for more intensive management programs for asthma or COPD.

Moderate-intensity educational approaches. Moderate-intensity educational approaches require a greater time commitment on the part of patients. The approaches also involve more implementation resources. The services include seminars for patients or providers, and call centers, referral services, or more targeted educational materials for patients. The goal of moderate-intensity approaches is to get everyone involved in the treatment and management of asthma—health care providers, pharmacists, and patients with asthma and their families—to do something to improve treatment of asthma. For example, involving people by having them attend a seminar or call a referral service is a positive step in the change process. The approaches are designed to encourage communication within and among groups of health care providers and patients.

High-intensity educational approaches. As the name implies, high-intensity educational approaches require a high degree of commitment from all involved in a program, including those who develop, implement, facilitate, receive, and evaluate the program. High-intensity programs typically produce the best outcomes, although the costs of such programs are higher than for other approaches. High-intensity approaches for people with asthma are designed to educate them about their disease, teach self-management skills, and promote behavior change. For example, an asthma disease management program could teach patients about the respiratory system and signs and symptoms of asthma, trigger identification and control, use of a peak flow meter and an asthma diary to monitor asthma, inhaler techniques, and types of medication to treat asthma, particularly the difference between quick-relief and controller medications (e.g., Lucas et al., 2001).

Critical design elements of a high-intensity program for asthma are as follows:

- The program is conducted over time so that participants can practice self-management skills, thereby increasing their confidence in managing their asthma.
- Outcomes data are collected so that the impact of the program can be evaluated and skills taught during the program can be reinforced.
- Support is provided to those in group and case management programs to promote discussion of personal experiences and permit feedback and expressions of empathy and encouragement.

High-intensity provider programs include preceptorships and formal education programs. Successful education programs are Continuing Medical Education (CME) accredited, are led by well-respected facilitators, involve peer discussion, and are oriented toward case studies. The primary method of teaching is by example; preceptorships provide an opportunity for hands-on experiences. A high-intensity educational program was used in the study by Clark and colleagues (1998), which taught physicians in an interactive seminar to examine ways to develop a partnership with their patients. The results were improvements in patients' compliance to controller medications and increased confidence in managing their asthma. A high-intensity educational program was also used in the study by the HIPPO Project (Heinrich & Homer, 1999), a program that used a consultative model in which the project staff worked closely with patients to teach them how to manage their asthma.

The key to the success of any type of educational program requires focusing on the details of implementation. Exhibit 8.3 provides a list of

EXHIBIT 8.3
Developing and Implementing a High-Intensity Educational Program

- Assign a leader who has the time, communication skills, and interpersonal skills to build support and maintain the momentum needed to design, implement, and evaluate a program.
- Prepare a realistic budget for conducting the program and analyzing outcome data.
- Build an implementation team, and identify the roles and responsibilities of each member. To gain cooperation and obtain maximum input, include people from each area involved in the program, regardless of what their involvement will be or when it will occur.
- Determine the program goals.
- Determine the outcomes measures to be used, as well as how and when they will be used.
- Determine the way the program will be delivered to patients. Program delivery types may include classroom sessions, the Internet, case management, telephones, and direct mail. For health care providers, types of program delivery may include seminars and courses, preceptorships, lunch-and-learn sessions, the Internet, and direct mail.
- Develop program content by considering the target population and any cultural issues that may need to be addressed.
- Determine and design tools necessary for the program, such as educational pieces and program announcements.
- Design outcomes surveys and an analysis plan.
- Determine and arrange for data management and analysis of collected data.
- Identify targets for the program: people with asthma and health care providers. Options include an analysis of medical and pharmacy claims data, surveys, or data on all members of a group.
- Design the recruitment and retention strategies.
- Determine the types of incentives needed to encourage participation and patient retention in the program.
- Identify and train the people conducting the program, if applicable.
- Prepare various materials, such as recruitment materials, educational materials, and surveys.
- Determine the cost of program for the participants, if applicable.
- Recruit participants, conduct the program, evaluate the outcomes, and modify the program as needed.

implementation issues to consider when developing an educational program for any chronic disorder, including asthma, COPD, or tuberculosis. These issues should be considered by behavioral scientists and all members of an interdisciplinary treatment team. An example of a high-intensity intervention program is patient self-management of a respiratory disorder. Components typically included in such programs for asthma are outlined in Exhibit 8.4. The summary of the components could easily serve as a backdrop for designing and implementing a self-management program for any chronic condition, including asthma, COPD, and tuberculosis.

In summary, numerous treatment strategies that focus on patients partnering with medical and behavioral scientists in the management of respiratory disorders, particularly asthma, have evolved in the past 25 years.

EXHIBIT 8.4
Components of Self-Management for Respiratory Disorders

Goal selection
Goal selection occurs after patient education.
- Goals are jointly set by health care workers and patients.
- Goal selection includes input by patients and health care providers and may involve negotiation between parties.
- A significant goal is a jointly developed action plan for treatment of the disorder.
- Goal selection also (a) establishes outcome preferences, (b) increases commitment, and (c) generates expectancies to trigger effort and performance.

Information collection
Information collection is based on self-monitoring.
- Information collection includes observation of selected events such as respiratory exacerbation or distress.
- Monitor behavior, particularly coughing and sneezing, to limit likelihood of infection when around others (tuberculosis).
- Record accurate information on a daily diary form.
- Record peak flow values to provide objective data on pulmonary functioning.
- Record use of chest physiotherapy techniques or oxygen (for those with chronic obstructive pulmonary disease [COPD]).
- Record information on daily exercise (for those with COPD).
- Record information on use of preventive and as-needed medications.
- Record effective methods of preventing exposing others to the tuberculosis bacterium.

Information processing and evaluation
Patients process and evaluate information they have gathered about themselves and their breathing.
- Patients detect changes in breathing from adaptation or baseline level.
- Patients evaluate and make judgments on the basis of collected information.
- Patients analyze antecedent events that may have led to breathing changes. They also analyze behaviors taken to manage the changes and consequences of these actions.
- Patients consider contextual events that may have contributed to breathing changes, as well as consider actions taken to manage such changes.
- Patients with tuberculosis process and evaluate the steps taken to prevent exposing others to the bacterium.

Decision-making
Patients make the most appropriate decisions to effectively manage breathing changes.
- Patients make the most appropriate decisions about being around others and exposing them to the tuberculosis bacterium.
- Patients use heuristics they have learned proven to be effective in the medical decision-making literature including thinking of specific actions to take, using a personal database of information, adjusting treatment in stepwise manner, perceiving actions in terms of probabilities, and not relying on memory.

Exhibit continues

EXHIBIT 8.4   (*Continued*)

Action

Patients perform the actions they have previously agreed on to manage daily breathing, exacerbations of their condition, breathing distress, or (for those with tuberculosis) unnecessary exposure of others to the tuberculosis bacterium.

- Patients use personal skills and techniques such as self-instruction to guide the performance of their actions.
- Self-reaction to the actions taken and their consequences.
- Patients should objectively evaluate their performance to establish realistic expectations of their actions.
- Patients become effective managers of their respiratory disorder.

The success of these approaches, particularly of asthma self-management, is a harbinger for the potential success of similar techniques for treatment of tuberculosis and COPD. In addition, the emergence of managed care has created several levels of treatment that are available to patients with respiratory diseases. The hierarchy of levels not only makes greater use of finite resources but also permits treatment approaches to be tailored for the needs and abilities of individual patients.

CONCLUSION

The chapter focused on three respiratory disorders: tuberculosis, COPD, and asthma. The discussion acknowledged that the conditions can be differentiated by physiological criteria and by the extent to which behavioral scientists have been involved in treating the conditions. Behavioral scientists can further delineate their role or potential role from the perspective of primary or secondary prevention. Kaplan (2000) pointed out that primary prevention "requires preventive maneuvers that reduce the chance that a health problem will develop" (p. 382). Primary prevention almost always requires behavior change. However, secondary prevention is medical prevention based on the diagnosis and treatment of an existing condition.

Behavioral scientists have generally been nonparticipating bystanders as tuberculosis has reemerged in the world. The role they have played in developing countries is somewhat understandable; tuberculosis and the association of tuberculosis with HIV and AIDS in some regions of the world have thus far defeated attempts at containment and control. Whether the two infections will ever be controlled is problematic. Like a wildfire, the infections may defy containment and run their slow and horrific course.

However, as exemplified by Japan, a renascence of tuberculosis is taking place in developed countries. The fact that almost a third of the world's population is infected with the tuberculosis bacterium combined with increased globalization brought on by air travel offers a frightening prospect. Yet any control over tuberculosis requires behavioral input for primary prevention (e.g., teaching patients with active tuberculosis how to prevent the spread of infection, teaching those without the infection to avoid becoming infected) and secondary prevention (e.g., developing adherence strategies for adherence to antituberculosis medications).

Psychologists and other behavioral scientists have become increasingly involved with the treatment of COPD. Behavioral techniques, which are often coupled with pharmacological tools (e.g., nicotine patches, bupropion), offer the best hope for the primary prevention of cigarette smoking, the greatest risk factor for COPD. COPD is usually not diagnosed until it is clinically apparent and moderately advanced; however, much of the prevention efforts will be through secondary prevention techniques—through smoking cessation methods and by promoting adherence to medication and exercise regimens.

This chapter focused heavily on asthma for two reasons. First, behavioral scientists have long been accepted as members of research and treatment teams for asthma, particularly for children. Usually, these teams are multidisciplinary and as such, behavioral scientists have often been unable to fully use their skills and expertise. However, the increasing use of interdisciplinary research and treatment teams may remedy this outcome. Second, because of behavioral scientists' acceptance as members of interdisciplinary research teams, they have been able to assist patients with asthma and conduct more research on the condition. The conclusion regarding children with asthma—that they are normal youngsters in abnormal situations—may not seem like a meaningful concept, but it took three decades of research for medical and behavioral sciences to reach the conclusion. In doing so, it shattered many of the persistent myths about asthma, including the perception that asthma was a psychological condition that occurred because of a faulty mother–child relationship (e.g., French & Alexander, 1941).

In conclusion, respiratory disorders will continue to be a major health concern throughout the world in the 21st century. Behavioral scientists must assume a leadership role in the primary and secondary prevention of these disorders. If behavioral scientists' knowledge and skills are fully used, they can help prevent disease—for example, by designing primary prevention strategies to prevent tuberculosis or applying secondary prevention techniques to smoking cessation programs for patients with COPD. Behavioral scientists have the proven skills and expertise to help people stop smoking or adhere to medication or exercise regimens. The future of respiratory diseases will be a function not only of refined medical care and treatment but also of how well behavioral scientists are able to change people's behavior. It is an awesome challenge.

REFERENCES

Abe, C., Hirano, K., Wada, M., & Aoyagi, T. (2001). Resistance of *Mycobacterium tuberculosis* to four first-line anti-tuberculosis drugs in Japan, 1997. *International Journal of Tuberculosis and Lung Disease, 5*, 46–52.

American Thoracic Society. (1995). Standards for the diagnosis and care of patients with chronic obstructive pulmonary disease. *American Journal of Respiratory and Critical Care Medicine, 152*, S77–S122.

Annett, R. D. (1996, May). *Psychological growth and development studies and characteristics of the Childhood Asthma Management Program (CAMP) participants.* Paper presented at the annual meeting of the American Thoracic Society, New Orleans, LA.

Annett, R. D., & Bender, B. G. (1994). Neuropsychological dysfunction in asthmatic children. *Neuropsychological Review, 4*, 91–115.

Austin, J. K. (1989). Comparison of child adaptation to epilepsy and asthma. *Journal of Child and Adolescent Psychiatric and Mental Health Nursing, 2*, 139–144.

Barry, M. J., & Walschlager, S. A. (1998). Exercise training and chronic obstructive pulmonary disease: Past and future research directions. *Journal of Cardiopulmonary Rehabilitation, 18*, 181–191.

Bender, B. (1996). Measurement of quality of life in pediatric asthma clinical trials. *Annals of Allergy, Asthma, and Immunology, 77*, 438–447.

Bender, B. (1998, April). *Is there a relationship between psychological dysfunction and disease severity in children with mild-to-moderate asthma?* Presented at the annual meeting of the American Thoracic Society, Chicago, IL.

Bender, B. G., Belleau, L., Fukuhara, J. T., Mrazek, D. A., & Strunk, R. C. (1987). Psychomotor adaptation in children with severe chronic asthma. *Pediatrics, 79*, 723–727.

Bender, B. G., Ilke, D., DuHamel, T., & Tinkelman, D. (1998). Neuropsychological and behavioral changes in asthmatic children treated with beclomethasone dipropionate versus theophylline. *Pediatrics, 101*, 355–360.

Bender, B. G., & Klinnert, M. D. (1998). Psychological correlates of asthma severity and treatment outcomes. In H. Kotses & A. Harver (Eds.), *Self-management of asthma* (pp. 63–88). New York: Marcel Dekker.

Bender, B. G., Lerner, J., & Kollasch, E. (1988). Mood and memory changes in asthmatic children receiving corticosteroids. *Journal of the American Academy of Child and Adolescent Psychiatry, 6*, 720–725.

Bender, B., Lerner, J., & Poland, J. (1991). Association between corticosteroids and psychological change in hospitalized asthmatic children. *Annals of Allergy, 66*, 414–419.

Bender, B., & Milgrom, H. (1992). Theophylline-induced behavior change in children: An objective evaluation of parent's perceptions. *Journal of the American Medical Association, 267*, 2621–2624.

Bender, B., & Milgrom, H. (1995). Neuropsychiatric effects of medications for allergic diseases. *Journal of Allergy and Clinical Immunology, 95*, 523–528.

Bender, B. G., Milgrom, H., & McCormick, D. (2001). Children's school performance is not impaired by short-term administration of diphenhydramine or loratadine. *Journal of Pediatrics, 138*, 656–660.

Bendstrup, K. E., Ingemann, J. J., Jensen, J., Holm, S., & Bengtsson, B. (1997). Out-patient rehabilitation improves activities of daily living, quality of life and exercise tolerance in chronic obstructive pulmonary disease. *European Respiratory Journal, 10*, 2801–2806.

Biederman, J., Milberger, S., Faraone, S. V., Guite, J., & Warburton, R. (1994). Associations between childhood asthma and ADHD: Issues of psychiatric comorbidity and familiarity. *Journal of the American Academy of Child and Adolescent Psychiatry, 33*, 842–848.

Bierman, C., Pierson, W., Shapiro, G., & Simons, E. (1975). Brain damage from asthma in children. *Journal of Allergy and Clinical Immunology, 55*, 126.

Blanc, P. D., Eisner, M. D., Israel, L., & Yelin, E. H. (1999). The association between occupation and asthma in general medical practice. *Chest, 115*, 1259–1264.

Broughton, W. A., & Bass, J. B., Jr. (1999). Tuberculosis and diseases caused by atypical mycobacteria. In R. K. Albert, S. G. Shapiro, & J. R. Jett (Eds.), *Comprehensive respiratory medicine* (pp. 29.1–29.16). St. Louis, MO: C. V. Mosby.

Burman, W. J., Cohn, D. L., Rietmeijer, C. A., Judson, F. N., Sbarbaro, J. A., & Reves, R. R. (1997). Noncompliance with directly observed therapy for tuberculosis. Epidemiology and effect on the outcome of treatment. *Chest, 111*, 1168–1173.

Burman, W. J., Dalton, C. B., Cohn, D. L., Butler, J. R., & Reves, R. R. (1997). A cost-effectiveness analysis of directly observed therapy vs. self-administered therapy for treatment of tuberculosis. *Chest, 112*, 63–70.

Busse, W. W., & Reed, C. E. (1988). Asthma: Definitions and pathogenesis. In E. Middleton, Jr., C. E. Reed, E. F. Ellis, N. F. Adkinson, Jr., & J. W. Yunginer (Eds.), *Allergy: Principles and practice* (pp. 969–989). St. Louis, MO: C. V. Mosby.

Bussing, R., Halfon, N., Benjamin, B., & Wells, K. B. (1995). Prevalence of behavior problems in U.S. children with asthma. *Archives of Pediatric and Adolescent Medicine, 149*, 565–572.

Cadman, D., Boyle, M., Szatmari, P., & Offord, D. R. (1987). Chronic illness, disability, and mental and social well-being: Findings of the Ontario Child Health Study. *Pediatrics, 79*, 805–813.

Cambach, W., Wagenaar, R. C., Koelman, T. W., van Keimpema, A. R., & Kemper, H. C. (1999). The long-term effects of pulmonary rehabilitation in patients with asthma and chronic obstructive pulmonary diseases: A research synthesis. *Archives of Physical Medical Rehabilitation, 80*, 103–111.

Caplin, D. L., & Creer, T. L. (2001). A self-management program for adult asthma. III. Maintenance and relapse of skills. *Journal of Asthma, 338*, 343–356.

Celli, B. R. (1998). Standards for optimal management of COPD: A summary. *Chest, 113*, 283S–287S.

Centers for Disease Control and Prevention. (1998a). Forecasted state-specific estimates of self-reported asthma prevalence—United States, 1998. *Morbidity and Mortality Weekly Report, 47*, 1022–1025.

Centers for Disease Control and Prevention. (1998b). Surveillance for asthma—United States, 1960–1995. *Morbidity and Monthly Weekly Report, 47*, 837–840.

Centers for Disease Control and Prevention. (1999). Primary multi-resistant tuberculosis—Ivanovo Oblast, Russia, 1999. *Morbidity and Mortality Weekly Report, 48*, 661–664.

Centers for Disease Control and Prevention. (2001). Preventing and controlling tuberculosis along the U.S.–Mexico border. *Morbidity and Mortality Weekly Report, 50*, No. RR-1.

Childhood Asthma Management Program Group. (1999). The Childhood Asthma Management Program (CAMP): Design, rationale and methods. *Controlled Clinical Trials, 20*, 91–120.

Clark, N. M., Gong, M., Schork, M. A., Evans, D., Roloff, D., Hurwitz, M., et al. (1998). Impact of education of physicians on patient outcomes. *Pediatrics, 101*, 831–836.

Creer, T. L. (1979). *Asthma therapy: A behavioral health-care system for respiratory disorders.* New York: Springer.

Creer, T. L. (1982). Asthma. *Journal of Consulting and Clinical Psychology, 50*, 912–921.

Creer, T. L. (1990). Strategies for judgment and decision-making in the management of childhood asthma. *Pediatric Asthma, Allergy, and Immunology, 4*, 253–264.

Creer, T. L. (1991). The application of behavioral procedures to childhood asthma: Current and future perspectives. *Patient Education and Counseling, 17*, 9–22.

Creer, T. L. (2000). Self-management of chronic diseases. In M. Boekaerts, P. R. Pintrich, & M. Zeidner (Eds.), *Self-regulation: Theory, research, applications* (pp. 601–629). Orlando, FL: Academic Press.

Creer, T. L., & Bender, B. G. (1995). Pediatric asthma. In M. C. Roberts (Ed.), *Handbook of pediatric psychology* (2nd ed., pp. 219–240). New York: Guilford Press.

Creer, T. L., & Holroyd, K. A. (1997). Self-management. In A. Baum, C. McManus, S. Newman, J. Weinman, & R. West (Eds.), *Cambridge handbook of psychology, health and medicine* (pp. 255–257). Cambridge, England: Cambridge University Press.

Creer, T. L., Holroyd, K. A., Glasgow, R. E., & Smith, T. W. (in press). Health psychology. In M. J. Lambert (Ed.), *Handbook of psychotherapy and behavior change* (5th ed.). New York: Wiley.

Creer, T. L., & Levstek, D. A. (1998). Respiratory disorder. In A. Bellack & M.

Hersen (Eds.), *Comprehensive clinical psychology* (pp. 339–359). New York: Pergamon.

Creer, T. L., Winder, J. A., & Tinkelman, D. (1999). Guidelines for the diagnosis and management of asthma: Accepting the challenge. *Journal of Asthma, 36*, 391–407.

Decker, J. L., & Kaliner, M. A. (1988). *Understanding and managing asthma.* New York: Avon.

DeFries, J. C., Olson, R. K., Pennington, B. F., & Smith, S. D. (1991). Colorado reading project: Past, present, and future. *Learning Disabilities, 2*, 37–46.

Donnelly, E. (1994). Parents of children with asthma: An examination of family hardiness, family stressors, and family functioning. *Journal of Pediatric Nursing, 9*, 398–408.

Donnelly, J. E., Donnelly, W. J., & Thong, Y. H. (1987). Parental perceptions and attitudes toward asthma and its treatment: A controlled study. *Social Science and Medicine, 24*, 431–437.

Dunleavy, R. A. (1981). Neuropsychological correlates of asthma: Effect of hypoxia or drugs? *Journal of Consulting and Clinical Psychology, 49*, 137.

Dunleavy, R. A., & Baade, L. F. (1980). Neuropsychological correlates of severe asthma in children 9–14 years old. *Journal of Consulting and Clinical Psychology, 48*, 214–221.

Dye, C., Scheele, S., Dolin, P., Pathania, V., & Raviglione, M. C. (1999). Global burden of tuberculosis. *Journal of the American Medical Association, 282*, 677–686.

Epstein, R. S., & Sherwood, L. M. (1996). From outcomes research to disease management: A guide for the perplexed. *Annals of Internal Medicine, 124*, 832–838.

Farmer, P. E., Becerra, M. C., & Kim, J. Y. (1999). *Conclusions and recommendations. The global impact of drug-resistant tuberculosis.* Boston, MA: Harvard University, Program in Infectious Disease and Social Change.

Ferguson, G. T. (1998). Management of COPD. Early identification and active intervention are crucial. *Postgraduate Medicine, 103*, 136–141.

Fish, J. E., & Peters, S. P. (1999). Airway remodeling and persistent airway obstruction in asthma. *Journal of Allergy and Clinical Immunology, 104*, 509–516.

Fisher, E. B. (in press). Smoking. In J. Raczynski, L. Bradley, & L. Leviton (Eds.), *Handbook of clinical health psychology: Volume 2. Disorders of behavior and health.* Washington, DC: American Psychological Association.

Fogio, K., Bianchi, L., Bruletti, G., Battista, L., Pagani, M., & Ambrosino, N. (1999). Long-term effectiveness of pulmonary rehabilitation in patients with chronic airway obstruction. *European Respiratory Journal, 13*, 125–132.

Fowler, M. G., Johnson, M. P., & Atkinson, S. S. (1985). School achievement and absence in children with chronic health conditions. *Journal of Pediatrics, 106*, 683–687.

French, T. M., & Alexander, F. (1941). Psychogenic factors in bronchial asthma. *Psychosomatic Medicine Monographs, 4*, 1–92.

Freudenberg, N., Feldman, C. H., Clark, N. M., Millman, E. J., Valle, I., & Wasilewski, Y. (1980). The impact of bronchial asthma on school attendance and performance. *Journal of School Health, 50,* 522–526.

Garb, H. N. (1998). *Studying the clinician.* Washington, DC: American Psychological Association.

Garmezy, N. (1985). Stress-resistant children: The search for protective factors. In J. E. Stevenson (Ed.), *Recent research in developmental psychopathology:* Journal of Child Psychology and Psychiatry, *Book* (Suppl. 4, pp. 213–233). Oxford: Pergamon.

Garner, P. (1998). What makes DOT work? *Lancet, 352,* 1326–1327.

Garrett, L. (1994). *The coming plague. Newly emerging diseases in a world out of bounce.* New York: Farrar, Straus, & Giroux.

Gasner, M. R., Maw, K. L., Feldman, G. E., Fujiwara, P. I., & Frieden, T. R. (1999). The use of legal action in New York City to ensure treatment of tuberculosis. *New England Journal of Medicine, 340,* 359–366.

Geschwind, N., & Galaburda, A. (1987). Cerebral lateralization: Biological mechanisms, associations and pathology: II. A hypothesis and program for research. *Archives of Neurology, 42,* 521–552.

Gilger, J. W., Pennington, B. F., Green, P., Smith, S. M., & Smith, S. D. (1992). Reading disability, immune disorders and non-right-handedness: Twin and family studies of their relations. *Neuropsychologia, 30,* 209–227.

Goldstein, R. S., Gort, E. H., Stubbing, D., Avendano, M. A., & Guyatt, G. H. (1994). Randomized controlled trial of respiratory rehabilitation. *Lancet, 344,* 1394–1397.

Gourevitch, M. N., Alcabes, P., Wasserman, W. C., & Arno, P. S. (1998). Cost-effectiveness of directly observed chemoprophylaxis of tuberculosis among drug users at high risk for tuberculosis. *International Journal of Tuberculosis and Lung Disease, 2,* 531–540.

Graham, P. J., Rutter, M., Yule, W., & Pless, I. B. (1967). Childhood asthma: A psychosomatic disorder? *British Journal of Preventive and Social Medicine, 21,* 78–85.

Gutstadt, L. B., Gillette, J. W., Mrazek, D. A., Fukuhara, J. T., LaBrecque, J. F., & Strunk, R. C. (1989). Determinants of school performance in children with chronic asthma. *American Journal of Diseases of Children, 143,* 471–475.

Hamlett, K. W., Pelligrini, D. S., & Katz, K. S. (1992). Childhood chronic illness as a family stressor. *Journal of Pediatric Psychology, 17,* 33–47.

Havard, J. D. (1975). Relationship between allergic conditions and language and/or learning disabilities. *Dissertation Abstracts International, 35,* 6940.

Heinrich, P., & Homer, C. J. (1999). Improving the care of children with asthma in pediatrics practice: The HIPPO project. *Pediatric Annals, 1999, 28,* 64–72.

Hermann, J., Florin, I., Dietrich, M., Rieger, C., & Hahlweg, K. (1989). Maternal criticism, mother–child interaction, and bronchial asthma. *Journal of Psychosomatic Research, 33,* 469–476.

Heyman, S. J., Sell, R., & Brewer, T. F. (1998). The influence of program acceptability on the effectiveness of public health policy: A study of directly observed therapy for tuberculosis. *American Journal of Public Health, 88,* 442–445.

Hugdahl, K., Synnevag, B., & Satz, P. (1990). Immune and autoimmune diseases in dyslexic children. *Neuropsychologia, 28,* 673–679.

Jajosky, R. A., Harrison, R., Reinisch, F., Flattery, J., Chan, J., Tumpowsky, C., et al. (1999). Surveillance of work-related asthma in selected U.S. states using surveillance guidelines for state health departments—California, Massachusetts, Michigan, and New Jersey, 1993–1995. *Morbidity and Mortality Weekly Report, 48,* 1–20.

Janelli, L. M., Schrer, Y. K., & Schmieder, L. E. (1991). Can a pulmonary health teaching program alter patients' ability to cope with COPD? *Rehabilitation Nursing, 16,* 199–202.

Joint ACCP/AACVPR Evidence-Based Guidelines. (1997). Pulmonary rehabilitation. *Chest, 112,* 1363–1396.

Kaplan, B. J., McNichol, J., Conte, R. A., & Moghadam, H. K. (1987). Sleep disturbance in preschool-aged hyperactive and nonhyperactive children. *Pediatrics, 80,* 839–844.

Kaplan, R. M. (2000). Two pathways to prevention. *American Psychologist, 55,* 382–396.

Kaptein, A. A. (1997). Behavioural interventions in COPD: A pause for breath. *European Respiratory Journal, 7,* 88–91.

Kashani, J. H., Konig, P., Shepperd, J. A., Wilfley, D., & Morris, D. A. (1988). Psychopathology and self-concept in asthmatic children. *Journal of Pediatric Psychology, 13,* 509–520.

Keeley, D. J., & Silverman, M. (1999). Issues at the interface between primary and secondary care in the management of common respiratory disease. 2: Are we too ready to diagnose asthma in children? *Thorax, 54,* 625–628.

Kim, S. P., Ferrara, A., & Chess, S. (1980). Temperament of asthmatic children. *Journal of Pediatrics, 97,* 483–486.

Klinnert, M. D. (1997a). Guest editorial: Psychosocial influences on asthma among inner-city children. *Pediatric Pulmonology, 24,* 234–236.

Klinnert, M. D. (1997b). The psychology of asthma in the school-aged child. In P. Kember & J. Bemporand (Eds.), *Handbook of child and adolescent psychiatry: The grade school child* (pp. 579–594). New York: Wiley.

Knight, W. (1998). *Managed care. What it is and how it works.* Gaithersburg, MD: Aspen Press.

Kombe, G. C., & Darrow, D. M. (2001). Revisiting emerging infectious diseases: The unfinished agenda. *Journal of Community Health, 26,* 113–122.

Kopp, C. B., & Krakow, J. B. (1983). The developmentalist and the study of biological risk, a view of the past with an eye toward the future. *Child Development, 54,* 1086–1108.

Kotses, H., Bernstein, I. L., Bernstein, D. I., Reynolds, R. V. C., Korbee, L., Wigal,

J. K., et al. (1995). A self-management program for adult asthma. Part I. Development and evaluation. *Journal of Allergy and Clinical Immunology, 95,* 529–540.

Lacasse, Y., Wong, E., Guyatt, G. H., King, D., Cook, D. J., & Goldstein, R. S. (1996). Meta-analysis of respiratory rehabilitation in chronic obstructive pulmonary disease. *Lancet, 348,* 1115–1119.

Lavigne, J. V., & Faier-Routman, J. (1992). Psychological adjustment to pediatric physical disorders: A meta-analytic review. *Journal of Pediatric Psychology, 17,* 133–157.

Lindgren, S., Lokshin, B., Stromquist, A., Weinberger, M., Nassif, E., McCubbin, M., et al. (1992). Does asthma or treatment with theophylline limit children's academic performance? *New England Journal of Medicine, 327,* 926–930.

Liu, B.-Q., Peto, R., Chen, Z.-M., Boreham, J., Wu, Y.-P., Li, J.-Y., et al. (1998). Emerging tobacco hazards in China: 1. Retrospective proportional mortality study of one million deaths. *British Medical Journal, 317,* 1411–1422.

Lucas, D. O., Zimmer, L. O., Paul, J. E., Jones, D., Slatko, G., Liao, W., et al. (2001). Two-year results from the asthma self-management program: Long-term impact on health care services, costs, functional status, and productivity. *Journal of Asthma, 38,* 321–330.

MacLean, W. E., Perrin, J. M., Gortmaker, S., & Pierre, C. B. (1992). Psychological adjustment of children with asthma: Effects of illness severity and recent stressful life events. *Journal of Pediatric Psychology, 17,* 159–171.

Mahler, D. A. (1998). Pulmonary rehabilitation. *Chest, 113,* 263S–268S.

Marder, D., Targonski, P., Orris, P., Persky, V., & Addington, W. (1992). Effect of racial and socioeconomic factors on asthma mortality in Chicago. *Chest, 101,* 426S–429S.

Mathison, D. A. (1998). Asthma in adults. In E. Middleton, Jr., C. E. Reed, E. F. Ellis, N. F. Adkinson Jr., J. W. Yuninger, & W. W. Busse (Eds.), *Allergy: Principles and practice* (5th ed., pp. 901–926). St Louis, MO: C.V. Mosby.

McCowan, C., Bryce, F. P., Neville, R. G., Crombie, I. K., & Clark, R. A. (1996). School absence valid morbidity marker for asthma? *Health Bulletin (Edinburgh), 54,* 307–313.

McGee, R., Stanton, W., & Sears, M. R. (1993). Allergic disorders and attention deficit disorder in children. *Journal of Abnormal Child Psychology, 21,* 79–89.

McLoughlin, J., Nall, M., Isaacs, B., Petrosko, J., Karibo, J., & Lindsey, B. (1983). The relationship of allergies and allergy treatment to school performance and student behavior. *Annals of Allergy, 51,* 506–510.

McNicol, K. N., Williams, H. E., Allan, J., & McAndrew, I. (1973). Spectrum of asthma in children: Psychological and social components. *British Medical Journal, 4,* 16–20.

Melvin, J. L. (1980). Interdisciplinary and multidisciplinary activities and the ACRM. *Archives of Physical Medicine and Rehabilitation, 61,* 379–380.

Mitchell, E. A., Aman, M. G., Turbott, S. H., & Manku, M. (1987). Clinical characteristics and serum essential fatty acid levels in hyperactive children. *Clinical Pediatrics, 26,* 406–411.

Murray, C. J. L., & Lopez, A. D. (1996). *The global burden of disease.* Geneva, Switzerland: World Health Organization.

National Institutes of Health. (1991). *Executive summary: Guidelines for the diagnosis and management of asthma* (NIH Publication No. 91-3042A). Washington, DC: U.S. Department of Health and Human Services.

National Institutes of Health. (1997). *Expert Panel Report 2: Guidelines for the diagnosis and management of asthma* (NIH Publication No. 97-4051A). Washington, DC: U.S. Department of Health and Human Services.

National Institutes of Health. (2001). *Expert summary: Global initiative for chronic obstructive lung disease* (NIH Publication No. 2701A). Washington, DC: U.S. Department of Health and Human Services.

Nellhaus, G., Newman, I., Ellis, E., & Pirnat, M. (1975). Asthma and seizures in children. *Pediatric Clinics of North America, 22,* 89–100.

Newacheck, P. W., & Halfon, N. (1998). Prevalence and impact of disabling chronic conditions in childhood. *American Journal of Public Health, 88,* 610–617.

Newacheck, P. W., & Stoddard, J. J. (1994). Prevalence and impact of multiple childhood chronic illnesses. *Journal of Pediatrics, 124,* 40–48.

Nocon, A., & Booth, T. (1989–1990). The social impact of asthma: A review of the literature. *Social Work and Social Science Review, 1,* 177–200.

Norrish, M., Tooley, M., & Godfrey, S. (1977). Clinical, physiological, and psychological study of asthmatic children attending a hospital clinic. *Archives of Disease in Childhood, 52,* 912–917.

Ockene, J. K., Emmons, K. M., Mermelstein, R. J., Perkins, K. A., Bonollo, D. S., Voorhees, C. C., et al. (2000). Relapse and maintenance issues for smoking cessation. *Health Psychology, 19*(Suppl.), 17–31.

Osler, W. (1892). *The principles and practice of medicine.* New York: Appleton.

Padur, J. S., Rapoff, M. A., Houston, B. K., Barnard, M., Danovsky, M., Olson, N. Y., et al. (1995). Psychosocial adjustment and the role of functional status for children with asthma. *Journal of Asthma, 32,* 345–353.

Palmer, C. S., Miller, B., Halpern, M. T., & Geiger, L. J. (1998). A model of the cost-effectiveness of directly observed therapy for treatment of tuberculosis. *Journal of Public Health Management Practice, 4,* 1–13.

Parcel, G. S., Gilman, S. C., Nader, P. R., & Bunce, H. (1979). A comparison of absentee rates of elementary school children with asthma and nonasthmatic schoolmates. *Pediatrics, 64,* 878–881.

Pearce, N., Beasley, R., Burgess, C., & Crane, J. (1998). *Asthma epidemiology. Principles and methods.* New York: Oxford University Press.

Pennington, B. G., Smith, S. D., Kimberling, W. J., Green, P. A., & Haith, M. M. (1987). Left-handedness and immune disorders in familial dyslexia. *Archives of Neurology, 44,* 634–639.

Perrin, J. M., MacLean, W. E., & Perrin, E. C. (1989). Parental perceptions of health status and psychologic adjustment of children with asthma. *Pediatrics, 83*, 26–30.

Pimental, D., Tort, M., D'Anna, L., Krawic, A., Berger, J., Rossman, J., et al. (1998). Ecology of increasing disease. *BioSciences, 48*, 817–826.

Purcell, K., Brady, K., Chai, H., Muser, J., Molk, L., Gordon, N., et al. (1969). The effect on asthma in children of experimental separation from the family. *Psychosomatic Medicine, 31*, 144–164.

Rachalefsky, G., Wo, J., Adelson, J., Mickey, M. R., Spector, S. L., Katz, R. M., et al. (1986). Behavior abnormalities and poor school performance due to oral theophylline use. *Pediatrics, 78*, 1133–1138.

Reed, C. E. (1999). The natural history of asthma in adults: The problem of irreversibility. *Journal of Allergy and Clinical Immunology, 103*, 539–547.

Renne, C. M., & Creer, T. L. (1985). Asthmatic children and their families. In M. L. Walraich & D. K. Routh (Eds.), *Advances in developmental and behavioral pediatrics* (6th ed., pp. 41–81). Greenwich, CT: JAI Press.

Ries, A. L., Kaplan, R. M., Limberg, T. M., & Prewitt, L. A. (1995). Effects of pulmonary rehabilitation on physiologic and psychosocial outcomes in patients with chronic obstructive pulmonary disease. *Annals of Internal Medicine, 122*, 823–832.

Rodriguez-Garcia, R. (2001). The health–developmental link: Travel as a public health issue. *Journal of Community Health, 26*, 93–112.

Roth, N., Beyreiss, J., Schlenzka, K., & Beyer, H. (1991). Coincidence of attention deficit disorder and atopic disorders in children: Empirical findings and hypothetical background. *Journal of Abnormal Child Psychology, 19*, 1–13.

Rutter, M. (1987). Psychosocial resilience and protective mechanisms. *American Journal of Orthopsychiatry, 57*, 316–331.

Scherer, Y. K., Schmieder, L. E., & Shimmel, S. (1998). The effects of education alone and in combination with pulmonary rehabilitation on self-efficacy in patients with COPD. *Rehabilitation Nursing, 23*, 71–77.

Schlieper, A., Adcock, C., Beaudry, P., Feldman, W., & Leikin, L. (1991). Effect of therapeutic plasma concentrations of theophylline on behavior, cognitive processing, and affect in children with asthma. *Journal of Pediatrics, 118*, 449–455.

Schobinger, R., Florin, I., Zimmer, C., Lindemann, H., & Winter, H. (1992). Childhood asthma: Paternal critical attitude and father–child interaction. *Journal of Psychosomatic Research, 36*, 743–750.

Senior, R. M., & Anthonisen, N. R. (1998). Chronic obstructive pulmonary disease (COPD). *American Journal of Respiratory and Critical Care Medicine, 157*, S139–S147.

Sly, R. M. (1988). Mortality from asthma, 1979–1984. *Journal of Allergy and Clinical Immunology, 82*, 705–717.

Sly, R. M., & O'Donnell, R. (1997). Stabilization of asthma mortality. *Annals of Allergy, Asthma, and Immunology, 78*, 347–354.

Smith, D. H., Malone, D. C., Lawson, K. A., Okamoto, L. J., Battista, C., & Saunders, W. B. (1997). A national estimate of the economic costs of asthma. *American Journal of Respiratory Care and Critical Care Medicine, 156*, 787–893.

Snyder, D. C., Paz, E. A., Mohle-Boetaini, J. C., Fallstad, R., Black, R. L., & Chin, D. P. (1999). Tuberculosis prevention in methadone maintenance clinics. Effectiveness and cost-effectiveness. *American Journal of Respiratory and Critical Care Medicine, 160*, 178–185.

Stanford, R., McLaughlin, T., & Okamoto, L. J. (1999). The cost of asthma in the emergency department and hospital. *American Journal of Respiratory and Critical Care Medicine, 160*, 211–215.

Stein, R. E., & Jessop, D. J. (1984). Relationship between health status and psychological adjustment among children with chronic conditions. *Pediatrics, 73*, 169–174.

Steinhausen, H., Schindler, H., & Stephan, H. (1983). Correlates of psychopathology in sick children: An empirical model. *Journal of the American Academy of Child Psychiatry, 22*, 559–564.

Stempel, D. A., Sturm, L. L., Hedblom, E. C., & Durcannin-Robbins, J. F. (1995). Total costs of asthma care. *Journal of Allergy and Clinical Immunology, 95*, 217.

Suess, W. M., & Chai, H. (1981). Neuropsychological correlates of asthma: Brain damage or drug effects? *Journal of Consulting and Clinical Psychology, 49*, 135–136.

Tiep, B. L. (1997). Disease management of COPD with pulmonary rehabilitation. *Chest, 112*, 1630–1656.

Toshima, M. T., Kaplan, R. M., & Ries, A. L. (1990). Experimental evaluation of rehabilitation in chronic obstructive pulmonary disease: Short-term effects on exercise endurance and health status. *Health Psychology, 9*, 237–252.

Tulsky, J. P., Pilote, L., Hahn, J. A., Zolopa, A. J., Burke, M., Chesney, M., et al. (2000). Adherence to isoniazid prophylaxis in the homeless. A randomized controlled trial. *Archives of Internal Medicine, 160*, 697–702.

U.S. Department of Health and Human Services. (2000). *Healthy people 2010: Understanding and improving health* (2nd ed.). Washington, DC: U.S. Government Printing Office.

Varni, J. W. (1983). *Clinical behavioral pediatrics*. New York: Pergamon.

Volmink, J., & Garner, P. (2001). Interventions for promotion adherence to tuberculosis management (Cochrane Review). In *The Cochranel Library, 2*. Oxford, England: Update Software.

Vuurman, E. F., Veggel, F. L., Uiterwijk, M. M., Leutner, D., & O'Hanlon, J. F. (1993). Seasonal allergic rhinitis and antihistamine effects on children's learning. *Annals of Allergy, 71*, 121–126.

Walley, J. D., Khan, M. A., Newell, J. N., & Khan, M. H. (2001). Effectiveness of the direct observation component of DOTS for tuberculosis: A randomized controlled trial in Pakistan. *Lancet, 356*, 664–669.

Wamboldt, F. S., Wamboldt, M. Z., Gavin, L. A., Roesler, T. A., & Brugman,

S. M. (1995). Parental criticism and treatment outcome in adolescents hospitalized for severe chronic asthma. *Journal of Psychosomatic Research*, 39, 995.

Weiss, K. B., Gergen, P. J., & Hodgson, T. A. (1992). An economic evaluation of asthma in the United States. *New England Journal of Medicine*, 326, 862–866.

Weitzman, M., Klerman, L. V., Lamb, G., Menary, J., & Alpert, J. J. (1982). School absence: A problem for the pediatrician. *Pediatrics*, 69, 739–746.

Wigal, J. K., Creer, T. L., Kotses, H., & Lewis, P. D. (1990). A critique of 19 self-management programs for childhood asthma. Part I. The development and evaluation of the programs. *Pediatric Asthma, Allergy, and Immunology*, 4, 17–39.

Wissow, L. S., Gittelsohn, A. M., Sazklo, M., Starfield, B., & Mussman, M. (1988). Poverty, race, and hospitalization for childhood asthma. *American Journal of Public Health*, 78, 777–782.

World Health Organization. (1999). *Making a difference*. Geneva, Switzerland: Author.

World Health Organization. (2001, June). TB–HIV. Fueling each other. *Stop TB News*, pp. 1–4.

Young, P., Dewse, M., Fergusson, W., & Kolbe, J. (1999). Improvements in outcomes for chronic obstructive pulmonary disease (COPD) attributable to a hospital-based respiratory rehabilitation programme. *Australian and New Zealand Journal of Medicine*, 29, 59–65.

Zwarenstein, M., Schoeman, J. H., Vundule, C., Lombard, C. J., & Tatley, M. (1998). Randomized controlled trial of self-supervised and directly observed treatment of tuberculosis. *Lancet*, 352, 1340–1343.

9

DISEASES OF THE DIGESTIVE SYSTEM

BRENDA B. TONER AND JOSEE CASATI

The ninth revision of the *International Classification of Diseases* (ICD–9; Practice Management Information Corporation, 1998) is a classification system that provides health care professionals with consistent and accurate diagnostic coding of medical and mental health disorders. Classification of these diseases is divided into 17 general categories, with subcategories being noted for each. Specifically, under the category *diseases of the digestive systems,* the *ICD*–9 lists several disorders, including diseases of the oral cavity, salivary glands, and jaws; diseases of the esophagus, stomach, and duodenum; appendicitis; hernia of the abdominal cavity; noninfectious enteritis and colitis; and other diseases of intestines and peritoneum.

Research in the area of digestive diseases has focused primarily on biological and medical aspects of these disorders. Little attention has been given to psychosocial complications of these medical conditions. However, a few disorders worth mentioning have received limited attention with respect to psychosocial aspects, including temporomandibular joint disorder (TMJ) and oral diseases. Additionally, the two general areas of *functional gastrointestinal disorders* (FGID) and *inflammatory bowel disease* (IBD) have received extensive attention. More specifically, these two disorders have been conceptualized using a biopsychosocial perspective (Drossman, 1998; Engel, 1977). This perspective provides a framework for understanding the biological and psychosocial components of these diseases and can provide models for other areas within the digestive system.

The purpose of this chapter is to provide an understanding of diseases of the digestive system. Because it is beyond the scope of this chapter to provide an extensive and detailed discussion of all the specific diseases of the digestive system, the discussion is limited to FGID and IBD. The first section of this chapter provides an overview of FGIDs. The second section addresses IBD. The biopsychosocial perspective as it relates to these two disorders is also outlined. The third section discusses how to integrate psychosocial issues into current treatment protocols. The final section briefly addresses future directions.

FGIDs

Definition and Symptoms

FGIDs are characterized by recurrent or current gastrointestinal symptoms that as yet have no identifiable structural or biochemical basis. The most common FGID is functional bowel disorder (FBD), which includes the following symptoms: functional constipation, functional diarrhea, irritable bowel syndrome (IBS), and chronic functional abdominal pain (CFAP). IBS is associated with abdominal pain or discomfort for at least 12 weeks or more that has two or three of the following features: (a) is relieved with defecation, (b) is associated with a change in frequency of bowel movements, (c) is associated with a change in stool form (appearance). Symptoms that are associated with IBS include abnormal bowel movement frequency (more than three per day, less than three per week), abnormal stool form (hard stool, loose and watery stool), abnormal stool passage (straining or urgency, feeling of incomplete evacuation), passage of mucus, and bloating or feelings of abdominal distension (Thompson et al., 2000).

Epidemiology

FGIDs are very common disorders, affecting 9% to 22% of all the Western populations. However, of those affected, very few seek medical consultations or treatment for their gastrointestinal symptoms (Whitehead, Bosmajian, Zonderman, Costa, & Schuster, 1988). According to Drossman, Whitehead, and Camilleri (1997), of those who seek treatment, FGID accounts for 28% of gastroenterological practice in Western societies and 12% of primary care. In the United States, FGID is associated with unnecessary procedures and surgeries (Burns, 1986; Thompson, Dotevall, Drossman, Heaton, & Kruis, 1989) and results in more than 2.2 million prescriptions per year (Sandler, 1990). In addition to these medical costs, FGID has a considerable economic impact because it results in decreased work capacity. Next to the common cold, it ranks as the second most common cause of work absenteeism (Young, Alpers, Norland, & Woodruff, 1976).

FGID is a disorder that affects mostly women (Drossman, Sandler, McKee, & Lovitz, 1982; Sandler, Drossman, Nathan, & McKee, 1984; Talley, Zinmeister, Van Dyke, & Melton, 1991; Thompson et al., 2000). Although men and women are affected by FGID, studies consistently demonstrate that women outnumber men within the nonpatient population (Drossman et al., 1993), within the patient population (Longstreth & Wolde-Tsadik, 1993), and within the tertiary care setting (Drossman, Creed, et al., 1995). To date, most of the information about FGID has been drawn from women participants.

A review of the literature by Toner and Akman (2000) noted that the majority of studies investigating FGID use only women in their samples. Moreover, of those studies that do include men, few perform a gender difference analysis. Studies that examine sex differences do so in a descriptive manner, do not test for statistically significant differences, and have small sample sizes. Of those studies that investigate sex differences and include both male and female participants in their samples, the focus has been in the areas of frequency of physician visits, psychological symptomatology, physical symptomatology, and abuse histories. Thus far, the literature suggests that there are few consistent sex differences. Because a significant percentage of patients with FGID are women, the issue of gender must be integrated into the conceptualization and treatment of these disorders (Toner, Segal, Emmott, & Myran, 2000).

Conceptualization: Brain—Gut Interactions

FGID is best conceptualized using a biopsychosocial model (Drossman, 1996). As summarized by Drossman et al. (1999), the biopsychosocial model may help to explain the reason patients have different symptoms such as both diarrhea and constipation, pain without dysmotility, or disturbed motility with pain. Additionally, histories of sexual, physical, and emotional abuse, unhelpful coping abilities, and other psychosocial distress and the varied impact of these factors on quality of life and clinical outcome are more easily explained by the biopsychosocial model. Moreover, other contributing factors such as environmental stress, emotions, and thoughts on gut function, which are affected through receptor activity and neurotransmitter release, profoundly affect daily function, symptom severity, and health outcome. Thus, the biopsychosocial model would address these issues and play an important role in the understanding and treatment of FGID.

FGID, and more specifically, IBS, are best explained as a dysregulation of brain–gut neuroenteric systems (Drossman et al., 1999). When patients with FGID are compared with healthy patients, physical and psychological stressors, food, balloon distention, and various peptides have contributed to the increased motility experienced by those with FGID (Drossman et al., 1994, 1997). Furthermore, in response to balloon distention and other stimuli (visceral hypersensitivity), patients with FGID experience decreased thresholds for gut pain. Therefore, it is no longer imperative that researchers try to assess whether pain or bowel symptoms are caused by physiological or psychological factors. Rather, the goal of investigators is to determine to what extent these factors contribute to FGID.

Several lines of evidence clearly support the role of the central nervous system (CNS) in modulating motility. For example, different electroencephalography (EEG) sleep patterns have been noted in patients with FGID (Kumar, Thompson, Wingate, Vesselinova-Jenkins, & Libby, 1992), with motility disturbances disappearing during sleep (Kellow, Gill, & Wingate, 1990). Additionally, alertness and arousal cause propagating velocity to increase and migrating motor complex (MMC) frequency to decrease (Kellow et al., 1990; Valori, Kumar, & Wingate, 1986). In addition, several studies have noted that patients with IBS experience increases in colonic motility and EEG beta power activity in response to experimental stressors (Fukudo, Nomura, Muranaki, & Taguchi, 1993).

Positron emission tomography (PET) studies indicate that patients with IBS differ from healthy people based on regional cerebral perfusion (Mayer & Gebhart, 1994). For example, compared with control patients, in response to rectal distension or anticipation of rectal distension, patients with IBS activate the prefrontal cortex rather than the anterior cingulate (Silverman et al., 1997). Therefore, in response to anticipated and incoming visceral pain, pain perception may be amplified because patients with IBS may fail to use CNS downregulating mechanisms and activate a part of the brain that amplifies pain.

Psychosocial Factors

Stigma and Myths

FGIDs such as IBS are associated with morally pejorative connotations. According to Kirmayer and Robbins (1991), the dualistic metaphysics that exists in Western society and particularly in Western medicine suggests that illness is the result of psychological factors that are mediated by and potentially under the person's voluntary control or an accident that befalls the patient and can be attributed to impersonal causes. Moreover, disorders disproportionately prevalent in women are quite often trivialized or described as psychological in origin (Lips, 1997). Therefore, it should not be surprising that patients who have FGIDs often feel that their prob-lems are treated as if they are not real and are caused by a moral or psy-chological weakness or defect (Kirmayer & Robbins, 1991). Thus, when referred to health care providers, people with FGID may think that the providers will consider their symptoms to be "all in their heads" and thus not serious. It is important that health care professionals validate and ap-preciate the reality of the symptoms, for example, by acknowledging and addressing psychosocial components and disease-related symptoms. In do-ing so, they can challenge the artificial dualism between functional and organic components of illness imposed by our society and enhance the therapeutic alliance (Toner et al., 2000).

Several other myths are also associated with FGIDs. One such myth is that some patients with FGID achieve some gain or benefit through their illness (e.g., are relieved of responsibilities, get increased attention). There are no empirical data to suggest that people with FGID benefit or take pleasure from this chronic and devastating illness. Rather, patients with FGID are interested in overcoming the psychosocial consequences of living with these chronic and potentially disabling diseases. This myth may have emerged because people with a chronic illness such as FGID often are relieved from some of their usual responsibilities and may receive social and financial compensation (Toner, 1998–1999).

An additional myth is that FGID is a psychiatric disorder or masked depression. Several studies have found that a substantial percentage of women with FGID, particularly in tertiary care settings, have a high prev-alence of depression or anxiety. It is unclear why such an association exists, but the following explanations have been proposed: (a) People who also have an associated anxiety or depressive disorder may have more difficulty coping with gastrointestinal problems and may seek specialized help for their pain at higher rates than people with FGID who do not have an associated anxiety or depressive disorder; (b) anxiety and depression are common in the general population, and their co-occurrence may simply be a result of this high frequency; or (c) depression or anxiety may be a con-sequence of living with a chronic, debilitating disorder such as FGID (Toner, 1998–1999).

Another myth is people with FGID are sometimes "difficult patients." Physicians and other health care providers are not adequately trained in the conceptualization or treatment of FGIDs such as IBS. The lack of information coupled with the shame and trivialization associated with hav-ing a so-called *functional disorder* leads to frustration, further distressing patients. For physicians, such patients may illicit uncomfortable feelings that might lead some health care professionals to feel helpless and frus-trated with the situation. Rather than referring to patients with FGID as difficult, it is more helpful to conceptualize the *disorder* as difficult, espe-cially in light of the fact that there is little information about and a great deal of stigma associated with these FGIDs (Toner, 1998–1999). An open and honest discussion acknowledging the frustration associated with this chronic and debilitating disorder is beneficial. To date, no effective medication or cure is available for FGID, so the focus of treatment is symptom management and improving coping strategies. As such, it is important to establish a collaborative environment in which patient and health care provider work together in attempting to understand the most effective strategies in managing the chronic, painful symptoms. Treatment plans must address and acknowledge an individual's needs and concerns. In doing so, physicians can help to improve coping abilities of patients with FGID, decrease their psychosocial distress, and potentially improve their quality of life.

Sexual, Physical, and Emotional Abuse

Studies suggest that there is a strong association between FGIDs and self-reported sexual and physical abuse (Drossman, Talley, Lesserman, Olden, & Barreiro, 1995; Drossman et al., 1990). According to Lesserman et al. (1996), poor health status is associated with rape, and abuse that was life threatening. However, it is important to note that a history of abuse is not etiological for FGID. Other chronic pain conditions are also associated with a high frequency of abuse history. As noted by Whitehead et al. (1988), people with a history of abuse are more likely to communicate psychological distress through physical symptoms. Moreover, they may be more likely to seek medical attention as a result of altered cognitions (e.g., feeling ineffective and unable to control symptoms).

A study by Ali et al. (2000) compared women who were treated in a tertiary care setting with a diagnosis of IBS with women who had a diagnosis of IBD on measures of emotional abuse, self-blame, and self-silencing. Women with IBS scored significantly higher on all three variables. Additionally, all three variables were significantly intercorrelated in both the IBS and IBD samples, suggesting that women who experience emotional abuse are more likely to self-silence and self-blame. The authors of this study concluded that emotional abuse, self-blame, and self-silencing are important constructs in the understanding of the role of psychosocial factors in IBS and should be investigated accordingly. It is important to understand that these factors do not cause IBS but may play a role, as do several other biopsychosocial factors, in the understanding and treatment of IBS.

Psychiatric Disorders

Currently, researchers are debating about the association between psychiatric disorders and FGID—in other words, whether psychiatric disorders are a cause of, a consequence of, or co-occur with FGID. Numerous studies have demonstrated that patients who are treated in tertiary care settings have a high prevalence (50%–100%) of psychiatric illness (Blanchard, Scarff, Schwarz, Suls, & Barlow, 1990; Colgan, Creed, & Klass, 1988; Corney & Stanton, 1990; Craig & Brown, 1984; Ford, Miller, Eastwood, & Eastwood, 1987; MacDonald & Bouchier, 1980; Toner, Garfinkel, Jeejeebhoy, 1990). Accounts of cormorbid conditions with IBS include (a) mood disorders (major depression and dysthymic disorder), (b) somatoform disorders (hypochondriasis and somatization disorders), and (c) anxiety disorders (panic and generalized anxiety disorders). (Possible explanations for this high association were discussed in the previous section on stigma and myths.)

Life Stress

Severe life stress has also been associated with FBDs (Creed, Craig, & Farmer, 1988). In the attempt to establish some control over their symptoms, many patients with FGID use social stress as an explanation for exacerbation of symptoms and treatment seeking. According to Drossman et al. (1997), when compared with people without health problems or the nonclinical (community sample) population with similar gastrointestinal complaints, patients with IBS tend to have higher psychosocial distress scores. Particularly in specialty clinics, people with IBS seeking health care (Drossman et al., 1988; Whitehead et al., 1988) are less likely to see an association between their IBS symptoms and stress (Thompson, Heaton, Smyth, & Smyth, 1996; Toner, 1994) and have more severe medical symptoms and more general anxiety, depression (Drossman et al., 1988; Heaton et al., 1992; Talley, Boyce, & Jones, 1997), and health anxiety (Drossman et al., 1988).

To date, investigators have not identified a personality profile unique to IBS. According to Toner et al. (1998), patients with IBS who go to specialty clinics commonly believe that their bowel symptoms are indicative of cancer or serious gut disease. As such, they pay particular attention to abdominal sensations, seeking out other information that is consistent with such beliefs (Toner et al., 1998). Patients with IBS report many nongastrointestinal complaints (Chabbra, Toner, Ali, & Stuckless, 1999), resulting in 2 to 3 times as many visits to physicians for these disorders (Drossman et al., 1993). These findings suggest that psychological treatment may help patients to reduce gastrointestinal symptoms, decrease subjective distress, and increase coping ability. Physiological and psychosocial components play an important role in the treatment of IBS; however, current treatment for IBS continues to focus on medications and dietary fiber (for a comprehensive review of physiological interventions, see Drossman et al., 1999).

Treatment

Overview of Psychotherapies

Psychological treatments for FGID have been well documented and include dynamic psychotherapy, cognitive–behavioral therapy (CBT), relaxation, and hypnotherapy (Drossman, Creed, Olden, Toner, & Whitehead, 2000). To date, the empirical literature suggests that no one treatment is superior for FGID.

An important component of dynamic psychotherapy is the close therapeutic relationship between patient and therapist. The relationship allows interpersonal issues to be highlighted, enabling the patients to gain insight into their problems and possibly reduce gastrointestinal symptoms (Drossman et al., 2000). Dynamic psychotherapy is similar to brief interpersonal psychotherapy (Guthrie, Creed, Dawson, & Tomenson, 1991).

CBT can also be used for FGID. The benefits of CBT are supported by several characteristics of those with FGID: (a) perfectionist attitudes, (b) a strong desire for social approval, and (c) a high prevalence of anxiety, depression, and assertion difficulties. All of these characteristics are amenable to treatment with CBT (Toner, 1994). CBT allows patients to control their gastrointestinal symptoms by helping them alter perceptions of their situation and learn new ways of thinking and behaving through practice and personal experience (Drossman et al., 2000).

Arousal reduction, or relaxation training, techniques include (a) progressive muscle relaxation training, (b) autogenic training, (c) biofeedback, and (d) yoga or transcendental meditation. These techniques consist of different procedures and strategies designed to teach patients to counteract the physiological consequences of stress and anxiety (Drossman et al., 2000).

Hypnotherapy can also be used for FGID. With the use of an audiotape, patients can practice autohypnosis at home. Patients learn how to give themselves suggestions of relaxation (Whorwell, 1991) and help to relax gastrointestinal smooth muscle and reduce striated muscle tension (Drossman et al., 2000).

Empirical Support for Psychotherapies

Most of the research in the area of FGID has focused on IBS. In a recent overview of this area, a multinational team including Drossman et al. (2000) reviewed 15 controlled studies to compare psychological treatment with conventional medical treatment. It was not possible to perform a meta-analysis because of the inadequate number of well-designed studies. The participation rate for two of the studies was less than 40%. Five of six studies that controlled for expectancy and time with the therapist demonstrated that patients in the psychological treatment groups showed significantly greater improvement in bowel symptoms. Ten of 13 studies showed psychological treatments as significantly superior to conventional medical treatment in terms of reducing bowel symptoms. Follow-up data were available for only nine studies and of these, eight showed psychological treatment to be superior to medical treatment.

One of the most challenging problems in reviewing the published literature is that surprisingly few controlled studies investigating psychological treatments for FGID have been conducted (Drossman, 1995a). Additionally, it is difficult to determine the efficacy of a specific theoretical approach because most of the controlled studies have used multicomponent treatment packages (e.g., cognitive–behavioral, psychodynamic, biofeedback, and relaxation approaches). As such, it is difficult to assess which aspects of and to what extent the treatments were beneficial. Moreover, therapeutic techniques and procedures are not described adequately and in specific detail.

The data thus far seem to indicate that when compared with conventional medical treatment, psychological interventions are consistently more effective. It is also important to note that when different treatment techniques were used, no differences in outcome were found.

IBD

IBD refers to two clinically similar and yet distinct disorders of the gastrointestinal tract: Crohn's disease (CD) and ulcerative colitis (UC). These chronic and potentially disabling disorders present a continuous challenge to the medical community and are associated with increased medical costs (Hay & Hay, 1992) and impaired quality of life (Gazzard, Price, Libby, & Dawson, 1978; Mallet, Lennard-Jones, Bingley, & Gilon, 1978; Schoenberg, 1983; Sorensen, Olsen, & Binder, 1987). It is estimated that IBD affects between 90 and 300 people per 100,000 in the United States (Mendeloff, 1975).

Scientific and clinical interest in IBD has been steadily increasing, as evidenced by the growing number of associated scientific publications and professional organizations. Initial scientific reports on IBD focused on the biological and medical aspects of this disorder, with little attention being given to psychosocial factors. In recent years and largely in part a result of the introduction of the biopsychosocial model of illness (Drossman, 1998; Engel, 1977), research has begun to shift away from a unidirectional and biologically based method of conceptualizing and treating IBD to a more integrative and comprehensive approach, incorporating biological and psychosocial factors. Several studies have discussed the importance of identifying psychosocial aspects of these painful and potentially debilitating diseases and integrating these factors into treatment protocols, potentially enhancing quality of life (Casati & Toner, 2000; Casati, Toner, de Rooy, Drossman, & Maunder, 2000; de Rooy et al., 1997; Drossman, Patrick, Mitchell, Zagami, & Appelbaum, 1989).

Psychosocial Factors

Psychosocial factors (e.g., life events that are particularly stressful for the patient, psychiatric diagnoses, a history of physical or sexual abuse) have been identified as possible contributors to the expression and maintenance of IBD (Drossman, 1995b). Researchers are currently debating about the relationship between stress and IBD; however, several studies have found a relationship between stressful life events and disease activity (Duffy et al., 1991; Garrett, Brantley, Jones, & McKnight, 1991; Gerbert, 1980). Psychiatric illness, particularly anxiety and depression disorders (Maunder & Cardish, 1996; North, Clouse, Spitznagel, & Alpers, 1990; Porcelli, Leoci, & Guerra, 1996), are highly prevalent in patients with IBD. Like patients with other gastrointestinal disorders, patients with IBD who have a history of physical and sexual abuse have difficulty coping with these chronic diseases (Drossman, 1995b).

A diagnosis of IBD means that a patient's life will be characterized by uncomfortable medical procedures and medications, the need to alter daily activities to account for loss of energy and pain, and psychosocial distress. Studies investigating specific fears and concerns of patients with IBD have noted that many of the concerns voiced by patients with IBD relate to loss of control and the unpredictability of these diseases. For example, a study by Drossman and colleagues in 1989 reported that the major fear of patients with IBD was the uncertainty caused by having the disease. In this study, the investigators used the Rating Form of IBD Patient Concerns (RFIPC) to identify and assess the major worries and concerns of patients with IBD (Drossman et al., 1991).

Other concerns were related to the effects of medication, change in energy levels, having surgery, loss of bowel control, being a burden on others, and developing cancer. Similar results were obtained by de Rooy et al. (1997). Additionally, differences were noted depending on the type of IBD that the patient had. For example, those with UC worried more about cancer whereas those with CD worried more about their energy level, being a burden on others, reaching full potential, having pain, and financial difficulties. Considering that the clinical course of IBD is uncertain and unpredictable, it should not be surprising that disease-related concerns reflect the uncertainty of these diseases. Difficulties in coping with these chronic and potentially debilitating diseases must be acknowledged and addressed by physicians. In doing so, physicians might alleviate much of the psychosocial distress experienced by patients with IBD.

Casati et al. (2000) reviewed several studies investigating health-related concerns and worries of patients with IBD. The following themes were identified: control, isolation and fear, loss of energy, concern with body image, not reaching full potential, feeling dirty, feeling of being a burden, and lack of information from the medical community. Case vignettes were used to describe the impact of these health-related concerns on patients' quality of life. Because it is beyond the scope of this chapter to provide an extensive discussion of these issues, this chapter includes a brief summary of disease-related concerns of patients with IBD (for a complete review, see Casati et al., 2000).

Loss of control is an important issue for people with IBD. As already stated, the disease process is uncertain and unpredictable. Consequently, the physical complications of these diseases, such as abdominal cramps and rectal incontinence, may contribute to the patients' sense of loss of control. The physicians' awareness of and willingness to acknowledge and thus address these issues will likely improve their patients' ability to cope with these diseases and improve clinical and treatment outcome.

Feelings of isolation and fear are also important issues that must be addressed by physicians (Casati et al., 2000; Drossman et al., 1989; Godber, 1989). The potential embarrassment and shame associated with IBD makes many patients feel isolated. Additionally, the complications of IBD (i.e., anemia, diarrhea) mean that planned meetings and day-to-day activities may have to be altered or cancelled at a moment's notice. It is difficult for people who do not have the disease to fully appreciate the day-to-day struggles endured by patients with IBD. Thus, patients with IBD may experience feelings of shame, embarrassment, and guilt, potentially compromising their ability to cope with their disease.

Another important issue that must be addressed by physicians is the possibility of cancer. Many patients express a fear of developing cancer. The risk of developing cancer is associated with duration of the disease and the extent of colon involvement (Mellemkjaer et al., 1995). It is important that physicians provide patients with accurate information about the risk factors for cancer (Gillan, Andrews, & Prior, 1994). The physicians' understanding of and willingness to address this issue helps to legitimize patients' concern and helps alleviate much of the fear that the patients may be experiencing. Additionally, patients should be reassured that the physician is listening to their worries and concerns.

Fatigue or loss of energy caused by complications of these diseases and medications is another concern for people with IBD (Casati et al., 2000; de Rooy et al., 1997; Drossman et al., 1989; Mallet et al., 1978; Maunder et al., 1997) and may result in decreased ability to participate in work (Sorensen et al., 1987; Wyke, 1988; Wyke, Edwards, & Allan, 1988) and leisure activities (Sorensen et al., 1987). Several studies have noted that 20% of patients with CD were unable to work because of CD-related symptoms (Duclos et al., 1990; Sorensen et al., 1987).

Another important issue for people with IBD is body image (Casati et al., 2000; de Rooy et al., 1997; Drossman et al., 1989; Maunder et al., 1997). Surgery and the side effects from medications may greatly alter the way one looks and compromise coping abilities. For example, facial bloating caused by steroid therapy may be particularly troubling for adolescents. It is important that physicians address the emotional concerns in addition to alleviating the physical complications of IBD such as diarrhea and bleeding. IBD is usually diagnosed during adolescence, when interpersonal identities are developing, so body image is a realistic and understandable concern.

Not reaching full potential is also a significant issue for people with IBD (Casati et al., 2000; de Rooy et al., 1997; Drossman et al., 1989; Maunder et al., 1997) and refers to the physical limitations placed on the individual because of these illnesses. Side effects of medications and complications from surgery may limit the academic aspirations or type of occupation the person pursues. Another problem that individuals with IBD experience is feeling dirty (Casati et al., 2000; de Rooy et al., 1997; Drossman et al., 1989). For many patients with IBD, rectal urgency may make them cautious about taking trips or outings where toilets may not be readily available. As such, rectal incontinence may compromise their ability to engage in social and leisure activities and may reinforce their need for social isolation.

Another concern is the fear of being a burden (Casati et al., 2000; de Rooy et al., 1997; Drossman et al., 1989; Maunder et al., 1997). The onset of IBD and disease-related stress places a strain on family, friends, and coworkers. Like many other chronic medical conditions, IBD results in family conflict, reduced socialization, and isolation. This may further compromise patients' ability to cope with their disease. Educating patients about IBD and its complications is likely to help patients increase their self-esteem, develop coping strategies, and possibly reduce their psychosocial distress. Additionally, supportive services (e.g., counselors, IBD support groups) can enable patients and their families to share their experiences and listen to others in similar situations.

Although researchers have expanded the understanding of IBD with respect to pathophysiology, knowledge of its etiology and treatment is limited. Patients may find that physicians are uncomfortable and unwilling to discuss psychosocial aspects of IBD. Additionally, the lack of information available from the medical community further adds to the uncertainty and fear experienced by patients. Consequently, coping abilities may be compromised and interfere with treatment compliance, resulting in decreased quality of life.

It becomes evident from the previous discussion that patients with IBD tend to have similar concerns. However, several studies have indicated that certain factors are relevant to the types of concerns expressed by patients with IBD. For example, Maunder, Toner, de Rooy, and Moskovitz (1999) demonstrated that people who do not seek psychotherapy have different concerns than people with IBD who seek counseling. Issues such as being a burden, pain and suffering, feeling out of control, financial difficulties, feeling alone, sexual performance, feeling dirty or smelly, and being treated as different were all discussed as important struggles when dealing with the complications of these diseases. Moreover, women expressed concerns related to body image and attractiveness. Another study by Maunder and colleagues (1999) noted that when compared to men with IBD, women with IBD were more likely to express concerns about their bodies, their attractiveness, having children, and feeling alone. Other studies have suggested that disease-related concerns vary across cultures, with greater concerns by being expressed by African Americans than White people. In France and Portugal, the most troublesome patient concerns were related to pain and suffering (Levenstein, Li, & Drossman, 1998).

Biopsychosocial Model

To date, the etiology of IBD is unknown. Environmental factors (Berstein, Blanchard, Rawsthorne, & Wajda, 1999; Lashner, 1995), genetic factors (Binder, 1998; Satsangi, Parkes, Jewell, & Bell, 1998; Tysk, Lindberg, Jarnerot, & Floderus-Myrhed, 1988), and dysregulation in immune function (Daruna & Morgan, 1990; Sartor, 1995; Shanahan & Anton, 1988) have been proposed as possible explanations for IBD. Although it is certainly important to identify biological determinants of IBD, the data thus far seem to suggest that it is equally as important to understand the role that psychosocial stressors play in the exacerbation and maintenance of IBD (Casati & Toner, 2000; Casati et al., 2000; Drossman, 1995b; Gazzard et al., 1978; Maunder et al., 1997; Schoenberg, 1983; Sorensen et al., 1987).

Thus, the data suggest that IBD is best conceptualized from a biopsychosocial perspective, incorporating the biological, social, and psychological perspectives of illness (Drossman, 1998). According to Drossman (1998), the way individuals respond to their disease and the way the disease influences their response is strongly influenced by psychosocial factors. Several studies have indicated that effective coping strategies and support systems are likely to alleviate the psychosocial demands of the disease and thus improve treatment and clinical outcome. For example, Kinash, Fisher, Lukie, and Carr (1993) noted that patients with IBD who experienced greater lifestyle satisfaction did so because of effective coping strategies. Another study by Schneider (1985) found that patients with IBD who had strong social support networks (e.g., family, friends, IBD support groups) demonstrated better overall adjustment to their disease. Similarly, Colcher (1984) found that the ability of the spouse and family to adapt to the complications of IBD, particularly its unpredictability and uncertainty, were important factors in how people with IBD adjust to their disease. In the absence of these modulating factors, referral to IBD support groups may be beneficial (Godber, 1989; Godber & Mayberry, 1988; Mayberry, 1987).

Treatment

No cure currently exists for IBD and as such, the goal of therapeutic interventions for these diseases is to reduce the physical complications and possibly achieve remission. Medical (Bitton & Peppercorn, 1995) and surgical interventions (Glotzer, 1995; Weiss & Wexner, 1995) for IBD have been well documented in the treatment literature. To date, no specific psychological mechanism for IBD has been identified; however, the literature does suggest that psychological factors play an important role in the exacerbation and maintenance of IBD. As such, investigations into psychological interventions for IBD have received extensive attention in the treatment literature (for an evaluative overview, see Schwarz & Blanchard, 1990).

Empirical Support for Psychotherapies

It is now widely accepted that several of the earliest studies investigating psychological treatments had severe methodological problems, namely small sample sizes and lack of control groups (Grace, Wolf, & Wolff, 1950; Joachim, 1983; Shaw & Ehrlich, 1987; Sperling, 1957; Weinstock, 1961).

Multicomponent treatment approaches have been used to treat IBD. In a study using a combination of personal planning skills, autogenics, and communication skills, Milne, Joachim, and Niedhardt (1986) randomized 80 patients with IBD to receive either treatment or a control treatment. Patients who received the combined treatment showed significant improvement. Additionally, the treatment group showed a significant decrease in scores on both the Inflammatory Bowel Disease Stress Index and the Crohn's Disease Activity Index (CDAI). Failure to match participants with respect to symptom severity limits the interpretation of this study. Further, it is unclear which treatment factors contributed to improvement and to what extent. In another study, Schwarz and Blanchard (1991) compared a combination of cognitive and behavioral techniques (education, progressive muscle relaxation, biofeedback, and cognitive techniques) to a symptom monitoring control condition. Patients in the control group did significantly better than the treated patients.

In a study by Jantschek et al. (1998), patients were randomized to receive short-term psychodynamic therapy as an adjunct to standardized corticosteroid treatment or a control treatment. No significant differences between the two groups were noted. Unfortunately, this study had a low participation rate. In another study, Maunder, Lancee, Esplen, and Greenberg (1998) used supportive–expressive group psychotherapy in a 20-week trial. Reductions were noted in IBD-related symptoms, and patients improved on measures assessing anxiety and depression.

Research in the area of IBD has advanced our ability to treat these diseases. However, as clearly outlined in this discussion, patients' current life situations, the psychosocial complications of these illnesses, and social support systems play an important role in the way patients with IBD adjust to these chronic and potentially disabling diseases. An integrative approach to treatment that acknowledges and addresses patients' worries and concerns will help patients cope with symptoms and improve their quality of life. The next section includes a brief description of how psychosocial issues can be integrated in treatment protocols.

Integrating Psychosocial Issues Into Treatment

Therapeutic relationship. Some patients with IBS and IBD may be reluctant to understand and accept the role of psychosocial issues in their disease. In particular, patients who have been sexually abused are often unable to understand the relationship between psychosocial factors and their illness. Facilitating a therapeutic relationship with the patient enables the physician to acknowledge the patient's worries, beliefs, and expectations. Moreover, a therapeutic relationship enables the physician to ease the patient's concerns and clarify misunderstandings. Through education and an empathetic rapport, physician and patient can work together to negotiate a plan of treatment (Drossman et al., 2000).

Associating bowel symptoms with psychosocial factors. To understand and assess the link between psychosocial factors and bowel symptoms, it is imperative that patients keep a record of their IBS symptoms; dietary, stress, or lifestyle changes; timing of menstruation; and timing of bowel movements. The information elicited through this daily record provides the basis for cognitive–behavioral techniques (Drossman et al., 2000).

Referral to a mental health professional. For some patients with IBS and IBD, a referral for a consultation is an important aspect in the overall treatment plan. For example, major depression, panic disorders, and other comorbid psychiatric illnesses might require specific treatments such as antidepressants, CBT, or another type of psychotherapy. Moreover, serious impairments in daily functioning might require specific treatment tailored to improving coping abilities. A history of abuse may also interfere with the patient's ability to adjust to the illness. It is important that the health professional acknowledge the importance of psychosocial issues as contributing factors to the illness. Doing so allows the gastroenterologist to address the perceived stigma or feelings of rejection that may prevent the patient from a seeking a referral (e.g., for those who think it is "just their nerves" when test results for other diseases come back negative; Drossman et al., 2000).

CONCLUSION

This chapter has provided an extensive discussion of FGIDs and IBDs. The data presented strongly support a biopsychosocial conceptualization of these disorders. Clearly, psychosocial factors play an important role in the exacerbation and maintenance of FGID- and IBD-related symptoms. Quality of life and coping abilities may be improved if psychosocial issues are addressed to the same degree as are physical issues. Conceptualizing FGID and IBD from a biopsychosocial perspective allows clinicians to better understand and treat individuals who are diagnosed with these disorders. Future research must examine how biopsychosocial factors affect other diseases of the digestive system. New models of conceptualizing other diseases of the digestive system are also needed.

Researchers of FGID and IBD have suggested that psychological treatments are valuable interventions for both FGID and IBD. Further research is needed to determine the effectiveness of psychological interventions for other diseases of the digestive system. Moreover, future studies should focus on determining which aspects of psychological treatment packages (e.g., relaxation, cognitive restructuring) account for their effectiveness and which patient characteristics predict response to specific psychological treatments. Long-term studies must also be conducted, and the role of sociocultural factors and gender on FGID and IBD should be explored as well.

REFERENCES

Ali, A., Toner, B. B., Stuckless, N., Gallop, R., Diament, N. E., Gould, M. I., et al. (2000). Emotional abuse, self-blame, and self-silencing in women with irritable bowel syndrome. *Psychosomatic Medicine, 62,* 76–82.

Berstein, C. N., Blanchard, J. F., Rawsthorne, P., & Wajda, A. (1999). Epidemiology of Crohn's disease and ulcerative colitis in a central Canadian province: A population based study. *American Journal of Epidemiology, 149*(10), 916.

Binder, V. (1998). Genetic epidemiology in inflammatory bowel disease. *Digestive Diseases, 16,* 351–355.

Bitton, A., & Peppercorn, M. A. (1995). Medical management of specific clinical presentations. *Gastroenterology Clinics of North America, 24*(3), 541–558.

Blanchard, E. B., Scarff, L., Schwarz, S. P., Suls, I. N., & Barlow, D. H. (1990).

The role of anxiety and depression in the irritable bowel syndrome. *Behavior Research and Therapy, 28,* 401–405.

Burns, D. G. (1986). The risk of abdominal surgery in irritable bowel syndrome. *South African Medical Journal, 70,* 91.

Casati, J., & Toner, B. B. (2000). Psychological aspects of inflammatory bowel disease. *Biomedicine & Pharmacotherapy, 54,* 388–393.

Casati, J., Toner, B. B., de Rooy, E. C., Drossman, D. A., & Maunder, R. G. (2000). Concerns of patients with inflammatory bowel disease: A review of emerging themes. *Digestive Diseases and Sciences, 45*(1), 26–31.

Chabbra, M., Toner, B. B., Ali, A., & Stuckless, N. (1999). *The relationship between somatic symptoms and the attribution of illness in irritable bowel syndrome patients.* Unpublished manuscript.

Colcher, S. D. (1984). Family structure, stress, and individual adjustment to ulcerative colitis. *Dissertation Abstracts International, 44*(11), 3520–3521.

Colgan, S., Creed, F. H., & Klass, S. H. (1988). Psychiatric disorder and abnormal illness behavior in patients with upper abdominal pain. *Psychological Medicine, 18,* 887–892.

Corney, R. H., & Stanton, R. (1990). Physical symptom severity, psychological and social dysfunction in a series of outpatients with irritable bowel syndrome. *Journal of Psychosomatic Research, 34,* 483–491.

Craig, T. K. G., & Brown, G. W. (1984). Goal frustration and life events in the aetiology of painful gastrointestinal disorder. *Journal of Psychosomatic Research, 28*(5), 411–421.

Creed, F., Craig, T., & Farmer, R. (1988). Functional abdominal pain, psychiatric illness, and life events. *Gut, 29,* 235–242.

Daruna, J. H., & Morgan, J. E. (1990). Psychosocial effects on immune function: Neuroendocrine pathways. *Psychosomatics, 31,* 4.

de Rooy, E. C., Toner, B. B., Greenberg, G. R., Cohen, Z., Baron, D., Steinhart, H. A., et al. (1997). *Concerns of outpatients with inflammatory bowel disease: Identification and impact.* Unpublished manuscript.

Drossman, D. A. (1995a). Psychosocial factors in the care of patients with gastrointestinal disorders. In T. Yamada (Ed.), *Textbook of gastroenterology.* Philadelphia: Lippincott.

Drossman, D. A. (1995b). Psychosocial factors in inflammatory bowel disease. In J. B. Kirsner & R. G. Shorter (Eds.), *Inflammatory bowel disease.* Baltimore: Williams & Wilkins.

Drossman, D. A. (1996). Gastrointestinal illness and the biopsychosocial model [Editorial]. *Journal of Clinical Gastroenterology, 22,* 252–254.

Drossman, D. A. (1998). Presidential address: Gastrointestinal illness and the biopsychosocial model. *Psychsomatic Medicine, 60,* 258–267.

Drossman, D. A., Creed, F. H., Fava, G. A., Olden, K. W., Patrick, D. L., Toner, B. B., et al. (1995). Psychosocial aspects of functional gastrointestinal disorders. *Gastroenterology International, 8,* 47–90.

Drossman, D. A., Creed, F. H., Olden, K. W., Svedlund, J., Toner, B. B., & White-head, W. E. (1999). Psychosocial aspects of the functional gastrointestinal disorders. *Gut, 45*(Suppl. 2), 1125–1130.

Drossman, D. A., Creed, F. H., Olden, K. W., Toner, B. B., & Whitehead, W. E. (2000). Psychosocial aspects of the functional gastrointestinal disorders. In D. A. Drossman, E. Corazziari, N. J. Talley, W. G. Thompson, & W. White-head (Eds.), *The functional gastrointestinal disorders* (2nd ed., pp. 157–245). Lawrence, KS: Allen Press, Inc.

Drossman, D. A., Lesserman, J., Li, Z., Mitchell, C. M., Zagami, E. A., & Patrick, D. L. (1991). The rating form of IBD patient concerns: A new measure of health status. *Psychosomatic Medicine, 53*, 701–712.

Drossman, D. A., Lesserman, J., Nachman, G., Li, Z., Gluck, H., Toomey, T. C., et al. (1990). Sexual and physical abuse in women with functional or organic gastrointestinal disorders. *Annals of Internal Medicine, 113*(11), 828–833.

Drossman, D. A., Li, Z., Andruzzi, E., Temple, R. D., Talley, N. J., Thompson, W. G., et al. (1993). U.S. householder survey of functional gastrointestinal disorders: Prevalence: Sociodemography and health impact. *Digestive Disease and Sciences, 38*, 1569–1580.

Drossman, D. A., McKee, D. C., Sandler, R. S., Mitchell, C. M., Cramer, E. M., Lowman, B. C., et al. (1988). Psychosocial factors in the irritable bowel syn-drome: A multivariate study of patients and non-patients with irritable bowel syndrome. *Gastroenterology, 95*, 702–708.

Drossman, D. A., Patrick, D. L., Mitchell, C. M., Zagami, E. A., & Appelbaum, M. I. (1989). Health-related quality of life in inflammatory bowel disease: Functional status and patient worries and concerns. *Digestive Diseases and Sci-ences, 34*(9), 1379–1386.

Drossman, D. A., Richter, J. E., Talley, N. J., Thompson, W. G., Corazziari, E., & Whitehead, W. E. (1994). *Functional gastrointestinal disorders: Diagnosis, path-ophysiology, and treatment.* Boston: Little, Brown.

Drossman, D. A., Sandler, R. S., McKee, D. C., & Lovitz, A. J. (1982). Bowel patterns among subjects not seeking health care. *Gastroenterology, 83*, 529–534.

Drossman, D. A., Talley, N. J., Lesserman, J., Olden, K. W., & Barreiro, M. A. (1995). Sexual and physical abuse and gastrointestinal illness. Review and recommendations. *Annals of Internal Medicine, 123*(10), 782–794.

Drossman, D. A., Whitehead, W. E., & Camilleri, M. (1997). Medical position statement: Irritable bowel syndrome. *Gastroenterology, 112*, 2118–2119.

Duclos, B., Planchon, F., Jouin, H., Chamouard, P., Schieber, J. P., Ubrich-Leuilliot, M., et al. (1990). Socioprofessional consequences of Crohn's disease. *Gastroenterologie Clinique et Biologique, 14*(12), 966–972.

Duffy, L. C., Zielezny, M. A., Marshall, J. R., Byers, T. E., Weiser, M. M., Phillips, J. F., et al. (1991). Relevance of major stress events as an indicator of disease activity prevalence in inflammatory bowel disease. *Behavioral Medicine, 17*, 101.

Engel, G. L. (1977). The need for a new medical model: A challenge for biomedicine. *Science, 196,* 129–136.

Ford, M. J., Miller, P. M., Eastwood, J., & Eastwood, M. A. (1987). Life events, psychiatric illness and the irritable bowel syndrome. *Gut, 28,* 160–165.

Fukudo, S., Nomura, T., Muranaka, M., & Taguchi, F. (1993). Brain–gut response to stress and cholinergic stimulation to irritable bowel syndrome. A preliminary study. *Journal of Clinical Gastroenterology, 17*(2), 133–141.

Garrett, V. D., Brantley, P. J., Jones, G. N., & McKnight, G. T. (1991). The relation between daily stress and Crohn's disease. *Journal of Behavioral Medicine, 14,* 87.

Gazzard, B. D., Price, H. L., Libby, G. W., & Dawson, A. M. (1978). The social toll of Crohn's disease. *British Medical Journal, 2,* 1117–1119.

Gerbert, B. (1980). Psychological aspects of Crohn's disease. *Journal of Behavioral Medicine, 3,* 41.

Gillan, C. D., Andrews, H. A., & Prior, P. (1994). Crohn's disease and colorectal cancer. *Gut, 35,* 651.

Glotzer, D. J. (1995). Surgical therapy for Crohn's disease. *Gastroenterology Clinics of North America, 24*(3), 577.

Godber, D. (1989). Lay counselling and inflammatory bowel disease. *Stress Medicine, 5,* 211–212.

Godber, D., & Mayberry, J. F. (1988). A preliminary report on the role of lay counselling amongst patients with inflammatory bowel disease. *Journal of the Royal Society of Medicine, 81*(9), 528–529.

Grace, W. J., Wolf, S., & Wolff, H. G. (1950). Life situations, emotions, and chronic ulcerative colitis. *Journal of the American Medical Association, 142,* 1044–1048.

Guthrie, E., Creed, F., Dawson, E., & Tomenson, B. (1991). A controlled trial of psychological treatment for the irritable bowel syndrome. *Gastroenterology, 100,* 450–457.

Hay, J. W., & Hay, A. R. (1992). Inflammatory bowel disease: Costs of illness. *Journal of Clinical Gastroenterology, 14,* 309–317.

Heaton, K. W., O'Donnell, L. J. D., Braddon, F. E. M., Mountford, R. A., Hughes, A. O., & Cripps, P. J. (1992). Symptoms of irritable bowel syndrome in a British urban community: Consulters and nonconsulters. *Gastroenterology, 102,* 1962–1967.

Jantschek, G., Zeitz, M., Pritsch, M., Wirching, M., Klor, U., Studt, H., et al. (1998). Effect of psychotherapy on the course of Crohn's disease. *Scandinavian Journal of Gastroenterology, 33,* 1289–1296.

Joachim, G. (1983). The effects of two stress management techniques on patients with IBD. *Nursing Papers, 15,* 5–18.

Kellow, J. E., Gill, R. C., & Wingate, D. L. (1990). Prolonged ambulant recordings of small bowel motility demonstrate abnormalities in the irritable bowel syndrome. *Gastroenterology, 98,* 1208–1218.

Kinash, R. G., Fisher, D. G., Lukie, B. E., & Carr, T. L. (1993). Coping patterns and related characteristics in patients with IBD. *Rehabilitation Nursing, 18,* 12–19.

Kirmayer, L. J., & Robbins, J. M. (1991). Functional somatic syndromes. In L. J. Kirmayer & J. M. Robbins (Eds.), *Current concepts of somatization* (pp. 79–105). Washington, DC: American Psychiatric Association Press.

Kumar, D., Thompson, P. D., Wingate, D. L., Vesselinova-Jenkins, C. K., & Libby, G. (1992). Abnormal REM sleep in the irritable bowel syndrome. *Gastroenterology, 103,* 12–17.

Lashner, B. A. (1995). Epidemiology of inflammatory bowel disease. *Gastroenterology Clinics of North America, 24*(3), 467.

Lesserman, J., Drossman, D. A., Li, Z., Toomey, T. C., Nachman, G., & Glogau, L. (1996). Sexual and physical abuse history in gastroenterology practice: How types of abuse impact health status. *Psychosomatic Medicine, 58,* 4–15.

Lips, H. M. (1997). *Sex and gender: An introduction.* Mountain View, CA: Mayfield.

Longstreth, G. F., & Wolde-Tsadik, G. (1993). Irritable bowel type symptoms in HMO examinees: Prevalence, demographics, and clinical correlates. *Digestive Diseases and Sciences, 38,* 1581–1589.

MacDonald, A. J., & Bouchier, P. A. (1980). Non-organic gastrointestinal illness: A medical and psychiatric study. *British Journal of Psychiatry, 136,* 1276–1283.

Mallet, S., Lennard-Jones, J., Bingley, J., & Gilon, E. (1978). Living with the disease. *Lancet, 2,* 619–621.

Maunder, R. G., & Cardish, R. J. (1996). Psychological factors affecting medical condition: Prevalence and difficulty applying the diagnosis of inflammatory bowel disease. *Psychosomatic Medicine, 58,* 91.

Maunder, R. G., de Rooy, E. C., Toner, B. B., Greenberg, G. R., Steinhart, A. H., McLeod, R. S., et al. (1997). Health related concerns of people who receive psychological support for inflammatory bowel disease. *Canadian Journal of Gastroenterology, 11*(8), 681–685.

Maunder, R., Lancee, W. J., Esplen, M. J., & Greenberg, G. R. (1998). Interim report on supportive–expressive group psychotherapy for inflammatory bowel disease. *Psychosomatic Medicine, 60,* 127.

Maunder, R., Toner, B. B., de Rooy, E., & Moskovitz, D. (1999). Influence of sex and disease on illness-related concerns in inflammatory bowel disease. *Canadian Journal of Gastroenterology, 13*(9), 728–732.

Mayberry, J. F. (1987). The role of local self-help groups for patients with inflammatory bowel disease. *International Journal of Colorectal Diseases, 2,* 15.

Mayer, E. A., & Gebhart, G. F. (1994). Basic and clinical aspects of visceral hyperalgesia. *Gastroenterology, 107*(1), 271–293.

Mellemkjaer, L., Olsen, J. H., Frisch, M., Johansen, C., Gridley, G., & McLaughlin, J. K. (1995). Cancer in patients with ulcerative colitis. *International Journal of Cancer, 60,* 330.

Mendeloff, A. (1975). The epidemiology of idiopathic inflammatory bowel disease.

In J. B. Kirsner & R. G. Shorter (Eds.), *Inflammatory bowel disease* (pp. 3–19). Philadelphia: Lea & Febiger.

Milne, B., Joachim, G., & Niedhardt, J. (1986). A stress management programme for inflammatory bowel disease patients. *Journal of Advanced Nursing, 11,* 561–567.

North, C. S., Clouse, R. E., Spitznagel, E. L., & Alpers, D. H. (1990). The relation of ulcerative colitis to psychiatric factors: A review of findings and methods. *American Journal of Psychiatry, 147,* 974.

Practice Management Information Corporation. (1998). *International classification of diseases, ninth revision.* USA: Author.

Porcelli, P., Leoci, C., & Guerra, V. (1996). A prospective study of the relationship between disease activity and psychologic distress in patients with inflammatory bowel disease. *Scandinavian Journal of Gastroenterology, 31*(8), 792.

Sandler, R. S. (1990). Epidemiology of irritable bowel syndrome in the United States. *Gastroenterology, 99,* 409–415.

Sandler, R. S., Drossman, D. A., Nathan, H. P., & McKee, D. C. (1984). Symptoms complaints and health care seeking behavior in subjects with bowel dysfunction. *Gastroenterology, 87,* 314–318.

Sartor, R. B. (1995). Current concepts of the etiology and pathogenesis of ulcerative colitis and Crohn's disease. *Gastroenterology Clinics of North America, 24*(3), 475–507.

Satsangi, J., Parkes, M., Jewell, D. P., & Bell, J. L. (1998). Genetics of inflammatory bowel disease. *Clinical Science, 94,* 473–478.

Schneider, A. P. (1985). Coping with Crohn's disease: Some factors contributing to the appraisal of a chronic stressor. *Dissertation Abstracts International, 46*(3), 970B.

Schoenberg, P. (1983). An experience of ulcerative colitis. *British Journal of Psychiatry, 143,* 517–518.

Schwarz, S. P., & Blanchard, E. B. (1990). Inflammatory bowel disease: A review of the psychological assessment and treatment literature. *Annals of Behavioral Medicine, 12,* 95–105.

Schwarz, S. P., & Blanchard, E. B. (1991). Evaluation of a psychological treatment for inflammatory bowel disease. *Behavior Research and Therapy, 29*(2), 167–177.

Shanahan, F., & Anton, P. (1988). Neuroendocrine modulation of the immune system: Possible implications for inflammatory bowel disease. *Digestive Diseases and Sciences, 33,* 41S.

Shaw, L., & Ehrlich, A. (1987). Relaxation training as a treatment for chronic pain caused by ulcerative colitis. *Pain, 29*(3), 287–293.

Silverman, D. H. S., Munakata, J. A., Ennes, H., Mandelkern, M. A., Hoh, C. K., & Mayer, E. A. (1997). Regional cerebral activity in normal and pathologic perception of visceral pain. *Gastroenterology, 112*(1), 64–72.

Sorensen, V. Z., Olsen, B. G., & Binder, V. (1987). Life prospects and quality of life in patients with Crohn's disease. *Gut, 28,* 382–385.

Sperling, M. (1957). The psychoanalytic treatment of ulcerative colitis. *International Journal of Psychoanalysis, 38,* 341.

Talley, N. J., Boyce, P. M., & Jones, M. (1997). Predictors of health care seeking for irritable bowel syndrome: A population based study. *Gut, 41,* 394–398.

Talley, N. J., Zinmeister, A. R., Van Dyke, C., & Melton, L. (1991). Epidemiology of colonic symptoms and irritable bowel syndrome. *Gastroenterology, 101,* 927–934.

Thompson, W. G., Dotevall, G., Drossman, D. A., Heaton, K. W., & Kruis, W. (1989). Irritable bowel syndrome: Guidelines for the diagnosis. *Gastroenterology International, 2,* 92–95.

Thompson, W. G., Heaton, K. W., Smyth, T., & Smyth, C. (1996). Irritable bowel syndrome: The view from general practice [Abstract]. *Gastroenterology, 110,* 705.

Thompson, W. G., Longstreth, G., Drossman, D. A., Heaton, K., Irvine, E. J., & Muller-Lissner, S. (2000). Functional bowel disorders and functional abdominal pain. In D. A. Drossman, E. Corazziari, N. J. Talley, W. G. Thompson, & W. E. Whitehead (Eds.), *The functional gastrointestinal disorders* (pp. 360–361). Lawrence, KS: Allen Press, Inc.

Toner, B. B. (1994). Cognitive–behavioral treatment of functional somatic syndromes: Integrating gender issues. *Cognitive and Behavioral Practice, 1,* 157–178.

Toner, B. B. (1998–1999). Challenging myths associated with IBS [Four-part series]. *Participate, 7*(4), 8(1), 8(2), 8(3).

Toner, B. B., & Akman, D. (2000). Gender issues in irritable bowel syndrome. *American Journal of Gastroenterology, 95*(1), 11–16.

Toner, B. B., Garfinkel, P. E., & Jeejeebhoy, K. N. (1990). Psychological factors in irritable bowel syndrome. *Canadian Journal of Psychiatry, 35,* 158–161.

Toner, B. B., Segal, Z. V., Emmott, S. D., & Myran, D. (2000). *Cognitive–behavioral treatment of irritable bowel syndrome: The brain–gut connection.* New York: Guilford Publications.

Toner, B. B., Segal, A. V., Emmott, S., Myran, D., Ali, A., DiGasbarro, I., et al. (1998). Cognitive–behavioral group therapy for patients with irritable bowel syndrome. *International Journal of Group Psychotherapy, 38,* 215–243.

Tysk, C., Lindberg, E., Jarnerot, G., & Floderus-Myrhed, B. (1988). Ulcerative colitis and Crohn's disease in an unselected population of monozygotic and dizygotic twins. A study of heritability and the influence of smoking. *Gut, 29,* 990–996.

Valori, R. M., Kumar, D., & Wingate, D. L. (1986). Effects of different types of stress and/or "prokinetic" drugs on the control of the fasting motor complex in humans. *Gastroenterology, 90,* 1890–1900.

Weinstock, H. (1961). Hospital psychotherapy in severe ulcerative colitis. *Archives of General Psychiatry, 4,* 509.

Weiss, E. G., & Wexner S. D. (1995). Surgical therapy for ulcerative colitis. *Gastroenterology Clinics of North America, 24*(3), 559–596.

Whitehead, W. E., Bosmajian, L., Zonderman, A. B., Costa, P. T., Jr., & Schuster, M. M. (1988). Symptoms of psychologic distress associated with irritable bowel syndrome: Comparison of community and medical clinic sample. *Gastroenterology, 95,* 709–714.

Whorwell, P. J. (1991). Use of hypnotherapy in gastrointestinal disease. *British Journal of Hospital Medicine, 45,* 27–29.

Wyke, R. J. (1988). Capacity for work and employment record of patients with inflammatory bowel disease. *International Disability Study, 10,* 176.

Wyke, R. J., Edwards, F. C., & Allan, R. N. (1988). Employment problems and prospects for patients with inflammatory bowel disease. *Gut, 29,* 1229.

Young, S. J., Alpers, D. H., Norland, C. C., & Woodruff, R. A. (1976). Psychiatric illness and the irritable bowel syndrome. *Gastroenterology, 70,* 162–166.

10

GENITOURINARY DISEASES

CYNTHIA D. BELAR AND STEVEN M. TOVIAN

The genitourinary (GU) system refers to the reproductive and urinary systems. In men and women, the GU system includes the bladder, ureters, urethra, and kidneys. In women, it also includes the ovaries, uterus, vagina, labia, fallopian tubes, and clitoris. In men, it also includes the penis, testes, prostate gland, and vas deferens.

The diseases classified in the ninth revision of the *International Classification of Diseases* (*ICD–9*, 1999) under the GU system are heterogeneous, with widely different etiologies, pathophysiologies, treatments, and psychological issues. For example, chronic renal failure, infertility, urinary incontinence, and endometriosis are all classified within this section. Rather than integrating the research from all diseases in such a heterogeneous classification, this chapter provides a brief description of each condition and reviews pertinent contributions of health psychology research.

CHRONIC RENAL FAILURE

Nature of the Problem

The irreversible failure of the excretory and regulatory functions of the kidneys is end-stage renal disease (ESRD). According to the 1999 *An-*

nual Data Report of the U.S. Renal Data System, 304,083 patients were treated for ESRD in 1997, with a growth rate of approximately 6% per year over the previous 5 years. Incidence and prevalence rates increase with age, and ESRD is more common in men than in women. African American and Native Americans have rates 3 to 5 times higher than White and Asian American populations. Indeed, African Americans constitute 32% of patients with ESRD, although they make up only about 12% of the U.S. population. The most common overall cause of ESRD is diabetes, followed by hypertension and glomerulonephritis (inflammation of capillary loops inside the kidney); hypertension is the most common cause for African Americans. Total spending for ESRD in 1997 was $15.64 billion.

Loss of kidney functioning is fatal. The uremic syndrome appears when renal functioning decreases to 20% to 25% of normal levels; it produces systemic biochemical imbalance and multiple organ dysfunction as toxins accumulate and electrolytes go awry. Treatment for renal failure consists of hemodialysis, peritoneal dialysis, or kidney transplantation. Transplantation is considered the best option, both medically and in terms of quality of life, but the need for kidneys has expanded disproportionately to the availability of donor organs. Hence, hemodialysis is the most common treatment, although it does not correct all ESRD imbalances. Sexual dysfunction, cognitive impairment, anemia, hypocalcemia (reduction of calcium in blood causing muscle cramping), pruritus (itching), and septicemic infections can often result. Hemodialysis requires 3 to 6 hours to complete and is provided 3 times per week. It can be conducted at home but is most often provided on an outpatient basis. The other form of dialysis, continuous ambulatory peritoneal dialysis, does not require blood removal because it uses peritoneal membranes as artificial kidneys. Patients infuse and remove a dialysate solution several times daily in 30- to 60-minute cycles; thus, the treatment is more self-directed and less restrictive.

Adherence to medical regimens is an important feature of all treatments. Patients receiving dialysis have severe fluid restrictions as well as significant dietary restrictions. The required phosphate-binding medication often has unpleasant gastrointestinal side effects. The dialysis treatment itself is time consuming and, if done at home, is quite demanding. Those who receive kidney transplants have a strict immunosuppressive regimen and must be attentive to signs of rejection. Nonadherence in patients with ESRD is estimated at 30% to 50%. Nonadherence is a direct cause of a significant number of deaths among patients receiving dialysis (e.g., through fluid overload) and has been related to renal graft failure in transplant recipients (for a review, see Christensen, Benotsch, & Smith, 1997).

Contributions of Health Psychology

Before the development of renal dialysis, ESRD was fatal. Even after its introduction in the 1960s, dialysis was not widely available to all those with ESRD. Thus, multidisciplinary teams were established to identify which candidates were best suited to undertake this demanding treatment. Psychological evaluations addressed issues of emotional stability, intellectual capacity, and motivation and ability to adhere to complex regimens. After dialysis became more accessible through the 1973 Medicare entitlement program, psychologists were still involved in decision-making regarding candidacy for renal transplant.

However, throughout this period researchers were learning more about the psychological factors that were predictive of morbidity and mortality in ESRD and the significant associated psychological stressors and quality-of-life issues. As the role of psychological factors became increasingly recognized, psychologists provided direct services to patients with ESRD and became consultants in program development for dialysis units and transplant teams (e.g., Kirschenbaum, 1991). In fact, given the intrusiveness and side effects of treatments, ESRD has been described as a "living stress laboratory" for the study of chronic illness effects (Devins et al., 1990). Research has shown that the burden of family adaptation is shouldered more by women and spouses than men and patient counterparts (Devins, Hunsley, Mandin, Taub, & Paul, 1997) and that poor vocational functioning may be partly caused by cognitive deficits associated with ESRD (Bremer, Wert, Durica, & Weaver, 1997).

Psychological problems associated with hemodialysis have included those associated with uremia (e.g., memory deficits, concentration problems), as well as anxiety and depression. Reviews of the literature have suggested that the prevalence of clinical depression in those with ESRD is 12% to 45%, although it is often undetected (Christensen & Moran, 1998). Rates are highest for in-center dialysis patients, and some evidence has shown that depression is related to earlier mortality and morbidity. Although the mediational mechanisms for the relationship between depression and survival are not clear, both behavioral (nonadherence) and biological (impaired immunocompetence) pathways have been postulated. It may also be that some of the depressive symptoms represent the incomplete control of uremia and anemia. However, a report revealed that 47% of patients who were receiving dialysis and had major depressive episodes received no psychological treatments (Hong, Smith, Robson, & Wetzel, 1987). Moreover, systematic studies of psychological interventions to improve psychological adjustment and quality of life are lacking (Symister & Friend, 1996).

Most psychological research has focused on determinants of patient nonadherence and has produced mixed results, although greater levels of family support are usually associated with better adherence (for reviews, see Brantley & Hitchcock, 1995; Christensen et al., 1997). Christensen and Moran (1998) attributed this finding to a failure to consider interactions among patient attributes, disease characteristics, and treatment variables. These authors argued that adherence is better explained by the degree of congruency between patient coping style and the demands of the treatment (e.g., "active copers" are more adherent to self-directed treatments such as at-home dialysis). As knowledge in this area develops, psychological data will be increasingly useful in medical decision-making regarding treatment alternatives. With respect to psychological interventions, some evidence has suggested that behavioral strategies such as behavioral contracting, token economies, and positive reinforcement can improve adherence, but it is also clear that management is within a chronic maintenance model and relapse prevention components are essential. It is also noteworthy that in-center dialysis is done in group settings, which could allow the use of group interventions. Preliminary work by Tucker, Mulkerne, and Ziller (1982) suggested using such an approach to facilitate global psychosocial adjustment.

CHRONIC INTERSTITIAL CYSTITIS

Nature of the Problem

Interstitial cystitis (IC) is a chronic bladder disease of unknown cause. IC probably represents a spectrum of disorders, one of which is an autoimmune disease. Other postulated causes include infection, vascular alterations, toxic agents, and neurological disorders. Stress-induced bladder mast cell activation has been demonstrated in animal research (Spanos et al., 1997); thus, psychological factors may be relevant through a neuroimmunoendocrine pathway. According to the Interstitial Cystitis Association (www.ichelp.org), 450,000 people may be affected by the disease; it is most commonly found in women. Symptoms include urinary frequency and urgency and suprapubic pain. It can be debilitating with respect to work, recreation, and sexual functioning, and it is incurable. Oral medications include anti-inflammatory drugs, antihistamines, muscle relaxants, and antispasmodic drugs. Other treatments available are bladder distention methods and instillation of medications such as dimethyl sulfoxide directly into the bladder. In severe cases, surgical treatment such as urinary diversion has been used.

Contributions of Health Psychology

The psychosocial difficulties associated with IC have long been recognized. Hanno and Wein (1987) noted the hopeless attitude seen in many patients with IC. Research has documented the prominence of sexual problems, as well as patients' feelings of helplessness and inadequacy while they try to cope with the disease (Keltikangas-Jarvinen, Auvinen, & Lehtonen, 1988). Chapters in Volume 2 of this series that focus on coping with chronic illness and pain management are most relevant to this disorder (Raczynski, Bradley, & Leviton, in press).

URETHRAL SYNDROME

Nature of the Problem

In women, urethral syndrome consists of urinary urgency and frequency, painful urination (dysuria), low back pain, and other voiding difficulties (i.e., weak stream and hesitancy) in the absence of definable organic pathology. Urethral syndrome accounts for more than 5 million doctors' office visits per year in the United States (Scotti & Ostergard, 1984). The syndrome discussed in this section is either chronic or recurrent.

Irritation in the urethra, particularly in the area of the external (striated) sphincter, is thought to be the cause of the urethral syndrome (Kellner, 1991). Most women (15% to 75%) with urethral syndrome have evidence of bacterial infection. Even though they may have no evidence of concurrent infection, about 15% have histological evidence of previous infection (Scotti & Ostergard, 1984). Causes other than infections involving musculature and sphincter dysfunction have been suggested. Dynamic studies have shown that spasticity of the smooth muscle sphincter may account for additional reports of urethral syndrome. In such cases, treatments with alpha-receptor-blocking drugs, surgical dilation procedures, or both may be helpful (Bergman, Karram, & Bhatia, 1989). A more thorough

TABLE 10.1
Etiology and Treatment of Urethral Syndrome

Etiology	Treatment
Infection	Antibiotics
Obstruction (anatomical and spasm)	Dilatation
	Alpha-blocker medication
	Benzodiazepines
Chronic inflammatory urethritis	Dilatation
	Steroids
Neurological	Anesthetic injections
Dermatological	Estrogen and steroid creams
Allergic	Steroids
	Antihistamines
	Avoidance of allergens
Psychogenic	Psychotherapy

listing of causes and treatments of the urethral syndrome is presented in Table 10.1.

Because the etiology of urethral syndrome is obscure, medical treatment has been and remains very empirical. Antibiotics, bladder neck opening, internal urethrotomy, urethral dilation, local steroid injections, estrogens, and general tranquilizers (e.g., diazepam) have all been used (Scotti & Ostergard, 1984). Because obstruction and infection are the most frequent etiologies, antibiotics (mainly tetracyclines) and urethral dilation have become the most popular treatment modalities (Kellner, 1991). Urethral syndrome that is based on psychogenic factors remains a diagnosis of exclusion of any physical disease.

Contributions of Health Psychology

Behavioral and Psychological Assessment

The urethral syndrome is a diagnosis of exclusion of treatable physical disease. A large proportion of women who seek medical treatment because of urethral symptoms have acute as well as chronic or recurrent infections that contribute to this syndrome. Women who are anxious or have other psychopathological symptoms and who have a tendency to perceive bodily sensations seem to perceive their urethral symptoms more, may be more distressed by the symptoms, or both. Anxiety may contribute to selective perception or induce hypochondriacal concerns (Kellner, 1991).

Reiter, Shakerin, Gambone, and Milburn (1991) studied 52 women with a probable somatic cause of their urological dysfunction and 47 women without somatic abnormalities and a diagnosis of urethral syndrome. The authors found the psychosocial profile of women with urethral syndrome differed from that of women with a somatic etiology and that previous sexual abuse was a significant predisposing risk for urethral syndrome. This study highlights the crucial need for evaluation of past sexual abuse and possible past traumatic stress for women with urethral syndrome.

Psychometric Assessment

Anxiety and concerns about health may exacerbate lower urinary tract symptoms of some patients with urethral syndrome and cause them to seek medical care more often. Carson, Osborne, and Segura (1979) studied 57 women with urethral syndrome. Using the Minnesota Multiphase Personality Inventory (MMPI; Hathaway & McKinley, 1967) as part of their psychosocial evaluation, they found these patients demonstrate a "classic V conversion" on Hypochondria, Hysteria, and Depression scales, which is consistent with other research findings on chronic pain, lower back pain, and patients with somatoform complaints and supports the likelihood of involvement of psychophysiological processes.

Treatment

No adequately controlled studies in the literature have suggested the most appropriate psychological treatment of urethral syndrome. Kellner (1991) reported that diazepam was found to relieve symptoms in 13 of 15 women with urethral syndrome in several uncontrolled studies. If organic causes of the syndrome are identified and treated but the symptoms persist, or if psychological factors (e.g., past sexual abuse) seem to play a substantial role, the patient should be referred for individual psychotherapy in accordance with treatment for psychophysiological or posttraumatic disorders. If the urethral symptoms occur predominantly in certain situations, treating the patients with cognitive–behavioral approaches may be helpful, as it is for other phobias and anxiety disorders.

PROSTATITIS

Prostatitis is characterized by painful, reduced urine flow in men caused by inflammation of the prostate gland. Located just below the bladder and next to the rectum, the prostate gland is apple shaped, with the urethra running through its center. If the prostate gland swells, the urethra is pinched off, obstructing the flow of urine and causing a reflux of urine, potentially damaging the kidneys (Tanagho & McAninch, 1995).

It is estimated more than 500,000 men experience prostatitis every year in the United States (Tanagho & McAninch, 1995). Prostatitis can occur at any age. Several types of prostatitis exist, but all have similar symptoms: fever; urination problems, including burning or bleeding; decreased urine flow; and a steady pain in the lower back, pelvis, or upper thighs. If bacteria or viruses enter the urethra and spread to the prostate, inflammation, or prostatitis, results. In younger men, prostatitis is usually caused by a bacterial infection and responds to antibiotics. However, in older men (older than age 50 years), the prostate may enlarge to more than 50% of its normal size because of the aging process, not because of an infection. This type of prostatitis in older men is often treated with the surgery transurethral resection (TUR), which involves trimming the gland down to normal size. About 20% of the men who have this operation experience impotence after surgery (Tanagho & McAninch, 1995).

Contributions of Health Psychology

As is discussed in the next section of this chapter, clinical health psychologists can treat these patients.

Nature of the Problem

According to the American Society for Reproductive Medicine (ASRM), *infertility* is defined as the inability to conceive after 1 year of sexual intercourse with no birth control. It is a problem that is more widespread than customarily thought, affecting 6.1 million American women and their partners, or about 10% of those of reproductive age (ASRM, 1998b). Although the rate of infertility has been relatively stable over time, the numbers of couples seeking services has dramatically increased (Office of Technology Assessment [OTA], 1988). This increase has been attributed to increased public awareness of the problem as well as advances in medical technology and treatment. Certain age groups also have increased infertility rates, perhaps because of the number of couples who have delayed childbearing and the large cohort of baby boomers who recently passed through their reproductive years.

The cause of infertility can be identified in approximately 84% of couples, although for approximately 16% the infertility is unexplained (ASRM, 1997). When diagnosed, infertility is attributable to female factors in approximately 40% of cases, to male factors in approximately 40%, and to both male and female factors in 20%. Exhibit 10.1 lists common causes of infertility. Approximately 25% of couples have more than one factor causing infertility (ASRM, 1995b). It is also noteworthy that numerous behavior-mediated factors (e.g., cigarette smoke, marijuana, caffeine, alcohol, exercise, being underweight or overweight) can have adverse effects on human eggs and sperm and thus may negatively affect fertility.

Pregnancy is possible for more than half of couples seeking treatment (ASRM, 1997). Medical treatments offer hope, but they are expensive, are

EXHIBIT 10.1
Common Causes of Infertility

Male factors	Female factors
Azoospermia	Tubal factors (blockage, scarring)
Oligospermia	Anovulation
Sperm motility or morphology	Ovulation problems
Sperm antibodies	Endometriosis
Varicocele	Luteal phase defects
Duct obstruction	Inflammatory factors
Endocrine problems	Sperm antibodies
Inflammatory factors	Cervical mucus problems
Substance abuse	Uterine factors
Testicular heat	Strenuous exercise
Medications	Age
Radiation	

demanding, and can be psychologically stressful. Moreover, they involve complex issues concerning the couple, the family, religion, and culture, and an understanding of concomitant legal and ethical issues has been outpaced by the advances in biotechnology. Current treatments include intrauterine insemination (IUI) and ovulation induction methods as well as a number of assisted reproductive technologies (ARTs). Accounting for more than 70,000 babies born in the United States, current ARTs include in vitro fertilization (IVF), gamete intrafallopian transfer, zygote intrafallopian transfer, and intracytoplasmic sperm injection. Cryopreservation is available to maintain embryos for use after failed trials or at a later date to provide siblings for children born of ART. Moreover, third-party reproduction is available through donor sperm, donor eggs, donor embryos, and surrogacy. In fact, a child can now have five parents: the genetically related mother (the egg donor), a genetically related father (the sperm donor), the gestational mother (the woman who physically has the baby), and the social mother and father (the couple who rears the child). With new techniques in ovum donation, a child could have two genetically linked mothers as well.

Although a review of medical treatments is outside the scope of this chapter, excellent resources for up-to-date information regarding infertility and its treatments are the ASRM (http://www.ASRM.org) and the national support group Resolve (http://www.Resolve.org). The national success rate reports of the Society for Assisted Reproductive Technology (SART) are available through the Division of Reproductive Health at the Centers for Disease Control and Prevention (http://www.cdc.gov/nccdphp/drh). It is widely accepted that psychological counseling should be available for infertile couples in treatment. ASRM (1998a) practice guidelines for oocyte and embryo donation include psychological evaluation as an integral component.

Contributions of Health Psychology

Early psychological work focused on infertility as caused by intrapsychic conflicts. Explanations included formulations of underlying conflicts such as those about parenthood, sexuality, or one's mother. These psychogenic models were largely refuted by psychological research and advances in knowledge regarding medical causes of infertility, although this does not mean that psychological factors never play an etiological role. In fact, psychological distress may be a risk factor for reduced fertility in some women (Hjollund et al., 1999). Stress may affect prolactin secretion in women, sperm count in men, and immunological conditions necessary for embryo implantation.

Current research has adopted a more biopsychosocial model focusing on the interaction of multiple systems. Health psychology has enhanced the understanding of psychological reactions to infertility, gender differences in stress and coping, psychophysiological components, psychological aspects of medical treatments, and the relationships between stress and outcomes. Psychological interventions have been designed to help manage the stress of infertility, and behavioral research on sexually transmitted diseases furthers efforts of prevention because they are the primary preventable cause of infertility. Excellent reviews of health psychology research have been conducted by Stanton and colleagues (Stanton & Burns, 1999; Stanton & Dunkel-Schetter, 1991). A brief summary of their work follows.

Many women describe infertility as the worst experience of their lives. Moreover, infertility is generally a problem for a couple, not for an individual. Most people remain psychologically resilient, but response varies widely, with some demonstrating clinically significant levels of anxiety and depression. For most, infertility is a major stressor that is associated with significant distress and life disruption. Greater distress is associated with the use of coping strategies such as avoidance and self-blame, whereas seeking emotional support is related to more positive adjustment. A meta-analysis by Jordan and Revenson (1999) revealed gender differences in coping strategies, with women using social support, escape and avoidance, planful problem-solving, and positive reappraisal more than men. However, the research on dyadic components in coping and adjustment and how these might be related to specific interventions is limited.

The development of ARTs has presented new stressors for couples in terms of decision-making and the inherent stress of the procedures. The treatment process has been described as an "emotional roller coaster" and is often associated with short-term clinically significant depression and anxiety. Women report higher treatment-related distress (Beutel et al., 1999). Egg retrieval and the period after embryo transfer when patients are waiting for pregnancy results are two of the most stressful times. Moreover, the stress of infertility treatment itself may influence treatment success. For example, Boivin and Takefman (1995) found a lower IVF success rate in women who reported more daily stress during the treatment cycle as compared with their less stressed counterparts.

It has also been noted that patients tend to overestimate their chances of success with ARTs, despite the fact that the majority of attempts are unsuccessful. Although this has been of some concern given the assumption that unrealistic expectations are associated with poorer adjustment to treatment failure, increased risk associated with overestimation has not been documented. In fact, considering the significant investment of emotional and financial resources in treatment, overestimation may be a buffer against negative affect. The long-term psychological effects of multiple failed attempts with ARTs are not known, although some evidence has suggested more negative effects with more failures. Little information is available about the impact of decisions to disclose or not to disclose the use of gamete donors.

Psychological interventions for patients with infertility involve those aimed at managing negative affect, promoting coping and stress management, and facilitating treatment decision making, although most treatment research has been uncontrolled. Nevertheless, as noted previously, ASRM guidelines call for the availability of psychological counseling for infertile couples; some infertility treatment programs actually require it. O'Moore and colleagues (1983) found that couples who received autogenic training had significant reductions in state anxiety and that women had lower plasma prolactin levels. Benefits from emotion-focused and problem-focused coping skills training have also been documented (McQueeney, Stanton, & Sigmon, 1997).

Perhaps the most widely cited intervention studies are those by Domar and colleagues (1990, 1992, 1998). These authors developed a 10-week cognitive–behavioral treatment group with components of relaxation training, cognitive restructuring, group support, stress management, nutritional and exercise advice, and partner involvement. Women who participated in these groups reported less anxiety and depression, as well as increased vigor. The preliminary results from a randomized controlled trial of this treatment also revealed a higher viable pregnancy rate when compared to controls. However, given a variety of alternate hypotheses, it is impossible to conclude from this work that psychological interventions definitively improve conception rates. Nevertheless, this research and that of Poehl and colleagues (1999) in Austria has suggested that this possibility is worthy of further study.

IMPOTENCE OF ORGANIC ORIGIN

Nature of the Problem

Definition and Prevalence

Impotence, or erectile dysfunction (ED), is a persistent or recurrent, partial or complete failure to attain or maintain sufficient penile erections for satisfactory sexual functioning with subsequent marked distress and interpersonal difficulty (American Psychiatric Association, 1994). It is estimated that more than 10 million American men experience ED. The prevalence of ED increases with age as physical and mental illnesses and concomitant prescription drug use increase, which is common during the middle and later years of life. The incidence of ED is approximately 10% of men at age 50, 20% at age 60, 30% at age 70, and 40% at age 80 (Ackerman, 1992). Using a biopsychosocial model, ED is considered neither organic nor psychogenic but rather is considered to be influenced by an interacting set of variables. It therefore requires assessment of cognitive, behavioral, affective, and interpersonal factors as well as of physical factors for effective treatment. The psychological consequences of ED include depression, performance anxiety, and relationship distress (Ackerman, 1995; Ackerman & Carey, 1995).

Etiology

ED can occur as a result of malfunction in any one or more of the physiological processes discussed previously. Vascular inadequacy is the most frequent cause, and hormonal abnormalities are the least likely cause. Neurological, structural, and psychological factors are responsible for the remaining portion of male sexual difficulties (Ackerman, Montague, & Morgenstern, 1994). ED is not a result of natural aging.

Many medications prescribed for various physical and psychiatric disorders can impair erectile functioning and sexual desire. Medications such as antihypertensive agents, anticholinergics, and drugs used in the treatment of psychiatric disorders (i.e., phenothiazines, benzodiazepines, and antidepressants) can be associated with ED (Ackerman, 1995).

Current Medical Treatments

Options for medical treatment depend on the suspected cause of the ED. For example, testosterone replacement therapy is used to treat hormonal insufficiency. If ED developed after medications were prescribed for a primary medical condition, cessation or substitution of those medications may be helpful. Ackerman and colleagues (1994) reviewed possible medicinal approaches with yohimbine-HCl and Frental, and they concluded that these drugs provide nothing more than placebo effects at best. The authors also thoroughly described and reviewed additional medical options such as injection methods with papaverine-HCl, vascular surgery, and both internal and external implant prosthesis. Surgical approaches attempt to correct vascular insufficiency by blocking venous return or increasing arterial inflow. Arterial reconstruction and bypass grafting may improve blood inflow. Intracavernous injection of vasoactive agents such as papaverine-HCl is considered first-line therapy and can be self-administered. However, potential side effects such as painful erections, hypotension, and liver enzyme abnormalities have been reported. The reliability and effectiveness of penile implants have improved over the years and may be considered second-line therapies, should injections and vacuum devices prove unsuccessful. (Vacuum devices have an external vacuum chamber that pulls blood into the penis, producing an erection. Elastic is slipped on the base of the penis to maintain the erection after the chamber is removed.)

Patients undergoing any invasive procedure or who are using medication (e.g., Sildenafil, Viagra) to treat ED often require adjunct psychological support and psychoeducational therapy to ensure success. Sildenafil enhances the effect of sexual stimulation with smooth muscle relaxation and inflow of blood to corpus cavernosum in the penis. Prevalence rates of the side effects of the medication, which is taken 30 minutes to 4 hours before sexual activity, are severe headaches (10%), rapid heart rate (10%), abnormal vision (1%–10%), dizziness (1%–10%), skin rash (1%–10%), and nasal congestion (1%–10%). Outcome studies have suggested that one third of the men using Sildenafil have no positive effects (Lacy, Armstrong, & Goldman, 1999). Because Sildenafil does not cause penile erections, foreplay and relationship factors play a major role in the use of this medication.

Contributions of Health Psychology

Psychological and Behavioral Assessment

Ackerman and Carey (1995) recommended a thorough evaluation of past and current ED (i.e., description of the presenting complaint and its duration, frequency, and nature of onset), once rapport has been established. Other relevant information includes masturbatory fantasies, sexual drive, sexual techniques, and sexual knowledge. Frequency and outcome attempts at intercourse should be reviewed, as well as coping effort for unsuccessful attempts. Questions pertaining to sexual orientation, sexual deviations, and past sexual abuse should be included. Occasionally, special treatment circumstances, such as vasoactive injection therapy or penile implant surgery, require the psychologist to assess misconceptions, attitudes, or unrealistic expectations to maximize treatment outcome.

The Miami Sexual Dysfunction Protocol (MSDP; Ackerman, Helder, & Antoni, 1989) is a broad, semistructured interview format designed for use in medical settings to help organize information taken from the man with sexual dysfunction and his partner. Another important skill that the psychologist brings to the evaluation of ED is the ability to elicit concise information regarding sexual functioning while creating a relaxed, trusting atmosphere (Ackerman & Carey, 1995). Having an organized protocol such as the MSDP helps facilitate the collection of baseline data for clinical training and research purposes in a relaxed atmosphere.

Psychophysiological Factors

As with all other urological disorders, before any referral to the health psychologists, all patients with ED should undergo a medical and urological examination, including blood chemistry testing and specialized urodynamic studies. For example, the patient may return to the urologist for overnight, inpatient Rigiscan diagnostic monitoring. Rigiscan monitoring involves the assessment of erectile functioning, including assessment of rigidity and tumescence at the base and tip of the penis and the duration of these events throughout the sleep cycle (Ackerman, 1992).

Ackerman and colleagues (1994) outlined treatment options for ED. Treatment options depend on the suspected cause of the ED, the quality of the patient's relationships, his premorbid sexual satisfaction, and his acceptance and mastery of any medical approach. If the causes are psychological or behavioral, individual, sex therapy, or both are an important aspect of or the sole method of treatment (for comprehensive sex therapy texts, see Schover & Jensen, 1988; Wincze & Carey, 1991). If relationship problems exist, conjoint therapy is recommended with or before sex therapy. For invasive therapeutic options such as injection methods, vascular surgery, or an implantable prosthesis, referral for adjunct psychoeducational and supportive psychotherapy may be indicated. Problems such as performance anxiety, reduced orgasmic intensity, or relationship conflicts can emerge secondary to invasive medical procedures and often respond to cognitive–behavioral interventions (Ackerman & Carey, 1995). Psychological interventions with ED are listed in Exhibit 10.2.

ENDOMETRIOSIS

Nature of the Problem

Endometriosis occurs when the endometrial tissue that lines the uterus grows outside the uterine cavity. It is common disorder, found in approximately 7% of women of reproductive age, yet many women are asymptomatic (ASRM, 1995a). Other women have mild to severe symptoms of dysmenorrhea, dyspareunia, pelvic pain, infertility, or all of these.

Endometriosis is an unpredictable disorder. Endometrial tissue can implant anywhere in the abdominal cavity or migrate to distant sites such as the lungs. The tissue responds to cyclical changes in estrogen and pro-

---

EXHIBIT 10.2
Psychological Interventions for Impotence or
Erectile Dysfunction

Conjoint therapy
- Relationship and communication skill training
- Sex therapy

Individual therapy
- Psychoeducational (postinvasive medical procedure)
- Cognitive–behavioral therapy
- Sex therapy

---

gesterone, and its growth can irritate surrounding tissue, causing inflammation. This process may produce adhesions (scar tissue) that can bind pelvic organs and cause severe pain. The cause of endometriosis is not fully understood. One theory involves retrograde menstruation (i.e., when menstrual discharge flows backward into the pelvis, depositing endometrial cells that implant themselves). Another explanation involves failure of the immune system to clear the errant cells from retrograde menstruation.

Contributions of Health Psychology

Although pain is not a valid indicator of the extent of endometriosis, pain is the primary symptom for which patients seek relief. Chapter 9 in Volume 2 provides a review of psychological factors in the understanding, assessment and treatment of pain (Raczynski et al., in press). Refer to the following section on dyspareunia and the previous section on infertility; endometriosis can be a significant contributor to these disorders.

DYSPAREUNIA

Nature of the Problem

Dyspareunia refers to painful sex. The pain can occur before, during, or after intercourse and can be experienced as superficial, deep, intermittent, sharp, or aching. Although rare in men, prevalence rates in women range from 8% to 34% (Wincze & Carey, 1991). Glatt, Zinner, and McCormack (1990) found that more than 60% of a community sample of women had experienced dyspareunia, and almost half of the 33.5% who reported a current problem had experienced it throughout their entire sex lives. Many with the problem had never reported it to a professional, although painful intercourse has been described as the most common sexual complaint in obstetrics and gynecology practices (Steege, 1984). Physical findings are often absent, and women are sometimes informed that their problem is psychological, despite a lack of scientific evidence for a psychological basis. However, dyspareunia can affect sexual behavior, relationship adjustments, and the general sense of well-being. It can also result in the development of vaginismus, which is itself associated with dyspareunia. Physical conditions that can cause dyspareunia are pelvic infections, urinary tract infections, endometriosis, ovarian cysts, hymenal remnants, estrogen deficiencies, vaginal atrophy, previous traumas (including sexual abuse), and scarring following episiotomy.

Vulvar vestibulitis syndrome is a distinct condition in which a burning or incisive pain is experienced during attempted penetration or stimulation of the vulvar vestibule. Goetsch (1991) reported rates up to 15%

in general gynecology practices. Theories of etiology include recurrent candidiasis or human papilloma virus infections, use of vaginal creams, problems of autoimmunity, and hormonal factors. Bergeron and Binik (1999a) described this syndrome as a neglected women's health problem.

Contributions of Health Psychology

Psychologists have elucidated the impact of dyspareunia on sexual functioning and psychological well-being. In some patients, prior sexual abuse or conflicts about sexuality have been implicated in its etiology (Leiblum, 1996). As in other pain conditions, cognitive, affective, and behavioral factors have been related to pain perception and coping. Even when organic factors are being successfully treated, cognitive–behavioral treatments can help cope with past experiences that cause the patient to associate sex with pain. Treatment components include progressive muscle relaxation, Kegel exercises, vaginal dilators, cognitive restructuring of past sexual experiences and values, coping skills training, interpersonal adjustment and communication interventions, and management of anxiety and depression (Bergeron & Binik, 1999b; Leiblum, 1996; Wincze & Carey, 1991).

Bergeron and Binik (1999b) reported on a randomized trial comparing cognitive–behavioral therapy, electromyographical biofeedback, and vestibulectomy for treatment of vulvar vestibulitis. All treatments resulted in reductions in pain and improvements in psychological adjustment and sexual function 6 months later. Surgery was superior to the two psychological interventions but was also associated with numerous reports of a worsened condition. When considering the usefulness of psychological interventions, it is important to acknowledge that many patients are hesitant to undergo an invasive procedure such as vestibulectomy and would prefer other options. Moreover, Schover, Youngs, and Cannata (1992) reported that success rates of vestibulectomy increase when combined with psychological interventions.

VAGINISMUS

Nature of the Problem

Vaginismus is a condition in which the muscles of the outer third of the vagina spasm involuntarily, making sexual intercourse difficult or impossible. Vaginismus is thought to be a conditioned response caused by painful intercourse or psychosexual trauma. Vaginismus often begins with dyspareunia, which can be the result of numerous organic factors described in the previous section. Vaginismus is thought to be a major cause of unconsummated marriage. It can prevent pregnancy, provide a barrier to gynecological exams, and thus negatively affect a woman's health. Vaginismus is not necessarily associated with sexual unresponsiveness; many women with this problem can achieve orgasms alone or with their partners. Prevalence in the general population is not known, but it is estimated that 5% to 42% of patients who seek sex therapy have problems with vaginismus. Higher rates have been found in Irish women (for a discussion of related issues, see Wincze & Carey, 1991).

Contributions of Health Psychology

Psychology has contributed the major etiological model for vaginismus— a problem of behavioral conditioning. In this model, dyspareunia is the unconditioned stimulus that leads to the unconditioned response of self-protective tightening of the vaginal muscles. Over time, stimuli associated with the painful sex (e.g., thoughts of intercourse, stimulation by a partner) lead to a conditioned response (i.e., the muscle spasm). The classical conditioning is strengthened by operant conditioning because the avoidance behaviors reduce pain and anticipatory anxiety. This model is supported by research of women with vaginismus; fear of pain is the factor most commonly stated as the cause of their problem (Ward & Ogden, 1994). Psychosexual trauma and conflicts as well as cultural conditioning have also been implicated in the etiology of vaginismus. In addition, patients feel embarrassed and frustrated, and relationships can be stressed (Wincze & Carey, 1991.

Treatment of vaginismus is primarily psychological. Cognitive–behavioral components include cognitive restructuring of negative sexual messages and inaccurate beliefs about self and sexual behavior along with in vivo desensitization, including relaxation training and systematic vaginal dilation using fingers or a graduated set of dilators.

Findings from Ogden and Ward (1995) related to the usefulness of psychological services. Their study of 89 women with vaginismus revealed that although most had contacted their general practitioner for help, the physician was considered the least helpful when compared with other providers. Specifically, only 23% of those women who sought services from general practitioners believed it helpful, compared with 56% who sought help from a gynecologist, 62% who sought help from a sex therapist, and 76% who sought help from a psychotherapist.

DYSMENORRHEA

Nature of the Problem

Dysmenorrhea is difficult or painful menstruation that may accompany otherwise normal ovulation cycles. The symptoms associated with dysmenorrhea are many and vary among individuals. Most often, central lower abdominal pain is accompanied by discomfort in the lower back, thighs, or both. This pain may be accompanied by some combination of nausea, vomiting, diarrhea, headache, dizziness, and an emotional component that may include irritability, tension, and depression (Warrington, Cox, & Evans, 1988). As is discussed in the next section, the latter complaints may be differentiated from similar symptoms that may accompany the premenstrual syndrome (PMS).

A summary of the research by Warrington, Cox, and Evans (1988) indicated about half of all women experience dysmenorrhea, although it is debilitating in only approximately 3% to 4%. The primary physiological mechanism for these symptoms seems to involve excess prostaglandins or hormones involved in the hypothalamic–pituitary–ovarian–uterine systems. Psychosocial influences appear to involve childbirth, birth control, familial experiences, religious upbringing, and stress (social readjustment or change).

Contributions of Health Psychology

The Moos (1985a) Menstrual Distress Questionnaire has better internal consistency and test–retest reliability than other assessment questionnaires. This questionnaire consists of a 47-item retrospective version and a 48-item prospective version. It measures eight subscales, including pain, fluid retention, autonomic reactions, negative affect, impaired concentration, behavior changes, arousal, and control.

Treatment is determined after a thorough physical exam and diagnosis that rules out PMS and other pelvic disorders that cause dysmenorrhea. Physical treatments include oral contraceptives and medications that are prostaglandin inhibitors. Psychological treatments include some form of physical coping strategies (e.g., relaxation training; Fleischauer, 1977), some form of systematic desensitization (Cox & Meyer, 1978), and cognitive reframing (Quillen & Denney, 1982).

PMS

Nature of the Problem

The vast majority of women experience changes associated with fluctuating hormone levels during their menstrual cycle and thus can report premenstrual symptoms, which are symptoms experienced in the late luteal phase that remit with onset of menses (see Exhibit 10.3). Many women experience bloating and breast tenderness, but symptoms vary across women and sometimes within women across cycles. For example, a woman

EXHIBIT 10.3
Commonly Reported Premenstrual Symptoms

Physical	Behavioral	Emotional
Bloating	Insomnia	Depression
Breast tenderness	Agitation	Anxiety
Weight gain	Impaired concentration	Anger
Acne	Carbohydrate cravings	Tension
Gastrointestinal distress	Increased sexual drive	Crying spells
Headaches	Diminished sexual interest	Irritability
Rashes	Increased energy	Emotional lability
Muscle and joint pains	Forgetfulness	Oversensitivity
Gingivitis	Social withdrawal	
Swelling in extremities		

may report bursts of energy one month but increased emotional sensitivity and tearfulness the next. In addition, different symptoms across ethnic groups may reflect cultural attitudes toward menses and symptom reporting. For example, in the United States, African American women reported more food cravings, weight gain, swelling, and headaches but less severe cramping and negative emotions than did White women (Stout, Grady, & Steege, 1986; Woods, Most, & Dery, 1982).

When symptoms are severe enough to impair normal functioning, PMS is considered a disorder, although the validity of this syndrome has been a topic of substantial controversy since it was first named nearly 70 years ago. The majority of women with PMS are diagnosed in their 30s or 40s, and estimates from community sampling are that 6% to 10% experience PMS (Deuster, Adera, & South-Paul, 1999). Definition and measurement problems have been common in research in the field, which is itself embedded in cultural attitudes toward menstrual phenomena.

Severe premenstrual symptoms can result in a psychiatric diagnosis of premenstrual dysphoric disorder (PDD). Approximately 24% of women receiving psychiatric services have PDD, and approximately 50% of patients seeking services for PMS have had a history of psychiatric illness (Hurt, Freeman, Gise, Rivera-Tovar, & Steege, 1992; Rivera-Tovar & Frank, 1990). Bancroft (1993) suggested that recurrent premenstrual mood changes may actually increase risk for depression. In the general population, it is estimated that 5% of women have PDD (Rivera-Tovar & Frank, 1990). However, there is continuing controversy about the classification of PPD itself. Some are concerned that categorizing PDD as a psychiatric disorder will restrict research on PMS to psychiatric areas and thus misrepresent the full nature of the problem, which has numerous biopsychosocial components.

The etiology of PMS and PDD remains unclear, although numerous hypotheses have been offered, including progesterone deficiency, vitamin B6 deficiency, prostaglandin deficiency, neurotransmitter abnormalities (particularly serotonin and γ-aminobutyric acid), estrogen excess, hyperprolactinemia, mineral imbalances (particularly of calcium and magnesium), sociocultural factors, menstrual attitudes and expectations, and unresolved psychosexual conflicts. No definitive linkage has been established between psychological experiences and menstrual cycle physiology or pathophysiology. However, Derry, Gallant, and Woods (1997) noted that, despite this lack of success, the pursuit of an endocrinopathology of PMS has been relentless. They attribute this search to its consistency with cultural views of PMS as a "hormone imbalance" and the "age-old search for the supposed negative effect of reproductive functioning on women's well-being" (p. 205). However, it is likely that biological components play a significant role. It is known that other medical and psychological problems are often exacerbated by menstrual cycle phases (e.g., migraines, diabetes, asthma, depression, multiple sclerosis, irritable bowel syndrome).

Contributions of Health Psychology

Health psychology research has furthered the understanding of the psychological factors related to PMS and provided methodological improvements in its assessment and diagnosis. Hamilton and Gallant (1993) have provided an excellent critique of the biomedical literature from a health psychology perspective. Moreover, some research has supported the use of psychological interventions in the treatment of PMS.

Psychological Factors

One line of research has suggested that expectancies can affect report of premenstrual symptoms, thus the impact of social learning in PMS warrants further study (Derry et al., 1997). Other research has demonstrated the importance of perceptual processes such as appraisal of stressors in those with PMS (e.g., Fontana & Badawy, 1997; Fontana & Palfai, 1994). With respect to coping with premenstrual symptoms, active–behavioral and active–cognitive methods have been described as the most helpful (Choi & Salmon, 1995).

Another focus of research has been the relationship between stress and symptoms. Although women with PMS often report a higher level of life stress, research has not been able to demonstrate a cause-and-effect relationship between stress and PMS. However, stress may exacerbate symptoms and make it more difficult for women to cope with them. Woods and colleagues offered another perspective, suggesting that those women with PMS have heightened arousal and increased stress reactivity. These factors affect life stressors and attitudes toward menstruation and promote the interpretation of premenstrual arousal as negative. Their work has suggested a complex reciprocal relationship between stress and symptoms (Woods et al., 1998).

Diagnosis

Early diagnoses of PMS were based on retrospective self-reports. Subsequent psychological research has demonstrated self-reports to be an unreliable and inaccurate method for the report of menstrual cycle symptoms (Gallant, Popiel, Hoffman, Chakraborty, & Hamilton, 1992; Hurt et al., 1992). Indeed, the importance of more sound psychometric methods has been so well established that it has actually been incorporated into diagnostic criteria for PMS and PDD. For example, according to the fourth edition of the *Diagnostic and Statistical Manual of Mental Disorders (DSM–IV*; American Psychiatric Association, 1994), the diagnosis of PDD must be prospectively confirmed via daily symptom ratings for at least two cycles. In addition to daily ratings, measures such as the Moos Menstrual Distress Questionnaire (Moos, 1985b) and visual analog scales have also been used in the assessment process (Casper & Powell, 1986).

Treatment

Research using psychological interventions is limited but encouraging. Goodale, Domar, & Benson (1990) reported success in alleviating PMS symptoms with the relaxation response, which has repeatedly been shown to help with other symptoms of stress and pain. Kirkby (1994) reported significant reductions in PMS symptoms and irrational thinking at a 9-month follow-up after treatment with a cognitive–behavioral coping skills intervention. Although not randomly assigned, treated patients showed significant improvement as compared with those receiving a nonspecific treatment and those in a waiting-list control group.

Christensen and Oei (1995) found that anxiety, depression, negative thoughts, and physical changes could be successfully addressed using either a cognitive–behavior therapy intervention (cognitive restructuring and assertion training) or an information-focused therapy that included relaxation training, nutritional guidelines, lifestyle recommendations, and assertion training. The outcome of these interventions did not differ, yet both used cognitive and behavioral techniques, although the latter did not include a systematic focus on belief restructuring.

The most well-controlled research is a randomized controlled clinical trial of cognitive therapy for PMS conducted by Blake, Salkovskis, Gath, Day, & Garrod (1998). Treatment consisted of 12 weekly individual sessions focusing on links among thoughts, feelings, behaviors, and physical symptoms. Homework assignments included thought records and behavioral rehearsals, and researchers paid significant attention to the way PMS triggered panic, low self-esteem, or fear of failure. This study revealed significant reductions in psychological (e.g., irritability, tearfulness) symptoms, somatic (e.g., breast tenderness, bloating) symptoms, and self-rated impairment of functioning in the treatment group as compared with a waiting-list control group, even 4 months later.

INCONTINENCE

Nature of the Problem

Definition

Incontinence is a symptom, not a disease (Orzeck & Ouslander, 1987), and can result from pathological, anatomical, or physiological conditions within the urinary system or elsewhere in the body. Urinary incontinence is a condition in which involuntary loss of urine can be a social or hygienic problem and is objectively demonstrable (Ory, Wyman, & Yu, 1986). Many causes of urinary incontinence can be treated or changed, such as infection, atrophic vaginitis, acute confusional states, mobility restrictions, fecal impaction, and the side effects of drugs. Longer term or permanent causes of urinary incontinence include diabetes, stroke, cerebral palsy, multiple sclerosis, prostate enlargement, prostate cancer, spinal cord injuries, and birth defects such as spinal bifida (American Association of Retired Persons & Simon Foundation for Continence, 1993). This section focuses on only adult urinary incontinence. The types of urinary incontinence are listed in Table 10.2.

Prevalence, Costs, and Impact

Approximately 13 million Americans experience urinary incontinence (Agency for Health Care Policy and Research [AHCPR], 1996). Urinary incontinence may be underreported because of the stigma attached to the disorder and because of the inherent difficulty in measuring its oc-

TABLE 10.2
Types of Urinary Incontinence

Type	Definition
Urge	Detrusor overactivity with sudden and intense desire to urinate and inability to suppress urge
Stress	Physical stress on the abdomen causing excess pressure on the bladder
Overflow	Leakage of urine without the urge to void
Reflex	Complete absence of bladder control (total)
Functional	Inability or unwillingness to use the toilet appropriately
Iatrogenic	Postsurgical incontinence or incontinence due to the effects of medication combinations
Complex	More than one type of incontinence occurring simultaneously (mixed)

currence. Among those between ages 15 and 64 years, the prevalence of urinary incontinence in men ranges from 1.5% to 5% and in women ranges from 10% to 25% (Thomas, Plymat, Blannin, & Meade, 1980). In one series of randomly selected women (ages 30–59 years), 26% reported having experienced urinary incontinence as a social or hygienic problem (Elving, Foldspang, Lain, & Mommens, 1989).

Among the more than 1.5 million U.S. nursing-facility residents, the prevalence of urinary incontinence is 50% or higher, with episodes generally occurring more than once per day (AHCPR, 1996). Direct costs of caring for people with urinary incontinence are $11.2 billion annually in the community and $5.2 billion in nursing homes (AHCPR, 1996). Indirect costs for bladder disorders are unknown but likely extend into the billions. Indirect costs include costs for protective garments, medication, and loss of income (Tries & Brubaker, 1996). In addition, urinary incontinence is associated with a reduction in self-esteem, circumscribed social interactions, a decrease in quality of life, depression, and increasing dependence on caregivers, and it is aggravated with the effects of institutionalism and declining medical conditions (Tovian, 1998).

Etiology

Urinary incontinence has many predisposing factors and is associated with impaired physiological or psychological functioning (Resnick & Yalla, 1985). Urinary incontinence affects individuals of all ages but is most prevalent among older adults. As a result, urinary incontinence is commonly and mistakenly attributed to the aging process. Older adults are more likely to have conditions that predispose them to incontinence or contribute to the causes of incontinence. For example, conditions such as decreased bladder capacity, decreased capacity of the urethral muscle to keep the bladder neck closed, increased frequency of bladder contractions, and increased postvoid residuals can contribute to urinary incontinence and are seen in older adults (American Association of Retired Persons & Simon Foundation for Continence, 1993; Burgio & Engel, 1987). However, many of these conditions can be controlled or avoided when properly identified. Other risk factors include child bearing—the overall delivery experience and number of children delivered vaginally, which weakens the muscles of the pelvic floor; prostate surgery, with removal of all or part of the prostate gland because of prostate cancer or benign prostatic hyperplasia; and disease processes such as those in multiple sclerosis, stroke, Parkinson's disease, and cerebral palsy. In addition, birth defects affecting the bladder or nervous system (i.e., spinal bifida) can be associated with urinary incontinence (American Association of Retired Persons & Simon Foundation for Continence, 1993).

Urinary incontinence is not a normal aspect of aging nor is it irreversible. Some transient or temporary causes of urinary incontinence include delirium; urinary tract infections; vaginitis; use of certain drugs, such as sedative hypnotics or diuretics; severe depression; excessive urine production; restricted mobility; and stool impaction (AHCPR, 1996). Current medical treatments include pharmacological agents, hormonal treatments, and surgery.

Contributions of Health Psychology

Assessment

Psychological assessment with urinary incontinence includes characterization of the incontinence, identification of urine loss, and evaluation of the emotional and behavioral responses to urinary incontinence and its causes. A possible psychological treatment regimen may be used if appropriate (Tovian, 1996).

Behavioral and psychological. Burgio and Engel (1987) provided a thorough review of behavioral assessment techniques that can be used by the psychologist when working in collaboration with physicians and nurses to address urinary incontinence. Although the authors limited their discussion to geriatric populations, their methods can be generalized to other populations as well. The authors used techniques involving interview guidelines, mental status evaluations, bladder records or symptom diaries, and assessment of mobility and toileting skills. Interview guidelines need to take into account antecedents of incontinence, descriptions of incontinent episodes, and the consequences of incontinence.

Each individual who experiences incontinence feels differently about it and reacts with varying degrees of emotional distress. Tovian (1996, 1998) summarized numerous studies that identify the psychological reactions to urinary incontinence. Psychological responses such as depression, shame, and embarrassment from public accidents or odor; anxiety; agoraphobia; sexual dysfunction; irritability; frustration; and anger have all been identified among those with incontinence and need to be assessed in the interview. Urinary incontinence results in changes in quality of life, with possible loss of self-esteem, loss of a job, isolation, and increased dependency. Reactions of institutional and home caregivers can be assessed in keeping with the biopsychosocial model of assessment.

Psychometric. Shumaker, Wyman, Uebersax, McClish, and Fantl (1994) developed a life impact assessment instrument for urinary incontinence in women—the Incontinence Impact Questionnaire (IIQ)—and a symptom inventory specifically addressing symptoms associated with lower urinary tract and genital dysfunction—the Urogenital Distress Inventory (UDI). Data on the reliability, validity, and sensitivity to change of these measures demonstrated that they are psychometrically strong and can be self-administered. Uebersax, Wyman, Shumaker, McClish, and Fantl (1995) further reduced the 30-item IIQ and the 19-item UDI to 7- and 6-item short forms, respectively, supporting the use of these instruments in clinical and research applications.

Treatment

The treatment of urinary incontinence can be divided into four categories: (a) behavioral techniques, (b) pharmacological treatment, (c) surgery, and (d) supportive devices (including catheters and absorbent pads and garments). A combination of interventions may be used, depending on the patient's needs and physician's diagnosis.

Behavioral techniques. Behavioral techniques include bladder training, habit training (timed voiding), prompted voiding, pelvic muscle exercises, and biofeedback. Behavioral techniques show improvement ranging from complete cessation of incontinence to reductions of number of episodes (AHCPR, 1996). Behavioral techniques have no reported side effects, do not limit future treatment options, and can be used in combination with other therapies for urinary incontinence. Behavioral interventions seem to be most effective for urge and stress incontinence and least effective for patients with overflow urinary incontinence (AHCPR, 1996).

- *Bladder training.* Bladder training (or bladder retraining) consists of three primary components: education, scheduled voiding, and positive reinforcement. The education program usually combines written, visual, and verbal instructions that address physiology and pathophysiology. The voiding schedule incorporates a progressively increased interval between mandatory voidings, with concomitant distraction or relaxation techniques. The person is taught to consciously delay voiding. If the patient is unable to delay voiding between schedules, the person can adjust the schedule and start the timing from the last void. The person could also keep the prearranged schedule and disregard the unscheduled void. Finally, positive reinforcement is provided. In a randomized controlled study, Fantl et al. (1991) reported that 12% of the women who underwent bladder training became continent, and 75% improved to at least a 50% reduction in the number of incontinent episodes. This form of training has been used to manage urinary incontinence due to bladder instability.
- *Habit training.* Habit training, or timed voiding, is scheduled toileting on a planned basis. Unlike bladder training, there is no systematic effort to have the patient delay voiding and resist the urge to urinate. The goal is to decrease incontinent episodes by telling patients to void at regular intervals. At-

tempts are made to match the voiding intervals to the person's natural voiding schedule. In one controlled study on habit training (Jarvis, 1981), 51 nursing home residents were identified with an electronic monitoring device. Jarvis found that 86% of the participants improved their urinary incontinence over baseline levels when compared with control groups.

- *Prompted voiding.* Prompted voiding is a supplement to habit training and attempts to teach people to be aware of their incontinence status and request toileting assistance from caregivers. Three elements comprise prompted voiding: (a) monitoring (being checked by caregivers on a regular basis and reporting whether wet or dry), (b) prompting (being prompted to try to use the toilet), and (c) reinforcement (being praised for maintaining continence and for attempting to toilet). Prompted voiding has been shown to be effective for nursing home patients with incontinence who are dependent or cognitively impaired (Tovian, 1996).

- *Pelvic muscle exercises.* Pelvic muscle exercises, or Kegel exercises, improve urethral resistance through active exercise of the pubococcygeus muscle. The exercises strengthen the voluntary periurethral and pelvic muscles. The contraction inherent in the exercise exerts a closing force on the urethra and increases muscle support to the pelvic visceral structures (AHCPR, 1996). Pelvic muscle exercises have been shown to be effective for women with stress incontinence, for men after prostate surgery, and for women who have had multiple pelvic surgeries. This exercise is often coupled with pharmacological therapy and biofeedback (Burgio & Engel, 1990; Burns, Mareck, Duttmar, & Bullogh, 1985).

- *Biofeedback.* Tries and Brubaker (1996) critically reviewed 13 major studies using biofeedback and reported overwhelming effectiveness (an overall 76% to 87% reduction in incontinent episodes) in the treatment of stress and urge incontinence, especially when used in conjunction with other behavioral techniques, surgery, and pharmacological interventions. The sampled studies by Tries and Brubaker were highly heterogeneous in terms of etiology, age, and gender. The authors concluded that, on the basis of efficacy, low invasiveness, and cost effectiveness, biofeedback should be offered as an integral part of any multidisciplinary evaluation and treatment program.

- *Behavioral techniques in outpatient adults.* Combined analyses were conducted of 22 studies that dealt with all behavioral interventions on an outpatient basis (AHCPR, 1996). The studies were standardized along measures of efficacy, reflecting the percentage of wetness and dryness. Results indicated that the average percentage reduction in incontinence frequency at the end of behavioral treatments was 64.6%, with a 95% confidence interval range from 58.8% to 70.4%. Additional randomized controlled trials and a randomized but not controlled study, all of women in outpatient settings, suggested that behavioral techniques result in subjective cure and improvement rates of 70% to 77%, with improvements maintained for at least 6 months (AHCPR, 1996).

- *Behavioral techniques in the nursing home.* The severity of urinary incontinence in nursing home residents is often aggravated by the effects of institutionalization, declining medical conditions, and inconsistent nursing care. Nevertheless, a similar combined analysis of 428 persons studied in nursing homes using habit training and prompted voiding (AHCPR, 1996) suggested that patients were dry 70% of the time at baseline; this percentage rose to 81% after behavioral treatments during daytime hours only.

Additional psychological treatments. In addition to those mentioned above, there are several more psychological treatments to consider.

- *Self-help and patient education.* "I Will Manage" is a Simon Foundation program based on the principles of self-help. It is hosted by laypeople and professionals. The program's format is designed to accomplish two goals: (a) to present practical, multidisciplinary information on incontinence and (b) to encourage people to share their experiences and develop the confidence to make changes in their life ("I Will Manage" self-help groups; Simon Foundation for Continence, 1991). This patient education approach assumes that much of the psychosocial distress accompanying incontinence is largely a result of a lack of knowledge concerning incontinence, its causes and treatment, and the health care system. Empirical evidence of the efficacy of this approach would be useful.

- *Coping skills approach.* The coping skills approach involves structured training in specific cognitive, behavioral, and affective competencies for managing the disruptive effects of urinary incontinence. The coping skills approach assumes that the distress experienced in managing the effects of illness and disability is partially caused by a limited or ineffective skills repertoire. For example, Lewis and Gonzales (1994) reported the successful use of systematic desensitization to eliminate urethral catheter dependence of a 69-year-old male with urge incontinence caused by a cerebrovascular accident. Psychological interventions for urinary incontinence are summarized in Exhibit 10.4.

FUTURE RESEARCH

In this chapter we have assumed that an adequate understanding and treatment of GU diseases is based on a biopsychosocial perspective. As a result, health psychologists can play a crucial role in research, intervention, patient and professional education, and public policy toward these diseases. However, several research and clinical areas require future consideration.

More extensive research is needed about the ways psychosocial factors affect and are affected by understudied areas of GU disorders (e.g., menopausal disorders). Additional research is needed in specific content areas (e.g., the role of stress in infertility). Research in areas described in this chapter would benefit from an emphasis on life-span perspectives and cultural diversity. However, because GU diseases are best understood in the context of a biopsychosocial model, more integrative research is needed to simultaneously examine relationships among biological markers of disease activity (e.g., infertility and stress response systems), psychological parameters (e.g., coping patterns), and socioenvironmental (e.g., social support) parameters. Professionals working with GU disorders can no longer assume that a linear relationship exists between biology and behavior or culture and behavior.

For clinicians, empirically validated treatments must be made widely known and implemented within the general health care system. In addition, the limitations in the previously described positive results for urinary incontinence behavioral interventions are noteworthy. The results discussed involve the use of different outcome criteria, variability, and fre-

EXHIBIT 10.4
Psychological Interventions for Urinary Incontinence

Behavioral techniques
- Bladder training
- Habit training
- Prompt voiding
- Kegel exercises
- Biofeedback

Self-help and patient education group (*I Will Manage*; Simon Foundation)

Coping skills training

---

quency of treatment sessions; variability of comprehensiveness in training procedures; absence or variability in follow-up data; use of heterogenous samples; and a lack of standardized terminology for various "behavioral techniques." These remain crucial issues when considering outcome measures for treatment interventions with GU disorders.

In the changing health care milieu of managed care and capitated markets, the health psychologist based in or consulting with programs in obstetrics and gynecology or urology must have data on outcome parameters, quality assurance, and cost effectiveness of psychological services. The use of normed psychological assessment measures (Tovian, 1998) and empirically validated treatment interventions will also assist clinical health psychologists in their interactions with physicians and nurses in obstetrics, gynecology, and urology. Program development is also facilitated when clinical health psychologists are aware of the issues most salient to physicians in these specialties (e.g., time demands, cost-effectiveness) and attempt to speak a common language (e.g., avoid psychological jargon; Adams, 1992; Tovian, 1998).

Health psychologists can also be instrumental in the important efforts needed to inform and educate the public, policymakers, and medical professionals about GU diseases. An example of this would be health psychologists' involvement in various reputable national organizations outside the health care system (e.g., the National Kidney Disease Foundation, the Simon Foundation for Continence) that promote awareness and advocacy for GU disorders. Patient referrals to these same organizations can also promote improved psychosocial treatment.

CONCLUSION

This chapter has demonstrated that the health psychologist can offer a full spectrum of research and specialized clinical services to programs involved in the diagnosis and treatment of GU disorders. Health psychologists should continue to develop effective research assessment and treatment models and strategies and take the steps necessary to ensure that these models and strategies are more widely available and implemented. Such a goal can only improve patient care and enhance healthy psychologists' professional contributions in medical settings.

REFERENCES

Ackerman, M. D. (1992). Consultation with clinical urology: Expanded roles for health psychologists. *The Health Psychologist, 14,* 3–4.

Ackerman, M. D. (1995). Behavioral approaches to assessing erectile dysfunction. *The Behavior Therapist, 18,* 31–34.

Ackerman, M. D., & Carey, M. P. (1995). Psychology's role in the assessment of erectile dysfunction: Historical precedents, current knowledge, and methods. *Journal of Consulting and Clinical Psychology, 63,* 862–876.

Ackerman, M. D., Helder, L. H., & Antoni, M. H. (1989, March). *The Miami sexual dysfunction protocol.* Poster presented at the Tenth Annual Scientific Session of the Society of Behavioral Medicine, San Francisco.

Ackerman, M. D., Montague, D. K., & Morgenstern, S. (1994, March). Impotence: Help for erectile dysfunction. *Patient Care,* pp. 22–56.

Adams, D. B. (1992). Medical and surgical interface: Problems with philosophy and nosology. *Psychotherapy Bulletin, 27*(2), 23–25.

Agency for Health Care Policy and Research, Public Health Service, U.S. Department of Health and Human Services. (1996, March). *Urinary incontinence in adults: Clinical practice guidelines* (AHCPR Pub. No. 96-0682). Rockville, MD: Author.

American Association of Retired Persons, & Simon Foundation for Continence. (1993). *Promoting continence: Educating older Americans about incontinence.* Washington, DC: Author.

American Psychiatric Association. (1994). *Diagnostic and statistical manual of mental disorders* (4th ed.). Washington, DC: Author.

American Society for Reproductive Medicine. (1995a). *Endometriosis.* Birmingham, AL: Author.

American Society for Reproductive Medicine. (1995b). *Infertility: An overview.* Birmingham, AL: Author.

American Society for Reproductive Medicine. (1997). *Unexplained infertility.* Birmingham, AL: Author.

American Society for Reproductive Medicine. (1998a). Guidelines for gamete and embryo donation. *Fertility and Sterility, 70*(Suppl. 3), 1–13.

American Society for Reproductive Medicine. (1998b). *Infertility fact sheet.* Birmingham, AL: Author.

Bancroft, J. (1993). The premenstrual syndrome—A reappraisal of the concept and the evidence. *Psychological Medicine,* (Suppl. 24), 1–47.

Bancroft, J. (1995). The menstrual cycle and the well being of women. *Social Science and Medicine, 41,* 785–791.

Beck, J. G. (1993). Vaginismus. In W. O'Donohue & J. H. Geer (Eds.), *Handbook of sexual dysfunctions: Assessment and treatment* (pp. 381–397). Boston, MA: Allyn & Bacon.

Bergeron, S., & Binik, I. (1999a). Vulvar vestibulitis syndrome: A neglected women's health problem: Part I. *The Health Psychologist, 21*(2), 4.

Bergeron, S., & Binik, I. (1999b). Vulvar vestibulitis syndrome: A neglected women's health problem: Part II. *The Health Psychologist, 21*(3), 18.

Bergman, A., Karram, M., & Bhatia, N. N. (1989). Urethral syndrome: A comparison of different treatment modalities. *Journal of Reproductive Medicine, 3*, 157–161.

Beutel, M., Kupfer, J., Kirchmeyer, P., Kehde, S., Kohn, F. M., Schroeder-Printzen, I., et al. (1999). Treatment-related stresses and depression in couples undergoing assisted reproductive treatment by IVJ or ICSI. *Andrologia, 31*, 27–35.

Blake, F., Salkovskis, P., Gath, D., Day, A., & Garrod, A. (1998). Cognitive therapy for premenstrual syndrome: A controlled trial. *Journal of Psychosomatic Research, 45*, 307–318.

Boivin, J., & Takefman, J. E. (1995). Stress level across stages of in vitro fertilization in subsequently pregnant and nonpregnant women. *Fertility and Sterility, 64*, 802–810.

Brantley, P. H. J., & Hitchcock, P. B. (1995). Psychological aspects of chronic-maintenance hemodialysis patients. In A. J. Goreczny (Ed.), *Handbook of health and rehabilitation psychology* (pp. 497–511). New York: Plenum Press.

Bremer, B. A., Wert, K. M., Durica, A. L., & Weaver, A. (1997). Neuropsychological, physical and psychosocial functioning of individuals with end-stage renal disease. *Annals of Behavioral Medicine, 19*, 348–352.

Burgio, K. L., & Engel, B. T. (1987). Urinary incontinence: Behavioral assessment and treatment. In L. L. Carstensen & B. A. Edelstein (Eds.), *Handbook of clinical gerontology* (pp. 252–266). New York: Pergamon Press.

Burgio, K. L., & Engel, B. T. (1990). Biofeedback-assisted behavioral training for elderly men and women. *Journal of the American Geriatrics Society, 38*, 338–340.

Burns, P. A., Mareck, M. A., Duttmar, S. S., & Bullogh, B. (1985). Kegel exercises with biofeedback therapy for stress incontinence. *Nurse Practitioner, 4*, 28–33.

Carson, C. C., Osborne, D., & Segura, J. W. (1979). Psychologic characteristics of patients with female urethral syndrome. *Journal of Clinical Psychology, 35*, 312–314.

Casper, R., & Powell, A. M. (1986). Premenstrual syndrome: Documentation by linear analog scale compared with two descriptive scales. *American Journal of Obstetrics and Gynecology, 155*, 862–863.

Choi, P. Y., & Salmon, P. (1995). How do women cope with menstrual cycle changes? *British Journal of Clinical Psychology, 34*, 139–151.

Christensen, A. J., Benotsch, E. G., & Smith. T. W. (1997). Determinants of regimen adherence in renal dialysis. In D. S. Gochman (Ed.), *Handbook of health behavior research II: Provider determinants* (pp. 231–244). New York: Plenum Press.

Christensen, A. J., & Moran, P. J. (1998). Psychosomatic research in end-stage renal disease: A framework for matching patient to treatment. *Journal of Psychosomatic Research, 44*, 523–528.

Christensen, A. P., & Oei, T. P. (1995). The efficacy of cognitive behaviour therapy in treating premenstrual dysphoric changes. *Journal of Affective Disorders, 33*, 57–63.

Cox, D. J., & Meyer, R. G. (1978). Behavioral treatment parameters with primary dysmenorrhea. *Journal of Behavioral Medicine, 1*, 297–310.

Derry, P. S., Gallant, S. J., & Woods, N. F. (1997). Premenstrual syndrome and menopause. In S. J. Gallant, G. P. Keita, & R. Royak-Schaler (Eds.), *Health care for women: Psychological, social and behavioral influences* (pp. 203–220). Washington, DC: American Psychological Association.

Deuster, P. A., Adera, T., & South-Paul, J. (1999). Biological, social and behavioral factors associated with premenstrual syndrome. *Archives of Family Medicine, 8*, 122–128.

Devins, G. M., Hunsley, J., Mandin, H., Taub, K. J., & Paul, L. C. (1997). The marital context of end-stage renal disease: Illness intrusiveness and perceived changes in family environment. *Annals of Behavioral Medicine, 19*, 325–332.

Devins, G. M., Mandin, H., Hons, R. B., Burgess, E. D., Klassen, J., Taub, K., et al. (1990). Illness intrusiveness and quality of life in end-stage renal disease: Comparison and stability across treatment modalities. *Health Psychology, 9*, 117–142.

Domar, A. D., Freizinger, M., Clapp, D., Slawsby, E., Mortola, J., Kessel, B., et al. (1998, October). *The impact of group psychological interventions on pregnancy rates in infertile women.* Paper presented to the annual meeting of the American Society of Reproductive Medicine, San Francisco, CA.

Domar, A. D., Seibel, M. M., & Benson, H. (1990). The mind/body program for infertility: A new behavioral treatment approach for women with infertility. *Fertility and Sterility, 53*, 246–249.

Domar, A. D., Zuttermeister, P. C., Seibel, M., & Benson, H. (1992). Psychological improvement in infertile women after behavioral treatment: A replication. *Fertility and Sterility, 58*, 144–147.

Elving, L. B., Foldspang, A., Lain, G. W., & Mommens, S. (1989). Descriptive epidemiology of urinary incontinence in 3,100 women age 30–59. *Scandinavian Journal of Urology and Nephrology, 125*, 37–43.

Fantl, J. A., Wyman, J. F., McClish, D. K., Harkins, S. W., Elswick, K. K., Taylor, J. R., et al. (1991). Efficacy of bladder training in older women with urinary incontinence. *Journal of the American Medical Association, 265*, 609–613.

Fleischauer, M. L. (1977). A modified Lamaze approach in the treatment of primary dysmenorrhea. *Journal of American College Health Associations, 25*, 273–275.

Fontana, A. M., & Badawy, S. (1997). Perceptual and coping processes across the menstrual cycle: An investigation in a premenstrual syndrome clinic and a community sample. *Behavioral Medicine, 22*, 152–159.

Fontana, A. M., & Palfai, T. G. (1994). Psychosocial factors in premenstrual dysphoria: Stressors, appraisal and coping processes. *Journal of Psychosomatic Research, 38*, 557–567.

Gallant, S. J., Popiel, D. A., Hoffman, D. M., Chakraborty, P. K., & Hamilton, J. A. (1992). Using daily ratings to confirm premenstrual syndrome/late luteal phase dysphoric disorder: Part II. What makes a "real" difference? *Psychosomatic Medicine, 54,* 167–181.

Glatt, A. E., Zinner, S. H., & McCormack, W. M. (1990). The prevalence of dyspareunia. *Obstetrics and Gynecology, 75,* 433–436.

Goetsch, M. F. (1991). Vulvar vestibulitis: Prevalence and historic features in a general gynecologic practice population. *American Journal of Obstetrics and Gynecology, 161,* 1609–1617.

Goodale, I. L., Domar, A. D., & Benson, H. (1990). Alleviation of premenstrual syndrome with the relaxation response. *Obstetrics and Gynecology, 75,* 649–655.

Hamilton, J. A., & Gallant, S. (1993). Premenstrual syndromes: A health psychology critique of biomedically oriented research. In R. J. Gatchel & E. B. Blanchard (Eds.), *Psychophysiological disorders: Research and clinical applications* (pp. 383–438). Washington, DC: American Psychological Association.

Hanno, P. M., & Wein, A. M. (1987). *Interstitial cystitis: Part I* (American Urological Association Update). Houston, TX: American Urological Association.

Hathaway, S., & McKinley, J. (1967). *The Minnesota Multiphasic Personality Inventory manual.* New York: Psychological Corporation.

Hjollund, N. H., Jensen, T. K., Bonde, J. P., Henricksen, T. B., Andersson, A., Kolstad, H. A., et al. (1999). Distress and reduced fertility: A follow-up study of first-pregnancy planners. *Fertility and Sterility, 72,* 47–53.

Hong, G. A., Smith, M. D., Robson, A. M., & Wetzel, R. D. (1987). Depressive symptomatology and treatment in patients with end-stage renal disease. *Psychological Medicine, 17,* 185–190.

Hurt, S. W., Freeman, E., Gise, L., Rivera-Tovar, A., & Steege, J. (1992). Late luteal phase dysphoric disorder in 670 women evaluated for premenstrual complaints. *American Journal of Psychiatry, 149,* 525–530.

International classification of diseases, ninth revision. (1999). Los Angeles, CA: Practice Management Information Corp.

Jarvis, G. J. (1981). A controlled trial of bladder drill and drug therapy in the management of detrusor instability. *British Journal of Urology, 53,* 565–566.

Jordan, C., & Revenson, T. A. (1999). Gender differences in coping with infertility: A meta-analysis. *Journal of Behavioral Medicine, 22,* 341–358.

Kellner, R. (1991). *Psychosomatic syndromes and somatic symptoms.* Washington, DC: American Psychiatric Press.

Keltikangas-Jarvinen, L., Auvinen, L., & Lehtonen, T. (1988). Psychological factors related to interstitial cystitis. *European Urology, 15,* 69–72.

Kirkby, R. J. (1994). Changes in premenstrual symptoms and irrational thinking following cognitive–behavioral coping skills training. *Journal of Consulting and Clinical Psychology, 62,* 1026–1032.

Kirschenbaum, D. S. (1991). Integration of clinical psychology into hemodialysis programs. In J. J. Sweet, R. H. Rozensky, & S. M. Tovian (Eds.), *Handbook of clinical psychology in medical settings* (pp. 567–586). New York: Plenum Press.

Lacy, C. F., Armstrong, L. L., & Goldman, M. P. (1999). *Drug information handbook* (7th ed.). Hudson, OH: Lexi-Comp Press.

Leiblum, S. R. (1996). Sexual pain disorders. In G. O. Gabbard & S. D. Atkinson (Eds.), *Synopsis of treatments of psychiatric disorders* (2nd ed., pp. 805–810). Washington, DC: American Psychiatric Press.

Leiblum, S. R. (Ed.). (1997). *Infertility: Psychological issues and counseling strategies.* New York: Wiley.

Lewis, L., & Gonzales, L. R. (1994). Treatment of urethral catheter dependence: A case study of intervention in the interdisciplinary geriatric setting. *Journal of Clinical Psychology in Medical Settings, 1,* 363–373.

McQueeney, D. A., Stanton, A. L., & Sigmon, S. (1997). Efficacy of emotion-focused and problem-focused group therapies for women with fertility problems. *Journal of Behavioral Medicine, 20,* 313–331.

Moos, R. H. (1985a). *Perimenstrual symptoms: A manual and overview of research with the Menstrual Distress Questionnaire.* Palo Alto, CA: Stanford University and Veterans Affairs Hospital.

Moos, R. H. (1985b). *Premenstrual symptoms: A manual and overview of research with the Menstrual Distress Questionnaire.* Palo Alto, CA: Social Ecology Laboratory, Stanford University School of Medicine.

Office of Technology Assessment. (1988). (Publication No. OTA-BA-358). Washington, DC: U.S. Government Printing Office.

Ogden, J., & Ward, E. (1995). Help-seeking behaviour in sufferers of vaginismus. *Sexual and Marital Therapy, 10,* 23–30.

O'Moore, A. M., O'Moore, R. R., Harrison, R. F., Murphy, G., & Carruthers, M. E. (1983). Psychosomatic aspects in idiopathic infertility: Effects of treatment with autogenic training. *Journal of Psychosomatic Research, 27,* 145–151.

Ory, M. G., Wyman, J. F., & Yu, L. C. (1986). *Clinics in Geriatric Medicine, 2,* 657–671.

Orzeck, S., & Ouslander, J. G. (1987). Urinary incontinence: An overview of causes and treatment. *Journal of Enterostomal Therapy, 14,* 20–27.

Poehl, M. A., Bichler, K., Wicke, V., Dorner, V., & Feichtinger, W. (1999). Psychotherapeutic counseling and pregnancy rates in in vitro fertilization. *Journal of Assisted Reproduction and Genetics, 16,* 302–305.

Quillen, M. H., & Denney, D. R. (1982). Self-control of dysmenorrhea symptoms through pain management training. *Journal of Behavior Therapy and Experimental Psychiatry, 13,* 123–130.

Raczynski, J., Bradley, L., & Leviton, L. (Eds.). (in press). *Handbook of clinical health psychology: Volume 2. Disorders of behavior and health.* Washington, DC: American Psychological Association.

Reiter, R. C., Shakerin, L. R., Gambone, J. C., & Milburn, A. K. (1991). Psychological profiles of women with urethral syndrome. *American Journal of Obstetrics and Gynecology, 6,* 104–109.

Resnick, N. M., & Yalla, S. V. (1985). Management of urinary incontinence in the elderly. *New England Journal of Medicine, 313,* 800–805.

Rivera-Tovar, A., & Frank, E. (1990). Late luteal phase dysphoric disorder in young women. *American Journal of Psychiatry, 147,* 1634–1636.

Schover, L. R., & Jensen, S. B. (1988). *Sexuality and chronic illness: A comprehensive approach.* New York: Guilford Press.

Schover, L. S., Youngs, D. D., & Cannata, R. (1992). Psychosexual aspects of the evaluation and management of vulvar vestibulitis. *American Journal of Obstetrics and Gynecology, 167,* 630–636.

Scotti, R. J., & Ostergard, D. R. (1984). The urethral syndrome. *Clinical Obstetrics and Gynecology, 27,* 515–529.

Shumaker, S. A., Wyman, J. F., Uebersax, J. S., McClish, D. K., & Fantl, J. A. (1994). Health-related quality of life measures for women with urinary incontinence: The Incontinence Impact Questionnaire and The Urogenital Distress Inventory. *Quality of Life Research, 3,* 291–306.

Simon Foundation for Continence. (1991). *"I Will Manage" self-help groups.* Wilmette, IL: Author.

Spanos, C., Pang, X., Ligris, K., Letourneau, R., Alferes, L., Alexacos, N., et al. (1997). Stress-induced bladder mast cell activation: Implications for interstitial cystitis. *Journal of Urology, 157,* 669–672.

Stanton, A. L., & Burns, L. H. (1999). Behavioral medicine approaches to infertility counseling. In L. H. Burns & S. N. Covington (Eds.), *Infertility counseling: A comprehensive handbook for clinicians* (pp. 129–147). New York: Parthenon.

Stanton, A. L., & Dunkel-Schetter, C. D. (1991). *Infertility: Perspectives from stress and coping research.* New York: Plenum Press.

Steege, J. F. (1984). Dyspareunia and vaginismus. *Clinical Obstetrics and Gynecology, 27,* 750–759.

Stout, A. L., Grady, T. A., & Steege, J. F. (1986). Premenstrual symptoms in Black and White community samples. *American Journal of Psychiatry, 143,* 1436–1439.

Symister, P., & Friend, R. (1996). Quality of life and adjustment in renal disease: A health psychology perspective. In R. J. Resnick & R. H. Rozensky (Eds.), *Health psychology through the life span: Practice and research opportunities* (pp. 265–287). Washington, DC: American Psychological Association.

Tanagho, E. A., & McAninch, J. W. (1995). *Smith's general urology* (14th ed.). Norwalk, CT: Appelton-Lange.

Thomas, T. M., Plymat, K. R., Blannin, J., & Meade, T. W. (1980). Prevalence of urinary incontinence. *British Medical Journal, 21,* 1243–1245.

Tovian, S. M. (1996). Health psychology and the field of urology. In R. J. Resnick & R. H. Rozensky (Eds.), *Health psychology through the life span: Practice and research opportunities* (pp. 289–312). Washington, DC: American Psychological Association.

Tovian, S. M. (1998). Urological disorders. In P. M. Camic & S. J. Knight (Eds.), *Clinical handbook of health psychology: A practical guide to effective interventions* (pp. 439–480). Seattle, WA: Hogrefe & Huber.

Tovian, S. M., & Rozensky, R. H. (1985). Building inner confidence. In C. B. Gartley (Ed.), *Managing incontinence* (pp. 48–57). Ottowa, IL: Jameson Books.

Tovian, S. M., Rozensky, R. H., Sloan, T. B., & Slotnik, G. M. (1995). Adult urinary incontinence: Assessment, intervention, and the role of clinical health psychology in program development. *Journal of Clinical Psychology in Medical Settings, 1,* 339–362.

Tries, J., & Brubaker, L. (1996). Application of biofeedback in the treatment of urinary incontinence. *Professional Psychology: Research and Practice, 27,* 554–560.

Tucker, C. M., Mulkerne, D. J., & Ziller, R. C. (1982). An ecological and behavioral approach to outpatient dialysis treatment. *Journal of Chronic Diseases, 35,* 21–27.

Uebersax, J. S., Wyman, J. F., Shumaker, S. A., McClish, D. K., & Fantl, J. A. (1995). Short forms to assess life quality and symptom distress for urinary incontinence in women: The Incontinence Impact Questionnaire and the Urogenital Distress Inventory. *Neurology and Urodynamics, 14,* 131–139.

United States Renal Data System. (1999). *United States Renal Data System 1999 annual data report.* (Available online at www.med.umich.edu/usrds/)

Walker, A. (1995). Theory and methodology in premenstrual syndrome research. *Social Science and Medicine, 41,* 793–800.

Ward, E., & Ogden, J. (1994). Experiencing vaginismus: Sufferers' beliefs about causes and effects. *Sexual and Marital Therapy, 9,* 33–45.

Warrington, C. S., Cox, D. J., & Evans, W. S. (1988). Dysmenorrhea. In E. A. Blechman & K. D. Brownell (Eds.), *Handbook of behavioral medicine for women* (pp. 70–79). New York: Pergamon Press.

Wincze, J. P., & Carey, M. P. (1991). *Sexual dysfunction: A guide for assessment and treatment.* New York: Guilford Press.

Woods, N., Lentz, M. J., Mitchell, E. S., Heitkemper, M., Shaver, J., & Henker, R. (1998). Perceived stress, physiologic stress arousal, and premenstrual symptoms: Group differences and intra-individual patterns. *Research in Nursing Health, 21,* 511–523.

Woods, N., Most, A., & Dery, G. (1982). Estimating the prevalence of perimenstrual symptoms. *Research in Nursing Health, 5,* 81–91.

SUGGESTED READING

Chronic Renal Failure

Brantley, P. H. J., & Hitchcock, P. B. (1995). Psychological aspects of chronic-maintenance hemodialysis patients. In A. J. Goreczny (Ed.), *Handbook of health and rehabilitation psychology* (pp. 497–511). New York: Plenum Press.

Christensen, A. J., Benotsch, E. G., & Smith. T. W. (1997). Determinants of regimen adherence in renal dialysis. In D. S. Gochman (Ed.), *Handbook of* health behavior research II: Provider determinants (pp. 231–244). New York: Plenum Press.

Christensen, A. J., & Moran, P. J. (1997). Psychological aspects of renal disease. In M. Johnston & D. Johnston (Eds.), *Health psychology* (Vol. 8). New York: Wiley & Sons.

Symister, P., & Friend, R. (1995). Quality of life and adjustment in renal disease: A health psychology perspective. In R. J. Resnick & R. H. Rozensky (Eds.), *Health psychology through the life span: Practice and research opportunities* (pp. 265–287). Washington, DC: American Psychological Association.

Infertility

American Society for Reproductive Medicine. (1996). *Bibliography from the Mental Health Professional Group*. Birmingham, AL: Author.

Hammer Burns, L., & Covington, S. N. (Eds.). (1999). *Infertility counseling: A comprehensive handbook for clinicians*. Pearl River, NY: Parthenon.

Leiblum, S. R. (Ed.). (1997). *Infertility: Psychological issues and counseling strategics*. New York: Wiley.

Stanton, A. L., & Dunkel-Schetter, C. D. (1991). *Infertility: Perspectives from stress and coping research*. New York: Plenum Press.

Dyspareunia

Bergeron, S., & Binik, I. (1999a). Vulvar vestibulitis syndrome: A neglected women's health problem: Part I. *The Health Psychologist, 21*(2), 4.

Bergeron, S., & Binik, I. (1999b). Vulvar vestibulitis syndrome: A neglected women's health problem: Part II. *The Health Psychologist, 21*(3), 18.

Wincze, J. P., & Carey, M. P. (1991). *Sexual dysfunction: A guide for assessment and treatment*. New York: Guilford Press.

Vaginismus

Beck, J. G. (1993). Vaginismus. In W. O'Donohue & J. H. Geer (Eds.), *Handbook of sexual dysfunctions: Assessment and treatment* (pp. 381–397). Boston, MA: Allyn & Bacon.

Wincze, J. P., & Carey, M. P. (1991). *Sexual dysfunction: A guide for assessment and treatment*. New York: Guilford Press.

Premenstrual Syndrome

Bancroft, J. (1993). The premenstrual syndrome—A reappraisal of the concept and the evidence. *Psychological Medicine* (Suppl. 24), 1–47.

Hamilton, J. A., & Gallant, S. (1993). Premenstrual syndromes: A health psychology critique of biomedically oriented research. In R. J. Gatchel & E. B. Blanchard (Eds.), *Psychophysiological disorders: Research and clinical applications* (pp. 383–438). Washington, DC: American Psychological Association.

Walker, A. (1995). Theory and methodology in premenstrual syndrome research. *Social Science and Medicine, 41,* 793–800.

Incontinence

Rozensky, R. H., & Tovian, S. M. (1985). Strategies for a full life. In C. B. Gartely (Ed.), *Managing incontinence* (pp. 58–69). Ottowa, IL: Jameson Books.

Tovian, S. M., & Rozensky, R. H. (1985). Building inner confidence. In C. B. Gartely (Ed.), *Managing incontinence* (pp. 48–57). Ottowa, IL: Jameson Books.

Tovian, S. M., Rozensky, R. H., Sloan, T. B., & Slotnik, G. M. (1995). Adult urinary incontinence: Assessment, intervention, and the role of clinical health psychology in program development. *Journal of Clinical Psychology in Medical Settings, 1,* 339–362.

Tries, J., & Eisman, E. (1995). Biofeedback for the treatment of urinary incontinence. In M. E. Schwartz (Ed.), *Biofeedback: A practitioner's guide* (pp. 597–631). New York: Guilford Press.

11

COMPLICATIONS OF PREGNANCY, CHILDBIRTH, AND THE PUERPERIUM

DEBORAH N. ADER

In 1997, 3,880,894 babies were born in the United States, yielding a fertility rate of 65 women per 1,000 among women ages 15 to 44 years (Centers for Disease Control [CDC] and Prevention, 1999). Most pregnancies progress normally without major threats to maternal health. Nevertheless, complications of pregnancy, childbirth, and the puerperium are common and constitute an important women's health issue. Extensive medical research results detail these complications, but a definitive understanding of etiology, successful prevention, or optimal management remains elusive for many serious obstetrical problems. Furthermore, health psychology's potential to contribute to the understanding and management of obstetrical complications has barely begun to be realized. A search for "obstetrical complications" in the PsycLIT database produced 345 references from 1984 to March 1999, providing a simple, albeit somewhat superficial, example of the state of affairs. Only 25% of the references address maternal health

The opinions or assertions contained herein are those of the author and are not to be construed as official or reflecting the views of the National Institutes of Health. The author gratefully acknowledges Willem J. Kop, PhD, and LTC Matrice W. Browne, MD, for their helpful comments on a previous draft of this chapter.

topics, and the majority address fetal and infant outcomes or long-term mental health outcomes of children.

Because research incorporating psychosocial or behavioral variables in obstetrical complications is relatively limited, this chapter focuses primarily on common complications of pregnancy that have been the subject of most biopsychosocial research: spontaneous abortion (SAB), preterm delivery, excessive nausea and vomiting, and hypertension. Issues in obstetrical hemorrhage, chronic medical disorders in pregnancy, and labor and delivery complications are briefly mentioned as well. Finally, some suggestions regarding future directions in research on these important health issues are discussed. Each section includes discussion of incidence and general risk factors, psychosocial factors, health-related behaviors, and intervention approaches (if data were available). The distinction between psychosocial factors and health-related behaviors is somewhat arbitrary, and such factors are often closely intertwined. In this context, constructs or general (i.e., not specifically health-related) factors are classified as *psychosocial* (e.g., stress, social support, work), whereas classic health psychology topics such as substance use, weight change, and exercise are classified as *health-related behaviors*.

Although this book emphasizes health psychology applications, research on psychological, behavioral, and social interventions in obstetrical complications is sparse. Thus, this chapter devotes equal or greater attention to what is known about biopsychosocial risk factors, on the premise that knowledge about such factors should enrich approaches to prevention and treatment. Detailed discussion of the known or theorized physiological mechanisms causing or contributing to obstetrical disorders is beyond the scope of this chapter, but the most prominent or relevant processes are briefly mentioned. These putative processes must be incorporated into conceptual models from which both research and practice evolve.

An overview of the chapter is provided in Table 11.1, which lists the obstetrical complications discussed and their incidence and some of the factors associated with elevated risk.

SAB

Incidence and General Risk Factors

Spontaneous termination of pregnancies at less than 20 weeks of gestation occurs in an estimated 12% to 20% of pregnancies (Gannon, 1994; O'Hare & Creed, 1995). Most SABs are associated with abnormalities of the embryo (American College of Obstetrics and Gynecology [ACOG], 1995). Additional risk factors for SAB include exposure to anesthetic gases, antineoplastic drugs, ionizing radiation, lead, and ethylene oxide (used for

TABLE 11.1
Complications of Pregnancy, Childbirth, and the Puerperium

Complication	Incidence per 1,000	Psychosocial/behavioral risk factors
Spontaneous abortion	120–200	Alcohol, smoking, cocaine
Preterm birth	114	Low SES, perceived stress, depression, job strain, pattern of weight gain, smoking
Hyperemesis gravidarum	5–10	Overweight, high dietary fat
Hypertension Chronic Pregnancy-induced Eclampsia	6.9 24–37 3.3	Low SES, work factors, duration of cohabitation, overweight, excessive pregnancy weight gain, >4 cups of coffee/day
Premature rupture of membranes	80	Smoking
Abruptio placentae	4–13	Smoking, alcohol, cocaine
Placenta previa	3–5	Smoking

sterilization of hospital equipment; Gabbe & Turner, 1997). In addition, some evidence has suggested elevated risk for miscarriage with occupational exposures to noise (85 db or higher), solvents, and pesticides (Lindbohm, 1995; Nurminen, 1995a, 1995b).

Psychosocial Factors

Very little empirical research has been conducted on the role of psychosocial factors in SAB. Studies of women with recurrent miscarriages have failed to find any unique associated personality or emotional features (Gannon, 1994). A few psychoanalytic case studies have suggested potential psychological causes of miscarriage (e.g., rejection of motherhood), but larger, more systematic studies have not found anxiety or personality characteristics to be significantly associated with SAB (Madden, 1988).

Studies examining the effects of work on pregnancy outcome have found that being employed does not put women at increased risk for miscarriage. However, Bryant and Love (1991) found that working primarily because of financial need is associated with increased risk of SAB, with an odds ratio (OR) of 1.8 to 2.1. Schenker, Eaton, Green, and Samuels (1997) found that lawyers working more than 45 hours a week during the first trimester of pregnancy were three times more likely to have SAB than those working fewer hours. In addition, rotating shift work has been associated with miscarriage (Lindbohm, 1995).

A few studies have examined the association between self-reported stress and SAB (O'Hare & Creed, 1995; Schenker et al., 1997) and have suggested that stressful life events or high-demand job situations may increase risk for SAB. However, retrospective methodology and equivocal results in the literature make it impossible to draw firm conclusions about the role of stress. It seems likely that stressful life events, work-related stress, social support, coping style, and other stress-relevant factors may play some role in SAB. Numerous studies have suggested that psychotherapy, particularly supportive therapy, may be effective in improving pregnancy outcomes in women with recurring miscarriages (see Gannon, 1994). However, more and better-designed studies are needed to establish the relationship of stress and social support to SAB.

Health-Related Behavior: Alcohol, Tobacco, and Cocaine

In a prospective study, Russell and Skinner (1988) assessed self-reported prepregnancy alcohol consumption and indications of problem drinking in a large group of obstetrical patients. Every ounce of absolute alcohol consumed per day was associated with a 25% increased risk of SAB. Positive associations between alcohol consumption and SAB have been reported by other researchers as well (Plant, 1984; Schenker et al., 1997). However, Cavallo, Russo, Zotti, Camerlengo, and Ruggenini (1995) found no association between alcohol consumption and SAB. Abel (1997) reported that American studies tend to find a positive association between alcohol consumption and SAB, whereas European studies tend to find no association. Accurate assessment of alcohol intake is difficult; self-reports probably underestimate true consumption. Russell and Skinner (1988) advocated assessing indications of prepregnancy drinking rather than heavy drinking during pregnancy to reduce defensiveness among obstetrical patients and obtain more accurate reporting of potentially harmful alcohol-related behavior.

Epidemiological and case control studies have found smoking is related to increased risk for SAB (with relative risks ranging from 1.2 to 1.8). In vitro fertilization studies have demonstrated that smokers have a significantly increased risk of SAB compared with nonsmokers, with a higher likelihood that the aborted embryos are chromosomally normal (ACOG, 1993). Cocaine has also been associated with increased risk of SAB (Chasnoff, Burns, Schnoll, & Burns, 1985).

EARLY OR THREATENED LABOR

Incidence and General Risk Factors

Delivery between 20 and 37 weeks of gestation is considered preterm and occurred in 11.4% of U.S. pregnancies in 1997 (CDC, 1998). Extremes of maternal age are associated with increased risk of preterm delivery (Bennedsen, 1998; Kyrklund-Blomberg & Cnattingius, 1998), as are extremes of prepregnancy weight, Black race, small stature, previous poor pregnancy outcomes, low education, low socioeconomic status, and occupational exposure to lead (Carmichael, Abrams, & Selvin, 1997; Copper et al., 1996; Hedegaard, Henriksen, Secher, Hatch, & Sabroe, 1996; Nordentoft et al., 1996; Peacock, Bland, & Anderson, 1995).

Psychosocial Factors

The role of psychosocial factors, most commonly stress, distress, work, and social support, have frequently been investigated in preterm delivery.

Stress

In studies of preterm labor, stress is most often assessed in terms of life events that occur during, or before and during, the pregnancy. Stress related to life events is assessed in one or more of the following three ways in each study: (a) life event counts—a simple sum of the number of specified life events that occurred during the time period assessed, (b) objectively weighted life events—use of a priori weighting of events to obtain a stress severity score, and (c) subjectively rated life events—individuals' perceptions of severity of events, yielding subjective stress severity scores.

In a population-based prospective study, 5,834 Danish women completed questionnaires during the 16th and 30th weeks of gestation; 207 (3.5%) delivered preterm. No association was found between count of major life events and preterm delivery; however, the number of life events rated as highly stressful, especially those that occurred later in pregnancy, was associated with preterm delivery (Hedegaard et al., 1996). In another large Danish study, women completed a questionnaire on general health, psychosocial stressors, and sociodemographic characteristics at the 20th week of gestation. Controlling for maternal age, cohabitation with partner, and education, perceived stress (but not objective stressful life events) was significantly associated with preterm delivery ($OR = 1.9$). The authors suggested that, given the lack of support for a causal relationship between objective life events and preterm delivery, coping strategies must be essential in influencing length of gestation in women who experience major life events during pregnancy (Nordentoft et al., 1996). Similarly, Copper et al. (1996) obtained subjectively weighted stress scores at 25 through 29 weeks of gestation in 2,593 women. After controlling for race, maternal age, marital status, government insurance, education, and tobacco, alcohol, and drug use, stress was significantly associated with preterm birth.

Lobel, Dunkel-Schetter, and Scrimshaw (1992) defined prenatal stress as a factor comprising chronic state anxiety, chronic perceived stress, and subjectively weighted life events stress. (The first two components were measured prospectively, and the last was measured postpartum.) After controlling for parity and medical risk, prenatal stress was found to be a significant predictor of early delivery.

In a review of the research on stress and preterm delivery, Lobel (1994) suggested that the number of life events may also have a significant effect on birth outcome, although results are not consistent across all studies. She argued that failure to find effects of prenatal life events on gestational age may be a result of the timing of stress assessments, the events, or both. In at least one study, no life events occurring in the latter half of pregnancy were included. The temporal relationship of stress to pregnancy outcome has not been systematically studied.

Hoffman and Hatch (1996) reviewed 11 studies on life events stress published since 1984; only one study found a positive association (unadjusted $OR = 3.2$, with exposure to a severe life event or ongoing difficulty). Life events did not predict preterm delivery in biologically high-risk women (i.e., women with a previous poor pregnancy outcome) in a study conducted by Honnor, Zubrick, and Stanley (1994).

Numerous physiological mechanisms and behaviors related to stress can be postulated to affect pregnancy. Wadhwa, Sandman, Porto, Dunkel-Schetter, and Garite (1993) suggested several possibilities. First, elevated levels of pituitary hormones such as oxytocin and prostaglandins may result in premature uterine contractions and contribute to the initiation of premature labor. Second, vasoconstriction may reduce uteroplacental perfusion and exchange and contribute to intrauterine growth retardation. Third, opiate or β-endorphin elevations in maternal plasma and placental opiate release in response to hypothalamic–pituitary–adrenal (HPA) activation could cause dysregulation of the developing fetal nervous system and have neurodevelopmental consequences. Finally, the immunosuppressive effects of HPA activation may leave a woman more susceptible to infection, which is a risk factor for preterm labor. Indirect effects of stress on gestation may include an increased tendency to engage in risky health behaviors such as alcohol use, smoking, drug use, and consuming a poor diet. For example, Copper et al. (1996) found that a poor overall psychosocial state in pregnant women was significantly associated with smoking and drug use, and increased anxiety was significantly associated with alcohol use.

In summary, the pattern of results in the literature suggests that perceived, or subjectively weighted, life events stress is the most likely life events stress measure to be related to preterm delivery. Simple life event counts are possibly related to preterm birth, and objectively weighted stress scores are not related. Other forms of assessment are notably absent in this research. Chronic stress and hassles have not been investigated, and variables that may moderate or mediate stress effects have not been thoroughly explored. There is a need for systematic research into the temporal association between stress and pregnancy outcome, studies investigating the ways physiological reactivity and reactions to stress affect pregnancy, and examination of the extent to which stress modifies health-related behaviors in ways that may be detrimental to pregnancy.

Distress

Emotional distress, most commonly depression and anxiety, have been studied in relation to preterm delivery. Hoffman and Hatch (1996) reported that most research in this area fails to find any association between anxiety and preterm delivery, but several studies have found an association with depression symptoms. Steere, Scholl, Hediger, and Fischer (1992) found that women with Beck Depression Inventory scores of 16 or higher (dysphoria) had increased odds of preterm birth ($OR = 2.5$) relative to those with lower scores; women with scores of 21 or higher (depression) had even higher risk ($OR = 3.4$). Another study found depressive symptoms were associated with preterm delivery among African American women but not White women. Several studies have found no difference in gestational duration related to use of antidepressants, but at least one reported that fluoxetine exposure late in pregnancy was associated with increased risk of preterm delivery (Bennedsen, 1998). In general, the current evidence regarding effects of psychotropic drugs on preterm delivery is inconclusive.

Additional research has suggested that depressed mood is related to poor health behaviors such as cigarette, alcohol, and cocaine use and insufficient weight gain during pregnancy. As with stress research, studies have been inconsistent with respect to timing of assessments during pregnancy, and mechanisms have not been investigated.

Social Support

Two observational studies reported associations of social support with gestational duration. In one study, being married and having more frequent contact with neighbors was associated with lower rates of preterm delivery (Peacock et al., 1995). In another study, among African Americans only, availability of partner support and being married were each associated with increased gestational age (Norbeck & Anderson, 1989). Social support seems to exert a main effect, rather than buffering effect, on preterm delivery. However, randomized controlled trials in which social support was provided have found no effect on preterm delivery (Hoffman & Hatch, 1996). Hoffman and Hatch offered two possible reasons for the different results obtained in observational studies versus controlled trials. First, participants recruited into controlled trials are generally women who obtain early prenatal care, not women who delay obtaining care (who are also at more risk for high stress). Second, the observational studies suggested ongoing, intimate support may be critical; randomized controlled trials provide support in the form of relatively few contacts by a nurse or lay educator. Interventions designed to enhance support from a woman's existing social network need to be developed and tested.

Work

Gabbe and Turner (1997) reviewed the literature on working outside the home during pregnancy and concluded that women with uncomplicated pregnancies can safely work during pregnancy. Working in itself does not seem to increase the risk of preterm birth. However, working long hours, working long shifts, standing or walking for 5 or more hours per day, and physically strenuous work have all been associated with higher rates of preterm delivery (Gabbe & Turner, 1997).

It has been suggested that job stress, job strain, or attitude toward working may contribute to preterm delivery. Homer, James, and Siegel (1990) found that high job stress, defined as having a high-demand and low-control working situation, was confounded with high physical exertion. When the exertion level was controlled, the initial association found between job stress and preterm delivery disappeared. However, for the 70 women in the sample who stated they did not want to be working outside the home after age 35, stressful work significantly worsened pregnancy outcome:

> Women working in jobs characterized by high levels of psychological demand with little control over the pace and style of response to those demands were somewhat more likely to deliver a preterm, low-birth-weight infant than women in other jobs, if they were not motivated to continue working. (p. 175)

Similarly, one retrospective case-control study found a small effect size for the association between job strain and preterm delivery in women who worked more than 30 weeks during pregnancy (Brett, Strogatz, & Savitz, 1997).

In postpartum interviews with 2,663 Mexican women, Ceron-Mireles, Harlow, and Sanchez-Carrillo (1996) found occupation, working conditions, and job stress to be unassociated with preterm delivery. However, women who did not have prenatal leave benefits (i.e., the usual prenatal leave in Mexico of 6 weeks) were almost three times more likely to deliver prematurely.

Health-Related Behavior

Weight Gain

Carmichael et al. (1997) reported on patterns of weight gain and preterm delivery in a sample of more than 7,000 women whose prepregnancy body mass index (BMI) was less than 29. (Obesity is defined as a BMI of 30 or higher.) The authors found that patterns of gain deviating from the general pattern of slow gain in early pregnancy and faster, approximately linear gain later are associated with increased risk of spontaneous preterm delivery.

Alcohol, Tobacco, and Caffeine

Most studies have found no association between alcohol intake during pregnancy and preterm delivery (e.g., Peacock et al., 1995). Reviews have suggested an effect of alcohol on gestation duration is unlikely (Bennedsen, 1998). However, Lundsberg, Bracken, and Saftlas (1997) found that light and mild-to-moderate drinking during month 7 of pregnancy, controlling for alcohol consumption during month 1, was a significant risk factor for preterm delivery. This study is flawed by reliance on postpartum reporting of third-trimester alcohol consumption. (Consumption during the first trimester was reported within the first 16 weeks of gestation.) Nevertheless, period of alcohol exposure, as well as amount of alcohol consumed, warrant further investigation to establish whether alcohol consumption is truly unrelated to preterm delivery.

Despite some conflicting results, convincing evidence of an effect of maternal smoking on preterm delivery exists. Smokers seem to have a relative risk of preterm delivery between 1.2 and 2 compared with nonsmokers (Bennedsen, 1998). One study found that smoking increased the risk of preterm delivery only among women with a high intake of caffeine (>400 mg/day) (Wisborg, Henriksen, Hedegaard, & Secher, 1996). Other studies have found no overall effect on preterm delivery but an association with very early birth (<32 weeks) (Peacock et al., 1995; Vitoratos et al., 1997). Risk of spontaneous preterm delivery consistently increases with the amount smoked (Kyrklund-Blomberg & Cnattingius, 1998), and an association between number of cigarettes smoked per day and premature rupture of membranes has also been reported (Vitoratos et al., 1997). Smoking cessation during the first trimester has been shown to reduce rates of preterm delivery (Mainous & Hueston, 1994). No association has been found between caffeine intake and preterm birth (Peacock et al., 1995).

Exercise

Participating in sports or exercise is associated with lower rates of preterm delivery. Lack of leisure-time physical activity during pregnancy may increase risk (Gabbe & Turner, 1997). In one study, 557 women were monitored during each trimester and birth outcomes were recorded. Heavier exercise (at levels higher than 1,000 kcal/week) seemed to reduce risk of preterm birth. Low to moderate exercise showed no association with gestational length (Hatch, Levin, Shu, & Susser, 1998). Healthy women who engage in regular physical activity during pregnancy do not seem to be at increased risk for preterm delivery and may be at significantly lower risk than sedentary women.

Intervention

The most common medical approaches to preventing preterm delivery for women with high medical risk or after premature labor occurs are medication, bed rest, or both. Some research on preterm labor, as on other pregnancy complications, has raised doubts about the efficacy of bed rest (e.g., al-Najashi & al-Mulhim, 1996). Considering problems with adherence and the inconvenience, discomfort, and distress prolonged bed rest may cause women, more research is needed to determine whether or under which circumstances this intervention is warranted.

Behavioral approaches to preventing preterm delivery have focused on either training women to detect early signs of preterm labor using relaxation and hypnotic suggestion or providing social support. Smith, Weinman, Reeves, Wait, & Hinckley (1993) trained 41 pregnant adolescents how to detect premature labor; 21 detected early contractions and obtained treatment, of whom 18 delivered at term. However, this study included no control group. In contrast, the Collaborative Group on Preterm Birth Prevention (1993) randomized 2,395 pregnant women at high risk for preterm labor into intervention and control groups at each of five centers. Women in the intervention group were instructed to recognize early signs of preterm labor and notify staff if they occurred. No reliable benefit was shown.

Beckmann, Beckmann, Stanziano, Bergauer, and Martin (1996) analyzed uterine activity records from 778 women and found participants were able to identify only 17.2% of all contractions recorded by tocodynamometry. The authors concluded that, even when patients are provided with ongoing feedback regarding perceptive accuracy, palpation is not a reliable tool for accurate identification of uterine contractions in women at risk for preterm labor. Nevertheless, insufficient data exist to conclude that women cannot be trained to detect premature onset of labor. The training techniques used in this study may not have been adequate for this task. Better self-detection might result from training using biofeedback techniques.

Omer (1987) conducted a trial of hypnosis as an adjunct to medication in 39 women hospitalized for preterm labor. The initial hypnosis session lasted 1.5 hours and was followed by approximately another 1.5 total hours on subsequent days, for an average of 3 total hours. In addition, each woman was given a hypnotic exercise on audiocassette and instructed to practice with the cassette twice daily during her hospitalization and once daily at home until the end of the 37th week. Hypnotic suggestions included relaxation of the body and uterus, time progression and visualization of the pregnancy continuing to term, suggestions for a positive emotional attitude, and "therapeutic anecdotes embodying indirect suggestions" (p. 212). Hypnosis significantly prolonged pregnancy in these women compared with a control group receiving medication only. However, the author conceded that it is not clear that the hypnosis created the therapeutic effect; this intervention also attempted to improve patients' motivation for pregnancy prolongation, perhaps enhancing cooperation with the medical regimen. Alternately, the "active ingredient" of the intervention may have been the social support provided by the extra attention and interaction received by the hypnosis group. However, randomized clinical trials of enhanced psychosocial support during pregnancy have not shown a reduction in premature delivery (Copper et al., 1996).

EXCESSIVE VOMITING IN PREGNANCY

Incidence and General Risk Factors

Nausea, with or without vomiting, is the most common complaint during the first trimester of pregnancy; 50% to 80% of women experience some nausea and vomiting during early pregnancy. The physiological changes that cause "morning sickness" generally subside by 14 to 16 weeks of gestation. However, an estimated 0.5 to 10 pregnant women in 1,000 experience severe, intractable nausea and vomiting that continues past this point and may be severe enough to require hospitalization (Iancu, Kotler, Spivak, Radwan, & Weizman, 1994; Lub-Moss & Eurelings-Bontekoe, 1997). This condition, hyperemesis gravidarum (HG), is characterized by disturbed nutrition, electrolyte imbalance, ketosis, acetonuria, and extreme weight loss (>5% of body weight). Associated symptoms include sleep disturbances, fatigue, and irritability. The condition tends to resolve by the 20th week of pregnancy but can persist throughout gestation and can ultimately lead to neurological disturbances, renal and liver damage, retinal hemorrhage, and termination of pregnancy. Modern standard-of-care fluid and electrolyte replacement has virtually eliminated death, which previously was not an uncommon result of HG (Lub-Moss & Eurelings-Bontekoe, 1997). During the 1980s, more than 50,000 women were hospitalized annually for HG, with an average hospital stay of 4 days (Signorello, Harlow, Wang, & Erick, 1998). Risk of developing HG is highest among primigravida women, women who have had prior unsuccessful pregnancies or abortions, and women with a history of HG in previous pregnancies (Hod et al., 1996). Young age, low education, and high body weight have also been implicated (Signorello et al., 1998).

Psychosocial Factors

There has been much theorizing but relatively little empirical work on the possible etiological role of psychosocial factors in excessive nausea and vomiting during pregnancy. Various psychiatric disorders, personality pathology, problematic interpersonal relationships, and stress have been suggested as causal or at least associated with elevated risk, but research results have been equivocal (Lub-Moss & Eurelings-Bontekoe, 1997). Psychoanalytically oriented theorizing has been common but difficult to substantiate (e.g., strong maternal dependence, infantile personality associated with hysteria, intrapsychic conflict, conversion reaction, rejection of pregnancy) (El-Mallakh, Liebowitz, & Hale, 1990; Hod et al., 1996). Interestingly, it has been observed that excessive nausea and vomiting in pregnancy is unknown in primitive cultures but begins to develop as these cultures come into contact with Western civilization (Iancu et al., 1994). Iancu et al. supported the argument that psychosocial factors are important in the etiology of HG by citing evidence that (a) symptoms have been shown to disappear when the patient is separated from her family, and relapse often occurs when she returns to the family environment; (b) HG is seen only in humans; (c) HG is treatable by hypnosis and suggestion; and (d) the incidence of HG decreases markedly during war time.

Health-Related Behavior

Signorello et al. (1998) hypothesized that dietary fat, which has been shown to influence estrogen production and metabolism, influences risk of developing HG. Retrospective reports of average dietary intake for the prepregnancy year were obtained from 44 women who had been hospitalized for severe HG and from 87 control patients. Dietary fat was positively associated with HG; risk of HG tripled with each 25-g increase in prepregnancy total fat intake. When saturated fat intake alone was examined, the odds ratio increased to 5.4 for each 15-g increase. This study is consistent with one theory regarding the etiology of HG, which suggests metabolic or nutritional deficiencies are involved. Some research has shown changes in serum lipids and lipoproteins related to HG and associated with autonomic nervous dysfunction, but results have been mixed (Lub-Moss & Eurelings-Bontekoe, 1997). Additional research on the role of diet, nutritional status, and metabolic factors in HG could contribute to our understanding of this disorder.

Intervention

Standard treatment of severe HG involves hospitalization, withholding oral feeding, and delivery of intravenous fluids (Iancu et al., 1994). In addition, ondansetron (Zofran), a 5-HT$_3$ antagonist used as an antiemetic for chemotherapy-associated nausea and vomiting and postoperative nausea, has been used successfully (Tincello & Johnstone, 1996). Naef et al. (1995) found that providing medical treatment in the patient's home produced results no different from those obtained in hospitalized patients, but a higher rate of rehospitalization occurred among the hospitalized women.

Some evidence has suggested that hypnosis may be an effective treatment for HG (Iancu et al., 1994). Torem (1994) reported successfully treating HG in a small series of cases using various techniques of suggestion under hypnosis. The women were all rated high in hypnotic susceptibility. The author stressed the importance of assessing susceptibility to hypnosis when considering hypnosis as a treatment. In a larger study, Fuchs (1989) treated 138 women with severe HG (vomiting 15 to 20 times per day) using hypnotic relaxation, hypnosis with imagery, or group hypnotherapy. He reported a relatively high success rate: 69% of women had an "excellent" response (no vomiting or nausea), and 19% had a "good" response (no vomiting but continued nausea) after, in most cases, one to three 45 to 60 minute sessions. A "poor" response (vomiting less than 6 times per day, improvement in nausea) was significantly less common in women who received group hypnotherapy than in those treated individually. As promising as these results seem, this study and the few other studies in this area suffer from inadequate control groups, nonrandom assignment to treatment, no standardization of treatment techniques, and unblinded assessments. Hypnosis may be a useful therapeutic tool for hyperemesis, but the limited and methodologically flawed research to date has provided insufficient scientific support for such therapy and insufficient information regarding the necessary or sufficient parameters of successful hypnotherapy. Well-controlled studies are needed.

Behavior therapy approaches to treating hyperemesis have incorporated the relaxation component of hypnotherapy (and sometimes imagery) and have added self-monitoring, functional analysis of behavior, and stimulus control. For example, Callahan, Burnette, DeLawyer, and Brasted (1986) used patient reports regarding episodes of vomiting to identify idiosyncratic triggering cues in 4 women hospitalized for hyperemesis. These triggering stimuli were removed, counterconditioning was used, or a problem-solving approach was taken, as appropriate. Vomiting was eliminated or reduced in all cases. Similar behavioral techniques and findings were reported by another group (Long, Simone, & Tucher, 1986; Simone & Long, 1985).

Like most hypnotherapy studies, the behavior therapy studies have relied on small samples, are not well controlled or blinded, and are not designed to enable identification of the "active" component of treatment. Relaxation is common to both hypnotherapy and behavioral treatment and in some cases seems sufficient to reduce or eliminate vomiting. Social interaction and social support are also common to both approaches and have not been controlled for. No studies have been reported on social support as an intervention for hyperemesis.

HYPERTENSION

Incidence and General Risk Factors

Hypertension in pregnancy is the second most common cause of maternal death in the United States and the leading cause in many parts of the world (Sibai et al., 1997). Pregnancy-induced hypertension (PIH) occurs in 2.4% to 3.7% of pregnancies annually in the United States (CDC, 1998; Sibai et al., 1997). The majority of cases occur in healthy, nulliparous women, with an incidence of 6% to 7% in this group (Sibai, 1998). Hypertension in the absence of proteinuria is referred to as *gestational hypertension*, whereas hypertension in the presence of proteinuria is defined as *preeclampsia* (Misra & Kiely, 1995).

Risk factors for PIH include extremes of maternal age, non-White race, low socioeconomic status, elevated systolic and diastolic blood pressure early in pregnancy, presence of gestational diabetes, and obesity (Dekker & Sibai, 1998; Sibai et al., 1997). Incidence and severity are also markedly increased in women with multifetal gestation, vascular or renal disease, previous severe preeclampsia or eclampsia, or abnormal uterine artery Doppler velocimetry measurements (Sibai, 1998).

Psychosocial Factors

Stress and Distress

In a review of the research on psychosocial factors and pregnancy outcomes, Paarlberg, Vingerhoets, Passchier, Dekker, and Van Geijn (1995) reported that studies investigating the association between stressful life events and preeclampsia have produced conflicting results, and design differences make the studies difficult to compare. Poland, Giblin, Lucas, and Sokol (1986) examined anxiety and trait-at-ease in women at prenatal visits occurring during weeks 28 to 32 of pregnancy. Trait-at-ease was associated with increased risk of developing PIH after the 28th week of pregnancy. The authors explain this counterintuitive finding as follows:

> That women who reported themselves to be generally at ease were more likely to develop PIH is consistent with the hypothesis that these individuals may maintain that perception by denying stressful experiences and expressing anxiety covertly through physiological means, e.g., hypertension. (p. 90)

Further understanding of the relationship of stress or distress to PIH is obscured by the fact that many researchers studying these constructs lump pregnancy complications together to form one or two outcome variables. Thus, numerous reports indicate a relationship between life event stress and the occurrence of pregnancy complications but fail to report whether a relationship exists between stress and PIH specifically.

Work

A few studies in the last decade have investigated work or work stress in relation to PIH. In 1990, Klebanoff, Shiono, and Rhoads (1990) compared pregnancy outcomes between residents and wives of medical residents; residents had a significantly higher incidence of preeclampsia. Wergeland and Strand (1997) found increased incidence of preeclampsia in women whose work involved lifting heavy loads, who had a hectic work pace, or who worked with their hands above shoulder level. Shift work was also associated with increased risk but for parous women only. In a postpartum survey, a large sample of women who continued employment beyond the first trimester rated their perceived control over work pace. A small but significant effect was found. The odds ratio for women perceiving no control over their work pace was 1.6 compared with women who reported a high level of perceived control (Wergeland & Strand, 1998).

Landsbergis and Hatch (1996) compared employed women and women not working outside the home, and they also examined various job characteristics relevant to job stress (e.g., job complexity, job pressures, control level, job decision latitude). All cases of PIH occurred in the employed women. Neither gestational hypertension nor preeclampsia showed a clear association or consistent dose–response relation with the measured variables. However, gestational hypertension of women in low-status jobs increased with reported low job decision latitude or low job complexity.

Duration of Sexual Cohabitation

Several studies have suggested that becoming pregnant by a man who is different than the biological father of a prior pregnancy increases risk of developing PIH in women who have had several pregnancies (multigravidae) (Robillard et al., 1994). These findings are consistent with the hypothesis that PIH results from an immunological reaction of the mother against placental tissue that is incompatible with maternal tissue. Assuming that PIH has an immunological etiology, Robillard et al. (1994) reasoned that the incidence of the disorder might be related to the duration of exposure to antigens from the father. During a protracted sexual relationship, women may develop an immune response that protects them from the father's antigens in a subsequent pregnancy. Postpartum interviews were conducted with 1,101 women in Guadalupe; 11.9% of primigravidae, 4.7%

of multigravidae, and 24.0% of multigravidae who had a new partner developed PIH. Duration of sexual cohabitation was significantly shorter for women with PIH. Overall incidence of PIH dropped from 10.6% to 5.1% (from 11.9% to 3.3% in primigravidae) in women with more than 12 months of sexual cohabitation before conception, and there was an inverse dose–response effect of duration of cohabitation on risk. Logistic regression controlling for maternal age, level of education, partnership status, gravidity, and race did not alter the odds ratios.

Health-Related Behavior

Weight and Physical Activity

High prepregnancy BMI, higher than recommended weight gain during pregnancy, and deviation from recommended rate of weight gain during pregnancy have been associated with PIH (Ogunyemi, Hullett, Leeper, & Risk, 1998; Poland et al., 1986; Sibai et al., 1997). Marcoux, Brisson, and Fabia (1989) retrospectively assessed leisure-time physical activity for the first 20 weeks of pregnancy in women with gestational hypertension or preeclampsia and control groups a few days after delivery. Women who reported some physical activity were at lower risk for both conditions. Relative risk of preeclampsia was inversely related to maximal intensity of leisure-time physical activity; no such effect was found for gestational hypertension. In addition, frequent walking at work or at home significantly reduced risk of preeclampsia. Physical activity levels before pregnancy were not examined.

Smoking and Caffeine

Some evidence has shown that smoking is associated with reduced risk of developing PIH. Misra and Kiely (1995) found that women who smoked during the 3 months after learning they were pregnant had a significantly reduced risk of gestational hypertension; this effect was stronger for multiparous than primiparous women. Another study of more than 6,000 women in Norway found that those who smoked had lower weights, lower pregnancy weight gains, and less PIH. Incidence of PIH among smokers was 4% compared with 7.5% for nonsmokers (Rasmussen & Oian, 1998). On the other hand, Sibai et al. (1997) did not find cigarette smoking beyond the last menstrual period to be associated with reduced incidence of preeclampsia. According to Rasmussen and Oian, the lower incidence of PIH in smokers cannot be explained by the effect of nicotine on thromboxane or prostacyclin activity. Smoking affects hemoglobin levels, which in turn are associated with PIH. However, if smoking indeed reduces the risk of developing PIH, the mechanisms by which it does so are unknown.

Little research has been conducted on the effects of alcohol or caffeine consumption on PIH, although Sibai et al. (1997) listed alcohol consumption as a risk factor for developing the disorder. Wergeland and Strand (1997) reported that consuming more than four cups of coffee per day is associated with increased risk of preeclampsia.

Intervention

Numerous approaches to preventing PIH have been studied and not found effective, including antihypertensives, magnesium, calcium, zinc, fish oil supplementation, and low doses of aspirin. The current literature indicates that neither dietary supplementation nor pharmacological therapy is effective in preventing preeclampsia. For treatment of PIH, physicians most commonly prescribe some form of restricted activity, from complete hospital bed rest to bed rest at home. As mentioned previously, few well-controlled studies have investigated the efficacy of bed rest, and patient adherence can be problematic.

Somers, Gevirtz, Jasin, and Chin (1989) studied 45 women with mild PIH between 30 and 36 weeks of gestation who had been prescribed restricted activity or bed rest. Women were randomly assigned either bed rest alone, compliance enhancement training, or a biobehavioral intervention. Compliance enhancement training consisted of 4 contact hours, including PIH education, behavioral contracting, self-monitoring, problem identification and problem-solving skills, time management, self-reinforcement, stimulus cueing, and attention to compliance-enhancing cognitions. The biobehavioral intervention was designed to cultivate a low state of arousal while enhancing compliance with bed rest and careful obstetrical monitoring. It consisted of 4 contact hours, including components of the compliance training in addition to self-monitoring of blood pressure and thermal biofeedback relaxation training. Women in the biobehavioral intervention group were instructed to practice procedures twice daily and complete at least three relaxation breaks daily. This group experienced a significant decrease in mean arterial pressure, whereas the other two groups had trends toward increasing mean arterial pressure. The number of hours of bed rest was uncorrelated with blood pressure, raising the question of whether bed rest has any efficacy in the treatment of PIH or at least of relatively mild PIH. Effects of the intervention on proteinuria and edema were not measured, and it is not clear to what extent these results are generalizable to more severe cases of hypertension or preeclampsia. These results are consistent with previous, less well-controlled research using relaxation and biofeedback (Little et al., 1984).

Hypertension complicating pregnancy, childbirth, and the puerperium seems to be a clinical syndrome rather than a single disease and has an unknown but likely multifactorial, etiology. Preexisting medical conditions;

immunological, genetic, or dietary factors; vasospasm associated with sympathetic nervous system hyperactivity; or any combination of these factors may play a role in any individual case of PIH. The complexity of the etiology and the disappointing results of medical prevention efforts suggest it is unlikely that any single intervention will effectively prevent PIH (Sibai, 1998; Somers et al., 1989). However, some promising early results of behavioral interventions such as relaxation and biofeedback support developing a biopsychosocial approach to the prevention and treatment of PIH.

ABRUPTIO PLACENTAE AND PLACENTA PREVIA

Incidence and General Risk Factors

Disorders of placental attachment are associated with potentially life-threatening prenatal hemorrhage. In a patient with abruptio placentae, or placental abruption, the normally implanted placenta detaches prematurely. Preterm delivery, ischemic damage to maternal organs, and cesarean section are among the possible consequences (Andres, 1996). Reported incidence of abruptio placentae ranges from 0.4 to 1.3% of deliveries (Cunningham, MacDonald, Gant, Leveno, & Gilstrap, 1993). In women with placenta previa, the placenta implants in the lower part of the lower uterine segment, presenting before the fetus; premature, usually cesarean delivery can result. Incidence of placenta previa is 0.3 to 0.5% (Cunningham et al., 1993). Risk factors for both complications include older maternal age and multiparity. In addition, prior abruption, external trauma, and African American ethnicity are associated with increased risk of placental abruption. Previous cesarean section or induced abortion is associated with increased risk of placenta previa (Cunningham et al., 1993).

Health-Related Behavior

Smoking has been implicated in both abruptio placentae and placenta previa. Reported odds ratios range from 1.5 to 4.4 for placenta previa; the association is dose dependent (Andres, 1996; Chelmow, Andrew, & Baker, 1996; McMahon, Li, Schenck, Olshan, & Royce, 1997). Similarly, reported odds ratios range from 1.5 to 3.0 for placental abruption, with a dose-dependent relationship (Andres, 1996; Cnattingius, Mills, Yuen, Eriksson, & Salonen, 1997; Spinillo et al., 1994; Wong & Bauman, 1997).

Some evidence has suggested alcohol consumption and cocaine use increase the risk for placental abruption (ACOG, 1994; Cunningham et al., 1993). Potential effects of other behavioral or psychosocial factors have not been studied in patients with these obstetrical complications.

CHRONIC MEDICAL DISORDERS IN PREGNANCY

Chronic medical disorders, especially anemia and diabetes, are common during pregnancy and are associated with various adverse outcomes. Successful management of many of these diseases depends on good adherence; for example women with anemia must take prescribed iron supplements, and women with diabetes must adhere to a more complex set of behaviors. Adherence has been widely studied in medicine and in diabetes research specifically, but very little systematic research into behavioral management of these disorders during pregnancy can be found in the literature. Also largely absent from the literature are biopsychosocial approaches to managing other chronic diseases that continue into or occur during pregnancy, such as cardiopulmonary disease, asthma and allergies, and rheumatic diseases. Given the potential adverse effects of many medications on the pregnancy or the fetus, development of nonmedical interventions designed to decrease chronic disease activity in pregnant women could be a valuable contribution of health psychology.

COMPLICATIONS OF LABOR AND DELIVERY

Behavioral research on complications of labor and delivery is virtually nonexistent. Studies examining effects of childbirth preparation have focused on pain, satisfaction with the childbirth experience, and psychological outcomes rather than on medical complications. Lobel (1994) concluded that little evidence supports a relationship of number of life events to labor and delivery complications, but some evidence has suggested subjectively weighted life event stress may be associated with labor and delivery complications. Some intervention studies using relaxation, hypnosis, social support, or a combination of these during labor have found decreased labor duration and perinatal complications (Dreher, 1996; Dunkel-Schetter & Lobel, 1998; Paarlberg et al., 1995).

CONCLUSION

The body of published research on complications of pregnancy, childbirth, and the puerperium does not provide clear guidelines for health psychology interventions. Relaxation, hypnosis, and social support are promising modalities for preventing or managing many obstetrical complications, but further well-controlled research is needed if practice is to be based on a firm scientific foundation. The use of behavioral techniques to aid in eliminating risky behaviors such as smoking, substance abuse, or inappropriate patterns of weight gain seems desirable given the prevalence and scope of adverse consequences associated with these behaviors. In 1996, approximately 13.6% of women in the United States smoked during pregnancy (CDC, 1998). Health care costs attributable to smoking-related increases in obstetrical complications have been estimated at $135 to $167 million per year (Adams & Melvin, 1998). Tobacco use is among the most modifiable risk factors for obstetrical complications, and smoking cessation falls squarely within the domain of applied health psychology. Considering the dearth of research on smoking cessation and other behavioral interventions during pregnancy, such interventions should be conducted systematically in a way that can be reported in the literature, ultimately enhancing psychologists' ability to tailor techniques for optimal effectiveness.

Development of successful health psychology interventions for obstetrical complications depends to a large extent on identifying psychosocial and behavioral factors important in the etiology and course of these complications and establishing the relevant mechanisms. Postulated mechanisms underlying effects on obstetrical complications of psychosocial factors such as stress, social support, socioeconomic status, or coping include direct physiological effects of stress hormones, indirect effects via increased high-risk behaviors, and psychoneuroimmune processes. The extent to which these physiological mechanisms operate in complications of pregnancy remains to be established.

More well-designed health psychology research on obstetrical complications is needed. The current literature suffers from methodological limitations, inconsistencies in operationalization and measurement of variables, and heterogeneity or noncomparability of samples in terms of parity, important sociodemographic variables, or other relevant variables. The common practice of collapsing birth outcomes into one dependent variable hampers understanding what are likely the unique effects of different stressors or sets of psychosocial variables on different outcomes.

Substantively, a wide variety of questions remains to be addressed in biopsychosocial research on obstetrical complications. Most research to date has focused on stress, physical- or work-related strain, social support, and risk behaviors. Stress research has focused on life events and directed little attention toward chronic stressors or hassles, and measurement of the physiological stress response is usually lacking. Physical strain at work seems related to pregnancy risk, but leisure-time exercise does not. Related issues of controllability, attitudes, and perceived work stress have begun to be examined but need more thorough investigation. Social support studies vary in the timing of support and in the way support is defined and measured, and controlled studies tend to yield results that differ from naturalistic studies. More systematic exploration of social support, coping, and related issues seems warranted.

Furthermore, little is known about the importance of temporal issues in obstetrical complications. Are there critical periods of exposure to high levels of stress, risky behavior, or physical strain? How important is chronicity of exposure or behavior? Finally, most complications of pregnancy, childbirth, and the puerperium have simply not been investigated from a biopsychosocial perspective. Psychosocial factors may be relatively unimportant in some of these complications but are likely to play some role in others.

Complications of pregnancy, childbirth, and the puerperium have received an increasing amount of attention from a biopsychosocial perspective during the past two decades. Interesting patterns of findings have emerged, but more work remains to be done, making this area exciting and full of interesting possibilities for health psychologists.

REFERENCES

Abel, E. L. (1997). Maternal alcohol consumption and spontaneous abortion. *Alcohol and Alcoholism, 32*(3), 211–219.

Adams, E. K., & Melvin, C. L. (1998). Costs of maternal conditions attributable to smoking during pregnancy. *American Journal of Preventive Medicine, 15*(3), 212–219.

al-Najashi, S. S., & al-Mulhim, A. A. (1996). Prolongation of pregnancy in multiple pregnancy. *International Journal of Gynaecology and Obstetrics, 54*(2), 131–135.

American College of Obstetrics and Gynecology. (1993). Smoking and reproductive health. *ACOG Technical Bulletin*, No. 180.

American College of Obstetrics and Gynecology. (1994). Substance abuse in pregnancy. *ACOG Technical Bulletin*, No. 195.

American College of Obstetrics and Gynecology. (1995). Early pregnancy loss. *ACOG Technical Bulletin*, No. 212.

Andres, R. L. (1996). The association of cigarette smoking with placenta previa and abruptio placentae. *Seminars in Perinatology, 20*(2), 154–159.

Beckmann, C. A., Beckmann, C. R., Stanziano, G. J., Bergauer, N. K., & Martin, C. B. (1996). Accuracy of maternal perception of preterm uterine activity. *American Journal of Obstetrics and Gynecology, 174*(2), 672–675.

Bennedsen, B. E. (1998). Adverse pregnancy outcome in schizophrenic women: Occurrence and risk factors. *Schizophrenia Research, 33*(1–2), 1–26.

Brett, K. M., Strogatz, D. S., & Savitz, D. A. (1997). Employment, job strain, and preterm delivery among women in North Carolina. *American Journal of Public Health, 87*(2), 199–204.

Bryant, H. E., & Love, E. J. (1991). Effect of employment and its correlates on spontaneous abortion risk. *Social Science and Medicine, 33*(7), 795–800.

Callahan, E. J., Burnette, M. M., DeLawyer, D., & Brasted, W. S. (1986). Behavioral treatment of hyperemesis gravidarum. *Journal of Psychosomatic Obstetrics and Gynaecology, 5*(3), 187–195.

Carmichael, S., Abrams, B., & Selvin, S. (1997). The association of pattern of maternal weight gain with length of gestation and risk of spontaneous preterm delivery. *Paediatric Perinatology and Epidemiology, 11*(4), 392–406.

Cavallo, F., Russo, R., Zotti, C., Camerlengo, A., & Ruggenini, A. (1995). Moderate alcohol consumption and spontaneous abortion. *Alcohol and Alcoholism, 30*(2), 195–201.

Centers for Disease Control and Prevention. (1998). Births, marriages, divorces, and deaths for November 1997. *Monthly Vital Statistics Report, 46*(11, Suppl.).

Centers for Disease Control and Prevention. (1999). Births: Final data for 1997. *National Vital Statistics Reports, 47*(18).

Ceron-Mireles, P., Harlow, S. D., & Sanchez-Carrillo, C. I. (1996). The risk of prematurity and small-for-gestational-age birth in Mexico City: The effects of working conditions and antenatal leave. *American Journal of Public Health, 86*(6), 825–831.

Chasnoff, I. J., Burns, W. J., Schnoll, S. H., & Burns, K. A. (1985). Cocaine use in pregnancy. *New England Journal of Medicine, 313*, 666–669.

Chelmow, D., Andrew, D. E., & Baker, E. R. (1996). Maternal cigarette smoking and placenta previa. *Obstetrics and Gynecology, 87*(5, Pt. 1), 703–706.

Cnattingius, S., Mills, J. L., Yuen, J., Eriksson, O., & Salonen, H. (1997). The paradoxical effect of smoking in preeclamptic pregnancies: Smoking reduces the incidence but increases the rates of perinatal mortality, abruptio placentae, and intrauterine growth restriction. *American Journal of Obstetrics and Gynecology, 177*(1), 156–161.

Collaborative Group on Preterm Birth Prevention. (1993). Multicenter randomized, controlled trial of a preterm birth prevention program. *American Journal of Obstetrics and Gynecology, 169*(2), 352–366.

Copper, R. L., Goldenberg, R. L., Das, A., Elder, N., Swain, M., Norman, G., et al. (1996). The preterm prediction study: Maternal stress is associated with spontaneous preterm birth at less than thirty-five weeks' gestation. National Institute of Child Health and Human Development Maternal–Fetal Medicine Units Network. *American Journal of Obstetrics and Gynecology, 175*(5), 1286–1292.

Cunningham, F. G., MacDonald, P. C., Gant, N. F., Leveno, K. J., & Gilstrap, L. C. (1993). *William's obstetrics* (19th ed.). Norwalk, CT: Appleton-Lange.

Dekker, G. A., & Sibai, B. H. (1998). Etiology and pathogenesis of preeclampsia: Current concepts. *American Journal of Obstetrics and Gynecology, 179*(5), 1359–1375.

Dreher, H. (1996). Can hypnosis rotate a breech baby before birth? *Advances, 12*(3), 46–50.

Dunkel-Schetter, C., & Lobel, M. (1998). Pregnancy and childbirth. In E. A. Blechman & K. D. Brownell (Eds.), *Behavioral medicine and women: A comprehensive handbook* (pp. 475–482). New York: Guilford Press.

El-Mallakh, R. S., Liebowitz, N. R., & Hale, M. S. (1990). Hyperemesis gravidarum as conversion disorder. *Journal of Nervous and Mental Disease, 178*(10), 655–659.

Fuchs, K. (1989). Treatment of hyperemesis gravidarum by hypnosis. *Australian Journal of Clinical Hypnotherapy and Hypnosis, 10*(1), 31–42.

Gabbe, S. G., & Turner, L. P. (1997). Reproductive hazards of the American lifestyle: Work during pregnancy. *American Journal of Obstetrics and Gynecology, 176*(4), 826–832.

Gannon, K. (1994). Psychological factors in the aetiology and treatment of recurrent miscarriage: A review and critique. *Journal of Reproductive and Infant Psychology, 12*(1), 55–64.

Hatch, M., Levin, B., Shu, X. O., & Susser, M. (1998). Maternal leisure-time exercise and timely delivery. *American Journal of Public Health, 88*(10), 1528–1533.

Hedegaard, M., Henriksen, T. B., Secher, N. J., Hatch, M. C., & Sabroe, S. (1996). Do stressful life events affect duration of gestation and risk of preterm delivery? *Epidemiology, 7*(4), 339–345.

Hod, M., Rabinerson, D., Kaplan, B., Peled, Y., Bar, J., Shindel, B., et al. (1996). Perinatal complications following gestational diabetes mellitus: How "sweet" is ill? *Acta Obstetrica and Gynecologica Scandinavia, 75*(9), 809–815.

Hoffman, S., & Hatch, M. C. (1996). Stress, social support and pregnancy outcome: A reassessment based on recent research. *Paediatric Perinatology and Epidemiology, 10*(4), 380–405.

Homer, C. J., James, S. A., & Siegel, E. (1990). Work-related psychosocial stress and risk of preterm, low birthweight delivery. *American Journal of Public Health, 80,* 173–177.

Honnor, M. J., Zubrick, S. R., & Stanley, F. J. (1994). The role of life events in different categories of preterm birth in a group of women with previous poor pregnancy outcome. *European Journal of Epidemiology, 10*(2), 181–188.

Iancu, I., Kotler, M., Spivak, B., Radwan, M., & Weizman, A. (1994). Psychiatric aspects of hyperemesis gravidarum. *Psychotherapy and Psychosomatics, 61*(3–4), 143–149.

Klebanoff, M. A., Shiono, P. H., & Rhoads, G. G. (1990). Outcomes of pregnancy in a national sample of resident physicians. *New England Journal of Medicine, 323,* 1040–1045.

Kyrklund-Blomberg, N. B., & Cnattingius, S. (1998). Preterm birth and maternal smoking: Risks related to gestational age and onset of delivery. *American Journal of Obstetrics and Gynecology, 179*(4), 1051–1055.

Landsbergis, P. A., & Hatch, M. C. (1996). Psychosocial work stress and pregnancy-induced hypertension. *Epidemiology, 7*(4), 346–351.

Lindbohm, M. L. (1995). Effects of parental exposure to solvents on pregnancy outcome. *Journal of Occupational and Environmental Medicine, 37*(8), 908–916.

Little, B. C., Benson, P., Beard, R. W., Hayworth, J., Hall, F., Dewhurst, J., et al. (1984). Treatment of hypertension in pregnancy by relaxation and biofeedback. *Lancet, 19,* 865–867.

Lobel, M. (1994). Conceptualizations, measurement, and effects of prenatal maternal stress on birth outcomes. *Journal of Behavioral Medicine, 17*(3), 225–272.

Lobel, M., Dunkel-Schetter, C., & Scrimshaw, S. C. M. (1992). The role of prenatal maternal stress on infant prematurity. *Health Psychology, 11*, 32–40.

Long, M. A., Simone, S. S., & Tucher, J. J. (1986). Outpatient treatment of hyperemesis gravidarum with stimulus control and imagery procedures. *Journal of Behavior Therapy and Experimental Psychiatry, 17*(2), 105–109.

Lub-Moss, M. M. H., & Eurelings-Bontekoe, E. H. M. (1997). Clinical experience with patients suffering from hyperemesis gravidarum (severe nausea and vomiting during pregnancy): Thoughts about subtyping of patients, treatment and counseling models. *Patient Education and Counseling, 31*(1), 65–75.

Lundsberg, L. S., Bracken, M. B., & Saftlas, A. F. (1997). Low-to-moderate gestational alcohol use and intrauterine growth retardation, low birthweight, and preterm delivery. *Annals of Epidemiology, 7*(7), 498–508.

Madden, M. E. (1988). Internal and external attributions following miscarriage. *Journal of Social and Clinical Psychology, 7*(2–3), 113–121.

Mainous, A. G., & Hueston, W. J. (1994). The effect of smoking cessation during pregnancy on preterm delivery and low birthweight. *Journal of Family Practice, 38*, 262–266.

Marcoux, S., Brisson, J., & Fabia, J. (1989). The effect of leisure time physical activity on the risk of pre-eclampsia and gestational hypertension. *Journal of Epidemiology and Community Health, 43*(2), 147–152.

McMahon, M. J., Li, R., Schenck, A. P., Olshan, A. F., & Royce, R. A. (1997). Previous cesarean birth. A risk factor for placenta previa? *Journal of Reproductive Medicine, 42*(7), 409–412.

Misra, D. P., & Kiely, J. L. (1995). The effect of smoking on the risk of gestational hypertension. *Early Human Development, 40*(2), 95–107.

Naef, R. W., III, Chauhan, S. P., Roach, H., Roberts, W. E., Travis, K. H., & Morrison, J. C. (1995). Treatment for hyperemesis gravidarum in the home: An alternative to hospitalization. *Journal of Perinatology, 15*(4), 289–292.

Norbeck, J. S., & Anderson, N. J. (1989). Psychosocial predictors of pregnancy outcomes in low-income Black, Hispanic, and White women. *Nursing Research, 38*(4), 204–209.

Nordentoft, M., Lou, H. C., Hansen, D., Nim, J., Pryds, O., Rubin, P., et al. (1996). Intrauterine growth retardation and premature delivery: The influence of maternal smoking and psychosocial factors. *American Journal of Public Health, 86*(3), 347–354.

Nurminen, T. (1995a). Female noise exposure, shift work, and reproduction. *Journal of Occupational and Environmental Medicine, 37*(8), 945–951.

Nurminen, T. (1995b). Maternal pesticide exposure and pregnancy outcome. *Journal of Occupational and Environmental Medicine, 37*(8), 935–942.

Ogunyemi, D., Hullett, S., Leeper, J., & Risk, A. (1998). Prepregnancy body mass index, weight gain during pregnancy, and perinatal outcome in a rural Black population. *Journal of Maternal Fetal Medicine, 7*(4), 190–193.

O'Hare, T., & Creed, F. (1995). Life events and miscarriage. *British Journal of Psychiatry, 167*(6), 799–805.

Omer, H. (1987). A hypnotic relaxation technique for the treatment of premature labor. *American Journal of Clinical Hypnosis, 29*(3), 206–213.

Paarlberg, K. M., Vingerhoets, A. J., Passchier, J., Dekker, G. A., & Van Geijn, H. P. (1995). Psychosocial factors and pregnancy outcome: A review with emphasis on methodological issues. *Journal of Psychosomatic Research, 39*(5), 563–595.

Peacock, J. L., Bland, J. M., & Anderson, H. R. (1995). Preterm delivery: Effects of socioeconomic factors, psychological stress, smoking, alcohol, and caffeine. *British Medical Journal, 311*, 531–535.

Plant, M. L. (1984). Drinking amongst pregnant women: Some initial results from a prospective study. *Alcohol and Alcoholism, 19*(2), 153–157.

Poland, M. L., Giblin, P. T., Lucas, C. P., & Sokol, R. J. (1986). Psychobiological determinants of pregnancy-induced hypertension. *Journal of Psychosomatic Obstetrics and Gynaecology, 5*(2), 85–92.

Rasmussen, S., & Oian, P. (1998). Smoking, hemoglobin concentration and pregnancy-induced hypertension. *Gynecological and Obstetrical Investigation, 46*(4), 225–231.

Robillard, P. Y., Hulsey, T. C., Perianin, J., Janky, E., Miri, E. H., & Papiernik, E. (1994). Association of pregnancy-induced hypertension with duration of sexual cohabitation before conception. *Lancet, 344*, 973–975.

Russell, M., & Skinner, J. B. (1988). Early measures of maternal alcohol misuse as predictors of adverse pregnancy outcomes. *Alcoholism: Clinical and Experimental Research, 12*(6), 824–830.

Schenker, M. B., Eaton, M., Green, R., & Samuels, S. (1997). Self-reported stress and reproductive health of female lawyers. *Journal of Occupational and Environmental Medicine, 39*(6), 556–568.

Sibai, B. (1998). Prevention of preeclampsia: A big disappointment. *American Journal of Obstetrics and Gynecology, 179*(5), 1275–1278.

Sibai, B. M., Ewell, M., Levine, R. J., Klebanoff, M. A., Esterlitz, J., Catalano, P. M., et al. (1997). Risk factors associated with preeclampsia in healthy nulliparous women. *American Journal of Obstetrics and Gynecology, 177*(5), 1003–1010.

Signorello, L. B., Harlow, B. L., Wang, S., & Erick, M. A. (1998). Saturated fat intake and the risk of severe hyperemesis gravidarum. *Epidemiology, 9*(6), 636–640.

Simone, S. S., & Long, M. A. (1985). The behavioral treatment of hyperemesis gravidarum. *Behavior Therapist, 8*(7), 128–129.

Smith, P. B., Weinman, M., Reeves, G. C., Wait, R. B., & Hinkley, C. M. (1993). Educational efforts in preventing preterm delivery among inner city adolescents. *Patient Education and Counseling, 21*(1–2), 71–75.

Somers, P. J., Gevirtz, R. N., Jasin, S. E., & Chin, H. G. (1989). The efficacy of biobehavioral and compliance interventions in the adjunctive treatment of mild pregnancy-induced hypertension. *Biofeedback and Self-Regulation, 14*(4), 309–318.

Spinillo, A., Capuzzo, E., Colonna, L., Solerte, L., Nicola, S., & Guaschino, S. (1994). Factors associated with abruptio placentae in preterm deliveries. *Acta Obstetrica Gynecologica Scandinavia, 73*(4), 307–312.

Steere, R. A., Scholl, T. O., Hediger, M. L., & Fischer, R. L. (1992). Self-reported depression and negative pregnancy outcome. *Journal of Clinical Epidemiology, 45*(10), 1093–1099.

Tincello, D. G., & Johnstone, M. J. (1996). Treatment of hyperemesis gravidarum with the 5-HT$_3$ antagonist ondansetron (Zofran). *Postgraduate Medical Journal, 72*(853), 688–689.

Torem, M. S. (1994). Hypnotherapeutic techniques in the treatment of hyperemesis gravidarum. *American Journal of Clinical Hypnosis, 37*(1), 1–11.

Vitoratos, N., Botsis, D., Grigoriou, O., Bettas, P., Papoulias, I., & Zourlas, P. A. (1997). Smoking and preterm labor. *Clinical and Experimental Obstetrics and Gynecology, 24*(4), 220–222.

Wadhwa, P. D., Sandman, C. A., Porto, M., Dunkel-Schetter, C., & Garite, T. J. (1993). The association between prenatal stress and infant birth weight and gestational age at birth: A prospective investigation. *American Journal of Obstetrics and Gynecology, 169*(4), 858–865.

Wergeland, E., & Strand, K. (1997). Working conditions and prevalence of pre-eclampsia, Norway 1989. *International Journal of Gynaecology and Obstetrics 58*(2), 189–196.

Wergeland, E., & Strand, K. (1998). Work pace control and pregnancy health in a population-based sample of employed women in Norway. *Scandinavian Journal of Work, Environment, & Health, 24*(3), 206–212.

Wisborg, K., Henriksen, T. B., Hedegaard, M., & Secher, N. J. (1996). Smoking during pregnancy and preterm birth. *British Journal of Obstetrics and Gynaecology 103*(8), 800–805.

Wong, P. P., & Bauman, A. (1997). How well does epidemiological evidence hold for the relationship between smoking and adverse obstetric outcomes in New South Wales? *Australia New Zealand Journal of Obstetrics and Gynaecology 37*(2), 168–173.

12

DISEASES OF THE SKIN AND SUBCUTANEOUS TISSUE

STEVEN M. TOVIAN

Skin is the one suit we never remove but, like everything else we wear, we change it to fit our mood or occasion. At times intimately private and other times blatantly public, skin is the ultimate interface between the self and others, between our inner being and the outer world. It is both the means by which we feel the world and the screen on which we project our personal feelings for the world to see (Grossbart, 1993).

Dermatological diseases represent a broad range of disorders with wide-ranging implications. In 1990, it was estimated that there were more than 44 million annual visits for dermatological complaints and more than $5 billion was spent for dermatological services, hospitalizations, and drugs for skin diseases. In that same year, it was estimated that more than 2 million people in the United States, from ages 1 to 74, had a skin condition that severely limited their employment or daily activities at home or school (Zanolli, 1990). Given these implications, comprehensive understanding and treatment of dermatological disorders requires a biopsychosocial perspective in which health psychologists can play an important role.

The main purpose of this chapter is to facilitate a greater understanding of dermatological disorders from a health psychology perspective. The first section of this chapter discusses the importance of psychological factors in dermatological diseases. The second section examines several models describing the psychosomatic aspects of dermatological disorders. The third section reviews contributions of health psychologists to assessment and treatment of specific dermatological diseases. The concluding section considers future clinical and research areas.

OVERVIEW OF THE SKIN

Although the skin is often conceptualized as a mere outer coating of the body, it actually contains a wide variety of cells, including sense organs that constantly react to pressure, temperature, and noxious stimulation (Pinkerton, Hughes, & Wenrich, 1982). A section of skin about the size of a quarter contains an average of 3 feet of blood vessels, 12 feet of nerves, 25 nerve endings, 100 sweat glands, and more than 3 million cells. It is the largest of human organs. Spread flat, it would cover 20 square feet. Skin provides the first line of defense against microbes, physical trauma, and environmental irritants. The skin maintains roaming immune system cells that engulf invading microorganisms and protect vulnerable tissues against attack (Grossbart, 1993). Further, the skin contains numerous glands, blood vessels, and smooth muscle elements, many of which come under autonomic nervous system (ANS) control. Therefore, emotional stimuli are able to precipitate various skin reactions through autonomic arousal (Pinkerton et al., 1982).

The ANS mediates external and internal stimuli into experienced emotionality, affecting various cutaneous components such as vascular blood flow and sweat glands. Some of the more common emotionally induced skin reactions include *blushing*—a reddening of the skin surface of the face and neck caused by dilatation of cutaneous blood vessels, *pallor* —a paling or whitening of the skin surface caused by constriction of cutaneous blood vessels, and *perspiration*—the exudation of fluid by the sweat glands. It has been shown that perspiration directly affects the electrodermal response, which is a change in resistance of the skin to the passage of an electrical current. This phenomenon, the galvanic skin response (GSR), is considered to be an indicator of emotional activity and is familiar to psychologists (Pinkerton et al., 1982).

PSYCHOLOGICAL FACTORS

The importance of psychological factors in dermatological conditions is illustrated in several studies. Sanborn, Sanborn, Cimbolic, and Niswander (1972) found that 2.7% of admissions to a U.S. Veterans Affairs hospital were for skin disorders. They found that 6 of 64 patients (9.4%) who had committed suicide experienced dermatological disorders and associated anxiety and depression. The authors also reported that the occurrence of dermatological flare-ups were associated with emotional distress for these patients.

Gould and Gragg (1983) examined the incidence of psychiatric disorders in 60 patients admitted to a dermatology–psychiatry liaison clinic and found the three most common psychiatric diagnoses were depression, anxiety, and obsessive–compulsive disorder (OCD). The investigators did not use any structured interviews, report reliability checks on their diagnoses (either dermatological or psychiatric), or use standardized psychological tests.

However, Hatch, Paradis, Friedman, Popkin, and Shalita (1992) evaluated 34 patients with dermatological problems with a structured psychiatric interview. The patients were diagnosed with several pruritic or itching conditions (i.e., atopic dermatitis [AD], eczema, psoriasis, and prurigo nodularis). Twenty-six percent of the patients had one or more anxiety disorders. Of five patients (14%) diagnosed with OCD, four of them had contamination obsessions, with washing as their primary obsessive–compulsive problem. They described washing anywhere from 1 to 12 hours per day, often using abrasive cleansers that affected their dermatological conditions. Of the five patients with OCD, one patient had panic disorder and generalized anxiety disorder (GAD) and one had GAD only. Two of these patients had a primary diagnosis of panic disorder, one had GAD, and one had posttraumatic stress disorder. This study suggests that many patients with anxiety disorders, especially OCD, are seeking care from dermatologists.

Skin disease can also be associated with severe emotional reactions and functional handicaps. Jowett and Ryan (1985) analyzed the effects of three skin disorders on patients' overall emotional, social, and functional relationships. Using a semistructured interview, they interviewed 100 patients older than age 16 years who had experienced dermatological disorders for at least 12 months. Patients included 30 with acne, 38 with psoriasis, and 32 with eczema. Eighty-two percent of the patients had noticeable skin lesions on their faces, hands, and other visible areas. In terms of psychiatric dysfunction, 61% of the patients experienced anxiety and 27% experienced depression. In addition, 64% of the patients reported that their skin conditions adversely affected their socioeconomic activities, and 40% said that their social life was adversely affected as well. Forty-seven percent of the patients with eczema, 3% with acne, and 26% with psoriasis reported family discord. The authors found 80% of the patients reported severe shame and embarrassment, but those patients who developed their skin condition later in life or developed it during infancy reported less shame and embarrassment.

These data suggest that psychological disturbances are prevalent in patients with dermatological problems but may be rarely diagnosed, treated, or referred for psychological treatment (Friedman, Hatch, & Paradis, 1993). Patients with dermatological problems may be reluctant to take a referral to a mental health professional because of the significant stigma associated with mental illness. Such patients prefer to consult a dermatologist and define themselves as having a medical condition rather than a psychological disorder. In addition, dermatologists may lack sufficient understanding of the role of health psychologists in the assessment and treatment of their patients or the role psychological factors play in the etiology and maintenance of dermatological diseases. To this end, one goal of this chapter is to familiarize the health psychologist with the range of disorders that are treated by dermatologists and influenced by psychological factors.

MODELS OF PSYCHOSOMATIC DERMATOLOGICAL DISORDERS

Three basic theories have influenced the understanding of the etiology and course of psychosomatic dermatological diseases. These include (a) the psychoanalytic model, (b) the behavioral model, and (c) the diathesis–stress model.

Freud and his followers in the psychoanalytic movement viewed psychosomatic conditions as the outward expression of inner conflict (Koblenzer, 1987). For example, conversion symptoms were viewed as a representation of the patient's unconscious conflicts and the compromise made when unacceptable thoughts or wishes were repressed. The location of the dermatological lesion was hypothesized as having symbolic meaning for the patient; for example, dermatitis on the hand could reflect a possible conflict about masturbation. Although the psychoanalytic approach has been both the oldest and most dominant approach in the literature, few if any empirical or experimental studies have validated these theories (Friedman et al., 1993).

The second important model of psychosomatic disorders, the behavioral model, has focused more on the course of a dermatological disorder than on its etiology. In this model, psychosomatic dermatological conditions are thought to be influenced by learning principles and reinforcement of maladaptive behaviors. Much of the research on this approach has focused on patients who scratch compulsively (Friedman et al., 1993). Welkowitz, Held, and Held (1989) described a multicomponent behavioral program to reduce the frequency of scratching in a patient with neurotic excoriation. The program included self-monitoring procedures such as daily records designed to separate automatic behavior—scratching—from its controlling stimuli. Ratliff and Stein (1968) used aversive procedures (i.e., electric shock and verbal yells) to treat excessive scratching and used progressive relaxation as a competing response. Friedman et al. (1993) noted that the limits of the behavioral approach include that they have consisted mostly of case studies with little or no follow-up. They also noted that, although behavioral therapy has guided many interventions, it does not offer a comprehensive approach to understanding the etiology of these disorders.

The third model is the diathesis–stress model. According to this model, genetically vulnerable individuals may develop dermatological diseases under specific conditions such as exposure to allergens and psychosocial stressors (Arnetz, Fjellner, Eneroth, & Kallner, 1991). Stress can alter physiological processes and lead to disease. Stress may be categorized as resulting from major life events (e.g., marriage, divorce, death of a loved one) or an excess of minor events (i.e., daily hassles). However, research to date has tended to focus on measuring stress levels and the way various stressors may affect bodily processes and influence the onset and course of certain dermatological disorders.

Stress has been shown to affect bodily processes, causing increased sympathetic arousal, peripheral vascular changes, release of histamine into the skin, and a lowered itch threshold (Fjellner & Arnetz, 1985). Arnetz et al. (1991) compared patients with psoriasis and AD with control patients on a test of skin reactivity within each group. They found there were individual variations, rather than group differences in dermatological reactivity, within each group. For example, skin reactivity seemed to be associated more with the differences in coping style and mood than with specific dermatological conditions. Although various bodily changes have been linked to stress, no long-term prospective studies link stress with a specific dermatological disease (Friedman et al., 1993).

Other clinicians have linked psychosocial stress with the onset and course of psoriasis and AD. Faulstich, Williamson, Duchman, Conerly, and Brantley (1985) hypothesized that flares of AD resulted from stress. Graham and Wolf (1953) found that emotional stress causes blood vessel dilation, which they hypothesized could lead to the onset of eczema, hives, or pruritus.

Another link between mind and body has been shown with hypnosis, which aids in the treatment of viral warts, dermatitis, and hives (Surman, Gottlieb, Hackett, & Silverberg, 1973). Hypnotic inhibition of the flare reaction to a histamine prick test and of pain perception (Zachariare & Bjerring, 1990) further suggests that stress may not only lead to changes in bodily processes and itch perception but also to changes in immune functioning, inflammation, and pain processes as well.

CLASSIFICATION OF DISORDERS

Despite previous arbitrary attempts to classify skin disorders in which psychological factors are involved, Koblenzer (1987) proposed a three-part classification system that is based on presumed common etiology, with categories including (a) conditions that are strictly psychological in origin (e.g., dermatitis artefacta, neurotic excoriations, prurigo nodularis), (b) dermatological conditions that, although initially caused by biological or environmental factors, are believed to be perpetuated by psychological factors (e.g., urticaria [hives], alopecia [hair loss], hyperhidrosis [excessive sweating], erythema [blushing]), and (c) conditions dependent on both genetic or environmental factors and stress factors (e.g., AD [eczema], psoriasis, acne). This chapter includes discussions of skin diseases from the 9th revision of the *International Classification of Diseases* (*ICD–9*; 1996). Discussions have been limited to diseases with relevant research on the role of health psychology. Disorders involving solely psychological conditions are thoroughly reviewed by Friedman et al. (1993). The conditions include several pruritic disorders (reviewed later in this chapter) and several other conditions, including parasitosis (delusions about skin infestation of parasites), body dysmorphic disorders (dermatological hypochondriasis), trichotillomania (pulling of hair resulting in hair loss), and psychogenic pain syndromes such as glossodynia (painful tongue) and glossopyrosis (burning tongue). Although these conditions are not classified in the *ICD* codes for skin disorders and are classified as mental disorders (see chapter 5, in this volume), clinical health psychologists often receive referrals from dermatologists who have attempted to treat these disorders. Reviews indicate that behavior modification approaches help control trichotillomania (Friman, Finney, & Christopherson, 1984); the use of neuroleptics assist in the control of parasitosis, and serotoninergic agents control body dysmorphic disorders (Friedman et al., 1993). Rumsey (1997) provided an in-depth review of issues involving facial scarring and facial disfigurement and outlined a cognitive problem-solving approach for patients and their families with these unique dermatological problems.

In the following sections, each disorder is defined and listed according to the *ICD–9*. The contributions of health psychology in assessment and treatment are presented. Limited empirically or experimentally collected evidence is available. Dermatological disorders have often been defined in idiosyncratic ways. Standardized assessment tools have not been developed for either the medical and dermatological or psychological aspects of skin disorders, and the treatment literature consists mostly of unreplicated clinical single cases with little follow-up and poor controls. Nevertheless, enough data exist to suggest that clinical health psychology interventions can affect the etiology and course of skin disorders.

PRURITUS

Pruritus refers to the conditions that are characterized by itching, scratching, or rubbing, often to the degree of a compulsion, as the primary symptoms. Itching is associated with the corticothalamic pain system. There exist subliminal stimuli, which evoke itching outside consciousness, and liminal stimuli, in which the afferent pathways are sensorial. Medical scientists lack sufficient knowledge about the way itching develops, the way it is experienced, and the reason it finally ends. However, like pain perception, clear individual differences may exist for the itching perception threshold. Pruritus often plays a role in many dermatological disorders (e.g., eczema, psoriasis), but it can also be an isolated condition.

Other medical disorders that can cause itching include diabetes mellitus, nephritis, gout, liver disease, leukemia, and Hodgkin's disease. Itching can also be caused by pregnancy and senility (Musaph, 1977). It is clear from this list that it is crucial for dermatologists to rule out all possible medical etiologies of any pruritic condition. It is also crucial that health psychologists have a close working relationship with dermatologists and understand the terms used in the specialty. In this section, several pruritic disorders with clear psychological etiologies are described. These disorders are not caused by a medical condition.

Neurotic Excoriations

Neurotic excoriations are characterized by skin lesions that develop because of severe burning or itching sensations that cause patients to knowingly and repetitively scratch themselves. Neurotic excoriations are typically reported in women in their 20s and 30s (Doran, Roy, & Wolkowitz, 1985). Lesions are frequently located on the upper body, face, legs, and arms. Doran et al. concluded that these patients have inhibited, repressed, and internally directed rage and difficulties overcoming problematic life situations. Psychoanalytic clinicians have long hypothesized that repressed rage and guilt feelings can trigger scratching and that the function of excessive scratching and the subsequent psychical damage is either self-punitive or a physiological release for psychological tension, such as rage, repression, or denial of needed love. However, in their thorough review of dermatological disorders, Friedman et al. (1993) found no empirical evidence to support this hypothesis.

Dermatitis Artefacta

Dermatitis artefacta involves self-inflicted dermatological lesions. Patients consciously or unconsciously withhold information about their behavior and strenuously deny to health care professionals that they are responsible for the lesions (Doran et al., 1985). The wide spectrum of symptoms range from unconscious picking at small skin irregularities to uncontrolled picking that causes severe lesions. These lesions often have a bizarre configuration and are confined to areas that are easily accessible to the hands. Clinically, it has been reported that if not actively psychotic, these patients have borderline personality structures (Friedman et al., 1993).

Sneddon and Sneddon (1975) reported a long-term follow-up study of 43 patients with dermatitis artefacta. Their sample consisted primarily of young women who had the dermatological disorder and many other psychogenic problems. Thirty percent of the patients in the study continued to injure themselves or were disabled as a result of other psychiatric disorders more than 12 years after the onset of dermatitis artefacta. When the patients recovered, the recovery was associated with a change in life circumstances rather than medical treatments, psychological treatments, or both.

Musaph (1977) presented two single-case studies of anogenital pruritus (itching in the genital areas); patients experienced itching long after the skin disorder was treated with medication. In lieu of any physical cause in either case, strong repressed emotions were hypothesized as the reason for the continuous itching. No treatment approach was attempted.

Prurigo Nodularis

Prurigo nodularis is characterized by itching lesions of single or multiple nodules of skin in a linear arrangement located predominantly on the extremities, especially on the anterior surface of the legs. The etiology of this disorder is obscure, although bouts of extreme pruritus occur when patients are under extreme emotional stress. Although medical treatments typically include corticosteroids, patients complain of physical exhaustion, so rest and nutrition are often additional treatments (Pinkerton et al., 1982).

Lamontagne (1978) treated a 61-year-old woman with a 25-year history of prurigo nodularis. Dermatological treatments alone were ineffective. The woman had insomnia because of the severe itching. Medications (diazepam, chlorpromazine, and trimeprazine) were used combined with autogenic relaxation training and electromyography (EMG) frontalis biofeedback. Relaxation training consisted of listening to a tape at home 30 minutes daily for 3 weeks. Practice continued in Weeks 4 through 6 without the tape. By the end of Week 6, EMG results improved, and pruritus and scratching decreased. An estimated 40% of the nodules were gone at the end of treatment and were still gone at the 6-month follow-up.

ATOPIC DERMATITIS

Occurrence and Etiology

AD, or *eczema*, the most common form of neurodermatitis, is characterized by itching (pruritus), erythema (redness), oozing and crusting, excoriation (skin loss caused by scratching), and lichenification (thickening of the skin). AD affects 7 to 24 people per 1,000 and accounts for 20% of all patients treated by dermatologists. Sleep problems often develop as a result of the itching. AD occurs in two clinical forms: infantile/child and adolescent/adult. The infantile/child form is characterized by blisters, oozing, and crusting with excoriation. The adolescent/adult form is characterized by marked dryness, thickening, excoriation, and possible scarring. The infantile/child form is found on the face, scalp, arms, and legs. The adolescent/adult form is distributed on the elbows and knees, hands and feet, and ears. Other terms for this disorder include *neurodermatitis*, *prurigo*, and *atopic eczema* (Friedman et al., 1993).

The prognosis of AD has been primarily examined in cross-section studies of risk factors and a limited number of longitudinal or follow-up studies. For example, Vickers (1980) studied 2,000 children for 2 to 21 years and had excellent response rates to his survey. He found that for this sample, AD cleared up in about 90% of cases and recurred in about 7%. Such factors as severity of the AD, birth order, method of infant feeding, and other allergies had no prognostic value. Early onset, patterns of spread, and being male seemed to be better prognostic signs. Late onset, AD on elbows and knees as well as on wrists and hands, comorbid asthma, severity of itching, and poor socioeconomic status seemed to negatively affect prognosis. Vickers offered no theoretical discussion for his findings.

Sleep disturbances may be an issue in those with severe AD; patients with itching tend to have a pattern of light, interrupted sleep (Charman & Horne, 1997). Although sleep patterns in patients with AD resemble those of patients with depression and generalized emotional constriction, scratching behavior may certainly arouse patients with AD from deeper stages of sleep (Tantum, Kalvey, & Brown, 1982). Jordan and Whitlock (1974) demonstrated that patients with AD developed a conditioned itch–scratch response more readily than control patients, and these responses were not quickly extinguished.

It seems that the chronicity of AD is perpetuated by the habit of scratching, which could be brought on by stress and anxiety. Other etiologies are thought to be antigen–antibody reactions and external irritants. Determination of the specific causes is influenced by the age of the patient, the season, and local milieu. Sensitization to foods and inhalants and bacteria and fungi are common in middle-age patients. With older patients the chief causes include focal infections, psychosomatic disorders, and metabolic abnormalities (Pinkerton et al., 1982).

The course of AD varies from mild, single episodes to severe, chronic, recurrent episodes. The infantile form usually becomes milder or disappears after the age of 3 or 4. At puberty and in the late teenage years, recurrences can occur. Of patients with AD, 30% eventually develop allergic asthma or rhinitis (hay fever). Such patients usually have a family history of AD, asthma, or rhinitis. AD is usually worse in the winter because of the decrease in humidity. Wool and lanolin commonly irritate the skin of patients with AD, and food allergies can affect them as well (Pinkerton et al., 1982).

Medical treatment for AD usually involves antihistamines, calcium gluconate injections, medicated gauze compresses, and corticosteroids. Prolonged use of steroids may cause immunosuppression and further skin damage. Drug therapy improves about 50% of cases of AD; most medications, except for those for AD exacerbations, are palliative. These medications do not tend to break the vicious cycle of tension–skin irritation/irritation–skin irritation–tension that is common among patients with AD (Charman & Horne, 1997).

Psychological Antecedents

Brown (1967) found patients with AD reported significantly more separation experiences in the year previous to the onset of their symptoms compared with a control sample of dental patients. Of the patients with AD, 48% had experienced severe shock, worry, or emotional upset in the 6 months preceding the onset of AD. The AD group also reported significantly more frustration and anger when under stress as compared with the control group. This finding suggests that a combination of both objective life situations and reaction to stress generated by these situations may relate to AD.

Similarly, an early study using a large sample of patients with AD (n = 100) found that more than 70% reported antecedent emotional stressors related to AD onset (Wittkower & Russell, 1953). Two more studies reported higher state and trait anxiety ratings for patients with AD compared with clinical groups and groups with no disease (Faultisch et al., 1985; Garrie, Garrie, & Mote, 1974). However, these studies would have been more useful if they had used dermatological disorder controls that had a biological etiology such as fungal infection (Friedman et al., 1993).

It has been speculated that emotional reactions in those with dermatological conditions such as AD may lead to altered autonomic activity, resulting in peripheral vascular changes and a lowering or raising of itch thresholds, leading to the vicious itch–scratch cycle. Jordan and Whitlock (1974) tested this hypothesis with 18 patients with AD, using a classical conditioning paradigm in which an itch stimulus was applied to each person's hand, and the skin reaction (GSR) and scratching behaviors were measured to determine itch thresholds. Results indicated that patients with dermatological problems developed a conditioned scratch response much sooner than healthy control patients, supporting the hypothesis that stress and anxiety may mediate AD.

It has long been hypothesized in the clinical literature that environmental factors are especially important variables in childhood dermatological disorders. Clearly, dermatological disorders developing in childhood and adolescence have a great potential to inhibit normal developmental processes. A comprehensive review and assessment of childhood dermatological disorders is beyond the scope of this chapter, but some relevant findings are worth noting.

Gil et al. (1988) provided support for the idea that environment and social learning are important in the maintenance of scratching behavior. In the presence of one parent, the authors examined the scratching behavior of 33 children with severe AD using an observational system that recorded scratching requests, actual behaviors of the child and parent, and parental prevention of scratching. Results indicated that parent behavior predicts a large and significant amount of variance in scratching-related behaviors, even after controlling for demographic and medical status variables. Parental attention, which was typically provided after the child scratched, seemed to reinforce scratching behavior. This was true even when the attention was in the form of scratching prevention. In contrast, noncontingent attention was related to a lower incidence of scratching.

Gil and Sampson (1989) also examined the relationship of stress and family environment to symptom severity in children with AD. Chronic problems associated with AD, such as lifestyle adjustments (e.g., not being able to eat certain foods) and home treatments (e.g., taking frequent baths), were found to be strongly related to AD symptom severity. Children from well-organized families that allowed their members to be relatively autonomous had fewer and less severe dermatological symptoms than children in enmeshed and chaotic families. The authors speculated that some families' emphasis on self-reliance, planning, and regular routines may serve as a buffer against stress for children with AD. Compliance with treatment recommendations also seemed greater in such families (Friedman et al., 1993).

Interventions

Insight-oriented and behavioral therapies for patients with AD have been studied. Brown and Bettley (1971) randomly assigned 72 patients with AD to either a medication group or a medication and traditional psychotherapy group for 4 months. Psychotherapy consisted of a focused approach on awareness and verbalization of resentment and hostility, with an aim of changing life situations involving conflict and frustrations. Change in all groups was measured by the Cornell Medical Index (Brodman, Erdman, Lorge, Wolff, & Broadbent, 1949) and a symptom rating scale devised by the investigators. Although the difference between groups was not statistically significant in general, a subset of patients who received psychotherapy had significantly clearer skin than the patients who received medication alone. This subgroup included those whose onset of psychological symptoms occurred within 1 year of getting AD (i.e., those who had an emotional disturbance that was "highly relevant" to the AD) and those with high motivation for psychological treatment. These patients' improvements in psychological symptoms were maintained over a 14-month period. This study provides evidence of the effectiveness of psychological treatment for skin disorders that are linked to emotional disturbance, particularly when the disturbance is temporally related to the dermatological condition and the patient is amenable to this type of treatment (Friedman et al., 1993).

Cataldo, Varni, Russo, and Estes (1980) successfully used a combination of techniques, including verbal remedies, incompatible responses, distraction, and differential social attention from the therapist, to treat a patient with chronic dermatitis. Allen and Harris (1966) successfully trained a mother to use reinforcement procedures to eliminate her 5-year-old daughter's scratching. The child's body had no sores after 6 weeks and at a 4-month follow-up. Manuso (1977) reported success in treating a 60-year-old woman with chronic AD on her hands by using biofeedback-assisted vasodilation training. However, all these single-case studies lacked random assignments to well-defined treatment protocols, checks on the reliability of ratings to control for potential investigator bias, and adequate follow-up. Additional single-case studies were reviewed by Pinkerton et al. (1982).

Haynes, Wilson, Jaffe, and Britton (1979) studied 12 patients with AD who received frontal EMG biofeedback and relaxation training. Patients were exposed to a no-treatment baseline, a phase using nonspecific treatment factors (listening to a tone in the biofeedback room), and relaxation training with EMG biofeedback. Photo analysis of the skin, which consisted of subjective severity ratings by two independent raters and an inch-by-inch determination of affected skin before and after treatment, revealed significant decreases in dermatological problems. Ratings of itching levels decreased within but not across treatment sessions. Haynes et al. interpreted their findings as offering mixed support for the hypothesis that AD is amenable to psychobiological procedures. Their study is also important in that they carefully assessed actual skin changes reliably and objectively. Unfortunately, subsequent studies have not used this type of well-controlled methodology.

ERYTHEMATOUS CONDITIONS

General Factors

Erythema (blushing) is a dermatological condition characterized by persistent redness of the cheeks, neck, and chest. It occurs only in White people and is seen in people of all ages from adolescents to older adults.

Psychological factors are strongly implicated in symptomatic erythema. Clinicians who work with patients with symptomatic erythema describe them as having psychological problems similar to those of patients with hyperhidrosis (excessive sweating), which is discussed later in this chapter. The patients have been described as socially phobic and inhibited, and they have difficulty describing emotions (Friedman et al., 1993). Initially caused by biological or environmental factors, symptomatic erythema can be perpetuated by psychological factors. Erythematous conditions are common in patients with specific dermatological disorders such as rosacea, lupus erythematosus, actinic reticuloid, and psoriasis.

Interventions

Bar and Kuypers (1973) have shown the usefulness of a paradoxical approach to erythema. Patients were instructed to try to blush as many times as possible, and the reports suggest that patients were able to voluntarily control previously involuntary blushing. In a single-case report with a 6-month follow-up, Gibbs (1969) described the successful use of assertiveness training and interpersonal skills training to control blushing. No further controlled studies have been carried out on this disorder.

PSORIASIS

Prevalence

Psoriasis is a chronic, noncontagious skin disease characterized by thick, dry, red patches of skin covered by shiny or grayish-white scales. These skin plaques, which result from an abnormal proliferation of epidermal cells, often hurt and itch and occasionally bleed (Zanolli, 1990). Psoriasis can severely affect an individual's physical, psychological, and social functioning (Rapp et al., 1996), and these difficulties are often exacerbated by medical treatments for the disease, many of which are inconvenient, messy, or odoriferous (Leary, Rapp, Herbst, Exum, & Feldman, 1998).

The prevalence in the general population varies geographically from 1% to 2.8% and is estimated to affect 1 to 3 million people in the United States. Approximately 30% of monozygotic twins have psoriasis. Environmental and genetic factors are believed to cause the disorder. In 60% of the cases reported, psoriasis begins before age 30 and is found equally in men and women, but it is rare in children younger than age 15 years (Friedman et al., 1993).

Psychosocial Factors

In an examination of psychosocial factors in psoriasis, Gupta et al. (1988, 1989) studied the psychocutaneous characteristics of patients who reported that stress exacerbated their disorder. Compared with a group of patients with psoriasis who reported that stress was not a factor in their illness, the high-stress reactors had a more clinically disfiguring disease and more frequent flare-ups. These patients were judged to rely more on the approval of others and experience more stress related to having psoriasis.

Most attempts to delineate specific personality characteristics with psoriasis have failed to yield significant results. Summarizing these studies, Friedman et al. (1993) found that patients with psoriasis had high levels of aggression, depression, anxiety, and obsessiveness. From their thorough review, the authors concluded that some of the abnormal psychological characteristics reported in patients with psoriasis are typical reactions to any chronic, cosmetically disfiguring disease.

In addition to coping with the physical discomforts of psoriasis and its treatment, patients must also contend with the reactions of others to their skin lesions. Indeed, patients in one study ranked "embarrassment over one's appearance" as the worst thing about having psoriasis (Baughman & Sobel, 1970), and 90% of a sample of outpatients with psoriasis reported experiencing shame and embarrassment because of their skin appearance (Jowett & Ryan, 1985). Of the inpatients with psoriasis studied by Ramsey and O'Reagan (1988), 50% reported that psoriasis had interfered with sexual relationships, and 84% of Jobling's (1976) sample reported having trouble forming social relationships. Most startling, 19% of the patients in one study reported incidents of blatant rejection in which they were asked to leave a restaurant, swimming pool, health club, hairdresser, or other public place (Ginsburg & Link, 1993). As a result, many people with psoriasis avoid activities that expose their lesions, such as swimming and sunbathing, even though exposure to the sun's ultraviolet radiation is known to improve psoriasis (Ramsey & O'Reagan, 1988).

Given that the psychological distress reported by patients with psoriasis seems to be tied to their concerns about how they are perceived and evaluated by other people, a fear of negative evaluation seems to be important to understanding reactions to psoriasis. Indeed, Leary et al. (1998) demonstrated that psoriasis severity and fear of negative evaluation predicted perceptions of being stigmatized, interpersonal discomfort, distress regarding observable symptoms of the disease, and the degree to which psoriasis interfered with the quality of life of 318 patients with psoriasis.

Interventions

Using a single subject design, Waxman (1973) examined treatments including hypnosis, relaxation, insight therapy, and behavioral techniques (counterconditioning and assertiveness training) for a 38-year-old woman with a 10-year history of psoriasis. Although he reported disappearance of the psoriasis and improvement in psychological functioning, the author was not able to identify the improving factor in treatment because of the research design.

To determine effective treatment, Gaston, Crombez, Lassorde, Bernier-Buzzanga, and Hodgins (1991) used a time-series research design to assign 18 patients with psoriasis to one of four groups: meditation, meditation plus imagery, waiting-list, and no treatment control. Treatment lasted 12 weeks, with 4-week prebaseline and postbaseline periods. The severity of psoriasis was determined by a dermatologist on a four-point scale on three dimensions (thickness, erythema, and silvery plaques) and on the basis of the amount of the scalp covered with lesions. Results revealed a significant difference between the mean ratings of treatment and the control groups after treatment. No additional impact was associated with the use of imagery techniques. Patients' continuing use of dermatological medication while participating in the study was not found to be a significant factor in improvement. Despite the small sample size, this study's sound methodological design and adequate controls are good examples for future research.

In a rare study of group therapy with patients with dermatological problems, Bremer-Schulte, Cormane, Van Dijk, and Wuite (1985) investigated the effects of a 10-week group didactic program with 42 patients with psoriasis. The investigators also looked at differences using a trained patient and a professional as group coleaders. The group's treatment consisted of lectures, discussion, and relaxation and deep breathing exercises. The treatment focused on the following aspects of psoriasis: somatic information about causes and medical treatments, emotional consequences (e.g., anxiety, depression, shame), and social factors (e.g., lack of understanding by others, isolation). Compared with a group of waiting-list control individuals, the experimental group required significantly less medication, reported less shyness and shame, and rated their psoriasis less important in their daily lives. In addition, group participants developed better interaction and problem-solving skills. Follow-up data after two years showed an overall continuation of these effects. The authors also found the coleader format produced a better outcome than did formats with groups led by laypeople or professionals.

ALOPECIA

Alopecia, or hair loss, is a dermatological condition characterized by a single or multiple areas of nonscarring hair loss that affects the scalp, beard area, or other body areas (alopecia universalis). The onset of hair loss can be accompanied by increased hair shedding, or it can be slow or insidious. The classic lesion is round or oval. The skin surface may appear pink and be associated with itching, tingling, burning, or painful sensations. Alopecia varies greatly in etiology, response to treatment, and prognosis. It has been associated with endocrine disorders (i.e., hypothalamic dysfunction), oral infections, metabolic disorders, and sexually transmitted diseases (Friedman et al., 1993).

Alopecia begins at any age and affects men and women equally. The overall lifetime incidence is approximately 1.7%; the prevalence is estimated to be about 0.1%. About 30% of patients have a family history of alopecia. Multiple episodes, hair loss in addition to loss of scalp margins, and having an alopecia episode that has lasted more than 2 years are all correlated with poor prognosis. Medical treatment typically involves topical steroids, corticosteroids, and cyclosporine (Folks & Kinney, 1995).

Etiological Factors

The exact etiology of alopecia is still unknown. Many dermatologists believe alopecia is an autoimmune disease. However, a major subset of people with alopecia has a primarily psychosomatic cause, such as stressful life events and premorbid personality factors. Folks and Kinney (1995) supported a diathesis–stress model in the etiology of alopecia. The authors hypothesized that fewer catecholamines, initially produced by and maintained by stress, are broken down, resulting in a larger quantity of certain catecholamines free to act and cause enzymatic destabilization, resulting in alopecia.

Lyketsos, Stratigos, Tawil, Psaras, and Lyketsos (1985) performed a well-controlled study of 26 patients diagnosed with alopecia and urticaria (which is discussed later in this chapter). The study involved a large sample group, included appropriate controls, and used reliable psychological measures. The study included 38 nonpsychosomatic patients with dermatological problems and patients with conditions such as herpes zoster, genital warts, chicken pox, and impetigo as a control group. The results indicated that patients with alopecia had significantly lower scores on measures of dominance and higher scores on measures of extrapunitiveness, intrapunitiveness, anxiety, and depression when compared with the control group.

Perini et al. (1984) compared the life circumstances of 48 patients with alopecia, 30 patients with common baldness, and 30 patients with fungal infections. Life events were measured by the Paykel Revised Interview for Recent Events (Paykel, Emms, Fletcher, & Rassaby, 1980), which included 64 life events and was administered in a semistructured interview. Events were recorded only when they occurred 6 months before the onset of various dermatological conditions. Patients with alopecia experienced significantly more life events than patients with common baldness and fungal infections. Life events included losses of loved ones, marital problems, car accidents, and financial difficulties. The authors hypothesized that alopecia resulted from stress, which in turn affected immune functions.

These studies support the notion that although initially caused by biological or environmental factors, urticaria (hives), hyperhidrosis (excessive sweating), and symptomatic erythema (blushing) can be perpetuated by psychological factors. No empirical studies on psychological interventions with alopecia were found.

HYPERHIDROSIS

General Factors

Hyperhidrosis (excessive sweating) typically occurs on the palms, soles, and armpits but can be generalized over the entire body. It is associated with physiological activity, climactic conditions, emotional arousal (i.e., shame, anxiety), and the ingestion of certain foods and medications. Individuals with this disorder may experience excessive sweating of the forehead, upper lip, or sternal region a few moments after eating spicy foods, chocolate, or tomato sauce or after drinking tea. Patients with hyperhidrosis often fear physical intimacy and other physical contact such as handshakes. Congenital factors involving functional or physiological disturbances of the central nervous system, dysfunction of internal secretion glands, obesity, poor circulation, and allergies have been shown to contribute to this disorder. Medical treatment has involved reserpine, x-rays, a bland diet, exercise moderation, tonic baths containing sea salt or alum, prepared lotions, creams and dusting powders, and surgery involving severing nerves (Pinkerton et al., 1982). Hyperhidrosis affects 1 in 200 people in the general population (Friedman et al., 1993).

Interventions

Most of the research on hyperhidrosis is limited to single-case treatment studies. Lerer and Jacobowitz (1981) described the psychological treatment of a 19-year-old woman who had experienced hyperhidrosis since age 5. Results of psychological testing indicated that before treatment she experienced excessive anxiety, fearfulness, and difficulty in interpersonal relationships and coping, in addition to deficits in ego functioning and a hysterical personality organization. After insight-oriented psychotherapy, testing indicated that she had decreased anxiety and aggression and improved assertiveness and coping skills. Two, 12-month follow-up measures revealed that she continued to show clinical improvements in hyperhidrosis and psychological symptoms.

Bar and Kuypers (1973) used assertiveness training and desensitization to assist another 19-year-old woman with severe palmar hyperhidrosis that had lasted for several years. She had a history of feeling rejected and found it difficult to express negative feelings. Her low self-esteem produced anxiety in social situations that produced severe sweating in her palms. Although palmar sweating did not cease altogether, assertiveness training and desensitization aided in remission of the hyperhidrosis. A 12-month follow-up revealed control of the hyperhidrosis and no relapse of the former behavior pattern.

Based on studies that demonstrated the effectiveness of instrumental conditioning in lowering the rate of sweating in normal participants, Koblenzer (1987) recommended the use of GSR biofeedback techniques and psychotherapy for patients with hyperhidrosis. However, controlled studies documenting the effectiveness of biofeedback techniques with this clinical sample do not seem to exist.

ACNE

Etiology and Psychological Factors

The term *acne* is used in conjunction with at least 10 types of conditions, referring to the size, shape, color, and extent of pimples (papules). The most common forms of acne are acne vulgaris, which begins in puberty, and acne rosacea, which involves adult-onset acne. Severe acne vulgaris is found in 0.5% to 7% of adolescents. The effects of acne on psychological states vary extensively and are often mediated by severity of the disease, coping ability, age, family and peer support systems, and the patient's perception of the disease (Fried & Shalita, 1992).

Studies have documented the fact that acne may significantly interfere with social activities, such as dating and sports participation, academic functioning, and unemployment among adolescents (Jowett & Ryan, 1985). Perhaps related to social impairments, a correlation has been found between acne severity and the extent of self-image impairment (Wu, Kinder, Trunnel, & Fulton, 1988) and clinical depression (Cunliffe, Hull, & Hughes, 1989). In addition, several well-controlled studies reviewed by Friedman et al. (1993) have shown increased levels of anxiety and anger in patients with acne when compared with patients with erythematosus but no other skin condition.

Interventions

The sparse research on psychological treatment for severe acne has focused on stress reduction techniques. For example, Hughes, Brown, Lawlis, and Fulton (1983) successfully used a combination of biofeedback, relaxation techniques, and cognitive imagery to treat a single case of severe acne. Using a multiple baseline design, they showed that patients experienced increased acne severity when the relaxation component was temporarily suspended.

Like psoriasis and AD, acne can be considered a pruritic skin disorder dependent on both genetic–environmental and stress factors. Research on these conditions tends to be more methodologically sound than research of other dermatological disorders, which likely reflects the greater interest and longer history of research on acne (Friedman et al., 1993). However, an important task for health psychologists working with people with dermatological disorders remains the development of reliable and valid assessment instruments.

URTICARIA

Urticaria (hives) is a dermatological condition characterized by white or red wheals and slightly elevated papules or welts that are usually surrounded by a halo and associated with itching, stinging, and prickling sensations. The commonly affected areas are the torso, buttocks, and chest (Pinkerton et al., 1992). Acute cases may be mild, have a gradual onset, or have a sudden onset, but the condition usually disappears with or without treatment in a few hours or days. When symptoms occur daily and extend beyond a few weeks, the condition may be considered to be influenced by psychological factors. The chronic form (symptoms persisting for more than 8 weeks) has remissions and exacerbations for months or years (Friedman et al., 1993). In the United States, 15% to 20% of the population, children and adults, experiences urticaria on at least one occasion (Folks & Kinney, 1995).

Urticaria can have an allergic or a nonallergic basis. Allergic causes include infections, food, drugs, inhaled pollen or dust, and physical stressors such as cold water, heat, and ultraviolet radiation. Nonallergic causes of what is often termed *cholinergic urticaria* include psychological stress, endocrine imbalance, exercise, and warming of the body. Chronic urticaria is difficult to treat. The removal of focal infections, control of psychological stressors, and relief of fatigue are important treatments. Other medical treatments include a variety of pharmacological remedies, tepid or cold baths, and ice-cold compresses. The use of local antipruritic lotions and antihistamine drugs often relieves the itching and stinging (Pinkerton et al., 1992). Tricyclic antidepressants such as doxepin are used by dermatologists for the treatment of chronic urticaria (Folks & Kinney, 1995).

Etiological Factors

Lyketsos et al. (1985) studied 28 patients diagnosed with nonallergenic and noninfectious urticaria and compared them with a control group of 38 nonpsychosomatic patients with dermatological problems who were diagnosed with conditions such as herpes zoster, genital warts, chicken pox, or impetigo. The results indicated that the patients with urticaria scored significantly lower than the control group on measures of dominance and higher on measures of extrapunitiveness, intrapunitiveness, anxiety, and depression. Werth (1978) examined the relationship between emotional conflict and recurrent urticaria in five patients. She concluded the patients' outbreaks of urticaria were related to experiencing an insoluble dilemma or conflict.

Interventions

Daniels (1973) treated a 23-year-old woman who had urticaria covering her face and entire body and who also had interpersonal problems with her husband and in-laws. She was trained in deep muscle relaxation with accompanying anxiety hierarchies pertaining to her relationship with her husband and family. Hypnosis was also used to reduce her anxiety. Covert reinforcement that was based on the woman's response to a reinforcement survey schedule was used. Her hives disappeared after 12 weeks and had not recurred after 23 months.

Keegan (1976) used a combination of approaches in treating four patients with urticaria. Treatment involved patient education about various physical and psychological etiologies: avoidance of specific allergens, use of antihistamines, short-term use of minor tranquilizers for anxiety, and a combination of problem-oriented psychotherapy, family therapy, hypnosis, and relaxation training. Three of the four patients had complete remission of their hives.

Moan (1979) used GSR-assisted relaxation and biofeedback in treating a 28-year-old woman's urticaria. It covered her entire body, and she had been affected for 3 years. During the 2 months preceding treatment, the hives occurred and subsided twice daily, lasting from 1 to 2 hours, and were correlated with perceived levels of anxiety by the patient. Treatment consisted of 8 weekly sessions of autogenic relaxation training with GSR biofeedback. When treatment was terminated, her skin level conductivity was reduced 8%, and her anxiety levels were reportedly decreased. She experienced no recurrence during the final 5 weeks of treatment and still had no hives at an 8-month follow-up.

In their review of the literature on psychological interventions with urticaria, Friedman et al. (1993) noted that most of the clinical data on urticaria have relied on clinical reports and case studies. These reports have significant limitations, including a failure to randomly choose patients, a lack of control groups, and evaluators who were not blind to diagnoses and hypotheses being tested.

FUTURE RESEARCH

Medical interventions have been widely considered to be the treatment of choice for dermatological conditions. However, a growing body of research suggests that the efficacy of current medical approaches is too often palliative, and the combination of medical and psychological approaches should be the treatment of choice (Faulstich & Williamson, 1985). Additional well-designed, sophisticated research is necessary to identify the kinds of psychological interventions that are effective for treating dermatological conditions and refine the interventions already in use.

Although psychological factors have long been implicated in the etiology, exacerbation of, and reaction to dermatological conditions, the current empirical evidence is modest at best (Friedman et al., 1993). Historically, approaches that have emphasized purely psychological (primarily psychodynamic or behavioral) or biological factors have failed to convincingly explain the onset, exacerbation, or alleviation of dermatological disorders and symptoms. The complexity of dermatological disorders requires an integrated, biopsychosocial approach that considers biological vulnerability, personality, individual coping styles, and familial support systems.

Clinical Implications

This chapter has shown that clinical health psychologists have much to offer patients with dermatological disorders. However, dermatologists may fail to recognize the importance of the effects of psychological stress and distress on their patients' symptoms. This may be a result of the dermatologists' inexperience with these issues, the orientation and focus solely on "disease states" in medical education, or office time constraints (Friedman et al., 1993).

Clinical health psychologists interested in dermatology would be in a better market niche if they were based in a dermatologist's office or clinic. As a member of the dermatology team, such close proximity could generate more referrals for the psychologists and possibly help patients overcome their resistance to being treated by a psychologist because of their medical diagnosis. Additional steps in overcoming this common problem in tertiary medical care are outlined by Rozensky, Sweet, and Tovian (1997).

Collaboration with the dermatologist also requires a familiarity with the wide range of dermatological disorders affected by psychological factors. Practical and timely solutions facilitate collaboration with physicians (Rozensky et al., 1997). The ability to offer a concise treatment plan for a specific behavior with a particular diagnosis is optimal. When discussing goals of psychological interventions with dermatologists, it is best to emphasize the attempt to lower, change, or control stress and problem behaviors using behavioral or stress–diathesis models rather than psychoanalytical paradigms.

The health care arena is undergoing radical economic change, so clinical health psychologists in dermatology must provide evidence of the efficacy and cost effectiveness of their assessments and interventions to patients and insurers. Support for the effectiveness of empirically based treatments could help accomplish this goal.

New areas of clinical intervention could involve prevention of skin diseases and skin cancer. For example, Mickler, Rodrigue, and Lescano (1999) examined various self-examination paradigms for early identification and treatment of skin cancer. Clinical health psychology, with its understanding of adherence, compliance, self-control, and behavior change, should continue to be involved in this crucial aspect of dermatology.

Research Implications

Health psychology researchers need to focus on understudied areas of dermatological disorders, taking life-span perspectives and highlighting ethnic and cultural issues. Research needs to focus on more biopsychosocial paradigms and comprehensive stress–diathesis models with skin diseases. Researchers cannot assume a linear relationship exists between biology and behavior or culture and behavior.

More controlled assessment and treatment studies with specificity and matching of patient variables to treatment outcome (e.g., outcome of contingency management of scratching behavior in highly anxious children with AD) are needed. Studies with better defined control groups, measures of dermatological change, intervention techniques, and follow-up are needed. Finally, psychological instruments that have standardized assessments normed with patients who have dermatological problems are needed. With such instruments, researchers and clinicians may be able to determine whether all patients with the same disorder (e.g., eczema) are necessarily the same.

CONCLUSION

Dermatological diseases are often caused by, exacerbated by, and result in numerous adverse psychological effects. Health psychologists have much to offer patients with skin diseases. In addition to providing a comprehensive understanding of the dermatological disease experience, health psychologists can be critical in the successful treatment of these conditions. Health psychologists need to continue to develop effective assessment and treatment modalities for the range of skin disorders and take the necessary steps to ensure that these skills are available and implemented. Such a strategy will have a major impact on countless patients and at the same time contribute to psychology, health, and medicine.

REFERENCES

Allen, K. E., & Harris, F. R. (1966). Elimination of a child's excessive scratching by training the mother in reinforcement procedures. *Behavior Research and Therapy, 4,* 79–84.

Arnetz, B. B., Fjellner, B. O., Eneroth, P., & Kallner, A. (1991). Endocrine and dermatological concomitants of mental stress. *Acta Dermato–Venereologica, 156,* 9–12.

Bar, L. H., & Kuypers, B. R. (1973). Behavior therapy in dermatological practice. *British Journal of Dermatology, 88,* 591–598.

Baughman, R. D., & Sobel, R. (1970). Psoriasis: A measure of severity. *Archives of Dermatology, 101,* 390–393.

Bremer-Schulte, M., Cormane, R. H., Van Dijk, E., & Wuite, J. (1985). Group therapy of psoriasis. *Journal of American Academy of Dermatology, 12,* 61–66.

Brodman, K., Erdman, A. J., Lorge, I., Wolff, H. G., & Broadbent, T. H. (1949). The Cornell Medical Index: An adjunct to medical interviewing. *Journal of the American Medical Association, 140,* 530–534.

Brown, D. G. (1967). Emotional disturbance in eczema: A study of symptom reporting behavior. *Journal of Psychosomatic Research, 11,* 27–40.

Brown, D. G., & Bettley, F. R. (1971). Psychiatric treatment of eczema: A controlled trial. *British Medical Journal, 2,* 729–734.

Cataldo, M. F., Varni, J. W., Russo, R. C., & Estes, S. A. (1980). Behavior therapy techniques in the treatment of dermatitis. *Archives of Dermatology, 116,* 919–922.

Charman, D., & Horne, D. L. (1997). Atopic dermatitis. In A. Baum, S. Newman, J. Weinman, R. West, & C. McManus (Eds.), *Cambridge handbook of psychology, health, and medicine* (pp. 372–375). Cambridge, England: Cambridge University.

Cunliffe, W. J., Hull, S. M., & Hughes, B. R. (1989). Psychiatric syndromes with dermatologic expression. *Clinics in Dermatology, 104,* 611–619.

Daniels, L. K. (1973). Treatment of urticaria and severe headache by behavior therapy. *Psychosomatics, 14,* 347–351.

Doran, A. R., Roy, A., & Wolkowitz, O. M. (1985). Self-destructive dermatoses. *Psychiatric Clinics of North America, 8,* 291–298.

Faulstich, M. E., & Williamson, D. A. (1985). An overview of atopic dermatitis: Toward a biobehavioral integration. *Journal of Psychosomatic Research, 29,* 647–654.

Faulstich, M. E., Williamson, D. A., Duchman, E. G., Conerly, S., & Brantley, P.

(1985). Psychophysiological analysis of atopic dermatitis. *Journal of Psychosomatic Research, 29,* 415–417.

Fjellner, B. O., & Arnetz, B. B. (1985). Psychological predictors of pruritus during mental stress. *Acta Dermato–Venereologica, 65,* 504–508.

Folks, D. G., & Kinney, F. C. (1995). Dermatologic conditions. In A. Stoudemire (Ed.), *Psychological factors affecting medical conditions* (pp. 123–140). Washington, DC: American Psychiatric Association.

Fried, R. G., & Shalita, A. R. (1992). The reciprocal interaction between acne and the psyche. *Focus on Cutis and Psyche, 2,* 28–33.

Friedman, S., Hatch, M., & Paradis, C. (1993). Dermatological disorders. In R. J. Gatchel & E. B. Blanchard (Eds.), *Psychophysiological disorders: Research and clinical applications* (pp. 205–244). Washington, DC: American Psychological Association.

Friman, P. C., Finney, J. W., & Christopherson, E. R. (1984). Behavioral treatment of trichotillomania: An evaluation review. *Behavior Therapy, 15,* 249–264.

Garrie, E. V., Garrie, S. A., & Mote, T. (1974). Anxiety and atopic dermatitis. *Journal of Consulting and Clinical Psychology, 42,* 742–753.

Gaston, L., Crombez, J., Lassorde, M., Bernier-Buzzanga, J., & Hodgins, S. (1991). Psychological stress and psoriasis: Experimental and prospective correlational studies. *Acta Dermato–Venereologica, 156,* 37–43.

Gibbs, D. (1969). Reciprocal inhibition therapy of a case of symptomatic erythema. *Behavior Research and Therapy, 3,* 261.

Gil, K. M., Keefe, F. J., Sampson, H. A., McCaskill, C. C., Rodin, J., & Crisson, J. E. (1988). Direct observation of scratching behavior in children with atopic dermatitis. *Behavior Therapy, 19,* 213–227.

Gil, K. M., & Sampson, H. A. (1989). Psychological and social factors of atopic dermatitis. *Allergy, 44,* 84–98.

Ginsburg, I. H., & Link, B. G. (1993). Psychosocial consequences of rejection and stigma feelings in psoriasis patients. *International Journal of Dermatology, 32,* 587–591.

Gould, W. M., & Gragg, T. M. (1983). A dermatology–psychiatry liaison clinic. *Journal of the American Academy of Dermatology, 9,* 73–77.

Graham, D. T., & Wolff, S. (1953). The relation of eczema to attitude and to vascular reaction of the human skin. *Journal of Clinical Medicine, 42,* 238–254.

Grossbart, T. A. (1993). The skin: Matters of the flesh. In D. Goleman & J. Gurin (Eds.), *Mind–body medicine: How to use your mind for better health* (pp. 145–160). New York: Consumer Reports.

Gupta, M. A., Gupta, A. K., Kirby, S., Schork, N. J., Gorr, S. K., Ellis, C. N., et al. (1989). A psychocutaneous profile of psoriasis patients who are stress reactors: A study of 127 patients. *General Hospital Psychiatry, 11,* 166–173.

Gupta, M. A., Gupta, A. K., Kirby, S., Weiner, H. K., Mace, T. M., Schork, N. J., et al. (1988). Pruritus in psoriasis: A prospective study of some psychiatric and dermatologic correlates. *Archives of Dermatology, 124,* 1052–1057.

Hatch, M. L., Paradis, C., Friedman, S., Popkin, M., & Shalita, A. R. (1992). Obsessive–compulsive disorder in patients with chronic pruritic conditions: Case studies and discussion. *Journal of the American Academy of Dermatology, 26*, 549–551.

Haynes, S. N., Wilson, C. C., Jaffe, P. G., & Britton, B. T. (1979). Biofeedback treatment of atopic dermatitis. *Biofeedback and Self-Regulation, 4*, 195–209.

Hughes, H., Brown, B. W., Lawlis, G. F., & Fulton, J. E. (1983). Treatment of acne vulgaris by biofeedback, relaxation and cognitive imagery. *Journal of Psychosomatic Research, 27*, 185–191.

International classification of diseases, 9th revision, clinical modification (4th ed.). (1996). Los Angeles, CA: Practice Management Information Corporation.

Jobling, R. G. (1976). Psoriasis—A preliminary questionnaire study of sufferer's subjective experience. *Clinical Experimental Dermatology, 1*, 233–236.

Jordan, J. M., & Whitlock, F. A. (1974). Atopic dermatitis anxiety and conditioned scratch responses in cases of atopic dermatitis. *British Journal of Dermatology, 86*, 574–585.

Jowett, S., & Ryan, T. (1985). Skin disease and handicap: An analysis of the impact of skin conditions. *Social Science and Medicine, 20*, 425–429.

Keegan, D. L. (1976). Chronic urticaria: Clinical psychophysiological and therapeutic aspects. *Psychosomatics, 17*, 160–163.

Koblenzer, C. S. (1987). *Psychocutaneous disease.* New York: Grune & Stratton.

Lamontagne, Y. (1978). Treatment of prurigo nodularis by relaxation and EMG biofeedback training. *Behavior Analysis and Modification, 8*, 246–249.

Leary, M. R., Rapp, S. R., Herbst, K. C., Exum, M. L., & Feldman, S. R. (1998). Interpersonal concerns and psychological difficulties of psoriasis patients: Effects of disease severity and fear of negative evaluation. *Health Psychology, 17*, 530–536.

Lerer, B., & Jacobowitz, J. (1981). Treatment of essential hyperhidrosis by psychotherapy. *Psychosomatics, 22*, 536–538.

Lyketsos, G. C., Stratigos, J., Tawil, G., Psaras, M., & Lyketsos, C. G. (1985). Hostile personality characteristics, dysthymic states and neurotic symptoms in urticaria, psoriasis, and alopecia. *Psychotherapy and Psychosomatics, 44*, 122–131.

Manuso, J. S. (1977). The use of biofeedback-assisted hand warming training in the treatment of chronic eczema dermatitis of the hands: A case study. *Journal of Behavioral Therapy and Experimental Psychiatry, 43*, 120–125.

Mickler, T. J., Rodrigue, J. R., & Lescano, C. M. (1999). A comparison of three methods of teaching skin self-examination. *Journal of Clinical Psychology in Medical Settings, 6*, 273–286.

Moan, E. R. (1979). GSR biofeedback assisted relaxation training and psychosomatic hives. *Journal of Behavior Therapy and Experimental Psychiatry, 10*, 157–158.

Musaph, H. (1977). Itching and other dermatoses. In E. P. Wittkower & H. Warnes

(Eds.), *Psychosomatic medicine: Its clinical applications* (pp. 307–316). New York: Harper and Row.

Paykel, E. S., Emms, E. M., Fletcher, J., & Rassaby, E. S. (1980). Life events and social support in puerperal depression. *British Journal of Psychiatry, 136,* 339–346.

Perini, G. I., Fornasa, C. V., Cipriani, R., Bettin, A., Zecchino, F., & Peserico, A. (1984). Life events and alopecia areata. *Psychotherapy Psychosomatics, 41,* 48–52.

Pinkerton, S., Hughes, H., & Wenrich, W. W. (1982). Skin disorders. In S. Pinkerton, H. Hughes, & W. W. Wenrich (Eds.), *Behavioral medicine: Clinical implications* (pp. 248–260). New York: Wiley.

Ramsey, B., & O'Reagan, M. (1988). A survey of the social and psychological effects of psoriasis. *British Journal of Dermatology, 118,* 195–201.

Rapp, S. R., Exum, M. L., Feldman, S. R., Reboussin, D., Fleisher, A., & Clarke, A. (1996). *Suicidal ideation, distress, and disability associated with psoriasis: A profile of high risk patients.* Manuscript submitted for publication, Department of Psychiatry and Behavioral Sciences, Bowman Gray School of Medicine, Wake Forest University, Winston-Salem.

Ratliff, R. G., & Stein, N. H. (1968). Treatment of neurodermatitis by behavior therapy: A case study. *Behavior Research and Therapy, 6,* 397–399.

Rozensky, R. H., Sweet, J. J., & Tovian, S. M. (1997). *Psychological assessment in medical settings.* New York: Plenum Press.

Rumsey, N. (1997). Dysmorphology and facial disfigurement. In A. Baum, S. Newman, J. Weinman, R. West, & C. McManus (Eds.), *Cambridge handbook of psychology, health and medicine* (pp. 450–452). Cambridge, England: Cambridge University.

Sanborn, P. E., Sanborn, C. J., Cimbolic, P., & Niswander, G. P. (1972). Suicide and stress-related dermatoses. *Behavior Research and Therapy, 19,* 313–318.

Sneddon, I., & Sneddon, J. (1975). Self-inflicted injury: A follow-up study of 43 patients. *British Medical Journal, 3,* 527–530.

Surman, O. S., Gottlieb, S. K., Hackett, T. P., & Silverberg, E. L. (1973). Hypnosis in the treatment of warts. *Archives of General Psychiatry, 28,* 439–441.

Tantum, D., Kalvey, R., & Brown, D. G. (1982). Sleep, scratching, and dreams in eczema. *Psychotherapy Psychosomatics, 37,* 26–38.

Vickers, C. H. (1980). The natural history of atopic eczema. *Acta Dermatologia Venereologia* (Suppl.), *92,* 113–115.

Waxman, D. (1973). Behavior therapy of psoriasis: A hypnoanalytic and counter-conditioning technique. *Postgraduate Medical Journal, 49,* 591–595.

Welkowitz, L. A., Held, J. L., & Held, A. L. (1989). Management of neurotic scratching with behavioral therapy. *Journal of the Academy of Dermatologists, 21,* 802–804.

Werth, G. R. (1978). The hives dilemma. *American Family Physician, 17,* 139–143.

Wittkower, E., & Russell, B. (1953). *Emotional factors in skin disease*. New York: Harper.

Wu, S. F., Kinder, B. N., Trunnel, T. N., & Fulton, J. E. (1988). Role of anxiety and anger in acne patients: A relationship with the severity of the disorder. *Journal of American Academy of Dermatology, 18*, 325–332.

Zachariare, R., & Bjerring, P. (1990). The effect of hypnotically induced analgesia on flare reaction of the cutaneous histamine prick test. *Archives of Dermatological Research, 282*, 539–543.

Zanolli, M. D. (1990). Psoriasis and Reiter's disease. In W. M. Sams & P. S. Lynch (Eds.), *Principles and practice of dermatology* (pp. 307–323). New York: Churchill-Livingstone.

13

RHEUMATIC DISEASES

BRUCE A. HUYSER AND JERRY C. PARKER

Diseases of the musculoskeletal system and connective tissue, or rheumatic diseases, are the most prevalent chronic conditions in the United States (Callahan, 1996). Moreover, the economic, social, and psychological consequences of rheumatic conditions are enormous (Yelin & Callahan, 1995). For example, rheumatic conditions are the leading cause of being absent from work, and they also have been associated with increased psychological distress, decreased functional abilities, and high utilization of medical services (Callahan, 1996). Given these wide-ranging implications, comprehensive understanding and treatment of rheumatic conditions requires a biopsychosocial perspective. As such, rheumatic diseases are an area in which health psychologists can play a pivotal role. The overarching purpose of this chapter is to promote a greater understanding of rheumatological disorders from a health psychology perspective.

Because it is important for psychologists in health care settings to have at least a rudimentary understanding of relevant medical conditions, the first section of this chapter provides a basic classification scheme for rheumatic conditions, in addition to an overview of prototypical disorders. The second section examines primary symptoms and correlates of rheumatic disease from a biopsychosocial perspective. The third main section addresses pertinent assessment and treatment issues. The final section briefly discusses areas of future research and clinical challenges.

BASIC DEFINITIONS AND PROTOTYPES

The rheumatic diseases represent a wide range of disorders. For example, the ninth revision of the *International Classification of Diseases, Clinical Modification* (*ICD–9–CM*; World Health Organization [WHO], 1989) includes more than 200 discrete disorders and many more subtypes under the general category of "diseases of the musculoskeletal system and connective tissue." In addition to commonly known arthropathies such as osteoarthritis (OA), this general category also includes acquired deformities and arthropathies associated with endocrine and metabolic disorders. Clearly, a discussion of all these specific diseases is beyond the scope of this chapter. Fortunately, numerous classification systems organize these myriad disorders into manageable categories. Because it is both simple and relatively comprehensive, this chapter adapts an eight-category scheme outlined by Fries (1995) and adds two, age-specific categories for children and older adults.

Overview of the Joint

Because many rheumatic diseases attack different parts of the joint, a brief overview of joint anatomy is warranted (see Figure 13.1). The two main types of joints in the human body are the synarthrodial and diarthrodial (or synovial) joints; the latter are of primary concern in rheumatic conditions. In diarthrodial joints the adjoining surfaces of bones are protected by cartilage, a virtually frictionless covering. A synovial membrane surrounds this joint space; the surrounding membrane contains synovial fluid, which lubricates cartilage surfaces. Ligaments, which are composed of fibrous tissue, connect bone to bone, thereby stabilizing joints. Finally, muscles taper down to form connective tissue, or tendons, which attach muscle to bone, generally just above or below the joint (Fries, 1995).

Synovitis: Inflammation of the Joint Membrane

Synovitis refers to inflammation of the synovial membrane. This class of disorders is characterized by red, warm, tender, or swollen joints. It affects women more than men, and it can occur at any age (Fries, 1995). The primary example of synovitis is rheumatoid arthritis (RA). Other disorders such as systemic lupus erythematosus (SLE) and psoriatic arthritis often have a synovitis component.

RA affects up to 2% of the U.S. population, with women three times

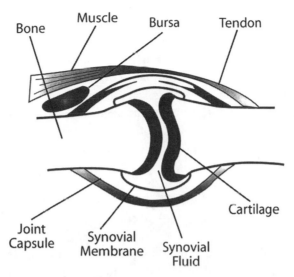

Figure 13.1. Major joint components. Different rheumatic conditions affect various parts of the joint. For example, cartilage degeneration characterizes osteoarthritis. Inflammation of the synovial membrane characterizes rheumatoid arthritis. Inflammation within the joint space characterizes both infectious arthritis and crystal-related conditions like gout. Inflammation of the tendon, where it connects to bone, characterizes ankylosing spondylitis. Inflammation of muscle fiber characterizes conditions like polymyalgia rheumatica. Finally, inflammation of the bursa, a small sac of tissue that eases muscle movement, characterizes bursitis.

more likely to be affected than men (Wilder, 1993). Although the etiology of RA is unclear, this disorder has an autoimmune component. Over time inflammatory processes can gradually digest cartilage and bone in affected joints. RA can attack any joint, although the wrists and knuckles are almost always affected, with the knees and feet often becoming involved as well. Generally, joints are affected bilaterally (Fries, 1995). Although synovitis is the hallmark feature of RA, other common symptoms include fatigue, muscle aches, and a low-grade fever. RA also can have systemic effects, including damage to the eyes, the nervous system, and the cardiovascular system. RA generally manifests in three patterns. The *monocyclic type* is characterized by its brief duration of no more than a few months and minimal disability. The *polycyclic type* is intermittent and usually causes little disfigurement or disability. The *chronic type* can be very debilitating; unfortunately, most individuals with RA have this type (Fries, 1995). Current pharmacological treatment of RA is often characterized by an early aggressive approach geared toward controlling the underlying synovitis (Pincus, 1996). To this end, drugs of choice are disease-modifying antirheumatic drugs (DMARDs) such as Plaquenil, gold shots, and methotrexate.

Spondyloarthropathies: Inflammation of the Joint Attachments

In *spondyloarthropathies*, the primary inflammation occurs in ligaments and tendons that attach to bones. Such conditions affect men more than women and typically begin between ages 15 and 40 (Fries, 1995). Ankylosing spondylitis (AS) is the prototypical spondyloarthropathy. Other examples include Reiter's syndrome, enteropathic arthritis (i.e., arthritis associated with inflammatory bowel disease), and psoriatic arthritis with a spinal component (Taurog, 1993).

AS generally affects the central parts of the body, causing pain and stiffness, particularly at the sacroiliac joints—the point at which the sacrum (at the bottom of the spine) is connected to the pelvic bones. AS typically affects young men and begins as an insidious low back pain that spreads to other fibrous joints, including rib–spine and rib–breastbone connections. After a period of pain and stiffness, a bony bridge often grows across affected joints, which fuses bones together but relieves pain. AS is usually a relatively minor condition, although it can cause serious disability in a minority of patients (Fries, 1995). It has no known cure, and management strategies focus on minimizing disability through exercise and pharmacological interventions such as indomethacin and naproxen to control inflammation and pain (Gall, 1996).

Crystal Arthritis: Inflammation in the Joint Space

In *crystal arthritis*, crystals form within the joint space or other connective tissues, causing painful inflammation. Crystal arthritis occurs more often in men than women and typically begins in middle or later years. The prime example, gout, is caused by uric acid crystals. A similar condition, pseudogout, is caused by calcium crystals (Schumacher, 1996).

Gout begins with an asymptomatic stage characterized by high blood levels of uric acid. In the second stage, acute gouty arthritis, a painful inflammatory reaction to crystals develops and then typically resolves within 2 weeks. Acute gout generally affects one joint at a time, usually the base of the great toe. The subsequent stage is also asymptomatic, although the patient has an increased chance of having another attack. A final stage, chronic tophaceous gout, is characterized by widespread distribution of crystals, possible damage to the joints, and adverse effects on the kidneys (Fries, 1995). Several drugs help effectively manage gout (e.g., cholchicine), and resting inflamed joints also helps facilitate recovery. Gout can be better managed by decreasing body weight, increasing exercise, and restricting alcohol and foods high in uric acid (Schumacher, 1996).

Infectious Arthritis: Infections in the Joint Space

Infectious arthritis results in swelling and the formation of pus within the joint space, warm red skin around the joint, and considerable pain. Acute joint infection can be caused by virtually any microbial agent, including a wide range of bacteria, viruses, and fungi (Schumacher, 1996). These infections occur in either sex and can begin at any age, although young people are infected with the gonococcus bacterium, and older individuals are more frequently infected by the staphylococcus germ. Single joint involvement is most common, although there may be multiple joints affected, particularly in patients with predisposing conditions such as RA. Risk factors for infectious arthritis include infection somewhere else in the body, extremes of age, other systemic diseases, recent surgery, and IV drug use. Although gonococcal arthritis is probably the most common form of infectious arthritis, nongonococcal bacterial infections are generally the most serious (Schumacher, 1996). If untreated, staphylococcus infections can result in bone destruction and even death. The prognosis for infectious arthritis is excellent if identified and treated early enough (Fries, 1995). Treatment typically consists of antibiotics and joint aspiration if needed. In light of possible complications resulting from insufficiently treated infectious arthritis, strict adherence to treatment regimens is critical.

OA: Cartilage Degeneration

OA, also known as *osteoarthrosis* or *degenerative joint disease* and the most common arthritis (Felson, 1990), is a progressive condition characterized by loss of articular cartilage and the formation of bone spurs, leading to pain and sometimes deformity. Rates of OA increase significantly with age, with typical onset between 45 and 70 years. Although most individuals in their 70s show radiographical evidence of OA, less than half are actually symptomatic (Bagge, Bjelle, Eden, & Svanborg, 1991). Increased risk for OA is associated with female gender, obesity, trauma, and certain genetic factors (Stein, Griffin, & Brandt, 1996). The three common OA subtypes are as follows: One form, the mildest form, causes a largely benign enlargement of finger joints; another form is characterized by bony growths on the spine, which can wear away spinal disks and irritate nerves or other back structures; and a third form, which is generally the most severe, involves degeneration of weight-bearing joints such as the hips and knees (Fries, 1995). No established cure exists for OA. Pharmacological interventions merely control symptoms and do not affect underlying disease processes. In addition, long-term use of drugs such as nonsteroidal anti-inflammatory drugs (NSAIDs) may foster adverse side effects such as renal toxicity. Current treatment focuses on nonpharmacological management, including exercise to maintain function, weight loss to decrease joint load, and protective measures such as avoiding heavy lifting (Brandt, 1998). Surgical interventions, particularly those for hip or knee replacements, also can result in profound relief and functional improvements.

Connective Tissue Diseases: Not Quite Arthritis

The term *connective tissue disease* describes a group of systemic rheumatic syndromes that have an autoimmune component, which is characterized by a loss of tolerance to self-antigens. The connective tissue diseases include SLE, scleroderma, Sjörgren's syndrome, polyarteritis, and inflammatory myopathies such as polymyositis and dermatomyositis (Fries, 1995). Connective tissue diseases are much more common in women, with female: male ratio distributions ranging from 3:1 for inflammatory myopathies to 10:1 for SLE (Klippel, 1996).

SLE is the most common connective tissue disease (Mills, 1994). SLE ranges from being a relatively easily treated disorder characterized by rash, fatigue, and arthritic manifestations to a life-threatening condition characterized by kidney failure and irreversible central nervous system (CNS) damage. Many individuals with SLE experience musculoskeletal symptoms such as synovitis, and affected joints tend to be similar to those affected by RA. However, in contrast to RA, SLE-related synovitis does not generally cause articular degeneration and instead results in inflammation of the surrounding tendons (Klippel, 1996). Interestingly, patients with SLE-related arthritis tend to have a better prognosis than the average patient with lupus. Because of the highly variable nature of the disease, treatment regimens may vary considerably; some patients may require potentially dangerous corticosteroids and immunosuppressants, whereas others may do best without any pharmacological agents (Fries, 1995).

Polymyositis and dermatomyositis are closely related connective tissue diseases characterized by muscle destruction, pain, and weakness. The skin also can be involved, with rashes and changes in surrounding blood vessels. Another complication is muscular degeneration in the chest wall, leading to difficulty breathing or correctly swallowing food. The onset of these disorders may be insidious or sudden. Moreover, disease course is highly variable. Some individuals die within 5 years of disease onset, whereas others make an almost complete recovery (Fries, 1995). Standard treatment involves high doses of corticosteroids, most typically oral prednisone (Klippel, 1996).

Localized Conditions: Injury, Inflammation, and Repair

The general category of rheumatic diseases also includes various localized conditions, usually those resulting from injury or irritation. These common conditions consist of lower back problems, bursitis, carpal tunnel syndrome, tendinitis, and tennis elbow (Fries, 1995).

Low back pain is the second most common medical condition (Frymoyer, 1988). For approximately 90% of those with low back pain, the pain is a result of trauma or overuse, whereas the remaining 10% have pain that is a function of a systemic illness such as AS (Borenstein, 1996). Pain is usually most pronounced in the concave portion of the lower back and may radiate downward. Excluding back pain caused by AS, common low back syndrome may be relieved somewhat with activity but generally gets worse from overactivity if healing is not complete. *Acute back pain* is defined as pain that lasts less than 12 weeks; most back pain disappears within this time. Effective treatment for an acute injury generally requires adequate rest to allow healing (Fries, 1995). Unfortunately, for a smaller but nevertheless substantial subgroup of patients, back pain develops into a chronic syndrome which, by definition, lasts more than 12 weeks (Borenstein, 1996). Although chronic low back pain usually cannot be cured completely, therapy can decrease pain and improve function. Recent evidence-based approaches generally discourage surgery, the prescription of bed rest, and extensive use of analgesics. Rather, therapy involves promoting correct posture and addressing contributing psychosocial variables (Hadler, 1996).

General Conditions: Overall Aching and Tenderness

General rheumatic conditions are characterized by global aching and stiffness. Although they can affect either sex at any age, this class of disorders affects women more than men, usually those between ages 30 and 50. Moreover, these conditions cannot be unambiguously identified through a physical examination or laboratory markers (Fries, 1995). The prime example in this class is *fibromyalgia (FM) syndrome,* also known as *fibrositis* and *fibromyositis.*

FM is an increasingly recognized condition that affects approximately 3.4% of women and 0.5% of men (Wolfe, Ross, Anderson, Russell, & Hebert, 1995). This syndrome is characterized by widespread pain and the presence of at least 11 of 18 specified tender point sites, both of which have lasted for at least 3 months. Moreover, sleep is typically light and nonrestorative. Approximately one third of patients with FM also have overlapping conditions such as chronic fatigue syndrome, irritable bowel syndrome, tension headaches, and Raynaud's phenomenon. FM also may be concomitant with other rheumatic conditions such as RA and SLE (Clark, 1996). Pain levels in those with FM often vary considerably and may last for many years, even for life. Although FM is not a degenerative condition, it has no known cure. Patients rarely respond fully to treatment with NSAIDs or corticosteroids, although antidepressants may improve sleep and reduce pain.

Rheumatic Diseases of Aging

Many rheumatic diseases affect older individuals. Diseases such as osteoporosis, polymyalgia rheumatica (PMR), and giant cell arteritis develop predominantly in individuals older than age 60 (Maricic, 1996).

Osteoporosis is characterized by deteriorating bone tissue and decreased bone mass, which promote bone fragility and increase the risk of fracture. Osteoporosis affects more than 25 million Americans, 80% of whom are women (Renfro & Brown, 1998). Moreover, each year an estimated 1.2 million fractures are attributable to osteoporosis among Americans 45 years or older. Approximately 50% of older patients with hip fractures never regain the same level of functional independence, and 25% require long-term institutional care (Maricic, 1996). Although genetics account for 40% to 60% of the variance in bone mass, numerous other factors have been implicated in the etiology of osteoporosis, including postmenopausal estrogen deficiency, calcium deficiency, chronic alcohol and nicotine use, insufficient exercise, and various medications. Supplements such as calcium, vitamin D, and androgens can help prevent osteoporosis (Riggs & Melton, 1992). Moreover, an appropriate exercise regimen is a significant part of the prevention and management of osteoporosis (Tinetti et al., 1994).

PMR is characterized by pain, particularly in the neck and shoulder muscles, and in the hip area. PMR is most commonly diagnosed after age 60, and the mean age of onset is 70. The precise etiology is unknown. About 20% of individuals diagnosed with PMR also develop *giant cell arteritis*, a systemic vasculitis that causes inflammation and occlusion of involved arteries (Maricic, 1996). If not diagnosed early, the condition tends to get progressively worse and is characterized by chronic low-grade fevers, increasing fatigue, significant weight loss, and synovitis. Prednisone is the standard treatment for PMR, and it often has rapid and striking results. However, because patients with PMR and giant cell arteritis are often treated with high doses of prednisone, they are at risk to experience adverse corticosteroid-induced side effects such as myopathy and osteoporotic fractures (Fries, 1995). Consequently, physical therapy is especially important for helping maintain range of motion and counteracting steroid-induced muscle loss and osteoporosis (Maricic, 1996).

Rheumatic Diseases of Childhood

There are more than 110 forms of arthritis or related musculoskeletal syndromes that affect children (Singsen, 1990). These diseases can be separated into various clusters, including inflammatory diseases, noninflammatory disorders, heritable disorders of connective tissue, metabolic disorders, and systemic diseases with musculoskeletal manifestations. The age of onset tends to be disease specific. Moreover, these childhood diseases are generally more common among girls. Race seems to play a role in some conditions. For example, African Americans have higher rates of childhood SLE than do White people (Erlandson, 1996).

Juvenile rheumatoid arthritis (JRA) is the most common childhood inflammatory rheumatic disease (Erlandson, 1996). JRA is not the same as adult RA, and the clinical manifestations, pathophysiology, and treatment approaches are often quite distinct. Three subtypes of JRA are recognized (Fries, 1995). The first type most commonly affects one joint, particularly large joints such as the knee, which become swollen and sore. The second type includes systemic manifestations such as high fever (up to 106 °F), fatigue, and skin rash, along with possible enlargement of the liver, spleen, and lymph nodes. Episodes may remit and return, with frank joint involvement more likely in later episodes. The final type, polyarticular arthritis, most closely resembles adult RA. It generally has an insidious onset around adolescence and includes multiple bilateral joint involvement and intense inflammation of the joint membrane. Although the prognosis for a near complete recovery is quite good for the first two types of JRA, about half of children with polyarticular JRA require arthritis treatment as adults. Treatment for JRA is typically multifaceted. Although pharmacological treatment approaches are increasingly aggressive to minimize joint destruction, they are not curative. The focus is on alleviating inflammation with anti-inflammatory or cytotoxic medications. Physical therapy also plays a major role in preserving function, eliminating pain, and improving motion and strength (Erlandson, 1996).

BIOPSYCHOSOCIAL PERSPECTIVE ON SYMPTOMS AND CORRELATES OF RHEUMATIC DISEASE

Although significant differences exist among the categories of rheumatic disease, they do have some common characteristics. One significant theme is the notion that these disorders often are highly variable. Rheumatic disorders may cause few symptoms in some individuals but significant distress and disability in others (Rice & Pisetsky, 1999). Thus, having a rheumatic condition can be marked by chronicity, fluctuating disease severity, and relative resistance to treatment. In turn, the experience of having a rheumatic disease takes place within the context of interrelated psychosocial factors. In the next section, frequent symptoms and correlates of rheumatic disease are examined from the perspective of a biopsychosocial model. Because the relationships among such factors are often bidirectional, the discussions may overlap.

Pain

Pain is one of the most important consequences of rheumatic conditions (Bradley, 1993). For example, self-reported pain among individuals with RA has been associated with a wide range of demographic, medical, and psychological factors (Parker, Frank, Beck, Finan, et al., 1988). Correlatively, epidemiological studies have suggested that individuals with chronic pain tend to have higher levels of affective distress (e.g., anxiety and depression) than those without pain (Von Korff, Dworkin, Le Resche, & Kruger, 1988). These lines of evidence rightly indicate that pain is a multidimensional phenomenon. On a physiological level, pain sensations and inhibition are related to interactions of the CNS and peripheral mechanisms (Crofford & Casey, 1999). Nevertheless, because pain is unpleasant, it invariably has an affective component combined with its behavioral effects.

In general, pain in rheumatic disorders has not been reliably associated with standard measures of disease activity, physical examinations, or current methods of imaging (Merskey, 1996). Increasing lines of evidence have suggested that in people with RA, pain levels are relatively independent of disease activity measures such as joint counts (Huyser et al., 1998). In contrast, in people with varying rheumatic diseases, higher pain levels have been associated with psychosocial variables such as increased distress, decreased social support, and decreased coping skills (Bradley & Alberts, 1999). However, even the relationships between pain and psychosocial variables can be complicated. For example, emotional disorders such as depression may cause pain but conversely, chronic pain conditions may predispose individuals to experience depression. In addition, the relationship between anxiety and pain seems to be curvilinear; anxiety tends to increase pain if an individual is at rest, whereas those in dangerous, high-anxiety situations (e.g., soldiers in battle) have decreases in perceived pain levels (Merskey, 1996). Regardless of the hypothesized direction of the association, these examples highlight the critical ways that psychosocial variables can affect the experience of pain.

Although a strong relationship exists between pain levels and psychosocial variables, the previous discussion is not intended to suggest that pain in rheumatic disorders does not have at least some significant physiological basis. A greater understanding of such physiological pathways may help illuminate psychosocial aspects of pain in rheumatic disease.

One potentially problematic aspect of chronic pain in rheumatic conditions involves the common clinical observation that perceived pain sometimes seems to spread well beyond parts of the body clearly affected by the disease. In fact, a physiological basis for this phenomenon of "spreading pain" is described by Wall (1989). In a review, Wall outlined the way chronic pain can alter receptive fields for afferent neurons in the dorsal horn of the spine, thereby expanding the range of stimuli that elicit sensations of pain. Similarly, the possibility of dual physiological pathways for pain and rheumatic disease activity may account for the relative disjunction between pain and disease activity (Affleck et al., 1997). Thus, health care workers should be cautious about inferring malingering or psychosomatic etiologies (e.g., suggesting "it's all in your head") of pain that does not clearly correspond with physical examinations or available laboratory findings.

Individuals with chronic pain may have a physiologically based predisposition for experiencing negative affective states such as anger, depression, and anxiety—without the clear mediation of psychosocial factors. Fernandez and Milburn (1994) suggested that in response to aversive stimuli such as pain, humans are physiologically "prewired" to experience negative affect, which in turn motivates adaptive processes. They argued that anger and anxiety motivate the fight-or-flight response, whereas depression motivates a submissive response. This notion is supported by the identification of a direct subcortical pathway through which pain receptors transmit afferent signals to the thalamus and the amygdala, which are responsible for releasing anger responses (LeDoux, 1987).

Fatigue

Fatigue also is a troublesome problem for many individuals with rheumatic diseases. Fatigue has objective physiological manifestations (e.g., increased lactate levels), behavioral manifestations (e.g., decreased physical and mental performance), and a subjective dimension. However, objective measures of fatigue have not been unambiguously correlated with subjective measures among clinical populations; thus, most studies about fatigue and rheumatic disease focus on subjective fatigue (Piper, 1989).

Although the prevalence and severity of fatigue varies among types of rheumatic diseases, levels of fatigue can be high. For example, rates of fatigue have been found to be 80% and higher among individuals with RA, FM, and SLE and at least 50% in individuals with AS (Belza, 1996). Given FM's high association with chronic fatigue syndrome (Bennett, 1998), it is not surprising that FM is strongly associated with fatigue. However, even in those with RA, which does not include fatigue as a diagnostic criterion, up to 57% have indicated that fatigue is the most problematic aspect of their disease (Tack, 1990).

As with pain, available research has suggested that fatigue may be relatively independent of actual disease activity and more strongly associated with psychosocial variables. Two studies with RA samples found that fatigue was most strongly associated with psychosocial variables such as higher levels of pain and depression and lower levels of social support (Huyser et al., 1998; Riemsma et al., 1998). Other studies have suggested that fatigue in those with SLE also is more strongly associated with psychosocial factors than with disease activity (Bruce, Mak, Hallett, Gladman, & Urowitz, 1999; Wang, Gladman, & Urowitz, 1998).

Negative Affect

Estimates about the prevalence of mood disorders among those with rheumatic diseases are complicated by the fact that symptoms for rheumatic disorders such as RA, FM, AS, and SLE often overlap with the somatic symptoms of mood disorders. Nevertheless, negative affect seems to be common in people with rheumatic disease. Some evidence also has suggested that people who are middle age or younger may be at greater risk for experiencing negative affect than older individuals with rheumatic disease (Wright et al., 1998).

Depression symptoms often overlap anxiety among individuals with rheumatic conditions; clinically noteworthy levels of anxiety have been found among large rheumatic disease samples (Frank & Hagglund, 1996). Rates of depression and anxiety seem to be highest in those with FM, with frequencies ranging between 26% and 71%. Frequencies of depression and anxiety in those with RA range between 14% and 42%, and frequencies of depression in OA range from 14% to 23% (for a review, see Bradley & Alberts, 1999). Moreover, clinically significant rates of depression range from 20% to 55% in those with SLE and higher than 31% in those with AS (Frank & Hagglund, 1996).

Many studies have examined the relationships between depression and anxiety and other relevant variables. This research has suggested that mood disturbance often is associated with increased pain, increased functional impairment, and overutilization of medical services (Frank & Hagglund, 1996). Moreover, although evidence has suggested that measures of disease activity are associated with psychological distress (Parker et al., 1991, 1992), other measures such as pain severity, age, neuroticism, daily stressors, work demands, self-efficacy, and functional ability are better predictors of anxiety and depression (Bradley & Alberts, 1999). A recent RA study suggested that these types of relationships remain within the first year of disease onset (Evers, Kraaimaat, Geenen, & Bijlsma, 1997). Interestingly, another study suggested that a prior episode of major depression, even if antecedent to RA onset, leaves a "scar" that subsequently predisposes people to higher levels of pain at times when they concurrently experience subthreshold depression symptoms (Fifield, Tennen, Reisine, & McQuillan, 1998).

Although depression and anxiety in those with rheumatic conditions have been fairly well studied, there is an unfortunate relative dearth of empirical studies about the role of another type of negative affect—namely, anger (Huyser & Parker, 1999). Nevertheless, anger often has been observed among individuals with chronic illnesses such as rheumatic disease (Moldofsky & Chester, 1970). Moreover, Feuerstein (1986) found higher levels of anger (along with depression and anxiety) among patients with low back pain than in asymptomatic controls. Some evidence also has suggested that the experience and expression of anger may affect chronic pain (Kinder & Curtiss, 1988). Of particular note is anger management style. An "anger-in" (i.e., suppressed anger) management style was found to be more prevalent among patients with chronic pain than among healthy control patients (Hatch et al., 1991), and this same type of anger management style has been inversely related to adjustment level (Kerns, Rosenberg, & Jacob, 1994). In addition, a recent study found that both anger-in and "anger-out" (i.e., expressed anger) management styles were associated with pain exacerbation, suggesting that poorly managed anger, whether expressed or suppressed, is associated with higher pain levels (Burns, 1997).

Sleep

Although the research base about the relationship between sleep and the rheumatic disorders is not extensive, high frequencies of sleep disturbances have been associated with various rheumatic disorders. Pain is the most commonly cited cause of sleep disturbance among individuals with rheumatic conditions (Wegener, 1996). Conversely, poor sleep may increase pain and fatigue. Of course, these options are not mutually exclusive. Finally, increased rates of depression and anxiety among those with rheumatic conditions also may contribute to sleep problems.

Sleep disturbances have been most consistently found in people with FM, and several lines of evidence have suggested increased nocturnal vigilance, high levels of subjective sleep disturbance, nonrestorative sleep, and intrusion of alpha waves during non-REM sleep in individuals with FM (Wegener, 1996). Sleep disturbances have been linked with other rheumatic diseases. For example, individuals with RA often experience sleep fragmentation (i.e., light, easily disrupted sleep with multiple awakenings), and this disturbance has been associated with various symptoms including increased disease activity (Crosby, 1991). Sleep disturbances also have been documented in individuals with OA (Moldofsky, Lue, & Saskin, 1987) and Sjögren's syndrome (Gudbjornsson, Roman, Hetta, & Hallgren, 1993).

Stress

Having a rheumatic disease may create stress in an individual's life; conversely, stress may exacerbate rheumatic disease. Stress can be conceptualized at three distinct but related levels: (a) situational factors that act as stressful stimuli, (b) stress-related physiological systems, and (c) psychological factors (e.g., perceived coping) that moderate how stressors are experienced (Cohen, Kessler, & Gordon, 1995). Although all three levels are germane to rheumatic disease, the current section focuses on the first two types.

Rheumatic disorders often produce pain and psychological distress, which are themselves significant stressors. Having a rheumatic condition also can create numerous other stressors, including reductions in home- and work-related activities and corresponding financial hardship caused by decreased earnings and increased health care costs (Yelin, 1995). The effects on social relationships of having a rheumatic condition also may contribute to stress. For example, approximately half of individuals with RA reported problems with social interactions and communication with others (Bradley, 1994). Perhaps not surprisingly, evidence has suggested that higher perceived levels of positive social support tend to buffer the adverse effects of environmental stressors (Penninx et al., 1997). Conversely, lower levels of social support have been associated with increased physical disability (Weinberger, Tiermey, Booher, & Hiner, 1990), and negative social interactions have been associated with increased depression (Revenson, Schiaffino, Majerovitz, & Gibofsky, 1991).

Extant evidence has suggested that environmental stressors can affect rheumatic disease processes. Overall, current studies do not unequivocally associate environmental stressors with the etiology of rheumatic diseases such as RA (Huyser & Parker, 1998). However, some evidence has suggested that psychosocial stressors affect the progression of acute back pain into chronic back pain syndrome (Weiser & Cedraschi, 1992). Moreover, external stressors and disease progression have been linked with other rheumatic disorders. For example, daily hassles have been associated with increased inflammation in patients with RA (Affleck, Tennen, Urrows, & Higgins, 1994; Thomason, Brantley, Jones, Dyer, & Morris, 1992). Another RA study found that minor stressors are associated with disease exacerbation but somewhat paradoxically, major life stressors such as the death of a family member are associated with decreases in disease activity (Potter & Zautra, 1997). Numerous daily hassles and poor social support also have been associated with poorer mental and physical health for SLE patients (Dobkin et al., 1998).

A significant body of research has explicitly examined the relationship between stress-related physiological mechanisms and rheumatic disease. Although various physiological systems are involved in stress responses, most relevant research has focused on two primary stress systems: (a) the hypothalamic–pituitary–adrenal (HPA) axis and (b) the sympathetic–adrenal–medullary (SAM) system (see Figure 13.2). A review provides evidence that dysregulation of both the HPA axis and the SAM

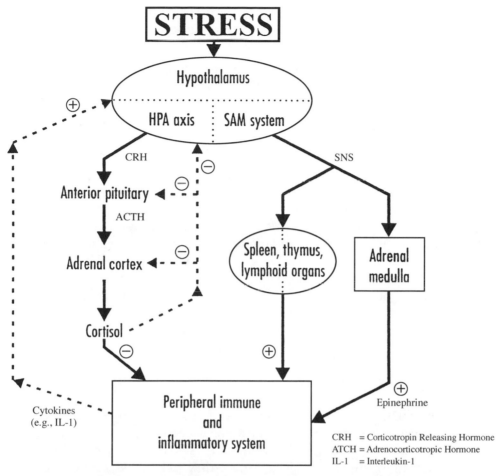

Figure 13.2. Stress responses mediated by the hypothalamic–pituitary–
adrenal (HPA) axis and the sympathetic–adrenal–medullary (SAM) system.
The minus (−) symbols represent activation; the plus (+) symbols represent
inhibition. Dashed lines on the HPA axis represent negative feedback loops.
The hypothalamus coordinates the stress-related action of the HPA axis and
the SAM system. Sympathetic nervous system action generally elicits immune
and inflammatory activity via direct innervation of the spleen, thymus and
lymphoid organs, and adrenal medulla. The HPA axis ultimately produces
cortisol, which down-regulates SAM-mediated peripheral immune and
inflammatory action. *Note.* From "Stress and Rheumatoid Arthritis: An
Integrative Review," by B. A. Huyser & J. C. Parker, 1998, *Arthritis Care and
Research, 11*(2), pp. 135–145. Copyright 1998 by Wiley-Liss, Inc., a
subsidiary of John Wiley & Sons, Inc. Adapted with permission.

system may underlie the association between environmental stress and increases in RA disease activity (Huyser & Parker, 1998). Other evidence
has suggested the HPA axis and the SAM system also are dysregulated in
FM, and these perturbations may influence the extreme pain sensitivity
that characterizes FM (Crofford et al., 1994; Weigent, Bradley, Blalock, &

Alarcon, 1998). HPA axis abnormalities also have been identified in a variety of other rheumatic conditions, including SLE (Gutierrez, Garcia, Rodriquez, Rivero, & Jacobelli, 1998), Sjörgren's syndrome (Johnson, Vlachoyiannopoulos, Skopouli, Tzioufas, & Moutsopoulos, 1998), and even low back pain (Griep et al., 1998).

Other multilevel studies have provided particularly valuable information about the relationships between various aspects of stress and rheumatic disease. For example, one study examined the relationships among daily stressors, negative mood, joint pain, and markers of inflammation and immune activity in an RA sample (Affleck et al., 1997). Increases in daily event stressors were directly associated with increased pain but indirectly associated with decreased joint inflammation, thereby suggesting a dual pathway for pain and inflammation. Another RA study found that increased interpersonal stress was associated with short-term immune changes and increased disease activity 1 week later (Zautra et al., 1997). In addition, increases in pain from inflammatory processes predicted lower stress levels during the following week. The authors hypothesized that either the patient's social network had responded to the pain by decreasing negative social interactions or, alternatively, patients had intentionally decreased social interactions to reduce the risk of negative encounters.

Cognitive and Coping Factors

The relationship between rheumatic disease and two cognitive factors, learned helplessness and self-efficacy, has been fairly well studied, at least in regard to rheumatic conditions such as RA. *Helplessness* refers to a global state in which individuals believe they lack viable ways to eliminate or alleviate sources of stress (DeVellis & Callahan, 1993). Because symptoms of many rheumatic diseases wax and wane unpredictably, helplessness may develop. Correspondingly, existing research has suggested that individuals reporting high levels of helplessness are more likely to report higher pain levels, greater depression, and greater functional impairment (for a review, see Keefe & Bonk, 1999). Baseline levels of helplessness have been found to predict greater RA disease activity (Nicassio et al., 1993), although disease activity also has been found to increase helplessness (Schoenfeld-Smith et al., 1996).

Self-efficacy tends to be more behavior specific and refers to the confidence individuals have regarding their own ability to perform specific goal-directed tasks (Bandura, 1977). For example, individuals with low self-efficacy are less likely to persist and comply with treatment regimens, regardless of their beliefs about the potential helpfulness of the intervention. In a sample with FM, higher self-efficacy beliefs regarding pain control have been associated with higher pain threshold and pain tolerance levels and lower frequencies of pain behavior, even after controlling for demographic factors and disease activity (Buckelew et al., 1994). Higher self-efficacy also has been associated with decreased low back pain (Lin, 1998). Finally, increases in self-efficacy have been associated with decreased depression, pain, and disease activity (Lefebvre et al., 1999; Smarr et al., 1997), and increased treatment adherence (Brus, van de Laar, Taal, Rasker, & Wiegman, 1999) in RA.

Coping refers to behaviors that use available resources to manage internal or external demands. Important distinctions in the research on coping include problem- versus emotion-focused coping and passive versus active coping. Generally, emotion-focused and passive coping approaches have been found to be the most maladaptive. For example, passive strategies characterized by catastrophic thinking or hoping "things will just get better" have been associated with greater pain and psychological distress (for a review, see Bradley & Alberts, 1999) and poorer functional outcome (Evers, Kraaimaat, Geenen, & Bijlsma, 1998) across different rheumatic conditions. Conversely, active problem-focused coping responses have been consistently associated with positive affect and improved psychological adjustment (Young, 1992).

Work Disability

Rheumatic disease is the leading cause of work loss and the second leading cause of work disability payments (Allaire, 1996). For example, roughly 25% to 50% of individuals with RA and OA are disabled after having the disease for one decade (Pincus, Mitchell, & Burkhauser, 1989), and about the same amount in an SLE sample were disabled after approximately 5.5 years (Clarke et al., 1993).

Numerous risk factors for work disability have been identified. Poor disease status is a strong predictor of disability for individuals with RA, JRA, and AS (for a review, see Allaire, 1996). Time off work also seems to be an important factor. For example, the probability that people with low back problems will return to work is 70% after 2 months away from work, 50% after 6 months, 30% after 12 months, and 10% after 2 years (Waddell, 1992). Other psychosocial variables also seem to be involved. For example, significant risk factors for RA-related disability include little education, little social support, and depression (Allaire, 1996); poor psychological status and high pain levels have been linked with decreased work productivity in individuals with SLE (Clarke, Bloch, Danoff, & Esdaile, 1994).

Preliminary Conclusions

The foregoing section highlights the notion that rheumatic diseases are expressed and experienced within a web of interconnected psychosocial factors. From research already discussed, one could readily conceive of a situation in which a rheumatic condition such as RA could produce painful joints, which would limit function and initiate a chain of events: potential depression, which could result in work disability and therefore exacerbate marital problems—further increasing disease activity. Thus, one can reasonably infer that at least for a subset of individuals with chronic rheumatic conditions such as RA, SLE, OA, and FM, effective management necessarily involves adequate assessment and treatment of relevant psychosocial factors. Moreover, psychosocial assessment and intervention can be potentially relevant for any individual with a rheumatic condition. For example, gout is usually an easily treated disease that readily responds to pharmacological intervention. However, even in this case, key psychosocial concepts such as adherence to prescribed medication regimens are relevant to effective management. Similarly, the efficacy of interventions such as exercise, which can be essential to the management of rheumatic conditions (Minor, 1996), hinges on patient adherence to prescribed regimens.

BIOPSYCHOSOCIAL ASSESSMENT OF RHEUMATIC DISEASE

The first part of this section focuses on a range of assessment tools for rheumatic diseases. Of course, much valuable information can be derived from a well-structured clinical interview. Thus, health psychologists should routinely question patients about relevant topics such as symptom profile, mood difficulties, marital or other family problems, employment, other environmental stressors, adherence to prescribed regimens, substance abuse, and medicolegal issues. However, formal assessment tools can serve as valuable adjuncts in this process. Subsequent discussion in this section concentrates on identifying select psychometrically sound assessment measures; it is not intended to be fully comprehensive. This discussion begins with global assessment measures and then examines specific areas such as pain, fatigue, negative affect, stress, coping and cognitive factors, social support, marital functioning, and personality.

Global Assessment Measures

Health psychologists working with patients who have rheumatic disease may use numerous broad-spectrum measures that assess various problems in daily living as well as other dimensions of health status such as pain and psychosocial adjustment. One such measure, the Arthritis Impact Measurement Scale (AIMS), was specifically designed for individuals with arthritis (Meenan et al., 1984; Meenan, Gertman, & Mason, 1980). This multidimensional index is grouped into nine component subscales: mobility, physical activity, dexterity, household activities, activities of daily living, pain, anxiety, depression, and social activities. A similar measure, the Health Assessment Questionnaire (HAQ), also has been widely used for those with rheumatic disease (Fries, Spitz, Kraines, & Holman, 1980). The HAQ evaluates outcomes on five dimensions: death, discomfort, disability, drug toxicity, and dollar cost. A modified version of the HAQ, the MHAQ (Pincus, Summey, Soraci, Wallston, & Hummon, 1983), is shorter and takes less time. The Sickness Impact Profile (SIP), a generic measure that provides a profile of disability across 12 domains (Bergner, Bobbitt, Carter, & Gilson, 1981), can be validly used with rheumatic disease populations (Sullivan, Ahlmen, & Bjelle, 1990). Finally, the Multidimensional Pain Inventory was developed as a broad-based measure of the cognitive and behavioral factors that influence pain (Kerns, Turk, & Rudy, 1985). This 52-item self-report measure is divided into three parts: Part I measures pain severity, interference, social support, life control and affective distress; Part II assesses patients' perceptions of spousal responses; and Part III assesses overall activity levels.

Pain

As mentioned previously, pain is a multidimensional construct that includes an intensity component, an affective component, and a behavioral dimension. Pain intensity is typically measured by verbal rating scales, numeric rating scales, or visual analogue scales—all of which have been found to be reliable and valid for pain populations (Jensen & Karoly, 1992). The affective dimension of pain can be measured with numerous different instruments. One valid and reliable means involves the use of visual analogue scales about pain unpleasantness (Price, Harkins, & Baker, 1987). Another well-validated option involves using the McGill Pain Questionnaire (MPQ), which yields three pain-related subscales: affective, evaluative, and sensory (Melzack, 1975). Pain behavior such as grimacing, guarded movements, and rubbing also can be effectively evaluated. Keefe and Williams (1992) developed a standardized protocol for sampling and recording pain behavior for individuals with OA, and the protocol also has been successfully used with individuals with other rheumatic diseases such as RA, JRA, and FM (Keefe & Bonk, 1999).

Instruments are also available specifically for pediatric assessments. The Varni/Thompson Pediatric Pain Questionnaire (PPQ) is a multidimensional measure that uses structured interviews of the parents and the child, respectively (Varni, Thompson, & Hanson, 1987); unfortunately, this measure is rather long. Other more clinically useful instruments for pediatric assessments include the Oucher facial scale (Beyer, Denyes, & Villarruel, 1992)—an easily understood self-report measure of pain affect —and the 100-mm thermometer (Abu-Saad & Uiterwijk, 1995)—a visual analog measure of pain intensity.

Fatigue

Two-multidimensional measures of subjective fatigue have been successfully used with RA samples: the Piper Fatigue Self-Report Scale (Piper et al., 1989) and the Multidimensional Assessment of Fatigue (Belza, Henke, Yelin, Epstein, & Gilliss, 1993). The Fatigue Severity Scale, a one-dimensional nine-item scale, is based on the characteristics of fatigue in those with SLE (Schwartz, Jandorf, & Krupp, 1993). Finally, the Profile of Mood States (POMS) contains a seven-item subscale for fatigue (McNair, Lorr, & Dropplemen, 1992) and has been used with various clinical populations.

Negative Affect

A sensitive and specific way of assessing mood is via structured and semistructured interviews such as the Diagnostic Interview Schedule (Robbins, Helzer, Croughan, & Ratcliff, 1981). However, numerous self-report measures also are used to assess mood in those with rheumatic disease. One approach involves the use of global measures. The AIMS, the previously mentioned global health status scale, has subscales for depression and anxiety. The Symptom Checklist–90–Revised (SCL–90–R) is a global measure of psychological distress with nine subscales, including scales for anxiety and depression (Derogatis, 1977). Both the Center for Epidemiological Studies Depression Scale (Radloff, 1977) and the State–Trait Anxiety Inventory (Spielberger, Gorsuch, & Luchene, 1970) often have been used with individuals who have rheumatic diseases.

Stress

Various measures assess stressful environmental stimuli over different time frames. For example, the Life Events Survey (Sarason, Johnson, & Siegel, 1978) examines a wide variety of major life stressors (e.g., death in the family, marriage, legal troubles) that have occurred during the previous year. The Hassles Scale measures stressors (i.e., events related to work or health) that have occurred within the previous month (Kanner, Coyne, Schaeger, & Lazarus, 1981). The Daily Stress Inventory measures the source and impact of stressful events (e.g., arguments with a spouse) that have occurred during the previous 24 hours (Brantley, Waggoner, Jones, & Rappaport, 1987). All these measures have been used successfully with individuals who have rheumatic diseases.

Coping

Coping instruments typically assess general coping skills, or more specifically, pain coping strategies. The most widely used scale for problem-versus emotion-focused coping is the Ways of Coping Scale (Folkman, Lazarus, Dunkel-Schetter, DeLongis, & Gruen, 1986). This 66-item measure yields subscales for various types of coping (e.g., seeking social support, accepting responsibility, escape avoidance). An alternative form of the scale, the Arthritis Appraisal and Ways of Coping Scale (Regan, Lorig, & Thoreson, 1988), was designed specifically for those with rheumatic disease. Regarding the assessment of specific pain coping strategies, one of the most widely used instruments is the Coping Strategies Questionnaire (Rosenthiel & Keefe, 1983). Factor analyses have yielded two primary factors: The first measures the frequency of a broad range of coping strategies, whereas the second measures the perceived effectiveness of coping and the tendency to avoid cognitive distortions.

Self-Efficacy

Self-efficacy among those with rheumatic disease can be measured with the Arthritis Self-Efficacy Scale (ASES), a brief 20-item self-report measure (Lorig, Chastain, Ung, Shoor, & Holman, 1989). Three factor analytically derived subscales provide information about self-efficacy for pain (e.g., "How certain are you that you can decrease your pain quite a bit?"), function (e.g., "As of now, how certain are you that you can walk 100 feet on flat ground in 20 seconds?"), and controlling other symptoms (e.g., "How certain are you that you can control your fatigue?").

Helplessness

Because individuals with rheumatic diseases may perceive themselves as helpless and having minimal control over their disease, it may be important to formally assess levels of helplessness. To this end, two short psychometrically sound instruments can be fairly easily integrated into clinical practice settings. The Arthritis Helplessness Index (AHI) is a 15-item self-report instrument that measures individuals' levels of helplessness regarding various aspects of arthritis (Nicassio, Wallston, Callahan, Herbert, & Pincus, 1985). The Rheumatology Attitudes Index (RAI) represents a modification of the AHI and was specifically designed for general rheumatology practice (Callahan, Brooks, & Pincus, 1988).

Other Cognitive Factors

Because cognitive distortions can affect various domains such as depression, helplessness, and self-efficacy, formal assessment of cognitive distortions in individuals with rheumatic conditions can be useful. To this end, the Cognitive Error Questionnaire was originally developed for patients with chronic low back pain (Lefebvre, 1981), and a modified version applies to other types of arthritis (Smith, Peck, Milano, & Ward, 1988). The Inventory of Negative Thoughts Related to Pain (INTRP) is a 21-item measure that pertains to three types of factor analytically derived distortions: negative self-statements (e.g., "I am useless"), negative social cognitions (e.g., "No one cares about my pain"), and self-blame (e.g., "It is my own fault I hurt like this"; Gill, Williams, Keefe, & Beckham, 1990).

Social Support

Although initial social support measures focused on the quantity of social support (i.e., number of potentially supportive individuals), recent measures have more carefully examined the quality of such support. Keefe and Bonk (1999) identify the Social Support Questionnaire (SSQ) as the measure of choice for assessing both the quantity and quality of social support (Sarason, Levine, Basham, & Sarason, 1983). Because this original measure is rather long, clinicians may prefer to use the short version of the SSQ (Sarason, Shearin, Pierce, & Sarason, 1987). Another option that has been used with individuals with rheumatic diseases is the Social Relationships Questionnaire, a 14-item measure of perceived social support (Heitzman & Kaplan, 1988).

Marital and Family Functioning

Rheumatic diseases can affect both the individual with the disease as well as spouse and family members. One widely used measure of marital satisfaction is the Dyadic Adjustment Scale (Spanier, 1976). This 32-item self-report measure has four subscales: dyadic consensus, dyadic satisfaction, dyadic cohesion, and affectional expression. The previously mentioned MPI also can be useful in assessing social support, particularly in regard to patient perceptions of spousal response to complaints or displays of pain.

Sleep

Although no well-established sleep measures exist for those with rheumatic diseases, a review of sleep parameters should be included in a psychosocial assessment (Wegener, 1996). Short-term complaints should be distinguished from chronic difficulties. Sleep diaries may be helpful and often include a daily record of bedtime, rising time, mid-sleep awakenings, daytime fatigue and drowsiness, pain, mood (e.g., anxiety and depression), and medications. Clinicians also may want to gather information about other factors that may affect sleep, including eating, substance use, exercise habits, sleep schedule, presleep activities, and the sleep environment.

Personality Measures

A careful evaluation of personality factors and general psychological functioning may be important, especially when serious psychological problems seem to be involved. A wide variety of standard personality measures (e.g., the MMPI–2) could be used. However, because personality instruments generally have not been normed on rheumatic populations and because these instruments often overlap with rheumatic disease symptoms, they should be used with caution.

BIOPSYCHOSOCIAL TREATMENT

Pharmacological management of rheumatic disease is usually geared toward control of underlying disease processes (e.g., with DMARDs) and pain management (e.g., with NSAIDs). Such medical interventions are generally a necessary component of treatment, and many individuals with rheumatic conditions respond adequately to such treatment. However, these interventions are not sufficient for many other patients. As with assessment, effective management of rheumatic conditions requires appropriate and individualized attention to psychosocial variables. Increasing evidence has suggested that multimodal approaches (i.e., those that combine medical treatment, cognitive–behavioral interventions, and exercise under the auspices of appropriate professionals) are the most effective treatments for those individuals with rheumatic disease who do not respond adequately to conservative biomedical interventions (Crook & Tunks, 1996). The focus of this section is key components of effective psychosocial treatment for individuals with rheumatic conditions. The section begins with review of general treatment approaches and then includes a discussion of interventions for specific problem areas.

General Treatment Approaches

Widespread evidence has suggested that education-based interventions for individuals with rheumatic disease are associated with positive outcomes. However, although many individuals with rheumatic disease are not adequately informed about their conditions (Daltroy, 1993), most evidence also has suggested that merely providing information has limited value (DeVellis & Blalock, 1993). In contrast, more comprehensive and action-oriented interventions such as cognitive–behavioral therapy (CBT) and self-management approaches have been associated with various positive outcomes, including decreased pain, depression, and anxiety and increased self-efficacy, function, and work levels (for a review, see Boutaugh & Lorig, 1996). In fact, CBT and the Arthritis Self-Management Program

(ASMP; Lorig, Mazonson, & Holman, 1993) have satisfied the American Psychological Association's criteria for empirically validated treatment for pain among those with RA and OA (Compass, Haaga, Keefe, Leitenberg, & Williams, 1998). Evidence has suggested that these treatment gains tend to be long term (i.e., last for more than 12 months) for many individuals (Parker et al., 1995), particularly among those who continue to practice coping skills regularly (Parker, Frank, Beck, Smarr, et al., 1988). Some studies have suggested that similar treatment approaches also are effective for other rheumatic conditions such as FM (Buckelew et al., 1998; Turk, Okifuji, Sinclair, & Starz, 1998).

Other promising interventions include telephone counseling, which has been associated with positive outcomes on psychological measures (Maisiak, Austin, & Heck, 1996), functional ability (Weinberger, Tiermey, Booher, & Katz, 1989), and mail-delivered self-management programs, which have been associated with positive outcomes on both psychological and disease-related parameters (Fries, Carey, & McShane, 1997). In addition, emotional disclosure of stressful events has been associated with improved psychological functioning (Kelly, Lumley, & Leisen, 1997) and disease status parameters (Smyth, Stone, & Kaell, 1999) in individuals with RA. Finally, although data on the effectiveness of psychotherapy and mutual support groups for individuals with rheumatic disorders is inconclusive (DeVellis & Blalock, 1993; Hawley, 1995), interventions that involve family members and friends as an adjunct to other programs often have better outcomes (Lanza & Revenson, 1993).

Because they have already been identified as empirically validated treatments, this section includes a more in-depth discussion of CBT and the ASMP. This discussion relies heavily on outlines developed by Keefe and Caldwell (1996) and Boutaugh and Lorig (1996), respectively.

Extant CBT for those with rheumatic disease generally feature group sessions taught by psychologists for 1–2 hours per week for 5 to 10 weeks. CBT is characterized by three basic elements: (a) education about and rationale for treatment (e.g., explaining pain theories and the interrelationships between psychosocial factors and rheumatic disease), (b) coping skills training (e.g., relaxation and cognitive restructuring), and (c) relapse prevention.

Self-management strategies such as the ASMP are similar to standard CBT interventions. This standardized group intervention is usually taught by trained professionals or laypeople and generally lasts about 2 to 2.5 hours per week for 5 to 7 weeks. The course content provides a combination of disease-related information and training in adaptive behaviors such as exercise, relaxation, and problem-solving. The ASMP also may include a social support component (e.g., involving family), and more recent versions have explicitly concentrated on improving self-efficacy. Following is an elaboration of essential components of these interventions.

Education and Rationale

A key component of education involves teaching patients the way psychosocial factors can influence pain and other rheumatic disease symptoms. To personalize this process, patients can be asked to describe how their rheumatic condition has affected their own functioning in behavioral, cognitive, and affective domains. In turn, this exercise can increase patient awareness of the connections among thoughts, feelings, and behaviors and help elucidate the way problematic coping patterns may develop over time. Of course, patients also are taught that old patterns can be changed by learning new cognitive and behavioral skills. These processes encourage a philosophy of self-management so that patients can begin to take active roles in controlling their rheumatic condition and secondary sequelae as much as possible.

Education efforts are more likely to be successful if the clinician takes time to identify the patients' major concerns and tailor interventions accordingly (Daltroy, 1993). Similarly, to correct misunderstandings, set acceptable treatment priorities, and maximize motivation to change, it is important to first elicit patients' attributions about their disease and their treatment goals. Finally, clinicians should provide specific instructions in easily understood language.

Coping Skills Training

Patients with rheumatic disease can learn various coping skills to help them better manage pain and other disease-related problems. Effective coping skills training generally progresses from the least difficult skills (e.g., relaxation) to the most difficult (e.g., cognitive restructuring) and requires guided practice and sufficient feedback (Keefe & Caldwell, 1996).

Relaxation training. Relaxation is a fundamental coping skill that can provide several benefits, including reducing muscle tension that may cause pain, decreasing physiological stress responses that may exacerbate disease activity, diverting attention from unpleasant symptoms, and improving sleep. Although myriad methods exist for teaching relaxation (e.g., biofeedback, autogenic training), most CBT uses progressive muscle relaxation training. Imagery training (e.g., imagining a pleasant scene) is often used as an adjunct to relaxation training. After patients have used practice sessions to consistently elicit relaxation in a quiet, controlled environment, training typically shifts to using abbreviated relaxation methods (e.g., 30-second body scans) during more demanding activities of daily living.

Activity–rest cycling. Patients with rheumatic disease frequently have difficulty efficiently pacing activities. Whereas some patients tend to overdo activities, thus greatly increasing pain and fatigue and the length of recovery sessions, others do too little and become deconditioned, which also increases pain and disability. Activity–rest cycling is designed to break these maladaptive patterns by helping each patient identify and implement individualized activity–rest patterns that maximize functional activity and minimize pain and fatigue. A common way of facilitating this process is through self-monitoring of activities and examining subsequent effects on mood and disease symptoms.

Cognitive restructuring. Individuals with rheumatic disease and depression, anxiety, or high pain levels often have negative thoughts about themselves and others. These thoughts may result in higher levels of pain, greater negative affect, and decreased functioning. The overall purpose of cognitive restructuring is to help patients identify such thoughts and consciously replace them with more adaptive ones, thereby decreasing negative affect and increasing adaptive coping. To this end, patients are often instructed to monitor the relationships among situations, associated thoughts, and associated affect. After identifying thought patterns, patients are taught to examine these thoughts for cognitive distortions (e.g., "My RA gives me pain, so I must be defective") and replace the negative thought with a more positive reframe (e.g., "Having pain may slow me down, but I'm still a good person").

Relapse Prevention

Daily use of cognitive–behavioral strategies has been associated with better long-term outcomes (Parker, Frank, Beck, Smarr, et al., 1988). Nevertheless, when individuals with rheumatic conditions are faced with increased life stress or disease flares, they may feel overwhelmed, use the counterproductive strategy of curtailing or terminating effective coping practices, and thereby precipitate greater increases in pain, distress, and disability. Patients also may decrease practice of cognitive–behavioral skills when rheumatic symptoms diminish, setting the stage for maladaptive coping if rheumatic symptoms intensify. Relapse prevention is intended to counteract these outcomes. Primary components of relapse prevention include (a) identifying potential high-risk relapse situations (e.g., disagreements with spouse), (b) learning to identify early signs of relapse (e.g., increased pain or depression), (c) rehearsing more adaptive responses to such situations, and (d) providing self-rewards for effective coping in response to potential relapse triggers (Keefe & Van Horn, 1993). Although early CBT interventions had relapse prevention training at the end of the program, most current interventions provide such training throughout the course of the protocol (Bradley & Alberts, 1999).

Other Treatment Issues

Exercise Interventions

A comprehensive discussion of exercise interventions is beyond the scope of this chapter and more appropriately written by specialists in disciplines such as physical therapy or occupational therapy. Nevertheless, it is important to briefly discuss the critical role that exercise can play in rheumatic disease management. Multimodal management of rheumatic conditions frequently includes exercise interventions; health psychologists should be aware of this option and consider referring patients when exercise has not been adequately addressed.

Poor physical health contributes to various problems, including excess fatigue, low functional status, low pain threshold, sleep disturbances, and depression. Moreover, low levels of physical fitness have been reported in those with various rheumatic diseases (RA, OA, JRA, FM, and SLE; Falconer, 1996). Fortunately, increased physical fitness in young and older individuals with inflammatory or noninflammatory rheumatic disease has been associated with improved outcomes without disease exacerbation (Kovar et al., 1992; Minor, Hewett, Webel, Anderson, & Kay, 1989). Appropriate regular exercise can improve range of motion, muscle strength, general conditioning, and functional abilities and help reduce pain, fatigue, and depression (Minor & Sanford, 1999).

Adherence

For medication, exercise, or cognitive–behavioral interventions to be fully effective, patients must adhere to treatment recommendations. However, adherence rates for various chronic conditions are often quite low. For example, adherence rates among individuals with RA range from 16% to 84% for medications and 39% to 65% for therapeutic exercise (Belcon, Haynes, & Tugwell, 1984; Bradley, 1989). Evidence from individuals with rheumatic diseases has suggested that young children (Kroll, Barlow, & Shaw, 1999) and busy, middle-age adults (Huyser, Buckelew, Hewett, & Johnson, 1997; Park et al., 1999) may be at particularly high risk for nonadherence. Numerous factors have been generally correlated with nonadherence, including patient–family factors (e.g., helplessness, poor coping, family dysfunction), disease factors (e.g., a patient who is asymptomatic or in remission, increased number of symptoms), and regimen factors (e.g., complex and demanding regimens, lack of continuity of care, negative side effects; Rapoff, 1996).

The research on increasing adherence among populations with rheumatic diseases is rather limited; however, a few general recommendations are in order. On a "process level," health care providers can maximize adherence by providing the patient with sufficient support and understanding, eliciting patient attributions about treatment recommendations, and helping patients explicitly consider the pros and cons of adherence and nonadherence (DiMatteo, 1994). Moreover, numerous content-oriented strategies for improving adherence to rheumatic disease regimens exist (Rapoff, 1996), including educational strategies (e.g., providing clear verbal and written information, emphasizing the importance of adherence), organization strategies (e.g., reducing regimen complexity, minimizing treatment costs), and behavioral strategies (e.g., increasing self-management skills, involving family members in the supervision of regimens).

Negative Affect

One study found that primary risk factors for depression in RA (e.g., average daily stressors, self-efficacy) were preventable and modifiable to a large degree (Wright et al., 1996). However, although studies of those with rheumatic disease reported mood improvements after psychological interventions such as CBT, these studies generally tended to focus on improving rheumatic disease symptoms rather than directly examining treatment effects on psychiatric disorders. In addition, although numerous studies have examined the effects of antidepressant medications on rheumatic disease variables and the studies suggested that such medications produce analgesic effects independent of mood (Frank & Hagglund, 1996), these studies usually used subtherapeutic doses; one cannot make clear inferences about the effects of medications on mood disturbance. Clearly, more research in this area is warranted. Because no obvious contraindications are known, a commonsense approach to treating diagnosable depressive disorders and other psychiatric disturbances among individuals with rheumatic diseases is to simply treat their condition as one would treat them in the general populations; that is, provide them with or refer them for empirically validated psychological treatment, pharmacological treatment, or both.

Self-Efficacy

As mentioned previously, self-efficacy seems to moderate numerous important outcomes in those with rheumatic conditions. Fortunately, self-efficacy seems to be a modifiable variable. CBT interventions have been associated with increased self-efficacy in patients with FM (Buckelew et al., 1996) and patients with RA (Smarr et al., 1997). Moreover, studies about the ASMP showed that adding strategies specifically designed to enhance self-efficacy improved health outcomes. Techniques for enhancing self-efficacy include breaking down desired skills and behaviors into easily mastered components, helping patients set realistic short-term goals, and setting up situations in which individuals similar to the identified patient can model successful behavior and provide praise and positive feedback (Lorig & Gonzalez, 1992).

Sleep

No well-controlled studies of sleep-enhancing interventions exist for individuals with rheumatic disease. Therefore, current recommendations are based on studies of nonrheumatic diseases (Wegener, 1996). Effective treatment of sleep disturbance begins with identifying and addressing relevant medical, psychiatric, or environmental problems. If such changes do not effectively promote desired changes in sleeping, implementation of effective sleep hygiene principles (see Exhibit 13.1) or specialized behavioral treatment for sleep may be warranted (Lacks, 1987). Finally, pharmacological interventions may be necessary. When primary rheumatic disease processes such as pain and inflammation militate against sleep, adequate doses of NSAIDs or other analgesic medications may be warranted. Short-term use of hypnotic medication may be useful for some sleep problems, particularly those of recent onset. Especially in individuals with FM, small doses of tricyclic antidepressants such as amitriptyline have been shown to reduce both sleep disturbance and pain (Carette, McCain, Bell, & Fam, 1986).

FUTURE DIRECTIONS

This chapter has been predicated on the notion that adequate understanding and treatment of rheumatic conditions requires a biopsychosocial perspective. As such, health psychologists can play a critical role in this endeavor. However, numerous research and clinical areas require continued efforts by psychologists.

Although conditions such as RA, OA, and FM are relatively well studied, more extensive research about the ways psychosocial factors affect many other rheumatic conditions (e.g., childhood rheumatic disorders) is needed. Also needed is additional research in specific content areas. For example, as mentioned previously, there is a dearth of focused research about interventions for sleep problems or diagnosable psychiatric disturbance in all rheumatic diseases. Another area that needs more study is the use of behavioral interventions for the secondary prevention of chronic musculoskeletal pain (Linton & Bradley, 1996).

Existing research identifies CBT and self-management programs as empirically validated treatments for OA- and RA-related pain. Further research should examine the degree to which these interventions are effective for many other rheumatic conditions. Moreover, numerous other intervention directions show promise, including telephone counseling and emotional disclosure of stressful events. These treatment approaches require further study both within and across rheumatic diseases. Finally, in addition to answering general questions about the efficacy of such interventions, effectiveness of these interventions as they are applied to general community settings needs to be evaluated.

Precisely because rheumatic disease is best understood within the context of a biopsychosocial model, more integrative research that simultaneously examines relevant biological (e.g., stress response systems, markers of disease activity), psychological (e.g., coping patterns), and socioen-

EXHIBIT 13.1
Sleep Hygiene Principles

Regular sleep patterns
Go to bed and wake up the same time each day.
Avoid naps, except for brief 10 to 15 minute period 8 hours after waking.
Take a hot bath to raise temperature 2°C within 2 hours of bedtime.
A hot drink may help.
Establish a bedtime ritual.

Environmental factors
Avoid large meals 2 to 3 hours before bedtime.
Avoid bright light if you have to get up during the sleep period.
Keep clock face turned away.
Make sure sleeping environment is dark, quiet, and comfortable.

Exercise
Exercise regularly each day.
Avoid vigorous exercise 2 hours before bedtime.

Drug effects
Give up smoking entirely, or avoid smoking several hours before bedtime.
Do not smoke if you experience a mid-sleep awakening.
Limit consumption of alcoholic beverages.
Discontinue caffeine.
Avoid use of over-the-counter sleep medications.
Use prescribed sleep medication only occasionally.

Aging
Learn about changes in sleep parameters that occur with age to reduce unrealistic expectations and anxiety.

Note. Adapted from *Clinical Care in the Rheumatic Diseases* (p.123), by S. T. Wegener, B. L. Belza, and E. P. Gall (Eds.), 1996, Atlanta, GA: The American College of Rheumatology. Copyright 1996. Used by permission of the American College of Rheumatology.

vironmental (e.g., social support, short and long-term stressors) parameters is needed (Huyser & Parker, 1998). Previously mentioned studies (e.g., Affleck et al., 1997; Zautra et al., 1997) illustrate this general approach with RA. Similar studies with other populations could greatly increase understanding of many aspects of rheumatic disease and in turn lead to more effective prevention and intervention. For example, given recent evidence that emotional disclosure may actually decrease disease activity in individuals with RA, multilevel studies that examine potential physiological mechanisms in this process could be extremely illuminating.

To reach maximum utility, "biopsychosocial understandings of rheumatic disease" and "empirically validated treatments" must become more widely known and implemented within the general health care system. Continued effort on numerous fronts may help increase access to biopsychosocial assessment and treatment for individuals with rheumatic conditions.

Especially in today's managed care environment, "good care" is care that works and cuts costs. Thus, as suggested, it is incumbent on psychologists to empirically demonstrate that psychosocial interventions actually improve outcomes across a variety of domains for different rheumatic conditions. Of course, such interventions must be affordable—or better, accompanied by direct and indirect cost offsets. Although psychologists should be cautious about promoting more than they can deliver (Fraser, 1996), a growing body of literature suggests that psychosocial interventions for individuals with rheumatic conditions produce economic benefits. For example, a 4-year follow-up study of the Arthritis Self-Management Program showed significant savings for patients with RA and patients with OA (Lorig et al., 1993); another 3-year study demonstrated significant cost offsets regarding psychosocial interventions for those with OA (Cronan et al., 1998). Finally, a third study showed that the most important predictors of short-term direct medical costs among patients with RA are modifiable variables such as global well being, pain, and functional disability (Clarke et al., 1999). As this body of information grows, psychologists should make concerted efforts to communicate the information to physicians, hospital administrators, health care executives, and relevant governmental bodies.

In a similar vein, effective psychosocial assessment and treatment of rheumatic conditions are largely dependent on primary care physicians or rheumatology specialists. In other words, these health care providers must either provide such services or refer patients to professionals who can provide these services. Although recent trends in medical training foster a greater interaction between physicians and psychologists, many physicians remain unaware of evidence-based psychological interventions for various disorders (Pace, Chaney, Mullins, & Olson, 1995). In the current medical environment, the responsibility to make this information available often lies with psychologists. Efforts toward this end are more likely to be successful when psychologists remain cognizant of the issues that are most important to physicians (e.g., time demands) and attempt to use familiar terms (e.g., avoid terminology unique to psychology and address discrete measurable outcomes; McDaniel, 1995).

Finally, psychologists can promote improved psychosocial treatment of rheumatic conditions by increasing awareness of and referral to reputable organizations outside the formal health care system. For example, the Arthritis Foundation (*www.arthritis.org*) provides many types of information and resources for individuals with rheumatic conditions, including self-management programs specifically designed for SLE and FM.

CONCLUSION

Rheumatic diseases often are characterized by numerous adverse effects including chronic pain, fatigue, poor sleep, interpersonal stress, and decreased functioning. Nevertheless, psychologists have much to offer patients with rheumatic conditions. In addition to providing a comprehensive understanding of the rheumatic disease experience, psychosocial approaches are critical in the management of these conditions. Health psychologists have the tools to conduct a thorough assessment of relevant psychosocial factors and provide effective intervention strategies such as CBT. The discipline of health psychology should continue to develop effective assessment and treatment modalities for a range of rheumatic conditions and take needed steps to ensure that this information is more widely available and implemented. This strategy will improve patient care and enhance the contributions of the profession of psychology.

REFERENCES

Abu-Saad, H. H., & Uiterwijk, M. (1995). Pain in children with juvenile rheumatoid arthritis: A descriptive study. *Pediatric Research, 38,* 194–197.

Affleck, G., Tennen, H., Urrows, S., & Higgins, P. (1994). Personal and contextual features of daily stress reactivity: Individual differences in relations of undesirable daily events with mood disturbance and chronic pain intensity. *Journal of Personality and Social Psychology, 66,* 329–340.

Affleck, G., Urrows, S., Tennen, H., Higgins, P., Pav, D., & Aloisi, R. (1997). A dual pathway model of daily stressor effects on rheumatoid arthritis. *Annals of Behavioral Medicine, 19,* 161–170.

Allaire, S. H. (1996). Work disability. In S. T. Wegener, B. L. Belza, & E. P. Gall (Eds.), *Clinical care in the rheumatic diseases* (pp. 141–145). Atlanta, GA: American College of Rheumatology.

Bagge, E., Bjelle, A., Eden, S., & Svanborg, A. (1991). Osteoarthritis in the elderly: Clinical and radiological findings in 79–85 year olds. *Annals of Rheumatic Disease, 50,* 535–539.

Bandura, A. (1977). Self-efficacy: Toward a unifying theory of behavioral change. *Psychology Review, 84,* 191–215.

Belcon, M. C., Haynes, R. B., & Tugwell, P. (1984). A critical review of compliance studies in rheumatoid arthritis. *Arthritis and Rheumatism, 27,* 1227–1233.

Belza, B. L. (1996). Fatigue. In S. T. Wegener, B. L. Belza, & E. P. Gall (Eds.), *Clinical care in the rheumatic diseases* (pp. 117–120). Atlanta, GA: American College of Rheumatology.

Belza, B., Henke, C., Yelin, E., Epstein, W., & Gilliss, C. (1993). Correlates of fatigue in older adults with rheumatoid arthritis. *Nursing Research, 42,* 93–99.

Bennett, R. (1998). Fibromyalgia, chronic fatigue syndrome, and myofascial pain. *Current Opinion in Rheumatology, 10*(2), 95–103.

Bergner, M., Bobbitt, R. A., Carter, W. B., & Gilson, B. S. (1981). The Sickness

Impact Profile: Development and final revision of a health status measure. *Medical Care, 19,* 787–805.

Beyer, J. E., Denyes, M. J., & Villarruel, A. M. (1992). The creation, validation, and continuing development of the Oucher: A measure of pain intensity in children. *Journal of Pediatric Nursing, 7*(5), 335–346.

Borenstein, D. G. (1996). Chronic low back pain. *Rheumatic Disease Clinics of North America, 22*(3), 439–456.

Boutaugh, M. L., & Lorig, K. R. (1996). Patient education. In S. T. Wegener, B. L. Belza, & E. P. Gall (Eds.), *Clinical care in the rheumatic diseases* (pp. 53–58). Atlanta, GA: American College of Rheumatology.

Bradley, L. A. (1989). Adherence with treatment regimens among adult rheumatoid arthritis patients: Current status and future directions. *Arthritis Care and Research, 2*(Suppl.), 33–39.

Bradley, L. A. (1993). Introduction: The challenges of pain in arthritis. *Arthritis Care and Research, 6,* 169–170.

Bradley, L. A. (1994). Psychological dimensions of rheumatoid arthritis. In F. Wolfe & T. Pincus (Eds.), *Rheumatoid arthritis: Critical issues in etiology, assessment, prognosis, and therapy* (pp. 273–295). New York: Marcel Dekker.

Bradley, L. A., & Alberts, K. R. (1999). Psychological and behavioral approaches to pain management for patients with rheumatic disease. *Rheumatic Disease Clinics of North America, 25*(1), 215–232.

Brandt, K. D. (1998). The importance of nonpharmacologic approaches in management of osteoarthritis. *American Journal of Medicine, 105*(1B), 39S–44S.

Brantley, P. J., Waggoner, C. D., Jones, G. N., & Rappaport, N. B. (1987). A Daily Stress Inventory: Development, reliability, and validity. *Journal of Behavioral Medicine, 10,* 61–74.

Bruce, I. N., Mak, V. C., Hallett, C. C., Gladman, D. D., & Urowitz, M. B. (1999). Factors associated with fatigue in patients with systemic lupus erythematosus. *Annals of Rheumatic Disease, 58*(6), 379–381.

Brus, H., van de Laar, M., Taal, E., Rasker, J., & Wiegman, O. (1999). Determinants of compliance with medication in patients with rheumatoid arthritis: The importance of self-efficacy expectations. *Patient Education and Counseling, 36*(1), 57–64.

Buckelew, S. P., Conway, R., Parker, J., Deuser, W. E., Read, J., & Witty, T. E. (1998). Biofeedback/relaxation training and exercise interventions for fibromyalgia: A prospective trial. *Arthritis Care and Research, 11,* 196–209.

Buckelew, S. P., Huyser, B., Hewett, J. E., Parker, J. C., Johnson, J. C., & Conway, R. (1996). Self-efficacy predicting outcome among fibromyalgia subjects. *Arthritis Care and Research, 9*(2), 97–104.

Buckelew, S. P., Parker, J. C., Keefe, F. J., Deuser, W. E., Crews, T. M., & Conway, R. (1994). Self-efficacy and pain behavior among subjects with fibromyalgia. *Pain, 59,* 377–384.

Burns, J. W. (1997). Anger management style and hostility: Predicting symptom-specific physiological reactivity among chronic low back pain patients. *Journal of Behavioral Medicine, 20,* 505–522.

Callahan, L. F. (1996). Impact of rheumatic disease on society. In S. T. Wegener, B. L. Belza, & E. P. Gall (Eds.), *Clinical care in the rheumatic diseases* (pp. 209–213). Atlanta, GA: American College of Rheumatology.

Callahan, L. F., Brooks, R. H., & Pincus, T. (1988). Further analysis of learned helplessness in rheumatoid arthritis using "Rheumatology Attitudes Index." *Journal of Rheumatology, 15,* 418–426.

Carette, S., McCain, G. A., Bell, D. A., & Fam, A. G. (1986). Evaluation of amitriptyline in primary fibrositis: A double-blind placebo-controlled study. *Arthritis and Rheumatism, 29,* 655–659.

Clark, S. (1996). Common soft tissue rheumatic disorders: Bursitis, tendinitis, carpal tunnel, myofascial pain, and fibromyalgia. In S. T. Wegener, B. L. Belza, & E. P. Gall (Eds.), *Clinical care in the rheumatic diseases* (pp. 197–202). Atlanta, GA: American College of Rheumatology.

Clarke, A. E., Bloch, D. A., Danoff, D. S., & Esdaile, J. M. (1994). Decreasing costs and improving outcomes in systemic lupus erythematosus: Using a regression tree to develop health policy. *Journal of Rheumatology, 21,* 2246–2253.

Clarke, A. E., Esdaile, J. M., Bloch, D. A., Lacaille, D., Danoff, D. S., & Fries, J. F. (1993). A Canadian study of the total medical costs for patients with systemic lupus erythematosus and predictors of costs. *Arthritis and Rheumatism, 36,* 1548–1559.

Clarke, A. E., Levinton, C., Joseph, L., Penrod, J., Zowall, H., & Sibley, J. T. (1999). Predicting the short-term direct medical costs incurred by patients with rheumatoid arthritis. *Journal of Rheumatology, 26*(5), 1068–1075.

Cohen, C., Kessler, R. C., & Gordon, L. U. (1995). Strategies for measuring stress in studies of psychiatric and physical disorders. In C. Cohen, R. C. Kessler, & L. U. Gordon (Eds.), *Measuring stress: A guide for health and social scientists* (pp. 3–28). New York: Oxford University Press.

Compass, B. E., Haaga, D. A., Keefe, F. J., Leitenberg, H., & Williams, D. A. (1998). Sampling of empirically supported psychological treatments for health psychology: Smoking, chronic pain, cancer, and bulimia nervosa. *Journal of Consulting and Clinical Psychology, 66,* 89–112.

Crofford, L. J., & Casey, K. L. (1999). Central modulation of pain perception. *Rheumatic Disease Clinics of North America, 25*(1), 1–13.

Crofford, L. J., Pillemer, S. R., Kalogeras, K. T., Cash, J. M., Michelson, D., & Kling, M. A. (1994). Hypothalamic–pituitary–adrenal axis perturbations in patients with fibromyalgia. *Arthritis and Rheumatism, 37,* 1583–1592.

Cronan, T. A., Hay, M., Groessl, E., Bigatti, S., Gallagher, R., & Tomita, M. (1998). The effects of social support and education on health costs after three years. *Arthritis Care and Research, 11*(5), 326–334.

Crook, J., & Tunks, E. (1996). Pain clinics. *Rheumatic Disease Clinics of North America, 22*(3), 599–611.

Crosby, L. F. (1991). Factors which contribute to fatigue associated with rheumatoid arthritis. *Journal of Advanced Nursing, 16*, 974–981.

Daltroy, L. H. (1993). Doctor–patient communication in rheumatological disorders. *Baillieres Clinical Rheumatology, 7*, 221–239.

Derogatis, L. R. (1977). *SCL–90–R administration, scoring, and procedures manual.* Towson, MD: Clinical Psychometric Research.

DeVellis, R. F., & Blalock, S. J. (1993). Psychological and educational interventions to reduce arthritis disability. *Baillieres Clinical Rheumatology, 7*, 397–416.

DeVellis, R. F., & Callahan, L. F. (1993). A brief measure of helplessness in rheumatic disease: The helplessness subscale of the Rheumatology Attitudes Index. *Journal of Rheumatology, 20*, 866–869.

DiMatteo, M. R. (1994). Enhancing patient adherence to medical recommendations. *Journal of the American Medical Association, 271*(1), 79–83.

Dobkin, P. L., Fortin, P. R., Joseph, L., Esdaile, J. M., Danoff, D. S., & Clarke, A. E. (1998). Psychosocial contributors to mental and physical health in patients with systemic lupus erythematosus. *Arthritis Care and Research, 11*(1), 23–31.

Erlandson, D. M. (1996). Rheumatic diseases in childhood. In S. T. Wegener, B. L. Belza, & E. P. Gall (Eds.), *Clinical care in the rheumatic diseases* (pp. 157–163). Atlanta, GA: American College of Rheumatology.

Evers, A. W. M., Kraaimaat, F. W., Geenen, R., & Bijlsma, J. W. (1997). Determinants of psychological distress and its course in the first year after diagnosis in rheumatic arthritis patients. *Journal of Behavioral Medicine, 20*, 489–504.

Evers, A. W. M., Kraaimaat, F. W., Geenen, R., & Bijlsma, J. W. (1998). Psychosocial predictors of functional change in recently diagnosed rheumatoid arthritis patients. *Behavior Research and Therapy, 36*(2), 179–193.

Falconer, J. A. (1996). Deconditioning. In S. T. Wegener, B. L. Belza, & E. P. Gall (Eds.), *Clinical care in the rheumatic diseases* (pp. 131–135). Atlanta, GA: American College of Rheumatology.

Felson, D. T. (1990). Osteoarthritis. *Rheumatic Disease Clinics of North America, 16*(3), 499–512.

Fernandez, E., & Milburn, T. W. (1994). Sensory and affective predictors of overall pain and emotions associated with affective pain. *Clinical Journal of Pain, 10*, 3–9.

Feuerstein, M. (1986, March). *Ambulatory monitoring of paraspinal skeletal muscle, autonomic and mood–pain interaction in chronic low back pain.* Paper presented at the Seventh Annual Meeting of the Society of Behavioral Medicine, San Francisco, CA.

Fifield, J., Tennen, H., Reisine, S., & McQuillan, J. (1998). Depression and the long-term risk of pain, fatigue, and disability in patients with rheumatoid arthritis. *Arthritis and Rheumatism, 41*(10), 1851–1857.

Folkman, S., Lazarus, R. S., Dunkel-Schetter, C., DeLongis, A., & Gruen, R. J. (1986). The dynamics of a stressful encounter: Cognitive appraisal, coping, and encounter outcomes. *Journal of Personality and Social Psychology, 50,* 992–1003.

Frank, R. G., & Hagglund, K. J. (1996). Mood disorders. In S. T. Wegener, B. L. Belza, & E. P. Gall (Eds.), *Clinical care in the rheumatic diseases* (pp. 125–130). Atlanta, GA: American College of Rheumatology.

Fraser, J. S. (1996). All that glitters is not always gold: Medical offset effects and managed behavioral health care. *Professional Psychology: Research and Practice, 21*(4), 335–344.

Fries, J. F. (1995). *Arthritis: A take care of yourself health guide for understanding your arthritis* (4th ed.). Reading, MA: Perseus Books.

Fries, J. F., Carey, C., & McShane, D. J. (1997). Patient education in arthritis: Randomized controlled trial of a mail-delivered program. *Journal of Rheumatology, 24*(7), 1378–1383.

Fries, J. F., Spitz, P., Kraines, R. G., & Holman, H. R. (1980). Measurement of patient outcomes in arthritis. *Arthritis and Rheumatism, 23,* 137–145.

Frymoyer, J. W. (1988). Back pain and sciatica. *New England Journal of Medicine, 318,* 291–300.

Gall, V. (1996). Spondyloarthropathies. In S. T. Wegener, B. L. Belza, & E. P. Gall (Eds.), *Clinical care in the rheumatic diseases* (pp. 171–175). Atlanta, GA: American College of Rheumatology.

Gill, K. M., Williams, D. A., Keefe, F. J., & Beckham, J. C. (1990). The relationship of negative thoughts to pain and psychological distress. *Behavior Therapy, 21,* 349–362.

Griep, E. N., Boersma, J. W., Lentjes, E. G., Prins, A. P., van der Korst, J. K., & de Kloet, E. R. (1998). Function of the hypothalamic–pituitary–adrenal axis in patients with fibromyalgia and low back pain. *Journal of Rheumatology 25*(7), 1374–1381.

Gudbjornsson, B., Roman, J. E., Hetta, J., & Hallgren, R. (1993). Sleep disturbance in patients with primary Sjogren's syndrome. *British Journal of Rheumatology, 32,* 1072–1076.

Gutierrez, M. A., Garcia, M. E., Rodriquez, J. A., Rivero, S., & Jacobelli, S. (1998). Hypothalamic–pituitary–adrenal function and prolactin secretion in systemic lupus erythematosus. *Lupus, 7*(6), 404–408.

Hadler, N. M. (1996). Regional illness: Managing musculoskeletal predicaments. In S. T. Wegener, B. L. Belza, & E. P. Gall (Eds.), *Clinical care in the rheumatic diseases* (pp. 203–207). Atlanta, GA: American College of Rheumatology.

Hatch, J. P., Schoenfeld, L. S., Boutros, N. N., Seleshi, E., Moore, P. J., & Cyr-Provist, M. (1991). Anger and hostility in tension-type headache. *Headache, 31,* 302–304.

Hawley, D. J. (1995). Psycho-educational intervention in the treatment of arthritis. *Baillieres Clinical Rheumatology, 9,* 803–823.

Heitzman, C. A., & Kaplan, R. M. (1988). Assessment of methods for measuring social support. *Health Psychology, 7,* 75–109.

Huyser, B., Buckelew, S. P., Hewett, J. E., & Johnson, J. C. (1997). Factors affecting adherence to rehabilitation interventions for individuals with fibromyalgia. *Rehabilitation Psychology, 42*(2), 75–91.

Huyser, B. A., & Parker, J. C. (1998). Stress and rheumatoid arthritis: An integrative review. *Arthritis Care and Research, 11*(2), 135–145.

Huyser, B. A., & Parker, J. C. (1999). Negative affect and pain in arthritis. *Rheumatic Disease Clinics of North America, 25*(1), 105–121.

Huyser, B. A., Parker, J. C., Thoreson, R., Smarr, K. L., Johnson, J. C., & Hoffman, R. (1998). Predictors of subjective fatigue among individuals with rheumatoid arthritis. *Arthritis and Rheumatism, 41*(12), 2230–2237.

Jensen, M. P., & Karoly, P. (1992). Self-report scales and procedures for assessing pain in adults. In D. C. Turk & R. Melzack (Eds.), *Handbook of pain assessment* (pp. 135–151). New York: Guilford Press.

Johnson, E. O., Vlachoyiannopoulos, P. G., Skopouli, F. N., Tzioufas, A. G., & Moutsopoulos, H. M. (1998). Hypofunction of the stress axis in Sjogren's syndrome. *Journal of Rheumatology, 25*(8), 1508–1514.

Kanner, A., Coyne, J., Schaeger, L., & Lazarus, R. (1981). Comparison of two modes of stress management: Daily hassles and uplifts versus major life events. *Journal of Behavioral Medicine, 4*, 1–29.

Keefe, F. J., & Bonk, V. (1999). Psychosocial assessment of pain in patients having rheumatic diseases. *Rheumatic Disease Clinics of North America, 25*(1), 81–103.

Keefe, F. J., & Caldwell, D. S. (1996). Cognitive–behavioral interventions. In S. T. Wegener, B. L. Belza, & E. P. Gall (Eds.), *Clinical care in the rheumatic diseases* (pp. 59–63). Atlanta, GA: American College of Rheumatology.

Keefe, F. J., & Van Horn, Y. (1993). Cognitive–behavioral treatment of rheumatoid arthritis pain: Maintaining treatment gains. *Arthritis Care and Research, 6*, 213–222.

Keefe, F. J., & Williams, D. A. (1992). Assessment of pain behaviors. In D. C. Turk & R. Melzack (Eds.), *Handbook of pain assessment* (pp. 277–292). New York: Guilford Press.

Kelly, J. E., Lumley, M. A., & Leisen, J. C. (1997). Health effects of emotional disclosure in rheumatoid arthritis patients. *Health Psychology, 16*, 331–340.

Kerns, R. D., Rosenberg, R., & Jacob, M. C. (1994). Anger expression and chronic pain. *Journal of Behavioral Medicine 17*, 57–67.

Kerns, R. D, Turk, D. C., & Rudy, T. E. (1985). The West Haven–Yale Multidimensional Pain Inventory (WHYMPI). *Pain, 23*, 345–356.

Kinder, B. N., & Curtiss, G. (1988). Assessment of anxiety, depression and anger in chronic pain patients: Conceptual and methodological issues. In C. D. Spielberger & J. N. Butcher (Eds.), *Advances in personality assessment* (pp. 161–174). Hillsdale. NJ: Erlbaum.

Klippel, J. H. (1996). Connective tissue diseases. In S. T. Wegener, B. L. Belza, & E. P. Gall (Eds.), *Clinical care in the rheumatic diseases* (pp. 165–170). Atlanta, GA: American College of Rheumatology.

Kovar, P. A., Allegrante, J. P., MacKenzie, C. R., Peterson, M. G. E., Gutin, B.,

& Charlson, M. E. (1992). Supervised fitness walking in patients with osteoarthritis of the knee. *Annals of Internal Medicine, 116*, 529–533.

Kroll, T., Barlow, J. H., & Shaw, K. (1999). Treatment adherence in juvenile arthritis—A review. *Scandinavian Journal of Rheumatology, 28*(1), 10–18.

Lacks, P. (1987). *Behavioral treatment for persistent insomnia.* New York: Persimmon Press.

Lanza, A. F., & Revenson, R. A. (1993). Social support interventions for rheumatoid arthritis patients: The cart before the horse? *Health Education Quarterly, 20*, 97–117.

LeDoux, J. E. (1987). Emotion. In F. Plum (Ed.), *Handbook of physiology* (Section 1, Vol. 5). Bethesda, MD: American Psychological Association.

Lefebvre, J. C., Keefe, F. J., Affleck, G., Raezer, L. B., Starr, K., & Caldwell, D. S. (1999). The relationship of arthritis self-efficacy to daily pain, daily mood, and daily pain coping in rheumatoid arthritis patients. *Pain, 80*(1–2), 425–435.

Lefebvre, M. F. (1981). Cognitive distortion and cognitive errors in depressed psychiatric and low back pain patients. *Journal of Consulting and Clinical Psychology, 49*, 517–525.

Lin, C. C. (1998). Comparison of the effects of perceived self-efficacy on coping with chronic cancer pain and coping with chronic low back pain. *Clinical Journal of Pain, 14*(4), 303–310.

Linton, S. J., & Bradley, L. A. (1996). Strategies for the prevention of chronic pain. In R. J. Gatchel & D. C. Turk (Eds.), *Psychological treatments for pain: A practitioner's handbook* (pp. 438–457). New York: Guilford Press.

Lorig, K., Chastain, R. L., Ung, E., Shoor, S., & Holman, H. (1989). Development and evaluation of a scale to measure perceived self-efficacy in people with arthritis. *Arthritis and Rheumatism, 32*(1), 37–44.

Lorig, K., & Gonzalez, V. (1992). The integration of theory with practice: A 12-year case study. *Health Education Quarterly, 19*, 355–368.

Lorig, K. R., Mazonson, P. D., & Holman, H. (1993). Evidence suggesting that health education for self-management in patients with chronic arthritis has sustained health benefits while reducing health care costs. *Arthritis and Rheumatism, 36*(4), 439–446.

Maisiak, R., Austin, L., & Heck, L. (1996). Health outcomes of two telephone interventions for patients with rheumatoid arthritis or osteoarthritis. *Arthritis and Rheumatism, 39*, 1391–1399.

Maricic, M. J. (1996). Rheumatic diseases of aging: Osteoporosis and polymyalgia rheumatica. In S. T. Wegener, B. L. Belza, & E. P. Gall (Eds.), *Clinical care in the rheumatic diseases* (pp. 191–195). Atlanta, GA: American College of Rheumatology.

McDaniel, S. H. (1995). Collaboration between psychologists and family physicians: Implementing the biopsychosocial model. *Professional Psychology: Research and Practice, 26*(2), 117–122.

McNair, D., Lorr, R., & Dropplemen, L. (1992). *Edits manual for the Profile of Mood States*. San Diego, CA: Education and Industrial Testing Service.

Meenan, R. F., Anderson, J. J., Kazis, L. E., Egger, M. A., Samuelson, C. O., & Wilkins, R. F. (1984). Outcome assessment in clinical trials. Evidence for the sensitivity of a health status measure. *Arthritis and Rheumatism, 27*(12), 1344–1352.

Meenan, R. F., Gertman, P. M., & Mason, J. H. (1980). Measuring health status in arthritis. The arthritis impact measurement scales. *Arthritis and Rheumatism, 23*(2), 146–152.

Melzack, R. (1975). The McGill Pain Questionnaire: Major properties and scoring methods. *Pain, 1*, 277–299.

Merskey, H. (1996). Psychological medicine, pain, and musculoskeletal disorders. *Rheumatic Disease Clinics of North America, 22*(3), 623–637.

Mills, J. A. (1994). Systemic lupus erythematosus. *New England Journal of Medicine, 330*, 1871–1890.

Minor, M. A. (1996). Rest and exercise. In S. T. Wegener, B. L. Belza, & E. P. Gall (Eds.), *Clinical care in the rheumatic diseases* (pp. 73–78). Atlanta, GA: American College of Rheumatology.

Minor, M. A., Hewett, J. E., Webel, R. R., Anderson, S. K., & Kay, D. R. (1989). Efficacy of physical conditioning exercise in patients with rheumatoid arthritis and osteoarthritis. *Arthritis and Rheumatism, 32*, 1396–1405.

Minor, M. A., & Sanford, P. T. (1999). The role of physical therapy and physical modalities in pain management. *Rheumatic Disease Clinics of North America, 25*(1), 233–248.

Moldofsky, H., & Chester, W. (1970). Pain and mood patterns in patients with rheumatoid arthritis: A prospective study. *Psychosomatic Medicine, 32*, 309–318.

Moldofsky, H., Lue, F. A., & Saskin, P. (1987). Sleep and morning pain in primary osteoarthritis. *Journal of Rheumatology, 14*, 124–128.

Nicassio, P. M., Radojevic, V., Weisman, M. H., Culbertson, A. L., Lewis, C., & Clemmey, P. (1993). The role of helplessness in the response to disease modifying drugs in rheumatoid arthritis. *Journal of Rheumatology, 20*, 1114–1120.

Nicassio, P. M., Wallston, K. A., Callahan, L. F., Herbert, M., & Pincus, T. (1985). The measurement of helplessness in rheumatoid arthritis: The development of the Arthritis Helplessness Index. *Journal of Rheumatology, 12*, 462–467.

Pace, T. M., Chaney, J. M., Mullins, L. L., & Olson, R. A. (1995). Psychological consultation with primary care physicians: Obstacles and opportunities in the medical setting. *Professional Psychology: Research and Practice, 26*(2), 123–131.

Park, D. C., Hertzog, C., Leventhal, H., Morrell, R. W., Leventhal, E., & Birchmore, D. (1999). Medication adherence in rheumatoid arthritis patients: Older is wiser. *Journal of the American Geriatric Society, 47*(2), 172–183.

Parker, J. C., Frank, R. G., Beck, N. C., Finan, M., Walker, S., & Hewett, J. E. (1988). Pain in rheumatoid arthritis: Relationship to demographic, medical, and psychological factors. *Journal of Rheumatology, 15*(3), 433–437.

Parker, J. C., Frank, R. G., Beck, N. C., Smarr, K. L., Buescher, K. L., & Phillips, L. R. (1988). Pain management in rheumatoid arthritis patients: A cognitive–behavioral approach. *Arthritis and Rheumatism, 31*, 593–601.

Parker, J. C., Smarr, K. L., Anderson, S., Hewett, J. E., Walker, S., & Bridges, A. (1992). Relationship of changes in helplessness and depression to disease activity in rheumatoid arthritis. *Journal of Rheumatology, 19*, 1901–1905.

Parker, J. C., Smarr, K. L., Buckelew, S. P., Stucky-Ropp, R. C., Hewett, J. E., & Johnson, J. C. (1995). Effects of stress management on clinical outcomes in rheumatoid arthritis. *Arthritis and Rheumatism, 38*(12), 1805–1818.

Parker, J. C., Smarr, K. L., Walker, S. E., Hagglund, K. J., Anderson, S. K., & Hewett, J. E. (1991). Biopsychosocial parameters of disease activity in rheumatoid arthritis: A prospective study of 400 patients. *Arthritis Care and Research, 4*, 73–80.

Penninx, B. W., van Tilburg, T., Deeg, D. J., Kriegsman, D. M., Boeke, A. J., & van Eijk, J. T. (1997). Direct and buffer effects of social support and personal coping resources in individuals with arthritis. *Social Science Medicine, 44*, 393–402.

Pincus, T. (1996). Rheumatoid arthritis. In S. T. Wegener, B. L. Belza, & E. P. Gall (Eds.), *Clinical care in the rheumatic diseases* (pp. 147–155). Atlanta, GA: American College of Rheumatology.

Pincus, T., Mitchell, J., & Burkhauser, R. V. (1989). Substantial work disability and earnings losses in individuals less than age 65 with osteoarthritis: Comparisons with rheumatoid arthritis. *Journal of Clinical Epidemiology, 42*, 449–457.

Pincus, T., Summey, J. A., Soraci, S. A., Wallston, K. A., & Hummon, N. P. (1983). Assessment of patient satisfaction in activities of daily living using a modified Stanford Health Assessment Questionnaire. *Arthritis and Rheumatism, 26*, 1346–1353.

Piper, B. F. (1989). Fatigue: Current bases for practice. In S. Funk, E. Tornquist, M. Champagne, L. Copp, & R. Wiese (Eds.), *Key aspects of comfort* (pp. 187–198). New York: Springer.

Piper, B. F., Lindsey, A. M., Dodd, M. J., Ferketich, S., Paul, S. M., & Weller, S. (1989). The development of an instrument to measure the subjective dimension of fatigue. In S. Funk, E. Tornquist, M. Champagne, L. Copp, & R. Wiese (Eds.), *Key aspects of comfort* (pp. 199–208). New York: Springer.

Potter, P. T., & Zautra, A. J. (1997). Stressful life events' effects on rheumatoid arthritis disease activity. *Journal of Consulting and Clinical Psychology, 65*(2), 319–323.

Price, D. D., Harkins, S. W., & Baker, C. (1987). Sensory–affective relationships among different types of clinical and experimental pain. *Pain, 28*, 291–299.

Radloff, L. S. (1977). The CES–D scale: A self-report depression scale for research in the general population. *Applied Psychological Measurement, 1*(3), 385–401.

Rapoff, M. A. (1996). Adherence. In S. T. Wegener, B. L. Belza, & E. P. Gall

(Eds.), *Clinical care in the rheumatic diseases* (pp. 137–140). Atlanta, GA: American College of Rheumatology.

Regan, C. A., Lorig, K., & Thoreson, C. E. (1988). Arthritis appraisal and ways of coping: Scale development. *Arthritis Care and Research, 1,* 139–150.

Renfro, J., & Brown, J. B. (1998). Understanding and preventing osteoporosis. *American Association of Occupational Health Nurses Journal, 46*(4), 181–191.

Revenson, T. A., Schiaffino, K. M., Majerovitz, S. D., & Gibofsky, A. (1991). Social support as a double-edged sword: The relation of positive and problematic support to depression among rheumatoid arthritis patients. *Social Science and Medicine, 33,* 807–813.

Rice, J. R., & Pisetsky, D. S. (1999). Pain in the rheumatic diseases: Practical aspects of diagnosis and treatment. *Rheumatic Disease Clinics of North America, 25*(1), 15–30.

Riemsma, R. P., Rasker, J. J., Taal, E., Griep, E. N., Wouters, J. M., & Wiegman, O. (1998). Fatigue in rheumatoid arthritis: The role of self-efficacy and problematic social support. *British Journal of Rheumatology, 37*(10), 1042–1046.

Riggs, B. L., & Melton, L. J. (1992). The prevention and treatment of osteoporosis. *New England Journal of Medicine, 327,* 620–627.

Robbins, L. N., Helzer, J. E., Croughan, J., & Ratcliff, K. S. (1981). National Institute for Mental Health Diagnostic Interview: Its history, characteristics, and validity. *Archives of General Psychiatry, 38,* 381–389.

Rosenthiel, A. K., & Keefe, F. J. (1983). The use of coping strategies in chronic low back pain patients: Relationship to patient characteristics and current adjustment. *Pain, 17,* 33–44.

Sarason, I. G., Johnson, J. H., & Siegel, J. M. (1978). Assessing the impact of life changes: Development of the life experiences survey. *Journal of Consulting and Clinical Psychology, 46,* 932–946.

Sarason, I. G., Levine, H. M., Basham, R. B., & Sarason, B. R. (1983). Assessing social support: The social support questionnaire. *Journal of Personality and Social Psychology, 44,* 127–139.

Sarason, B. R., Shearin, E. N., Pierce, G. N., & Sarason, I. G. (1987). Interrelations of social support measures: Theoretical and practical implications. *Journal of Personality and Social Psychology, 52,* 813–832.

Schoenfeld-Smith, K., Petroski, G. F., Hewett, J. E., Johnson, J. C., Wright, G. E., & Smarr, K. L. (1996). A biopsychosocial model of disability in rheumatoid arthritis. *Arthritis Care and Research, 9,* 368–375.

Schumacher, H. R. (1996). Acute inflammatory arthritis. In S. T. Wegener, B. L. Belza, & E. P. Gall (Eds.), *Clinical care in the rheumatic diseases* (pp. 183–189). Atlanta, GA: American College of Rheumatology.

Schwartz, J. E., Jandorf, L., & Krupp, L. B. (1993). The measurement of fatigue: A new instrument. *Journal of Psychosomatic Research, 37,* 753–762.

Singsen, B. H. (1990). Rheumatic diseases of childhood. *Rheumatic Disease Clinics of North America, 16*(3), 581–597.

Smarr, K. L., Parker, J. C., Wright, G. E., Stucky-Ropp, R. C., Buckelew, S. P., &

Hoffman, R. W. (1997). The importance of enhancing self-efficacy in rheumatoid arthritis. *Arthritis Care and Research, 10*(1), 18–26.

Smith, T. W., Peck, J. R., Milano, R. A., & Ward, J. R. (1988). Cognitive distortion in rheumatoid arthritis: Relation to depression and disability. *Journal of Consulting and Clinical Psychology, 56,* 412–416.

Smyth, J. M., Stone, A. A., Hurewitz, A., & Kaell, A. (1999). Effects of writing about stressful experiences on symptom reduction in patients with asthma or rheumatoid arthritis: A randomized trial. *Journal of the American Medical Association, 281*(14), 1304–1309.

Spanier, G. B. (1976). Measuring dyadic adjustment: New scales for assessing the quality of marriage and similar dyads. *Journal of Marriage and Family Therapy, 38,* 15–28.

Spielberger, D., Gorsuch, R., & Luchene, R. (1970). *State–trait anxiety inventory manual.* Palo Alto, CA: Consulting Psychologists Press.

Stein, C. M., Griffin, M. R., & Brandt, K. D. (1996). Osteoarthritis. In S. T. Wegener, B. L. Belza, & E. P. Gall (Eds.), *Clinical care in the rheumatic diseases* (pp. 177–181). Atlanta, GA: American College of Rheumatology.

Sullivan, M., Ahlmen, M., & Bjelle, A. (1990). Health status assessment in rheumatoid arthritis. I. Further work on the validity of the Sickness Impact Profile. *Journal of Rheumatology, 17,* 439–447.

Tack, B. B. (1990). Self-reported fatigue in rheumatoid arthritis: A pilot study. *Arthritis Care and Research, 3,* 154–157.

Taurog, J. D. (1993). Seronegative spondyloarthropies: Epidemiology, pathology, and pathogenesis. In H. R. Shumaker, J. H. Klipp, & W. J. Koopman (Eds.), *Primer on the rheumatic diseases* (10th ed., pp. 151–168). Atlanta, GA: Arthritis Foundation.

Thomason, B. T., Brantley, P. J., Jones, G. N., Dyer, H. R., & Morris, J. L. (1992). The relation between stress and disease activity in rheumatoid arthritis. *Journal of Behavioral Medicine, 15,* 215–220.

Tinetti, M. E., Baker, D. I., MacAnvay, G., Claus, E. B., Garrett, P., & Gottschalk, M. (1994). A multifactorial intervention to reduce the risk of falling among elderly people living in the community. *New England Journal of Medicine, 331,* 821–827.

Turk, D. C., Okifuji, A., Sinclair, J. D., & Starz, T. W. (1998). Interdisciplinary treatment for fibromyalgia syndrome: Clinical and statistical significance. *Arthritis Care and Research, 11*(3), 186–195.

Varni, J. W., Thompson, K. L., & Hanson, V. (1987). The Varni/Thompson pediatric pain questionnaire. I. Chronic musculoskeletal pain in juvenile rheumatoid arthritis. *Pain, 28*(1), 27–38.

Von Korff, M., Dworkin, S. F., Le Resche, L., & Kruger, A. (1988). An epidemiological comparison of pain complaints. *Pain, 32,* 173–183.

Waddell, G. (1992). Biopsychosocial analysis of low back pain. *Baillieres Clinical Rheumatology, 6,* 523–557.

Wall, P. D. (1989). The dorsal horn. In P. D. Wall & R. Melzack (Eds.), *Textbook of pain* (2nd ed., pp. 80–87). London: Churchill Livingstone.

Wang, B., Gladman, D. D., & Urowitz, M. B. (1998). Fatigue in lupus is not correlated with disease activity. *Journal of Rheumatology, 25*(5), 892–895.

Wegener, S. T. (1996). Sleep disturbance. In S. T. Wegener, B. L. Belza, & E. P. Gall (Eds.), *Clinical care in the rheumatic diseases* (pp. 121–124). Atlanta, GA: American College of Rheumatology.

Weigent, D. A., Bradley, L. A., Blalock, J. E., & Alarcon, G. S. (1998). Current concepts in the pathophysiology of abnormal pain perception in fibromyalgia. *American Journal of Medical Science, 315*(6), 405–412.

Weinberger, M., Tiermey, W. M., Booher, P., & Hiner, S. L. (1990). Social support, stress, and functional status in patients with osteoarthritis. *Social Science and Medicine, 30*, 503–508.

Weinberger, M., Tiermey, W. M., Booher, P., & Katz, B. P. (1989). Can the provision of information to patients with osteoarthritis improve functional status? A randomized, controlled trial. *Arthritis and Rheumatism, 32*(12), 1577–1583.

Weiser, S., & Cedraschi, C. (1992). Psychosocial issues in the prevention of chronic low back pain—A literature review. *Baillieres Clinical Rheumatology, 6*(3), 657–684.

Wilder, R. L. (1993). Rheumatoid arthritis: Epidemiology, pathology, and pathogenesis. In H. R. Shumaker, J. H. Klipp, & W. J. Koopman (Eds.), *Primer on the rheumatic diseases* (10th ed.). Atlanta, GA: Arthritis Foundation.

Wolfe, F., Ross, K., Anderson, J., Russell, I. J., & Hebert, L. (1995). The prevalence and characteristics of fibromyalgia in the general population. *Arthritis and Rheumatism, 38*, 19–28.

World Health Organization. (1989). *International classification of diseases, ninth revision, clinical modification (ICD–9–CM)*. Geneva: Author.

Wright, G. E., Parker, J. C., Smarr, K. L., Johnson, J. C., Hewett, J. E., & Walker, S. E. (1998). Age, depressive symptoms, and rheumatoid arthritis. *Arthritis and Rheumatism, 41*(2), 298–305.

Wright, G. E., Parker, J. C., Smarr, K. L., Schoenfeld-Smith, K., Buckelew, S. P., & Slaughter, J. (1996). Risk factors for depression in rheumatoid arthritis. *Arthritis Care and Research, 9*(2), 264–272.

Yelin, E. (1995). Musculoskeletal conditions and employment. *Arthritis Care and Research, 8*, 311–317.

Yelin, E., & Callahan, L. (1995). For the national arthritis data work group: The economic cost and social and psychological impact of musculoskeletal conditions. *Arthritis and Rheumatism, 38*, 1351–1362.

Young, L. D. (1992). Psychological factors in rheumatoid arthritis. *Journal of Consulting and Clinical Psychology, 60*, 416–427.

Zautra, A. J., Hoffman, J., Potter, P., Matt, K. S., Yocum, D., & Castro, L. (1997). Examination of changes in interpersonal stress as a factor in disease exacerbations among women with rheumatoid arthritis. *Annals of Behavioral Medicine, 19*, 279–286.

14

CONGENITAL ABNORMALITIES

ALAN M. DELAMATER AND CATHERINE L. GRUS

Many congenital abnormalities may be associated with impairments in cognitive, psychological, and social functioning. Congenital abnormalities include various anomalies of physical development, including the brain and nervous system, eyes, ears, heart and circulatory system, respiratory system, cleft palate and lip, upper alimentary tract, digestive system, genital organs, urinary system, musculoskeleton and limbs, diaphragm, integument, and chromosomes.

Congenital anomalies such as tracheoesophageal fistula, imperforate anus, Hirschsprung's disease, biliary atresia, diaphragmatic hernia, gastroschisis, ambiguous genitalia, and hypospadia, are typically repaired by pediatric surgeons during infancy or early childhood. Although surgical outcomes are generally good, many of these disorders require extensive medical follow-up and ancillary services including physical and occupational therapy and may be associated with significant psychological morbidity. However, relatively little psychological research has been conducted with these patient populations.

Psychologists have made many contributions to understanding how health care professionals can best manage individuals with several specific congenital anomalies. This chapter focuses on a few of these disorders, including congenital heart disease (CHD), craniofacial anomalies, spina bifida, hydrocephalus, and Down syndrome. For each disorder, the epidemiology, associated deficits and psychological factors, and opportunities for future research are discussed.

CHD

Many studies have examined the cognitive and psychosocial sequelae associated with CHD in children. Because of medical and surgical advances in the treatment of CHD, the majority of pediatric patients who would have previously died as a result of their illness are now surviving. Consequently, researchers have paid increased attention to the long-term cognitive and psychosocial sequelae of these disorders and their treatments.

Epidemiology and Medical Treatment

Approximately 8 children in 1,000 are born with CHD (Gersony, 1987). CHD includes disorders involving structural defects of the heart or the coronary blood vessels. Most cases are diagnosed during infancy and are thought to be caused by a combination of genetic and environmental factors. CHD is divided into cyanotic and acyanotic subtypes, each having a distinctive clinical presentation. It is only in the cyanotic type of CHD that oxygenation of the blood is significantly reduced; cyanosis has been implicated as one important factor in deficits in cognitive and psychosocial functioning.

Cyanotic CHD

In cyanotic CHD the blood is shunted away from the lungs as a consequence of a communication between the systemic and pulmonary circulations. The result is cyanosis, a reduction in blood oxygenation. Examples of these defects include tetralogy of Fallot (TOF) and pulmonary atresia, each accounting for about 10% of CHD cases. Another 5% of CHD cases involve transposition of the great arteries (TGA), in which the aorta and pulmonary arteries reverse, leading to mixing of oxygenated and deoxygenated blood.

Acyanotic CHD

In acyanotic CHD the blood is shunted away from the body and to the lungs because of holes in the walls of the heart chambers. This is the most common type of CHD and includes ventricular septal defects (about 28% of CHD cases), patent ductus arteriosus (about 10% of CHD), atrial septal/atrioventricular canal defects (about 10% of CHD), and coarctation of the aorta (about 5% of CHD). Valvular lesions obstruct blood flow at the valves and may result in either pulmonic stenosis (about 10% of CHD) or aortic stenosis (about 7% of CHD). Disease of the heart muscle, or cardiomyopathy, is another type of acyanotic CHD (Gersony, 1987).

Medical Treatment

The most severe defects are now corrected surgically during infancy. Even though mortality rates are low, the surgery itself may result in adverse changes in functioning, including mental retardation, language and learning disorders, and movement and seizure disorders (Fallon, Aparicio, Elliott, & Kirkham, 1995; Ferry, 1987). As an alternative to open-heart surgery, interventional catheterization is increasing in use for repair of certain types of CHD (Lock, Keane, Mandell, & Perry, 1992). For cases in which neither open-heart repairs nor interventional catheterization are feasible, heart transplantation has become an accepted approach to treatment (Addonizio, 1996; Baum & Bernstein, 1993).

Effects of Cognitive Development

Numerous studies have compared the cognitive development of children with cyanotic heart disease to the development of children with acyanotic heart lesions. The results of these studies have demonstrated significantly lower cognitive functioning in the cyanotic group (Aram, Ekelman, Ben-Shakhar, & Levinsohn, 1985; DeMaso, Beardslee, Silbert, & Fyler, 1990; Linde, Rasof, & Dunn, 1967; Silbert, Wolff, Mayer, Rosenthal, & Nadas, 1969). DeMaso et al. (1990) found that 14% of children with TGA and 22% of children with TOF had IQ scores of less than 79, compared with only 3% of the children with acyanotic heart disease. Moreover, 40% of children with TGA and 45% of children with TOF had clinically significant central nervous system (CNS) impairment. Some evidence has suggested that children with acyanotic heart disease perform more poorly than typically developing children (Linde et al., 1967; Yang, Liu, & Townes, 1994), although they perform better than children with cyanotic CHD.

For children with cyanotic heart disease, evidence has shown that surgery conducted at younger ages is associated with improved cognitive functioning (Newburger, Silbert, Buckley, & Fryler, 1984; O'Dougherty, Wright, Garmezy, Loewenson, & Torres, 1983). The results of these studies found a significant inverse correlation between age at repair (reflecting duration of hypoxia) and IQ for children with cyanotic CHD; no relationship was noted between age at repair and IQ for children with acyanotic disease.

Investigators have also examined the effects of cyanotic CHD on children's school performance. For example, O'Dougherty et al. (1983)

found 42% of the children studied required special educational programming. Wright and Nolan (1994) found children with cyanotic heart disease performed significantly worse on measures of academic achievement and intelligence. Although the mean IQ score fell within the average range, mean performance on academic measures was lower than average.

Several studies have shown that perceptual–motor skills are adversely affected by CHD (Linde, Rasof, & Dunn, 1970; Newburger et al., 1984; Silbert et al., 1969). As cyanosis has become linked with greater intellectual impairment, cognitive processes thought to be more sensitive to hypoxia such as attention, vigilance, and information-processing capacity have been investigated. Studies have shown deficits in attention processes in children with cyanotic heart disease (O'Dougherty, Wright, Loewenson, & Torres, 1985). However, findings from another study revealed no association between medical or surgical parameters and measures of attention and processing difficulties, suggesting that the cognitive and academic difficulties displayed by children with CHD are not fully explained by chronic hypoxia (Wright & Nolan, 1994).

The effects of surviving a cardiac arrest on the functioning of children with CHD have also been examined. Morris, Krawiecki, Wright, and Walter (1993) found that more children than expected scored less than one standard deviation below the normative means for the various tests used in the study. In addition, a longer duration of cardiac arrest was associated with worse performance. Bloom, Wright, Morris, Campbell, and Krawiecki (1997) compared children with CHD who had sustained a cardiac arrest in the hospital to a medically similar group of children with CHD to examine the additive impact of cardiac arrest on the functioning of children with CHD. The children in the cardiac arrest group had significantly lower scores on measures of general cognitive, motor, and adaptive behavior functioning and had greater disease severity. Forty-four percent of the cardiac arrest group performed at least one standard deviation below the mean on the general cognitive index, compared with only 6% of the children who had not sustained a cardiac arrest. These findings suggest that children surviving a cardiac arrest may be at increased risk for cognitive and academic difficulties.

Effects of Newer Medical Interventions

Because surgical repair is now routinely being performed during infancy (thereby reducing the impact of chronic hypoxia), increased attention has been focused on the neurological sequelae related to surgical and support techniques such as low-flow cardiopulmonary bypass, extracorporeal membrane oxygenation (ECMO), and heart transplantation.

Hypothermic Circulatory and Low-Flow Cardiopulmonary Bypass

The use of low-flow cardiopulmonary bypass has been associated with reduced neurological sequelae (Bellinger et al., 1995; Bellinger, Rappaport, Wypij, Wernovsky, & Newburger, 1997; Newburger et al., 1993). Bellinger et al. (1995) conducted a randomized clinical trial of 171 children with TGA repaired by an arterial switch operation that used either predominantly total circulatory arrest or predominantly continuous low-flow cardiopulmonary bypass. Developmental and neurological evaluations were performed at age 1 year. Infants who received circulatory arrest, as compared with those assigned to low-flow bypass, had lower mean scores on the Psychomotor Development Index of the Bayley Scales of Infant Development (a 6.5-point deficit) and a higher proportion had scores of less than 80 (27% vs. 12%). The score on the Psychomotor Development Index was inversely related to the duration of circulatory arrest. Neurological abnormalities were more common among the children receiving circulatory arrest, and the risk of neurological abnormalities increased with the duration of the arrest.

In a follow-up study, Bellinger et al. (1997) examined the children's developmental status that was based on parent-completed questionnaires. Results obtained when the children were age 2.5 years indicated that the children in the circulatory arrest group had poorer expressive language.

Oates, Simpson, Turnbull, and Cartmill (1995) compared children who had their defects repaired with deep hypothermia and circulatory arrest with those who had repair with cardiopulmonary bypass. Children's cognitive abilities were examined at an average of 9 to 10 years after the operation. The bypass group had reaction times 2 to 3 seconds shorter on average than those of the hypothermic circulatory arrest group. Although no significant differences in intelligence scores between the two groups were found, a relationship was observed between IQ scores and arrest time, indicating a significant decrease in IQ with increasing arrest time.

ECMO

ECMO is a relatively new life-saving surgical procedure involving cardiopulmonary bypass of blood via cannulation of the right common carotid artery and right internal jugular vein (Klein, 1988). ECMO is now considered a standard therapy for neonatal respiratory failure that is unresponsive to other interventions; it has also been used to treat children whose cardiopulmonary status deteriorated rapidly after surgery for CHD repair (Klein, Shaheen, Whittlesey, Pinsky, & Arciniegas, 1990).

Studies have generally shown that the growth and intellectual functioning until age 3 years of children without CHD treated with ECMO during the neonatal period are equal to or just below age-expected levels (Andrews, Nixon, Cilley, Roloff, & Bartlett, 1986; Taylor, Glass, Fitz, &

Miller, 1987). Longer term follow-up studies into middle childhood have also indicated that most children grow and develop normally, but neurological complications occur in almost 20% of cases (Hofkosh et al., 1991).

However, little is known about children who have received ECMO after cardiac surgery. Tindall, Tothermel, Delamater, Pinsky, and Klein (1999) examined neurodevelopment in children ages 4 to 6 who had ECMO after cardiac surgery almost 4 years before the study and compared them with cardiac control groups (children without ECMO) and healthy children. Compared with the cardiac and healthy control children, the ECMO group exhibited deficits in left-hand motor skills and lower visual memory and visuo–spatial constructive skills.

Heart Transplantation

Children with very severe CHD and those with acquired cardiac disease or intractable arrhythmias may need a heart transplantation. This operation was first performed successfully in children more than 25 years ago. Survival rates and quality of life have improved dramatically in recent years as more transplants have been performed and techniques refined. Heart transplantation is now considered an accepted treatment for patients whose disease is in the final stages and who have no alternative treatments. However, approximately 20% of children may have neurological complications following heart transplantation (Baum & Bernstein, 1993).

Little systematic data are available concerning cognitive development of children after heart transplantation. However, clinical descriptive reports have suggested that children do not have major abnormalities, and rehabilitation is very good as children return to school and engage in age-appropriate activities (Backer et al., 1992).

Trimm (1991) evaluated the development of 29 infants who received heart transplants before age 4 months. Although only 2 children had Bayley Mental Development Index scores of less than 84, 12 patients had scores of less than 84 on the Psychomotor Development Index. However, in another report of neurodevelopmental outcomes of children receiving transplants during infancy, Baum et al. (1993) found a mean Bayley Mental Developmental Index of 87 and a Psychomotor Developmental Index of 90, with 67% of the children having scores in the normal range.

Wray and Yacoub (1991) compared developmental functioning of children who received heart transplants with children who had corrective open-heart surgery and healthy control children. Children who received transplants had lower developmental scores than the healthy control children, but their mean scores were within normal limits. However, older children who had transplants scored significantly lower than both groups on developmental and academic achievement scores, and those with a history of cyanotic CHD did worse regardless of whether they had a transplant or an open-heart surgery.

The results of another study indicated that children given heart transplants had significantly lower scores on several developmental parameters, compared with a cardiac control group (receiving other surgery) and normal children (Wray, Pot-Mees, Zeitlin, Radley-Smith, & Yacoub, 1994). Among children younger than age 5 years, the children in the transplant and cardiac groups did not differ significantly from each other, but both groups performed significantly below the healthy control children in all developmental areas. Among older children, the transplant group had significantly lower intelligence than the two comparison groups and also performed significantly worse than the healthy group on tests of short-term memory, nonverbal reasoning, and information processing speed. Their short-term memory was also significantly lower than the cardiac control group.

Behavioral and Emotional Functioning

Numerous studies have examined the behavioral and emotional functioning of children with CHD. Early studies suggested that CHD had a negative impact on behavior and emotions (e.g., Aurer, Senturia, Shopper, & Biddy, 1971) and family functioning (e.g., Apley, Barbour, & Westmacott, 1967). More recent studies have also identified some specific problems during early childhood, such as difficult temperament (Marino & Lipshitz, 1991), and some emotional or behavioral problems later in childhood, particularly in children with decreased functional status.

DeMaso et al. (1990) examined psychological functioning of children with cyanotic CHD and found they had lower levels of psychological functioning than a control group of healthy children spontaneously recovered from their heart problem. Psychological functioning was predicted by degree of CNS impairment and IQ. In another study, the investigators found maternal perceptions accounted for the majority of variance in child adjustment, with medical severity explaining only 3% of the variance (DeMaso et al., 1991). The mean T score for total behavior problems for this sample of children with CHD was 52.2, indicating good overall functioning. Similarly, Morris et al. (1993) found little evidence suggesting significant behavioral problems in children with CHD who survived cardiac arrest.

Spurkland, Bjornstad, Lindberg, and Seem (1993) examined behavioral functioning and physical capacity in adolescents with cyanotic CHD and compared it with a healthy group who had repaired atrial septal defects. Results showed those adolescents with cyanotic CHD had significantly lower physical capacity, greater behavioral problems, and more psychiatric diagnoses, with overanxious disorder and dysthymic disorder being the most common diagnoses. Only one third of the youths with cyanotic CHD were functioning normally; one third had minor to moderate problems, and another third had serious dysfunction. Psychopathology was associated with more severe physical impairments.

Casey, Sykes, Craig, Power, and Mulholland (1996) examined the behavioral adjustment of children with surgically palliated complex CHD compared to children with innocent heart murmurs. Behavior ratings by teachers indicated that children with CHD were more withdrawn and more likely to have academic achievement problems. Degree of family strain and exercise tolerance were significant predictors of teacher-rated school performance. Ratings by parents indicated that children with CHD were more withdrawn, had more social problems, and engaged in fewer activities.

Few studies are available on the longer term behavioral and emotional adjustment of children with CHD. Available studies have suggested that young adults with CHD may be more dependent, reserved, and anxious (Baer, Freedman, & Garson, 1984; Garson, Williams, & Redford, 1974). However, the results of another study found no differences in the long-term psychosocial outcomes (emotional and social functioning and occupational attainment) between young adults who received childhood surgery for CHD and the control sample (Utens et al., 1994). However, the young adults with CHD were more likely to be living with their parents.

Uzark et al. (1992) examined the psychosocial adjustment 2 years after transplantation of a group of children who were a mean age of 10 years at the time of study. Parent behavior ratings indicated these children had significantly lower levels of social competence and more behavior problems than the normative population, with depressive symptoms noted to be the most common psychological problem. Psychosocial problems were associated with greater family stress and fewer family coping resources.

The posttransplantation regimen can be very stressful. It may consist of daily doses of immunosuppressive medications with considerable side effects and extensive medical follow-up treatments including endomyocardial biopsy. Regimen adherence problems may be clinically important, yet few studies have addressed this issue. One report indicated that 20% of pediatric patients had significant adherence problems, which increased the chances of graft rejection (Douglas, Hsu, & Addonizio, 1993). In a study of adult patients, those with adherence problems had a higher incidence of hospital readmission and higher total medical costs (Paris, Muchmore, Pribil, Zuhdi, & Cooper, 1994).

Mai, McKenzie, and Kostuk (1990) examined the psychosocial adjustment of adult patients prior to and 12 months after heart transplantation. Psychosocial adjustment and quality of life improved significantly at follow-up, with relatively few patients receiving a psychiatric diagnosis. Patients with psychiatric problems before the transplant were more likely to have postoperative regimen adherence problems.

Future Research

Although most children with CHD can be expected to function in the normal range, studies of cognitive development have shown that children with severe forms of CHD are at risk for lower levels of intellectual functioning and academic achievement. Increased neurological involvement and cyanosis and surgical repairs done later in childhood could cause more serious deficits in cognitive development. Further studies are needed of specific areas of cognitive functioning that may be affected by congenital cardiac disorders.

Many children with CHD can be expected to function within the normal range on measures of behavioral and emotional functioning, but if surgical repair is made later in childhood or their functional status diminished, the risk for behavioral or emotional difficulties increases. Future studies are needed that focus on social competence, social anxiety, feelings of vulnerability, and autonomy issues because these psychological factors may play an important role in the behavioral and emotional adjustment of children with CHD.

Although advances in medical and surgical management have improved survival and quality of life for children with congenital cardiac disorders, more studies of the developmental effects of such approaches are needed, particularly for children receiving ECMO and heart transplants.

More intervention research is also needed. Significant contributions could be made by developing and evaluating interventions to improve academic functioning, social competence, and autonomy. In addition, studies are needed to improve regimen adherence problems for patients after heart transplantation.

CRANIOFACIAL ANOMALIES

The most common craniofacial anomalies are cleft lip, cleft palate, and cleft lip and palate. However, facial clefts also occur as part of several craniofacial syndromes such as Aperts syndrome, Crouzons disease, and Pierre Robin syndrome. Among these anomalies, cleft lip and cleft palate have been studied most extensively and therefore are the focus of this section.

Epidemiology

Congenital craniofacial anomalies are among the most common birth defects. Cleft lip, cleft palate, or cleft lip and palate are the most common of these defects, with an overall prevalence rate of 1 in every 750 neonates (Berkowitz, 1994; Cleft Palate Foundation, 1996). Cleft lip with or without cleft palate is more common than cleft palate only. Gender is a factor; males are more likely to have a cleft of the lip with or without cleft of the palate, and females are more likely to have clefts of the palate. Incidence varies by racial and ethnic groups as well, with clefts being most common in Native Americans (1 in every 400 to 500 live births) and Asians (1 in 500), followed by White people of European descent (1 in 750). Clefts are the least common in African Americans (1 in 2,000; Berkowitz, 1994; Lettieri, 1997; Tolarova & Cervenka, 1998). The etiology of clefts is thought to be multifactorial, although in 44% to 64% of children, clefts are associated with a craniofacial syndrome (Berkowitz, 1994).

Clefts occur when the right and left segments of the palate and/or the lip elements fail to come together during fetal development (Berkowitz, 1994). Clefts can be unilateral or bilateral. Left-sided clefts are more common and account for 70% of all unilateral clefts (Berkowitz, 1994). Clefts are also classified as complete or incomplete. As such, a great deal of individual variation in presentation with clefting conditions occurs.

Medical Treatment

Treatment of cleft lip, cleft palate, and cleft lip and palate involves surgical repair of the structures affected. A child with a cleft is likely to undergo several surgeries, often beginning in infancy and extending into adolescence or young adulthood. Orthopedic devices are used in some cases before surgery to move the palatal segments into a better relationship.

Surgical repair of a cleft lip generally occurs at some time between ages 2 and 6 months (Berkowitz, 1994). The goal of lip closure is to bring the separated lip muscle parts into a normal relationship to minimize scarring, make the appearance pleasing, and facilitate normal facial development. Additional lip and nose surgeries are common and occur over several years.

Palatal repair typically occurs between ages 12 and 18 months, although individual factors affect timing. Repair of the palate may involve more than one surgical procedure. Repair includes moving the soft tissue covering the bone toward the middle of the palate over the cleft space. In addition, the muscles that comprise the soft palate are joined together either at the same time or before the hard palate is closed. A follow-up procedure (a pharyngeal flap) may be required when the child is about age 4 years to improve speech by controlling airflow (Berkowitz, 1994).

Associated Deficits

Clefting conditions affect multiple functional domains and require ongoing management throughout a child's development. Associated areas of deficit include dentition, feeding, speech and language development, audiological development, cognitive development, and psychosocial functioning. Children with clefts of the lip and palate typically experience dental problems such as missing or improperly positioned teeth that require ongoing orthodontic management. Feeding difficulties can also occur, particularly in infants with a cleft of the hard palate because their cleft makes it difficult for them to put adequate pressure on a nipple (Cleft Palate Foundation, 1989).

Speech deficits are a frequent and significant functional impairment associated with clefts of the palate (Berkowitz, 1994). The most common speech problem in children with cleft palate, occurring in 10% to 25% of children, is caused by velopharyngeal insufficiency, or inadequate closure of the oral–nasal orifice (Berkowitz, 1994). This structural abnormality makes it very difficult to control and direct the air stream during speech. Speech of children with a cleft palate is often characterized by hypernasality or excessive escape of speech sounds through the nose. Surgical repair improves this problem; however, the children need to learn to coordinate the sounds of normal speech (Berkowitz, 1994). Language disorders can also occur (Cleft Palate Foundation, 1989).

Young children with clefts of the palate are also at increased risk for otitis media, as the palatal muscles do not effectively allow the Eustachian tubes to open. Poor air circulation can allow fluid to form and accumulate in the middle ear and then become infected (Cleft Palate Foundation, 1989). As a result, children with clefts of the palate are more likely to experience hearing loss than children without cleft palate (Berkowitz, 1994).

Psychological Factors

Psychological issues associated with cleft lip and cleft palate have received considerable research attention. Areas of focus that are reviewed in the following sections include cognitive and academic functioning, attachment, emotional adjustment, and social skills.

Cognitive and Academic Functioning

Research findings have indicated that children with cleft conditions may be at greater risk for learning disabilities and poor academic performance. In one of the few published studies of school-age children with either isolated cleft palate or cleft lip and palate, Broder, Richman, and Matheson (1998) found 46% had a learning disability and 47% were functioning below grade level. For those with isolated cleft palate, males were significantly more likely to have a learning disability and to have repeated a grade. For those with cleft lip and palate, females were more likely than males to have repeated a grade. The type of learning disability was not presented. Although this study is limited because a control group was not used and demographic variables were not addressed, it does suggest that children with cleft conditions are at increased risk for learning disorders.

Studies examining the developmental functioning of infants with craniofacial conditions have also suggested that some children with clefts experience delays in development. Kapp-Simon (1997) compared infants ages 5 to 25 months on the Bayley Scale of Infant Development, including infants with isolated cleft lip, isolated cleft palate, cleft lip and palate, Pierre Robin syndrome, and craniosynostosis. Performance on the mental Bayley scale was two standard deviations below the mean in 12% of the isolated cleft palate group, 15% of the cleft lip and palate group, and 20% of the Pierre Robin group. Risk for developmental delay increased with an increase in number of other medical problems.

Similar findings were reported by Neiman and Savage (1997), who examined caregiver reports of development in 186 children with isolated cleft lip or palate or cleft lip and palate. Using cross-sectional ratings, differences emerged as a function of age. When compared to norms, a greater proportion of infants who were age 5 months were classified as "at risk" or "developmentally delayed." For infants with isolated cleft lip, this finding was observed on the total scale score and the motor score. Isolated cleft palate was associated with at risk and delayed development classifications more often in the domains of motor skills, self-help, and language. For infants with cleft lip and palate, this was observed on the total scale score, motor, self-help, and cognitive scores. At age 13 months, infants were within normal limits in all domains with the exception of infants with isolated cleft palate, who were more likely to show delays in the motor domain. Toddlers age 25 months were noted to be functioning significantly better than those age 36 months in the areas of fine motor skills, gross motor skills, and expressive language. At age 36 months, toddlers with cleft palate met criteria more frequently for at-risk and developmentally delayed classifications in the area of expressive language. Moreover, toddlers ages 25 and 36 months with cleft palate tended to have lower expressive language scores than those with cleft lip.

Cognitive and learning deficits have been consistently associated with some craniofacial syndromes. Caouette-Laberge, Bayet, and Larocque (1994) studied a sample of 108 children with Pierre Robin syndrome and found that 23% were classified as having mental retardation. However, mental retardation was more likely to be associated with other complications such as neurological problems or syndromes than specifically with the cleft.

Studies have indicated that not all craniofacial conditions are associated with cognitive or learning problems. Speltz, Endriga, and Mouradian (1997) compared 19 healthy, typically developing infants with 19 infants who had nonsyndromic sagittal synostosis. Groups were matched on demographic variables. Development was assessed at three time points. Mean cognitive and motor development as assessed by the Bayley Scales of Infant Development was within normal limits for both groups at all assessment points. None of the infants with sagittal synostosis received scores in the mental retardation or borderline range, and only one had a borderline motor score at the second assessment.

Overall, studies assessing cognitive and academic development have suggested that some children with clefting conditions may experience developmental delays and learning disabilities or show poor academic performance. However, these findings are limited by a lack of comparisons of children who have clefts with control children matched for demographic variables that may influence cognitive and academic outcomes. Some evidence has shown that children who have clefts associated with a craniofacial syndrome are at increased risk for cognitive and learning problems but again, findings vary by type of syndrome.

Social Functioning and Self-Esteem

The social functioning and self-esteem of children with cleft conditions have received considerable attention. Although the majority of studies of social functioning in children with clefts have focused on adolescents, research has examined the effects of these conditions at different ages. Krueckeberg, Kapp-Simon, and Ribordy (1993) compared the social skills of preschoolers with and without clefts. Control children were found to give friendlier responses to hypothetical social situations than children with clefts, although overall girls were more assertive than boys. Social skills in children with clefts were found to be significantly predicted by facial encoding ability and friendliness of response in a social situation. On an overall measure of self-competence, girls with clefts were found to have higher total scores than boys with clefts or control girls. However, it is important to note that ratings for boys with clefts were within normal limits.

Social competence was examined by Pope and Ward (1997a) in a sample of preadolescents with clefts including cleft palate only, cleft lip and palate, and craniofacial syndromes. Self-report measures of social functioning were completed by participants and their parents. When scores for the sample were compared with normative scores on the measures, no differences emerged for the sample. Regression equations to predict social competence indicated that it was associated with more companionship experiences; positive self-concept in the areas of scholastic, athletic, and physical appearance; and active orchestration of social activities by the parent. Lower social competence was associated with higher levels of social anxiety and loneliness, greater withdrawal behavior, and greater parental concern.

Extending their work with this sample, Pope and Ward (1997b) noted that dissatisfaction with facial appearance in preadolescents is associated with problematic peer relationships but generally not with other types of psychosocial adjustment problems. Perceived facial appearance was related to loneliness, parent advice and support, high parental concern, and parent-rated social problems. Preadolescents' reports of number of same-sex close friends and self-perceptions of social acceptance and global self-worth were positively related to self-perceived facial appearance.

Studies with adolescents have suggested differences between children with a cleft and children without clefts in social interactions. In one of the few studies to use a comparison group, Kapp-Simon and McGuire (1997) observed adolescents with and without clefts in the school lunch room and noted differences in social interactions. Comparison adolescents initiated more contact with peers, responded more frequently to peer initiation, and were more likely to have an initial contact become a conversation. Adolescents with clefts were approached by peers less often and engaged in fewer extended conversations, and peers were less likely to respond when addressed by them.

King, Shultz, Steel, Gilpin, and Cathers (1993) compared adolescents with cerebral palsy, cleft lip or palate only and cleft lip and palate, and spina bifida on measures of self-concept and social functioning. The only significant group difference that emerged was that adolescents with cleft lip, palate, or both reported higher levels of athletic competence than those in the other groups.

Thomas, Turner, Rumsey, Dowell, and Sandy (1997) measured facial satisfaction from participants with cleft lip or palate ranging in age from 10 to 20 years; those with craniofacial syndromes were excluded. Less satisfaction with facial appearance was reported by younger children. Facial satisfaction was significantly related to psychosocial functioning of younger children.

Children with cleft conditions have been shown to experience problems with social functioning such as inhibition, shyness, and withdrawal compared with peers in a natural setting (Kapp-Simon & McGuire, 1997). In contrast, studies relying on self-reports or parental reports of social skills have been less consistent in their findings and have reported impairment in some cases, no differences in others, and improved skills in some areas. It has been suggested that level of disfigurement does not relate to the extent of problems experienced (Kapp-Simon, 1997). Instead, self-esteem and satisfaction with facial appearance seems to be more important (Pope & Ward, 1997b; Thomas et al., 1997). In addition, cleft conditions may affect social functioning because children with clefts may not be able to accurately identify emotions being conveyed or produce a response that is recognized because of their facial differences (Krueckeberg et al., 1993).

Behavioral Functioning

Studies investigating the behavioral functioning of children with clefts have suggested that gender and age play a role in the type and severity of difficulty observed. Richman and Millard (1997) completed one of the few longitudinal studies of the behavioral functioning of children with cleft lip, palate, or both. Their sample included children with either cleft lip only or cleft lip and palate, as well as control children with no clefts. No differences in behavioral functioning were noted between the clinical groups, so results were combined for longitudinal analysis. As the girls got older, they had significantly higher rates of internalizing behaviors and conduct problems. Boys displayed higher rates of externalizing behaviors at younger ages.

Richman (1997) investigated the relationship of speech and facial variables to the behavioral functioning of children with cleft lip and palate or cleft palate only at ages 6, 9, and 12 years. No differences were noted between the two cleft conditions. Findings from a behavior rating scale revealed that boys and girls had higher scores than normal on the internalizing scale, whereas scores on the externalizing scale were comparable to normative values. Younger boys and those with lower intelligence were more likely to exhibit externalizing behavior problems. Older girls with greater intelligence were more likely to display internalizing behavior problems. When the effects of gender, IQ, and socioeconomic status were removed, older children with greater facial disfigurement had more internalizing behavior problems.

Speltz, Morton, Goodell, and Clarren (1993) compared the behavioral functioning of children with cleft lip only, cleft lip and palate, and craniosynostosis to control children with no clefts. Girls with a cleft had more mother-rated behavior problems (both internalizing and externalizing) than girls in the comparison group and boys with clefts, although their mean scores were within normal limits. No differences were noted on teacher ratings of child behavior. However, nearly 20% of the children with clefts were noted to have clinically significant behavior problems according to the mother and teacher. No significant differences in functioning were noted across the three craniofacial subgroups.

These findings suggest that children with clefts may be at risk for behavioral problems. Results also support a gender effect and different patterns of behavioral functioning at different ages. Girls with clefts seem to be at greater risk for internalizing behavioral problems, although they may also exhibit significant externalizing behavior problems as they get older. Attempts to relate behavioral functioning to features associated with having a cleft suggest that intelligence, speech functioning, and facial disfigurement may all be significant predictors, although different impacts of these variables have been noted at different ages. Unfortunately, little attention has been paid to the behavioral functioning of children with craniofacial syndromes, making it difficult to assess independently any behavioral impact of these disorders.

Attachment

Children with cleft lip, palate, or both have been hypothesized to be at risk for attachment difficulties. Risk factors include feeding difficulties, surgical and medical needs, and familial difficulty with adjustment and coping to having a child with a craniofacial difference (Eliason, 1991; Speltz, Greenberg, Endriga, & Galbreath, 1994). In one study to assess attachment directly, Speltz, Endriga, Fisher, and Mason (1997) compared infants with isolated cleft palate, infants with cleft lip and palate, and a comparison group. Although rates of secure attachment were similar across all groups, girls with a cleft of any type were at a twice greater risk than boys with a cleft for insecure attachment. In the cleft group, insecure attachment was predicted by several maternal variables, including younger age, primiparity, and depression.

Studies examining mother–child interactions during feeding also indicated that children with clefts are at an increased risk for attachment difficulties. Speltz, Goodell, Endriga, and Clarren (1994) have shown that the facial appearance in an infant with an unrepaired cleft lip may affect the ability to communicate emotions, which in turn affects interaction during feeding. Mothers of infants with cleft lip and palate were found to be less sensitive to the cues of their infants than mothers of infants with cleft palate only or a group of comparison mothers. Endriga and Speltz (1997) noted few differences between infants with and without clefts during mother–infant feeding interactions, although mothers of infants with cleft palate were less involved when their infant was looking at them.

Family Functioning

Few studies have examined the impact of craniofacial differences on family functioning. Speltz et al. (1993) noted that mothers of children with clefts reported poorer emotional health than control mothers. In addition, mothers of children with a cleft lip and palate reported less social support and satisfaction than mothers of children with cleft palate or synostosis, although many more of these mothers were single parents.

Campis, DeMaso, and Twente (1995) examined the relationship between maternal and child behavioral adjustment. Maternal self-reported levels of depression, anxiety, and parenting stress were within normal limits, as were maternal ratings of child behavior problems. Maternal adjustment and parenting stress were unrelated to the medical severity of their child's condition but were associated with maladjustment in the child. In addition, children with more comorbid medical conditions had more behavior problems.

In summary, findings indicate that mothers of children with craniofacial problems may have poorer emotional health. Maternal emotional adjustment, mother–child relationship stress, social support, and the severity of the medical condition have been identified as factors that are associated with the adaptation of children.

Future Research

Although cleft lip, cleft palate, and cleft lip and palate are the most common of the craniofacial conditions, they still occur relatively infrequently. Thus, much of the published research has used small, heterogeneous samples of children with different types of clefts (e.g., lip, palate, or both) or isolated clefting conditions mixed together with craniofacial syndromes. Future research should be conducted with larger, more homogeneous samples to improve understanding of the impact of clefts on children, which would most likely require collaborative, multicenter studies. Gender seems to be an important variable in many of the studies assessing the impact of clefting conditions. However, due to prevalence rates, boys tend to be represented more often in samples, so conclusions about the impact of clefts on girls are made from samples with limited numbers of girls. Finally, studies assessing the impact of craniofacial anomalies on adults are notably lacking.

SPINA BIFIDA

Spina bifida is caused by a neural tube defect and consists of a class of congenital anomalies that are the most commonly occurring congenital malformations. Several disorders are related to spina bifida and are associated with varying degrees of neurological impairment and associated disability.

Epidemiology and Clinical Presentation

The overall prevalence rate of spina bifida is approximately 1 to 5 of 1,000 live births (De Vivo, 1991), with relatively more White Americans than African Americans affected (Sarwark, 1996). More girls than boys have spina bifida, with a ratio of 1.5:1 (Jones, 1997). However, it is not known whether this is a true finding or that girls are simply more likely to survive it (Hunter, 1993b). Most neural tube defects occur in families with no prior history of affected individuals.

Spina bifida is a posterior spinal defect involving bone closure

(Hunter, 1993b). The defect can occur at any point along the spine, and the resulting lesion can be open or closed and visible or invisible (White, 1993). The major types of spina bifida include spina bifida occulta and spina bifida cystica. When the defect is covered by essentially normal skin, it is referred to as *spina bifida occulta*. Spina bifida occulta is the mildest and most common type. *Spina bifida cystica* typically refers to meningoceles and myelomeningoceles, which are lesions that occur as a result of defective closure of the neural tube in the vertebral column (Tolmie, 1997b). In the case of a meningocele, only the meninges are incorporated into the surrounding skin. In a myelomeningocele, both the meninges and spinal cord tissue are incorporated into the skin. A meningocele is a closed lesion and is not typically associated with a neurological deficit. However, when neural tissue is exposed, a neurological deficit is almost always present (Tolmie, 1997b).

The lesion can vary in size as well and can affect a single vertebra or the entire neuraxis (Hunter, 1993b). Most spina bifida can be treated by surgical closure during infancy. Untreated, open spina bifida has a mortality rate of 90% to 100% (Sarwark, 1996). Neurological impairment is present at birth and is related to the type, severity, and level of the lesion (Hunter, 1993b). Typically, the nerve leading to the bowel and bladder is damaged (White, 1993).

A multifactorial model has been proposed to describe the etiology of these disorders. Spina bifida occurs early in fetal development; closure of the neural tube occurs at approximately 22 to 26 days after conception. Neural tube defects can be detected prenatally by measurement of maternal serum alpha-fetoprotein levels at 16 to 18 weeks of gestation (Hunter, 1993b). Folic acid deficiency has been described as accounting for up to 50% of neural tube defects (Sarwark, 1996). Moreover, maternal folic acid supplementation before and during conception has been found to prevent the majority of recurrences of neural tube defects. Maternal diabetes mellitus and use of valproic acid or other anticonvulsants have been associated with neural tube defects, as has maternal hyperthermia during pregnancy (e.g., from a high fever, hot tub baths, sauna use). Lower socioeconomic status may also be related to increased risk (Hunter, 1993b).

Associated Deficits

Hydrocephalus, scoliosis, dilated urinary tract, and club foot are associated with neural tube defects. The obstruction caused by a myelomeningocele often results in hydrocephalus or an accumulation of cerebrospinal fluid (CSF) in the ventricles of the brain. Often the insertion of an intraventricular shunt is required to aid in drainage. Hydrocephalus occurs in 90% of those with lumbosacral spina bifida and can typically be detected in the neonatal period. Cervical, thoracic, and sacral lesions are less often associated with hydrocephalus. The development of ventriculoperitoneal shunts has significantly improved outcomes for children with spina bifida, and survival rates have increased during the past 15 years (Hunter, 1993b).

Physical therapy and orthopedic management are also often used for those with spina bifida to maintain flexibility, align the spine, and adjust the relationship of the hip, knee, and ankle. Renal abnormalities are also associated with spina bifida. Incontinence is caused by lack of normal rectal sensation and voluntary control of the external sphincter, which occur because of neurosensory and neuromotor impairments. Surgical management of club foot may also be required (Hunter, 1993b).

Psychological Factors

Cognitive Functioning

Research has shown that children with spina bifida, particularly those with hydrocephalus, are at risk for cognitive deficits. Minchom et al. (1995) noted that children with spina bifida and hydrocephalus had significantly lower cognitive functioning (mean IQ of 75.8) than those without hydrocephalus (mean IQ of 90.3). Hurley, Dorman, Laatsch, Bell, and D'Avignon (1990) found an average IQ score of 77.1 in a sample of individuals with spina bifida and hydrocephalus. Appleton et al. (1997) also noted that children with spina bifida had lower IQ scores than control children (78.6 vs. 100.5), although those with hydrocephalus were not separated out.

Increased risk for nonverbal learning disabilities in children with spina bifida has been suggested as well. Bier, Morales, Liebling, Geddes, and Kim (1997) studied factors associated with cognitive outcomes in 106 children and young adults with spina bifida. Eighty percent of the participants had shunted hydrocephalus. The average level of cognitive functioning as assessed on a brief intelligence test was 78, with a range of 40 to 116. Only 28% of the participants had scores within or above the average range; 15% had scores of less than 50, indicating significant cognitive impairment. Regression analyses showed that the lesion level and number of shunts accounted for more than half of the variance in cognitive total score. Those participants with shunt revisions had significantly lower nonverbal and total scores and also had a significant difference between their scores on the verbal and nonverbal tasks.

Hurley et al. (1990) studied what has been termed the *cocktail party syndrome*, which is a pattern of hyperverbal behavior and low cognitive functioning in individuals with spina bifida. The content of such verbalizations is noted to be superficial and frequently includes jargon the speaker does not even understand. Hurley et al. (1990) demonstrated that individuals with the cocktail party syndrome had significantly lower verbal and nonverbal cognitive abilities and academic achievement than healthy individuals and those with spina bifida but few symptoms. When compared with those who did not have the cocktail party syndrome but had a low IQ, no differences were measured on the cognitive factors, although academic functioning was significantly lower.

In summary, deficits in cognitive functioning seem to be associated with spina bifida; however, research findings have indicated this relationship is related to the presence of hydrocephalus.

Self-Concept

The self-concept of children with spina bifida is an area that has also received research attention. Appleton et al. (1994) compared a sample of children with spina bifida to a control group matched for age, gender, classroom, and housing neighborhood. Older girls with spina bifida had the lowest overall self-worth scores. With respect to academic functioning, children with spina bifida rated themselves as significantly less competent in reading, writing, math, and general intellectual ability than control groups. Those with spina bifida also rated themselves as lower in athletic competence and social acceptance. Social support by parents, teachers, and classmates was associated with global self-worth for children with spina bifida.

Appleton et al. (1997) examined self-image in children with spina bifida and a comparison group matched for age, gender, classroom, and housing neighborhood. Significant group differences were noted, with children with spina bifida reporting lower global self-worth. However, frequency of hydrocephalus, shunting, or degree of lesion was not reported.

Minchom et al. (1995) found a significant relationship between increased severity of disability and higher global self-worth and satisfaction with physical appearance. Presence of hydrocephalus had no independent effect on global self-worth. One possible reason suggested for the relationship between increased disability and increased self-worth was that children with milder disabilities are more likely to be interacting with peers who do not have disabilities and thus are subject to more comparisons.

Landry, Robinson, Copeland, and Garner (1993) compared children with spina bifida and matched control groups. None of the children were functioning in the mental retardation range, and all of the children with spina bifida had shunts because of hydrocephalus. Groups were matched on age and nonverbal intellectual functioning. No group differences were noted on a measure of self-competence. However, parent ratings revealed children with spina bifida had lower scores on the scholastic/cognitive competence and athletic/physical competence scales. Fletcher et al. (1995) also studied children who had shunts as a result of hydrocephalus and excluded children with mental retardation. Those with spina bifida and hydrocephalus had lower physical competence scores than control groups.

Behavioral and Emotional Functioning

Results of studies of the behavioral and emotional functioning of children with spina bifida have suggested an increased risk for difficulties. Wallander, Feldman, and Varni (1989) studied children with spina bifida, some of whom had shunts for hydrocephalus. Overall scores on a standardized measure of behavioral functioning revealed scores within normal limits on the internalizing, externalizing, and social competence scales. However, analyses comparing these scores to normative means indicated that children with spina bifida had more internalizing and externalizing problems and lower social competence than children who had not been referred for behavior problems but displayed fewer problems and greater social competence than children who had been referred. Overall, 16% of the children had significant internalizing problems, 19% had externalizing problems, and 23% had social competence problems. Adjustment was not related to an overall measure of disability. A small but significant relationship was detected between number of surgeries and internalizing problems.

Zurmohle et al. (1998) also examined the behavioral functioning of children with spina bifida. The study sample included children with spina bifida, most of whom had hydrocephalus, and a control group matched for age and gender. Intelligence was significantly lower in the children with spina bifida. There were no differences between the groups on an overall measure of behavior problems, but older girls with spina bifida had more problems with depression and social withdrawal, and older boys with spina bifida had higher scores on a scale measuring immaturity. Although no group differences were found on anxiety, children with spina bifida demonstrated a greater concern for social acceptance. A relationship approaching significance was found between psychosocial difficulties and medical severity.

A study by Appleton et al. (1997) provided more support for the findings of increased risk for psychological difficulties in children with spina bifida. Psychological functioning in children with spina bifida was compared with a group of children matched for age, gender, classroom, and housing neighborhood. Children with spina bifida had a more depressed mood, lower energy, and greater suicidal ideation. However, frequency of hydrocephalus, shunting, or degree of lesion was not reported for the sample.

Family Functioning

One of the few studies to assess psychological functioning in parents of children with spina bifida was conducted by Holmbeck et al. (1997). Compared with control mothers of healthy children, mothers of children with spina bifida reported less parenting satisfaction and competence and more social isolation and role restriction. They also used more denial and less active coping and planning and were less adaptable to change. Fathers reported more symptoms of psychological distress and less parenting satisfaction and were more likely to cope with stress by venting emotions. Nineteen percent of mothers and 26% of fathers of children with spina bifida had psychological symptom scores in the clinical range. Differences were not found between the groups on ratings of marital satisfaction. Fletcher et al. (1995) did not find any difference among families of children with spina bifida with or without hydrocephalus, those with hydrocephalus from other causes, and control families on measures of family environment, psychological resources, and material resources.

Family environment variables have also been examined in relation to social adjustment in adults with spina bifida. Loomis, Javornisky, Monahan, Burke, and Lindsay (1997) examined the relationship between perceptions of family functioning and social adjustment in adults with spina bifida. Participants rated their families as lower in cohesion, expressiveness, intellectual and cultural orientation, and active–recreational orientation when compared with normative values for the measure. Perceived family achievement orientation, encouragement of independence, and family organization were positively related to employment, community mobility, and social activity.

Future Research

Although significant advances have been made in the understanding of the psychological impact of spina bifida, several methodological issues are important for future research, such as the need to control for level of cognitive functioning, presence of hydrocephalus, shunting for hydrocephalus, and level and type of neurological impairment. Given that study samples have often included very broad age ranges, more developmental consideration in the design of future studies is also needed.

HYDROCEPHALUS

Hydrocephalus is excessive fluid within the cranium and is associated with increased pressure (Tolmie, 1997b). Hydrocephalus can be the result of increased production or decreased absorption of CSF, although it is usually caused by a mechanical obstruction to the circulation of CSF at one or more levels (Hunter, 1993a).

Epidemiology and Medical Issues

Isolated hydrocephalus is reported to occur in 0.5 to 0.8 of 1,000 births (Hunter, 1993a). Males are affected more frequently than females

(1.45:1) (Tolmie, 1997b). Hydrocephalus frequently occurs as part of a congenital malformation such as aqueductal stenosis.

Hydrocephalus can be identified during pregnancy using ultrasound, although most cases of congenital hydrocephalus are identified in early childhood. However, as many as 50% of cases of pediatric hydrocephalus may be asymptomatic. Isolated hydrocephalus is associated with lower risk of neurological disability (Tolmie, 1997b).

A ventriculoperitoneal shunt is commonly used in the management of hydrocephalus. The shunt is typically placed in one of the lateral ventricles; in the case of a ventriculoperitoneal shunt the other end flows into the peritoneal cavity.

Psychological Factors

Cognitive Functioning

Hydrocephalus has been associated with cognitive and motor deficits. Impairment in nonverbal abilities relative to verbal skills has been associated with hydrocephalus as well. Fletcher et al. (1995) found that among individuals with one of three different types of etiologies of hydrocephalus, all had lower overall cognitive abilities than those without hydrocephalus, although mean scores were lower than average to average. The lowest scores for overall cognitive abilities as well as visuo–perceptual and motor skills were found for children who had hydrocephalus associated with spina bifida.

Casey et al. (1997) examined academic functioning in children with hydrocephalus. Of a sample of 155 children with hydrocephalus, 36% required special school placement. The origin of hydrocephalus was a significant factor, with 29% of children with congenital hydrocephalus attending special education classes as compared with 60% with an infectious etiology and 52% with intraventricular hemorrhage. The number of shunt revisions was not associated with academic placement.

These cognitive deficits may be pervasive across the life span as suggested by the findings of Hommet et al. (1999). Their sample consisted of adolescents and adults, some with spina bifida and others with aqueductal stenosis. All had shunts for their hydrocephalus, and none were functioning in the mental retardation range. No differences were noted between those with and without spina bifida with regard to verbal comprehension abilities, which were in the average range. However, those individuals with spina bifida performed at lower levels on measures of perceptual–organizational abilities and tests of verbal and visual memory.

Behavioral and Emotional Functioning

Research findings have suggested that children with hydrocephalus have an increased risk for behavioral problems. Fernell, Gillberg, and von

Wendt (1991) compared children with and without hydrocephalus on numerous parent report measures of behavioral functioning. Mental retardation was present in 42% of children with hydrocephalus. Children with hydrocephalus were consistently rated as having more behavioral problems than the control groups; however, this difference was found in children with hydrocephalus and mental retardation, particularly when accompanied by a neurological impairment. The prevalence of behavior problems was 41% for those with hydrocephalus and mental retardation, 2% for those without mental retardation, and 5% for those in the comparison group. The origin of the hydrocephalus, having a shunt, and experiencing shunt dysfunction were factors not associated with the presence of behavior problems.

Although the presence of mental retardation may be associated with behavior problems in children with hydrocephalus, research findings of Fletcher et al. (1995) suggested an independent effect of the presence of hydrocephalus. In one of the few studies to consider the etiology of hydrocephalus, six groups of children were studied, including three distinct etiologies of hydrocephalus (spina bifida, prematurity, aqueductal stenosis) and three nonhydrocephalic comparison groups (spina bifida, prematurity, normal); children functioning in the mental retardation range were excluded from study. Children in the hydrocephalic groups were more likely to have significant internalizing behavior problems (29% compared with 12%). Behavior problems were more likely in boys and children who had shunts or shunt revisions, but the etiology of the hydrocephalus was unrelated to behavior problems.

Donders, Rourke, and Canady (1992) also examined the emotional functioning of children with hydrocephalus, some of whom also had spina bifida. Significant emotional adjustment problems were reported in 16% of the children. Parent ratings also indicated problems with cognitive development, physical independence, delays in reaching developmental milestones, and social isolation.

Adaptive Behavior

Fletcher et al. (1995) also assessed adaptive behavior and found that the three groups with hydrocephalus as well as the group with prematurity had lower composite adaptive behavior ratings. Daily living skills ratings were lower in those with both spina bifida and hydrocephalus. Similarly, Hommet et al. (1999) found lower adaptive behavior among children with hydrocephalus related to spina bifida or aqueductal stenosis; communication and daily living skills ratings were less than age level in these children.

Family Functioning

Donders et al. (1992) found parental adjustment difficulties in 44% of their sample of parents of children with hydrocephalus. Parents had higher assessed depression, hostility, and interpersonal sensitivity. Parental distress was not associated with medical or demographic variables.

Future Research

Similar to research examining psychological factors associated with spina bifida, future research assessing psychological factors in hydrocephalus must address several methodological issues. It is essential to carefully ascertain the medical etiology of the hydrocephalus and determine the neurological and intellectual functioning of the patients to reduce the heterogeneity of study samples. In addition, future studies should better address developmental issues, both in terms of defining study samples and examining the psychosocial impacts of hydrocephalus at various ages throughout the life span.

DOWN SYNDROME

Health psychologists have made many contributions to the understanding of psychological functioning of individuals with mental retardation. Prenatal, perinatal, and postnatal etiologies of mental retardation involving chromosomal, metabolic, infectious, and environmental factors and their interactions can be identified. Among the most common prenatal causes with a known genetic etiology is Down syndrome.

Epidemiology and Clinical Presentation

Down syndrome, or trisomy 21, is a genetic disorder in which the person has an extra copy of the 21st chromosome. Down syndrome has an overall prevalence rate of approximately 1 in 800 live births and is more likely to occur with increasing maternal age (Tolmie, 1997a). Up to 85% of infants live past 1 year of age, and more than 50% live longer than 50 years (Tolmie, 1997a).

Down syndrome is typically diagnosed at birth after confirmation by chromosome analysis, although prenatal diagnosis is also possible through amniocentesis. Features of Down syndrome include a poor Moro's reflex, hypotonia, a flat facial profile, upward-slanting palpebral fissures, redundant loose neck skin, and hyperextensible large joints (Jones, 1997; Tolmie, 1997a).

Individuals with Down syndrome have many related health problems. CHD is the most frequent health complication associated with Down syndrome and is a major cause of mortality for the infants (Tolmie, 1997a). Growth delays are also associated with Down syndrome. Puberty usually occurs normally (Tolmie, 1997a), although sexual development may be less complete than normal (Jones, 1997). Children with Down syndrome are likely to be overweight, and obesity is also a common problem in adults with the syndrome (Tolmie, 1997a). Gastrointestinal problems such as duodenal atresia and Hirschsprung's disease are also associated with Down syndrome. Hearing loss is common, occurring in 40% to 75% of children and adults with Down syndrome. Ocular abnormalities, including congenital cataract glaucoma, strabismus, and major refractive errors also occur frequently. Risk for leukemia is also greater for those with Down syndrome than for those in the general population, and people with Down syndrome have an increased susceptibility to infections. Hypothyroidism is also common. Seizure disorders occur in approximately 5% to 10% of individuals with the syndrome.

In addition, adults with Down syndrome are at increased risk for developing Alzheimer's disease, with prevalence rates of approximately 8% by age 49 years and more than 75% for those older than age 60 years. Although not all adults develop Alzheimer's, it has been suggested that adults with Down syndrome who are older than age 60 are likely to lose functional abilities more quickly than people with disorders such as cerebral palsy or epilepsy (Tolmie, 1997a).

Psychological Factors

Cognitive Functioning

Cognitive delays are associated with Down syndrome; functioning typically ranges from moderate to severe mental retardation (Jones, 1997). Cognitive skills generally decline from levels noted in infancy as demands for complex cognitive skills increase. Periods of developmental progress alternating with plateaus in development may also occur (Tolmie, 1997a).

Adaptive Behavior

Delays in adaptive functioning are also associated with Down syndrome. Although the range of delays observed can be broad, studies have suggested that children with Down syndrome have particular deficits in expressive language. Dykens, Hodapp, and Evans (1994) examined adaptive functioning as a function of age in their study of children with Down syndrome. Overall, their results indicated the children had a relative weakness in expressive communication skills. In contrast, receptive communication was noted to be an area of relative strength. Adaptive functioning was most strongly related to age among younger children. Weaker associations were found for children during middle childhood, suggesting some children with Down syndrome experience a plateau in the development of adaptive behavior skills.

Because adults with Down syndrome are living longer, assessments of changes in functioning across the life span are more significant. Studies such as those by Das, Divis, Alexander, Parrila, and Naglieri (1995) involving an older population with Down syndrome have found differences in functioning with increasing age. Four groups with mental retardation were compared: older adults with or without Down syndrome and younger adults with or without Down syndrome. Differences were noted in tasks involving planning, attention skills, simultaneous processing, and successive coding. Participants with Down syndrome had a greater cognitive decline with increasing age than participants without, with older adults with Down syndrome displaying the poorest performance on many of the measures. Young and Kramer (1991) also studied language skills and adaptive behavior in adults with Down syndrome. After controlling for hearing acuity, increasing age was associated with lower performance on measures of receptive language and self-help skills.

Behavioral Functioning

Studies of the behavioral functioning of children with Down syndrome have indicated they are at increased risk for behavior problems. Jones (1997) found that 13% of children with Down syndrome exhibited significant emotional problems. Gath and Gumley (1986) compared a large sample of children with Down syndrome to a control group of children matched for degree of verbal and motor disability. Overall means for the two groups were not different according to a parental measure of behavior problems, whereas teacher ratings indicated problems more frequently in the control group. However, 38% of those with Down syndrome and 46% of control children were rated as having significant behavior problems. Children in the Down syndrome group were rated as having significantly more behavior problems than their siblings. In addition, the presence of serious behavior problems was associated with low scores on a measure of adaptive functioning.

Parent ratings of behavior in a study by Dykens and Kasari (1997) found that children with Down syndrome function relatively better than children with Prader–Willi syndrome. Increasing age was associated with more behavior problems in the Down syndrome group, especially for internalizing behaviors such as anxiety, depression, and withdrawal. Although children with Down syndrome had less behavior problems than those with Prader–Willi syndrome, 23% of the Down syndrome group had higher total behavior problem scores. Specific behaviors occurring more frequently in the Down syndrome group were speech problems, preferring to be alone, being stubborn, having difficulty concentrating, and disobedience.

Other studies have also shown that behavior problems increase with age in those affected by Down syndrome. For example, Prasher, Chung, and Haque (1998) studied a large sample of older adolescents and adults with Down syndrome over three years. Declines in overall adaptive functioning, independent functioning, knowledge of numbers and time, self-direction, and responsibility were noted over the course of the study. However, when the sample was divided into those with dementia and those without, declines in independent functioning were observed only for those with dementia. Higher maladaptive behavior scores were found in the group with dementia, and a trend toward a positive relationship between increasing maladaptive scores and progression of dementia was noted.

Intellectual ability has been suggested as a moderating variable in age-related decline in individuals with Down syndrome. Burt et al. (1995) examined the neuropsychological and behavioral functioning of adults with Down syndrome for a 3-year-period. Participants who displayed clinical features of dementia were excluded from the study. Intellectual functioning at entry to the study had the largest association with performance in all areas, particularly on adaptive behavior.

In summary, research findings have indicated that it is important to consider the impact of Down syndrome throughout the life span. In addition to the health problems noted in adults with Down syndrome, research has shown that declines in cognitive, adaptive, and behavioral functioning occur with age. However, level of intellectual functioning and the presence of dementia and IQ level seem to be significant factors affecting outcomes.

Family Functioning

Caring for a child with Down syndrome has been associated with increased levels of family stress. Sanders and Morgan (1997) compared mothers' and fathers' perceptions of family stress and coping for a child with a developmental disability and coping with typically developing children. Three groups were compared: parents of children with Down syndrome, parents of children with autism, and parents of typically developing children. Both mothers and fathers of children with Down syndrome reported more pessimism about their child's future and that their child had more negative characteristics than typically developing children. Mothers also described their child as being more physically incapacitated. Few group differences were found on a measure of family functioning. The differences that did emerge were related to the family having free time to pursue activities. Mothers of children with Down syndrome reported the family as engaging in fewer recreation and sporting activities and fewer cultural, political, social, or intellectual activities than mothers of typically developing children.

Future Research

A strength in the research literature of individuals with Down syndrome is that development throughout the life span has been addressed. However, studies of adults with Down syndrome have not consistently controlled for variables such as intellectual ability and the presence of dementia, which have been shown to affect psychosocial functioning. Research studies on the impact of Down syndrome on children have typically been descriptive. Fewer studies have been designed to intervene with children and families of children with Down syndrome to reduce their behavioral problems and improve their adaptive functioning. Future research should focus on interventions to improve behavioral functioning and reduce the stress associated with caring for children with Down syndrome.

OTHER CONGENITAL ANOMALIES

Although a thorough discussion is beyond the scope of this chapter, it is worth noting that substantial psychological research has been conducted on some other congenital anomalies, and certain areas have had very little psychological research. Among the sex chromosome abnormalities, Turner syndrome has been fairly well studied. For example, research findings have indicated girls (McCauley, Kay, Ito, & Treder, 1987) and women (Delooz, Van den Berghe, Swillen, Kleczkowska, & Fryns, 1993; Downey et al., 1991) with Turner syndrome are more likely to have visuo–spatial deficits and psychosocial problems than girls without Turner syndrome. The cognitive and psychosocial functioning of individuals with various sex chromosome abnormalities has been reviewed by Bender, Puck, Salbenblatt, and Robinson (1990) and Berch and McCauley (1990).

Relatively little psychological research exists on children who have other types of congenital anomalies. For example, research by Tarnowski, King, Green, and Pease (1991) examined psychosocial functioning in children with congenital gastrointestinal anomalies including imperforate anus, gastroschisis, and omphalocele. Few studies have examined psychological adjustment in children with biliary atresia (e.g., Bradford, 1994), despite the continuing physical morbidities associated with this disorder (Ohi et al., 1990). Long-term outcomes for children with esophageal atresia or a tracheoesophageal fistula include a fairly high rate of morbidities that may impair quality of life (Somppi et al., 1998), yet psychological research for this patient population is lacking. Results of the few psychological studies available on hypospadias indicate many boys and men have concerns about their psychosexual development (Mureau, Slijper, Nijman, et al., 1995; Mureau, Slijper, van der Meulen, Verhulst, & Slob, 1995). Psychological adjustment has also been infrequently studied in children with congenital limb deformities (Bond, Kent, Binney, & Saleh, 1999; Bradbury, Kay, & Hewison, 1994) and port-wine stains (Sheerin, MacLeod, & Kusumakar, 1995).

CONCLUSION

Health psychologists have made many contributions to the understanding of issues affecting the care of individuals with congenital anomalies. This review has focused on research findings for CHD, craniofacial anomalies, spina bifida, hydrocephalus, and Down syndrome.

Research has shown that children with CHD are at risk for deficits in cognitive functioning and attention abilities, require more special educational placements, and have higher rates of behavioral and emotional problems—particularly when they have cyanotic heart disease, later surgical repair, and a lower functional status. Neurodevelopmental research has demonstrated that low-flow cardiopulmonary bypass is associated with better outcomes for children and has led to the discontinuation of circulatory arrest procedures during surgery. Although life-saving, the use of ECMO has been associated with visuo–spatial, visual memory, and left-hand motor deficits.

Children with cleft lip and palate are at risk for developmental delay, learning disabilities, and academic underachievement. In addition, they are at risk for psychosocial adjustment problems, particularly when they are dissatisfied with their facial appearance. Studies have indicated that girls are more likely to have emotional problems later in childhood, whereas boys are more likely to have behavioral problems earlier in childhood. Families are affected as well; parents of children with cleft lip and palate have increased rates of emotional distress.

Studies have shown that children with spina bifida are at risk for cognitive deficits and may require more special educational services, especially those with more severe lesions and more shunts. Behavioral problems, low self-esteem, and depression have also been documented in children with spina bifida. Mothers of these children have reported less parenting satisfaction and more social isolation. Similarly, research findings from studies of children with hydrocephalus have indicated they are at increased risk for cognitive delays, need more special education services, and are more likely to have psychosocial adjustment problems. Parents of children with hydrocephalus also have higher rates of psychosocial adjustment difficulties.

Research has demonstrated that individuals with Down syndrome have deficits in expressive communication skills, higher rates of behavioral problems, and have a greater decline in cognitive abilities with age. Studies have also shown greater stress in families of children with Down syndrome.

These findings indicate that health psychologists have important roles to play in the management of these congenital abnormalities. Given their increased risk for problems in cognitive development and psychosocial adjustment, children with these anomalies should have their developmental progress monitored as part of routine care. Interventions are needed to facilitate academic achievement and reduce the risk of psychosocial adjustment problems in children with these disorders. Psychological interventions are also needed for parents because of their increased stress and psychosocial adjustment difficulties. More research on the effectiveness of behavioral and psychosocial interventions is needed for all of these disorders.

Considerable psychological research has been conducted on disorders involving other congenital anomalies (e.g., Turner syndrome), but relatively little work has focused on the majority of other conditions. Given the extensive surgical interventions and medical follow-up required for conditions such as biliary atresia, Hirschsprung's disease, imperforate anus, gastroschisis, diaphragmatic hernia, and hypospadias and the expected psychological morbidity associated with these conditions, more research examining psychological issues and interventions to improve quality of life is needed. More psychological research is also needed in the areas of congenital limb deformities and skin deformities such as port-wine stain. Health psychologists have the opportunity to provide needed clinical services for patients and to conduct new research studies to elucidate the importance of psychological factors in many congenital abnormalities.

REFERENCES

Addonizio, L. J. (1996). Current status of cardiac transplantation in children. *Current Opinions in Pediatrics, 8,* 520–526.

Andrews, A. F., Nixon, C. A., Cilley, R. E., Roloff, D. W., & Bartlett, R. H. (1986). One-to three-year outcome for 14 neonatal survivors of extracorporeal membrane oxygenation. *Pediatrics, 78,* 692–698.

Apley, J., Barbour, R. F., & Westmacott, F. (1967). Impact of congenital heart disease on the family: A preliminary report. *British Medical Journal, 1,* 103–105.

Appleton, P. L., Ellis, N. C., Minchom, P. E., Lawson, V., Boell, V., & Jones, P. (1997). Depressive symptoms and self-concept in young people with spina bifida. *Journal of Pediatric Psychology, 22*(5), 707–722.

Appleton, P. L., Minchom, P. E., Ellis, N. C., Elliott, C. E., Boell, V., & Jones, P. (1994). The self-concept of young people with spina bifida: A population-based study. *Developmental Medicine and Child Neurology, 36,* 198–215.

Aram, D. M., Ekelman, B. L., Ben-Shakhar, G., & Levinsohn, M. W. (1985). Intelligence and hypoxemia in children with congenital heart disease: Fact or artifact? *Journal of the American College of Cardiology, 6,* 889–893.

Aurer, E. T., Senturia, A. G., Shopper, M., & Biddy, R. (1971). Congenital heart disease and child adjustment. *Psychiatric Medicine, 2,* 210–219.

Backer, C. L., Zales, V. R., Idriss, F. S., Lynch, P., Crawford, S., Benson, D. W., Jr., et al. (1992). Heart transplantation in neonates and children. *Journal of Heart and Lung Transplantation, 11,* 311–319.

Baer, P. E., Freedman, D. A., & Garson, A., Jr. (1984). Long-term psychological follow-up of patients after corrective surgery for tetralogy of Fallot. *Journal of the American Academy of Child Psychiatry, 23,* 622–625.

Baum, D., & Bernstein, D. (1993). Heart and lung transplantation in children. In I. H. Gessner & B. E. Victoria (Eds.), *Pediatric cardiology: A problem oriented approach* (pp. 245–252). Philadelphia: Saunders.

Baum, M., Chinnock, R., Ashwal, S., Peverini, R., Trimm, F., & Bailey, L. (1993). Growth and neurodevelopmental outcome of infants undergoing heart transplantation. *Journal of Heart and Lung Transplantation, 12*(Suppl.), 211–217.

Bellinger, D. C., Jonas, R. A., Rappaport, L. A., Wypij, D., Wernovsky, G., Kuban, K. C., et al. (1995). Developmental and neurologic status of children after heart surgery with hypothermic circulatory arrest or low-flow cardiopulmonary bypass. *New England Journal of Medicine, 332,* 549–555.

Bellinger, D. C., Rappaport, L. A., Wypij, D., Wernovsky, G., & Newburger, J. W. (1997). Patterns of developmental dysfunction after surgery during infancy to correct transposition of the great arteries. *Journal of Developmental and Behavioral Pediatrics, 18,* 75–83.

Bender, B., Puck, M., Salbenblatt, J., & Robinson, A. (1990). Cognitive development of children with sex chromosome abnormalities. In C. S. Holmes (Ed.), *Psychoneuroendocrinology* (pp. 138–163). New York: Springer-Verlag.

Berch, D., & McCauley, E. (1990). Psychosocial functioning of individuals with sex chromosome abnormalities. In C. S. Holmes (Ed.), *Psychoneuroendocrinology* (pp. 164–183). New York: Springer-Verlag.

Berkowitz, S. (1994). *The cleft palate story.* Carol Stream, IL: Quintessence.

Bier, J. B., Morales, Y., Liebling, J., Geddes, L., & Kim, E. (1997). Medical and social factors associated with cognitive outcome in individuals with myelomeningocele. *Developmental Medicine and Child Neurology, 39,* 263–266.

Bloom, A. A., Wright, J. A., Morris, R. D., Campbell, R. M., & Krawiecki, N. S. (1997). Additive impact of in-hospital cardiac arrest on the functioning of children with heart disease. *Pediatrics, 99,* 390–398.

Bond, J. M., Kent, G. G., Binney, V. A., & Saleh, M. (1999). Psychological adjustment of children awaiting limb reconstruction treatment. *Child Care, Health, and Development, 25,* 313–321.

Bradbury, E. T., Kay, S. P., & Hewison, J. (1994). The psychological impact of microvascular free toe transfer for children and parents. *Journal of Hand Surgery, 19,* 689–695.

Bradford, R. (1994). Children with liver disease: Maternal reports of their adjustment and the influence of severity on outcomes. *Child Care, Health, and Development, 20,* 393–407.

Broder, H. L., Richman, L. C., & Matheson, P. B. (1998). Learning disability, school achievement, and grade retention among children with cleft: A two-center study. *Cleft Palate–Craniofacial Journal, 35*(2), 127–131.

Burt, D. B., Loveland, K. A., Chen, Y., Chuang, A., Lewis, K. R., & Cherry, L. (1995). Aging in adults with Down syndrome: Report from a longitudinal study. *American Journal on Mental Retardation, 100*(3), 262–270.

Campis, L. B., DeMaso, D. R., & Twente, A. W. (1995). The role of maternal factors in the adaptation of children with craniofacial disfigurement. *Cleft Palate–Craniofacial Journal, 32*(1), 55–61.

Caouette-Laberge, L., Bayet, B., & Larocque, Y. (1994). The Pierre Robin sequence: Review of 125 cases and evolution of treatment modalities. *Plastic and Reconstructive Surgery, 93*(5), 934–942.

Casey, A. T. H., Kimmings, E. J., Kleinlugtebeld, A. D., Taylor, W. A. S., Harkness, W. F., & Hayward, R. D. (1997). The long-term outlook for hydrocephalus in childhood. *Pediatric Neurosurgery, 27,* 3–70.

Casey, F. A., Sykes, D. H., Craig, B. G., Power, R., & Mulholland, H. C. (1996). Behavioral adjustment of children with surgically palliated complex congenital heart disease. *Journal of Pediatric Psychology, 21,* 335–352.

Cleft Palate Foundation. (1989). *Cleft lip and cleft palate. The first four years.* Pittsburgh, PA: Author.

Cleft Palate Foundation. (1996). *The genetics of cleft lip and palate: Information for families.* Pittsburgh, PA: Author.

Das, J. P., Divis, B., Alexander, J., Parrila, R. K., & Naglieri, J. A. (1995). Cognitive decline due to aging among persons with Down syndrome. *Research in Developmental Disabilities, 16*(6), 461–478.

Delooz, J., Van den Berghe, H., Swillen, A., Kleczkowska, A., & Fryns, J. (1993). Turner syndrome patients as adults: A study of their cognitive profile, psychosocial functioning, and psychopathological findings. *Genetic Counseling, 4,* 169–179.

DeMaso, D. R., Beardslee, W. R., Silbert, A. R., & Fyler, D. C. (1990). Psychological functioning in children with cyanotic heart defects. *Developmental and Behavioral Pediatrics, 11,* 289–293.

DeMaso, D. R., Campis, L. K., Wypij, D., Bertram, S., Lipshitz, M., & Freed, M. (1991). The impact of maternal perceptions and medical severity on the adjustment of children with congenital heart disease. *Journal of Pediatric Psychology, 16,* 137–149.

De Vivo, D. C. (1991). The nervous system. In A. M. Rudolph (Ed.), *Rudolph's pediatrics* (pp. 1861–1888). Norwalk, CT: Appleton & Lange.

Donders, J., Rourke, B., & Canady, A. I. (1992). Emotional adjustment of children with hydrocephalus and their parents. *Journal of Child Neurology, 7,* 375–380.

Douglas, J. F., Hsu, D. T., & Addonizio, L. J. (1993). Noncompliance in pediatric heart transplant patients. *Journal of Heart and Lung Transplantation, 12*(Suppl.), 92.

Downey, J., Elkin, E., Ehrhardt, A., Meyer-Bahlburg, H., Bell, J., & Morishima, A. (1991). Cognitive ability and everyday functioning in women with Turner syndrome. *Journal of Learning Disabilities, 24,* 32–39.

Dykens, E. M., Hodapp, R. M., & Evans, D. W. (1994). Profiles and development of adaptive behavior in children with Down syndrome. *American Journal on Mental Retardation, 98*(5), 580–587.

Dykens, E. M., & Kasari, C. (1997). Maladaptive behavior in children with Prader–Willi syndrome, Down syndrome, and nonspecific mental retardation. *American Journal on Mental Retardation, 102*(3), 228–237.

Eliason, M. J. (1991). Cleft lip and palate: Developmental effects. *Journal of Pediatric Nursing, 6*(2), 107–113.

Endriga, M. C., & Speltz, M. L. (1997). Face-to-face interaction between infants with orofacial clefts and their mothers. *Journal of Pediatric Psychology, 22*(4), 439–453.

Fallon, P., Aparicio, J. M., Elliott, M. J., & Kirkham, F. J. (1995). Incidence of neurological complications of surgery for congenital heart disease. *Archives of Disease in Childhood, 72,* 418–422.

Fernell, E., Gillberg, C., & von Wendt, L. (1991). Behavioral problems in children with infantile hydrocephalus. *Developmental Medicine and Child Neurology, 33,* 388–395.

Ferry, P. C. (1987). Neurological sequelae of cardiac surgery in children. *American Journal of Diseases of Children, 141,* 309–312.

Fletcher, J. M., Brookshire, B. L., Landry, S. H., Bohan, T. P., Davidson, K. C., Francis, D. J., et al. (1995). Behavioral adjustment of children with hydrocephalus: Relationships with etiology, neurological, and family status. *Journal of Pediatric Psychology, 20,* 109–125.

Garson, A., Williams, R. B., & Redford, T. (1974). Long-term follow up of patients with tetralogy of Fallot: Physical health and psychopathology. *Journal of Pediatrics, 85,* 429–433.

Gath, A., & Gumley, D. (1986). Behavior problems in retarded children with special reference to Down's syndrome. *British Journal of Psychiatry, 149,* 156–161.

Gersony, W. M. (1987). The cardiovascular system. In R. E. Behrman & V. C. Vaughan (Eds.), *Nelson textbook of pediatrics* (13th ed., pp. 943–1026). Philadelphia: Saunders.

Hofkosh, D., Thompson, A. E., Nozza, R. J., Kemp, S. S., Bowen, A., & Feldman, H. M. (1991). Ten years of extracorporeal membrane oxygenation: Neurodevelopmental outcome. *Pediatrics, 87,* 549–555.

Holmbeck, G. N., Gorey-Ferguson, L., Hudson, T., Seefeldt, T., Shapera, W.,

Turner, T., et al. (1997). Maternal, paternal, and marital functioning in families of preadolescents with spina bifida. *Journal of Pediatric Psychology, 22*(2), 167–181.

Hommet, C., Billard, C., Gillet, P., Barthez, M. A., Lourmiere, J. M., Santini, J. J., et al. (1999). Neuropsychological and adaptive functioning in adolescents and young adults shunted for congenital hydrocephalus. *Journal of Child Neurology, 14*(3), 144–150.

Hunter, A. G. W. (1993a). Brain. In R. E. Stevenson, J. G. Hall, & R. M. Goodman (Eds.), *Human malformations and related anomalies* (Vol. II, pp. 62–73, 102–107). Oxford, England: Oxford University Press.

Hunter, A. G. W. (1993b). Brain and spinal cord. In R. E. Stevenson, J. G. Hall, & R. M. Goodman (Eds.), *Human malformations and related anomalies* (Vol. II, pp. 109–137). Oxford, England: Oxford University Press.

Hurley, A. D., Dorman, C., Laatsch, L., Bell, S., & D'Avignon, J. (1990). Cognitive functioning in patients with spina bifida, hydrocephalus, and the "cocktail party" syndrome. *Developmental Neuropsychology, 6*(2), 151–172.

Jones, K. L. (1997). *Smith's recognizable patterns of human malformation.* Philadelphia: Saunders.

Kapp-Simon, K. (1997, January). *Psychological issues in cleft palate and craniofacial treatment.* Presentation at the 1997 Winter Symposium and Annual Meeting of the Florida Cleft Palate–Craniofacial Association, Tampa.

Kapp-Simon, K. A., & McGuire, D. E. (1997). Observed social interaction patterns in adolescents with and without craniofacial conditions. *Cleft Palate–Craniofacial Journal, 34*(5), 380–384.

King, G. A., Shultz, I. Z., Steel, K., Gilpin, M., & Cathers, T. (1993). Self-evaluation and self-concept of adolescents with physical disabilities. *American Journal of Occupational Therapy, 47*(2), 132–140.

Klein, M. D. (1988). Neonatal ECMO. *TransAmerican Society of Artificial Internal Organs, 34,* 39–42.

Klein, M. D., Shaheen, K. W., Whittlesey, G. C., Pinsky, W. W., & Arciniegas, E. (1990). Extracorporeal membrane oxygenation (ECMO) for the circulatory support of children after repair of congenital heart disease. *Journal of Thoracic and Cardiovascular Surgery, 100,* 498–505.

Krueckeberg, S. M., Kapp-Simon, K. A., & Ribordy, S. C. (1993). Social skills of preschoolers with and without craniofacial anomalies. *Cleft Palate–Craniofacial Journal, 30*(5), 475–481.

Landry, S. H., Robinson, S. S., Copeland, D., & Garner, P. W. (1993). Goal-directed behavior and perception of self-competence in children with spina bifida. *Journal of Pediatric Psychology, 18*(3), 389–396.

Lettieri, J. (1997). Lips and oral cavity. In R. E. Stevenson, J. G. Hall, & R. M. Goodman (Eds.), *Human malformations and related anomalies* (pp. 367–381). Oxford, England: Oxford University Press.

Linde, L. M., Rasof, B., & Dunn, O. J. (1967). Mental development in congenital heart disease. *Journal of Pediatrics, 71,* 198–203.

Linde, L. M., Rasof, B., & Dunn, O. J. (1970). Longitudinal studies of intellectual and behavioral development in children with congenital heart disease. *Acta Paediatrica Scandinavica, 59,* 169–176.

Lock, J. E., Keane, J. F., Mandell, V. S., & Perry, S. B. (1992). Cardiac catheterization. In D. C. Fyler (Ed.), *Nadas' pediatric cardiology* (pp. 187–224). Philadelphia: Hanley & Belfus.

Loomis, J. W., Javornisky, J. G., Monahan, J. J., Burke, G., & Lindsay, A. (1997). Relations between family environment and adjustment outcomes in young adults with spina bifida. *Developmental Medicine and Child Neurology, 39,* 620–627.

Mai, F. M., McKenzie, F. N., & Kostuk, W. J. (1990). Psychosocial adjustment and quality of life following heart transplantation. *Canadian Journal of Psychiatry, 35,* 223–227.

Marino, B. L., & Lipshitz, M. (1991). Temperament in infants and toddlers with cardiac disease. *Pediatric Nursing, 17,* 445–448.

McCauley, E., Kay, T., Ito, J., & Treder, R. (1987). The Turner syndrome: Cognitive deficits, affective discrimination, and behavior problems. *Child Development, 58,* 464–473.

Minchom, P. E., Ellis, N. C., Appleton, P. L., Lawson, V., Boll, V., Jones, P., et al. (1995). Impact of functional severity on self concept in young people with spina bifida. *Archives of Disorders of Children, 73,* 48–52.

Morris, R. D., Krawiecki, N. S., Wright, J. A., & Walter, L. W. (1993). Neuropsychological, academic, and adaptive functioning in children who survive in-hospital cardiac arrest and resuscitation. *Journal of Learning Disabilities, 26,* 46–51.

Mureau, M., Slijper, F., Nijman, R., van der Meulen, J., Verhulst, F., & Slob, A. (1995). Psychosexual adjustment of children and adolescents after different types of hypospadias surgery: A norm-related study. *Journal of Urology, 154,* 1902–1907.

Mureau, M., Slijper, F., van der Meulen, J., Verhulst, F., & Slob, A. (1995). Psychosexual adjustment of men who underwent hypospadias repair: A norm-related study. *Journal of Urology, 154,* 1351–1355.

Neiman, G. S., & Savage, H. E. (1997). Development of infants and toddlers with clefts from birth to three years of age. *Cleft Palate–Craniofacial Journal, 34*(3), 218–225.

Newburger, J. W., Jonas, R. A., Wernovsky, G., Wypij, D., Hickey, P. R., Kuban, C. K., et al. (1993). A comparison of the perioperative neurologic effects of hypothermic circulatory arrest versus low-flow cardiopulmonary bypass in infant heart surgery. *New England Journal of Medicine, 329,* 1057–1064.

Newburger, J. W., Silbert, A. R., Buckley, L. P., & Fryler, D. C. (1984). Cognitive function and age at repair of transportation of the great arteries in children. *New England Journal of Medicine, 310,* 1495–1499.

Oates, R. K., Simpson, J. M., Turnbull, J. A., & Cartmill, T. B. (1995). The relationship between intelligence and duration of circulatory arrest with deep hypothermia. *Journal of Thoracic and Cardiovascular Surgery, 110,* 786–792.

O'Dougherty, M., Wright, F. S., Garmezy, N., Loewenson, R. B., & Torres, F. (1983). Later competence and adaptation in infants who survive severe heart defects. *Child Development, 54,* 1129–1142.

O'Dougherty, M., Wright, F. S., Loewenson, R. B., & Torres, F. (1985). Cerebral dysfunction after chronic hypoxia in children. *Neurology, 35,* 42–46.

Ohi, R., Nio, M., Chiba, T., Endo, N., Goto, M., & Ibrahim, M. (1990). Long-term follow-up after surgery for patients with biliary atresia. *Journal of Pediatric Surgery, 25,* 442–445.

Paris, W., Muchmore, J., Pribil, A., Zuhdi, N., & Cooper, D. K. C. (1994). Study of the relative incidences of psychosocial factors before and after heart transplantation and the influence of posttransplantation psychosocial factors on heart transplantation outcome. *Journal of Heart and Lung Transplantation, 13,* 424–432.

Pope, A. W., & Ward, J. (1997a). Factors associated with peer social competence in preadolescents with craniofacial anomalies. *Journal of Pediatric Psychology, 22*(4), 455–496.

Pope, A. W., & Ward, J. (1997b). Self-perceived facial appearance and psychosocial adjustment in preadolescents with craniofacial anomalies. *Cleft Palate–Craniofacial Journal, 34*(5), 396–401.

Prasher, V. P., Chung, M. C., & Haque, M. S. (1998). Longitudinal changes in adaptive behavior in adults with Down syndrome: Interim findings from a longitudinal study. *American Journal on Mental Retardation, 103*(1), 40–46.

Richman, L. C. (1997). Facial and speech relationships to behavior of children with clefts across three age levels. *Cleft Palate–Craniofacial Journal, 34*(5), 390–395.

Richman, L. C., & Millard, T. (1997). Brief report: Cleft lip and palate: Longitudinal behavior and relationships of cleft conditions to behavior and achievement. *Journal of Pediatric Psychology, 22*(4), 487–494.

Sanders, J. L., & Morgan, S. B. (1997). Family stress and adjustment as perceived by parents of children with autism or Down syndrome: Implications for intervention. *Child and Family Behavior Therapy, 19*(4), 15–32.

Sarwark, J. F. (1996). Spina bifida. *Pediatric Clinics of North America, 43*(5), 1151–1158.

Sheerin, D., MacLeod, M., & Kusumakar, V. (1995). Psychosocial adjustment in children with port-wine stains and prominent ears. *Journal of the American Academy of Child and Adolescent Psychiatry, 34,* 1637–1647.

Silbert, A., Wolff, P. H., Mayer, B., Rosenthal, A., & Nadas, A. S. (1969). Cyanotic heart disease and psychological development. *Pediatrics, 43,* 192–200.

Somppi, E., Tammela, O., Ruuska, T., Rahnasto, J., Laitinen, J., Turjanmaa, V., et al. (1998). Outcome of patients operated on for esophageal atresia: 30 years' experience. *Journal of Pediatric Surgery, 33,* 1341–1346.

Speltz, M. L., Endriga, M. C., Fisher, P. A., & Mason, C. (1997). Early predictors of attachment in infants with cleft lip and/or palate. *Child Development*, 68(1), 12–25.

Speltz, M. L., Endriga, M. C., & Mouradian, W. E. (1997). Presurgical and post-surgical mental and psychomotor development of infants with sagittal synostosis. *Cleft Palate–Craniofacial Journal*, 34(5), 374–379.

Speltz, M. L., Goodell, E. W., Endriga, M. C., & Clarren, S. K. (1994). Feeding interactions of infants with unrepaired cleft lip and/or palate. *Infant Behavior and Development*, 17(2), 131–139.

Speltz, M. L., Greenberg, M. T., Endriga, M. C., & Galbreath, H. (1994). Developmental approach to the psychology of craniofacial anomalies. *Cleft Palate–Craniofacial Journal*, 31(1), 61–67.

Speltz, M. L., Morton, K., Goodell, E. W., & Clarren, S. K. (1993). Psychological functioning of children with craniofacial anomalies and their mothers: Follow-up from late infancy to school entry. *Cleft Palate–Craniofacial Journal*, 30(5), 482–489.

Spurkland, I., Bjornstad, P. G., Lindberg, H., & Seem, E. (1993). Mental health and psychosocial functioning in adolescents with congenital heart disease. A comparison between adolescents born with severe heart defect and atrial septal defect. *Acta Paediatrics*, 82, 71–76.

Tarnowski, K., King, D., Green, L., & Pease, M. (1991). Congenital gastrointestinal anomalies: Psychosocial functioning of children with imperforate anus, gastroschisis, and omphalocele. *Journal of Consulting and Clinical Psychology*, 59, 587–590.

Taylor, G. A., Glass, P., Fitz, C. R., & Miller, M. K. (1987). Neurologic status in infants treated with extracorporeal membrane oxygenation: Correlation of imaging findings with developmental outcome. *Radiology*, 165, 679–682.

Thomas, P. T., Turner, S. R., Rumsey, N., Dowell, T., & Sandy, J. R. (1997). Satisfaction with facial appearance among subjects affected by a cleft. *Cleft Palate–Craniofacial Journal*, 34(3), 226–231.

Tindall, S., Tothermel, R. R., Delamater, A., Pinsky, W. W., & Klein, M. D. (1999). Neuropsychological abilities of children with cardiac disease treated with extracorporeal membrane oxygenation. *Developmental Neuropsychology*, 16, 101–115.

Tolarova, M., & Cervenka, J. (1998). Classification and birth prevalence of orofacial clefts. *American Journal of Medical Genetics*, 75, 126–137.

Tolmie, J. (1997a). Down syndrome and other autosomal trisomies. In D. L. Rimoin, J. M. Connor, & R. E. Pyeritz (Eds.), *Emery and Rimoin's principles and practice of medical genetics* (3rd ed., pp. 925–971). New York: Churchill-Livingstone.

Tolmie, J. (1997b). Neural tube defects and other congenital malformations of the central nervous system. In D. L. Rimoin, J. M. Connor, & R. E. Pyeritz (Eds.), *Emery and Rimoin's principles and practice of medical genetics* (3rd ed., pp. 2145–2176). New York: Churchill-Livingstone.

Trimm, F. (1991). Physiologic and psychological growth and development in pediatric heart transplant recipients. *Journal of Heart and Lung Transplantation*, 10, 848–855.

Utens, E. M., Verhulst, F. C., Erdman, R. A., Meijboom, F. J., Duivenvoorden, H. J., Bos, E., et al. (1994). Psychosocial functioning of young adults after surgical correction for congenital heart disease in childhood: A follow-up study. *Journal of Psychosomatic Research*, 38, 745–758.

Uzark, K. C., Sauer, S. N., Lawrence, K. S., Miller, J., Addonizio, L., & Crowley, D. C. (1992). The psychosocial impact of pediatric heart transplantation. *Journal of Heart and Lung Tranplantation*, 11, 1160–1167.

Wallander, J. L., Feldman, W. S., & Varni, J. W. (1989). Physical status and psychosocial adjustment in children with spina bifida. *Journal of Pediatric Psychology*, 14(1), 89–102.

White, M. (1993). Spina bifida: The personal and financial cost of incontinence. *British Journal of Nursing*, 2(22), 1123–1124, 1126–1130.

Wray, J., Pot-Mees, C., Zeitlin, H., Radley-Smith, R., & Yacoub, M. (1994). Cognitive function and behavioral status in paediatric heart and heart–lung transplant recipients: The Harefield experience. *British Medical Journal*, 309, 837–841.

Wray, J., & Yacoub, M. (1991). Psychosocial evaluation of children after open heart surgery versus cardiac transplantation. In M. Yacoub & J. R. Pepper (Eds.), *Annals of cardiac surgery*, 90–91 (pp. 50–55). London: Current Science.

Wright, M., & Nolan, T. (1994). Impact of cyanotic heart disease on school performance. *Archives of Disease in Childhood*, 71, 64–70.

Yang, L., Liu, M., & Townes, B. (1994). Neuropsychological and behavioral status of Chinese children with acyanotic congenital heart disease. *International Journal of Neuroscience*, 74, 109–115.

Young, E. C., & Kramer, B. M. (1991). Characteristics of age-related language decline in adults with Down syndrome. *Mental Retardation*, 29(2), 75–79.

Zurmohle, U., Homann, T., Schroeter, C., Rothgerber, H., Hommel, G., & Ermet, J. A. (1998). Psychosocial adjustment of children with spina bifida. *Journal of Child Neurology*, 13(2), 64–70.

15

CERTAIN CONDITIONS ORIGINATING IN THE PERINATAL PERIOD

FONDA DAVIS EYLER

The classification of conditions originating in the perinatal period, leading to the *International Classification of Diseases,* ninth revision (*ICD–9*), codes for diseases and disorders, are likely to catch patients off guard. Pregnancy, labor, and delivery are not disease states and are usually normal, natural events in the lives of childbearing women. Otherwise healthy women and their families expect (as they should, given the statistics) that all stages will occur without problems, although not without some effort and discomfort. Therefore, in the minority of cases in which perinatal events do seriously affect the outcome of the newborn infant, women and their families experience a generally unanticipated crisis that may center around a critically ill neonate or a long-term illness or disability. Health psychologists can be helpful to families through research on best practices, by providing assessments and interventions for neonates and through support and counseling during and after the family's crisis.

This chapter provides an overview of some of the most common maternal conditions associated with adverse neonatal outcomes. A few neonatal problem areas in which health psychologists can be most helpful to infants and families are highlighted. Case histories illustrative of families' needs or concerns and suggested strategies for psychologists are discussed.

OVERVIEW OF MATERNAL CONDITIONS AFFECTING NEONATAL OUTCOMES

Exhibit 15.1 includes the rates of some of the common maternal and infant *ICD–9* conditions originating in the perinatal period (National Vital Statistics Report, 1999). Numerous toxins, diseases, or disorders of organs or systems that can affect a pregnant woman and also maternal surgeries or injuries can have a range of effects on the developing fetus— from worrisome but short-term consequences to death. In addition to life- and health-sustaining oxygen and nutrients from the pregnant mother, most other substances also cross the placenta into the fetal blood circulation. Thus, environmental toxins with which the pregnant woman comes in contact or noxious substances she ingests or inhales can potentially harm her child as well. Furthermore, developing fetuses are susceptible to infections carried by their mothers that can be life and health threatening, such as the human immunodeficiency virus (HIV) and genital herpes, and to infections that may have little effect on the mother but can have lifelong consequences for the infant, such as rubella (which may cause loss of vision) and cytomegalovirus (CMV, which may cause hearing loss or have other possible central nervous system [CNS] effects).

Any maternal conditions that alter, temporarily block, or chronically reduce the flow of oxygen or nutrients to the fetus can, in extreme conditions, result in fetal loss (spontaneous abortion, miscarriage, or stillbirth). Less extreme cases can result in intrauterine growth retardation, asphyxia, premature birth, or all of these.

Occasionally, premature birth is also associated with maternal conditions such as multiple gestation (because the uterus is crowded), incompetent cervix (in which the mouth of the uterus fails to remain closed), premature rupture of membranes (in which labor is triggered or a resulting infection forces immediate delivery), or abruption of the placenta from the wall of the uterus (which forces immediate delivery and can be life threatening if abruption is complete). Complications of labor and delivery can also create problems for the neonate. Umbilical cords can prolapse or become compressed during delivery, cutting off fetal blood supply and placing the infant at risk for asphyxia. Delivery can also be complicated by failure of the labor to progress, abnormal presentation of the fetus (e.g., breech), and an infant whose size is disproportionate to that of the mother. Especially large infants with shoulder dystocia can have nerve injury or Erb's palsy. Intracranial hemorrhage may also be associated with the trauma of difficult deliveries.

EXHIBIT 15.1

Rates of Common Medical and Health Conditions Originating in the Perinatal Period

Maternal risk factors	Complications of labor and delivery	Abnormal conditions of the newborn
Pregnancy-associated hypertension: 36.8 (Eclampsia: 3.3)	Meconium-stained fluid, moderate to heavy: 56	Need assisted ventilation <30 min: 21.5 ≥30 min: 9.1
Diabetes: 26.4	Fetal distress: 40.4	Hyaline membrane disease/respiratory distress syndrome: 6.4
Anemia: 20.2	Breech/malpresentation: 38.3	Birth injury: 3.1
Hydramnios/oligohydramnios: 13	Premature rupture of membranes: 28.3	Meconium aspiration syndrome: 2.3
Previous preterm or small-for-gestational-age infant: 12	Dysfunctional labor: 27.6	Anemia: 1.1
Previous infant 4000+ g: 10.9	Cephalopelvic disproportion: 21.1	Preterm birth: 114[a]
Genital herpes: 9	Precipitous labor: 20.8	Seizures: 0.6
Uterine bleeding: 7	Maternal fever or infection: 15.7	Fetal alcohol syndrome: 0.1
Chronic hypertension: 6.9	Prolonged labor: 8.5	Apgar score at 5 minutes <7: 14[a]
Rh sensitization: 6.5	Abruptio placentae: 5.7	
Renal disease: 2.7	Placenta previa: 3.2	
Incompetent cervix: 2.7	Other excessive bleeding: 5.7	
Smoking: 132[a]	Cord prolapse: 2	
Weight gain <16 lb: 111[a]	Cesarean delivery 208[a]	
Late or no prenatal care: 39[a]		
Drinking: 12[a]		

Note. Rates reflect the number of live births with each specified condition per 1,000 live births. National Vital Statistics Report, *47*(18), April 29, 1999, 51–79.

[a]Extrapolated to rate per 1,000 births from data on percentages of all births.

Infants who experience stress during pregnancy, labor, or delivery often pass meconium before delivery. Thus, meconium-stained amniotic fluid is a risk factor for aspiration and its possible respiratory complications, which include pneumonia.

Any of the conditions described that place the life of an otherwise viable fetus in jeopardy may involve medical assistance for rapid delivery, including the use of forceps, vacuum extraction, or caesarian (surgical) delivery. The interventions themselves can occasionally result in iatrogenic trauma or injury.

In the following discussion of health psychologists' role in treating conditions originating in the perinatal period, one of the most common neonatal problems is highlighted: infants born prematurely. In the examination of prematurity, emphasis is placed on the most worrisome developmental sequelae of an infant with a very low birthweight, or those born weighing less than 1,500 g (Eyler, 1993).

PREMATURELY BORN, VERY LOW-BIRTHWEIGHT NEONATES

Prevalence

According to U.S. statistics (Guyer, MacDorman, Martin, Peters, & Strobino, 1998), the percentage of infants born with a low birthweight (<2,500 g) has increased (especially among White women) to 7.5% of all births. The rate of infants born with very low birthweights (<1,500 g) has increased slightly to 1.4% of births. Rates of prematurity and low birthweights commonly have been shown to vary considerably by state and by racial groups (Blackmore et al., 1993). Furthermore, teenage girls are more likely to have low-birthweight infants for various reasons (Roth, Hendrickson, Schilling, & Stowell, 1998). Although still a significant factor in the incidence of prematurity, births to teenage mothers have begun to decrease in the past few years (Guyer et al., 1998). Some of the latest increases in the rate of prematurity can be attributed to the recent increase in births to women older than age 30, as well as a significant increase in the treatment of infertility and the resulting increase in higher order multiple births, which are generally premature. Research shows a positive trend toward earlier use of prenatal care. When timely and comprehensive, early prenatal care has been shown to promote healthier pregnancies (Strobino, O'Campo, & Schoendorf, 1995).

Effects of Improved Medical Care

With the advent of regionalized perinatal intensive care in the 1960s, the medical care and outcomes of prematurely born infants changed dramatically (Stahlman, 1984; Stewart, Reynolds, & Lipscomb, 1981). Transport vehicles and highly trained medical teams now routinely move critically ill newborn infants to regional centers for specialized neonatal intensive care. Pregnant women at high risk for delivering premature, low-birthweight, or critically ill infants are triaged to receive prenatal care and deliver at centers with high-risk obstetrics and neonatal intensive care. With more recent advances in perinatal medicine and sophisticated technology, survival of the premature, low-birthweight infant has continued to increase significantly; in some cases, survival has more than doubled in the lowest birthweight categories. The majority of studies have demonstrated that morbidity has also decreased or stabilized (for reviews, see Eyler, 1993; Vohr & Msall, 1997). A meta-analysis (Lee et al., 1995) using data from 32 developmental studies of very low-birthweight infants born from 1947 to 1987 also concluded that increased survival has been accompanied by a decrease in the incidence of disabilities.

However, some researchers have reported that the increased survival of infants with complications of prematurity has been accompanied by an increase in the long-term developmental deficits or functional limitations of these infants (Saigal & O'Brodovich, 1987; Vohr & Msall, 1997). One study reported an increased rate of cerebral palsy but not in the overall incidence of disabilities (Tudehope et al., 1995). A review (Bhushan, Paneth, & Kiely, 1993) estimated the incidence of cerebral palsy has risen 20% with the increased survival of low-birthweight infants. In another review of the world literature and their own experiences, Hack and Fanaroff (1999) found that the survival rate of the most extremely low-birthweight infants (<800 g) has changed little in recent years, but they found a high incidence of and apparent increase in the medical and neuro-developmental problems for infants of that size. They concluded that, with current levels of care, the limits of viability have been reached and that professionals should be seriously concerned with the major morbidity experienced by these extremely low-birthweight infants.

Mortality Associated With Birthweight

Mortality has been consistently related to birthweight. In 1996, 64% of all infant deaths occurred among those born with a low birthweight. Two of 100 low-birthweight infants and one of four very low-birthweight infants are not likely to survive the first year (Guyer et al., 1998). With some exceptions, studies have shown that overall morbidity has also increased as birthweight has decreased (for a review, see Eyler, 1993; Hack et al., 1995; Horwood, Mogridge, & Darlow, 1998; Klebanov, Brooks-Gunn, & McCormick, 1994b).

Disabilities Associated With Birthweight

Several studies (Bylund et al., 1998; Regev, Dolfin, Ben-Nun, & Herzog, 1995; Roussounis, Hubley, & Dear, 1993; Sethi & Macfarlane, 1996; Weisglas-Kuperus, Baerts, & Sauer, 1993) of very low-birthweight infants (<1,500 g) have reported an overall disability rate (that has not changed much during the past two decades) of 15% to 33%, of which 4% to 13% was reported as a major disability. Other reports also have demonstrated that 7- to 12-year-olds who were very low-birthweight infants (compared with matched or randomized control groups or the general population of full-term or heavier birthweight infants) performed less well on measures of neurological status; motor, cognitive or intellectual ability; and educational achievement and also had more attention, behavior, social, emotional, and psychiatric problems (Botting, Powls, Cooke, & Marlow, 1997, 1998; Hack et al., 1995; Hille et al., 1994; Horwood et al., 1998; Klebanov, Brooks-Gunn, & McCormick, 1994a, 1994b; Marlow, Roberts, & Cooke, 1993; Rickards et al., 1993; Taylor, Klein, Schatschneider, & Hack, 1998).

Disabilities Associated With Extremely Low Birthweight

Among extremely low-birthweight infants (<1,000 g), early studies reported that up to 50% had some sort of impairment (for a review, see Eyler, 1993). More recent studies of 1- to 5-year-old children have shown some neurodevelopmental impairment in up to 50%, with some researchers reporting 7% to 28% as severe (Blitz, Wachtel, Blackmon, & Berenson-Howard, 1997; Bourchier, 1994; Bowen et al., 1993; Dezoete, MacArthur, & Aftimos, 1997; Finnstrom et al., 1998; Piecuch, Leonard, Cooper, & Sehring, 1997; Tudehope et al., 1995; Victorian Infant Collaborative Study Group, 1997).

A study of 7- and 8-year-old children reported that those who were less than 1,000 g at birth had poorer motor, visual–motor integration, IQ, achievement, and adaptive behavior scores than did matched, full-term or heavier weight infants (Saigal, Szatmari, Rosenbaum, Campbell, & King, 1991). When infants with neurological problems and IQs of less than 1 SD were removed, academic achievement and learning disability were similar to control groups, but infants who were less than 1,000 g at birth had poorer motor skills and required more special education assistance (Saigal, Rosenbaum, Szatmari, & Campbell, 1991). Ornstein, Ohlsson, Edmonds, and Asztalos (1991) reviewed the 25 studies that were published in the previous decade of very or extremely low-birthweight infants who had been monitored until school age. They concluded that, although the majority of the children had age-appropriate IQs, they had a higher rate of special education placement and more motor coordination, visual–motor integration, and behavior problems. However, poor outcome was most often predicted by low socioeconomic status (SES). Another study of extremely low-birthweight infants also found that they had an increased need for special education services, poorer performance on cognitive/language and motor tests, and a 20% major disability rate (Halsey, Collin, & Anderson, 1996).

Early studies found 30% to 60% of infants with birthweights of (a) less than 750 g or (b) less than 800 g had some sort of disability (for a review, see Eyler, 1993). Later studies (Blaymore-Bier et al., 1994; La Pine, Jackson, & Bennett, 1995) reported a prevalence of neurological impairments of between 19% and 47%, which has changed little during the previous 10 to 15 years. Compared with term control children, heavier weight control children, or both, problems identified in school-age children who were (a) less than 800 g or (b) less than 750 g at birth include decreased psychomotor and visual–memory ability, academic achievement, and social and adaptive behavior and increased attention problems and learning disorders—even for those who as infants were neurologically intact, of average IQ, or both (Hack et al., 1994; Taylor, Hack, Klein, & Schatschneider, 1995; Whitfield, Grunau, & Holsti, 1997).

Disabilities Associated With Gestational Age

With little exception, decreased gestational age historically has been related to increased morbidity (Eyler, 1993), including language impairments (Briscoe, Gathercole, & Marlow, 1998). One study of infants born after less than 20 weeks gestation but who were greater than 500 g at birth reported that the majority of infants were stillborn. Of the live infants, 30% received care from the neonatal intensive care unit (NICU); of those, 11% survived and 69% had one or more major disabilities. The investigators concluded that at the edge of viability, survival without an associated major disability is possible but rare (Sauve, Robertson, Etches, Byrne, & Dayer-Zamora, 1998).

Birthweight and gestational age seem to be markers of risk, reflecting the level of maturity of infants and therefore their likely complications. Some investigators have shown that when they adjusted for medical risk variables, gestational age and birthweight categories were no longer significantly related to outcome (e.g., Piecuch et al., 1997; Tudehope et al., 1995). Similarly, other researchers have shown that very low-birthweight infants with severe complications had persistent abnormalities and poorer development over the first year, whereas those with milder complications were more similar to infants born at term (Anderson et al., 1996).

Outcomes Related to Respiratory Illness

Most follow-up studies of low-birthweight infants have demonstrated that about 12% to 50% had long-term neuromuscular and developmental problems that were related to the severity of their respiratory illness or its complications (see Eyler, 1993, for a review, and Bowen et al., 1993; deRegnier, Roberts, Ramsey, Weaver, & O'Shea, 1997; Tudehope et al., 1995; Yeo, Choo, & Ho, 1997). Similar findings have been reported in several early studies (for a review, see Eyler, 1993) and more recent studies that prospectively entered infants with specific respiratory diagnoses (Cheung, Barrington, Finer, & Robertson, 1999; Singer, Yamashita, Lilien, Collin, & Baley, 1997). In those who were followed up (from age 1 to 8 years), 12% to 50% of the preterm infants with respiratory problems demonstrated evidence of developmental or neurological sequelae that were related to transport status, birthweight, gestational age, sepsis, the severity of their respiratory illness, or all of these.

With rare exception, prospective studies that have included infants with the more serious respiratory ailment of bronchopulmonary dysplasia (BPD) have reported that at 1 to 3 years follow-up, more infants with BPD had severe delays and growth retardation and poorer cognitive, sensorimotor, and language scores (Goldson, 1984; Meisels, Plunkett, Roloff, Pasick, & Stiefel, 1986; Singer et al., 1997; Vohr, Bell, & Oh, 1982).

Outcomes Related to Intracranial Hemorrhage

One of the most problematic potential effects of prematurity on neurodevelopmental outcome is intracranial hemorrhage (ICH). This bleeding in the brain is usually documented by a cranial ultrasound or computerized tomography (CT) brain scans. Severity is scored from grade 1 to 4 using the system of Papile and colleagues (Papile, Munsick-Bruno, & Schaefer, 1983). Grade 1 is an isolated hemorrhage only in the germinal matrix; Grade 2 is an intraventricular hemorrhage (IVH) with a normal ventricular size; Grade 3 is an IVH with ventricular dilation; and Grade 4 is an IVH that extends into the parenchymal areas. Furthermore, extensive IVH can result in brain swelling and fluid buildup, or hydrocephalus. Often, classification includes this distinction (e.g., "Grade 4 bleed, with [or without] hydrocephalus").

ICH prevalence is highest among infants with the youngest gestational ages, ranging from less than 6% in infants born after more than 30 weeks of gestation to 60% in infants born after 23 to 28 weeks (Catto-Smith, Yu, Bajuk, Orgill, & Astbury, 1985; Papile et al., 1983; Sauve & Singhal, 1985; TeKolste, Bennett, & Maack, 1985). The prevalence is also highest among those with the lowest birthweights, from 40% in infants with birthweights of less than 1,500 g to 57% in those born weighing less than 801 g (Hack et al., 1995; Hawgood, Spong, & Yu, 1984; Kilbride, Daily, Matiu, & Hubbard, 1989; Ment et al., 1982; Stewart et al., 1983). However, Bylund et al. (1998) found ICH in only 19% of infants with birthweights of less than 1,000 g. Studies have shown ICH to be associated with respiratory problems, fluctuating cerebral blood velocity, and systemic hypotension (Bada et al., 1990; Beverley, Chance & Coates, 1984; Low et al., 1986; Mehrabani, Gowen, & Kopelman, 1991; Perlman, McMenamin, & Volpe, 1983; Scott, Ment, Ehrenkranz, & Warshaw, 1984; Stewart et al., 1983; Welch & Bottoms, 1986).

Very low-birthweight infants with documented ICH are more likely to have other perinatal problems as well (Ment et al., 1982; Palmer, Dubowitz, Levene, & Dubowitz, 1982; Stewart et al., 1983; Williams, Lewandowski, Coplan, & D'Eugenio, 1987). In several cases, those most at risk for a poor outcome were the infants with IVH who also had BPD, chronic lung disease, progressive hydrocephalus, or asphyxia (Dezoete et al., 1997; Landry et., 1984; Skouteli, Dubowitz, Levene, & Miller, 1985).

In numerous studies of low-birthweight infants, IVH has been shown to be related to poor developmental outcome, including cerebral palsy and other motor abnormalities (Catto-Smith et al., 1985; Krishnamoorthy et al., 1990; Papile et al., 1983; Regev et al., 1995; Scott et al., 1984; TeKolste et al., 1985; Williams et al., 1987). In one study of preterm 2-year-olds, subependymal and mild intraventricular hemorrhages, which are likely to affect subcortical and frontal brain areas, were shown to be associated with poorer performance on cognitive tasks specific to those areas (Ross, Boatright, Auld, & Nass, 1996).

With little exception (Bylund et al., 1998), the graded severity of ICH has been shown to be related to mortality (Ment et al., 1982; Williamson et al., 1983) and neurological, motor, and developmental problems (Bendersky & Lewis, 1995; Bowen et al., 1993; Cheung et al., 1999; Finnstrom et al., 1998; Ford, Steichen, Steichen Asch, Babcock, & Fogelson, 1989; Hanigan et al., 1991; Papile et al., 1983; Piecuch et al., 1997; TeKolste et al., 1985; Vohr, Garcia Coll, Flanagan, & Oh, 1992; Williamson et al., 1983). With rare exception, studies have shown an increase in neurological and developmental problems, including cerebral palsy, when IVH was accompanied by dilation or hydrocephalus (Ishida et al., 1997; Kilbride et al., 1989; Msall et al., 1994; Palmer, Dubowitz, Levene, et al., 1982; Roth et al., 1993; Stewart et al., 1983; Tudehope et al., 1995), or by other medical variables (Msall et al., 1991; Tudehope et al., 1995).

Outcomes Related to Periventricular Leukomalacia

Although it is less common, periventricular leukomalacia (PVL) can be a devastating sequela of IVH or other brain injury such as that resulting from asphyxia. PVL refers to the structural damage from loss of gray matter in the brain that is inferred from low-density areas observed on CT scans. Studies of preterm or low-birthweight infants with PVL have reported death rates from 20% (of infants born weighing less than 1,200 g) to 94% (of those born weighing less than 1000 g) and rates of cerebral palsy from 83% to 100% (Bozynski et al., 1985; DeVries et al., 1985; McMenamin, Shackelford, & Volpe, 1984). Several studies reported a relationship of PVL to poor development outcome in low-birthweight infants (Blitz et al., 1997; McCarton-Daum, Danziger, Ruff, & Vaughn, 1983; Piecuch et al., 1997), even when gestational age and other risk variables were controlled (Finnstrom et al., 1998; McMenamin et al., 1984). Some studies found 100% of survivors of PVL developed major disabilities or mental retardation; in one study, 50% were blind (DeVries et al., 1985; McMenamin et al., 1984; Regev et al., 1995). Vohr and Ment (1996) have reviewed IVH and its associated risk and protective factors as well as possible outcomes in the preterm infant.

Outcomes Related to Retrolental Fibroplasia

Another complication of prematurity that can have lifelong consequences for children and their families is vision loss. Retrolental fibroplasia (RLF) is a disorder related to oxygen treatment that is common in extremely low-birthweight infants with respiratory disease. Because of this association, RLF is also referred to as retinopathy of prematurity (ROP). Similar to ICH, ROP has a commonly used grading system that describes the progression of retinal changes resulting in various stages (I–V) of retinal detachment. In the early stages of the disorder, spontaneous regression of changes is common; with minor scarring, those with the disorder may have almost normal vision. Some studies have found that an ROP grade of III or higher is related to severe impairments (Bowen et al., 1993; Finnstrom et al., 1998; Msall et al., 1993). The individuals usually have residual neurological damage from the more progressive Stages IV and V. Ultimately, when retinas are thickened, heavily scarred, and detached, total blindness results.

In studies of very low-birthweight infants, blindness has been reported in 3% of infants born weighing less than 1,000 g (Hoskins, Elliot, Shennan, Skidmore, & Keith, 1983; Yu et al., 1992) and in 1.2% of infants born weighing 1,000 to 1,500 g, all but one of whom received ventilatory assistance (Campbell et al., 1983). Another investigation reported a 20% incidence of ROP, 9% of whom were diagnosed with Grade V, and one of whom (<1%) progressed to blindness. RLF was related to birthweight and apnea episodes during which 100% oxygen was required (Merritt & Kraybill, 1986). A large study of infants with birthweights of 600 to 1,500 g showed that birthweight predicted RLF. Duration of ventilatory assistance was related to RLF only for those infants born weighing less than 1,000 g (Flynn, 1983).

Outcomes Related to Sensorineural Hearing Loss

Hearing loss is also commonly associated with prematurity. Even isolated from other problems, hearing loss can affect the course of development and the type of interventions needed. From several studies the overall incidence of sensorineural hearing loss has been estimated to range from 1.3% of infants without perinatal risk factors to 28.6% of infants born weighing 1,500 g who were also diagnosed with seizures; in one of the studies, 3% were deaf at age 5 years. Hearing impairments were also related to other neurological problems; the severity of illness, including chronic lung disease requiring prolonged respiratory assistance; and drug therapies. In follow-up studies of those with hearing loss, 40% were reported to score below normal on developmental assessments, and 48% had short-term auditory memory problems (related to newborn bilirubin concentrations), with accompanying lower IQs and reading ability (Bergman et al., 1985; Doyle et al., 1992; Kileny & Robertson, 1985; Neild, Schrier, Ramos, Platzker, & Warburton, 1986; Yu et al., 1992).

ROLE OF THE HEALTH PSYCHOLOGIST

Individualized Developmental Assessment of Infants

Although some of the discussed complications associated with prematurity or very low birthweight are easily identifiable by the medical team in the neonatal period (e.g., early evidence of severe brain injury such as PVL or vision loss following ROP), their precise consequences may not be known. Other problems are even less obvious and may not manifest for a year or more (e.g., cerebral palsy or global developmental delay). Understanding the general prevalence and potential sequelae of being born prematurely with very low birthweight can be helpful in designing follow-up programs or protocols to triage those infants most at risk for delays in their growth and development, one of the many tasks well suited for health psychologists. However, group data are of limited help in predicting the outcome of any one child, counseling the child's family about the course to expect, or designing individualized interventions. These require the psychologist to provide appropriate, individual developmental assessment of children when they are medically stable and the health care team and family are ready to make plans for developmental interventions.

The overall positive news that can be shared with families is that their child may beat the odds. There is great individual variation in how well infants with similar perinatal histories of illnesses and treatments, even those with identified abnormalities, can withstand their effects and recover (another way of stating that group data on outcomes do not allow psychologists to predict the outcome well for any individual). Recovery may be related to the resilience to insults and compensation possible in the immature but rapidly growing brain of the preterm neonate; the strengths inherent in the individual organism; the effects of a stimulating, enriching environment; or all of these. To better understand a given infant's potential for recovery and developmental progress, it is important for the health psychologist to consider the contribution of the needs and strengths of the specific baby, the unique caregiving environment in which the infant is found, and the infant's ability to control and organize his or her behavior to adapt and adjust to that environment (Sameroff & Chandler, 1975). Neonatal behavioral assessments can help in those determinations.

Given the many factors affecting development, there are obvious limitations to how well outcome can be predicted for a neonate or young infant, even with use of appropriate, individualized assessments by skilled clinicians. For example, the types of cognitive reasoning and problem-solving abilities so important for normal adult functioning cannot be measured in a young child. The rapid changes during infancy and individual styles and rates of development can affect the accuracy of an assessment at any one point in time. However, most infants do develop skills in a similar order and at a similar rate so that norms can be developed for behaviors expected at each age. Thus, tests are available that can indicate whether even a young infant is on target compared with same-age peers, and repeated evaluations can better assess the rate of developmental progression. Studies have suggested that prediction may be more accurate when infants show delayed development. Low developmental scores were found to be related to low intelligence test scores and poorer academic achievement, but average and high scores were not predictive (Rubin & Balow, 1979).

Initially, assessments for newborn infants were static neurological exams that included measures of reflexes, movement, and tone. About the time that advances in neonatology were being translated into regionalized perinatal care, developmental psychologists were reporting physiological measures of heart rate and brain wave activity in the neonate that gave evidence of the type of attention and memory abilities that are prerequisites to learning. Behavioral correlates of those physiological measures also indicated an organism that actively oriented to sensory stimuli in the surrounding environment. In contrast to the former notion of a more passive newborn controlled by reflexes, these observations gave way to the view of a sophisticated repertoire of newborn behavior (Friedman, 1972; Graham, Clifton, & Halton, 1968; Self, Horowitz, & Pagan, 1972; Siqueland & Lipsitt, 1966). For example, not only could neonates track visually and localize auditory stimuli, but investigators demonstrated they could make fine discriminations and show preferences, generally for those stimuli likely to be associated with their caregivers (e.g., faces, voices, cuddling; Goren, Sarty, & Wu, 1975; Trehub & Chang, 1977). This interest has been shown to be reciprocated by adults' responses to infants' cries (Formby, 1967) and the baby-face look of helplessness (Fullard & Reiling, 1976). It has been hypothesized that this relationship or mutual attraction has evolved by enabling infants to gain the attention they need for nurturing (Bowlby, 1969). Whatever its origin and development, this dynamic role of the newborn infant—the capacity to elicit a response and facilitate an interaction so that caregivers can learn to read the infant's cues and respond appropriately—has become a critical part of newborn assessment (Brazelton, 1984).

The Brazelton (1984) Neonatal Behavioral Assessment Scale (NBAS) was one of the first tests designed to measure not only static newborn reflexes but also the more adaptive, regulatory, and interactive abilities of the neonate. It has come to be considered by many as the gold standard of newborn assessments. NBAS summary, or cluster, scores have been correlated with many perinatal risk factors including prematurity and low birthweight. The clusters have been related to changes during the first month of life, treatment effects, parental behavior, and later development (Brazelton & Nugent, 1995).

The NBAS can aid psychologists in identifying early concerns, designing interventions for needy infants and their families, and planning follow-up care. Arranging for parents to observe the examination and receive feedback about their infants' strengths and needs can be an effective intervention strategy and has been shown to have positive effects on parental attitudes and caregiving, as well as subsequent effects on infant development (Eyler, 1980; Widmayer & Field, 1980, 1981; Worobey & Belsky, 1982).

Another commonly used newborn assessment, the Dubowitz Neurological Assessment of Term and Preterm Newborns (Dubowitz & Dubowitz, 1981) includes a neurological assessment and a few behavioral items similar to those assessed by the NBAS. Although this descriptive measure provides no summary scores, its advantages include the ease with which it can be learned and administered, even for use with preterm and ill neonates in intensive care nurseries.

Palmer and colleagues (Palmer, Dubowitz, Verghote, & Dubowitz, 1982) provided data on concurrent validity by demonstrating that responses of preterm infants improved as gestational age increased, but those tested at 40 weeks did less well overall than did infants born at term. Research performed at the University of Florida, which included a quantification of the descriptive items of the Dubowitz assessment, provided some support for the tool as a measure of development by demonstrating that older hospitalized infants responded better. When controlling for age, those born at earlier gestations performed less well, possibly reflecting their perinatal risk (Eyler, Delgado-Hachey, Woods, & Carter, 1991).

With regard to predictive ability of the assessment, the Dubowitzes reported that their clinical evaluations of more worrisome responses at term were related to poorer neurological status at 1 year (Dubowitz et al., 1984). We also demonstrated that clinical impressions of "normal" or "suspect" based on the Dubowitz assessment in the newborn period were significantly related to "normal" or "below-normal" categories on the Bayley Scales of Infant Development, Physical Developmental Index at 1 year. However, examination of the quantitative version of the assessment, controlling for the effects of birthweight and gestational age, demonstrated fewer than half of the items were significantly related to development after 2 years; findings were inconsistent across age groups, and most items were related only to the psychomotor, not mental, developmental index of the Bayley scales (Eyler et al., 1991).

In summary, when assessing high-risk neonates, psychologists should keep in mind that norms are not firmly established for the course and rate of neonatal development, especially the recovery growth of infants who have been born prematurely or have been critically ill as newborns. Thus, interpretations about the long-term implications of any one individualized assessment should be made cautiously. Parents can be told that neonatal assessments can identify infants whose performance is not typical for their age or who have specific problems that might benefit from individualized service plans and follow-up care. However, repeated developmental assessments are required to assess the ongoing developmental progress and potential for recovery (Gorski, Lewkowicz, & Huntington, 1987). Psychologists have not only the theoretical and applied background crucial for the development of skills in test administration and interpretation but also the research training needed to adapt current tests or develop new measures in cases in which existing assessments have limitations.

Assessment of the Caregiving Environment

The fact that it is difficult to predict outcome from neonatal developmental assessments has a positive aspect. In part, this difficulty is the result of individual recovery from perinatal problems that seems to be facilitated by a nurturing environment. It is well accepted that children do not develop in a vacuum; development involves a complex interaction between organisms and their environments. Even those infants without perinatal problems and with full potential for growth and development need the support of a caregiving environment. For those infants who begin life with problems, a developmentally enhancing environment may be even more important.

One of the most common predictors of development is the family's SES (Sameroff & Chandler, 1975), which may be a marker of some obvious aspect of the child's environment that is important for growth and development, such as access to health care or adequate nutrition. It may also reflect conditions associated with poverty and less education, such as a larger number of children in a home requiring attention or parents who do not have the ability or opportunity to provide a developmentally stimulating environment.

The importance of SES and other aspects of the caregiving environment for the development of high-risk neonates has been supported by several studies of children from infancy to school age. In some cases, participants have included large samples of those who were cared for in the NICU; in others, infants were defined as preterm, extremely preterm, very low birthweight, or extremely low birthweight. Most studies have reported decreased scores of ability or achievement (some of which declined over time) or an increased incidence of special education or grade retention. All of these studies found some outcome related to sociodemographic factors (e.g., income, maternal education, race, or gender), usually in addition to an association with perinatal risk variables (e.g., extremely low birthweight, IVH). However, in some children, social factors were better predictors or major determinants of outcome (Botting et al., 1998; Campbell et al., 1993; Carter, Resnick, Ariet, Shieh, & Vonesh, 1992; Cohen & Parmelee, 1983; Escalona, 1982; Hack et al., 1992; Hille et al., 1994; Msall et al., 1993, 1991, 1994; Piecuch et al., 1997; Resnick et al., 1990; Resnick et al., 1998; Vohr et al., 1992).

Some evidence also exists for an interactive model, with socioeconomic and cultural factors predicting poor performance on some measures to a greater degree among children with medical problems or only among those with lower birthweights (Levy-Schiff, Einat, Mogilner, Lerman, & Krikler, 1994; Monset-Couchard, de Bethmann, & Kastler, 1996; Resnick et al., 1990). Others similarly have demonstrated that children who were at double risk—had a low SES and very low birthweight or early cognitive problems—performed least well on ability or achievement tests (Ross, Lipper, & Auld, 1991; Smith, Ulvund, & Lindemann, 1994).

Maternal factors such as judgment of daily stress and education have also been shown to predict developmental scores of 2- to 5-year-olds who had very low birthweights; in one study, they accounted for more variance in outcome than a neurological risk score (Thompson et al., 1994, 1997). Other researchers (McCormick, Workman-Daniels, & Brooks-Gunn, 1996) also found maternal mental health and home environment, as well as lower birthweight related to school behavior problems.

The relationship between development and perinatal risk variables has also not held up in other studies in which there seemed to be compensating factors. In families with high SES or positive home environments, maternal education or the quality of the home rather than perinatal variables related to cognitive or academic outcomes (Beckwith & Parmelee, 1986; Schraeder, Heverly, & O'Brien, 1996; Wilson, 1985). In a large longitudinal study of very low-birthweight infants, development and language of the infants at age 2 to 3 years were related to SES, family functioning, and the severity of perinatal problems when compared to term infants matched on SES. However, risk status was reversed by a compensating family. Infants who were identified as high risk by early tests but were developing normally at age 2 years came from families with high family functioning scores. Conversely, infants who were designated as low risk but were later developmentally delayed had families with significantly lower family functioning scores (Siegel, 1981, 1982).

These studies can be discouraging and encouraging. An important contribution health psychologists could make would be to use research to identify those aspects of SES that make it such a powerful predictor. However, psychologists will not be able to cure poverty or directly affect the educational level of families, although referrals to social and educational services may be of significant help. Yet, to the extent that SES is a marker of the family's knowledge of child development, their beliefs about the importance of parenting, and other situations that affect their relationships with their children, intervention opportunities exist that may improve family functioning and caregiving behaviors. Thus, it is important that when determining which interventions may be helpful, health psychologists offer to assess the family's needs and concerns and their potential effects on their infant's outcome. The family may need crisis intervention and counseling to deal with issues resulting from their child's illness or developmental interventions and parenting skills to enhance their child's development.

For health psychologists working with very low-birthweight infants and their families, most interventions begin in the NICU. It is in the NICU that these preterm neonates and their family spend their first weeks together. Thus, the special circumstances of the NICU environment, its potential effects on the neonate and family, and interventions that may be needed also should be considered.

Care in the NICU

Because of their prematurity, the potential severity of their complications, and the life- and health-preserving medical interventions required, very low-birthweight infants may require lengthy hospitalization in NICUs, the length of which is often equal to the number of weeks premature the infants are born. By the end of a stay in the NICU, infants may have experienced weeks to months of probes, sticks, scans, and surgeries, often in lieu of consistent, positive interactions with their caregivers. Psychologists and others have been concerned about the possible adverse effects of the NICU on the immature infant's ability to adapt to the extrauterine environment. There has also been concern that it may be difficult for caregivers to provide developmentally enhancing care in the NICU environment.

With support from animal research, some have argued that the amount of sensory stimulation in a typical NICU may be stressful for the very low-birthweight or young preterm infant's immature coping system and adversely affect CNS organization while critical pathways are being developed (Brazelton, 1980). Studies have documented negative physiological and behavioral responses of preterm and ill infants in NICUs to frequent (sometimes continuous) episodes of high levels of sound, light, or handling (Anagnostakis, Petmezakis, Messaritakis, & Metsaniotis, 1980; Danford, Miske, Headley, & Nelson, 1983; Gorski, Hole, Leonard, & Martin, 1983; Gottfried & Hedgman, 1984; Gottfried et al., 1981; Long, Lucey, & Philip, 1980; Long, Philip, & Lucey, 1980; Newman, 1981; Parmelee, 1985). For example, sudden, loud noises, shown to penetrate plastic isolettes, have been related to measures or observations of decreased blood oxygenation and increased heart rate, respiration rate, intracranial pressure, startles, activity, and crying (Long, Lucey, et al., 1980; Newman, 1981).

Furthermore, to illuminate critical medical procedures, many NICUs have been designed with overhead cool, fluorescent lighting at levels shown to result in retinal damage in some species of animals (Gottfried & Hedgman, 1984). Also worrisome is the result of a controlled study of low-birthweight infants and light. The study that found infants whose eyes were not shielded to ambient light in the NICU had a greater incidence of retinopathy of prematurity (Glass et al., 1985).

Handling of young, sick infants in the NICU is as unavoidable as occasional loud noises and as necessary as good illumination. However, research has shown that routine nursery procedures can decrease measures of blood oxygenation and quiet sleep and increase active or rapid eye movement (REM) sleep, heart rate, disorganized breathing, apnea, hypertension, intracranial pressure, and hypoxemia (Danford et al., 1983; Eyler et al., 1989; Long, Philip, et al., 1980). Unfortunately, the most critically ill infants generally require the most medical and nursing interventions. It is these most vulnerable infants who were found to be more affected by the necessary but stressful procedures (Eyler et al., 1989; Gottfried & Hedgman, 1984).

On a more encouraging note, clinical researchers have demonstrated that staff could be trained to reduce noise in the NICU (Long, Lucey, et al., 1980) and alter procedures so that they can decrease periods when infants are hypoxemic (Long, Philip, et al., 1980). A staff education program in care protocols that was designed to decrease environmental stress to support infant development was also found to be successful; treated infants had more optimal feeding and respiratory statuses, less morbidity, improved behavioral organization, and shorter hospitalization (Becker, Grunwald, Moorman, & Stuhr, 1991). Furthermore, researchers have demonstrated that compared with the effects of medical interventions, behavioral assessments (Morrow et al., 1990) and developmental interventions (Eyler et al., 1989) can be provided with negligible decreases in blood oxygenation. Thus, the health psychologist may be able to create opportunities to educate and assist members of the health care team and families to reduce periods of stress for fragile infants while safely providing needed assessments and interventions.

The problem of sensory stimulation in the NICU is a complex one. Although the level of stimulation in many NICUs seems to have adverse effects, some hospitalized neonates may be deprived of the typical sensorimotor experiences that generally enhance development (Cornell & Gottfried, 1976). Because feedback is critical for the development of sensorimotor integration, it is likely inappropriate as well as impossible to completely protect immature infants from sound, light, and tactile stimulation.

Although isolettes may minimize startle responses to sudden, loud noises, they also muffle the sound of human voices (Gottfried & Hedgman, 1984; Long, Lucey, et al., 1980; Newman, 1981). Likewise, continuous exposure to bright light and use of eye shields that protect infants from intense lighting both eliminate face-to-face interaction with caregivers. Others also have voiced concern that the continuous nature of light and sound stimulation precludes development of the infant's sense of rhythm or diurnal pattern (Gottfried & Hedgman, 1984; Gottfried et al., 1981) and may result in habituation or shutting out, eliminating potential social interactions (Newman, 1981; Parmelee, 1985).

Controlled observations in our NICU (Eyler, Woods, Behnke, & Conlon, 1991) and the NICUs of other researchers (Gottfried & Hedgman, 1984) have shown that infants are frequently handled in the NICU. Most of the handling involved medically related treatments from nurses. Little social interaction was involved, and few of the contacts seemed appropriate for the infant's status or state—for example, talking to an awake, attentive infant or consoling an upset, crying one.

Some research has shown that even apparently gentle social interactions may be stressful for the youngest, sickest infants in the NICU (Gorski et al., 1983). Thus, it has been argued that poor timing of contacts may be as upsetting as those that seem inherently aversive (Gorski et al., 1983; Parmelee, 1985). A balance of the appropriate intensity and timing of stimulation may be achieved by the psychologist's work with the health care team and family to individualize the care of each very low-birthweight infant.

A review and discussion of interventions that may be appropriate for very low-birthweight infants in the NICU would not be complete without consideration of the involvement of the parent or other primary caregivers. Thus, it is important first to examine the potential effects on parents of having a premature, critically ill newborn in the NICU.

A family may live near a regional tertiary perinatal intensive care center; however, it is more likely that a high-risk, expectant mother would be triaged to deliver there or transported during labor, thus separating her from her family, perhaps by many miles. If she delivered elsewhere, it would be likely that her very low-birthweight infant would have to be transported without her to receive care in an NICU. When a mother has delivered somewhere else by caesarian section or is medically unstable, she may have to wait several days before traveling to a regional center to see her newborn. The child's father and other family members may feel torn between the needs to spend time with the infant, mother, other children or dependents and at their jobs. A single mother may not have the family support or child care that would enable her to visit her child often during an extended hospital stay. Many families undoubtedly feel the economic strain of transportation, child care, or missing work, which reduces the amount of time they can visit.

This difficult separation may result in less consistent contact between child and family. It may also compound any feelings of loss of control or isolation the family may have. Being an infrequent visitor may increase the difficulty of communicating with the health care team about the infant's condition and the family's concerns. Likewise, the staff may have little opportunity to offer the support that would boost the family's confidence and help them feel comfortable in providing care to their hospitalized neonate.

Even when families are able to visit their very low-birthweight infant, they may feel that the NICU is imposing and overwhelming. Real or perceived barriers to a family's contact with their baby can be created by the sense of importance given to washing and gowning before entering through large, automatic doors into what may appear to be a space-age facility, the bustling staff and constant noise of beepers, monitors, and alarms, and the vast amount of sophisticated equipment that is monitoring and supporting their tiny infant.

It may be difficult for families to identify with a small, frail-looking infant lying among many tubes, wires, lines, restraints, and covers (from plastic wrap to layette blankets). Some parents have expressed worry about the pain their child feels and are fearful that moving or even touching may hurt the infant or dislodge life-saving tubes or lines.

Usually the immature lungs of very low-birthweight newborns require respiratory assistance by mechanical ventilation. The oxygen and sometimes positive pressure an infant receives through a tube to the lungs precludes any sounds the infant might make; it is often disturbing to parents that they cannot hear their child cry or know for certain when the infant is upset. As infants improve and can breathe without assistance, they may be extubated and receive supplemental oxygen under a plastic hood. The oxygen hood over the infant's head is usually clouded with mist, making it difficult for the parents to see the infant's face.

In addition, very low-birthweight neonates have immature livers and often have jaundice. Ultraviolet lights are used to help break down the accumulating toxic bilirubin. This procedure requires that the infant wear protective eye patches because of the lights, preventing eye contact for the duration of the phototherapy.

The immature digestive system of very small preterm infants generally requires days or weeks of intravenous or parenteral feedings. Even when a preterm infant's gut can tolerate formula, the sucking effort of a weak infant may burn more calories than can be ingested by mouth. In this case, the infant receives feedings dripped through a tube in the infant's nose or mouth to the stomach. If complications such as necrotizing enterocolitis develop and require surgery, it may be many weeks before a mother can breast or bottle feed her own infant.

When infants are less critically ill, they may be moved from a more accessible open bed to an isolette. However, temperature instability may minimize the time the parents can open the portholes or remove their infant from the isolette. As the family delights in the infant's progress, it may not be apparent to them that they will face different barriers to their face-to-face interactions with their baby. In short, their infant's medical instability and treatments may delay for weeks the parent's opportunity to hold or cuddle the infant. Months may pass before parents have any quiet or private time with their infant.

Aside from these real and perceived physical barriers, parents may also have psychological barriers to positive interactions with a very low-birthweight infant in the NICU. Of all the members of the health care team, psychologists should find it easiest to understand the emotional responses that a family is likely to have after the birth of a critically ill newborn. It is common for parents to feel utter disappointment that their expectation of a normal, healthy child has not been fulfilled. Professionals understand that parents often grieve for a lost dream—the perfect child (Benfield, Leib, & Reuter, 1976; Kennell & Klaus, 1982).

Other clinicians (e.g., Moses, 1983) have described the experiences of families following the birth of a premature, critically ill infant. Parents often seem to be in a state of shock and generally report that they find it difficult to believe the situation. This early denial of the situation or lack of understanding of its seriousness can be an adaptive mechanism. With time, parents may be able to find the strength and support needed for them to accept and cope with their newfound reality. Sometimes the anxiety parents feel can also help them focus the energy and resources they need for coping. The frustration felt by most of the families often leads to repeated examination of the course of events. Sometimes parents turn inward (i.e., feel guilty), wondering what they should have done or not done to prevent their tragedy. Sometimes they turn the frustration outward (i.e., feel anger), trying to determine what role others may have played in the situation or what they should be currently doing to help. Most parents and families seem to experience the very understandable loss of control, although not all can identify or express the feelings. Most also continue to feel anxious and fearful about the life and well-being of their child. Over time, the ordeal can be depressing, especially for families of very low-birthweight infants who have a long hospitalization. In my experiences with families of critically ill newborns, parents have described the ordeal as an emotional roller coaster. They experience feelings of relief and hopefulness as their child improves, followed by increased feelings of fear and grief as the child has medical setbacks or complications. A few parents have shared with me their reluctance to let themselves become too attached to their baby, anticipate taking their infant home, or expect a good outcome for fear that this emotional involvement would simply increase the pain of losing the child if it died.

The intense emotions parents feel may help them change their attitudes and behaviors in ways that help them cope with loss. Psychologists understand this phenomenon and can provide the validation and support families may need during this stressful time (Moses, 1983). When infants do not survive, psychologists may be able to provide immediate support and counseling for parents and offer to refer them for ongoing intervention, to professional therapists, and to community parent support groups.

Intervention in the NICU

In the course of typical development, healthy newborns are able to provide information about their needs that helps their caregivers respond appropriately (Goldberg, 1977). This is the beginning of the neonate's process of interacting with and understanding the world (Watson, 1967). These early contingent interactions become the foundation of the positive caregiver–child relationship (Bell & Ainsworth, 1972) thought to be essential for a child's development of self-esteem and continued motivation to grow and learn (White, 1959).

Unfortunately, because of the circumstances described in the previous section, a very low-birthweight infant who is critically ill often may be deprived of these developmentally enhancing interactions. Even when infants are medically stable and parents are able to visit their infant in the NICU, parents have reported that they lack confidence in their caregiving skills and that their attempts to interact with their infants are not always rewarding (Kennell & Klaus, 1982).

Touching a small, fragile infant may illicit an infant startle response; a jerky movement or grimace may discourage further contact. With decreased interaction, the infant may be less likely to become attentive and responsive and provide the feedback that would encourage continued interaction with the caregiver. Although this situation is more likely to occur when an infant is very ill, it may continue even when the infant is older and more medically stable (Minde, Whitelaw, Brown, & Fitzhardinge, 1983).

Because of the concerns and needs expressed by families with critically ill newborns and the desire to optimize the development of infants at high risk for developmental problems, there were attempts in the late 1960s and early 1970s to facilitate parents' involvement in the care of their infants in NICUs (Leifer, Leiderman, Barnett, & Williams, 1972). Efforts to encourage early and extended contact between parents and preterm (and term) infants resulted in more positive parental attitudes and behaviors. This finding led investigators to suggest that an early period exists during which contact of the parent and newborn is critical for bonding, a discovery that has been found in other animal species (Kennell & Klaus, 1982). A later researcher challenged the notion of a critical bonding period in humans (Lamb, 1982). However, studies continue to demonstrate that parents have positive feelings about increased involvement with their infants in NICUs (Yu, Jamieson, & Astbury, 1981) and, with staff encouragement, may visit more often and be more realistic and hopeful about their infant's outcome (Zeskind & Iacino, 1984).

In addition to the studies focusing on parental involvement in the caregiving of their infants, others have attempted to provide developmentally enhancing experiences for neonates in NICUs. Based on the positive results of infant stimulation and early educational interventions with children from socially or economically deprived environments (Bronfenbrenner, 1976; Gordon, Lally, & Guinagh, 1976), early attempts were made to augment the experiences of infants in the NICU, generally using protocols that increased sensorimotor or tactile–kinesthetic stimulation.

Many of these early studies reported at least modest or short-term gains that included positive changes in state and activity and more optimal developmental performances. In a few studies, infants with intervention had increased norepinephrine and epinephrine urine levels, weight gain, less apnea and bradycardia, and a decreased length of hospital stay (Barnard & Bee, 1983; Field et al., 1986; Korner, Guilleminault, Van den Hoed, & Baldwin, 1978; Kuhn et al., 1991; Leib, Benfield, & Guidubaldi, 1980; Masi, 1979; Oehler, 1985; Rose, Schmidt, Riese, & Bridger, 1980; Rosenfield, 1980; Scafidi, Field, & Schanberg, 1993; Scott & Richards, 1979). In a recent study, developmental gains from early intervention with very low-birthweight infants were not observed compared with control groups, but parents reported fewer behavioral problems in their 2-year-old children (Matsuishi et al., 1998).

When studies have included parent participation or education or a home-based follow-up component, results generally have shown a more positive parental attitude, behavior, or parent–child interactions, or better growth and development (Barrera, Rosenbaum, & Cunningham, 1986; Field, Widmayer, Stringer, & Ignatoff, 1980; O'Reilly, O'Reilly, & Furuno, 1986; Rose et al., 1980; Widmayer & Field, 1980; Widmayer & Field, 1981; Yu et al., 1981; Zeskind & Iacino, 1984). A recent study that included hospital and home-based interventions found that the mental development of 7-year-old children who had low birthweights was significantly higher than low-birthweight control children and equal to normal-weight control children (Achenbach, Phares, Howell, Rauh, & Nurcombe, 1990).

More comprehensive, family-centered interventions have been designed that seem to have been more successful. The Infant Health and Development Program (1990) was a large multicenter study of low-birthweight infants that included birthweight stratification and random assignment to either a comprehensive intervention program for child and family including pediatric care or to only pediatric follow-up. The intervention group received home visits after NICU discharge until age 1 year and group parent meetings and center-based developmental services from ages 1 to 3 years. Investigators found higher intelligence scores at age 3 years and fewer behavioral problems among those in the comprehensive intervention group. At age 5 years, IQ, behavior, and health were similar in intervention and follow-up only groups; however, in the heavier low-birthweight stratum, the intervention group had significantly increased IQ scores (Brooks-Gunn et al., 1994). By age 8 years, there were only modest treatment-related improvements in the cognitive and academic achievement skills of the heavier low-birthweight children (McCarton et al., 1997).

Given the inconsistent findings in studies, it has been difficult to identify the type, amount, and timing of interventions that have been most effective, particularly for infants with differing problems. Of further concern is that many of the earlier studies of intervention included infants who were the least ill or were recovering from their illness. One study found that sick, preterm infants, especially the youngest, seemed more stressed by the interventions provided (Oehler, 1985). These results and the paucity of information about the most vulnerable neonates call to question the appropriateness of interventions for the youngest and sickest of very low-birthweight neonates.

Several researchers have proposed that the appropriateness of interventions for critically ill neonates (including protection from overstimulation as well as arousal for social interaction) be based on evaluation of the individual infant's maturation level, developmental status, temperament, processing ability, behavioral state and responses, and an assessment of the ecology of the environment (Cornell & Gottfried, 1976; Gorski et al., 1983; Parmelee, 1985).

Als et al. (1986) designed individualized developmental care plans for very low-birthweight infants with respiratory distress syndrome, which called for modifications in the NICU environment and in caregiving to minimize stress and respond to the infants' individual needs. Infants with individualized care plans fed orally sooner, had fewer days of assisted respiration, and had better developmental scores and parental interactions at 9 months than infants in a contrast group. In a similar randomized trial (Als et al., 1994), trained nurses and the infants' parents served as caregivers, and developmental specialists supported the caregiving by regularly observing the infants and updating their care plans. Infants with care plans again showed improved feeding and respiratory status, along with decreased frequency of IVH and shorter hospital stays. Treatment infants also had improved neurobehavioral functioning at 42 weeks postconceptional age (PCA) and at 9 months.

Other studies that have included individualized developmental care have shown at least short-term beneficial effects for very low-birthweight infants. In a randomized replication and extension of Als's studies, Ariagno et al. (1997) demonstrated treatment related improvement at 42 but not 36 weeks PCA. In addition, no treatment advantages were shown on development at 4, 12, or 24 months. Another randomized study found that infants who received treatment required fewer days of assisted respiration, began full feedings sooner, had shorter hospital stays, and demonstrated improved behavioral performance at 42 weeks PCA (Fleisher et al., 1995). In a phase lag study of 124 infants, those receiving developmental versus conventional interventions were more physiologically stable over time (Stevens, Petryshen, Hawkins, Smith, & Taylor, 1996). In addition, compared with control groups in a traditional NICU, low-birthweight infants in a nursery with decreased stimulation, diurnal cycles, and state-contingent nursing care had steadier and longer sleep states (Fajardo, Browning, Fisher, & Paton, 1990). Preterm infants also have been shown to seek contact with a "breathing bear," which provided rhythmic stimulation that was set to reflect their own respiratory patterns. Infants who were given the chance to self-regulate their stimulation had more quiet sleep than control infants with nonbreathing bears in their cribs (Thoman & Graham, 1986).

A longitudinal intervention study of low-birthweight infants and their families done at the University of Florida (Resnick, Eyler, Nelson, Eitzman, & Bucciarelli, 1987) demonstrated more long-term benefits of individualized developmental care combined with family-centered education. Developmental specialists provided interventions for children and caregivers during the infants' hospitalization. Soon after discharge, which is often a difficult adjustment period, a nurse practitioner visited the families' home to monitor the infants' general health status and demonstrate developmental activities that caregivers could provide at home. As an additional part of the intervention study, early childhood developmental specialists continued to visit the home twice a month until each child was age 2 years, providing family support and demonstrating educational activities chosen for each child's developmental age and needs. The goals of the home interventions included facilitating the families' involvement in promoting their children's development and becoming advocates for their children's health care and developmental services. In blinded evaluations at ages 1 and 2 years, the children in the special treatment group had significantly higher developmental scores and a lower rate of developmental delay than did control infants (Resnick et al., 1987).

Strategies used during the intervention show some of the opportunities that health psychologists may have to intervene with infants in the NICU and their families. Developmental activities can be provided to assist infants in adjusting to their environment, tolerating sensory input, adapting to social interaction, and eliciting positive responses from their caregivers. Individual interventions should be tailored to each infant's age, condition, and responses. Interventions may include reducing distress by protecting the infant from overstimulation, consoling upset infants, and providing sensitive and responsive interactions contingent on infant signals indicating tolerance of such contact (Eyler et al., 1989).

An equally important aspect of the program has involved interventions with the family, another role perfectly suited for psychologists. To establish their supportive, helping role, psychologists can make early contact with each parent, perhaps by offering congratulations on the birth of their child while acknowledging conflicting feelings of joy and fear. Not only do parents of critically ill newborns generally miss the celebration that normally surrounds a new birth, but some feel that loved ones are afraid to be involved, perhaps because they do not want to cause more distress. Ironically, the people who are trying to be the most helpful by not bothering the family may contribute to the family's feelings of isolation.

Efforts can be made to support parents wherever they may be in their grief process and to help them develop coping skills. Psychologists can validate parents' feelings and provide information needed to help decrease feelings of isolation and loss of control, a process that may involve good listening and reflecting skills and the facilitation of communication between families and the health care team.

At times, a member of the health care team who is trying to protect a family may instead seem patronizing or untrustworthy. For example, a hospital intern may choose to wait until morning to contact an infant's parents about a medical episode that occurred in the middle of the night. Although the intern may be doing this to help the family get more rest, the parents could end up angry and upset because they were not called immediately. The health psychologist may be able to explain that being called immediately, even if disturbed from sleep, could build parents' trust that they would be kept informed about any serious problems, perhaps allowing them to relax better between calls.

When emotionally ready, parents can be encouraged to participate in the care of their newborn. For example, a NICU nursing staff was concerned about a mother participating in the University of Florida intervention study (Resnick et al., 1987). The mother had not named her infant since his birth several days earlier and had only come to visit once. When a health psychologist spoke to the mother about her feelings, she said that she had previously given birth to a premature baby who died in the NICU. She was afraid that she would again become attached to and lose her baby. When the psychologist told her that her feelings were normal and understandable, she admitted wanting to be with her baby and was in fact thinking of little else. Within a few days, she had named her son, began visiting him daily, and became very involved in his care.

When parents are able to visit their newborns and after they have learned about their infant's condition and the equipment and procedures being used by the physicians and nurses, it is a good time to help parents connect with their baby and identify the child's individual strengths. Some parents think it is extremely difficult to relate to their baby in the middle of all the medical paraphernalia. Another child who was participating in the intervention research in our NICU was a very ill preterm infant with severe jaundice and needed constant phototherapy and to wear the associated eye patches. His parents hovered anxiously over the child and were fearful to touch their baby. Their son became calm as they spoke, and they were surprised when they were told by the study psychologist that he was listening to their voices. After the psychologist got permission to briefly turn off the lights and remove the eye patches, the parents began to cry as they saw their baby respond to them. Seeing his eyes for the first time made a connection for them; they told the psychologist that he finally seemed like their son. They were soon quite comfortable interacting with their baby and becoming involved in his care.

When parents are ready, health psychologists can then demonstrate ways they can safely interact with their infant. A goal could be to help parents recognize signals of distress and respond appropriately by protecting or soothing the infants. As their infant awakens, becomes alert, and seems able to tolerate more input, parents can gently engage in social interaction, supporting and encouraging growth and development. Health psychologists can be a great help to families by working with them on a developmental care plan incorporating their infant's typical patterns of response to stimuli, including signals of comfort and of distress. Caregivers can be taught ways to alter the environment for a vulnerable infant, decreasing stimulation and increasing restful periods, by minimizing the unnecessary procedures and clustering the necessary procedures. As infants become more self-regulated and responsive, psychologists can help caregivers understand the importance of their role: to sensitively read their infant's cues and respond with appropriate feedback and interact without stressing the infant by balancing arousal with rest. Care plans can be updated and strategies revised to reflect the increasing comfort and skills of caregivers and maturity of the infant. New interactive activities can be added to facilitate the infant's next level of development.

For very low-birthweight neonates, these contingent interactions with caregivers can provide opportunities for positive feedback for their behavior and the emerging feelings of competence that are essential for the development of self-esteem and the continued motivation to learn and grow. In addition, the participation of parents in the care of very low-birthweight infants can empower them as competent caregivers. When most other circumstances seem out of control, a parent's successful interventions with their critically ill newborn can increase their feelings of competence, providing the encouragement and motivation they may need for successful caregiving over the long term. Although this boost in confidence can be beneficial for all caregivers stressed by having a newborn in intensive care, it may be especially helpful for young parents with few experiences of success in their lives. Their new caregiving skills, the developing positive relationship with their newborn, and their emerging view of themselves as successful parents may signal a new beginning in their lives.

It may be important for health psychologists to realize caregivers' level of insecurity and help facilitate their success, not just model a level of competence that parents may feel they can never achieve. Psychologists can build parents' confidence by asking what the parents have observed about their baby, how they have responded, and then reinforcing positive behaviors or perhaps their close approximations to positive interactions.

Transition to Home Care

The final interventions that a psychologist working in the NICU may have with a child and family involve hospital discharge. Parents are commonly frightened of the transition to home; they wonder how they can possibly provide the same care that their infant received in the NICU. By the time of discharge, parents have usually watched their child learn to breathe unassisted, maintain normal temperatures without radiant heaters or isolettes, nipple feed and take in sufficient calories to maintain growth, begin to show some regular and approximately normal wake—sleep states, and perhaps engage in some limited social interaction. In spite of their child's recovery and the caregiving skills they have learned (which may include some fairly sophisticated medical procedures), the thought of being fully responsible for their child's care and the unknown future make the long-anticipated discharge a time as frightening as it is joyful.

The health psychologist can be most helpful to the family during this time of transition, validating their understandable fears, re-establishing a supportive connection, encouraging their efforts and plans, and providing the information and resources they need for the future. It may also be important to provide a realistic appraisal of what the family can expect for their child's future, given the assessed strengths and needs of the child, the research literature, and the best intervention efforts. It may be even more critical for the child's future to balance realism with encouragement that the family not give up hoping for the best possible outcome. The optimum development may be reached by expecting and striving for a miracle.

It is also important for the psychologist to recognize the ongoing stress families may experience during the following several years. Although some surveys of parents have found perceived impact on the family of very low-birthweight infants to be independent of sociodemographics or developmental delay of infants (Lee, Penner, & Cox, 1991), other studies have reported that parents perceived more family impact, personal strain, and higher burdens when they had lower incomes, when they had less education, and when their child had functional or developmental problems (Cronin, Shapiro, Casiro, & Cheang, 1995). A longitudinal, prospective study of high-risk and low-risk very low-birthweight infants and full-term control groups discovered that mothers of the preterm infants reported more psychological distress at 1 month than did mothers of the full-term infants. At 2 years, only mothers of high-risk very low-birthweight infants continued to report higher distress. At 3 years, their parenting stress continued to be higher. Investigators also found that the severity of the mother's depression was related to poorer developmental outcome of high- and low-risk very low-birthweight infants (Singer et al., 1999).

Even if the health psychologist is not personally involved with a developmental follow-up program, recommendations can be made based on the latest developmental assessment of the infant's progress and ongoing needs. In many states in the United States, very low-birthweight infants, especially those with significant medical complications and certainly those who already demonstrate signs of delay, are eligible for family-centered, comprehensive, individualized developmental services from birth to 3 years through the Individuals With Disabilities Education Act (IDEA; P.L. 99–457, Part C).

The NICU health psychologist may become part of the federally legislated multidisciplinary assessment of an infant who is eligible or referred for eligibility determination and perhaps a member of the child's required individualized family service plan (IFSP) team. The results of the multidisciplinary assessment of an infant's strengths and needs in each area of development must be presented in a meeting of the IFSP team that includes the family and any potential service providers.

Because being family centered is federally mandated recommendations for ongoing services are based on the family's concerns and priorities for their child and the results of the assessment and recommendations of the professionals on the team. Together, the family, evaluators, and service providers develop the IFSP. The IFSP documents the developmental goals set by the team, the services needed to meet those goals, the selection of a service coordinator or family advocate, and the ways everyone involved will work together to ensure those services can be provided.

Health Psychologist as Team Member and Leader in the NICU

Providing services to infants and their families in the NICU is always a team effort, a fact that should not be unfamiliar to a trained health psychologist. In a tertiary care center, the positions and levels of the medical team alone can be complicated to other professionals and often confusing for families. Neonatologists or neonatal fellows are the attending physicians and provide instruction and oversee care; pediatric residents or medical students and physician's assistants or nurse practitioners provide direct patient care and communicate with families; respiratory therapists are typically involved in the daily care of infants with breathing problems in the NICU; myriad other consulting services with various levels of teachers and students recommend treatment for problems with a particular organ or system—at times several individuals are involved with each child; and finally, bedside nurses carry out orders for treatment and usually work with families daily. It seems as soon as one learns the various players, it is time for a rotation and everyone changes. Parents are often frustrated about losing their doctor when the rotation ends in the midst of their infant's hospital stay.

Some NICU professionals also routinely consult other therapeutic services for specific issues. For example, they may consult occupational therapists to evaluate oral–motor functions when an infant has a feeding problem because of a cleft palate or lip, or they may consult physical therapists to treat an infant who is born with or develops muscle contractures. Often, clinical social workers are assigned to many if not all of the mothers with family difficulties, and many of these mothers (e.g., mothers who are not able to care for their child because of a disability, illness, or history of abuse or incarceration) interact with government agencies that may need to become involved.

Health psychologists must learn the staff hierarchies and job expectations in each NICU to determine how their skills can be used and what role they can play in the health care team. This may require formal negotiations with NICU medical or nursing directors during hiring or consultation. It may also require more informal on-the-job adaptations. Understanding the tendency of staff members in established positions to "guard their turf" and the importance of good communication, psychologists who are new members of a team should be able to reassure other health care personnel by word and deed of their professionalism and collegiality. It is also important for health psychologists to reassure those providing critical medical care that the role of the psychologist will not interfere with life or death procedures and treatments, nor will they provide or interpret medical information to families without consulting with physicians.

In recent years, there seems to be more emphasis on interdisciplinary collaboration, especially on clinical teaching and research teams within academic health care centers, supported in part by federal funding and legislation such as IDEA. Health care staffs may welcome health psychologists as an adjunct to medical decision-making teams.

Many NICUs also have their own or are affiliated with neonatal ethics committees. In most cases, these ethics committees consult with health care teams, providing advice on addressing ethical dilemmas that frequently arise in NICUs, such as whether to withhold or withdraw support in apparently futile cases (Edens, Eyler, Wagner, & Eitzman, 1990). Psychologists could play a vital role in a neonatal ethics committee as representatives or advocates for child development and family issues. As an outgrowth of collaboration on clinical teams or ethics committees, health psychologists may also find opportunities to be involved in the development and dissemination of best practices protocols that may affect the developmental or psychological well-being of infants or their families.

Developing rapport and collaboration within an interdisciplinary team can be productive and rewarding not only for patients but also for professionals. Psychologists should expect to find a unique role as a health care team member in the NICU. Those trained in infant developmental assessments are the most appropriate professionals to evaluate, recommend, and provide developmental interventions for at-risk infants. Although clinical social workers may be the professionals evaluating family systems, making referrals for community-based services, and interacting with child protection and legal services in some NICUs, those roles may be fulfilled by psychologists in others. In addition, psychologists may be needed to provide support and counseling for families who have a critically ill newborn or receive a disturbing diagnosis. Furthermore, psychologists who have assessed an infant's developmental status can best interpret the findings for parents and support them through any upsetting developmental diagnoses. In addition, as explained previously, psychologists can play a key role in helping families overcome physical and psychological barriers to bonding with their infant and facilitating their participation in the baby's care.

Psychologists may also develop opportunities for leadership in the

NICU environment by supervising or directing others who provide assessments and interventions for infants and their families in the hospital and during follow-ups. Perhaps a psychologist could develop the previous programs in facilities where they do not exist. In addition, in some NICUs, it may be most appropriate for the health psychologists to provide oversight or liaison with allied health providers and volunteers working with infants or families. Many hospitals have parent support groups that include "veteran" parents whose infants were cared for in the NICU. These parents volunteer to offer advice, empathy, and encouragement from the unique perspective of a family who has been through the experience. Some hospitals support a "cuddler" program, which is composed of volunteers who spend time with hospitalized infants whose families are unable to visit often. Health psychologists in the NICU would be well suited to orient, train, and oversee volunteers whose efforts complement the work of professionals intervening with very low-birthweight infants and their families.

Health Psychologist as Teacher and Researcher

Health psychologists working in the NICU may also encounter informal and formal teaching opportunities. As part of the health care team, psychologists may participate on clinical and teaching rounds in the NICU, during which they may have numerous opportunities to share information from a psychologist's perspective with physicians, nurses, and students. Psychologists can volunteer to provide lectures to or lead discussion groups for medical students, residents, or nursing staff members on specific topics relevant to the developmental or psychological care of infants and their families. Psychologists may also be involved in a more established rotation related to child development or family issues. Through such a program, medical students or residents in pediatrics may rotate and receive clinical instruction in or experience with assessments and interventions. Psychologists more formally affiliated with departments of pediatrics or divisions of neonatology may be asked or expected to present topics of general interest at grand rounds for pediatric residents, fellows, and faculty members or to share their research interests during division or departmental research seminars for fellows and faculty members.

Of all the professionals working in the NICU, health psychologists may be the most well trained in research methodology and statistical techniques and thus are uniquely suited to pursue support for research projects relevant to the care of infants and families in the NICU. They may have opportunities to collaborate on clinical trials or epidemiological studies directed by faculty members, and they may be of particular help in the research training of pediatric fellows involved in such research. Psychologists working in the interdisciplinary environment of the NICU should be very competitive as principal investigators in obtaining federal funding for grant proposals. The rapidly advancing science of neonatology continues to decrease mortality but presents multiple concerns about the short- and long-term morbidity of infants and the consequences on their families.

CONCLUSION

As reviewed in a previous section, very low-birthweight infants seem to be at risk for a range of neurological, growth, and developmental problems that may include sensorimotor and cognitive deficits. However, a few, large prospective investigations that were well-controlled studied outcomes related to specific medical problems or conditions. In the previously cited literature, complete information was not always available on population characteristics or adequate explanations of the sampling procedures and whether they included randomization of participants to treatment and control groups, matching of participants in various groupings, or any other treatment (e.g., statistical) of potentially confounding variables. It has been noted that potential bias in participant selection, consent, or attrition has rarely been reported by investigators (Bax, 1983; Kiely & Paneth, 1981; Mayes & Stahlman, 1982). In addition, many studies have not made comparisons of variables such as infant age, size at birth, or growth; type, severity, or complications of diseases that might relate to brain development; or family variables (e.g., SES, family functioning, the home environment), all of which might confound outcomes and lead to misinterpretations of findings (Kiely & Paneth, 1981; Mayes & Stahlman, 1982).

Health psychologists have the expertise to design and conduct more appropriate studies to determine which infants are most at risk and the nature of their developmental needs. Future research needs to include the variables listed and the effect of levels or standards of care, specific interventions, environmental conditions, and changes in treatment protocols over time. It is also important to investigate the type of child who benefits from interventions; the critical age to begin services; and the type, duration, intensity, and setting of the most effective treatments and persistence of any effects (McCarton, Wallace, & Bennett, 1995, 1996). Psychologists could ensure that a range of standardized assessments is considered and that the measures of neurological or developmental problems chosen are those that are most appropriate for the research hypotheses about outcome. They must also ensure that these outcome assessments be administered by professionally trained staff members who are unaware of any clinical conditions or treatments (Bax, 1983; Kiely & Paneth, 1981; Mayes & Stahlman, 1982). Psychologists will be able to choose the appropriate timing of assessments, which also reflects the research questions being asked (Davies, 1984).

Well-done research on the relationship of early problems and treatments to long-term developmental outcome can be of significant help to health care providers in adapting neonatal care, prioritizing the need for developmental follow-up care, and planning appropriate intervention strategies to optimize the outcome of very low-birthweight infants and all other at-risk infants.

The issue of prevention is particularly relevant to psychologists. The notion of prevention (of more long-term deficits) is inherent in the early interventions with infants and families discussed. However, a more primary prevention could include efforts to avoid pregnancy and birth-related problems through adequate prenatal care. Health psychologists are well trained to educate women on the importance of early access to health care during pregnancy and to facilitate adherence to nutritional and treatment regimens, some of which can prevent prematurity and neonatal illness. For example, psychologists are ideally suited to provide cessation interventions to encourage drug-, alcohol-, and tobacco-free pregnancies. Working within an interdisciplinary team, health psychologists can play an essential role in optimizing the health of pregnant women and their neonates.

REFERENCES

Achenbach, T. M., Phares, V., Howell, C. T., Rauh, V. A., & Nurcombe, B. (1990). Seven-year outcome of the Vermont Intervention Program for Low Birthweight Infants. *Child Development, 61,* 1672–1681.

Als, H., Lawhon, G., Brown, E., Gibes, R., Duffy, F. H., McAnulty, G., et al. (1986). Individualized behavioral and environmental care for the very low birth weight preterm infant at high risk for bronchopulmonary dysplasia: Neonatal intensive care unit and developmental outcome. *Pediatrics, 78,* 1123–1132.

Als, H., Lawhon, G., Duffy, F. H., McAnulty, G. B., Gives-Grossman, R., & Blickman, J. G. (1994). Individualized developmental care for the very low-birthweight preterm infants. Medical and neurofunctional effects. *Journal of the American Medical Association, 272,* 853–858.

Anagnostakis, D., Petmezakis, J., Messaritakis, J., & Metsaniotis, N. (1980). Noise pollution in neonatal units: A practical health hazard. *Acta Paediatrica Scandinavia, 69,* 771–773.

Anderson, A. E., Wildin, S. R., Woodside, M., Swank, P. R., Smith, K. E., Denson, S. E., et al. (1996). Severity of medical and neurologic complications as a determinant of neurodevelopmental outcome at 6 and 12 months in very low birth weight infants. *Journal of Child Neurology, 11,* 215–219.

Ariagno, R. L., Thoman, E. B., Boeddiker, M. A., Kugener, B., Constantinou, J. C., Mirmiran, M., et al. (1997). Developmental care does not alter sleep and development of premature infants. *Pediatrics, 100,* E9.

Bada, H. S., Korones, S. B., Perry, E. H., Arheart, K. L., Pourcyrous, M., Runyan,

I. W., III, et al. (1990). Frequent handling in the neonatal intensive care unit and intraventricular hemorrhage. *Journal of Pediatrics, 117,* 126–131.

Barnard, K. E., & Bee, H. L. (1983). The impact of temporally patterned stimulation on the development of preterm infants. *Child Development, 54,* 1156–1167.

Barrera, M. E., Rosenbaum, P. L., & Cunningham, C. E. (1986). Early home intervention with low-birthweight infants and their parents. *Child Development, 57,* 20–33.

Bax, M. (1983). Following up the small baby. *Developmental Medicine and Child Neurology, 25,* 415–416.

Becker, P. T., Grunwald, P. C., Moorman, J., & Stuhr, S. (1991). Outcomes of developmentally supportive nursing care for very low birth weight infants. *Nursing Research, 40,* 150–155.

Beckwith, L., & Parmelee, A. H. (1986). EEG patterns of preterm infants, home environment, and later IA. *Child Development, 57,* 777–789.

Bell, S. M. V., & Ainsworth, M. D. S. (1972). Infant crying and maternal responsiveness. *Child Development, 43,* 1171–1190.

Bendersky, M., & Lewis, M. (1995). Effects of intraventricular hemorrhage and other medical and environmental risks on multiple outcomes at age three years. *Journal of Developmental and Behavioral Pediatrics, 16,* 89–96.

Benfield, D. G., Leib, S. A., & Reuter, J. (1976). Grief response of parents after referral of the critically ill newborn to a regional center. *New England Journal of Medicine, 294,* 975–978.

Bergman, L., Hirsch, R. P., Fria, T. J., Shapiro, S. M., Holtzman, I., & Painter, J. J. (1985). Cause of hearing loss in the high-risk premature infants. *Journal of Pediatrics, 106,* 95–101.

Beverley, D. W., Chance, G. W., & Coates, C. F. (1984). Intraventricular hemorrhage—Timing of occurrence and relationship to perinatal events. *British Journal of Obstetrics and Gynaecology, 91,* 1007–1013.

Bhushan, V., Paneth, N., & Kiely, J. L. (1993). Impact of improved survival of very low birth weight infants on recent secular trends in the prevalence of cerebral palsy. *Pediatrics, 91,* 1094–1100.

Blackmore, C. A., Ferre, C. D., Rowley, D. L., Hogue, C. J., Gaiter, J., & Atrash, H. (1993). Is race a risk factor or a risk marker for preterm delivery? *Ethnicity and Disease, 3,* 372–377.

Blaymore-Bier, J., Pezzullo, J., Kim, E., Oh, W., Garcia-Coll, C., & Vohr, B. R. (1994). Outcome of extremely low-birth-weight infants: 1980–1990. *Acta Paediatrica, 83,* 1244–1248.

Blitz, R. K., Wachtel, R. C., Blackmon, L., & Berenson-Howard, J. (1997). Neurodevelopmental outcome of extremely low birth weight infants in Maryland. *Maryland Medical Journal, 46,* 18–24.

Botting, N., Powls, A., Cooke, R. W., & Marlow, N. (1997). Attention deficit hyperactivity disorders and other psychiatric outcomes in very low birthweight children at 12 years. *Journal of Child Psychology and Psychiatry and Allied Disciplines, 38*, 931–941.

Botting, N., Powls, A., Cooke, R. W., & Marlow, N. (1998). Cognitive and educational outcome of very-low-birthweight children in early adolescence. *Developmental Medicine and Child Neurology, 40*, 652–660.

Bourchier, D. (1994). Outcome at 2 years of infants less than 1000 grams: A regional study. *New Zealand Medical Journal, 107*, 281–283.

Bowen, J. R., Starte, D. R., Arnold, J. D., Simmons, J. L., Ma, P. J., & Leslie, G. I. (1993). Extremely low birthweight infants at 3 years: A developmental profile. *Journal of Paediatrics and Child Health, 29*, 276–281.

Bowlby, J. (1969). *Attachment and loss*. New York: Basic Books.

Bozynski, M. E. A., Nelson, M. N., Matalon, T. A., Genaze, D. R., Rosati-Skertich, C., Naughton, P. M., et al. (1985). Cavitary periventricular leukomalacia: Incidence and short-term outcome in infants weighing <1200 grams at birth. *Developmental Medicine and Child Neurology, 27*, 572–577.

Brazelton, T. B. (1980). Foreword. In E. J. Sell (Ed.), *Follow-up of the high risk newborn—A practical approach* (pp. xi–xx). Springfield, IL: Charles C Thomas.

Brazelton, T. B. (1984). Neonatal behavioral assessment scale. *Clinics in developmental medicine*. London: Spastics International Medical Publications.

Brazelton, T. B., & Nugent, J. K. (1995). *Neonatal behavioral assessment scale* (3rd ed., pp. 67–83). London: Mac Keith Press.

Briscoe, J., Gathercole, S. E., & Marlow, N. (1998). Short-term memory and language outcomes after extreme prematurity at birth. *Journal of Speech and Hearing Research, 41*, 654–666.

Bronfenbrenner, U. (1976). *Is early intervention effective?* (A report on longitudinal evaluations of preschool programs, Vol. 2). Washington, DC: Office of Human Development, Department of Health, Education and Welfare.

Brooks-Gunn, J., McCarton, C. M., Casey, P. H., McCormick, M. C., Bauer, C. R., Bernbaum, J. C., et al. (1994). Early intervention in low-birth-weight premature infants. Results through age 5 years from the Infant Health and Development Program. *Journal of the American Medical Association, 272*, 1257–1262.

Buckwald, S., Zorn, W. A., & Egan, E. (1984). Mortality and follow-up data for neonates weighing 500 to 800 g at birth. *American Journal of Diseases of Children, 138*, 779–782.

Bylund, B., Cervin, T., Finnstrom, O., Gaddlin, P. O., Kernell, A. Leijon, I., et al. (1998). Morbidity and neurological function of very low birthweight infants from the newborn period to 4 y of age. A prospective study from the southeast region of Sweden. *Acta Paediatrica, 87*, 758–763.

Campbell, M. K., Halinda, E., Carlyle, M. J., Fox, A. M., Turner, L. A., & Chance, G. W. (1993). Factors predictive of follow-up clinic attendance and developmental outcome in a regional cohort of very low birth weight infants. *American Journal of Epidemiology, 138*, 704–713.

Campbell, P. B., Bull, M. J., Ellis, F. D., Bryson, C. Q., Lemons, J. A., & Schreiner, R. L. (1983). Incidence of retinopathy of prematurity in a tertiary newborn intensive care unit. *Archives of Ophthalmology, 101,* 1686–1688.

Carter, R. L., Resnick, M. B., Ariet, M., Shieh, G., & Vonesh, E. F. (1992). A random coefficient growth curve analysis of mental development in low-birth-weight infants. *Statistics in Medicine, 11,* 243–256.

Catto-Smith, A. G., Yu, V. Y., Bajuk, B., Orgill, A. A., & Astbury, J. (1985). Effect of neonatal periventricular hemorrhage on neurodevelopmental outcome. *Archives of Disease in Childhood, 60,* 8–11.

Cheung, P. Y., Barrington, K. J., Finer, N. N., & Robertson, C. M. (1999). Early childhood neurodevelopment in very low birth weight infants with predischarge apnea. *Pediatric Pulmonology, 27,* 14–20.

Cohen, S. E., & Parmelee, A. H. (1983). Prediction of five-year Stanford–Binet scores in preterm infants. *Child Development, 54,* 1242–1253.

Cornell, E. H., & Gottfried, A. W. (1976). Intervention with premature human infants. *Child Development, 47,* 32–39.

Cronin, C. M., Shapiro, C. R., Casiro, O. G., & Cheang, M. S. (1995). The impact of very low-birth-weight infants on the family is long lasting. A matched control study. *Archives of Pediatrics and Adolescent Medicine, 149,* 151–158.

Danford, D. A., Miske, S., Headley, J., & Nelson, R. M. (1983). Effects of routine care procedures on transcutaneous oxygen in neonates: A quantitative approach. *Archives of Disease in Childhood, 58,* 20–23.

Davies, P. A. (1984). Follow up of low birthweight children. *Archives of Disease in Childhood, 59,* 794–797.

deRegnier, R. A., Roberts, D., Ramsey, D., Weaver, R. G., Jr., & O'Shea, T. M. (1997). Association between the severity of chronic lung disease and first-year outcomes of very low birth weight infants. *Journal of Perinatology, 17,* 375–382.

DeVries, L. S., Dubowitz, L. M., Dubowitz, V., Kaiser, A., Lary, S., Silverman, M., et al. (1985). Predictive value of cranial ultrasound in the newborn baby: A reappraisal. *Lancet, 1,* 137–140.

Dezoete, J. A., MacArthur, B. A., & Aftimos, S. (1997) Developmental outcome at 18 months of children less than 1000 grams. *New Zealand Medical Journal, 110,* 205–207.

Doyle, L. W., Keir, E., Kitchen, W. H., Ford, G. W., Rickards, A. L., & Kelly, E. A. (1992). Audiologic assessment of extremely low birth weight infants: A preliminary report. *Pediatrics, 90,* 744–749.

Dubowitz, L. M., & Dubowitz, V. (1981). *The neurological assessment of the preterm and full-term newborn infant.* London: Spastics International Medical.

Dubowitz, L. M., Dubowitz, V., Palmer, P. G., Miller, G., Fawer, C. L., & Levene, M. I. (1984). Correlation of neurologic assessment in the preterm newborn infant with outcome at 1 year. *Journal of Pediatrics, 105,* 452–456.

Edens, M. J., Eyler, F. D., Wagner, J. T., & Eitzman, D. V. (1990). Neonatal ethics: Development of a consultative group. *Pediatrics, 86,* 944–949.

Escalona, S. K. (1982). Babies at double hazard: Early development of infants at biologic and social risk. *Pediatrics, 70,* 670–676.

Eyler, F. D. (1980). Demonstration of premature infants' abilities to improve maternal attitude and facilitate mother–infant interaction. *Dissertation Abstracts International, 40,* 4521.

Eyler, F. D. (1993). Developmental outcomes. In P. B. Koff, D. V. Eitzman, & J. Neu (Eds.), *Neonatal and pediatric respiratory care* (pp. 440–501). St. Louis, MO: C. V. Mosby.

Eyler, F. D., Courtway-Meyers, C., Edens, M. J., Hellrung, D. J., Nelson, R. M., Eitzman, D. V., et al. (1989). Effects of developmental intervention on heart rate and transcutaneous oxygen in low birth-weight infants. *Neonatal Network, 8,* 17–23.

Eyler, F. D., Delgado-Hachey, M., Woods, N. S., & Carter, R. L. (1991). Quantifications of the Dubowitz neurological assessment of preterm neonates: Developmental outcome. *Infant Behavior and Development, 14,* 451–469.

Eyler, F. D., Woods, N. S., Behnke, M., & Conlon, M. (1991). Changes over a decade: Adult–infant interaction in the NICU. *Pediatric Research, 29,* 255A.

Fajardo, B., Browning, M., Fisher, D., & Paton, J. (1990). Effect of nursery environment on state regulation in very-low-birth-weight premature infants. *Infant Behavior and Development, 13,* 287–303.

Field, T. M., Schanberg, S. M., Scafidi, F., Bauer, C. R., Vega-Lahr, N., Garcia, R., et al. (1986). Tactile and kinesthetic stimulation effects on preterm neonates. *Pediatrics, 77,* 654–658.

Field, T. M., Widmayer, S. M., Stringer, S., & Ignatoff, E. (1980). Teenage, lower-class, Black mothers and their preterm infants: An intervention and developmental follow-up. *Child Development, 51,* 426–436.

Finnstrom, O., Otterblad, O. P., Sedin, G., Serenius, F., Svenningsen, N., et al. (1998). Neurosensory outcome and growth at three years in extremely low birthweight infants: Follow-up results from the Swedish national prospective study. *Acta Paediatrics, 87,* 1055–1060.

Fleisher, B. E., VandenBerg, K., Constantinou, J., Heller, C., Benitz, W. E., Johnson, A., et al. (1995). Individualized developmental care for very-low-birth-weight premature infants. *Clinical Pediatrics (Philadelphia), 34,* 523–529.

Flynn, J. T. (1983). Acute proliferative retrolental fibroplasia: Multivariate risk analysis. *Transactions of the American Ophthalmology Society, 81,* 549–591.

Ford, L. M., Steichen, J., Steichen Asch, P. A., Babcock, D., & Fogelson, M. H. (1989). Neurologic status and intracranial hemorrhage in very-low-birth-weight preterm infants. *American Journal of Diseases in Children, 143,* 1186.

Formby, D. (1967). Maternal recognition of infants' cry. *Developmental Medicine and Child Neurology, 9,* 293–298.

Friedman, S. (1972). Newborn visual attention to repeated exposure of redundant vs. "novel" targets. *Perception and Psychophysics, 12,* 291–294.

Fullard, W., & Reiling, A. M. (1976). An investigation of Lorenz's "babyness." *Child Development, 47,* 1191–1193.

Glass, P., Avery, G. B., Subramanian, K. N., Keys, M. P., Sostek, A. M., & Friendly, D. S. (1985). Effect of bright light in the hospital nursery on the incidence of retinopathy of prematurity. *New England Journal of Medicine, 313,* 401–404.

Goldberg, S. (1977). Social competence in infancy. *Merrill–Palmer Quarterly, 23,* 163–177.

Goldson, E. (1984). Severe bronchopulmonary dysplasia in the very low birth weight infant: Its relationship to developmental outcome. *Journal of Developmental and Behavioral Pediatrics, 5,* 165–168.

Gordon, I. J., Lally, R. J., & Guinagh, B. J. (1976). *Long-term results of early childhood education: A home learning center approach to early stimulation. Final report.* Bethesda, MD: National Institute of Mental Health, Department of Health, Education and Welfare.

Goren, C. C., Sarty, M., & Wu, P. Y. K. (1975). Visual following and pattern discrimination of face-like stimuli by newborn infants. *Pediatrics, 56,* 544–549.

Gorski, P. A., Hole, W. T., Leonard, C. H., & Martin, J. A. (1983). Direct computer recording of premature infants and nursery care: Distress following two interventions. *Pediatrics, 72,* 198–202.

Gorski, P. A., Lewkowicz, D. J., & Huntington, L. (1987). Advances in neonatal and infant behavioral assessment: Toward a comprehensive evaluation of early patterns of development. *Journal of Developmental and Behavioral Pediatrics, 8,* 39–50.

Gottfried, A. W., & Hedgman, J. E. (1984). How intensive is newborn intensive care? An environmental analysis. *Pediatrics, 74,* 292–294.

Gottfried, A. W., Wallace-Lande, P., Sherman-Brown, S., King, J., Coen, C., & Hodgman, J. E. (1981). Physical and social environment of newborn infants in special care units. *Science, 214,* 673–675.

Graham, F., Clifton, R. K., & Halton H. (1968). Habituation of heart rate responses to repeated auditory stimulation during the first five days of life. *Child Development, 39,* 35–52.

Greenough, A., & Roberton, N. R. (1985). Morbidity and survival in neonates ventilated for the respiratory distress syndrome. *British Medical Journal of Clinical Research, 290,* 597–600.

Gunn, T. R., Lepore, E., & Outerbridge, E. W. (1983). Outcome at school-age after neonatal mechanical ventilation. *Developmental Medicine and Child Neurology, 25,* 305–314.

Guyer, B., MacDorman, M. F., Martin, J. A., Peters, K. D., & Strobino, D. M. (1998). Annual summary of vital statistics—1997. *Pediatrics, 102,* 1333–1349.

Hack, M., Breslau, N., Aram, D., Weissman, B., Klein, N., & Borawski-Clark, E. (1992). The effect of very low birth weight and social risk on neurocognitive abilities at school age. *Journal of Developmental and Behavioral Pediatrics, 13,* 412–420.

Hack, M., & Fanaroff, A. A. (1999). Outcomes of children of extremely low birthweight and gestational age in the 1990s. *Early Human Development, 53,* 193–218.

Hack, M., Friedman, H., & Fanaroff, A. A. (1996). Outcomes of extremely low birth weight infants. *Pediatrics, 98,* 931–937.

Hack, M., Taylor, H. G., Klein, N., Eiben, R., Schatschneider, C., & Mercuri-Minich, N. (1994). School-age outcomes in children with birth weights under 750 g. *New England Journal of Medicine, 331,* 753–759.

Hack, M., Wright, L. L., Shankaran, S., Tyson, J. E., Horbar, J. D., Bauer, C. R., et al. (1995). Very-low-birth-weight outcomes of the National Institute of Child Health and Human Development Neonatal Network, November 1989 to October 1990. *American Journal of Obstetrics and Gynecology, 172*(2, Pt. 1), 457–464.

Halsey, C. L., Collin, M. F., & Anderson, C. L. (1996). Extremely low-birth-weight children and their peers. A comparison of school-age outcome. *Archives of Pediatrics and Adolescent Medicine, 150,* 790–794.

Hanigan, W. C., Morgan, A. M., Anderson, R. J., Bradle, P., Cohen, H. S., Cusack, T. J., et al. (1991). Incidence and neurodevelopmental outcome of periventricular hemorrhage and hydrocephalus in a regional population of very low birth weight infants. *Neurosurgery, 29,* 701–706.

Hawgood, S., Spong, J., & Yu, V. Y. H. (1984). Intraventricular hemorrhage incidence and outcome in a population of very-low-birth-weight infants. *American Journal of Diseases in Children, 138,* 136–139.

Hille, E. T., den Ouden, A. L., Bauer, L., van den Oudenrijn, C., Brand, R., & Verloove-Vanhorick, S. P. (1994). School performance at nine years of age in very premature and very low birth weight infants: Perinatal risk factors and predictors at five years of age. Collaborative Project on Preterm and Small for Gestational Age (POPS) Infants in The Netherlands. *Journal of Pediatrics, 125,* 426–434.

Hirata, T., Epcar, J. T., Walsh, A., Mednick, J., Harris, M., McGinnis, M. S., et al. (1983). Survival and outcome of infants 501 to 750 gm: A six year experience. *Journal of Pediatrics, 102,* 741–748.

Horwood, L. J., Mogridge, N., & Darlow, B. A. (1998). Cognitive, educational, and behavioural outcomes at 7 and 8 years in a national very low birthweight cohort. *Archives of Disease in Children Fetal Neonatal Edition, 79,* F12–F20.

Hoskins, E. M., Elliot, E., Shennan, A. T., Skidmore, M. B., & Keith, E. (1983). Outcome of very low birth weight infants born at a perinatal center. *American Journal of Obstetrics and Gynecology, 145,* 135–140.

Hutson, J. M., Driscoll, J. M., Fox, H. E., Driscoll, Y. T., & Steir, M. E. (1986). The effect of obstetric management on neonatal mortality and morbidity for infants weighing 700–1000 grams. *American Journal of Perinatology, 3,* 255.

Infant Health and Development Program. (1990). Enhancing the outcomes of low-birth-weight, premature infants: A multisite, randomized trial. *Journal of American Medical Association, 263,* 3035–3041.

Ishida, A., Nakajima, W., Arai, H., Takahashi, Y., Iijima, R., Sawaishi, Y., et al. (1997). Cranial computed tomography scans of premature babies predict their eventual learning disabilities. *Pediatric Neurology, 16,* 319–322.

Kennell, J. H., & Klaus, M. H. (1982). *Parental–infant bonding* (2nd ed.). St. Louis, MO: Mosby YearBook.

Kiely, J. L., & Paneth, N. (1981). Follow-up studies of low birth-weight infants: Suggestions for design, analysis, and reporting. *Developmental Medicine and Child Neurology, 23,* 96–100.

Kilbride, H. W., Daily, D. K., Matiu, I., & Hubbard, A. M. (1989). Neurodevelopmental follow-up of infants with birthweight less than 801 grams with intracranial hemorrhage. *Journal of Perinatology, 9,* 376–381.

Kileny, P., & Robertson, C. M. (1985). Neurological aspects of infant hearing assessment. *Journal of Otolaryngology, 14,* 34–39.

Kitchen, W. H., Ford, G., Orgill, A., Rickards, A., Astbury, J., Lissenden, J., et al. (1983). Collaborative study of very-low-birth-weight infants. *American Journal of Diseases of Children, 137,* 555–559.

Kitchen, W. H., Ford, G., Orgill, A., Rickards, A., Astbury, J., Lissenden, J., et al. (1984). Outcome in infants with birth weight 500–999 gm: A regional study of 1979 and 1980 births. *Journal of Pediatrics, 104,* 921–927.

Kitchen, W. H., Rickards, A. L., Doyle, L. W., Ford, G. W., Kelly, E. A., & Callanan, C. (1992). Improvement in outcome for very low birthweight children: Apparent or real? *Medical Journal of Austria, 157,* 154–158.

Klebanov, P. K., Brooks-Gunn, J., & McCormick, M. C. (1994a). Classroom behavior of very low birth weight elementary school children. *Pediatrics, 94,* 700–708.

Klebanov, P. K., Brooks-Gunn, J., & McCormick, M. C. (1994b). School achievement and failure in very low birth weight children. *Journal of Developmental and Behavioral Pediatrics, 15,* 248–256.

Korner, A. F., Guilleminault, C., Van den Hoed, J., & Baldwin, R. B. (1978). Reduction of sleep apnea and bradycardia in preterm infants on oscillating water beds: A controlled polygraphic study. *Pediatrics, 61,* 528–533.

Kraybill, E. N., Kennedy, C. A., Teplin, S. W., & Campbell, S. K. (1984). Infants with birth weights less than 1,001 g: Survival, growth, and development. *American Journal of Diseases of Children, 138,* 837–842.

Krishnamoorthy, K. S., Kuban, K. C., Leviton, A., Brown, E. R., Sullivan, K. F., & Allred, E. N. (1990). Periventricular–intraventricular hemorrhage, sonographic localization, phenobarbital, and motor abnormalities in low birth weight infants. *Pediatrics, 85,* 1027–1033.

Kuhn, C. M., Schanberg, S. M., Field, T., Symanski, R., Zimmerman, E., Scafidi, F., et al. (1991). Taactile-kinesthetic stimulation effects on sympathetic and adrenocortical function in preterm infants. *Journal of Pediatrics, 119,* 434–440.

Lamb, M. E. (1982). Early contact and maternal–infant bonding: One decade later. *Pediatrics*, *7*, 763–768.

Landry, S. H., Fletcher, J. M., Zarling, C. L., Chapieski, L., Francis, D. J., & Denson, S. (1984). Differential outcomes associated with early medical complications in premature infants. *Journal of Pediatric Psychology*, *9*, 385–401.

La Pine, T. R., Jackson, J. C., & Bennett, F. C. (1995). Outcome of infants weighing less than 800 grams at birth: 15 years' experience. *Pediatrics*, *96*(3, Pt. 1), 479–483.

Lee, K. S., Kim, B. I., Khoshnood, B., Hsieh, H. L., Chen, T. J., Herschel, M., & Mittendorf, R. (1995). Outcome of very low birth weight infants in industrialized countries: 1947–1987. *American Journal of Epidemiology*, *141*, 1188–1193.

Lee, S. K., Penner, P. L., & Cox, M. (1991). Impact of very low birth weight infants on the family and its relationship to parental attitudes. *Pediatrics*, *88*, 105–109.

Leib, S. A., Benfield, G., & Guidubaldi, J. (1980). Effects of early intervention stimulation on the development of preterm infants. *Pediatrics*, *66*, 83–90.

Leifer, A. D., Leiderman, P. H., Barnett, C. R., & Williams, J. A. (1972). Effects of mother–infant separation on maternal attachment behavior. *Child Development*, *43*, 1203–1218.

Levy-Shiff, R., Einat, G., Mogilner, M. B., Lerman, M., & Krikler, R. (1994). Biological and environmental correlates of developmental outcome of prematurely born infants in early adolescence. *Journal of Pediatric Psychology*, *19*, 63–78.

Long, J. G., Lucey, J. F., & Philip, A. G. S. (1980). Noise and hypoxemia in the intensive care nursery. *Pediatrics*, *65*, 143–145.

Long, J. G., Philip, A. G. S., & Lucey, J. F. (1980). Excessive handling as a cause of hypoxemia. *Pediatrics*, *65*, 203–207.

Low, J. A., Galbraith, R. S., Sauerbrei, E. E., Muir, D. W., Killen, H. L., Pater, E. A., et al. (1986). Maternal, fetal, and newborn complications associated with newborn intracranial hemorrhage. *American Journal of Obstetrics and Gynecology*, *154*, 345–351.

Markestad, T., & Fitzhardinge, P. M. (1981). Growth and development in children recovering from bronchopulmonary dysplasia. *Journal of Pediatrics*, *98*, 597–602.

Marlow, N., Roberts, L., & Cooke, R. (1993). Outcome at 8 years for children with birth weights of 1250 g or less. *Archives of Disease in Children*, *68*(3), 286–290.

Masi, W. (1979). Supplemental stimulation of the premature infant. In T. M. Field (Ed.), *Infants born at risk* (pp. 367–388). New York: S.P. Medical & Scientific Books.

Matsuishi, T., Ishibashi, S., Kamiya, Y., Shoji, J., Yamashita, Y., Fukuda, S., et al. (1998). Early intervention for very-low-birth-weight infants. *Brain Development*, *20*, 18–21.

Mayes, L. C., & Stahlman, M. T. (1982). Effect of hyaline membrane disease on outcome of premature infants. *American Journal of Diseases of Children, 136,* 885–886.

McCarton, C. M., Brooks-Gunn, J., Wallace, I. F., Bauer, C. R., Bennett, F. C., Bernbaum, J. C., et al. (1997). Results at age 8 years of early intervention for low-birth-weight premature infants. The Infant Health and Development Program. *Journal of the American Medical Association, 277,* 126–132.

McCarton, C. M., Wallace, I. F., & Bennett, F. C. (1995). Preventive interventions with low birth weight premature infants: An evaluation of their success. *Seminars in Perinatology, 19,* 330–340.

McCarton, C. M., Wallace, I. F., & Bennett, F. C. (1996). Early intervention for low-birth-weight premature infants: What can we achieve? *Annals of Medicine, 28,* 221–225.

McCarton-Daum, C., Danziger, A., Ruff, H., & Vaughan, H. G., Jr. (1983). Periventricular low density as a predictor of neurobehavioral outcome in very low-birth-weight infants. *Developmental Medicine and Child Neurology, 25,* 559–565.

McCormick, M. C., Brooks-Gunn, J., Workman-Daniels, K., Turner, J., & Peckham, G. J. (1992). The health and developmental status of very low-birth-weight children at school age. *Journal of the American Medical Association, 267,* 2204–2208.

McCormick, M. C., Workman-Daniels, K., & Brooks-Gunn, J. (1996). The behavioral and emotional well-being of school-age children with different birth weights. *Pediatrics, 97,* 18–25.

McMenamin, J. B., Shackelford, G. D., & Volpe, J. J. (1984). Outcome of neonatal intraventricular hemorrhage with periventricular ecodense lesions. *Annals in Neurology, 15,* 285–290.

Mehrabani, D., Gowen, C. W., & Kopelman, A. E. (1991). Association of pneumothorax and hypotension with intraventricular hemorrhage. *Archives of Disease in Childhood, 66,* 48–51.

Meisels, S. J., Plunkett, J. W., Roloff, D. W., Pasick, P. L., & Stiefel, G. S. (1986). Growth and development of preterm infants with respiratory distress syndrome and bronchopulmonary dysplasia. *Pediatrics, 77,* 345–352.

Ment, L. R., Scott, D. T., Ehrenkranz, R. A., Rothman, S. G., Duncan, C. C., & Warshaw, J. B. (1982). Neonates of <1250 grams birth weight and prospective developmental evaluation during the first year post-term. *Pediatrics, 70,* 292–296.

Merritt, J. C., & Kraybill, E. N. (1986). Retrolental fibroplasia: A five-year experience in a tertiary perinatal center. *Annals of Ophthalmology, 18,* 65–67.

Milligan, J. E., Shennan, A. T., & Hoskins, E. M. (1984). Perinatal intensive care: Where and how to draw the line. *American Journal of Obstetrics and Gynecology, 148,* 499–503.

Minde, K., Whitelaw, A., Brown, J., & Fitzhardinge, P. (1983). Effect of neonatal complications in premature infants on early parent–infant interactions. *Developmental Medicine and Child Neurology, 25*, 763–777.

Monset-Couchard, M., de Bethmann, O., & Kastler, B. (1996). Mid- and long-term outcome of 89 premature infants weighing less than 1,000 g at birth, all appropriate for gestational age. *Biology of the Neonate, 70*, 328–338.

Morrow, C. J., Field, T. M., Scafidi, F. A., Roberts, J., Eisen, L., Hogan, A. E., et al. (1990). Transcutaneous oxygen tension in preterm neonates during neonatal behavioral assessments and heelsticks. *Journal of Developmental and Behavioral Pediatrics, 11*, 312–316.

Moses, K. L. (1983). The impact of initial diagnosis: Mobilizing family resources. In J. A. Mulich & S. M. Pueschel (Eds.), *Parent professional partnerships* (pp. 11–41). Cambridge, MA: Academic Guild.

Msall, M. E., Buck, G. M., Rogers, B. T., Duffy, L. C., Mallen, S. R., & Catanzaro, N. L. (1993). Predictors of mortality, morbidity, and disability in a cohort of infants less than or equal to 28 weeks' gestation. *Clinical Pediatrics (Philadelphia), 32*, 521–527.

Msall, M. E., Buck, G. M., Rogers, B. T., Merke, D., Catanzaro, N. L., & Zorn, W. A. (1991). Risk factors for major neurodevelopmental impairments and need for special education resources in extremely premature infants. *Journal of Pediatrics, 119*, 606–614.

Msall, M. E., Buck, G. M., Rogers, B. T., Merke, D., Wan, C. C., Catanzaro, N. L., et al. (1994). Multivariate risks among extremely premature infants. *Journal of Perinatology, 14*, 41–47.

National Vital Statistics Report. (1999). *47*(18), 51–79.

Neild, T. A., Schrier, S., Ramos, A. D., Platzker, A. C., & Warburton, D. (1986). Unexpected hearing loss in high-risk infants. *Pediatrics, 78*, 417–422.

Newman, L. F. (1981). Social and sensory environment of low birth weight infants in a special care nursery. *Journal of Nervous and Mental Disease, 169*, 448–455.

Oehler, J. M. (1985, December). Examining the issue of tactile stimulation for preterm infants. *Neonatal Network*, pp. 25–33.

O'Reilly, K. A., O'Reilly, J. P., & Furuno, S. (1986). Predicting to 9-month performances of premature infants. *Physiotherapy, 66*, 508–515.

Ornstein, M., Ohlsson, A., Edmonds, J., & Asztalos, E. (1991). Neonatal follow-up of very low birthweight/extremely low birthweight infants to school age: A critical overview. *ACTA Paediatrica Scandinavica, 80*, 741–748.

Palmer, P. G., Dubowitz, L. M. S., Levene, M. I., & Dubowitz, V. (1982). Developmental and neurological progress of preterm infants with intraventricular hemorrhage and ventricular dilation. *Archives of Disease in Childhood, 57*, 748–753.

Palmer, P. G., Dubowitz, L. M. S., Verghote, M., & Dubowitz, V. (1982). Neurological neurobehavioral differences between preterm infants at term and full-term newborn infants. *Neuropediatrics, 13*, 183–189.

Papile, L. A., Munsick-Bruno, J., & Schaefer, A. (1983). Relationship of cerebral intraventricular hemorrhage and early childhood neurologic handicaps. *Journal of Pediatrics, 103*, 273–277.

Parmelee, A. H. (1985). Sensory stimulation in the nursery: How much and when? *Pediatrics, 6*, 242–243.

Perlman, J. M., McMenamin, J. B., & Volpe, J. J. (1983). Fluctuating cerebral blood-flow velocity in respiratory-distress syndrome. Relation to the development of intraventricular hemorrhage. *New England Journal of Medicine, 309*, 204–209.

Piecuch, R. E., Leonard, C. H., Cooper, B. A., & Sehring, S. A. (1997). Outcome of extremely low birth weight infants (500–999 grams) over a 12-year period. *Pediatrics, 100*, 633–639.

Piper, M. C., Kunos, I., Willis, D. M., & Mazer, B. (1985). Effects of gestational age on neurological functioning of the very low-birthweight infant at 40 weeks. *Developmental Medicine and Child Neurology, 27*, 596–605.

Regev, R., Dolfin, T., Ben-Nun, Y., & Herzog, L. (1995). Survival rate and 2 year outcome in very low birthweight infants. *Israel Journal of Medical Sciences, 31*, 309–313.

Resnick, M. B., Bauer, C. R., Cupoli, M., Ausbon, W. W., & Evans, J. (1983). Florida regional perinatal intensive care program developmental evaluation component—early developmental outcome. *Journal of the Florida Medical Association, 70*, 833–838.

Resnick, M. B., Eyler, F. D., Nelson, R. M., Eitzman, D. V., & Bucciarelli, R. L. (1987). Developmental intervention for low birth weight infants: Improved early developmental outcome. *Pediatrics, 80*, 68–74.

Resnick, M. B., Gomatam, S. V., Carter, R. L., Ariet, M., Roth, J., Kilgore, K. L., et al. (1998). Educational disabilities of neonatal intensive care graduates. *Pediatrics, 102*, 308–314.

Resnick, M. B., Stralka, K., Carter, R. L., Ariet, M., Bucciarelli, R. L., Furlough, R. R., et al. (1990). Effects of birth weight and sociodemographic variables on mental development of neonatal intensive care unit survivors. *American Journal of Obstetrics and Gynecology, 162*, 374–378.

Rickards, A. L., Kitchen, W. H., Doyle, L. W., Ford, G. W., Kelly, E. A., & Callanan, C. (1993). Cognition, school performance, and behavior in very low birth weight and normal birth weight children at 8 years of age: A longitudinal study. *Journal of Developmental and Behavioral Pediatrics, 14*, 363–368.

Rose, S. A., Schmidt, K., Riese, M. L., & Bridger, W. H. (1980). Effects of prematurity and early intervention on responsivity to tactual stimuli: A comparison of preterm and full-term infants. *Child Development, 51*, 416–425.

Rosenfield, A. G. (1980). Visiting in the intensive care nursery. *Child Development, 51*, 939–941.

Ross, G., Boatright, S., Auld, P. A., & Nass, R. (1996). Specific cognitive abilities in 2-year-old children with subependymal and mild interventricular hemorrhage. *Brain and Cognition, 32*, 1–13.

Ross, G., Lipper, E. G., & Auld, P. A. (1991). Educational status and school-related abilities of very low birth weight premature children. *Pediatrics, 88,* 1125–1134.

Roth, J., Hendrickson, J., Schilling, M., & Stowell, D. W. (1998). The risk of teen mothers having low birth weight babies: Implications of recent medical research for school health personnel. *Journal of School Health, 68,* 271–275.

Roth, J., Resnick, M. B., Ariet, M., Carter, R. L., Eitzman, D. V., Curran, J. S., et al. (1995). Changes in survival patterns of very low-birth-weight infants from 1980–1993. *Archives of Pediatrics and Adolescent Medicine, 149,* 1311–1317.

Roth, S. C., Baudin, J., McCormick, D. C., Edwards, A. D., Townsend, J., Stewart, A. S., et al. (1993). Relation between ultrasound appearance of the brain of very preterm infants and neurodevelopmental impairment at eight years. *Developmental Medicine and Child Neurology, 35,* 755–768.

Rothberg, A. D., Maisels, M. J., Bagnato, S., Murphy, J., Gifford, K., & McKinley, K. (1983). Infants weighing 1,000 gm or less at birth: Developmental outcome for ventilated and nonventilated infants. *Pediatrics, 71,* 599–602.

Rothberg, A. D., Maisels, M. J., Bagnato, S., Murphy, J., Gifford, K., McKinley, K., et al. (1981). Outcome for survivors of mechanical ventilation weighing less than 1,250 gm at birth. *Journal of Pediatrics, 98,* 106–111.

Roussounis, S. H., Hubley, P. A., & Dear, P. R. (1993). Five-year-follow-up of very low birthweight infants: Neurological and psychological outcome. *Child: Care, Health, and Development, 19,* 45–59.

Rubin, R. A., & Balow, B. (1979). Measures of infant development and socio-economic status as predictions of later intelligence and school achievement. *Developmental Psychology, 15,* 225–227.

Ruiz, M. P. D., LeFever, J. A., Hakanson, D. O., Clark, D. A., & Williams, M. L. (1981). Early development of infants of birth weight less than 1,000 grams with reference to mechanical ventilation in newborn period. *Pediatrics, 68,* 330–335.

Saigal, S., & O'Brodovich, H. (1987). Long-term outcome of preterm infants with respiratory disease. *Clinics in Perinatology, 14,* 635–650.

Saigal, S., Rosenbaum, P., Stoskopf, B., & Sinclair, J. C. (1984). Outcome in infants 501 to 1000 gm birth weight delivered to residents of the McMaster health region. *Journal of Pediatrics, 105,* 969–976.

Saigal, S., Rosenbaum, P., Szatmari, P., & Campbell, D. (1991). Learning disabilities and school problems in a regional cohort of extremely low birth weight (less than 1000 g) children: A comparison with term controls. *Journal of Developmental and Behavioral Pediatrics, 12,* 294–300.

Saigal, S., Szatmari, P., Rosenbaum, P., Campbell, D., & King, S. (1991). Cognitive abilities and school performance of extremely low birth weight children and matched term control children at age 8 years: A regional study. *Journal of Pediatrics, 118,* 751–760.

Sameroff, A. J., & Chandler, M. J. (1975). Reproductive risk and the continuum of caretaking casualty. In F. D. Horowitz (Ed.), *Review of child development research* (4th ed., pp. 187–244). Chicago: University of Chicago Press.

Sauve, R. S., Robertson, C., Etches, P., Byrne, P. J., & Dayer-Zamora, V. (1998). Before viability: A geographically based outcome study of infants weighing 500 grams or less at birth. *Pediatrics, 101*(3, Pt. 1), 438–448.

Sauve, R. S., & Singhal, N. (1985). Long-term morbidity of infants with bronchopulmonary dysplasia. *Pediatrics, 76,* 725–733.

Scafidi, F. A., Field, T., & Schanberg, S. M. (1993). Factors that predict which preterm infants benefit most from massage therapy. *Journal of Developmental and Behavioral Pediatrics, 14,* 176–180.

Schraeder, B. D., Heverly, M. A., & O'Brien, C. (1996). The influence of early biological risk and the home environment on nine-year outcome of very low birth weight. *Canadian Journal of Nursing Research, 28,* 79–95.

Scott, D. T., Ment, L. R., Ehrenkranz, R. A., & Warshaw, J. B. (1984). Evidence for late developmental deficit in very low birth weight infants surviving intraventricular hemorrhage. *Child's Brain, 11,* 261–269.

Scott, S., & Richards, M. (1979). Nursing low-birthweight babies on lambswool. *Lancet, 5,* 1028.

Self, P., Horowitz, F. D., & Pagan, L. Y. (1972). Olfaction in newborn infants. *Developmental Psychology, 1,* 349–363.

Sell, E. J., Gaines, J. A., Gluckman, C., & Williams, E. (1985). Early identification of learning problems in neonatal intensive care graduates. *American Journal of Diseases of Children, 139,* 460–463.

Sell, E. J., Hill, S., Poisson, S. S., Williams, E., & Gaines, J. A. (1985). Prediction of growth and development in intensive care nursery graduates at 12 months of age. *American Journal of Diseases of Children, 139,* 1198–1202.

Sethi, V. D., & Macfarlane, P. I. (1996). Neurodevelopmental outcome at age two years amongst very low birth weight infants: Results from a district general hospital. *Public Health, 110,* 211–214.

Shapiro, S., McCormick, M. C., Starfield, B. H., & Crawley, B. (1983). Changes in infant morbidity associated with decreases in neonatal mortality. *Pediatrics, 72,* 408–415.

Siegel, L. (1981). Infant tests as predictors of cognitive and language development at two years. *Child Development, 52,* 545–557.

Siegel, L. (1982). Reproductive, perinatal, and environmental factors as predictors of the cognitive and language development of preterm and full-term infants. *Child Development, 53,* 963–973.

Singer, L. T., Salvator, A., Guo, S., Collin, M., Lilien, L., & Baley, J. (1999). Maternal psychological distress and parenting stress after the birth of very low-birth-weight infants. *Journal of the American Medical Association, 281,* 799–805.

Singer, L., Yamashita, T., Lilien, L., Collin, M., & Baley, J. (1997). A longitudinal study of developmental outcome of infants with bronchopulmonary dysplasia and very low birth weight. *Pediatrics, 100,* 987–993.

Siqueland, E., & Lipsitt, L. P. (1966). Conditional head-turning behavior in the newborn. *Journal of Experimental Child Psychology, 3*, 356–376.

Skouteli, H. N., Dubowitz, L. M., Levene, M. I., & Miller, G. (1985). Predictors for survival and normal neurodevelopmental outcome of infants weighing less than 1001 grams at birth. *Developmental Medicine and Child Neurology, 27*, 588–595.

Smith, L., Ulvund, S. E., & Lindemann, R. (1994). Very low birth weight infants (<1501 g) at double risk. *Journal of Developmental and Behavioral Pediatrics, 15*, 7–13.

Stahlman, M. (1984). Newborn intensive care: Success or failure. *Journal of Pediatrics, 105*, 162–167.

Stevens, B., Petryshen, P., Hawkins, J., Smith, B., & Taylor, P. (1996). Developmental versus conventional care: A comparison of clinical outcomes for very low birth weight infants. *Canadian Journal of Nursing Research, 28*, 97–113.

Stewart, A. L., Reynolds, E. O. R., & Lipscomb, A. P. (1981). Outcome for infants of very low birthweight: Survey of world literature. *Lancet, 1*, 1038–1040.

Stewart, A. L., Thorburn, R. J., Hope, P. L., Goldsmith, M., Lipscomb, A. P., & Reynolds, E. O. (1983). Ultrasound appearance of the brain in very preterm infants and neurodevelopmental outcome at 18 months of age. *Archives of Disease in Childhood, 58*, 598–604.

Strobino, D., O'Campo, P., & Schoendorf, K. (1995). A strategic framework for infant mortality reduction: Implications for "Healthy Start." *Milbank Quarterly, 73*, 507–533.

Taylor, H. G., Hack, M., Klein, N., & Schatschneider, C. (1995). Achievement in children with birth weights less than 750 grams with normal cognitive abilities: Evidence for specific learning disabilities. *Journal of Pediatrics Psychology, 20*, 703–719.

Taylor, H. G., Klein, N., Schatschneider, C., & Hack, M. (1998). Predictors of early school age outcomes in very low birth weight children. *Journal of Developmental and Behavioral Pediatrics, 19*, 235–243.

TeKolste, K. A., Bennett, F. C., & Maack, L. A. (1985). Follow-up of infants receiving cranial ultrasound for intracranial hemorrhage. *American Journal of Diseases of Children, 139*, 299–303.

Thoman, E. B., & Graham, S. E. (1986). Self-regulation of stimulation by premature infants. *Pediatrics, 78*, 855–860.

Thompson, R. J., Jr., Goldstein, R. F., Oehler, J. M., Gustafson, K. E., Catlett, A. T., & Brazy, J. E. (1994). Developmental outcome of very low birth weight infants as a function of biological risk and psychosocial risk. *Journal of Developmental and Behavioral Pediatrics, 15*, 232–238.

Thompson, R. J., Jr., Gustafson, K. E., Oehler, J. M., Catlett, A. T., Brazy, J. E., & Goldstein, R. F. (1997). Developmental outcome of very low birth weight infants at four years of age as a function of biological risk and psychosocial risk. *Journal of Developmental and Behavioral Pediatrics, 18*, 91–96.

Trehub, S. E., & Chang, H. W. (1977). Speech as reinforcing stimulation for infants. *Developmental Psychology, 13,* 170–171.

Tudehope, D., Burns, Y. R., Gray, P. H., Mohay, H. A., O'Callaghan, M. J., & Rogers, Y. M. (1995). Changing patterns of survival and outcome at 4 years of children who weighted 500–999 g at birth. *Journal of Paediatrics and Child Healthcare, 31,* 451–456.

Victorian Infant Collaborative Study Group. (1997). Improved outcome into the 1990s for infants weighing 500–999 g at birth. *Archives of Disease in Childhood Fetal Neonatal Edition, 77,* 91–94.

Vohr, B. R., Bell, E. F., & Oh, W. (1982). Infants with bronchopulmonary dysplasia (growth pattern and neurological and developmental outcome). *American Journal of Diseases of Children, 136,* 443–447.

Vohr, B. R., Garcia Coll, C., Flanagan, P., & Oh, W. (1992). Effects of intraventricular hemorrhage and socioeconomic status on perceptual, cognitive, and neurologic status of low birth weight infants at 5 years of age. *Journal of Pediatrics, 121,* 280–285.

Vohr, B., & Ment, L. R. (1996). Intraventricular hemorrhage in the preterm infant. *Early Human Development, 44,* 1–16.

Vohr, B. R., & Msall, M. E. (1997). Neuropsychological and functional outcomes of very low birth weight infants. *Seminars in Perinatology, 21,* 202–220.

Watson, J. S. (1967). Memory and contingency analysis in infant learning. *Merrill–Palmer Quarterly, 13,* 55–76.

Weisglas-Kuperus, N., Baerts, W., & Sauer, P. J. (1993). Early assessment and neurodevelopmental outcome in very low-birth-weight infants: Implications for pediatric practice. *ACTA Paediatrica, 82,* 449–453.

Welch, R. A., & Bottoms, S. F. (1986). Reconsideration of head compression and intraventricular hemorrhage in the vertex very-low-birth-weight fetus. *Obstetrics and Gynecology, 68,* 29–34.

White, R. W. (1959). Motivation reconsidered: The concept of competence. *Psychological Review, 6,* 297–333.

Whitfield, M. F., Grunau, R. V., & Holsti, L. (1997). Extremely premature (< or = 800 g) schoolchildren: Multiple areas of hidden disability. *Archives of Disease in Childhood, Fetal Neonatal Edition, 77,* 85–90.

Widmayer, S. M., & Field, T. M. (1980). Effects of Brazelton demonstrations on early interactions of preterm infants and their teenage mothers. *Infant Behavior and Development, 3,* 79–89.

Widmayer, S. M., & Field, T. M. (1981). Effects of Brazelton demonstrations for mothers on the development of preterm infants. *Pediatrics, 67,* 711–714.

Williams, M. L., Lewandowski, L. J., Coplan, J., & D'Eugenio, D. B. (1987). Neurodevelopmental outcome of preschool children born preterm with and without intracranial hemorrhage. *Developmental Medicine and Child Neurology, 29,* 243.

Williamson, W. D., Desmond, M. M., Wilson, G. S., Murphy, M. A., Rozelle, J., & Garcia-Prats, J. A. (1983). Survival of low-birth-weight infants with neonatal intraventricular hemorrhage (outcome in the preschool years). *American Journal of Diseases of Children, 137,* 1181–1184.

Wilson, R. S. (1985). Risk and resilience in early mental development. *Developmental Psychology, 21,* 795–800.

Worobey, J., & Belsky, J. (1982). Employing the Brazelton scale to influence mothering: An experimental comparison of three strategies. *Developmental Psychology, 18,* 736–743.

Yeo, C. L., Choo, S., & Ho, L. Y. (1997). Chronic lung disease in very low birthweight infants: A 5-year review. *Journal of Paediatrics and Child Health, 33,* 102–106.

Yu, V. Y. H., Jamieson, G., & Astbury, J. (1981). Parents' reactions to unrestricted parental contact with infants in the intensive care nursery. *Medical Journal of Australia, 1,* 294–296.

Yu, V. Y. H., Manlapaz, M. L., Tobin, J., Carse, E. A., Charlton, M. P., & Gore, J. R. (1992). Improving health status in extremely low birthweight children between two and five years. *Early Human Deveopment, 30,* 229–239.

Zeskind, P. S., & Iacino, R. (1984). Effects of maternal visitation to preterm infants in the neonatal intensive care unit. *Child Development, 55,* 1887–1893.

16

SYMPTOMS, SIGNS, AND ILL-DEFINED CONDITIONS

MARK A. WILLIAMS AND MICHELLE Y. MARTIN

"Symptoms, Signs, and Ill-defined Conditions" in the ninth edition of the *International Classification of Diseases* (ICD–9; World Health Organization [WHO], 1991) is a collection of symptoms, signs, and laboratory findings that do not strictly represent a medical disorder that can be placed in the preceding sections of the classification system. In almost all instances, cases assigned diagnoses under this section of the *ICD–9* are cases (a) that have atypical clinical symptoms, preventing sufficient differential diagnosis that allows inclusion in one of the other sections; (b) in which the etiology is unknown at the time the diagnosis is given; or (c) in which the presentation is transient, and therefore the cause could not be determined. With additional medical evaluations, more specific diagnostic categories as described in the preceding sections of the *ICD–9* may become more appropriate.

The content of this *ICD–9* section does not focus on a specific body system. Therefore, the focus of this chapter is on the psychology of illness as a general area of research that has implications for clinical health psychology and medical practice. After reviewing research that provides support for the importance of psychological and social factors in understanding patients' presentation of illness, the chapter explores areas of application in research, assessment, and treatment.

PSYCHOLOGY OF PHYSICAL SYMPTOMS

Patients' ability to verbalize is an efficient and informative way to inform medical clinicians of their physical symptoms, which helps the clinicians make appropriate diagnoses, decide which medical tests may be needed, and prescribe appropriate treatments. Unfortunately, what experienced clinicians discover and empirical research illuminates is that at times, patients' self-reports of symptoms and functioning can be inadequate and misleading. Psychological research has demonstrated that patients' reports of symptoms are governed not just by "bottom-up" biosensory mechanisms but also by numerous "top-down" factors that can be characterized as psychological, social, and cultural influences (Cioffi, 1991). Barondess (1979) reserved the term *disease* to describe actual physical pathology, whereas he used the term *illness* to refer to individuals' subjective experience of suffering. Barondess suggested that self-report measures are more accurately viewed as measures of illness than disease. Although self-report measures can be helpful in making clinical diagnoses, it must be understood that they are subject to variability attributed to psychosocial and disease factors. Accurate assessment and treatment is more likely to be accomplished when clinicians understand their patients' disease states and their psychosocial makeup.

Cultural Influences

At the molar level, cultural factors have been shown to influence the nature and extent of symptom-reporting and treatment-seeking behavior (Harlap et al., 1975; Zola, 1966). In a particularly impressive example of cultural influences on symptom complaints, Raper (1958) observed that members of an African tribe rarely complained of upper gastrointestinal pains. He therefore hypothesized that peptic ulcers were a rare affliction among this group. However, autopsies later performed on members of this tribe found the prevalence of peptic ulcers to be similar to that found in England. Findings such as these are consistent with the hypothesis that psychosocial influences, which are often similar among groups of people, may influence the processes involved in symptom perception and reporting.

Learning Principles

Learning principles, including operant conditioning, classical conditioning, and modeling have been used to explain cultural and individual differences in symptom reporting and expression. For example, Whitehead, Winget, Fedoravicius, Wooley, and Blackwell (1982) reported that individuals characterized as displaying chronic illness behavior were more likely to recall receiving special treats when they had a cold or the flu as a child. Findings from the biofeedback literature have suggested that easily perceived physical symptoms (e.g., muscle contraction headaches, temporomandibular joint pain) are more likely to come under the control of operant reinforcers than symptoms that are more difficult to perceive (e.g., high blood pressure, gastric acid levels; Whitehead, Fedoravicius, Blackwell, & Wooley, 1979).

Attentional Processes

Attentional processes can influence symptom reporting. Numerous studies have demonstrated that by decreasing one's attentional focus toward internal somatic and cognitive cues, the subjective experience of pain can be decreased (McCaul & Malott, 1984). According to the competition of cues hypothesis, only a limited amount of sensory input can be consciously processed simultaneously, and sensory input competes for perceptual processing (e.g., Navon & Gopher, 1979). When demands for allocating attentional resources to external stimuli increase, it should result in a decreased perception of internal stimuli, including negative somatic sensations such as pain. Numerous studies have examined the efficacy of intentionally allocating attentional resources away from painful stimulation (e.g., using distraction procedures). In a review of this literature, McCaul and Malott (1984) concluded that distraction strategies are effective for reducing pain perception when the pain intensity is mild and the episode is relatively brief. In addition, distraction strategies requiring more sustained attention produce greater pain reduction.

Emotional Processes

Anxiety is an emotional process that can cause individuals to increase their monitoring of internal processes and become more self-conscious (e.g., Wegner & Giuliano, 1980). In a review of the literature examining the relationship among anxiety, attentional focus, and pain perception, Arntz, Dreessen, and Merckelbach (1991) concluded that when attentional focus is controlled, anxiety is not related to changes on physiological and subjective measures of pain. However, regardless of the presence of anxiety, the study found that attention to internal state resulted in increases on physiological and subjective measures of pain.

Not only can negative emotions increase one's concern and attentional focus on somatic functioning, but a growing body of research has indicated that negative emotions contribute to disease development and exacerbation, whereas positive emotions seem to protect a person from disease (e.g., Vaillant, 1976). Explaining the causal mechanisms behind the link between emotions and health is likely not a simple enterprise. One proposed explanation that has obtained empirical support is that emotional stress causes a reduction in the body's normal homeostasis and immunity from disease. The body is then less equipped to handle threats to health that are encountered on a daily basis.

Some studies have presented evidence that people who find it difficult to perceive and express emotions are also at increased risk for disease (Henry & Stephens, 1977). These studies have suggested that in certain situations, it is healthy to be able to perceive and express negative emotions. It is the inhibition of emotional expression under these circumstances that seems disruptive to physical health. In a series of studies, Pennebaker and colleagues (e.g., Pennebaker, Barger, Tiebout, 1989; Pennebaker & Beall, 1986; Pennebaker, Colder, & Sharp, 1990; Taylor, 1999) demonstrated that participants who disclose emotionally traumatic experiences through writing develop fewer somatic complaints and have fewer visits to health care professionals. Pennebaker and colleagues postulated that inhibition of emotionally traumatic experiences as a coping response leads to reduced immunity to disease. These studies suggest that it is healthier to confront emotionally upsetting experiences by talking or writing about them. Therefore, in this context, expression of negative emotion may be beneficial to physical health.

Symptom-Related Schemas

Perception is a constructive process in which one's sensory experiences, memories, expectations, and beliefs are actively involved in directing attention and organizing sensory input. These cognitive structures are collectively referred to as *schemas* (Williams, Watts, Macleod, & Matthews, 1991), or *top-down* influences (Cioffi, 1991). *Bottom-up* influences are those processes that activate sensory receptors that code information such as intensity, duration, and quality of the sensory input. *Perception* is the experiential output resulting from the combined influences of bottom-up and top-down influences.

Several laboratory-based and clinical studies have demonstrated the influence of symptom-related schemas on symptom perception and illness behavior (Pennebaker, 1982). For example, Pennebaker and Skelton (1981) deceived participants by telling them to expect that their finger temperature would become either higher or lower as a result of listening to ultrasonic noise. As predicted, the actual skin temperature did not change. However, participants' self-reports of finger temperature did change in a way that was consistent with the experimentally induced symptom-related schema. For participants led to expect increases in finger temperature, there was a positive correlation ($r = .48$) between self-reported finger temperature and the number of temperature fluctuations measured during the session. For participants led to expect decreases in finger temperature, there was a negative correlation between these two measures ($r = -.49$). Thus, subtle, brief changes in sensory information from the participants' fingers were interpreted in a way that was consistent with their experimentally induced symptom schemas.

The literature on the psychological consequences of heart attacks provides a clinical example of the influence of symptom-related schemas on behavior. Despite the fact that the majority of heart attacks do not cause permanent heart damage, many patients are reluctant to return to normal physical activities (Cohn & Duke, 1987). Physical arousal from exercise, sexual excitement, and emotional experiences may be labeled as evidence of heart malfunction and elicit fear cognitions (Taylor, Bandura, Ewart, Miller, & DeBusk, 1985). As a result, maladaptive patterns of avoidance of physical activity can develop.

As indicated previously, when painful stimulation is relatively mild and the episode is brief, distraction techniques can produce a decrease in pain perception. However, distraction techniques are difficult to sustain when a person is faced with moderate or severe levels of pain. Under these conditions, the literature has indicated that strategies emphasizing focused attention on the sensory aspects of pain (sensory monitoring) more effectively decrease pain perception than do distraction techniques. By encoding distressing sensations at their concrete, sensory–informational level, encoding at an emotional/threat–memory level may be reduced (Leventhal, Brown, Shacham, & Engquist, 1979). That is, patients are provided with a more adaptive schema, or top-down processing framework that competes with top-down processing of a less adaptive nature (e.g., focusing on the emotional aspects of the experience).

Leventhal, Leventhal, Shacham, and Easterling (1989) provided an example of the effectiveness of sensory monitoring as a schema framework for coping with pain. Pregnant women in labor were provided with either sensory-monitoring instructions or comments associated with distraction. Women in the sensory-monitoring condition were instructed as follows: "Pay close attention to specific aspects of your contractions." Sensory-monitoring reminders were given throughout Stage 1 of labor (before pushing contractions began) to be used in Stage 2 of labor. Women in the control condition were provided with messages associated with distraction. Postpartum interviews indicated that during Stage 2 of labor (the pushing contractions), patients who had received the sensory-monitoring instructions reported lower pain and anger scores than did the control patients.

Personality Traits

Researchers of emotion have concluded that stable individual differences exist that influence the nature of individuals' emotional experiences (e.g., Plutchik, 1980). Many studies have provided support for the idea that the dispositional mood domain is best represented by considering two relatively independent dimensions (e.g., Zevon & Tellegen, 1982). Watson and Tellegen (1985) have used the terms *positive affect (PA)* and *negative affect (NA)* to describe the two orthogonal dimensions of mood. PA reflects the extent to which one feels energized, active, or excited, whereas NA reflects the extent to which one experiences a broad range of negative mood states. High-NA individuals exhibit more distress in various situations and maintain a stable negative view of themselves. People with low NA are described as relatively content and secure (Watson & Clark, 1984).

Trait anxiety is considered a central feature of NA. However, NA includes a broader range of negative emotional experiences such as worry, anger, scorn, revulsion, guilt, self-dissatisfaction, and rejection (Watson & Clark, 1984). NA is primarily a measure of an individual's subjective experiences, such as measures of their mood and self-esteem.

Studies have found that individuals with high trait NA endorse more somatic complaints on symptom checklists than people with low trait NA (Watson & Pennebaker, 1989). Three hypotheses help account for these findings. The psychosomatic hypothesis asserts that NA is a personality construct associated with negative psychoneuroimmunological events that increase the incidence of disease. Although studies can be found suggesting that NA may increase disease risk, studies can also be found that do not support this explanation (Watson & Pennebaker, 1989).

The disability hypothesis asserts that NA and somatic complaints are moderately correlated because negative emotional experiences are the psychological consequence of the suffering produced by disease. Again, although some studies can be found in support of this hypothesis, many other studies do not support it (Watson & Pennebaker, 1989).

The symptom perception hypothesis is the third possible explanation for the moderate correlation between NA and somatic complaints (Watson & Pennebaker, 1989). This hypothesis asserts that differences in attentional and cognitive processes are responsible for variation in symptom reports (both psychological and physical). The self-conscious, hypervigilant style of high-NA individuals translates into an increased attentional focus on internal processes. Moreover, the anxious, negative cognitive style of high-NA individuals increases the likelihood that ambiguous physical sensations will be perceived as threatening. Thus, increased symptom reporting among high-NA individuals is proposed to be the result of differences in these psychological processes and not necessarily caused by differences in actual physical health.

Williams (1993) conducted a study that found support for the hypothesis that high-NA people are more internally focused than low-NA people. The participants were female college students categorized as being high or low NA. A dual-task, divided attention, laboratory-based paradigm was used. During the external–external condition, each participant simultaneously performed a choice reaction time task and a vowel cancellation task. As Williams predicted, the two groups did not differ on their dual-task performance during this condition. During the external–internal condition, each participant simultaneously performed a choice reaction time task (the external task) and a second task that required participants to focus their attention on internal somatic functions (the internal task). Specifically, they attempted to control the pitch of an auditory biofeedback signal by relaxing their stomach muscles. The auditory biofeedback was actually sham feedback. The high-NA participants showed a substantial performance deficit on the reaction time task (the external task) relative to the low-NA group. It seemed that the high-NA group was allocating a larger part of their attentional resources to the internal somatic-monitoring task, resulting in a relative decrement in their performance on the external reaction time task.

The importance of patients' symptom-related schemas and the hypothesis that high-NA individuals are more likely to endorse more somatic complaints because of an increased tendency toward negative or threat cognitions was supported in a study by Alexander (1998). Participants were recruited from a pool of patients diagnosed with fibromyalgia who were being monitored by a large university medical center. The participants were rank ordered on the basis of their scores on a measure of NA. A median split was used to assign participants to the high-NA and low-NA groups. Deception methodology was used to systematically manipulate participants' schemas regarding their pain levels. Participants had sham electrodes attached to the surface of the skin. They were told that a small amount of electricity would be passed through the electrodes and that they might feel mild discomfort. These instructions were deceptive. In fact, no electricity was flowing through the electrodes. Participants completed pain questionnaires before and after the sham manipulation. Compared with the low-NA group, the high-NA group had increased pain reports after the sham manipulation. These findings indicate that personality variables such as NA play a role in patients' perception and report of somatic functioning.

SOMATIZATION DISORDERS

Somatization is the report of somatic symptoms that have no apparent underlying organic explanation. Lipowski's (1988) definition of somatization, "a tendency to experience and communicate somatic distress and symptoms unaccounted for by pathological findings, to attribute them to physical illness, and to seek medical help for them," reflects the behavioral, cognitive, and experiential aspects of the disorder (p. 1358). According to the American Psychiatric Association's *Diagnostic and Statistical Manual of Mental Disorders*, fourth edition (*DSM–IV*, 1994), somatization is a "polysymptomatic disorder that begins before age 30 years, extends over a period of years, and is characterized by a combination of pain, gastrointestinal, sexual, and pseudoneurological symptoms" (p. 445). For symptoms that do not meet the criteria for a somatization disorder, undifferentiated somatoform disorder (i.e., "unexplained physical complaints, lasting at least 6 months, that are below the threshold for a diagnosis of somatization disorder") may be more appropriate (*DSM–IV*, 1994, p. 451). Unfortunately, neither definition provides a conceptual framework for understanding an individual who goes to the primary care clinician with transient, unexplained somatic concerns. Somatic distress lies along a continuum of severity. Excessive somatic concern can represent an important aspect of one's symptoms, even though the presentation does not necessarily meet criteria for a psychiatric disorder.

Somatization is a complex disorder. Critical analysis of theories of somatization is beyond the scope of this chapter. Instead, the chapter focuses on theories that have received attention in the literature: communication, anxiety and depression, and social learning theory.

Theories of communication are coincident with the commonly held belief that unexplained somatic distress reflects intrapsychic conflicts expressed in somatic form rather than as an emotional symptom. On the other hand, it is possible that a focus on one's somatic symptoms provides an acceptable diversion of one's attention away from distressing psychological events, such as an interpersonal conflict (Kellner, 1990). Alternatively, individuals may rely on somatic concerns to explain their shortcomings in other areas of their life.

Theories of anxiety and depression are supported by studies that consistently demonstrate a positive relationship between somatic symptoms and the presence of depression, anxiety, or both (Cadoret, Widmer, & Troughton, 1980; Katon, Kleinman, & Rosen, 1982; Kellner, 1986; Kellner, Simpson, & Winslow, 1972; Tyrer, 1976). Some researchers consider somatization to be a depressive equivalent. In other words, they contend that somatization has the same etiology and natural course as depression and would therefore respond to the same interventions. However, the evidence to support this hypothesis is not overwhelming (Kellner, 1990). Others have suggested that somatic symptoms may mask an underlying affective disorder, because some individuals respond to distress (e.g., a loss) with overt somatic concerns but no emotional symptoms (Kellner, 1990). Although the exact relationship between depression and somatic symptoms is not clear, it has been consistently found that patients with depression report more somatic concerns than their nondepressed peers and that individuals who somatize are more depressed than individuals with documented physical illness (e.g., Cadoret et al., 1980). Similarly, positive associations between anxiety and somatic symptoms have been found (Kellner et al., 1972).

Learning theories applied to somatization suggest that attention to bodily sensations may be a learned response. Somatic symptoms may reflect modeled behavior, serve the function of gaining attention, or merely reflect a learned response. Complaint behaviors, like other verbal behaviors, can come under the control of contingencies in the individual's environment. It has been suggested that the majority of the learning occurs in the family of origin (Kellner, 1990).

By considering somatization along a continuum, the clinician is actually accepting the idea that individuals express symptoms of disease and related behavioral dysfunction through the filter of their unique personality, psychopathology, and psychosocial situations. Understanding the patient in these terms allows the clinician to individually tailor the patient's treatment.

PLACEBO AND NOCEBO EFFECTS

Placebos and nocebos are powerful examples of the important role of personal beliefs and expectations on an individual's symptom perception, presentation, and overall health status. Although early theories of health and illness minimized or ignored the role of beliefs in understanding illness, a substantial body of evidence has shown the importance of expectations in one's health and recovery from sickness.

A *placebo* is an inactive substance or an intervention that influences a person's perceptions and behavior based on efficacy expectations (Brannon & Feist, 1997). Individuals become well or improve when they believe the treatment has curative properties. Placebo effects have been observed in the drug treatment of a range of disorders, including ulcers, coughing, dental pain, diabetes, postoperative pain, seasickness, colds, multiple sclerosis, headaches, radiation sickness, ulcers, asthma, parkinsonism, and more (Turner, Deyo, Loeser, Von Korff, & Fordyce, 1994).

In contrast, expectations of becoming sick and the consequent development of symptoms, illustrate the *nocebo* phenomenon. These negative expectations, whether specific or vague, can result in transient, chronic, or perhaps even fatal illness, regardless of the presence of objective findings (Hahn, 1997).

Placebo Effects

Inert pills (Wolf, 1950), sham surgeries (Beecher, 1961; Benson & McCallie, 1979) and psychological interventions (Schachter & Singer, 1962) have all produced placebo effects. The most powerful placebo effects have been observed in individuals who have been given inert medication. A pill's size, brand name, type (e.g., capsule, tablet), and delivery system (e.g., injections are more potent placebos than pills) all influence an individual's perception of curative ability (Buckalew & Coffield, 1982; Shapiro, 1970). In addition, color has been associated with specific treatment effects. For example, green Oxazepam pills more effectively treat anxiety than other colors, whereas a yellow pill of the same dosage is better for treating depression (Schapira, McClelland, Griffiths, & Newell, 1970).

To date, many hypotheses have been presented to explain the placebo response. In the 1950s, those individuals susceptible to the placebo effect —"placebo reactors"—were found to be more somatically preoccupied and anxious, more satisfied with their hospital stay, less mature, and more outgoing than individuals who were not labeled as placebo reactors (Straus & Cavanaugh, 1996). In general, however, attempting to identify a personality type that is consistently susceptible to placebos has been largely unsuccessful. Whether an individual succumbs to the placebo effect seems to depend on numerous contextual and situational factors (Brody, 1995).

Many researchers have suggested that the placebo response is a consequence of classical conditioning. This hypothesis is supported by studies that have shown the ability of a placebo to lower blood pressure after multiple pairings with an antihypertensive (Suchman & Ader, 1992). This hypothesis has also been proposed as an explanation of a placebo's ability to decrease pain (Staats, Hekmat, & Staats, 1998). Although classical conditioning is a plausible explanation of the placebo response, other studies have shown individuals can have the placebo response in the absence of any associative learning. For example, individuals who were told about the benefits of hand immersion in ice water had increased pain thresholds, pain endurance, and pain tolerance, whereas participants told of the negative effects of hand immersion showed the opposite effect (Staats et al., 1998). As this example illustrates, an intervention as simple as a suggestion may be sufficient to induce the placebo response.

Nocebo Effects

Like the placebo response, negative expectations about illness and subsequent symptoms have been demonstrated across numerous medical conditions. Women who believed they were at increased risk of dying from a heart attack were more likely to die of a coronary event than women who did not harbor negative expectations, a finding independent of the influence of traditional coronary disease risk factors (Eaker, Pinsky, & Castelli, 1992). In a group of patients with psychogenic seizures, the belief that a skin patch would induce seizures indeed caused seizures characterized by thrashing, nonresponsiveness, uncoordinated movements, auras, and postictal confusion, or sleepiness (Lancman, Asconape, Craven, Howard, & Penry, 1994). In a study by Luparello, Lyons, Bleecker, and McFadden (1968), almost 50% of patients with asthma developed asthmatic symptoms after exposure to an innocuous saline nebulized solution that was presented as an irritant or allergen. Remarkably, patients who had a full asthma attack experienced relief from their symptoms when the same innocuous solution was given as a treatment. Benedetti, Amanzio, Casadio, Oliaro, and Maggi (1997) showed that postoperative pain could be intensified with the administration of saline.

The role of expectations has also been demonstrated in a double-blind, within-subject, randomized study. Patients with asthma were given medications (a bronchodilator or a bronchoconstrictor) under four sets of conditions: (a) a bronchodilator described as such, (b) a bronchodilator described as a bronchoconstrictor, (c) a bronchoconstrictor described as such, and (d) a bronchoconstrictor described as a bronchodilator. Bronchodilators make it easier for a person to breathe because they open up the airway. In contrast, bronchoconstrictors make it more difficult for an individual to breathe because they tighten the airways. In this study, the airway reactivity to the medication was greater when the instructions were consistent with the pharmacological action of the medication than when instructions were inconsistent with the function of the substance. In other words, bronchodilators worked more effectively when patients were told they were bronchodilators than when told they were bronchoconstrictors. Similarly, bronchoconstrictors worked more effectively when patients were told they were bronchoconstrictors than when told they were bronchodilators (Luparello, Leist, Lourie, & Sweet, 1970). Benedetti and colleagues (1997) showed that saline could increase the pain of patients with mild postoperative pain and that the effect could be reversed with the administration of an anxiety-reducing drug.

A powerful example of the nocebo effect is also demonstrated when groups of people become mysteriously ill, a phenomenon that often occurs as a result of fears that they have been exposed to a contagion. This type of collective illness has been referred to as *sociogenic, assembly-line hysteria, mass hysteria,* and *psychogenic illness* (Hahn, 1997). An episode of mass psychogenic illness at a Tennessee high school (Jones et al., 2000) provides an illustrative example of collective illness. In 1998, a teacher at a high school reported a gasoline smell and subsequently experienced headaches, dizziness, nausea, and shortness of breath. Because of safety concerns, the school was evacuated. One hundred people were evaluated in the emergency room, and 38 were admitted and hospitalized overnight. The school was closed for 5 days, and on reopening, an additional 71 students and staff sought care at the hospital emergency room with symptoms severe enough that many were transported to the hospital via ambulance. The most common symptoms during the incident were nausea, headaches, drowsiness, dizziness, and chest tightness.

To determine the source of illness, numerous agencies became involved: the fire department, the gas company, representatives of the State Occupational Safety and Health Administration, the Centers for Disease Control and Prevention, the Environmental Protection Agency, the Tennessee Department of Health, the Agency for Toxic Substances and Disease Registry, the Tennessee Department of Agriculture, the National Institute for Occupational Safety and Health, private consultants, and local emergency personnel. Extensive investigations were conducted to identify possible sources of contamination, including analyses of the air, waste, water, caves in the area, school air system, plumbing, drilled core samples, surface areas in the school, and a range of additional environmental sources. Blood and urine samples were taken from those who had become ill and analyzed for the presence of various chemical compounds.

Although the majority of individuals who became sick believed that toxic substances or fumes had caused their symptoms, the reports from the group of individuals who were initially sick (before the school was closed) included at least 49 different locations of illness origination within the school. Interestingly, 36 of the locations were classrooms served by independent ventilation systems. In addition, more than 30 different words were used to describe the odor.

Despite the symptoms and the reports of the odor, no possible environmental causes for the odor or symptoms were found. Similarly, the results of the extensive toxicological studies preformed on the blood and urine were normal.

Given the normal findings of the toxicological screenings and evaluations of the environment, the cause of the mass illness remains unexplained. In a follow-up questionnaire administered 1 month after the mass illness, correlates of becoming ill included being female, smelling an unusual odor at school, observing another ill person, and knowing that a classmate was ill.

In addition to the emotional costs of mass illness, significant financial costs were involved. In addition to the hospitals and emergency service workers, 8 laboratories, 12 government agencies, and 7 private consulting firms were involved in the investigation. Medical expenses amounted to just higher than $90,000, a figure that includes the 178 emergency room visits and ambulance costs. An additional $5,000 was spent to perform the toxicological testing, and $9,000 was expended for the analysis of the samples taken from the environment. As a result of the school being closed, 18,000 person-days were lost, 3,000 person-hours were used to test environmental samples, and 200 person-hours were used to evaluate the clinical specimens.

APPLICATIONS IN CLINICAL HEALTH PSYCHOLOGY

Research Applications

Clinical research studies are typically conducted at tertiary care medical centers affiliated with a major research university. However, patients treated at such centers do not necessarily represent the general population in terms of illness severity and psychological makeup. This selection bias represents a limitation in the generalizability of research findings obtained from these studies. As an example, Bradley and colleagues (Aaron et al., 1996; Bradley, Alarcon, Alexander, et al., 1994; Bradley, Alarcon, Triana, et al., 1994) conducted studies of individuals with fibromyalgia from two settings. The first group, labeled "patients," were individuals who sought health care for their pain symptoms. The second group, labeled "nonpatients," were individuals who had symptoms consistent with the fibromyalgia diagnosis but were community residents who had not sought care for their pain symptoms. When patients were compared with nonpatients across numerous variables, patients were found to have more psychiatric diagnoses, poorer coping skills (e.g., more catastrophizing), and an overall greater self-reported disability. If these researchers had relied only on the patients who sought health care, they would have narrowly defined the psychological characteristics of patients with fibromyalgia.

A second implication of the psychology of symptoms on clinical research with medical patients surrounds the use of self-report data. Although self-reports can be a rich source of data about private, subjective information, they are no substitute for more objective measures of functioning. As found in the studies relating negative affectivity to somatic complaints, responses on self-report symptom questionnaires are related to many nonmedical characteristics of the patient including personality traits, mood state, illness related beliefs, and perceived response contingencies. Self-report data provide the patients' self-view of symptoms and functioning. Although the data are informative, they should not be accepted as necessarily an entirely valid reflection of the patients' true symptoms or functional capabilities. It is the interaction of the objective disease process and the individual's personal characteristics that determine the patient's experience of illness.

An illustration of one of the limitations of relying on self-reported symptoms in research is a study by Simon and Gureje (1999) in which they found relatively poor stability for the diagnosis of somatization disorder in primary care patients. Data were analyzed from the WHO study of psychological problems in general health care. A stratified sample of roughly 5,000 individuals completed the Composite International Diagnostic Interview (CIDI) at baseline and 12 months later. The CIDI has modules to assess several psychiatric disorders including somatization disorder. Results showed that 61% of lifetime, medically unexplained somatic symptoms reported at baseline were not reported at the 12-month follow-up interview. Close consideration of the findings suggests that errors in patient recall account for the majority of this instability.

This instability in symptom recall raises concerns about the validity of the *DSM–IV* approach to diagnosis of somatization disorder. The *DSM–IV* criteria defined *somatization disorder* as "a history of many physical complaints beginning before age 30 years that occur over a period of several years" (p. 445). From a practical perspective, research studies using these criteria will find a reliability confound. From a conceptual perspective, the *DSM–IV* criteria do not accommodate much of the data presented in this chapter, which views somatization along a continuum from normal to abnormal. For example, phenomena such as mass hysteria demonstrate that somatization can develop as an acute phenomenon that may not meet the durational criteria required by the *DSM–IV*.

Assessment Applications

The multimethod model of assessment has a long history in clinical psychology (Anastasi, 1982). The model takes into account that variability exists among different features of the psychological construct being measured but is also helpful in determining the extent to which one component of the construct is validated by other features that are measured using different techniques. For example, a man who rates his pain as a 10 on a scale of 1 to 10 is stating that his current pain is the worst that he could possibly imagine. Because the pain severity construct has other features, such as physiological changes expected to correlate with acute pain (e.g., heart rate, blood pressure, skin conductance) or overt behavioral indicators (e.g., postural changes, protective physical maneuvers, distressed affect, concentration difficulties), measurement of these combined with subjective self-reports lead to an analysis of the symptom complaint that is more valid than any one of these modalities alone.

Routinely making attempts to talk with informed third parties, such as a patient's spouse, parents, or children, can add substantial validity to the assessment enterprise. For example, at times, patients may be reluctant to discuss certain problems that nevertheless are important for an accurate understanding of the patient's difficulties. Third parties can be helpful with filling in gaps of information the patient is reluctant to discuss. In other instances, a patient may have numerous complaints that initially seem to be excessive for the presumed underlying disease. Discussion with third parties can provide a means for attempting to corroborate at least some of the overt functional impairments alleged by the patient. In addition, certain cultural or personal issues that influence the patient's symptom presentation may become more clearly understood when the clinician has the opportunity to talk with family members.

One of the major advantages of using self-report measures of symptoms is that a fairly comprehensive domain of content can be covered that is pertinent to the construct of interest (e.g., pain, cognitive deficits, psychiatric symptoms). However, self-report checklists are often affected by a patient's response-set bias—that is, a patient's tendency to underreport or overreport symptoms. They also reflect the self-view domain and may not be well corroborated by other sources of data. Self-report measures raise questions about the nature and severity of problems a patient may have. Follow-up assessments using interview techniques with the patient and others and a review of pertinent historical records are needed to more accurately understand the case. For example, individuals with somatization tendencies may not perceive that their emotional functioning affects their somatic symptoms. Therefore, merely using standard self-report measures to assess emotional problems may fail to uncover difficulties. It is only when adequate data are obtained using a multimethod framework that valid clinical assessments can be made about patients' symptoms and functional impairments.

Another example involves cognitive complaints. In one scenario a patient may become overly focused on concerns about losing cognitive functions. This concern may lead to a visit to the physician or other clinician with complaints of cognitive decline. Only after rather extensive questioning and formal cognitive testing can a valid assessment be made. There are many instances in which one's complaints about cognitive problems are not validated by objective assessment. Of course, the opposite scenario can also occur; a patient may be unaware of the extent of the cognitive deficits and therefore does not complain accurately about them. It is the formal cognitive testing and history from third parties that confirms the presence of the cognitive disorder.

Treatment Applications

By this point, we hope that we have presented a generally convincing argument to support our thesis that optimal and effective medical treatment partly depends on acquiring an accurate understanding of the patient's psychosocial situation. Clinicians can improve the effectiveness of patient care by finding ways of incorporating psychological interventions into their medical treatment.

One rather obvious conclusion that can be drawn from the research on the psychology of symptoms is that clinicians' behaviors toward their patients can have a powerful effect on the patient's illness (subjective experience of suffering and level of functioning) and disease (actual pathophysiological process). Several recommendations are given that may improve patient care by incorporating psychological interventions into medical practice.

First, treatment providers should be aware of their inherently powerful positions as they take on the role of expert and healer. This power should be used in an artfully therapeutic fashion so that the patient is encouraged, relieved of worry, and infused with hope and optimism. Numerous clinical observations and empirical studies have demonstrated that hope and optimism have beneficial effects on patients' general sense of well-being and physical health (Hafen, Karren, Frandsen, & Smith, 1996). Clinicians should make sure to discuss accurately with patients the nature of their medical problems, but they should present information in a way that fosters hope. At times, this hope may be focused specifically on obtaining a cure; at other times, it may be on improving functioning or helping the patient face death in a more peaceful fashion. In each instance, hope is couched in a pragmatic and goal-oriented attitude that helps the patient combat the negative effects of hopelessness and helplessness. Hope is generally experienced in relationship to someone else; therefore, the clinician's level of hope is contagious.

A second general strategy is to attempt to understand the patients' perspectives of their illness. All patients have their own commonsense understanding of their symptoms. Patients self-medicate, restrict activities, and experience emotional reactions as a result of their personal understanding of their symptoms. By asking patients about the concerns, worries, and beliefs that are related to their symptoms, the clinician can provide individualized information to the patient and make more specifically targeted recommendations. For example, a man who has chest pain may believe the pain is cardiac pain. He may spend more time focusing his attention on sensations from his chest, which could further increase his concern. Because of his belief that he has heart disease, he may avoid exercise and sexual relations because of the commonsense belief that exertion leads to a heart attack. After a medical assessment finds that the man has no evidence of heart problems, the man may continue to worry about his chest pains. His concern may be relieved by a physician who attempts to better understand his perception of his symptoms. The physician could attempt to reassure the patient that the chest pains are not indicative of cardiac disease, the patient could be taught how to determine the difference between cardiac pain and musculoskeletal pain, and a specific plan of exercise and stress reduction could be discussed and monitored.

Third, medical clinicians should routinely ask themselves about what role psychosocial factors play in each patient's illness symptoms and their capacity to manage different types of treatment. The psychosocial considerations should include factors that are likely to allow the patients to be adaptive copers rather than factors such as psychosocial characteristics that raise concern about coping abilities. Major areas of concern include social support, history of compliance to medical treatments, and the presence of psychiatric disorder. Several studies have demonstrated the importance of social support. People with stronger social ties and intimate relationships live longer, stay healthier, and cope better with life stressors (Hafen et al., 1996). Several studies have shown depression to be a risk factor for acquiring various diseases as well as increasing the morbidity and mortality of disease. This finding has been convincingly demonstrated among patients with coronary artery disease (Carney, Rich, & Jaffe, 1995). Many of these patients are likely reluctant to seek out mental health treatment or to seek help from a doctor with their chief complaint being psychiatric problems. Therefore, non-mental health care clinicians need to adequately explore these issues even when patients do not mention psychiatric symptoms as concerns in the initial assessment.

CONCLUSION

The psychology of physical symptoms poses a challenge to clinicians and researchers alike. Whether in a research setting or clinical context, cultural, psychological (e.g., learning, cognitive schemas, emotions, personality style, expectations), and social factors influence patients' symptom reports and illness experience. Although more research is needed to clarify the interactions among these variables, it is known that the management of somatic complaints requires a careful consideration of these factors. A disregard for the complexity of the psychology of symptoms will ultimately undermine efforts to deliver the best patient care.

REFERENCES

Aaron, L. A., Bradley, L. A., Alarcon, G. S., Alexander, R. W., Triana-Alexander, M., Martin, M. Y., et al. (1996). Psychiatric diagnosis in patients with fibromyalgia are related to health care-seeking behavior rather than to illness. *Arthritis and Rheumatism, 39,* 436–445.

Alexander, R. W. (1998). An investigation of relationships between negative affectivity, symptom reporting, and health care seeking in women with fibromyalgia (Doctoral dissertation, University of Alabama at Birmingham, 1998). *Dissertation Abstracts International–B, 58*(12), 6798.

American Psychiatric Association. (1994). *Diagnostic and statistical manual of mental disorders* (4th ed.). Washington, DC.

Anastasi, A. (1982). *Psychological testing.* New York: MacMillan.

Arntz, A., Dreessen, L., & Merckelbach, H. (1991). Attention, not anxiety, influences pain. *Behavior Research and Therapy, 29,* 41–50.

Barondess, J. A. (1979). Disease and illness—A crucial distinction. *American Journal of Medicine, 66,* 375–376.

Beecher, H. K. (1961). Surgery as placebo: A quantitative study of bias. *Journal of the American Medical Association, 176,* 1102–1107.

Benedetti, F., Amanzio, M., Casadio, C., Oliaro, A., & Maggi, G. (1997). Blockade of nocebo hyperalgesia by the cholecystokinin antagonist proglumide. *Pain, 71,* 135–140.

Benson, H., & McCallie, D. P. (1979). Angina pectoris and the placebo effect. *New England Journal of Medicine, 300,* 1424–1429.

Bradley, L. A., Alarcon, G. S., Alexander, R. W., Triana, M., Aaron, L. A., & Stewart, K. E. (1994). Pain thresholds, symptom severity, coping strategies, and pain beliefs as predictors of health care seeking in fibromyalgia patients. *Proceedings of the 7th World Congress on Pain, 2,* 167–176.

Bradley, L. A., Alarcon, G. S., Triana, M., Aaron, L. A., Alexander, R. W., Stewart, K. E., et al. (1994). Health care seeking behavior in fibromyalgia: Associations with pain thresholds, symptom severity, and psychiatric morbidity. *Journal of Musculoskeletal Pain, 3,* 79–87.

Brannon, L., & Feist, J. (1997). *Conducting health research.* New York: Brooks/Cole.

Brody, H. (1995). The placebo response. In D. Wedding (Ed.), *Behavior and medicine* (p. 345). St. Louis, MO: Mosby.

Buckalew, L. W., & Coffield, K. E. (1982). An investigation of drug expectancy as a function of capsule color and size and preparation form. *Journal of Clinical Psychopharmacology, 2,* 245–248.

Cadoret, R., Widmer, R. B., & Troughton, E. P. (1980). Somatic complaints: Harbinger of depression in primary care. *Journal of Affective Disorders, 2,* 61–70.

Carney, R. M., Rich, M. W., & Jaffe, A. S. (1995). Depression as a risk factor for cardiac events in established coronary heart disease. A review of possible mechanisms. *Annals of Behavioral Medicine, 17,* 142–149.

Cioffi, D. (1991). Beyond attentional strategies: A cognitive–perceptual model of somatic interpretation. *Psychological Bulletin, 109,* 25–41.

Cohn, K., & Duke, D. (1987). *Coming back: A guide to recovering from heart attack.* Reading, MA: Addison-Wesley.

Eaker, E. D., Pinsky, J., & Castelli, W. P. (1992). Myocardial infarction and coronary death among women: Psychosocial predictors from a 20-year follow-up of women in the Framingham Study. *American Journal of Epidemiology, 135,* 854–864.

Hafen, B. Q., Karren, K. J., Frandsen, K. J., & Smith, N. C. (1996). *Mind/body health.* Boston: Allyn and Bacon.

Hahn, R. A. (1997). The nocebo phenomenon: Concept, evidence, and implications for public health. *Preventive Medicine, 26,* 607–611.

Harlap, S., Davies, A. M., Harber, M., Samueloff, N., Rossman, H., & Prywes, R.

(1975). Ethnic group, immigration and infant morbidity in West Jerusalem. In L. Levi (Ed.), *Society, stress, and disease* (Vol. 2, pp. 323–335). New York: Oxford.

Henry, J. P., & Stephens, P. M. (1977). *Stress, health, and the social environment: A sociobiologic approach to medicine*. New York: Springer.

Jones, T. F., Craig, A. S., Hoy, D., Gunter, E. W., Ashley, D. L., Barr, D. B., et al. (2000). Mass psychogenic illness attributed to toxic exposure at a high school. *New England Journal of Medicine, 342*, 96–100.

Katon, W., Kleinman, A., & Rosen, G. (1982). Depression and somatization: A review, part I. *American Journal of Medicine, 72*, 127–153.

Kellner, R. (1986). *Somatization and hypochondriasis*. New York: Praeger-Greenwood.

Kellner, R. (1990). Somatization. Theories and research. *Journal of Nervous and Mental Disease, 178*, 150–160.

Kellner, R., Simpson, G. M., & Winslow, W. W. (1972). The relationship of depressive neurosis to anxiety and somatic symptoms. *Psychosomatics, 13*, 358–362.

Lancman, M. E., Asconape, J. J., Craven, W. J., Howard, G., & Penry, J. K. (1994). Predictive value of induction of psychogenic seizures by suggestion. *Annals of Neurology, 35*, 359–361.

Leventhal, H., Brown, D., Shacham, S., & Engquist, G. (1979). Effects of preparatory information about sensations, threat of pain, and attention on cold pressor distress. *Journal of Personality and Social Psychology, 37*, 688–714.

Leventhal, E. A., Leventhal, H., Shacham, S., & Easterling, D. V. (1989). Active coping reduces reports of pain from childbirth. *Journal of Consulting and Clinical Psychology, 57*, 365–371.

Lipowski, Z. J. (1988). Somatization: The concept and its clinical application. *American Journal of Psychiatry, 148*, 1358–1368.

Luparello, T. J., Leist, N., Lourie, C. H., & Sweet, P. (1970). The interaction of psychologic stimuli and pharmacologic agents on airway reactivity in asthmatic subjects. *Psychosomatic Medicine, 32*, 509–513.

Luparello, T., Lyons, H. A., Bleecker, E. R., & McFadden, E. R. (1968). Influences of suggestion on airway reactivity in asthmatic subjects. *Psychosomatic Medicine, 30*, 819–825.

McCaul, K. D., & Malott, J. M. (1984). Distraction and coping with pain. *Psychological Bulletin, 95*, 516–533.

Navon, D., & Gopher, D. (1979). On the economy of the human-processing system. *Psychological Review, 86*, 214–255.

Pennebaker, J. W. (1982). *The psychology of physical symptoms*. New York: Springer-Verlag.

Pennebaker, J. W., Barger, S. D., & Tiebout, J. (1989). Disclosure of traumas and health among holocaust survivors. *Psychosomatic Medicine, 51*, 577–589.

Pennebaker, J. W., & Beall, S. K. (1986). Confronting a traumatic event: Toward an understanding of inhibition and disease. *Journal of Abnormal Psychology,* *95,* 274–281.

Pennebaker, J. W., Colder, M., & Sharp, L. K. (1990). Accelerating the coping process. *Journal of Personality and Social Psychology, 58,* 528–537.

Pennebaker, J. W., & Skelton, J. A. (1981). Selective monitoring of physical sensations. *Journal of Personality and Social Psychology, 41,* 213–223.

Plutchik, R. (1980). *Emotion: A psychoevolutionary synthesis.* New York: Harper & Row.

Raper, A. (1958). The incidence of peptic ulceration in some African tribal groups. *Transactions of the Royal Society of Tropical Medicine and Hygiene, 152,* 525–546.

Schachter, W., & Singer, J. E. (1962). Cognitive, social, and physiological determinants of emotional state. *Psychological Review, 69,* 379–399.

Schapira, K., McClelland, H. A., Griffiths, N. R., & Newell, D. J. (1970). Study of the effects of tablet colour in the treatment of anxiety states. *British Journal of Medicine, 2,* 446–449.

Shapiro, A. K. (1970). Placebo effects in psychotherapy and psychoanalysis. *Journal of Clinical Pharmacology, 10,* 73–78.

Simon, G. E., & Gureje, O. (1999). Stability of somatization disorder and somatization symptoms among primary care patients. *Archives of General Psychiatry, 56,* 90–98.

Staats, P., Hekmat, H., & Staats, A. (1998). Suggestion/placebo effects on pain: Negative as well as positive. *Journal of Pain and Symptom Management, 15,* 235–243.

Straus, J. L., & Cavanaugh, S. (1996). Placebo effects: Issues for clinical practice in psychiatry and medicine. *Psychosomatics, 37,* 315–326.

Suchman, A. L., & Ader, R. (1992). Classical conditioning and placebo effects in crossover studies. *Clinical Pharmacology and Therapeutics, 52,* 372–377.

Taylor, C., Bandura, A., Ewart, C., Miller, N., & DeBusk, R. (1985). Raising spouse's and patient's perception of his cardiac capabilities after clinically uncomplicated myocardial infarction. *American Journal of Cardiology, 55,* 635–638.

Taylor, L. (1999). *Symptom management in older primary care patients: Feasibility of a laboratory-based, written self-disclosure protocol.* Unpublished master's thesis, University of Alabama at Birmingham.

Turner, J. A., Deyo, R. A., Loeser, J. D., Von Korff, M., & Fordyce, W. E. (1994). The importance of placebo effects in pain treatment and research. *Journal of the American Medical Association, 271,* 1609–1614.

Tyrer, P. (1976). *The role of bodily feelings in anxiety.* London: Oxford University Press.

Vaillant, G. E. (1976). Natural history of male psychological health. *Archives of General Psychology, 33,* 535–545.

Watson, D., & Clark, L. A. (1984). Negative affectivity: The disposition to experience aversive emotional states. *Psychological Bulletin, 96*, 465–490.

Watson, D., & Pennebaker, J. W. (1989). Health complaints, stress, and distress: Exploring the central role of negative affectivity. *Psychological Review, 96*, 234–254.

Watson, D., & Tellegen, A. (1985). Toward a consensual structure of mood. *Psychological Bulletin, 98*, 219–235.

Wegner, D. M., & Giuliano, T. (1980). Arousal-induced attention to self. *Journal of Personality and Social Psychology, 38*, 719–726.

Whitehead, W. E., Fedoravicius, A. S., Blackwell, B., & Wooley, S. (1979). A behavioral conceptualization of psychosomatic illness: Psychosomatic symptoms as learned responses. In J. R. McNamara (Ed.), *Behavioral approaches to medicine: Application and analysis* (pp. 65–99). New York: Plenum.

Whitehead, W. E., Winget, J., Fedoravicius, A. S., Wooley, S., & Blackwell, B. (1982). Learned illness behavior in patients with irritable bowel syndrome and peptic ulcer. *Digestive Diseases and Sciences, 27*, 202–208.

Wolf, S. (1950). Effects of suggestion and conditioning on the action of chemical agents in human subjects. The pharmacology of placebos. *Journal of Clinical Investigation, 29*, 100–109.

World Health Organization. (1991). *The international classification of diseases, ninth revision*. Salt Lake City, UT: Med-Index Publications.

Williams, J. M. G., Watts, F. N., Macleod, C., & Mathews, A. (1991). *Cognitive psychology and emotional disorders*. New York: Wiley.

Williams, M. A. (1993). *Evaluating the relationship between negative affectivity and symptom reporting: A test of the symptom perception hypothesis*. Unpublished doctoral dissertation, University of Mississippi.

Zevon, M. A., & Tellegen, A. (1982). The structure of mood change: An idiographic/nomothetic analysis. *Journal of Personality and Social Psychology, 43*, 111–122.

Zola, I. K. (1966). Culture and symptoms. An analysis of patients' presenting complaints. *American Sociological Review, 31*, 615–630.

17

INJURY AND POISONING

DAVID DILILLO, LIZETTE PETERSON, AND JANET E. FARMER

For more than three decades, unintentional injuries have been recognized as a significant public health problem in the United States. In 1966, the National Academy of Sciences referred to them as the "neglected disease of modern society." In 1985, the academy described unintentional injuries as the "principal public health problem in America," noting that "the study of injury represents unparalleled opportunities for reducing morbidity and mortality, and for realizing significant savings in both financial and human terms—all in return for a relatively modest investment" (p. v).

Today, more than 30 years since the academy first cited injury as a major public health concern, unintentional injuries continue to pose the most serious health risk in this country. The persistence of injuries as a significant social problem is reflected in morbidity and mortality statistics. Injuries are the leading cause of death among all Americans between ages 1 and 44, far surpassing the death rates attributable to ailments such as cancer and heart disease (Baker, O'Neill, Ginsburg, & Li, 1992). In 1995 alone, injuries accounted for 147,891 deaths, 2.6 million hospitalizations, and more than 36 million emergency room visits (Fingerhut & Warner, 1997). Children, who experience the greatest long-term consequences from injuries, are affected disproportionately. Each year, 16 million youths require emergency medical treatment for preventable injuries in the United

States; 600,000 are hospitalized, and 30,000 more are permanently disabled by injuries (Baker & Waller, 1989; Rodriguez, 1990). Between ages 5 and 34, injuries are the source of more deaths than all other causes combined (Baker et al., 1992). During the later stages of life, degenerative diseases account for a greater proportion of deaths than do injuries. Nevertheless, the per capita rates of injury among the elderly population are higher than among younger individuals. Finally, as if the individual human costs were not enough, the economic toll of injuries in society is also staggering. Estimates have found that more than $148 billion is spent to treat injuries in the United States each year (Rice & MacKenzie, 1989).

In addition to conveying the enormity of the problem, this chapter also provides an overview of common environmental and behavioral strategies used to prevent the most frequently occurring injuries, as well as a discussion of rehabilitation psychology, a subspecialty concerned with restoring the maximum quality of life to those who have been injured. Throughout this chapter, emphasis is placed on the contributions of psychologists to the areas of injury prevention and treatment with children. It is important at the outset to point out a fundamental premise that underlies the scientific study of injury—the assumption that injuries are not simply "accidents." In most cases, injuries are the product of predictable factors that are amenable to investigation and, therefore, to preventive intervention. The popular belief that injuries are chance events that are out of human control is a misconception antithetical to the notion that such events can be systematically investigated and prevented. In fact, the notion that injuries are the result of random environmental forces or reckless behavior has probably been the most influential factor delaying scientific attention to injury prevention (Barss, Smith, Baker, & Mohan, 1998). Thus, in the injury nomenclature, researchers and preventionists have eschewed the conventional term *accident* in favor of the more accurate descriptor *unintentional injury* to convey the conviction that most injuries are amenable to scientific investigation and ultimately can be prevented.

CLASSIFICATIONS OF INJURY

Within the World Health Organization's ninth edition of the *International Classification of Diseases (ICD–9)*, injuries and poisonings are the only disease category to encompass two separate sets of codes. The type of injury and body part affected are assigned a *nature of injury*, or *N*, code (e.g., N800.15 Closed Skull Fracture; N947.415 Burn of Vagina and Uterus). Although this classification shows extensive breadth and may be useful in the treatment of existing injuries, it is less useful in guiding the prevention of injuries. To assist in this endeavor, the *supplementary classification of external causes*, or *E*, codes, were devised and included beginning with the *ICD–9* to describe the etiology of an injury (e.g., E80.41 Fall From a Passenger Train; E90.50 Venomous Snake Bite). However, these codes seem weighted more toward adult injuries occurring in a military or industrial context and are less comprehensive in describing the range of possible pediatric injuries.

Other coding systems have also been derived for the purpose of describing the quantitative or qualitative characteristics of injuries. The best known of these is the Abbreviated Injury Scale (Association for the Advancement of Automotive Medicine, 1990), which yields a rating of severity of a range of traumatic injuries. Codes devised to assess specific types of injuries have also been devised. These include the Glasgow Coma Scale (Pettigrew, Wilson, & Teasdale, 1998), the Burn Grading System (Fisher, Wells, Fulwider, & Edgerton, 1977), and a system developed by the Committee on Medical Aspects of Automotive Safety (1972) to quantify the extent of road and highway injuries. All of these measures focus only on more severe (i.e., medically attended) injuries. However, some attempts have been made to measure the less severe yet stressful and much more ubiquitous injuries of children (Peterson, Heiblum, & Saldana, 1996).

UNINTENTIONAL INJURY: PATTERNS AND PREVENTIVE MEASURES

The occurrence of unintentional injuries often differs by the age and gender of the victim; geographical location; and, in some cases, race or ethnicity, socioeconomic status (SES), and time of year. Although intentionally inflicted injuries (e.g., homicide, suicide, child abuse) are of obvious importance and may share many risk factors with unintentional injury (Peterson & Brown, 1994), the breadth and complexity of these phenomena preclude inclusion in the current discussion. Considered here are several categories of injuries resulting from clearly unintentional acts. For each injury type, a brief description of the nature of the problem and some examples of common preventive measures are presented.

Injuries Related to Motor Vehicles

The Problem

Cars and other motorized vehicles are an integral part of everyday life in most countries. Although estimates vary, between 300,000 and 500,000 deaths and 10 to 15 million traffic-related injuries occur each year in the world (Transport and Road Research Laboratory, 1991). Per capita rates of traffic deaths in the United States are among the lowest in the world (Transport and Road Research Laboratory, 1991), yet they remain the leading cause of death among Americans between ages 1 and 34 (Karpf & Williams, 1983). Fatality rates vary significantly by age and gender, with increased incidence of death occurring during late adolescence and early adulthood, particularly among men (Baker et al., 1992). Impaired driving caused by alcohol consumption may be the most significant contributing factor in vehicle occupant deaths; 41% of all vehicle occupant fatalities involve drivers whose blood alcohol content exceeded the legal limits (Baker et al., 1992; National Highway Traffic Safety Administration [NHTSA], 1996).

Although the majority of people who die in vehicle crashes are car occupants, pedestrians make up the next largest category of deaths related to motor vehicles, accounting for approximately 8,000 fatalities annually (NHTSA, 1996). Pedestrian injury is a particular threat to young children and older adults. After cancer, pedestrian injuries are the leading cause of death of children ages 5 to 9 (National Safety Council, 1988). Given such figures, it is surprising that the number of child pedestrian injuries in recent years has dramatically decreased by 48%—a decline that is more likely attributable to children's reduction of walking as a means of transportation than to preventive measures per se (Hillman, Adams, & Whitelegg, 1991). Because they are more likely to experience slowed motor movements, diminished cognitive and memory capacities, and visual and auditory impairments, older adults are also at an increased risk for pedestrian injuries (Hogue, 1982).

Prevention

Most interventions to reduce occupant injuries have attempted to make vehicle interiors less dangerous to passengers during a crash. Regulatory actions such as the mandatory use of seat belts and infant car seats, modified vehicular front ends and steering columns, air bags, and added interior padding have all improved occupants' chances of surviving a collision. For example, the use of lap–shoulder belts and air bags have been found to decrease adult passenger fatality rates by 45% and 32%, respectively (Evans, 1990; Ferguson, 1996). Mandated behavioral interventions such as more stringent enforcement of drunk-driving laws, increased legal penalties, and public awareness campaigns may have also contributed to significant decreases in alcohol-related crashes in recent years (NHTSA, 1996).

As a whole, broad-based and purely educational interventions aimed at altering children's pedestrian behavior through individual training have met with only modest success (Rivara, 1990). It should be noted that the public has never provided sufficient support for behavioral and consequence-oriented training programs that have shown promise in promoting safe pedestrian behaviors among children (e.g., Yeaton & Bailey, 1978).

Researchers have expressed similar uncertainty about the prospects of affecting long-term behavioral change among older pedestrians (Baker, Robertson, & O'Neill, 1974). Current traffic-calming initiatives, which reduce the speed and volume of traffic in high-risk areas, hold perhaps the most promise for reducing pedestrian injuries among children and adults. These strategies include the use of one-way streets, speed reduction devices, and promotion of increased usage of public transportation.

Falls

The Problem

Falls are a major cause of serious injury, hospitalization, and disability in the United States and elsewhere. The severity of injuries resulting from falls is determined by several factors, including the distance fallen, the nature of the impact surface, and the specific body parts that must absorb the force of the fall. For children younger than age 5, falls are the most common injuries requiring emergency medical care (Wilson, Baker, Teret, Shock, & Garbarino, 1991). Common falls among children range from playground falls and falls from household furniture such as bookcases and bunk beds to relatively rare but potentially fatal falls from the windows of homes and buildings. The use of baby walkers for preambulatory infants is also associated with fall-related injuries, particularly because walkers can roll down stairs (Coats & Allen, 1991; Smith, Bowman, Luria, & Shields, 1996).

Despite the frequency of falls among children, 59% of those who are killed by falls are older than age 75 (Baker et al., 1992). Risk factors for older adult falls include a history of falls, cognitive impairment, chronic illness, difficulty with balance or gait, and usage of certain medications (Tinetti, Doucette, Clauss, & Marottoli, 1995). Nonfatal falls by older adults often result in serious injuries such as hip and other bone fractures (Fife & Barancik, 1985).

Prevention

Prevention measures for reducing injuries resulting from falls include those intended to alter fall-related behaviors among high-risk groups and approaches that stress environmental modifications to reduce the risk of falls. It has been shown that with minimal reinforcement school-age children can be taught to reduce improper and physically risky playground behaviors that can lead to falls (Heck, Collins, & Peterson, in press). For older adults, regular participation in weight-bearing exercise to increase bone strength may reduce the likelihood of falls that result in hip fractures (Province et al., 1995). Hip pads for older adults are another promising preventive measure. These pads are worn under clothing to absorb the impact of a fall and seem useful in preventing hip fractures. One clinical study found that nursing home residents randomly assigned to wear hip protectors were 53% less likely to sustain a hip fracture (Lauritzen, Petersen, & Lund, 1993). None of the participants who fell while wearing hip protectors had a fracture. However, concerns about comfort and low perceived probability of falling among older adults may reduce compliance with hip protector usage (Cameron & Quine, 1994).

Baker et al. (1992) suggested that additional attention should be paid to the design features of playgrounds, houses, and nursing homes to minimize risks. For instance, after realizing that open windows in New York City apartment buildings were a major cause of children's falls, legislation was enacted requiring the installation of protective bars on all upstairs windows, which led to a dramatic decrease in children's falls from windows (Barlow, Nicmirska, Gandhi, & Leblanc, 1983). However, because the bars may prevent occupants from escaping from a fire, other solutions continue to be sought.

Poisonings

The Problem

The *ICD* classifies acute poisonings along with injuries as external causes of morbidity and mortality. Almost 250,000 people are admitted to hospitals each year for poisonings that are either intentional (i.e., in a suicide) or unintentional (Rice & MacKenzie, 1989). Surprising perhaps is the fact that 99% of the 13,000 deaths from poisoning each year occur among adults, and nearly half of the deaths are considered suicides (Baker et al., 1992). Some of the most frequent agents involved in adult poisonings include carbon monoxide, opiates and cocaine, and psychotropic medications, particularly antidepressants.

The incidence of children's deaths from poisonings has declined markedly since child-resistant packaging was mandated by the Poison Prevention Packaging Act (PPPA) of 1970 (P.L. 91-601; Walton, 1982). However, poisonings continue to be a major cause of hospitalizations and medical treatment for children (Wilson et al., 1991). In many cases, cleaners and solvents that have previously poisoned a child remain accessible in cabinets and under sinks for weeks after the event, demonstrating that an incident does not automatically precipitate family change (Beautrais, Fergusson, & Shannon, 1987). For every poisoning that causes a child fatality, thousands more reports of toxin ingestions are received by poison control centers (Litovitz, Schmitz, & Holm, 1989).

Prevention

As noted, the PPPA, which requires that toxic, corrosive, or physically irritating household substances be stored in child-resistant containers, seems to have been quite successful in reducing the number of childhood deaths from poisonings (Clarke & Walton, 1979; Walton, 1982). Another study also supported this claim and further suggested that most poisonings occurring since the implementation of the PPPA have resulted from improperly secured caps and products not covered by the PPPA under certain circumstances (Rodgers, 1996).

In addition to the PPPA, prevention efforts have been directed toward educating children and caregivers about the dangers of poisons and what to do when someone ingests a toxin. One such intervention involved the use of stickers featuring "Mr. Yuk"—a small, green frowning face intended to warn children to stay away from poisonous substances. This campaign was abandoned when some children were apparently attracted to the colorful labels (Vernberg, Culver-Dickinson, & Spyker, 1984). Physician- and community-based interventions have also been attempted but have met with mixed results. One example involved a study that evaluated the efficacy of providing poisoning prevention education and a bottle of ipecac syrup to more than 5,000 Rhode Island families with newborn children (Cooper, Widness, & O'Shea, 1988). Although the intervention and control groups differed in the mean time between poisoning and the call for intervention, no significant differences were found between the groups in the number of calls made to a poison control center. (Only eight study families telephoned.)

Drownings

The Problem

For all ages, drowning is the third most common form of unintentional injury, with approximately 5,000 drownings occurring annually (Baker at al., 1992). Individuals between ages 1 and 18 have the greatest risk of drowning, and drowning is the leading cause of an injury fatality for children younger than age 5 (Wintemute, 1990). Infant drownings are most likely to occur in bathtubs. After age 1, drownings occur more frequently in home swimming pools and other open water sources such as rivers, lakes, and oceans (Quan, Gore, Wentz, Allen, & Novack, 1989; Wintemute, 1990). It is further estimated that for every child who actually drowns, nearly four more require medical care because of injuries from near drownings (Baker et al., 1992). About 1,000 of the total 5,000 annual drownings are boating related (Baker et al., 1992). Among adults and adolescents, alcohol usage has been established as a clear risk factor for drowning (Howland & Hingson, 1988; Howland et al., 1993).

Prevention

The primary preventive measures to reduce childhood drowning have involved environmental changes designed to "child proof" domestic swimming pools (Baker et al., 1992). Pool covers, alarms, and protective fencing are examples of strategies that have been used toward this end. Of these, fencing to keep children completely out of pool areas seems to be the most effective. Several studies have suggested that pools completely surrounded by sufficiently high fencing are less likely to be the source of a childhood drowning (Fergusson, Horwood, & Shannon, 1983; Pitt & Balanda, 1991; Present, 1987).

Of course, once children gain any access to a pool, the risk of drowning increases. Pool alarms detect motion on the water's surface but are problematic because they can be triggered by routine disturbances in the water such as those caused by weather or pool pumps. The protective value of pool covers varies depending on the type used. Soft, thermal covers seem deceptively safe to young children, who may try to walk on them, plunge below the water line, and become trapped under a cover after stepping off the pool's edge. Hard pool covers support the weight of a young child and, although less convenient, may pose a more formidable barrier to drownings.

It would be reasonable to expect that swimming lessons reduce children's risk of drowning. Lessons do seem to improve performance of specific skills related to swimming (e.g., floating, kicking, holding one's breath; Erbaugh, 1986), but it remains unclear whether swimming lessons decrease the risk of drowning. In addition, some parents may assume that swimming lessons will keep children from drowning. Such beliefs may lead to reduced supervision vigilance, which could lead to injury (DiLillo & Tremblay, 2001). Finally, although the design of personal flotation devices (e.g., life jackets) and their relative ability to keep users afloat has been studied (Hermann & Stormer, 1985; U.S. Coast Guard, 1995), it is unclear to what extent these devices actually reduce risk of drowning.

Burns and Smoke Inhalation

The Problem

The number of deaths caused by burns and smoke inhalation each year is exceeded only by those resulting from motor vehicle crashes and drownings. Most burns are caused by heat generated from open flames, hot liquids, or hot surfaces, although certain chemical agents cause burns as well. Household fires tend to be the most lethal type of burn-related danger, accounting for most of the approximately 5,000 fire-related deaths that occur annually in the United States (Division of Injury Control, 1990). Deaths from house fires are more common among children, older adults, African Americans, Native Americans, and individuals with a lower SES who rely more on dangerous heating methods (Baker et al., 1992). The geographical distribution of house-fire deaths reveals that a disproportionate number of fatalities occur in the southeastern United States (Baker et al., 1992). Burns that are nonfatal may require extensive, costly, and painful medical treatment. Medical hardships such as skin grafts and infections as well as permanent disfigurement and scarring may result from more serious but nonfatal burns.

Prevention

When maintained regularly, smoke detectors are probably the single most effective intervention to reduce injuries from building and residential fires; their usage has been directly linked to reduced risk of dying in a residential fire (Runyan, Bangdiwala, Linzer, Sacks, & Butts, 1992). Multicomponent community-based interventions to reduce burn injuries have also been evaluated. Of these programs, some have been shown to result in increases in knowledge, but few have demonstrated corresponding behavior changes. One exception was the Maine Burn Program (Clark, Katz, & Campbell, 1992), which targeted several types of burn injuries. This multifaceted program that included the establishment of statewide burn units, proper installation and use of wood stoves, mandated use of smoke detectors, and a burn education program for children resulted in a per capita decrease in the number of fire-related hospital admissions and deaths in the area during the time of intervention. Researchers have also developed training programs to teach children effective safety and escape behaviors in the event of a residential fire (e.g., Holmes & Jones, 1996; Jones, Kazdin, & Haney, 1981). These training programs have been successful at teaching fire safety skills, but insufficient funding and support has prevented population-level evaluations of children's abilities to perform newly acquired behaviors under the pressure and intensity of actual fire situations.

PASSIVE PREVENTION STRATEGIES: THE FIRST LINE OF DEFENSE

It is clear from this brief overview of the literature that the most common and effective methods of injury control involve the use of passive devices (e.g., safety belts, pool fencing, child-resistant medicine caps) designed to protect individuals from contacting potentially injurious objects in the environment. Indeed, considerably less effort is needed to make environmental or product modifications to promote safety than is required to motivate behavior changes that produce comparable levels of injury reduction. Clearly, manufacturing and selling household chemicals with child-resistant packaging is a more practical intervention than convincing millions of parents to store these substances out of reach of children (although this should be done also). This host–agent–environment model of injury, emphasizing the physical separation of individuals from hazards in the environment, has been widely adopted by medical and public health investigators and has traditionally dominated the field.

According to the model pioneered by Haddon (1970, 1980), the individual serves as the host of the injury, the agent is the injury-producing stimulus, and the environment is the setting in which the injury takes place. From this perspective, injury control can be likened to disease control in that the primary goal is to eliminate the injury agent from contact with the host, much the way one would attempt to prevent contact between virus and organism. Applied to injury control, this approach most often involves the use of passive protective barriers designed to prevent individuals from contacting a dangerous transfer of energy (e.g., heat, mechanical, chemical). For example, air bags are designed to absorb much of the energy transfer that results during an automobile collision.

As noted, many barrier-type interventions, which do not depend on individual action, have been remarkably successful. For example, children's poisonings plummeted when medicines and other toxic substances were placed in child-resistant containers (Walton, 1982). Child safety gates have drastically reduced the number of injuries sustained from falls (Wilson et al., 1991). Bicycle helmets can reduce the risk for children's head injuries by as much as 85% (Rivara, 1982).

Although barriers can be quite effective at family, community, and national levels, they have not been used to their fullest extent. Often, aesthetic, convenience, and economic factors take precedence over safety issues. Thus, shrubbery is planted next to roadways where unseen children can suddenly emerge into traffic. Plastic dry cleaner bags, which can suffocate children, are simply labeled with a warning rather than being eliminated altogether. Baby walkers contribute to thousands of injuries annually yet are still sold by the millions (Consumer Product Safety Commission, 1994; Karels, 1992).

In addition, barriers must be used carefully. Air bags are a highly effective way of protecting car occupants in crashes, as are rear-facing baby seats. However, when these two devices are combined, they can result in increased risk of injury for infants and children younger than age 10. It has been estimated that for every five lives saved by passenger-side air bags, one (usually a child's) is lost (Graham & Segui-Gomez, 1997). In reference to this situation, two prominent preventionists recently said,

> We are aware of no precedent in the history of preventive medicine where a mandatory measure was sustained with such a poor ratio of lifesaving benefit to fatal risk. Allowing young children to incur the bulk of this risk is particularly questionable. (Graham & Segui-Gomez, 1997, p. 2)

Speed humps are another example of a barrier intervention that must be used with caution, for they can cause speeding drivers to lose control of vehicles, threatening nearby pedestrians. Therefore, it is important that passive methods of injury prevention be evaluated for injury risk. Future advancements in air bag and speed hump engineering may render these devices safe for vehicle occupants and pedestrians under all circumstances.

The final and perhaps most significant issue is that passive interventions can protect individuals from only a fraction of the multitude of injury types. Many common injuries such as those sustained from near drownings in bathtubs, slips and falls, and choking on food can rarely be entirely prevented through barrier interventions. In situations in which passive environmental alterations and product modifications are not feasible, other more active methods of injury prevention must be used. This class of intervention strategies depends on the modification of human behavior and is discussed in subsequent sections.

BEYOND PASSIVE PREVENTION

The sheer variety of injuries and the complex and multifaceted nature of their etiologies call for the involvement of many disciplines if broad-based injury reduction efforts are to be effective. Toward this end, physicians, epidemiologists, biomechanical engineers, city planners, and economists have all made significant contributions to the injury control agenda in the United States. However, as a whole, psychologists have been slow to join this multidisciplinary cadre. This lack of involvement may reflect an historical divide that has existed between the behavioral sciences in general and the field of public health, which has consistently been in the forefront of injury prevention endeavors.

Although the field of psychology has traditionally been on the periphery of mainstream injury prevention and control efforts, the past two decades have included the dramatic expansion of the role of psychologists in identifying and modifying a broad spectrum of health-related behaviors (Belar, 1997). This growth into realms typically dominated by more overtly medical professions reflects an increasing appreciation of the significance of psychological and behavioral processes in the maintenance of physical health and well-being (Chesney, 1993). Just as psychology has made significant contributions to the prevention and treatment of other health-related behaviors (e.g., overeating, smoking, substance abuse), the field has much to offer to the area of unintentional injury prevention. More people are beginning to recognize that, for injury control to be effective, behavior must change among some groups, such as children, parents, legislators, manufacturers, and educators (Scheidt, 1988). Furthermore, many of the constructs with which psychologists are most conversant (e.g., motivation, perception, learning) are thought by many to be the key determinants of injury-related behaviors (Spielberger & Frank, 1992).

As noted, passive environmental modifications are the preferred front-line method of safety promotion. Yet even barriers such as safety belts, child-resistant lids, car seats, and child safety gates involve some behavioral component if they are to be implemented effectively. Safety belts must be buckled, children must be placed into car seats, and medicine caps must be properly replaced. The behavioral aspects and inherent limitations of passive interventions (most notably their applicability to a finite number of injuries) demonstrate that more active intervention strategies focusing on individual behavior change remain a crucial piece of the injury prevention puzzle. The point at which passive interventions become limited—when they are inapplicable or require human action to maintain—is the area in which health and clinical psychologists have the most to offer the field of injury prevention. Health psychologists in particular, whose training and expertise lie in the promotion of health-related behavior change, are uniquely qualified to design, implement, and evaluate behaviorally oriented interventions to reduce injuries or ameliorate their consequences.

PREVENTION OF CHILDHOOD INJURIES

Within the field of injury prevention to date, psychologists have made perhaps the most headway in creating programs that demonstrate the potential for reducing injuries of children, the most vulnerable segment of the population. Following is an overview and discussion of significant issues related to behavioral injury prevention for children. The concepts presented exemplify the potential contributions of psychology to the field of injury prevention as a whole. In addition to serving an informative purpose, it is hoped that explication of these issues might illuminate broader areas within the realm of injury prevention to which psychology can contribute.

Targeting Children

A small but consistent collection of studies has shown that children who undergo intensive behavioral rehearsal and receive modeling and consistent feedback and rewards can learn relevant safety skills such as child abduction prevention (Poche, Yoder, & Miltenberger, 1988), fire exiting (Jones & Haney, 1984), and broad-based home safety skills (Peterson, 1984). However, more widely used teaching interventions exist that have often been mislabeled as behavioral programs and have met with little success. In most cases, these approaches have been purely didactic, focusing almost exclusively on providing safety information to children. Such interventions have not required children to apply newly acquired knowledge through behavioral rehearsal of new skills. Children have been taught to memorize platitudes such as "stop, drop, and roll," which they are then expected to translate into safety behaviors during actual emergencies. Unfortunately, during emergencies, children tend to enact the very same behaviors they have practiced. This can lead to ineffective coping strategies, as in one dramatic anecdote involving a young girl whose only response to her clothes catching fire was to run and desperately yell "stop, drop, and roll!" just as she had been taught.

Most safety behaviors involve a series of surprisingly complex decisions that must be made quickly and under stress (see Jones & Haney, 1984). For example, a child attempting to escape a house fire encounters several difficult decision points. After realizing that a fire is burning, the child must crawl across the floor; then feel the door for heat; and then use that information to decide among multiple alternative actions, such as calling for help or choosing one of several possible escape routes. Another example is crossing a street at a busy intersection, which is not simply a matter of knowing what red, yellow, and green lights mean. Children must make a complex series of decisions and subtle judgments about the distance, speed, and direction of traffic. Cars turning right on red or suddenly making a left turn to avoid oncoming traffic must be seen and responded to effectively to avoid tragedy. It has been estimated that crossing a road can involve as many as 26 different tasks (Rivara, Booth, Bergman, Rogers, & Weiss, 1991). Unfortunately, too many youth safety programs are delivered in the form of classroom instruction with no active involvement from the children themselves. Expecting children to learn important safety behaviors solely from a lecture is like coaching a sports team solely by diagramming plays; neither endeavor can be successful if the participants do not practice the drills.

Effective teaching interventions may begin with a purely didactic component, such as the establishment of household safety rules (e.g., "No sharp objects are to be used without adult supervision"). Indeed, research on parental socialization of child safety behaviors has found that families with more safety rules have children with fewer injuries (Peterson & Schick, 1993). Of course, these families may be more safety conscious in general or have strong consequences for disobeying safety rules. To be maximally effective, household safety rules may need to be enforced with consequences. Unfortunately, the vast majority of parents of children in middle childhood (who are at an optimal age for learning) make no environmental changes following an injury and do not use the situation as a teaching opportunity (Peterson, Gillies, Cook, Schick, & Little, 1994). Data obtained from more than 1,000 minor injury reports revealed that after an injury, 80% of parents did nothing at all to prevent a reoccurrence of that injury. Giving an educational lecture with no associated consequences, which is perhaps the weakest of parental teaching methods, was the response to only 15% of injuries. To make matters worse, children reported hearing less than one of every seven lectures that parents said they had given. Both parents and children agreed that a real consequence (e.g., not allowing a child to play ball for several days if the child breaks the rules and plays ball near the street) was given after less than 3% of injuries.

Targeting Caregivers

Didactic interventions without specific consequences have directly targeted caregivers as well as children. Generally, the interventions that use population-wide distribution of information to induce individual behavior change are relatively ineffective—even those that are well planned and have good face validity. Although well intentioned, persuasive messages on television, educational brochures, and community meetings to teach skills have not been useful in increasing use of adult seat belts or child safety restraints or in decreasing the number of children's burns or home injuries (Pless & Arsenault, 1987; Robertson, Kelley, & O'Neill, 1974).

In contrast, behavior- and skills-based interventions targeting parents in high-risk groups can effectively reduce some hazards. Voluntary skills-based intervention programs for caregivers have successfully reduced environmental hazards such as lead paint and broken windows (Gallagher et al., 1982). With court-mandated contingencies, appropriate supervision has increased in neglectful and abusive families, and environmental hazards have decreased (Lutzker, Wesch, & Rice, 1984).

Caregiver interventions are particularly effective when delivered as milestone interventions (Roberts & Brooks, 1987). That is, teaching seems to be most effective when it occurs with important life transitions such as following a divorce or just before childbirth. It is during these periods that caregivers seem most receptive to safety interventions. For instance, physicians' advice to parents about the use of safety belts is more powerful just before the birth of a child than after the parents have already developed a pattern of riding without restraints (Christophersen, 1982).

Many of the leading injury-related killers of children, especially preschoolers, may be most effectively prevented by appropriate levels of parental supervision. Garbarino (1988) made an excellent case for the premise that parental negligence in the form of failure to provide acceptable supervision and care is responsible for a sizable proportion of children's injuries. Public health advocates have traditionally disregarded the possibility that intervening to improve caregiver supervision is a feasible goal of injury prevention. However, current contingencies such as bicycle helmet laws (Bergman, Rivara, Richards, & Rogers, 1990; Cote et al., 1992; Rivara et al., 1994), massive public education campaigns, and specific penalties (e.g., removing children from the home, terminating parental rights) when parents fail to comply with safety laws, and behavioral change strategies are increasingly likely to play a role in child injury prevention efforts.

It is clear that most parents care deeply about their children's safety.

Mothers have typically reported that they view themselves as being the primary parties responsible for their children's physical safety (Peterson, Farmer, & Kashani, 1990). But what exactly constitutes "appropriate supervision" to prevent the occurrence of injuries? To explore this issue, one investigation surveyed various respondents, including family service workers, physicians, and parents (Peterson, Ewigman, & Kivlahan, 1993). Each group was asked for how many minutes they would leave children of various ages alone in a particular location with no auditory or visual contact from an adult. This question was asked in reference to several locations that varied in degree of risk (e.g., the bedroom, the kitchen, the garage). Substantial variability was found within each group. For example, some respondents felt that a 10-year-old boy could not be left unsupervised in a neighborhood with hazards such as a pond, swimming pool, or creek for even 1 minute, whereas others felt that the same child could be left in the same neighborhood unsupervised for an entire day. The primary finding of this study was that no consistent beliefs exist concerning appropriate levels of supervision, especially for children during middle childhood. Note that extreme discrepancies were found even in the most rudimentary judgments —such as how much time to leave a child alone. Currently, there is great need for a tool to aid in the assessment of parental supervision in risky situations to explicate the crucial role that caregiver supervision plays in the injury process.

BEYOND TRADITIONAL MENTAL HEALTH TREATMENT MODELS

When primary prevention efforts fail and an injury occurs, the person affected may experience life-threatening bodily harm, sudden changes in everyday functioning, and even a permanent disability. In this way, injury outcome becomes more like an acute or even a chronic illness. Medical advances in the past several decades have produced a sharp decline in mortality following an injury, but morbidity has shown a corresponding increase (Keith, 1999). Although the vast majority of injuries require only acute medical treatment and short-term recuperation, more people are surviving catastrophic injuries such as severe traumatic brain injuries (TBIs), spinal cord injuries, amputation, and extensive burns or orthopedic injuries. These life-altering events place tremendous demands on the coping and adaptation abilities of the survivor and the family (Brandt & Pope, 1997).

The typical course of treatment after a serious injury involves emergency medical stabilization, intensive care services and acute hospitalization, rehabilitation, and a return to community living (Malec & Basford, 1996). Medical rehabilitation acts as a bridge between hospital treatment and community reintegration. An interdisciplinary team consisting of the family and physicians, nurses, therapists, psychologists, and other health professionals all work together to maximize the recovery of function and minimize the disabling effects of injury. Treatment is needed not only for physical impairments and medical concerns but also for cognitive, emotional, behavioral, and social difficulties that are associated with injury. For this reason, psychologists play a key role in health care delivery and program development for individuals after a physical trauma.

AFTER AN INJURY OCCURS

Rehabilitation psychology is a specialty area focused on assessment and treatment of people who experience injuries and health-related disabilities. Opportunities for rehabilitation psychologists have grown exponentially since the 1970s (Frank, 1999; Frank, Gluck, & Buckelew, 1990). Numerous factors have contributed to this trend, including the growing number of people living with disabilities and public policy mandates such as the Rehabilitation Act of 1973 (P.L. 93-112) and the 1975 Education for All Handicapped Act (P.L. 94-142). These landmark pieces of legislation shifted the focus of trauma treatment from medical outcomes to functional outcomes for consumers of disability-related services. Instead of prioritizing traditional medical goals such as absence of disease, these laws set a standard of improved capacity to function in everyday activities and enhanced quality of life. Given the expanded focus on behavioral adaptation, psychologists became important contributors to collaborative teams that provide comprehensive rehabilitation services. From early beginnings in the 1950s, rehabilitation psychology organized into Division 22 of the American Psychological Association in 1972 and recently obtained specialty accreditation through the American Board of Professional Psychology.

Founded in clinical and counseling psychology doctoral programs, training in rehabilitation psychology requires internships and postdoctoral fellowships that go beyond traditional mental health assessment, treatment, and consultation models (Elliott & Gramling, 1990). Patterson and Hanson (1995) outlined formal areas of expertise expected of rehabilitation psychologists. These areas include knowledge about biobehavioral aspects of injury (neuroanatomy, physiology, brain–behavior relationships, and chronic pain management), disability (handicapping myths, independent living supports, environmental barriers, and consumer advocacy), rehabilitation processes (interdisciplinary collaboration and team consultation), specialized assessment strategies (neuropsychological and vocational assessments) and treatment interventions (cognitive remediation, adaptation to injury, family adjustment, team consultation for behavioral management, and vocational and educational accommodations), and ethical–legal issues that arise as the result of injury (guardianship and competency). The knowledge base of this discipline draws heavily on content from the related specialty areas of health psychology and neuropsychology.

Enabling–Disabling Process

With such advanced training, psychologists are not only capable of contributing to each individual's adaptation following injury, but they are also well suited to advance a research and health policy agenda that improves quality of life for survivors and their families. For example, the influence of psychological research and theory is quite evident in a report by the Institute of Medicine (IOM) describing directions for rehabilitation science (Brandt & Pope, 1997). For the first time, the IOM clearly rejected the notion that outcome after injury can be understood simply in terms of the person's tissue damage, number of resulting impairments, and social role changes. Instead, the report described an enabling–disabling process model in which outcome is affected by multiple person–environment interactions. It acknowledged that individuals with similar physical injuries can experience very different outcomes because of complex interactions among the characteristics of the person injured (e.g., age, time since injury) and the nature of the social and physical environment (e.g., family support, accessibility of the workplace, adequacy of health care). The IOM report concluded that the best protection against unnecessary disability is to live in an enabling environment that supports positive adaptation, encourages health maintenance, and prevents secondary complications.

This conceptualization reflects basic tenets of health psychology and behavioral science that have long guided research and practice in clinical settings (e.g., Coie et al., 1993; Wallander & Thompson, 1995). A growing body of psychological research documents risk and resilience factors and person–environment relationships affecting outcomes after catastrophic injuries (Bigler, Clark, & Farmer, 1997; Eisenberg, Glueckauf, & Zaretsky, 1999; Frank & Elliott, 2000; Tarnowski, 1994). For example, after a spinal cord injury, studies indicated fewer secondary medical complications (e.g., decubitus ulcers, urinary tract infections) among people with more effective self-reported problem-solving abilities (Herrick, Elliott, & Crow, 1994) and among those with no history of alcohol problems before the injury (Hawkins & Heinemann, 1998). Such improved outcomes are presumably related to personal cognitive and behavioral attributes that mediate compliance with self-care regimens.

In addition, environmental factors influence risk for injury (Peterson & Brown, 1994; Peterson & Stern, 1997) and outcome after injury. Among the most studied variables are characteristics of the family environment. For example, married individuals with spinal cord injuries reported more positive coping styles and greater life satisfaction than unmarried adults

(Holicky & Charlifue, 1999); family cohesiveness and SES accounted for up to 50% of the variance in children's psychological adjustment after burn injuries (Blakeney, Portman, & Rutan, 1990; Tarnowski & Brown, 1999). The enabling–disabling model of disability fits well with previous psychological investigations showing the impact of contextual factors on injury outcome and establishes a framework to guide interdisciplinary rehabilitation research and practice.

Childhood TBI

TBI provides an excellent illustration of the unique role that psychologists play in the rehabilitation of serious injury. TBI is the leading cause of death and disability in children and young adults (National Institutes of Health [NIH], 1998). More than a million young people receive this type of injury annually in the United States, with a fatality rate of 10 per 100,000 and a prevalence rate of 180 to 200 per 100,000 (Kraus, 1995). Despite the common belief that the developing brain can recover fully from early injuries, children are actually quite vulnerable to the ill effects (Taylor & Alden, 1997). Initial acute medical problems and physical impairments may resolve, but hidden disabilities often remain in the form of persistent cognitive, behavioral, and personality changes as a result of more severe injuries. Psychologists have made extensive contributions to the understanding of brain–behavior relationships in children (Bigler, 1999), cognitive and behavioral sequelae (Ewing-Cobbs, Levin, & Fletcher, 1998), the effect of age at injury on outcome (Taylor & Alden, 1997), and family impact (Taylor et al., 1999; Waaland, 1998).

Until recently, the study of TBIs in children focused almost exclusively on the impact of injury-related variables, such as injury severity or outcome, rather than on the role of other childhood and environmental factors (Farmer & Peterson, 1995; Fletcher, Levin, & Butler, 1995). An emerging body of research literature has documented the substantial effects of preinjury and family functioning on children's recovery (Max et al., 1999; Ponsford et al., 1999; Taylor et al., 1999; Woodward et al., 1999; Yeates et al., 1997). In general, these studies confirmed that more severe injuries are associated with greater cognitive and behavioral impairments, but they also indicated that premorbid learning or behavioral problems and poor family adaptation are significant predictors of worse child outcomes. For instance, Yeates and colleagues (1997) found that measures of preinjury family functioning accounted for approximately 25% of the variance in cognitive and behavioral measures 1 year after the injury, whereas injury severity accounted for 20% of the variance. Subsequent analyses also identified similar associations between child outcome and postinjury family functioning (Taylor et al., 1999). These results are consistent with the IOM model that emphasizes person–environment interactions and suggests that comprehensive, multimodal approaches to treatment after a childhood TBI may be warranted.

In clinical practice, psychologists use a range of behaviorally based interventions to improve children's learning, adjustment, and social integration in rehabilitation, school, and community settings (Farmer & Muhlenbruck, 2000; Warshausky, Kewman, & Kay, 1999; Ylvisaker, 1998). However, very limited research has examined which interventions are most efficacious after TBI for either children or adults (NIH, 1998; Warshausky et al., 1999). The available data suggest that treatment is most effective when the goal is to provide a more structured and supportive physical and social environment rather than to shape self-initiated and self-sustained adaptive behaviors among those with more significant deficits. For example, Mateer, Kernes, and Eso (1997) reported that individuals with memory problems improve in everyday functioning after systematic instruction in the use of a memory notebook; however, this improvement is not sustained without regular external monitoring of the system. Similarly, disruptive behaviors can be decreased and appropriate social interactions increased, but these changes are not maintained when structured interventions are discontinued (Cooley, Glang, & Voss, 1997; Feeney & Ylvisaker, 1995). As it is during primary injury prevention, it may be challenging to achieve self-activated behavior changes during rehabilitative treatment after an injury. More research is needed to identify ways to establish and maintain compensatory behaviors that enable more effective daily functioning and social integration.

CONCLUSION

Injury prevention efforts span a continuum ranging from purely passive to purely active strategies. The key elements of passive approaches are product and environmental modifications that, once implemented, work relatively automatically, whereas the principal components of active strategies are education and behavior change (Shields, 1997). For much of its history, the field of injury prevention has focused on the development and evaluation of strategies on the passive end of this continuum. In fact, passive approaches so dominated the field for a time that some researchers seemed to have abandoned the notion that active strategies could serve as viable means of injury prevention (e.g., Baker, 1980). However, it has recently been asserted that the failure of many early educational programs may have led to unwarranted conclusions that behavior change interventions are futile (Shields, 1997). What does seem clear is that merely providing the public with information about particular injury risks may result in knowledge gains but is unlikely to engender the pervasive and lasting behavioral changes necessary for actual injury reduction. Successful behavioral interventions are more likely to be based on sound learning theory, including some combination of modeling, behavioral rehearsal, rewards, and feedback on performance—all skills with which psychologists are well acquainted (cf. Peterson, 1984; Roberts, Fanurik, & Wilson, 1988).

New injury prevention initiatives in the United States are being developed at many levels. At the national level, the CDC has now recognized that behavioral and social sciences can make contributions to injury prevention. The CDC is now beginning to fund behaviorally oriented research on the prevention of both unintentional and intentional injuries. The Safe Kids Foundation receives corporate support for safety from the private sector (e.g., Proctor and Gamble). On the local level, behavioral pediatrics, family and community medicine, and other areas of medicine are acknowledging and promoting a behavioral approach to injury prevention. Schools, police departments, and community centers are increasing their investments in safety. Simultaneously, parents are facing greater accountability for providing safe and appropriate supervision of children.

If psychologists are to make further inroads within the field of injury prevention, it will be because they devise, evaluate, and implement intervention strategies that will further the bottom-line objective: injury reduction. However interesting they may be, esoteric research endeavors that have little direct relevance to actual injury prevention will be of limited value to the broader field. To be a major player in the injury control arena, psychological research must be geared toward practical, cost-effective injury reduction strategies.

In the field of injury treatment, psychologists have made important contributions through interventions that decrease functional impairments after an acquired disability. Applications of behavioral science have resulted in improved approaches to cognitive assessment and remediation, behavioral management and self-regulation, and individual and family adaptation to life changes. Psychological research and theory have helped to shift the traditional medical focus on physical recovery from an injury to a more comprehensive examination of medical, behavioral, social, and environmental factors that interact to determine quality of life. However, what remains is a pressing need for well-designed clinical research that can guide rehabilitation practice and promote evidence-based decision making. Fortunately, granting agencies such as the National Institute on Disability and Rehabilitation Research (NIDRR) and the CDC continue to fund basic and clinical research that will lead to enhanced outcomes for people with injury-related disabilities.

In the changing world of health care, rehabilitation psychologists have had unique professional opportunities (Frank, 1999). As members of interdisciplinary health care teams, they have had some protection from the toll that managed care has taken on many mental health professionals in independent practice. In addition, training in the scientist–practitioner model promotes leadership skills that are valued by the interdisciplinary team. These skills include the ability to encourage effective team interactions, design and develop treatment programs, understand systems of care, and measure outcomes. Such organizational and managerial abilities create a special niche for psychology in health systems that extends beyond traditional therapeutic roles. Ultimately, whether the focus is on primary injury prevention or injury treatment, the aim of the psychologist is the same —to promote health and to enable optimal levels of functioning in everyday environments.

REFERENCES

Association for the Advancement of Automotive Medicine. (1990). *The abbreviated injury scale, 1990 revision.* Des Plaines, IL: Author.

Baker, S. P. (1980). Prevention of childhood injuries. *Medical Journal of Australia, 1,* 466–470.

Baker, S. P., O'Neill, B., Ginsburg, M. J., & Li, G. (1992). *The injury fact book* (2nd ed.). Lexington, MA: Lexington Books.

Baker, S. P., Robertson, L. S., & O'Neill, B. (1974). Fatal pedestrian collisions: Driver negligence. *American Journal of Public Health, 64,* 318–325.

Baker, S. P., & Waller, A. E. (1989). *Childhood injury: State-by-state mortality facts.* Washington, DC: National Maternal and Child Health Clearinghouse.

Barlow, B., Nicmirska, M., Gandhi, R. P., & Leblanc, W. (1983). Ten years of experience with falls from a height in children. *Journal of Pediatric Surgery, 18,* 509–511.

Barss, P., Smith, G., Baker, S., & Mohan, D. (1998). *Injury prevention: An international perspective: Epidemiology, surveillance, and policy.* Oxford, England: Oxford University Press.

Beautrais, A. L., Fergusson, D. M., & Shannon, D. T. (1987). Accidental poisoning in the first three years of life. *Australian Pediatric Journal, 18,* 328–342.

Belar, C. (1997). Clinical health psychology: A specialty for the 21st century. *Health Psychology, 16,* 411–416.

Bergman, A. B., Rivara, F. P., Richards, D. D., & Rogers, L. W. (1990). The Seattle children's bicycle helmet campaign. *American Journal of Diseases of Children, 144,* 727–731.

Bigler, E. D. (1999). Neuroimaging in pediatric traumatic head injury: Diagnostic considerations and relationships to neurobehavioral outcome. *Journal of Head Trauma Rehabilitation, 14,* 406–423.

Bigler, E. D., Clark, E., & Farmer, J. E. (Eds.). (1997). *Childhood traumatic brain injury.* Austin, TX: PRO-ED.

Blakeney, P., Portman, S., & Rutan, R. (1990). Familial values as factors influencing long term psychological adjustment of children after severe burn. *Journal of Burn Care and Rehabilitation, 11,* 472–475.

Brandt, E. N., & Pope, A. M. (1997). *Enabling America: Assessing the role of rehabilitation science and engineering.* Washington, DC: National Academy Press.

Cameron, I. D., & Quine, S. (1994). External hip protectors: Likely non-compliance among high risk elderly people living in the community. *Archives of Gerontology and Geriatrics, 19,* 273–281.

Chesney, M. A. (1993). Health psychology in the 21st century: Acquired immunodeficiency syndrome as a harbinger of things to come. *Health Psychology, 12,* 259–268.

Christophersen, E. R. (1982). Incorporating behavioral pediatrics into primary care. *Pediatric Clinics of North America, 29,* 261–296.

Clark, D. E., Katz, M. S., & Campbell, S. M. (1992). Decreasing mortality and morbidity rates after the institution of a statewide burn program. *Journal of Burn Care and Rehabilitation, 13,* 261–270.

Clarke, M. A., & Walton, W. W. (1979). Effect of safety packaging on aspirin ingestion by children. *Pediatrics, 63,* 687–693.

Coats, T. J., & Allen, M. (1991). Baby walker injuries—A continuing problem. *Archives of Emergency Medicine, 8,* 52–55.

Coie, J. D., Watt, N. F., West, S. G., Hawkins, J. D., Asarnow, J. R., Markman, H. J., et al. (1993). The science of prevention: A conceptual framework and some directions for a national research program. *American Psychologist, 48,* 1013–1022.

Consumer Product Safety Commission. (1994). Baby walkers: Advance notice of proposal rulemaking. *Federal Register, 59,* 39306–39311.

Cooley, E. A., Glang, A., & Voss, J. (1997). Making connections: Helping children with ABI build friendships. In A. Glang, G. H. S. Singer, & B. Todis (Eds.), *Students with acquired brain injury: The school's response* (pp. 255–275). Baltimore, MD: Paul H. Brookes.

Cooper, J. M., Widness, J. A., & O'Shea, J. S. (1988). Pilot evaluation of instructing parents of newborns about poison prevention programs. *American Journal of Disease in Childhood, 142*(6), 627–629.

Cote, T. R., Sacks, J. J., Lambert-Huber, D. A., Dannenberg, A. L., Kresnow, M. J., Lipsitz, C. M., et al. (1992). Bicycle helmet use among Maryland children: Effect of legislation and education. *Pediatrics, 89,* 1216–1220.

DiLillo, D., & Tremblay, G. C. (2001). Maternal and child reports of behavioral compensation in response to safety equipment usage. *Journal of Pediatric Psychology, 26,* 175–184.

Division of Injury Control. (1990). Childhood injuries in the United States. *American Journal of Diseases of Children, 144,* 627–646.

Eisenberg, M. G., Glueckauf, R. L., & Zaretsky, H. H. (Eds.). (1999). *Medical aspects of disability: A handbook for the rehabilitation professional* (2nd ed.). New York: Springer.

Elliott, T. R., & Gramling, S. E. (1990). Psychologists and rehabilitation: New roles and old training models. *American Psychologist, 45,* 762–765.

Erbaugh, S. J. (1986). Effects of aquatic training on swimming skill development of preschool children. *Perceptual and Motor Skills, 62,* 439–446.

Evans, L. (1990). Restraint effectiveness, occupant ejection from cars, and fatality reductions. *Accident Analysis and Prevention, 22,* 167–175.

Ewing-Cobb, L., Levin, H. S., & Fletcher, J. M. (1998). Neuropsychological sequelae after pediatric traumatic brain injury: Advances since 1985. In M. Ylvisaker (Ed.), *Traumatic brain injury rehabilitation: Children and adolescents* (2nd ed., pp. 11–26). Woburn, MA: Butterworth-Heinemann.

Farmer, J. E., & Muhlenbruck, L. (2000). Pediatric neuropsychology. In R. G. Frank & T. R. Elliott (Eds.), *Handbook of rehabilitation psychology* (pp. 377–397). Washington, DC: American Psychological Association.

Farmer, J. E., & Peterson, L. (1995). Pediatric traumatic brain injury: Promoting successful school reentry. *School Psychology Review, 24,* 230–243.

Feeney, T. J., & Ylvisaker, M. (1995). Choice and routine: Antecedent behavioral interventions for adolescents with severe traumatic brain injury. *Journal of Head Trauma Rehabilitation, 10,* 67–86.

Ferguson, S. A. (1996). *Update on airbag performance in the United States: Benefits and problems.* Washington, DC: Insurance Institute for Highway Safety.

Fergusson, D. M., Horwood, L. J., & Shannon, F. T. (1983). The safety standards of domestic swimming pools 1980–1982. *New Zealand Medical Journal, 96,* 93–95.

Fife, D., & Barancik, J. I. (1985). Northeastern Ohio Trauma Study III: Incidence of fractures. *Annals of Emergency Medicine, 14,* 244–248.

Fingerhut, L. A., & Warner M. (1997). *Injury chartbook. Health, United States, 1996–97.* Hyattsville, MD: National Center for Health Statistics.

Fisher, J. C., Wells, J. A., Fulwider, B. T., & Edgerton, M. T. (1977). Do we need a burn severity grading system? *Journal of Trauma, 17,* 252–255.

Fletcher, J. M., Levin, H. S., & Butler, I. J. (1995). Neurobehavioral effects of brain injury on children: Hydrocephalus, traumatic brain injury, and cerebral palsy. In M. C. Roberts (Ed.), *Handbook of pediatric psychology* (2nd cd., pp. 362–383). New York: Guilford Press.

Frank, R. G. (1999). Rehabilitation psychology: We zigged when we should have zagged. *Rehabilitation Psychology, 44,* 36–51.

Frank, R. G., & Elliott, T. R. (Eds.). (2000). *Handbook of rehabilitation psychology.* Washington, DC: American Psychological Association.

Frank, R. G., Gluck, J. P., & Buckelew, S. P. (1990). Rehabilitation: Psychology's greatest opportunity? *American Psychologist, 45,* 757–761.

Gallagher, S. S., Guyer, B., Kotelchuck, M., Bass, J., Lovejoy, F. H., Jr., McLoughlin, E., et al. (1982). A strategy for the reduction of childhood injuries in Massachusetts: SCIPP. *New England Journal of Medicine, 307,* 1015–1019.

Garbarino, J. (1988). Preventing childhood injury: Developmental and mental health issues. *American Journal of Orthopsychiatry, 58,* 25–36.

Graham, J. D., & Segui-Gomez, M. (1997). Airbags: Benefits and risks. *Risk in Perspective, 5,* 1–4.

Haddon, W. H., Jr. (1970). On the escape of tigers: An ecological note. *Technology Review, 72,* 3–7.

Haddon, W. H., Jr. (1980). Advances in the epidemiology of injuries as a basis for public policy. *Public Health Reports, 95,* 411–421.

Hawkins, D. A., & Heinemann, A. W. (1998). Substance abuse and medical complications following spinal cord injury. *Rehabilitation Psychology, 43,* 219–231.

Heck, A., Collins, J., & Peterson, L. (in press). Decreasing children's risk taking on the playground. *Journal of Applied Behavioral Analysis.*

Hermann, R., & Stormer, A. (1985). Results of recent research on life jackets. *Journal of Royal Naval Medical Services, 71,* 161–166.

Herrick, S., Elliot, T. R., & Crow, F. (1994). Self-appraised problem solving skills and the prediction of secondary complications among persons with spinal cord injuries. *Journal of Clinical Psychology in Medical Settings, 1,* 269–283.

Hillman, M., Adams, J., & Whitelegg, J. (1991). *One false move . . . : A study of children's independent mobility.* London: Policy Studies Institute.

Hogue, C. C. (1982). Injury in late life. Vol. 1. Epidemiology. *Journal of the American Geriatric Society, 30,* 183–190.

Holicky, R., & Charlifue, S. (1999). Aging and spinal cord injury: The impact of spousal support. *Disability and Rehabilitation, 21,* 250–257.

Holmes, G. A., & Jones, R. T. (1996). Fire evacuation skills: Cognitive behavior versus computer-mediated instruction. *Fire Technology, First Quarter,* 51–64.

Howland, J., & Hingson, R. (1988). Alcohol as a risk factor for drownings: A review of the literature (1950–1985). *Accident Analysis and Prevention, 20,* 19–25.

Howland, J., Smith, G. S., Mangione, T., Hingson, R., DeJong, W., & Bell, N. (1993). Missing the boat on drinking and boating. *Journal of the American Medical Association, 270,* 91–92.

Jones, R. T., & Haney, J. I. (1984). A primary preventive approach to the acquisition and maintenance of fire emergency responding: Comparison of external and self-instruction strategies. *Journal of Community Psychology, 12,* 180–191.

Jones, R. T., Kazdin, A. E., & Haney, J. I. (1981). Social validation and training of emergency fire safety skills for potential injury prevention and life saving. *Journal of Applied Behavior Analysis, 14,* 249–260.

Karels, T. R. (Ed.). (1992). *Briefing package—baby walker petition HP 92-2.* Washington, DC: U.S. Consumer Product Safety Commission.

Karpf, R. S., & Williams, A. F. (1983). Teenage drivers and motor vehicle deaths. *Accident Analysis and Prevention, 15,* 55–63.

Keith, R. A. (1999). Comprehensive rehabilitation: Themes, models, and issues. In M. G. Eisenberg, R. L. Glueckauf, & H. H. Zaretsky (Eds.), *Medical aspects of disability: A handbook for the rehabilitation professional* (2nd ed., pp. 3–25). New York: Springer.

Kraus, J. F. (1995). Epidemiological features of brain injury in children: Occurrence, children at risk, causes and manner of injury, severity, and outcomes. In S. H. Broman & M. E. Michel (Eds.), *Traumatic head injury in children* (pp. 22–39). New York: Oxford University Press.

Lauritzen, J. B., Petersen, M. M., & Lund, B. (1993). Effect of external hip protectors on hip fractures. *Lancet, 341,* 11–13.

Litovitz, T. L., Schmitz, B. F., & Holm, K. C. (1989). 1988 annual report of the American Association of Poison Control Centers National Data Collection System. *American Journal of Emergency Medicine, 7,* 495–545.

Lutzker, J. R., Wesch, D., & Rice, J. M. (1984). A review of Project "12-Ways": An ecobehavioral approach to the treatment and prevention of child abuse and neglect. *Advancement of Behavior Research and Therapy, 6,* 63–73.

Malec, J. F., & Basford, J. S. (1996). Postacute brain injury rehabilitation. *Archives of Physical Medicine and Rehabilitation, 77,* 198–207.

Mateer, C. A., Kerns, K. A., & Eso, K. L. (1997). Management of attention and memory disorders following traumatic brain injury. In E. D. Bigler, E. Clark, & J. E. Farmer (Eds.), *Childhood traumatic brain injury* (pp. 153–175). Austin, TX: PRO-ED.

Max, J. E., Roberts, M. A., Koele, S. L., Lindgren, S. D., Robin, D. A., Arndt, S., et al. (1999). Cognitive outcome in children and adolescents following severe traumatic brain injury: Influence of psychosocial, psychiatric, and injury-related variables. *Journal of the International Neuropsychological Society, 5,* 58–68.

National Academy of Sciences. (1985). *Injury in America: A continuing public health problem.* Washington, DC: National Academy Press.

National Highway Traffic Safety Administration. (1996). *Traffic safety facts 1995: A compilation of motor vehicle crash data from the Fatal Accident Reporting System and the General Estimates System.* Washington, DC: Author.

National Institutes of Health. (1998). *Consensus statement on rehabilitation of persons with traumatic brain injury* (Proceedings from the October 26–28, 1998 NIH Consensus Development Conference). Bethesda, MD: Author.

National Safety Council. (1988). *Accident facts, 1988.* Chicago: Author.

Patterson, D. R., & Hanson, S. L. (1995). Joint Division 22 and ACRM guidelines for postdoctoral training in rehabilitation psychology. *Rehabilitation Psychology, 40,* 299–310.

Peterson, L. (1984). The "Safe at Home" game: Training comprehensive prevention skills in latchkey children. *Behavior Modification, 8,* 474–494.

Peterson, L., & Brown, D. (1994). Integrating child injury and abuse–neglect research: Common histories, etiologies, and solutions. *Psychological Bulletin, 116,* 293–315.

Peterson, L., Ewigman, B., & Kivlahan, C. (1993). Judgments regarding appropriate child supervision to prevent injury: The role of environmental risk and child age. *Child Development, 64,* 934–950.

Peterson, L., Farmer, J., & Kashani, J. H. (1990). Parental injury prevention endeavors: A function of health beliefs? *Health Psychology, 9*, 177–191.

Peterson, L., Gillies, R., Cook, S., Schick, B., & Little, T. (1994). Developmental patterns of expected consequences for simulated bicycle injury events. *Health Psychology, 13*, 218–223.

Peterson, L., Heiblum, N., & Saldana, L. (1996). Validation of the Minor Injury Severity Scale: Expert and novice quantification of minor injury. *Behavior Therapy, 27*, 515–530.

Peterson, L., & Schick, B. (1993). Empirically derived injury prevention rules. *Journal of Applied Behavioral Analysis, 26*, 451–460.

Peterson, L., & Stern, B. L. (1997). Family processes and child risk for injury. *Behaviour Research and Therapy, 35*, 179–190.

Pettigrew, L. E., Wilson, J. T., & Teasdale, G. M. (1998). Assessing disability after head injury: Improved use of the Glasgow Outcome Scale. *Journal of Neurosurgery, 89*, 939–943.

Pitt, W. R., & Balanda, K. P. (1991). Childhood drowning and near-drowning in Brisbane: The contribution of domestic pools. *Medical Journal of Australia, 154*, 661–665.

Pless, I. B., & Arsenault, L. (1987). The role of health education in the prevention of injuries to children. *Journal of Social Issues, 43*, 87–104.

Poche, C., Yoder, P., & Miltenberger, R. (1988). Teaching self-protection to children using television techniques. *Journal of Applied Behavior Analysis, 21*(3), 253–261.

Ponsford, J., Willmott, C., Rothwell, A., Cameron, P., Ayton, G., Nelms, R., et al. (1999). Cognitive and behavioral outcome following mild traumatic head injury in children. *Journal of Head Trauma Rehabilitation, 14*, 360–372.

Present, P. (1987). *Child drowning study: A report on the epidemiology of drownings in residential pools to children under age five*. Washington, DC: U.S. Consumer Product Safety Commission.

Province, M. A., Hadley, E. C., Hornbrook, M. C., Lipsitz, L. A., Miller, J. P., Mulrow, C. D., et al. (1995). The effects of exercise on falls in elderly patients. A preplanned meta-analysis of the FICSIT Trials. Frailty and injuries: Cooperative studies of intervention techniques. *Journal of the American Medical Association, 273*, 1341–1347.

Quan, L., Gore, E. J., Wentz, K., Allen, J., & Novack, A. H. (1989). Ten-year study of pediatric drownings and near-drownings in King County, Washington: Lessons in injury prevention. *Pediatrics, 83*, 1035–1040.

Rice, D. P., & MacKenzie, E. J. (1989). *Cost of injury in the United States: A report to Congress*. San Francisco: Institute for Health and Aging, University of California & Injury Prevention Center, Johns Hopkins University.

Rivara, F. P. (1982). Epidemiology of childhood injuries. *American Journal of Diseases of Children, 136*, 399–405.

Rivara, F. P. (1990). Child pedestrian injury in the United States. *American Journal of Diseases of Children, 144*, 692–696.

Rivara, F., Booth, C., Bergman, A., Rogers, L., & Weiss, J. (1991). Prevention of pedestrian injuries to children: Effectiveness of a school training program. *Pediatrics, 88,* 770–775.

Rivara, F. P., Thompson, D. C., Thompson, R. S., Rogers, L. W., Alexander, B., Felix, D., et al. (1994). The Seattle Children's Bicycle Helmet Campaign: Changes in helmet use and head injury admissions. *Pediatrics, 93,* 567–569.

Roberts, M. C., & Brooks, P. H. (1987). Children's injuries: Issues in prevention and public policy. *Journal of Social Issues, 43,* 1–12.

Roberts, M. C., Fanurik, D., & Wilson, D. R. (1988). A community program to reward children's use of seat belts. *American Journal of Community Psychology, 16,* 395–407.

Robertson, L. S., Kelley, A. B., & O'Neill, B. (1974). A controlled study of the effect of television messages on safety belt use. *American Journal of Public Health, 64,* 1071–1080.

Rodgers, G. B. (1996). The safety effects of child-resistant packaging for oral prescription drugs: Two decades of experience. *Journal of the American Medical Association, 275*(21), 1661–1665.

Rodriguez, J. G. (1990). Childhood injuries in the United States: A priority issue. *American Journal of Diseases of Children, 144,* 625–626.

Runyan, C. W., Bangdiwala, S. I., Linzer, M. A., Sacks, J. J., & Butts, J. (1992). Risk factors for fatal residential fires. *New England Journal of Medicine, 37,* 859–863.

Scheidt, P. C. (1988). Behavioral research toward prevention of childhood injury. *American Journal of Diseases of Children, 142,* 612–617.

Shields, J. (1997). Have we become so accustomed to being passive that we've forgotten to be active? *Injury Prevention, 3,* 243–246.

Smith, G. A., Bowman, M. J., Luria, J. W., & Shields, B. J. (1996). Babywalker-related injuries continue despite warning labels and public education. *Pediatrics* [On-line serial], *100*(2). Retrieved from http://www.pediatrics.org/. Retrieved on March 30, 2000.

Spielberger, C. D., & Frank, R. G. (1992). Injury Control: A promising field for psychologists. *American Psychologist, 47,* 1029–1030.

Tarnowski, K. J. (Ed.). (1994). *Behavioral aspects of pediatric burns.* New York: Plenum Press.

Tarnowski, K. J., & Brown, R. T. (1999). Burn injuries. In A. J. Goreczny & M. Hersen (Eds.), *Handbook of pediatric and adolescent health psychology* (pp. 115–126). Boston, MA: Allyn & Bacon.

Taylor, H. G., & Alden, J. (1997). Age-related differences in outcomes following childhood brain insults: An introduction and overview. *Journal of the International Neuropsychological Society, 3,* 555–567.

Taylor, H. G., Yeates, K. O., Wade, S. L., Drotar, D., Klein, S. K., & Stancin, T. (1999). Influences on first-year recovery from traumatic brain injury in children. *Neuropsychology, 13,* 76–89.

Tinetti, M. E., Doucette, J., Claus, E., & Marottoli, R. (1995). Risk factors for serious injury during falls by older persons in the community. *Journal of the American Geriatric Society, 43*, 1214–1221.

Transport and Road Research Laboratory. (1991). *Towards safer roads in developing countries: A guide for planners and engineers.* Crowthorne, Berkshire, UK: Overseas Unit, Transport and Road Research Laboratory.

U.S. Coast Guard. (1995). *Draft regulatory evaluation: Recreational inflatable personal flotation device standards.* Washington, DC: Author.

Vernberg, K., Culver-Dickinson, P., & Spyker, D. A. (1984). The deterrent effect of poison-warning stickers. *American Journal of Disease in Childhood, 138,* 1018–1020.

Waaland, P. K. (1998). Families of children with traumatic brain injury. In M. Ylvisaker (Ed.), *Traumatic brain injury rehabilitation: Children and adolescents* (pp. 345–368). Boston, MA: Butterworth-Heinemann.

Wallander, J. L., & Thompson, R. J. (1995). Psychosocial adjustment of children with chronic physical conditions. In M. C. Roberts (Ed.), *Handbook of pediatric psychology* (2nd ed., pp. 124–141). New York: Guilford Press.

Walton, W. W. (1982). An evaluation of the Poison Prevention Packaging Act. *Pediatrics, 69*, 363–370.

Warshausky, S., Kewman, D., & Kay, J. (1999). Empirically supported psychological and behavioral therapies in pediatric rehabilitation of TBI. *Journal of Head Trauma Rehabilitation, 14*, 373–383.

Wilson, M. H., Baker, S. P., Teret, S. P., Shock, S., & Garbarino, J. (1991). *Saving children: A guide to injury prevention.* New York: Oxford University Press.

Wintemute, G. J. (1990). Childhood drowning and near-drowning in the United States. *American Journal of Diseases of Children, 144*, 663–669.

Woodward, H., Winterhalther, K., Donders, J., Hackbarth, R., Kuldanek, A., & Sanfilippo, D. (1999). Prediction of neurobehavioral outcome 1–5 years post pediatric traumatic head injury. *Journal of Head Trauma Rehabilitation, 14*, 351–359.

Yeates, K. O., Taylor, H. G., Drotar, D., Wade, S. L., Klein, S., Stancin, T., et al. (1997). Preinjury family environment as a determinant of recovery from traumatic brain injuries in school-age children. *Journal of the International Neuropsychological Society, 3*, 617–630.

Yeaton, W. H., & Bailey, J. S. (1978). Teaching pedestrian safety skills to small children: An analysis and one year follow-up. *Journal of Applied Behavior Analysis, 11*, 315–329.

Ylvisaker, M. (Ed.). (1998). *Traumatic brain injury rehabilitation: Children and adolescents.* Boston, MA: Butterworth-Heinemann.

AUTHOR INDEX

Numbers in italics refer to listings in the reference sections.

Bucciarelli, R. L., 506, *526*
Buchanan, I., 117, *131, 133*
Buchanan, L., 81, *90*
Bucher, H. C., 19, *35*
Buck, G. M., *525*
Buckalew, L. W., 542, *550*
Buckelew, S. P., 415, 422, 425, 426, *431, 434, 438, 439–440, 441,* 571, *577*
Buckley, L. P., 445, *478*
Buckloh, L., 112, *136*
Buckwald, S., *517*
Budzynski, T. H., 71, *90*
Buescher, K. L., 422, 424, *438*
Bukowski, W. M., 113, *136–137, 137*
Bulatovic, A., 85, 86, *90*
Bull, M. J., *518*
Bulloch, B., *337*
Bunce, H., 258, *279*
Burbach, D. J., 114, *139*
Burchett, B. M., 16, *35*
Burchinal, M., *140*
Burg, M., 206, *233*
Burgess, C., 248, *280*
Burgess, E. D., 309, *338*
Burghen, G. A., 71, *91*
Burgio, K. L., 329, 330, 332, *337*
Buring, J. E., *235*
Burish, T. G., 62, 105, *131*
Burke, G., 464, *478*
Burke, M., *281*
Burket, L. W., 14, *35*
Burket, R. C., 124, *131*
Burkhart, M. T., 69, 70, *89*
Burkhauser, R. V., 415, *438*
Burman, W. J., 242, 243, *273*
Burnette, M. M., 357, *365*
Burns, D. G., 284, *299*
Burns, J. W., 411, *431*
Burns, K. A., 348, *366*
Burns, L. H., 315, *341*
Burns, P. A., 332, *337*
Burns, W. J., 348, *366*
Burt, D. B., 470, *475*
Busse, W. W., 248, *273*
Bussing, R., 124, *131*, 254, 255, 257, *273*
Butler, A. C., 159, 160, *168*
Butler, G. E., 82, *96*
Butler, I. J., 572, *577*
Butler, J. R., 242, *273*
Butler, R., 112, *136*
Butow, P. N., 47, *57*

Butters, N., *200*
Buunk, B., 52, *63*
Byers, T. E., *300*
Bylund, B., 488, 491, *517*
Byrne, P. J., 489, *527*

Cacioppo, J. T., 48, *56*
Cadman, D., 256, *273*
Cadoret, R., 540, 541, *550*
Caine, E. D., 184, *197*
Caldwell, D. S., 422, 423, 435, *436*
Caldwell, S., 103, *135*
Caleman, R. E., *233*
Calhoun, K. S., *168*
Califf, R. M., *237–238*
Callahan, E. J., 357, *365*
Callahan, L., 399, 414, 419, *432, 433, 437, 441*
Callanan, C., 522, *526*
Cambach, W., 247, *273–274*
Camerlengo, A., 345, 348, 358, 364, *366*
Cameron, I. D., 560, 571, *576*
Cameron, P., 572, *580*
Camilleri, M., 284, 286, *300*
Camitta, B. M., 108, *135*
Campbell, D., 488, *527*
Campbell, M. K., 497, *517–518*
Campbell, P. B., 492, *518*
Campbell, R. M., 446, *474*
Campbell, S. K., *522*
Campbell, S. M., 77, 98, 563, *576*
Campis, L., 458, *475*
Canady, A. I., 466, *476*
Candelora, J., *34*
Cannata, R., 322, *341*
Canter, A., 7, 8, *27*
Cantwell, D., *169*
Capell, H., *230*
Capelli, M., 75, *90*
Capitano, J. P., 11, *27*
Caplin, D. L., 263, *273*
Cappello, N., *139*
Capuzzo, E., *370*
Cardish, R. J., 292, *302*
Carette, S., 427, *432*
Carey, M. P., 19, *27*, 105, *131*, 317, 319, 320, 322, 323, 336, *342*
Carlyle, M. J., *517–518*
Carmichael, S., 349, 352, *366*
Carney, R. M., 209, *230,* 232–230, 549, *550*

Chin, H. G., 361, 362, *370*
Chinnock, R., *474*
Chmiel, J., 10, *31*
Chodoff, P., 105, *133*
Choi, P. Y., 326, *337*
Choo, S., 490, *530*
Christensen, A., 308, 309, 310, 327, *337*
Christophersen, E. R., 76, *90*, 568, *576*
Christopherson, E. R., 376, *394*
Chuang, A., *475*
Chung, M. C., 469–470, *479*
Ciampi, A., *201*
Cibrorowski, J., 126, *140–141*
Cicchetti, D., 160, *168–169*
Cilley, R. E., 447, *473*
Cimbolic, P., 372, *396*
Cioffi, D., 534, 536, *550*
Cipriani, R., *396*
Cjakowski, S. M., 207, *237*
Clapp, D., *338*
Clark, C. M., 117, *137*
Clark, D. A., *527*
Clark, D. E., 563, *576*
Clark, E., 571, 572, *575*
Clark, L. A., 538, *553*
Clark, N. M., 267, *274, 276*
Clark, R. A., 258, *278*
Clark, S., 405, *432*
Clarke, A., 383, *396*, 415, 429, *432*
Clarke, G. N., 161, *170*
Clarke, M. A., 561, *576*
Clarke, W. L., 70, *90, 99*
Clarkson, T. B., 208, *234*
Clarren, S. K., 458, *480*
Claus, E. B., 440, 559, *581*
Cleary, P. D., 18, *32*
Cleft Palate Foundation, 451, 453, *475*
Clement, D. L., *230*
Clement, S., 68, *90*
Clemmey, P., 419, *437*
Cliff, L. D., *198*
Clifton, R. K., 494, *520*
Clopper, R. R., 85, 88, 93, *97*
Clouse, R. E., 72, 93, 292, *303*
Clover, R. D., 7, *27*
Cluff, L. E., 7, *27*
Cnattingius, S., 349, 353, 362, 366, *367*
Coates, A. S., 47, *57*
Coates, C. F., 491, *516*
Coates, T. J., 11, 18, 19, *27, 33*
Coats, T. J., 559, *576*
Cobb, J. L., *199*, 219, *235*

Cobb, S., 218, 219, *230*
Coda, R., 11, 12, *35*
Coddington, R. D., 123, *134*
Code, C., 182, *198*
Coen, C., *520*
Coffield, K. E., 542, *550*
Coffman, J. D., 224, 226, *230*
Cogen, R., 8, *28*
Cohen, C., 412, *432*
Cohen, D., 104, *141*
Cohen, F., 15, *31*
Cohen, H. J., 16, *35*
Cohen, H. S., *521*
Cohen, L., 43, 44, *56*
Cohen, M. J., 117, *132, 138*
Cohen, N., 50, *56*
Cohen, R. D., *231*
Cohen, S., 5, 7, 8, 13, 24, 27, 28, 30,
     40, 43, 50, 57, 59, 88, 90, 207,
     229, 230, 497, *518*
Cohen, Z., 292, *299*
Cohen-Cole, S., 8, *27*
Cohn, D. L., 242, *273*
Cohn, K., 537, *550*
Coie, J. D., 571, *576*
Colcher, S. D., 295, *299*
Colder, M., 536, *552*
Cole, J., 71, *89*
Cole, L. C., *198*
Cole, S. W., 11, 13, *28, 33*
Colegrove, R. W., Jr., 126, *132*
Coleman, R. E., *230*
Colgan, S., 289, *299*
Collaborative Group on Preterm Birth
     Prevention, 354, *366*
Collin, M., 490, *528*
Collins, J., 559, *578*
Colonna, L., *370*
Comite, F., *97*
Compass, B. E., 45, 58, 422, *432*
Compton, P. G., *97*
Conant, M., 15, 18, *28, 31*
Conerly, S., *393–394*
Conlon, M., 500, *519*
Conner, M., 43, *57*
Constantinou, J., *515, 519*
Consumer Products Safety Commission,
     564, *576*
Contant, C., *136*
Conte, P. M., 128–129, *131, 140*
Conte, R. A., 259, *277*
Conway, R., 415, *431*

Easterling, D. V., 537, *551*
Eastewood, M. A., 289, *301*
Eastwood, J., 289, *301*
Eaton, M., 347, 348, *369*
Eaton, W. W., 41, *58*
Eberly, S., 207, *230*
Eckl, C. L., 122, 124, *132, 133*
Eckman, J., 117, *131, 133*
Eden, S., 403, *430*
Edens, M. J., 512, *519*
Edgerton, M. T., 557, *577*
Edlund, B., 53, *63*
Edmonds, J., 488, *525*
Edwards, A. D., 491, *527*
Edwards, F. C., 293, *305*
Egan, E., *517*
Egger, M. A., *437*
Ehrenkranz, R. A., 491, 492, *524, 528*
Ehrhardt, A., 88, 90, *476*
Ehrlich, A., 296, *303*
Eiben, R., 489, *521*
Eigen, H., 75, *95*
Einat, G., 497, *523*
Eisenberg, D. M., 221, *231*
Eisenberg, M. G., 571, *576*
Eiser, C., 75, *90*
Eisner, M. D., 252, *273*
Eitzman, D. V., 506, 512, *519, 526, 527*
Ekelman, B. L., 445, *474*
Ekstrand, M., 11, *27*
Elashoff, R., *58*
Elbaz, M., *230*
Elbert, J. C., 156, *170*
Elder, N., *366*
Elder-Danda, C., *99*
Eliahou, H. E., 220, *236*
Eliason, M. J., 458, *476*
Elkin, E., *476*
Ell, K., 46, *58*
Ellenberg, J. H., 192, *200*
Elliot, E., 492, *521*
Elliott, C. H., 103–104, 104, *134, 134–135, 135*
Elliott, M. J., 445, *476*
Elliott, T. R., 570, 571, *576, 571, 577, 578*
Ellis, C. N., *394*
Ellis, E., 260, *279*
Ellis, F. D., *518*
Ellis, N. C., 461, 462, *473, 478*
Ellner, J., 14, *35*
El-Mallakh, R. S., 356, *366*

Elston, R. C., *232*
Elswick, K. K., *338*
Elving, L. B., 329, *338*
Elwood, M., 41, *61*
Embury, S. H., 111, *133*
Emery, C. F., 213, *230*
Emmons, K. M., 42, 43, 48, *57, 61, 279*
Emmott, S. D., 285, *304*
Emms, E. M., 386, *396*
Endo, N., 471, *479*
Endriga, M. C., 458, 476, *479–480, 480*
Eneroth, P., 375, *393*
Engel, B. T., 329, 330, 332, *337*
Engel, G. L., 144, *169, 283, 291, 301*
Engel, J., Jr., 189, 190, *197, 201*
Engle, R. G., 128–129, *140*
Engquist, G., 537, *551*
Engstrom, P. F., 48, *62*
Ennes, H., *303*
Ennis, M., *59*
Epcar, J. T., *521*
Epping-Jordan, J. E., 45, *58*
Epstein, L. H., 44, *60, 77, 78, 90, 91*
Epstein, R. S., 265, *275*
Epstein, W., 418, *430*
Erbaugh, S. J., 562, *577*
Erdman, A. J., 381, *393*
Erdman, R. A., *481*
Eremin, O., 50, *57*
Erfurt, J. C., *233*
Erhrlich, R. M., 83, *96*
Erick, M. A., 355, *369*
Erickson, B., 152, *169*
Eriksson, O., 362, *366*
Erkinjuntti, T., *200*
Erlandson, D. M., 417, *433*
Ernst, D., 40, *63*
Escalona, S. K., 497, *519*
Esdaile, J. M., 415, *432*
Eser, M., 219, *231*
Eshleman, S., 150, *170*
Esler, M., 218, *234*
Esplen, M. J., 297, *302*
Esterlitz, J., *369*
Estes, S. A., 382, *393*
Etches, P., 489, *527*
Eurelings-Bontekoe, E. H. M., 355, 356, *368*
Evans, A. E., 108, *136*
Evans, A. S., 8, *31*
Evans, D. A., 179, *198, 274*
Evans, D. L., 10, *28–29*

Hack, M., 487, 488, 489, 491, 497, *520–521, 529*

Hackbarth, R., *582*

Hackett, T. P., 375, *396*

Haddon, W. H., Jr., 564, *578*

Hadler, N. M., 405, *434*

Hadley, E. C., 559, *580*

Hafen, B. Q., 548, 549, *550*

Haggerty, R. J., 6, *33*

Hagglund, K. J., 410, 426, *434*

Hahlweg, K., 257, *277*

Hahn, J. A., *281*

Hahn, R. A., 541, 543, *550*

Haimes, A., 84, *91*

Hain, J., 8, *28*

Haith, M. M., 259, *280*

Hakami, M. K., *95*

Hakanson, D. O., *527*

Hale, M. S., 356, *366*

Halfon, N., 254, 256, *273, 279*

Halinda, E., *517–518*

Hall, F., 361, *367*

Hallett, C. C., 410, *431*

Hallgren, R., 411, *434*

Halliday, G. M., 182, *198*

Halmi, K. A., 152, *171*

Halpern, M. T., 242, *279*

Halsey, C. L., 489, *521*

Haltiner, A., 191, *198*

Halton, H., 494, *520*

Hamburg, D. A., 105, *133*

Hamburger, M. E., *30*

Hamilton, J. A., 326, 338, *339*

Hamilton, J. D., 16, *35*

Hamlett, K. W., 74, 75, 98, 254, 255, *276*

Hammersley-Maercklin, G., 75, *90*

Hammond, G. D., *137*

Hamovitch, M., 46, *58*

Hanahan, D., 37, *59*

Hance, M., 209, *232–230*

Handford, H. A., 125, *133, 136*

Haney, J. I., 563, 566, 567, *578*

Haney, T. J., *237–238*

Hanigan, W. C., 491, *521*

Hanno, P. M., 310, *339*

Hansen, D., *368*

Hansen, L. A., *200*

Hanson, C. L., 71, *91*

Hanson, M. M., *233*

Hanson, S., 71, *91*, 570, *579*

Hanson, V., 417, *440*

Haque, M. S., 469–470, *479*

Hara, K., 212, *230*

Harasty, J. A., 182, *198*

Harber, M., 534, *550–551*

Harburg, E., 218, 219, *231, 232, 233*

Hardy, D., *28*

Hariman, L. M. F., 117, *133–134*

Harkavy, J., *91*

Harkins, S. W., 338, 417, *438*

Harkness, W. F., *475*

Harlap, S., 534, *550–551*

Harlow, B. L., 355, *369*

Harlow, L. L., 19, *29*

Harlow, S. D., 352, *366*

Harrington, R., 162, *169*

Harris, D., 84, *93*

Harris, F. R., 382, *393*

Harris, M., *521*

Harrison, R. F., *277, 317, 340*

Hart, A. R., 48, *59*

Harvey, L. M., *99*

Hatch, J. P., 411, *434*

Hatch, M., 349, 350, 351, 353, 359, *367, 374, 375, 391, 394*

Hatch, M. L., 373, *395*

Hathaway, S., 312, *339*

Hauck, F., *90*

Hauenstein, L. S., *233*

Hauman, C. H., 9, *26*

Haupt, R., 109, *134*

Hauser, W. A., 189, 190, *198*

Havard, J. D., 259, *276*

Havermans, T., 75, *90*

Hawgood, S., 491, *521*

Hawkins, A., *136–137*

Hawkins, D. A., 571, *578*

Hawkins, J., 506, *529*, 571, *576*

Hawkins, N. G., 8, *30*

Hawkins, R. P., 147, *171*

Hawley, D. J., 422, *434*

Hay, A. R., 290, *301*

Hay, J. W., 290, *301*

Hay, M., *432*

Hayes, J., *90*

Haynes, R. B., 21, 22, 30, *35–36*

Haynes, S. B., 207, 208, *233*

Haynes, S. N., 372, *395*

Hays, R. D., 20, *28*

Haythornthwaite, J. A., 219–220, *233*

Hayward, R. D., *475*

Hayworth, J., 361, *367*

Headley, J., 499, *518*

Holicky, R., 572, *578*
Holland, J., 51, 53, *59–70*, 110, *134*
Holliday, J. E., 13, *29*
Hollingsworth, J. L., *95*
Hollis, J. F., 40, *63*
Hollon, S. D., 54, *57*, 159, *169*
Holm, K. C., 560, *579*
Holm, S., 247, *273*
Holman, H., 417, 419, 422, *434, 436*
Holman, R. C., 121, *134*
Holmbeck, G. N., 463, *476–477*
Holmes, G. A., 563, *578*
Holmes, G. I., 191, *199*
Holmes, T. H., 8, *30, 34*
Holroyd, K. A., 242, 263, *274, 274–275*
Holsti, L., 489, *530*
Holtzman, I., *516*
Homer, C. J., 267, *276–277, 367*
Hommet, C., 465, 466, *477*
Hong, G. A., *339*
Honig, G., *135*
Honnor, M. J., 350, *367*
Hons, R. B., 309, *338*
Hook, E. B., 81, *91*
Hook, R. J., 22, *29*
Hoon, E. F., 16, *34*
Hooper, S., *140*
Hope, P. L., *529*
Hopkins, K., *131*
Hopkins, M., 164, *168*
Hops, H., 161, *170*
Horbar, J. D., *521*
Horii, T., *230*
Horlock, P., *231*
Horn, M., 109, *130*
Horne, D. L., 379, 380, *393*
Hornrook, M. C., 559, *580*
Horowitz, F. D., 494, *528*
Horwitz, W. A., 105, 106, *134*
Horwood, L. J., 487, 488, *521*, 562, *577*
Hoskins, E. M., 492, *521, 524*
Hough, B. S., 70, *99*
Houts, A. C., 147, 148, 167, *169*
Howard, G., 543, *551*
Howell, C. T., 505, *515*
Howell, D. C., 45, *58*
Howell, R. H., *232*
Howland, J., 561, *578*
Hoy, D., 543, *551*
Hoyer, L., 120, 121, 122, *134, 140*
Hsieh, H. L., 487, *523*
Hsu, D. T., 450, *476*

Hsu, J., 76, *96*
Hsu, L., *131*
Hubbard, A. M., 491, *522*
Hubbard, J. R., 155, *169*
Hubley, P. A., 488, *527*
Hudson, S., 55, *61*
Hudson, T., 463, *476–477*
Hugdahl, K., 259, *277*
Hughes, A. O., *301*
Hughes, B. R., 388, *393*
Hughes, H., 372, 388, *395, 396*
Hughes, M., 150, *170*
Hughs, J., *29*
Hull, S. M., 388, *393*
Hullett, S., 360, *368*
Hulley, S. B., 208, *237*
Hulsey, T. C., 359, *369*
Humbert, J. H., 112, *135*
Hummon, N. P., 417, *438*
Hunkin, N. M., 227, *237*
Hunsley, J., 309, *338*
Hunter, A. G. W., *459–460*, 461, 464,
    477
Hunter, T. L., 19, *30*
Huntington, L., 496, *520*
Huntzinger, R. M., 126, *132*
Hurewitz, A., 422, *440*
Hurley, A. D., 461, *477*
Hurt, S. W., 325, 327, *339*
Hurtig, A. L., 115, 117, *133–134, 134*
Hurwitz, M., *274*
Huston, P., 211, *231*
Huszti, H. C., *94*
Hutson, J. M., *521*
Huxtable, K., 69, *99*
Huyser, B. A., 408, 410, 411, 412, 413,
    425, 428, *431, 434, 435*
Hyman, P., 52, *57*
Hynd, G. W., *138*
Hyun, C. S., *58*

Iancu, I., *168*, 355, 356, 357, *367*
Ianni, P., 223, 224, *232*
Iasiello-Vailas, L., 20, *28*
Ibrahim, M., 471, *479*
Ickovics, J. R., 11, *30*
Idress, F. S., *474*
Ievers, C. E., 75, 76, *91*, 106, *131*
Ignatoff, E., 505, *519*
Iijima, R., 491, *522*
Ikkala, E., 121, 122, *134*

Kop, W. J., 209, *232, 234*
Kopelman, A. E., 491, *524*
Kopp, C. B., 256, *277*
Korbee, L., *278*
Koritnick, D. R., 208, *234*
Korner, A. F., 504, *522*
Korones, S. B., 491, *516*
Korsch, B. M., 20, 21, 29, *32*
Korten, A. E., 179, *199*
Kostuk, W. J., 450, *478*
Kotelchuck, M., 568, *577*
Kotler, M., *367*
Kotses, H., 253, 263, *277–278, 282*
Kovacs, M., 72, *93*
Kovar, P. A., 425, *435–436*
Kovatchev, B., 70, *90*
Kovnar, E. H., *136*
Kozuma, K., *230*
Kraaij, V., 211, *231*
Kraaimaat, F. W., 410, 415, *433*
Kraemer, H. C., *63*
Kraines, R. G., 417, *434*
Krakow, J. B., 256, *277*
Kramer, B. M., 469, *481*
Kramer, J. C., 75, *90*
Kramer, M. E., *170*
Krantz, D. S., 204, 206, 207, 210, *230, 232, 233, 234*
Kraus, J. F., 572, *579*
Kravitz, R. L., *28*
Krawic, A., *280*
Krawiecki, N. S., 446, 474, *478*
Kraybill, E. N., 492, *522, 524*
Kresnow, M. J., 568, *576*
Krieger, N., 219, *234*
Kriegman, D. M., 412, *438*
Krikler, R., 497, *523*
Kril, J. J., 182, *198*
Krishnamoorthy, K. S., 491, *522*
Kroll, T., 425, *436*
Kronenberg, H. M., *98*
Kronenberger, W. G., 162, 164, 165, 166, 167, *170*
Kruekeberg, S. M., 445, 456, *477*
Kruger, A., 408, *440*
Kruis, W., 284, *304*
Krupp, L. B., 417, *439*
Kuban, C. K., 446, *478*
Kuban, K. C., 474, *522*
Kuczmarski, R. J., 44, 58, 77, *98*
Kugener, B., *515*
Kuhl, J., 221, *231*

Kuhn, C., *522*
Kuldanek, A., *582*
Kuller, L. H., 206, *231*
Kumanyika, S. K., 48, *60*
Kumar, D., 286, *302, 304*
Kumar, M., 14, *29–30, 35*
Kumar, N., *32*
Kun, L. E., 108, *135*
Kunos, I., *526*
Kupelnick, B., 221, *231*
Kupfer, J., 316, *337*
Kupst, M. J., 106, *135*
Kurtz, S. C., *90*
Kusumakar, V., 472, *479*
Kuttner, L., 103, *135*
Kutz, I., *235*
Kuypers, B. R., 387, *393*
Kwan, L., 222, *235*
Kyer, C. S., *31*
Kyrklund-Blomberg, N. B., 349, 353, *367*

Laakso, M. P., *198*
Laatsch, L., 461, *477*
LaBrecque, J. F., 257, *276*
Lacaille, D., 415, *432*
Lacasse, Y., 247, *278*
Lacks, P., 427, *436*
Lacy, C. F., 319, *340*
LaGreca, A., 71, 72, 90, 93, 96–97, 107, *135*
Lai, Z., *302*
Lain, G. W., 329, *338*
Laitinen, J., 471, *479*
Lally, R. J., 504, *520*
Lamb, G., 258, *282*
Lamb, M. E., 504, *523*
Lambert, H., *131*
Lambert, M. J., 157, *170*
Lambert, R. G., *131*
Lambert-Huber, D. A., 568, *576*
Lamenek, K. L., 21, *32*
Lamontagne, Y., 378, *395*
Lamparski, D., 70, *98–99*
Lancaster, W., 108, *130*
Lancee, W. J., 297, *302*
Lancman, M. E., 543, *551*
Landbergis, P. A., 359, *367*
Landis, K. R., 40, *60*
Landry, S. H., 462, 476, 477, 491, *523*
Landy, G., 82, *93*
Landzkowsky, P., 121, *135*

Martin, M. Y., 545, *549*
Martin, N. J., 118, 119, *133*
Masand, P., 160, *171*
Masdeu, J. C., *200*
Masi, W., 504, *523*
Maslak, P., 102, *138*
Masliah, E., *200*
Mason, C., 458, *479–480*
Mason, J. H., 416, *437*
Mason, J. W., 105, *133*
Massey, J. K., 16, *34*
Massie, M. J., 40, 51, 60, *62*
Mastri, A. R., 185, *199*
Matalon, T. A., *517*
Mateer, C. A., 572, *579*
Matheson, P. B., 453, *475*
Mathison, D. A., 253, *278*
Matiu, I., 491, *522*
Matsuishi, T., 505, *523*
Matt, K. S., 414, *441*
Matthews, K. A., 206, 208, 219, *231,*
    235
Mattsson, A., 124, *136*
Mauer, A., *137*
Maunder, R., 295, *302*
Maunder, R. G., 292, 293, 294, 295, 297,
    299, 302
Maunsell, E., 46, 52, 60, *61*
Maurer, H., *135*
Maurice, J., 213, *234*
Maw, K. L., 243, *276*
Max, J. E., 572, *579*
Maxwell, R. M., 48, *59*
Mayberry, J. F., 48, 59, 296, *301, 302*
Mayeaux, R., *201*
Mayer, E. A., 286, *302*
Mayes, L. C., 514, *524*
Mayes, S. D., 125, 127, *133, 136*
Mayne, T. J., 11, *33*
Mazer, B., *526*
Mazonson, P. D., 422, *436*
Mazur, T., 88, *93*
McAndrew, I., *278–279*
McAninch, J. W., 313, *341*
McAnulty, G., *515*
McAnulty, G. B., *515*
McArdle, S., 219, *231*
McAuliffe, T. L., 19, *31*
McCain, G. A., 427, *432*
McCallie, D. P., 542, *550*
McCallum, M., *91*
McCann, K. L., 79, *95*

McCarthy, S., 52, *57*
McCarton, C. M., 505, 514, *517, 524*
McCarton-Daum, C., 492, *524*
McCaskill, C. C., *394*
McCaul, K. D., 69, 90, 535, *551*
McCauley, E., 81, 89–90, *93,* 471, *474,*
    478
McClellan, P., 221, *234*
McClelland, H. A., 542, *552*
McClish, D. K., 330, 331, 338, *341, 342*
McCormack, W. M., 321, *339*
McCormick, D., 261, 273, 491, *527*
McCormick, M. C., 487, 488, 497, *522,*
    524, 528
McCowan, C., 258, *278*
McCubbin, H. I., 75, *93*
McCubbin, M. A., *93, 278*
McCurley, J., 78, *90*
McCutchan, J. A., *34*
McDaniel, J. S., 52, *61*
McDaniel, S. H., 429, *436*
McDermott, M., 207, *230*
McDonald, K., 126, *136*
McDonell, K., *99*
McDougal, S. S., 121, *133*
McGahee, T. W., 104, *131*
McGee, R., 41, *61,* 260, *278*
McGinnis, J., 42, *61*
McGinty, K., 104, *132*
McGlynn, E. A., *28*
McGonagle, K. A., 150, *170*
McGrath, P. J., 75, *90*
McGuire, D. E., 456, *477*
McGuire, L., 84, *94*
McKee, D. C., 285, 300, *303*
McKendry, R. J., *230*
McKenna, M. C., 40, 41, 42, *61*
McKenzie, F. N., *230,* 450, *478*
McKeown, T., 25, *33*
McKie, K. M., *138*
McKie, V. C., 117, *132*
McKinlay, J., 25, *33*
McKinlay, S., 25, *33*
McKinley, J., 312, *339*
McKinley, K., *527*
McKinnon, W., 14, *33*
McLarnon, L. D., 15, *33*
McLaughlin, J. K., *302*
McLaughlin, T., 252, *281*
McLeod, D. R., 162, *169*
McLeod, R. S., *302*
McLoughlin, E., 568, *577*

Oates, R. K., 447, 478–479
O'Brien, C., 498, 528
O'Brien, P. C., 199
O'Brodovich, H., 487, 527
Obrosky, D. S., 72, 93
O'Callaghan, M. J., 488, 529
O'Campo, P., 486, 529
Ochler, J., 504, 505, 525
Ochs, J., 108, 136, 137
Ockene, I. S., 204, 235
Ockene, J., 42, 43, 61, 204, 235, 246, 279
O'Cleirigh, C., 13, 26, 30, 33
O'Connor, G. T., 212, 235
O'Donnel, L. J. D., 301
O'Donnell, R., 252, 280
O'Dougherty, M., 445, 446, 479
Oehler, J. M., 529
Oei, T. P., 327, 337
Office of Technology Assessment, 340
Offord, D. R., 256, 273
Ogden, J., 323, 340, 342
Ogrocki, P., 31
Ogunyemi, D., 360, 368
Oh, W., 489, 490, 491, 516, 529–530, 530
O'Hanlon, J. F., 261, 281–282
O'Hare, T., 346, 347, 369
Ohata, J., 13, 26, 33
Ohi, R., 471, 479
Oian, P., 360, 369
Okamoto, L. J., 252, 281
O'Keefe, M. K., 19, 34
Okifuji, A., 422, 440
Olch, D., 126, 137
Olden, K. W., 285, 286, 288, 290, 297, 298, 299, 300
Olderma, F., 52, 63
O'Leary, A., 13, 35
O'Leary, B. J., 150, 171
Oliaro, A., 543, 550
Olmstead, E. M., 235
Olmsted, M. P., 219, 233
Olsen, B. G., 303
Olsen, J. H., 302
Olshan, A. F., 362, 368
Olson, R. A., 94, 103–104, 134–135, 429, 437
Olson, R. K., 259, 275
Omenn, G., 84, 94
Omer, H., 354, 369
O'Moore, A. M., 317, 340

O'Moore, R. R., 317, 340
O'Neil, B., 555, 559, 568, 575, 581
Ong, E. L. C., 12, 36
Oostveen, F. G., 9, 30
Opipari, L. C., 75, 76, 95
Orbach, C., 105, 131
Ordway, L., 28
O'Reagan, M., 384, 396
O'Reilly, J. P., 505, 525
O'Reilly, K. A., 505, 525
O'Reilly, P., 40, 61
Orenstein, D., 95
Orgill, A. A., 490, 491, 515, 518, 522
Orgill, A. L., 531
Orleans, C. T., 45, 61
Ornish, D., 216, 235–236
Ornstein, M., 488, 525
Orris, P., 257, 278
Ortega, J. A., 137
Ortiz-Valdes, J. A., 74, 98
Ory, M. G., 328, 340
Orzeck, S., 328, 340
Osborne, D., 312, 337
O'Shea, J. S., 561, 576
O'Shea, T. M., 490, 518
Osler, W., 251, 279
Ostergard, D. R., 311, 312, 341
Ostrow, J., 10, 31
O'Sullivan, G., 164, 166, 171
Otterblad, O. P., 519
Ouslander, J. G., 328, 340
Outerbridge, E. W., 520
Owen, N., 43, 61
Ozolins, M., 103–104, 134–135, 135

Paarlberg, K. M., 358, 363, 369
Pace, T. M., 429, 437
Pack, B., 114, 140
Padgett, D. A., 14, 34
Padur, J. S., 254, 255, 279
Paffebarger, R. S., 235
Pagan, L. Y., 494, 528
Pagani, M., 247, 275
Page, L., 220, 236
Pahor, M., 41, 62
Paik, M., 201
Painter, J. J., 516
Pais, R., 131
Palfai, T. G., 326, 338
Palmer, C. S., 242, 279
Palmer, P. G., 491, 495, 518, 525

SUBJECT INDEX

Learned helplessness, 158
  assessment, 419
  in rheumatic disease, 414
Leukemia, 101
  adjustment, 105–106
  bone marrow transplantation, 103
  causes, 102
  definition, 102
  epidemiology, 102
  managing treatment side effects, 104–105
  neuropsychological deficits in, 107–109
  pain management, 103–104
  prognosis, 103
  research needs, 109–110
  risk, 102
  role of health psychology, 109
  symptoms, 102
  treatment, 102–103
  treatment adherence, 106–107
Leukomalacia, periventricular, 491–492
Lewy body disease, 185, 186
Loss. *See* Bereavement and grief
Lou Gehrig disease. *See* Amyotrophic lateral sclerosis
Low-birthweight infants. *See* Premature, low-birthweight infants
Lumbar puncture, 103
Lung cancer mortality, 37
Lupus erythematosus, systemic, 400, 401, 404, 409, 412, 414
Lyme disease epidemiology, 6

Malaria, 6, 22
Malingering, 147
Managed care, 264–265, 335, 429
Marital satisfaction, 420
Measles, 6
Meditation, 385
Melanoma, 43
Memory, in dementia, 178–179
Meningitis, 175, 176
Menstruation problems
  dysmenorrhea, 323–324
  premenstrual syndrome, 324–328
Mental retardation
  hydrocephalus and, 466
  See also Down syndrome
Mesiotemporal sclerosis, 191

Metabolic disorders, 65. See also *specific disorder*
  research needs, 88–89
Methotrexate, 108
Migraine, 193
Miscarriage, 346–348
Monoamine oxidase inhibitors
  depression treatment, 160
  mechanism of action, 160, 163
  See also specific drug
Mononucleosis, 8
Motor vehicle accidents, 557–559, 564–565
Multiple sclerosis, 188–189
  role of health psychology, 175
Munchausen's syndrome by proxy, 147
Muscular dystrophy, 195–196
  role of health psychology, 174
Musculoskeletal disorders. *See* Rheumatic diseases
Myasthenia gravis, 195
  role of health psychology, 174
Myocardial infarction, 204
  psychosocial factors in, 205
Myocardial ischemia, 204, 206
Myotonic dystrophy, 195–196

Naive health theories, 20–21
Natural killer cells, 50
Nausea management, 104–105
  in pregnancy, 355–358
Neonatal Behavioral Assessment Scale, 495
Neurofibromatosis, 102
Neuromuscular disorders, 195–196
Neurotic excoriations, 377
Nifedipine, 224
Nocebo effects, 541, 542–545
Noradrenergic system, in anxiety, 163
Norepinephrine, 154–155, 160, 163

Obesity, 152
  cancer risk and, 43
  definition, 77
  epidemiology, 77
  hypertension risk, 220
  risk factors, 77–78
  treatment, 79–80

cancer, 44–45, 48–49
cardiac problems, 211–217
chronic obstructive pulmonary disease,
    271
coronary heart disease, 229
early detection strategies, 48–49
fall-related injuries, 559–560
hemophilia complications, 123
hemophilia transmission, 121–122
hypertension, 229
infectious disease, 5, 17–19, 22–25
motor vehicle-related injuries, 558–559
with premature/low-birthweight infant,
    515
preterm delivery, 354–355
rheumatic fever, 228
skin disorders, 392
smoking cessation programs, 246
stroke, 226
tuberculosis transmission, 244, 270–
    271
Prostatitis, 313
Prurigo nodularis, 378
Pruritis, 376–378
Pseudobulbar palsy, 178
Pseudodementia, 184
Psoriasis, 375
    prevalence, 383
    psychological interventions, 384–385
    psychosocial factors, 383–384
Psychoanalytic theory, 374
Psychogenic illness, 543–544
Psychological interventions
    atopic dermatitis, 381–382
    coronary heart disease, 213–217
    dyspareunia, 322
    efficacy/effectiveness, 156–157
    fertility problems, 317
    functional gastrointestinal disorder,
        290–291
    hyperemesis gravidarum, 357–358
    hypertension, 221–222
    inflammatory bowel disease, 296–298
    premenstrual syndrome, 327–328
    preterm delivery prevention, 354–355
    psoriasis, 384–385
    rheumatic disease, 421–427
    role in medical treatment generally,
        547–549
    stroke rehabilitation, 226–227

urethral syndrome, 313
urinary incontinence, 332–334
urticaria, 390
vaginismus, 323
Psychopathology
    asthma and, 254–255, 256
    classification, 145–149, 150
    clinical conceptualization, 143–144
    dementia assessment in, 184
    dermatological disorders and, 373
    epidemiology, 150
    in epilepsy, 191–192
    functional analysis, 147–148
    functional gastrointestinal disorders
        and, 287, 288–289
    health care utilization and, 148
    inflammatory bowel disease and, 292
    intersexuality disorders and, 86–87
    relationships with physical conditions,
        146–147, 148–149
    risk in cystic fibrosis, 74
    risk in diabetes, 72
    role of health psychology in treatment
        of, 167–168
    sickle cell disease and, 115
    sleep disorders in, 151
    treatment settings, 148
Psychosocial short stature, 85–86
Puberty, 87–88
Pulmonary atresia, 444
Pulmonary disease, Chronic obstructive.
        See Chronic obstructive pulmo-
        nary disease
Pulmonic stenosis, 445
Purpura, 101

Race/ethnicity
    cancer risk and management, 55
    cleft lip/palate risk, 452
    hypertension risk, 218
    patient concerns in inflammatory
        bowel disease, 295
Radiation therapy
    leukemia treatment, 103
    side effects, 107–108, 128
Raynaud's disease, 405
    clinical features, 223
    pathophysiology, 223–224
    treatment, 224–225

Stress (*Continued*)
  atopic dermatitis and, 380
  biological systems involved in, 154–155
  biopsychosocial model, 154–156
  cancer and, 41, 43, 46–47
  chronic, 205
  clinical significance, 23
  cognitive–mediational model, 155–156
  coronary heart disease and, 205–208, 210
  dermatological disorders and, 373
  diabetes management and, 70–71
  functional gastrointestinal disorders and, 289
  in hemophilia, 123
  hypertension in pregnancy and, 358–359
  hypertension risk, 218–219, 221–222
  infectious disease and, 10–13, 16–17
    disease susceptibility, 6–8
    implications for prevention, 17–19, 22–25
    implications for treatment, 16–17, 19–22
    inflammatory bowel disease and, 292–295
    and latent virus reactivation, 13–16
  measurement, 23–24
  miscarriage and, 347–348
  neuroimmune function and, 50–51
  occupational, 206–207
  premenstrual syndrome and, 326
  preterm delivery and, 349–351
  psoriasis and, 383–384
  rheumatic disease and, 411–414
  vaccine effectiveness and, 8–10
Stroke
  depression and, 227
  epidemiology, 225
  medical impairments, 226
  prevention, 226
  rehabilitation, 226–228
  risk factors, 225–226
  role of health psychology, 226–227
  sickle cell disease and, 111
  See also Cerebral vascular accidents
Substance use
  HIV infection risk, 18
  miscarriage risk, 348

in outpatient medical populations, 148
Suicides/suicidal behavior, 560
Sun exposure, cancer risk and, 43
Surgical interventions
  cleft lip/palate, 452
  congenital heart disease, 445, 446–449
  coronary heart disease, 211–212
  erectile dysfunction, 318
  psychological considerations, 149
Susceptibility to disease, psychosocial factors in
  cancer, 38, 39–45
  coronary heart disease, 204–211
  dermatological disorders, 375
  emotional processes in, 535–536
  infectious disease, 6–8
Sweating, excessive, 387–388
Sympathetic–adrenal–medullary system, 50
  in rheumatic disease, 412–413
  stress response, 154–155
Symptom analysis, 534–539, 545–546
Symptoms, signs and ill-defined conditions, 533
Synovitis, 400–401
Syphilis, 6

Teen pregnancy, 486
Tendinitis, 405
Tennis elbow, 405
Tetanus infection, 9
Tetralogy of Fallot, 444, 445
Theophylline, 261
Therapeutic relationship. *See* Physician–patient relationship
Thyroid disorders, 82–83
Tobacco use
  associated mortality, 42, 239–240
  cancer risk and, 42, 44–45
  hypertension in pregnancy and, 360
  initiation, 42
  miscarriage risk, 348
  mortality/morbidity, 246
  placental attachment disorders and, 362
  preterm delivery and, 353
  respiratory disorders associated with, 239, 245
  smoking cessation programs, 246, 271

trends, 44
Tourette's syndrome, 165
Toxic substance exposure
    in pregnancy, 484
    psychogenic illness, 543–544
    See also Poisoning
Transposition of great arteries, 444, 445
Transtheoretical model, 25
Treatment, generally
    infectious disease, 16–17, 19–22
    interdisciplinary teams, 240, 241
    multidisciplinary teams, 240–241
    role of health psychology, 149, 547–549
    See also Adherence; *specific diagnosis*
Trenchmouth, 8
Trichotillomania, 376
Tricyclic antidepressants, 160, 162
    mechanism of action, 160, 163
    See also specific drug
Trisomy 21. *See* Down syndrome
Tuberculosis
    drug resistant, 240
    epidemiology, 6, 240, 242, 244
    infection risk, 24
    mortality, 6, 240
    role of health psychology, 244–245, 270–271
    susceptibility, stress as factor in, 8
    transmission, 242, 244
    treatment, 242–243, 268
    treatment adherence, 243–244
Tularemia, 8
Turner syndrome, 80–81, 471
Type A behavior pattern, 208, 213–216

Ulcerative colitis. *See* Inflammatory bowel disease

Upper respiratory infection, 6–7
Urethral syndrome
    clinical features, 311
    etiology, 311–312
    psychological assessment, 312–313
    treatment, 311–312, 313
Urticaria, 389–390

Vaccination/immunization
    efficacy, 25
    stress effects, 8–10
Vaginismus, 322–323
Valium, 104
Varicella Zoster infection, 16
Viagra, 319
Vision problems, retinopathy of prematurity, 492–493
Vital exhaustion, 209–210
Vulvar vestibulitis syndrome, 321–322

Warts, genital, 6
Weight gain
    hypertension in pregnancy and, 360
    preterm delivery and, 352–353
Weight loss, for hypertension treatment, 221
Workplace problems
    complications of rheumatic disease, 415
    hypertension in pregnancy, 359
    miscarriage risk, 347
    occupational disorders, 206–207

Yohimbine, 318

ABOUT THE EDITORS

Editor-in-Chief

Thomas J. Boll, PhD, is director of the Neuropsychology Institute in Birmingham, Alabama. For 32 years, he was a professor at several universities and medical centers including the University of Washington; the University of Virginia; the Chicago Medical School; and for the past 20 years, the University of Alabama at Birmingham (UAB). He was a professor in the Departments of Psychology, Pediatrics, and Neurological Surgery. He is board certified in clinical psychology, clinical neuropsychology, and clinical health psychology. His research investigations in the areas of health and human behavior include issues related to heart and lung transplantations and chronic pediatric illnesses, including congenital cytomegalovirus, low birthweight, seizure disorders, and learning disabilities. He has written on various aspects of educational and curriculum design for health psychology and was the founding chairman of the Department of Medical Psychology at the Chicago Medical Center and the first director of clinical training for the Medical Psychology Program at UAB. He was the chair of the Doctoral Curriculum Committee at the Arden House Conference, which set the curriculum for health psychology doctoral training programs.

Volume Editors

Suzanne Bennett Johnson, PhD, is professor and director of the Center for Pediatric Psychology and Family Studies at the University of Florida–Gainesville. She has published widely in the areas of pediatric psychology, medical regimen adherence, psychosocial aspects of Type I diabetes, and the psychological impact of genetic testing. She is a Fellow of the American Psychological Association (APA), past president of APA's Division of Health Psychology (38), and past president of the Society of Pediatric

Psychology. She is board certified in clinical health psychology from the American Board of Professional Psychology. Recently she served as a Robert Wood Johnson Health Policy Fellow in the office of Sen. Hillary Rodham Clinton (D-NY).

Nathan W. Perry, Jr., PhD, is professor emeritus at the University of Florida, where he served as chair of the Department of Clinical and Health Psychology for more than 20 years. He is a past president of the Florida Psychological Association, past president of the Southeastern Psychological Association, and past president of the Clinical Psychology Division (12) of the American Psychological Association (APA). He is an APA Fellow and has served on the APA Board of Directors. He is a long-standing advocate of the scientist–practitioner training model and had a research career in the areas of vision and cognition. He is a Diplomate in clinical health psychology from the American Board of Professional Psychology.

Ronald H. Rozensky, PhD, is professor and chairman of the Department of Clinical and Health Psychology at the University of Florida. He has served as the chair of both the Board of Professional Affairs and the Board of Educational Affairs of the American Psychological Association (APA) and is a past president of the Illinois Psychological Association. He is an APA Fellow and has served two terms on the APA Council of Representatives. He has published in the areas of health psychology and professional practice. He is board certified in both clinical health psychology and clinical psychology from the American Board of Professional Psychology.

AAO-8887